INDIA

ANCIENT AND MODERN.

INDIA

ANCIENT AND MODERN.

GEOGRAPHICAL, HISTORICAL, POLITICAL, SOCIAL, AND RELIGIOUS;

WITH A PARTICULAR ACCOUNT OF THE STATE AND PROSPECTS OF CHRISTIANITY.

BY

DAVID O. ALLEN, D.D.

MISSIONARY OF THE AMERICAN BOARD FOR TWENTY-FIVE YEARS IN INDIA; MEMBER OF THE BOMBAY BRANCH OF THE ROYAL ASIATIC SOCIETY; AND CORRESPONDING MEMBER OF THE AMERICAN ORIENTAL SOCIETY.

BOSTON:

PUBLISHED BY JOHN P. JEWETT AND COMPANY.

CLEVELAND, OHIO:

JEWETT, PROCTOR AND WORTHINGTON.

NEW YORK: SHELDON, LAMPORT AND BLAKEMAN.

LONDON: TRÜBNER AND COMPANY.

1856.

CAMBRIDGE:
ALLEN AND FARNHAM, STEREOTYPERS AND PRINTERS.

PREFACE.

The writer, on returning to this country after his long residence in the East, observed in the frequent inquiries made concerning India, much desire for information, and a great want of accurate knowledge concerning that country and its inhabitants. And when asked what work he could recommend as containing the information which so many were desirous to obtain, he was constrained to reply that he knew of no such work suited to the people of the United States. Many works on India have been published in England, where the political relation of the two countries naturally creates a strong and general desire for information. But some of these works contain only the History of British India, and others contain only one period of history, or describe only one part of the country; all perhaps well suited to the class of people for whom they were designed in England, but not adapted for general reading in the United States; while no one work contains such a summary of general and particular information as to make it suitable for importation in any considerable number, or for republication in this country. The English Journals, reprinted in the United States, contain many well written articles upon India, but they were designed for England, and though well suited to the knowledge which the people there generally have concerning India and its inhabitants, they are not so well suited to the limited views of that country which people generally have in the United States. The religious journals in this country since the origin of Christian Missions to

India, have contained much interesting information concerning the social state of the inhabitants. They also contain frequent reference to the political state of the country, and various other matters which excite a desire for further knowledge, but they nowhere supply it, nor give information where it may be found.

A work on India suited to the people of the United States, appeared to be a *desideratum*, and in endeavoring to supply this want, the writer has aimed to include as much information concerning India, ancient and modern, as people generally would wish to read, and to which they could refer as often as they might have occasion. Newspapers and other journals often contain religious and political intelligence concerning India, which their readers can but imperfectly appreciate for want of more knowledge of the country and its inhabitants. And if this is so in respect to allusions, sketches, and extracts in American Journals, it is yet more so in respect to allusions, extracts, etc., contained in the English Reviews and Journals, as such articles were originally written for readers who have much more knowledge of India than the people of the United States generally have.

In no country have the inhabitants retained their religion, their superstitions, and their social and local usages for so long time, and with so little change, as in India. The religion of the ancient Egyptians, the Assyrians, the Persians, the Greeks, and the Romans, had great influence in forming the character of those nations. But they have all passed away, and their character and religion can now only be known from their history, and from those monuments and ruins of which the present generation in those countries, know neither the origin nor the meaning. But in India, the religious system which existed in the time of the Pharaohs, of Nebuchadnezzar, of Cyrus, of Solon, and of Romulus, still continues, and its influence is seen in the present state and character of the inhabitants. This remarkable fact invests the ancient history of India with great interest, and all who would understand the present state of the country and be able to appreciate the peculiar character of the people, must begin with their ancient history and primitive institutions.

The history of India contains a series of successive periods and changes. The first period was its state as indicated by fragments of its history and the state and character of the rude and uncivilized tribes, in some districts, who are the descendants of the aborigines. The first great change was the invasion of the power, religious or political, probably both united, which established Brahminism, or what is frequently called Hinduism. The second disturbing cause was Budhism, which originated in India, and after a long struggle with Brahminism, was expelled and took refuge in Ceylon and the countries east from India, as Burma, Siam, and China. The third cause was the invasion and conquest of the country by the Mohammedans, who were the predominant power for several hundred years. The fourth disturbing cause was the invasion of the country by the European nations, as the Portuguese, the Dutch, the French, and the English. These causes and their consequences appeared naturally to suggest the following order for this work, namely, Ancient India, or the Hindu Period, the Mohammedan Period, the European Period, the English Government of India, the Religion, Customs, Manners, etc. of the Inhabitants, the History of Christianity, and its Present State and Prospects. Nothing has been inserted without having what appeared to be sufficient authority, and in conflicting statements, those have been used which appeared to have the most evidence in their favor.

The work has been prepared with a view to exhibit the state and character of the people of India, and the causes now in operation to change their state and character. The history and state of the southern nations of Asia, at the commencement of this century, showed that there was little reason to hope for any improvement among them without some great political and moral changes. They had made but little progress for 2 or 3,000 years, and they appeared not to possess among themselves any power for political improvement, or for making any further progress in civilization. Within a century past great political changes have taken place, and are still in progress through the agency of foreign power and conquest. In these changes the people of the United States have had no direct agency, and no responsibility. Great moral changes have also commenced, and are in progress. In these changes, many in this country have taken an important part. The first missionaries who left the United States for the heathen world, proceeded to India, and there commenced the earliest American missions. From that time India has continued to share largely in the prayers and contributions of many people in the United States. And it is believed that more knowledge of that country and its inhabitants, and of the results of the missionary enterprise and of the facilities which now exist for promoting it, would excite increasing interest in this cause.

In 1827, the writer went to India, expecting to pass his life in the missionary cause in that country. And such continued to be his purpose till the failure of his health in 1853, made it necessary for him, if he would reserve himself for any thing more in life, to return to his native country. Compelled thus to relinquish his purpose of spending his life in the foreign missionary field, he has prepared this work in the hope of exciting feelings of more interest in the foreign missionary cause, and an increasing spirit of prayer and effort for the propagation of Christianity in India, and the other countries in the south part of Asia.

D. O. A.

BOSTON, OCT. 1, 1855.

CONTENTS.

PART I.

GEOGRAPHY.

PART II.

HISTORY.

CHAPTER I.—The Hindu Period.

CHAPTER II.—Mohammedan Period.

CHAPTER III.—European Period.

PART III.

THE GOVERNMENT OF INDIA.

PART IV.

PART V.

THE NATIVE POPULATION.

PART VI.

CHRISTIANITY IN INDIA.

CHAPTER I.

CHAPTER II.

CHAPTER III.

APPENDIX.

Appendix A.

Appendix B.

Appendix C.

Appendix D.

INDIA,

ANCIENT AND MODERN.

PART I.

GEOGRAPHY.

India has derived its name from the Indus, one of its largest rivers and generally considered part of its western boundary, separating it from Persia. This name was given to the country by the Persians, and thus it became known to the Greeks and Romans. The name of the country in the Sanscrit language and in ancient works generally, is *Bharat;* it is sometimes called *Bharatkhund,* and also *Jambhudwip.* The name of Hindustan, which is often given to India in Europe and America, is never applied to the whole country by Europeans living in India, nor by natives of the country. Hindustan is properly the name of that part of India which is north of the river Nerbudda or its latitude, excepting the provinces of Bengal on the east and of Gujerat on the west, which are generally known in the history of India by their respective names.

The name Hindustan, or Hindoostan, or Hindostan, was given to India by the Persians, and is composed of two Persian words, namely, *Hindu* signifying black, or in the plural, the blacks, or black people; and *stan* signifying a place or country. So Hindustan in the Persian language signifies the country of the black people; as Afghanistan is the country of the Afghans; as in English, Negroland means the country of the negroes.

The boundary of India on the south, is the ocean; on the

west, the ocean and the Indus; on the north, the Himalaya mountains; and on the east, the river Brahmaputra and the ocean, or the part of it called the Bay of Bengal.

The extreme length of India from Cape Comorin to the mountains which form the northern boundary of Cashmere, exceeds 1,900 miles, and its breadth from the mouth of the Indus to the Brahmaputra exceeds 1,500 miles. Its area is estimated at 1,280,000 square miles. Thus it is larger than all the United States which are east of the Mississippi, and as large as all Europe which is south of Russia and the Baltic Sea.

India at some period of its history was divided into different kingdoms corresponding in some degree to the names by which the different parts or provinces are now known, though the names were somewhat different in ancient times. Some of these names were given by Europeans in their first intercourse with the country, and having become thus known in Europe they have been retained, somewhat as the names of many places originated in America and have been perpetuated. These divisions, as Malabar, Mysore, Carnatic, Deckan, Gujerat, Bengal, Bahar, etc., have not very accurately defined limits, and they are not now recognized as civil divisions or provinces by the government. The divisions which have been introduced by the East India Company for economy and convenience in the affairs of government, have been often changed, and they are liable for the same reason to be changed again. The Mohammedans in establishing their power and administering the government of the country in many instances changed the names of provinces, cities, and villages. But the English have made no such changes, and the names of the districts, cities, and towns have been continued, and they are likely to continue as they have been for two or three centuries past, and as they are known in the modern history and geography of the country. The different parts of India will therefore be referred to by their usual names and these names will be in the usual orthography.

CLIMATE AND SEASONS.

A country extending nearly 2,000 miles in length in a line nearly north and south, must necessarily have great variety of climate and seasons. More than half of India is situated within the tropics; its northern limit is in the latitude of South Carolina, and nine tenths of it is further south than New Orleans. Thus situated, the climate of the country generally, as might be expected, is hot, — in some parts very hot. The temperature is affected by proximity to the sea-coast and elevation above the sea as well as by the latitude. In the provinces on the sea-shore on the eastern and western side of the peninsula, the heat is moderated by the sea-breezes, and the extremes of heat and cold are much less than inland places in the same latitude. In the provinces situated within the tropics or to the south of a line drawn from Calcutta to Cambay, the heat is everywhere severe in the hot months, and ice or frost is seldom seen in the cold months. The houses, whether European or native, with the exception of a few sanatory stations on the highest hills, have no chimneys or conveniences of any kind for using fire for comfort in any part of the year. In the great plains bordering on the Ganges and the Indus, which are low and remote from the sea, the heat is generally very severe in the hot months. The extremes here are greater than in the southern provinces. In the northern provinces snow and ice are frequent in the winter months.

The heat of the sun in India is more intense than in the United States when at the same altitude. The difference is also much greater there between the temperature in the sun and in the shade than it is in this country. Hence exposure to the rays of the sun is often injurious and is carefully to be avoided by all who have European constitutions, when no injury would be experienced from them in America. Europeans cannot endure the labor and continued exertion in India, which they can and do in their native climate. The injury and sufferings experienced vary according to the difference of temperature, peculiarity of constitution, habits of living, etc. But in all the hot districts such exposure, labor, and continued exertion soon produce prostration of strength, disease, and death.* This fact

* Perhaps the inquiry may occur how can this fact or opinion be reconciled with the conquest and government of the country by the English? An answer to this inquiry will be found when we come to treat of the British conquest and administration of India in another part of this work.

is as well established and as well known to all Europeans in India, as it is that they differ in complexion and personal appearance from the natives of the country. The native constitution has become adapted to the climate, and compared with Europeans they suffer but little from the heat. The lower classes will carry on their agricultural and other occupations daily, and will continue in their usual health in places and circumstances where Europeans generally would soon fail, sicken, and die.*

The sensation of cold and the suffering from it, are greater in India than in Europe and America at the same temperature. This soon becomes obvious to people on their first beginning to reside in that country, and such continues to be their experience. The native population are easily affected by the cold, and they suffer much from it. This arises in part from their peculiar constitution, adapted as it is to endure heat and *enjoy* a hot climate, and partly from their not having sufficient and suitable clothes, houses, etc.

The temperature of any place, as already remarked, depends upon its elevation and distance from the ocean as well as upon its latitude. This is more obvious in hot than in cold climates.

* While a change from the climate of Europe or of the United States at once to a tropical climate produces this effect on the same constitution, there can be no reasonable doubt that if the European constitution should be gradually subjected to the influence of a tropical climate through several generations, perhaps through several centuries, it would become as much adapted to the climate of India as the constitutions of the Hindus now are. Perhaps it would require as long to effect this change by each successive generation proceeding to a hotter climate, as it does to produce the complexion of the southern Asiatics. No one can proceed from England or any country in its latitude to the south cape of India or Ceylon, examining all the intermediate classes of people, without becoming satisfied that the difference in complexion is to be found in the climate and other coöperating causes. The complexion of the Jews wherever found confirms this opinion. When dispersed from Judea at the destruction of Jerusalem, the Jews being of common origin and living in a small country must have been of the same complexion. But now, wherever they have lived for several centuries and followed the occupations, customs, habits, etc., of the other classes of the inhabitants, they have become of the same complexion with them. The Jews in India, whose ancestors settled there many centuries ago, have become of the same complexion as other classes of the people of similar occupations and in similar circumstances. The same is true of the Jews settled in Arabia, Egypt, and western Asia, compared with other classes of the inhabitants in those places, as I saw when I was in those countries.

The mean temperature of January in Calcutta is 67°; in Madras it is 77°, and in Bombay 78°.

The mean temperature of May, which as it precedes the rainy season, is generally the hottest month of the year, in Calcutta is 83°; in Madras it is 87°; and in Bombay 85°. In New York, Philadelphia, and Boston, the mean temperature of July does not generally exceed 70°, thus showing the difference in the hottest weather to be 15°. These facts show that the average temperature of the coldest months in some of the largest cities in India, is several degrees higher than the average temperature of the hottest month in the large cities of the United States.

In the peninsular part of India fires are not generally necessary for comfort in houses, and chimneys are seldom seen. Cooking is usually done in out-houses. Various means are used in the hot months to mitigate the heat and to make houses comfortable. The more common way is to suspend a ventilator called *punka* in the rooms, which are generally high. Punkas are generally small frames covered with cloth and in the form of a board or plank, its length varying with the room or part to be ventilated, and its breadth from 18 to 36 inches. Punkas are suspended by ropes so that they can be swung just over the heads of persons standing, and when swung they produce an agreeable circulation of the air. These punkas are much used in houses, offices, churches, etc. Another method is to hang curtains of bamboo and other materials before doors and windows, and these being kept constantly wet, the air passing through them is cool. Another method is to place a ventilator constructed somewhat like a winnowing machine in some central part of the house, and by working it and hanging wet curtains over the doors, the air is kept moist and cool. Some such means for cooling the atmosphere are as necessary for people in health or in sickness in India, as fires in stoves and furnaces are for comfort in the United States in the winter season.

In the valleys and plains of the interior of the peninsula, and of the Ganges and the Indus, the temperature in the hot months is often greater than it is in Calcutta, or Madras, or Bombay, and in the cool months the cold is greater. The temperature also fluctuates more in such districts in any given time, as in a day or a week, and the extremes of heat and cold are greater in the course of a year.

In nothing does India differ more from Europe and America than in the seasons. The year is not divided there into seasons of spring, summer, autumn, and winter, and these words are seldom if ever used in reference to that country. Instead of the seasons current in the temperate climates, the common division of the year in India is into the rainy and fair seasons. In the central and northern provinces they sometimes speak of the rainy season, the cool season, and the hot season, or months. And in some provinces on the eastern side of the peninsula, they sometimes speak of the year as divided into the south-west monsoon and the north-east monsoon.

The rainy season, generally called the monsoon, is commonly reckoned to include four months, namely, June, July, August, and September. It comes from the south-west, and the clouds pour down the accumulated stores they have been gathering for some months over the Indian Ocean. The approach is indicated in the latter part of May by the atmosphere becoming hazy and moist, by large banks of watery-looking clouds in the afternoon, and by white fleecy clouds resting on the hills and mountains for some hours in the morning. These phenomena are so sure indications of its approach that people accustomed to observe them, are seldom overtaken by surprise. In some provinces, especially in the mountain districts and on the table-lands, there is much heavy thunder and vivid lightning at the commencement and again at the close of the rainy season. The monsoon commences at Cape Comorin and proceeds northward extending over all parts of India, except a tract on the Coromandel Coast. The greatest quantity falls in the low provinces near the sea and in mountainous districts. On the western coast of the peninsula the quantity varies from 70 to 100 inches. On the eastern coast the quantity is generally less. So also in the Deckan and in the great valley of the Ganges. On the Ghat mountains the quantity of rain that falls in the four months of the monsoon often exceeds 200 inches, and sometimes amounts to 300 inches. The tops of some of these high mountains are enveloped in thick fog and clouds, and have almost incessant rain for several months. The cascades formed by the floods of rain at this season are often sublime and beautiful.

The Coromandel Coast is so much sheltered by the mountains and high table-land of Mysore on the south-west that but little rain falls in the months, which in other parts of India are called the rainy reason. The provinces on this coast have their rain chiefly in the months of October and November, and it comes from the Bay of Bengal. Hence the inhabitants there speak of the south-west monsoon and of the north-east monsoon. In Bengal the rains come generally from the south, and the same clouds pass over the great valley of the Ganges, gradually turning to the north-west in the direction of the chain of the Himalaya mountains till they reach Cashmere and the Punjab, where the rains become comparatively light.

The rainy months are the natural season of production over all India. The earth, having become dry and hot, often to the depth of several feet, absorbs the first heavy rains. But the ground soon becomes saturated, and the warm state of the earth and of the atmosphere day and night adds force and vigor to the ordinary productive powers of nature. Vegetation springs up with a degree of rapidity and grows with a luxuriousness quite unknown in temperate climates. The change in the whole face of nature is great and surprising. In a few weeks all the tanks and ponds are full. Streams flow in channels where there had been no water for months, and rivers which had become almost dry, fill their channels, and bursting their banks occasion great damage. The rains close gradually, continuing longer in some provinces than in others. September is included in the rainy season, though generally on the sea-shore and in the large and low plains but little rain falls in this month. In the mountainous districts and on high table-land the rains often continue into October, and then close with heavy showers and much thunder and lightning.

From the close of the rainy season till June, the weather over the greater part of the country is fair. There is seldom a shower of rain or a cloudy day. The atmosphere, especially in the mornings, is often smoky and foggy. The ground is dry and parched, and the wind often raises clouds of dust. Vegetation except now and then in spots cultivated by irrigation, becomes dry and apparently dead. Cattle, horses, etc., graze wherever they can find any thing to eat, but they become lean and require fodder, which is provided for them in the rainy season, as provision is made in America in summer to supply the wants of winter. Trees, whether scattered or in forests, generally retain their leaves, but they have not the verdure and freshness of the rainy season. They must root deep in the ground and require little moisture, or they would dry up and perish during such a drought and heat of seven or eight months' duration. Those districts which have no forests and few trees, appear barren, dreary, and desolate. Water fit to drink often becomes very scarce, the springs, wells, and streams drying up. In the months of March, April, and May, the *mirage** often appears in great beauty for some hours in the middle of the day. In some districts hot winds blow for some hours in the middle of the day, and they are very withering and enervating. The change from the hot months to the rainy season is earnestly desired by all classes, Europeans and natives. The temperature then at once becomes cooler and humid, and the sky is overcast with clouds most of the time for several months.

DISEASES.

Cholera is believed to have originated in India and for many years its ravages were confined to that country, but it has now become known by sorrowful experience in nearly all parts of the

* The following is an extract from the writer's journal when on a tour in the Deckan in 1836. "To day at several places on the road the atmospherical phenomenon called *mirage*, appeared in great variety and beauty. Sometimes it appeared like a broad river, flowing with a rapid current and agitated by the wind. In another place it exhibited the appearance of a lake, several miles in extent, studded with islands and ruffled with waves. This phenomenon is not uncommon in the Deckan, in the dry season. I have several times seen it before, but never in such variety and beauty as I saw it to-day. The name in the native language is *mrugzul*, literally *deer-water*, and the people say it is so called because the deer, deceived in believing places exhibiting these phenomena to be streams and ponds of water, are often seen running to them, and then from one place to another, pursuing the floating vapor in the delusive hope of quenching their thirst."

world. It is generally committing its ravages in some parts of the country, and its appearance in any place does not excite much attention or anxiety, till cases of it have become frequent, and many of them have proved fatal. Great consternation then seizes all classes, and as many as can find means, escape for their lives, so that villages and even districts are for a while almost deserted. This disease has been a great scourge to India, and little progress has been made in ascertaining the causes, or discovering any remedy for it. Fevers, dysentery, hepatic affections, rheumatism, ophthalmia, and leprosy are frequent diseases. Of the last mentioned there are two or three different kinds. One of these, called sometimes the black leprosy, I have no doubt is the disease described by Moses in the laws given to the Jews.* It is a dreadful disease, hereditary, contagious, and incurable. I do not wonder at the strictness of the laws of Moses concerning it. When an attack of disease becomes a clearly developed case of this kind of leprosy, the unhappy subject is separated from his family and all society, almost as much as such an one would have been of old among the Jews. Such persons often live for several years, and it is not easy to conceive of human beings more diseased, distressed, helpless, and hideous than they become. There is another kind of leprosy which appears to be the same as is mentioned in several places in the Scriptures.† This disease makes its first appearance in a small white spot or spots on some part of the body, which increase till the skin over the greater part and sometimes over the whole body becomes changed into a dull, dirty white color, the person thus exhibiting a very singular appearance. This disease does not occasion much suffering, and sometimes does not appear to affect the general health. It is said to be incurable and is considered a great affliction, though it does not, like the black leprosy, debar the sufferer from all domestic and social intercourse. A disease called *elephantiasis*, very frequent in some districts, has been regarded by many, though perhaps not properly, as a kind of leprosy. It has the appearance of leprosy and dropsy combined. The disease is chiefly confined to the lower limbs, which become much

* See 13th and 14th chapters of Leviticus.

† See Ex. 4 : 6. Num. 12 : 10. 2 Kings 5 : 27.

swollen, heavy, and unwieldy, of very unsightly appearance, and are often in an inflamed and painful state. This disease is said to be incurable, but I am not aware that it occasions death.

The climate of India generally is not healthy for Europeans; indeed, to such persons some parts of the country are particularly unhealthy. But this is not the general character of the climate in respect to the native population. If the inhabitants of India could be as well supplied with wholesome food, have as comfortable clothing and houses, and when ill, could have as good medical attendance and care as the inhabitants of America and Europe have, perhaps they would generally have as good health, though probably the average duration of human life would still be some years less. In all classes both sexes arrive at puberty 2 or 3 years earlier than in Europe and America, and they appear to be as far advanced in life in their physical and mental faculties at 40 or 45 years of age, as the people of Europe and America do at 50 or 55; consequently the average duration of life among them must be considerably less.

MOUNTAINS, RIVERS, ETC.

Cape Comorin, the southern point of India, is the termination of the great mountain range commonly called in European geography the Ghats, but by the native population the Syadree mountains. They extend from Cape Comorin in a north-west direction nearly parallel with the coast at a distance varying from 30 to 50 miles to latitude 21° or nearly 1,000 miles. Their height varies from 2,000 to 4,000 feet; and in a few places it approaches 5,000 feet. These mountains rise abruptly on the west side from nearly the level of the sea, but on the east side the descent is small. They are generally covered with forests and their appearance adds much to the sublime and beautiful scenery visible from ships proceeding along the western coast. The Neilgherry Hills are east of the Ghats, between latitude 10° and 11°. They separate the table-land of Mysore from Travancore, and cover a considerable area. Some of these mountains rise to the height of 7,000 and 8,000 feet, and furnish scenery of great sublimity and beauty. Here are several important sanatory stations, which are much resorted to by Europeans.

The climate varies but little through the year, and is delightfully cool and invigorating, when compared with the low country and the sea-coast. The country of Mysore is bounded on the east by a range of mountains which extend to the river Krishna or Kistna, but they are not so high as the Ghats near the western coast.

In the north part of the Deckan is a range of high hills called the Sautpoora mountains, which are situated between the Taptee and Nerbudda rivers. The Nerbudda is generally regarded as the dividing line between the Deckan and Hindustan. On the north side of this river is a range of hills extending for several hundred miles, called the Vindya mountains. The Himalaya mountains form the northern boundary of India, separating it from Thibet. These mountains extend from the Brahmaputra to the Indus, more than 1,000 miles. They are the highest mountains in the world, in some places exceeding 27,000 feet.* As they rise from the valley of the Ganges to the regions of perpetual snow, they present every variety of climate, from the torrid to the frozen zone. The scenery of them from different places on the plain, and in ascending them, the views of the immense plains below and of the towering heights above surpass the expectations of all who have described them. Says Bishop Heber, "We could see one range of mountains after another, quite as rugged and generally speaking more bare than those we had left, till the horizon was terminated by a vast range of ice and snow, extending its battalion of white glittering spears from east to west as far as the eye could follow it, the principal points rising like towers on the glittering rampart, but all connected by a chain of humbler glaciers." Says Raper, "From the edge of the scarp the eye extended over 7 or 8 distinct ranges of hills, till the view was terminated by the Himalaya or Snowy Mountains. It is necessary for a person to place himself in our situation before he can form a just conception of the scene. The depth of the valley below, the progressive elevation of the intermediate hills and the majestic splendor of the cloud-capt Himalaya, formed

* Dhawalgiri is 27,462 feet, Juwahir is 25,740 feet, Jumnautri is 25,500. These mountains are higher than any other in the world, Chimborazo the highest peak of the Andes being only 21,464 feet.

so grand a picture that the mind was impressed with a sensation of dread rather than of pleasure." Says Elphinstone, "The stupendous height of those mountains, the numerous nations by whom they are seen, and who seem to be brought together by this common object, and the awful and undisturbed solitude which reign amidst their eternal snows, fill the mind with admiration and astonishment which no language can express."

Simla on the south-west side of the Himalaya, Darjeling in Bengal, Abu in Gujerat, Khandalla and Mahabuleshwur on the Ghats nearly east from Bombay, and Ootacummund, Khottagherry, and some other places on the Neilgherry and Pulney Hills in Mysore, are much resorted to as health-stations by Europeans, especially in the hot months. These hill-stations correspond in some degree to the watering places in America, as Saratoga, Newport, Cape May, etc. There is, however, this important difference. A large part of India is as hot upon an average through the year, as the cities in the United States are in the summer months. And so many of the people at these sanatory stations are persons, who, having become enervated by long residence in the low country, continue at these places especially at those in the southern part of the peninsula, for 1, 2, and 3 years. By these changes many are able to prolong their residence in India, and for some diseases the climate of these mountains is believed to be the best that could be found in any country, better than a voyage on sea, or a residence in Europe or America.

Bengal and the lands bordering on the Ganges, in some places for 100 miles and more on each side of the banks, are perfectly level. In ascending this noble river the country appears for some hundred miles like an unlimited prairie. A large extent of country bordering on the lower part of the Indus, is level, and between this river and Ajmere is a sandy barren desert, extending for several hundred miles almost without cultivation or inhabitants. Very little rain falls over this large region, and the districts bordering upon it frequently suffer from drought and consequent famine. Gujerat is generally level but is fertile. In some parts of the Deckan are plains nearly level, extending as far as the eye can reach, while in other places hills or mountains generally running in ranges diversify the face of the country.

The Indus rises in Thibet north of the Himalaya mountains, runs first north-west and then south-west for several hundred miles, and enters India west of Cashmere. It receives large tributaries as the Sutlege, the Hydrastes, the Chenab, and the Hydaspis in the Punjab, and then flows nearly south into the Indian Ocean. Its whole course is 1,700 miles. Steamboats and various kinds of river craft ply upon it, but its navigation is much obstructed by sand-banks, sudden changes in the channels, inundations, and rapids. The Ganges rises among the Himalayas on the south side, and flows through the most celebrated, fertile, and populous part of India for 1,600 miles into the Bay of Bengal. This river is held in great estimation by the Hindus, and particular places on it, as Hurdwar, Allahabad, and Benares, are among the most celebrated places of pilgrimage in India. There is much commerce on this river, but the sudden inundations, changes in the channel, etc., often make the navigation tedious and dangerous. The Brahmaputra is nearly as large and as long as the Ganges, but as it flows most of the distance through territories not subject to the English, it is not so well known, and is less used for commerce. The Nerbudda separates Hindustan from the Deckan. Its course is nearly west for 700 or 800 miles to the Gulf of Cambay. The channel of this river is very rocky. In the rainy season the current is so rapid, and in the hot season the water is so low, that there is but little commerce upon it. The same is true of the Taptee for most of its course of 500 miles into the Gulf of Cambay. The city of Surat is on this river a few miles from its mouth. All the large rivers of the peninsula, as the Godavery, the Krishna, and the Cavery, flow into the Bay of Bengal. These rivers are very useful for irrigating the lands on their banks for cultivation, but the inundations and currents are so great and sudden in the rainy season, and the water is reduced so low in the dry season, that they are little used for manufactures or for commerce. The mouths of these rivers are also much obstructed by shallows and sand-banks.

POPULATION.

India appears to have been a populous part of the world from its earliest authentic history. It probably had as large a population 1,500 and 2,000 years ago and even before that time, as it has had for 200 and 300 years past since it became known to the nations of Europe. A census of Bengal and of some other parts subject to the English has been taken, but there has never been any census of the whole of India, and so the population of all the country must be a matter of estimation. Hamilton in his large work on India has given a table of the different provinces, exhibiting the population of each, as enumerated and estimated, and makes the total to be 134,000,000. The authors of the Encyclopedia Britannica in an ably written and carefully prepared article on Hindustan, have also estimated the population at 134,000,000. Mr. McCulloch in his geography estimated the population at 131,750,000. Elphinstone in his late work on India estimates the population by the best information he could obtain, at 140,000,000. These estimates were made before the conquest of Scinde and the Punjab. In the debates, reports, etc., in Parliament when the renewal of the East India Company's charter, or the future government of India, was lately under consideration, the entire population was assumed to be 150,000,000. This number included Scinde and the Punjab. Of this population some estimates make one eighth and others make one tenth part to be Mohammedans.— A more particular description of the different classes comprising this great population, will be given in another part of this work.

ANIMALS, ETC.

The elephant, either wild or domestic, is found in all parts of India. In their wild state they are found chiefly in the forests on the Malabar Coast, in Assam and Rajpootana. An elephant at his birth is about 3 feet high, and is said to be from 20 to 30 years in attaining his full growth. Their common height is 9 and 10 feet. In some extreme cases they are said to reach 11 feet. They were formerly in great demand among the native powers for purposes of state, and were used in war. In the army of Porus, who resisted Alexander the Great in his invasion of India, were 200 war elephants. When Mahmoud of Ghizni invaded India, Jypal the Raja of Lahore came against him with a large army in which were "350 chain elephants." Ferishta says that Mahmoud of Ghizni had at one time 1,300 war elephants, obtained chiefly from India, and that Acber near the close of his reign had 5,000, which appears not improbable considering his great wealth and power. The changes which have taken place in the political state and government of the country, and in the tactics and instruments of war since the invention of fire-arms, have greatly diminished the number and value of elephants. Lions are not unfrequent in the north-western provinces. The male differs from the African lion, in having no mane. "The lion," says Bishop Heber, "which was long supposed to be unknown in India, is now ascertained to exist in considerable numbers in the districts of Saharunpore and Loodiana." Tigers are found in all parts of the country. The largest and fiercest tigers in the world are found in the lower part of Bengal in the large forests and jungles near the mouths of the Ganges and Brahmaputra. These are often called the royal Bengal tigers. The hunting of tigers was formerly a favorite sport of the emperors and princes of the country. It is a favorite and often very dangerous sport of Europeans. Leopards are common and are large and fierce. The rhinoceros is found in the forests in the eastern provinces of Bengal. The camel is frequent in all parts of India, and is much used for riding and carrying burdens. Horses are very common, but generally small. The best horses in India are brought from Arabia and Persia. Buffaloes are domesticated and kept for milk. Cattle are abundant. Bears, wolves, wild dogs, and hogs are abundant in some provinces; so also are antelopes and deer of various kinds; also hyenas, monkeys, porcupines, jackals, foxes, etc. Sheep and goats are kept in great abundance. The wool of sheep is coarse, generally black and of little value. The English have made repeated efforts to improve the quality of the wool of the Indian sheep, but with little effect. It has been found that if sheep with fine wool are taken from cold climates to India, their wool soon becomes coarse like the indigenous sheep and so is of little value.

Cross-breeding has not yet produced the results which were expected. The celebrated Cashmere shawls are made of the fine hair or wool of goats peculiar to that country.

Of serpents there are many kinds; the anaconda, or boa constrictor, grows to a great size in the forests; the much dreaded *cobra*, or *cobra de capello*, is very frequent; there are many other kinds of poisonous snakes. Scorpions of different kinds are frequent. Musquitoes are so numerous and venomous that it is necessary in nearly all parts of the country in the hot months, and in many places through the year, to sleep under gauze curtains. Vultures, eagles, buzzards, peacocks, ducks, etc., abound in different parts of the country. Fish are abundant, and fishermen are a numerous class on the sea-shore and along the large rivers. Alligators, turtles, etc., are found in the creeks and rivers.

MINERALS, ETC.

There are no gold or silver mines now wrought to any extent in India. Golconda was once celebrated for its diamonds, but these mines are not now wrought, and diamonds are seldom found. Cornelian and agates are found and exported in considerable quantities. Iron ore is abundant in several places, but the want or expense of fuel prevents these mines being wrought to any considerable extent, and so the country is chiefly supplied with iron from Europe. Marble is abundant in Rajpootana and rock salt in the Punjab. Saltpetre is produced in great quantities in Bengal, and much is exported to the European and American markets. Coal has been found in several places in Bengal, and is coming into extensive use. It has also been discovered on the banks of the Nerbudda, but for want of means of transportation it has been but little used. The railroads which have been projected and are now in the process of construction, will pass through these coal beds. The coal will then be available for manufactures and commerce, and its use for these purposes will form a new era in the history of India.

Cotton is indigenous and is produced in abundance over several provinces. Its cultivation might be extended almost indefinitely. The sugar-cane is cultivated, and large quantities of sugar are exported. Indigo and silk are produced and exported in large quantities to Europe and America. In some provinces the poppy is cultivated, and opium is one of the principal articles of export. Rice is cultivated in the low grounds of the peninsula, in Gujerat and in the great valley of the Ganges, and in all these provinces is the principal article of food. In districts where the nature of the soil or want of water will not admit of the cultivation of rice, wheat, barley, jowaree, bazaree and other kinds of grain are produced in abundance. The forests produce excellent wood for building and furniture. The teak, or Indian oak as it is sometimes called, has long been celebrated for its hardness and durability, and some of the best ships in the British navy and in their mercantile marine have been built in India. Elegant furniture is made of several different kinds of wood, among which is a kind of ebony called blackwood, and a species of mahogany called jack-wood. Of bamboos, there are several different kinds and all are applied to useful purposes. The palm and cocoa-nut tree are abundant, the groves or forests often extending in the southern provinces for miles in every direction.

It will be seen from the above that India is rich in natural productions and resources. Of its manufactures and commerce some account will be given in another part of this work.

PART II.

HISTORY.

CHAPTER I.

THE HINDU PERIOD.

THE early history of India is involved in much obscurity. There are no means of determining the date of any event previous to the invasion of Alexander the Great, which is generally reckoned to have been 325 years before the Christian era. India was then found to be a civilized and populous country, containing several separate and independent nations, and there was evidence that it had been such for several centuries.* Nor is it possible to find any authenticated facts, or to prepare any regular, connected, and consistent history of the country for some centuries after that invasion. From that great event till the Mohammedan invasion, a period of more than 1,000 years, the history of India is nearly as obscure and the want of materials for compiling it is nearly as great, as they are in respect to the period before that country became known to the nations of western Asia and Europe by that memorable invasion of the great hero of antiquity. Indeed, history is a department of

* "In reading any thing written about India, it is always necessary to bear in mind that India is only a name applied by Europeans to a great many countries, peopled by different nations and races of men, as different from each other in language, habits, and customs, as the various nations inhabiting modern Europe. The natives do not know what we mean by India, unless we inform them. They speak of countries and nations in which the Hindu religion is professed only in the same way that we speak of countries and nations professing Christianity. India as one country, is unknown to them, unless they have an idea of the lands where their religion prevails, similar to what we have when we speak of Christendom. The Bengalee, the Hindustanee, the Mahratta, and the Tamulian, are as much men of different nations, as the English, the French, the Germans, and the Italians."—*Buyers.*

literature which was quite unknown, or at least uncultivated, among the ancient nations of India — a remarkable fact concerning a people so much civilized, and who have left so much literature, and some of it of a high character on other subjects.

And yet the Hindus have what they believe to be genuine histories of their country, contained in works which claim to be of divine origin. These works are their Purans and poems, written long ago, and still held in great veneration. These works, if not of the nature of true history, yet show the state and character of the people of the ages when they were written. They have had much influence on the state and character of the people of modern India, and so are subjects of great interest.

The first thing that strikes us in examining these works, is their extravagant claims to great antiquity. In this respect however the Hindus have only done like other ancient nations, who were not compelled to connect their origin with definite facts and acknowledged events. The Athenians boasted that they were as ancient as the sun. The Arcadians pretended that they were older than the moon. The Lacedæmonians called themselves the sons of the earth. The Egyptians pretended that they were older than any other nation. The Chaldeans pretended that they could show their history for 150,000 years. The Burmese and the Chinese claim an origin yet more extravagant and incredible. But these pretensions to antiquity are supported by no well-authenticated facts or events, and they furnish no materials for connected and credible history.

The Hindu chronology, as contained in their sacred books, consists of four periods called yugas. The first period is called the Satya yuga, and continued for 1,728,000 years from the creation. The second period is called the Tret yuga, and continued for 1,296,000 years. The third period is called the Dwarpur yuga, and continued for 864,000 years. And the fourth period is called the Kalee yuga, which is the present age or period, and is to continue for 432,000 years. Of this last period, they believe nearly 5,000 years have passed. The amount of these four periods is 4,320,000 years.* They refer to longer periods than these, as 4,320,000,000 years make a kalpa

* There is some difference in this chronology in different works. I have given the one that appears to have the most authority.

or day of Brahm. Each kalpa contains 14 periods called manawantaras. Each manawantara contains 71 mota yugas, or great ages, and each mota yuga contains 4 yugas of unequal length. At the end of a kalpa the world is destroyed, but is to be renewed again. A comparison of these yugas with the Hindu astronomy, will show that they were fixed with reference to certain supposed retrospective astronomical conjunctions or events. Their astronomers were Brahmins, the hereditary priesthood, and their teachings and writings, whatever these might be, were received as true, and so these assumed eras became the generally believed chronology of the country.

The same sacred books contain other things yet more marvellous. Thus it is asserted that in the Satya yuga, human life was 100,000 years, and the human stature was 21 cubits, or about 37 feet high. In the Tret yuga, life was reduced to 10,000 years. In the Dwarpur yuga it was reduced to 1,000 years, and in the Kalee yuga — the present age — it has been reduced to 100 years. Some of the ancient heroes are declared to have had 10 and 12 faces, and 15 and 20 arms. A celebrated king by the name of Sagur had 60,000 sons, all born in a pumpkin, nourished in pans of milk, and all consumed and reduced to ashes by the curse of one Rishi. The sun is declared to be 800,000 miles from the earth, and the moon to be twice as far, or 800,000 miles beyond the sun. The earth is flat and circular, and its circumference is declared to be 4,000,000,000 miles. Mount Sumeru * is declared to be 600,000 miles high, and to descend 128,000 miles below the surface of the earth. The changes of day and night are believed to be caused by the sun revolving around this mountain. So when it is day in the countries on the south side, it is night in those on the opposite side, etc. Their astronomy † and geography contain numerous

* Probably this name was then given to the Himalaya mountains, which in that early age of the world were unexplored and little known, and when in the course of time and geographical research these mountains and the countries around them became so well known as to show that these descriptions could not be applied to them, the brahmins said that Sumeru was to the north of these mountains in countries yet unexplored. And such is still the opinion of brahmins and the great body of the Hindus who believe in the truth of these works.

† The Purans say that the sun is 800,000 miles, (100,000 yozuns) from the earth, and the moon is 800,000 miles beyond the sun. The constellations are 800,000 miles beyond the moon. Mercury is 1,600,000 miles (200,000 yozuns)

statements equally erroneous, absurd, and ridiculous. And as these rest on the same authority as their chronology, it is obvious that, as far as containing any authority of themselves, they are all to be regarded alike; that is, not as works of fact but of fancy and fiction; not as works of reason and revelation, but of romance and imagination.*

It is evident that no reliance can be put in works containing such statements in chronology, geography, and astronomy. Doubtless some of the kings and sages, whose names are mentioned and whose exploits and wisdom are celebrated in these works, were real personages, but the accounts of them are so intermixed with fancies and fables that no confidence can be put in them. The ancient history of India must be compiled from a discretionary use of such facts and fragments as can be gathered up, and these must be arranged according to the most approved chronology used in the history of other nations.

ABORIGINAL INHABITANTS.

The people we now commonly call Hindus and whose religion is called Hinduism or Brahminism, were not the first

beyond them, and Venus is at the same distance beyond Mercury. Mars is at the same distance beyond Venus. Jupiter is at the same distance from Mars, and Saturn at the same distance beyond Jupiter. From Saturn to Ursa Major is 800,000 miles, and from Ursa Major to Druv (the polar star) is 800,000 miles. The residence of the chief gods is 8,000,000 miles beyond Druv, etc.

* The following is from their Shasters: — Mount Meru or Sumeru is of the shape of an inverted cone, and is 128,000 miles in circumference at the base, and 256,000 miles at the top. On this mountain are the different heavens of Vishnu, Sheva, Indra, etc. The clouds ascend about one third the height of the mountain. There are great mountains around the base, on which are trees 8,800 miles high, and producing fruit as large as an elephant. Around this mountain are several countries, the farthest of which is surrounded by a salt sea. Beyond are six other seas, namely, the sea of sugar-cane juice, the sea of spirituous liquors, the sea of clarified butter, the sea of curds, the sea of milk, and the sea of fresh water. Beyond all these seas is a country of gold as large as the rest of the earth; beyond this are chains of mountains, and then a land of darkness supposed to be hell. — Strange as these notions appear, they have been believed in India for many hundred years past. I have often seen maps of the earth drawn by the Hindus according to these notions, with mount Sumeru in the centre of it, and then the different seas encircling it.

inhabitants of India. This is evident from the ancient history of the country (such facts and fragments as we have of it), and from the present state and character of the inhabitants. There are no means of ascertaining when the first inhabitants settled in the country. Probably it was soon after the dispersion of mankind from the great valley of the Euphrates. The climate, the fertility, and the rivers of India would naturally make it an inviting country for settlement. All records and all traditions refer to the west and the north-west, as the source whence the population flowed into the country. The first inhabitants of India were a rude people, who in the course of time became divided into different governments. The different languages still in use show the nations into which India was at some early period divided, while the rude tribes in different parts of the country, who have little or no knowledge of the Brahminical system are clearly the remains of the original population. The Bheels in central India, the Coolees in Gujerat, the Goands in Orissa, and the Shanars and other tribes or castes in the southern provinces of the peninsula, are scattered fragments of the aborigines, or earliest population of the country. They had not the distinctions of caste among them, and they had no sacred books. Their principal objects of worship were imaginary spiritual beings, who were believed to inhabit certain places, sometimes to appear in a visible form, and to interpose as they pleased in human affairs. They had priests of their own class, who pretended and were believed to have communication with these supposed spiritual beings and to be able, by incantations, prayers, offerings, and imprecations, to avert their displeasure and to secure their favor. Some of these beings were supposed to be benevolent, but they were generally believed to be malevolent. Hence fear and dread were the predominant feelings in their religion, and their worship was chiefly designed to secure themselves and their interests from injury. If they could be assured that these beings would let them entirely alone and in no way trouble or hurt them, they wished for nothing more. They would ask for no favors from them.

These beings were often supposed to be the spirits of persons who had died, and who from feelings of sympathy, or affection, or envy, or revenge haunted certain persons and places. Probably most of these beings were supposed to be spirits of this class. Accidents, misfortunes, calamities, insanity, and epidemics were ascribed to their agency.

There are no means for ascertaining how long the aborigines of India continued in this state, but probably such was their character for some centuries. Indeed, such is still the state and character of several tribes in different parts of the country, while in some districts the religion of the people is evidently a mixture of their primitive superstitions and the system commonly called Brahminism or Hinduism.

ORIGIN OF THE HINDUS AND HINDUISM.

It is now generally agreed among orientalists that the people, who are now commonly called the Hindus, were an invading and conquering nation, who came from the north-west into India. Sir William Jones was of the opinion that they came from Iran. Adelung was of the same opinion. Klaproth believed they came from the Caucasian Mountains. Schlegel ascribes their origin to some place on the border of the Caspian Sea, and Kennedy is of the opinion that the Brahmins first formed a community on the plains of the Euphrates. They brought with them the Hindu religion and the distinctions of caste. Or more probably they then instituted these distinctions by dividing themselves into the three higher castes, namely, the Brahmins to be the hereditary priesthood, the Kshatryas to be the military caste, and the merchants, traders, etc., who accompanied them to constitute the Vaishyas, while they included the lower people who accompanied them and the inhabitants of the country, in the Shudra caste. The distinctions of caste with the rights and privileges which the three highest shared in common among them, the degraded state of the whole Shudra caste, and the determination to keep them in the degraded state described in the Institutes of Menu, clearly indicate what parties were the conquerors and intended to rule, and what parties were the conquered and were to be ruled.

It is the general opinion of orientalists that the Vedas were compiled and put into their present form in the 14th century before the Christian era, and that this compilation was composed of notions, rites, etc., in previous use among them. According to this opinion the invasion of India by the nation or tribes who introduced the present system of Hinduism, took place as early as the exodus of the Israelites from Egypt. This invading and conquering nation had a much higher character of civilization than the inhabitants they found in India. They became settled on the banks of the Ganges and Jumna, and there they matured their civil and religious polity. According to the Institutes of Menu, supposed to be written 10 or 12 centuries before the Christian era, the three higher castes were to be invested with the sacred thread, and thence they are called the "twice born;" they were also to read the Vedas, and perform sacrifices. So these three castes must then have understood the Sanscrit language. Probably Sanscrit of the style of the Vedas was then the vernacular language of the conquerors. The first, or original inhabitants of the country, inferior in civilization, with no hereditary priesthood and no sacred books or clearly defined religious system, presented but a feeble barrier against a religious system thus introduced and supported. Still the progress of Hinduism in some parts of India was slow. The Deckan and the country south from it long continued to follow their original superstitions, and even now the knowledge and influence of Brahminism over the great body of the people in the southern parts of the peninsula is small when compared with what it is in the central and northern provinces.

The Hindu system of religion and government became first established in the central and northern parts of India, and for some centuries the chief seat of their power and influence was in those places. The actions and events described in their Purans chiefly took place there, and there most of these books were written. In the Purans and early poems two races of kings are described, called the Race of the Sun and the Race of the Moon, or the Solar and the Lunar race. The Solar race reigned in Ayodhya, the modern Oude; and the Lunar race in Pruyag, the modern Allahabad. These two capitals were near together, and the families were closely allied in their origin and by intermarriages. The names of the kings of these pretended dynasties are all that is known of most of them. Indeed, even these names are perhaps as really fictitious as the duration of their reigns, which in some cases are said to have exceeded 10,000 years. Fifty-seven kings of the Solar race are said to have reigned in Ayodhya previous to Rama or Ramchundra, who appears to have been a real personage, and who probably lived in the 12th or 13th century before the Christian era. This king was the most celebrated sovereign in the ancient history of India, and he is reckoned one of the incarnations of Vishnu. But there is no credible history of his reign. All is mixed with fictions and fables. His life and reign have been a fruitful subject for the poets, but the most celebrated work is an epic poem by Valmeeki, called the Ramayana. In early life Rama, whose father Dushuruth was king of Ayodhya, became the son-in-law of the king of Mithili, another branch of the Solar race. Family troubles soon followed his marriage, and he was compelled to retire with Seeta his wife into the forests. While there, Rawun, the king of Singul-Dwip, or Ceylon, then on a visit or expedition to the north part of India, carried off Seeta. Rama collected a large army, made an expedition into Ceylon, and recovered his wife. From various notices in this poem, the country on the Ganges appears to have been at that time in a much higher state of civilization than the Deckan and the other countries through which Rama passed in his expedition to Ceylon.

The next work that throws any light upon the dark field of Indian history is the Mahabharat, written probably about a century after the Ramayana. This work is also an epic poem, celbrating the wars which took place among the princes of the Lunar race. In the wars as well as the causes and circumstances connected with them, Krishna, one of the reputed incarnations of Vishnu, was a distinguished if not the most prominent actor. The Lunar race had at this time become divided into many different branches in the principal cities in the central and northern parts of India, who appear to have been more frequently in a state of war than of peace with each other. After a long series of complicated intrigues and family and personal quarrels, the parties rallied all their strength for a general conflict. Fifty-six royal tribes were then assembled on the field of Kuru. The battle continued (so the poets say) for 18 days and with prodigious slaughter on both sides before the contest was decided. It appears from this poem that India was then divided into a large number of small separate governments, which were often engaged in wars with each other, and now and then uniting for more general wars, as in the great war here celebrated.

The Hindus are fond of the marvellous, and are so credulous that they readily assent to almost any thing that took place long ago, or in some distant part of the world. Under the influence of such feelings the fictions of poetry in the course of time began to be considered as the facts of history. And as the exploits ascribed to Krishna exceeded mere human power, the difficulty was removed by placing him among the incarnations of Vishnu. There was much in his conduct at different times, which was pleasing to the taste and habits of the Hindus generally; and thus deified, Krishna soon became one of the favorite gods, and few if any of the Hindu deities have been more worshipped.

Buluram, or Buludeva, sometimes described as one of the brothers of Krishna, was one of the same age, and his exploits are celebrated in the Mahabharat. He is said to have founded a city called Palibothra, probably the modern Patna, which became one of the most magnificent cities in India. The foundation of two or three other cities is also ascribed to Buluram. He also was deified, and he is often reckoned among the incarnations of Vishnu.

It has been already stated that the first inhabitants of India entered the country from the west or north-west, and at some subsequent period another nation from the same source invaded and conquered them, introducing a higher state of civilization with the system of religion called Hinduism or Brahminism, and which still continues to be the religion of the great body of the people. There are traditions and fragmentary records of other invasions from the same source in remote antiquity. But the earliest invasion of which we have any authentic history, was made by Darius when he was king of Persia. This celebrated monarch became king of Persia 518 years before Christ. He extended his power from the Mediterranean Sea to the river Indus, and not satisfied with this magnificent empire, he resolved to extend his authority over India. With this view he directed admiral Scylax to construct a flotilla of boats in the Punjab, and descending the river to explore the country to the sea. These orders the admiral executed, and he gave such a glowing account of the beauty of the country and the wealth of the inhabitants, on the Indus, that Darius resolved to add it to his dominions. He invaded India with a large force, defeated and dispersed the armies sent against him, and extended his authority over the provinces on the Indus. There are no means of ascertaining how far he conquered the country, but the conquest must have been extensive, as it yielded the largest revenue of any Satrapy of the Persian empire. Indeed, it is said, that in some years one third of the revenue came from India, and that while the Persian provinces paid their revenues in silver, the Indian provinces paid theirs in gold. We are indebted for this information to the Grecian historians, who obtained their knowledge from the Persians, who had seen India, and who told them that the people of the country who lived beyond the Persian conquests, "were of black complexion, that they did not kill animals for food, but lived upon rice, grain, and fruits, that they exposed to death those who were so sick that they were not expected to recover, that their horses were of a small breed, and that the people manufactured the cotton of the country into fine clothing." The nations thus referred to were doubtless those living in the great valley of the Ganges, and this description shows that the inhabitants of India 2,300 years ago, much resemble their descendants of the present day.

Gaudama, the author of Budhism in its present form, and so much revered by all who profess that system, was born in India about the time of the Persian invasion. But his life and system properly belong to the religious history of India, to be considered hereafter.

ALEXANDER'S INVASION.

The next great event in the political history of the country was its invasion by Alexander the Great, about two centuries after the invasion of Darius. Of the state of the provinces which Darius had annexed to his own dominions during this period we have no particular information. But from the state in which Alexander found them, it appears that in the reigns of the later Persian monarchs, the provinces on the Indus, or at least all to the east of the Indus, had recovered their independence. Alexander having subverted the Persian empire, directed his course towards India. Some say his object was to take possession of the eastern provinces of the Persian empire, which had assumed their independence. But it is more probable that his object was to extend his dominions by the conquest of India, of whose power and riches he had heard such marvellous accounts from the Persians. Having obtained possession of Cabul and there rested awhile, he proceeded towards India, requiring and when refused enforcing the submission of all the chiefs and people along his march. He reached the Indus near Attock, and crossed the river on a bridge of boats. He found India divided into separate and independent kingdoms. Two princes, Arbissares and Taxiles submitted to Alexander without making any resistance, and friendly relations were formed between them. He then proceeded to Hydaspes, now called Jylum, one of the rivers of the Punjab. The rainy season had commenced and the river was much swollen. Porus, king of the country, was on the opposite bank of the river, to oppose his passage. The Indian army was arranged with much skill; a long range of elephants, used to war, was placed along the shore in front of the army. As often as Alexander made arrangements to cross the river, he saw corresponding arrangements made by his enemy to resist him. He saw it was necessary to devise some new way, and to elude the observation of his vigilant enemy. He had obtained information that the river could be more easily passed at an island, some miles above, and taking 11,000 veterans he left his camp in a dark and stormy night, and proceeding to the island, they crossed the river before morning. As Alexander's camp presented the usual appearance in the morning, Porus was not aware of what had been done, till informed that some of the Greeks had crossed the river, and were approaching him. Supposing it must be some small detachment, he despatched his son against it. But his son was defeated and slain. Porus then learned with surprise that Alexander had himself passed the river with a large body of his army. He at once proceeded against him with 30,000 foot, 4,000 horse, and many chariots and elephants. The battle continued for several hours. Alexander's army consisting, as already stated, of 11,000 men, was very inferior in numbers, but their cool courage, their skill in using their weapons, and their impetuosity in attack made them irresistible. The Indian army gave way before them, and flight soon became general. But Porus mounted on the largest elephant, and surrounded by a few chosen troops, continued the battle, apparently determined to die fighting. Alexander admiring his gallantry and anxious to save his life, sent messengers to beseech him to surrender on honorable terms. To this arrangement he at length consented. When conducted into the presence of the emperor, and asked how he wished to be treated, he replied with a noble dignity, "As a king." Alexander was so much pleased with his manners and conduct in such trying circumstances that he gave him his liberty and established or confirmed him in his kingdom. Porus showed that he could appreciate such conduct in Alexander, and continued to be his ally and friend.

Having made an amicable arrangement with Porus, Alexander proceeded through a rich and populous country to the Hyphasis, now called the Sutlege. The natives of India must by this time have become aware of the nature and object of his invasion, and of the valor and general character of his army. Such an victorious army already within the borders of their country must have produced great excitement, if not consternation throughout all the nations and tribes of northern India. This state of the country and the accounts concerning the power, resources, and riches of its kings,* were well calculated to raise the ambition of Alexander to the highest pitch. He

* Such as the following, "Here he heard of the kingdom of Magadi on the Ganges, the mighty sovereign of which could bring 600,000 foot into the field with 300,000 horse and 9,000 elephants. He heard of the splendor of its capital, Palibothra, nine miles long, and his ambition was kindled to plant his standard on its ramparts."

No city of the name of Palibothra is now known in India. Some orientalists believe it stood where Allahabad now is; others assign its location to Patna, and others again to Rajamahl. It appears probable that Patna is a contraction of the ancient Palibothra under its modern name.

was at this time just 30 years of age, and by inheritance or conquest had obtained possession of all parts of the world then known, and previously supposed to be worth conquering and governing. He was at the head of such an army as no monarch ever before had under his command—an army trained first by his father and then by himself, an army superior to any they had ever encountered, everywhere accustomed to victory, and every one of them able in the day of battle to take the command of the whole. He had now opening before him a dazzling career into parts of the world hitherto very imperfectly known, but of which marvellous accounts were current through the western world.

But Alexander's army generally did not share in these feelings. Many of them were becoming advanced in age and wished to exchange the active labors of war for a quiet life. They had been long absent from their own country and desired to return home. Their labors had been hard and their sufferings had been great. They had accomplished all the objects for which they at first engaged in the war. They saw no reason or propriety in pursuing an apparently interminable career of conquest in unknown parts of the world merely for the further glory of their leader, who had already acquired more renown than any man ever had before him. And further, they saw that they would have to endure a climate more severe, enervating and sickly than they had ever known. These things were well calculated to make the army hitherto invincible refuse to proceed any further. Alexander commanded, he entreated, he threatened, and he wept, but all was in vain. The army continued inflexible. He was compelled to yield and to limit his conquest and his dominions to the Indus. Unable to proceed any further into India, he resolved to make somewhat further examination of the country that was now in his power. He caused a flotilla of boats, one account says 2,000, to be prepared. When all were ready, solemn sacrifices were offered according to the Grecian and to the Indian rites. A part of the army embarked in the boats, and the rest made arrangements to proceed along the banks of the river. And then with great shoutings and rejoicings they commenced their return homewards. Their progress down the Indus was delayed by wars with some of the tribes on the banks, and they were nine months in reaching the sea. On arriving at the mouth of the river, Nearchus with a part of the fleet proceeded to the Persian Gulf, while Alexander proceeded with the army to Persia.

It was Alexander's intention to return to India, but his death which occurred in less than two or three years, put an end to all his plans. From the works of the Greek authors who accompanied him, we may learn much concerning the state of the country and manners of the people at that time. The people were divided into classes or *castes*, among whom the Brahmins, called by some of the Greeks, gymnosophists and philosophers, especially excited the curiosity and attention of Alexander and the learned men who accompanied him. In this account of India it is said that the people burned their dead, and that women sometimes voluntarily burned themselves with the bodies of their deceased husbands. Marriages were restricted to those of the same class, and often took place as early as 7 or 8 years of age. Indeed, the customs, manners, employments, etc., of the people of India 2,000 years ago, appear to have continued with little change till the present time.

STATE OF INDIA FROM THE INVASION OF ALEXANDER TO THE MOHAMMEDAN CONQUEST.

Alexander founded no colony in India and made no permanent changes in the government or institutions of the country. In the divisions and changes in the empire consequent upon his decease, Seleucus, one of his ablest generals, obtained the eastern part of his dominions, and established what has been called the Bactrian and Greco-Bactrian kingdom. He claimed those provinces which Alexander had conquered on the Indus, and resolved to carry into effect the scheme of conquest which his master so much desired. The history of the Bactrian kingdom is very obscure, but it appears that Seleucus invaded India and had somewhere a conflict with the army of Chandragupta, king of Magadi, called by the Greek historians Sandracottus, and described as sovereign of the greater part of central and northern India. The Greek historians say that Seleucus was victorious, but the result of the invasion does not show such success as he anticipated, for a treaty of peace was concluded, by which he relinquished all claim to any possession east of the Indus. A marriage connection was formed between the two royal families, and Seleucus appointed Magasthenes to reside as his minister at Palibothra. The Bactrian kingdom under a succession of Greek sovereigns continued for several reigns. From some fragments of Grecian and Indian history, and from numerous ancient ruins, it appears that there were three different dynasties of Bactrian kings, who had much intercourse with the princes of northern India. It appears that sometimes their dominions included provinces east of the Indus, and perhaps one of them for a while made his capital in some of these provinces. It appears not unlikely that the Purans refer to this kingdom when they say that eight Yuwun kings once reigned in some of the northern parts of India. Yuwuns is believed to be a corruption of Ionians, the name given to the Greeks by the people of India.

The Magadi sovereigns appear at this time to have been the most powerful in India. Of these Chandragupta was the most celebrated. He died about 300 years before the Christian era, and was succeeded by his son Mitragupta, and this kingdom under different dynasties continued till about A.D. 450, or for more than eight centuries. At one time, either as compensation for territory relinquished, or to purchase exemption from invasion, these sovereigns paid to the Bactrian monarchs annually, "a tribute of 50 elephants and a considerable sum of money." The state of India is described as prosperous and happy under the Magadi dynasty. Commerce, the arts, literature, and husbandry, all flourished. A royal road is said to have extended from the capital Palibothra to the Indus, and another to Broach in Gujerat. These sovereigns patronized learned men and supported a brilliant court. It appears to have been in this reign that the Sanscrit language attained its highest state of polish and refinement.

The religion professed by the last sovereigns of the Magadi kingdom was Budhism. The long continued controversy between those professing the Brahminical system, or common Hinduism, and those professing Budhism appears at this time to have come to a crisis, and probably the religious wars which terminated in the expulsion of the Budhists from India, were connected with the subversion of this kingdom. There is no connected and authentic history of these events, but only scattered fragments and poetic allusions to them in the Purans, and notices of them in inscriptions, ruins, etc. Some of the large cave-temples were made in these dynasties.

Thus the religion of India previous to the Mohammedans' establishing their power in the country, was of three kinds, namely:—

1. The religion of the first inhabitants which consisted in the worship of numerous local deities, many of them supposed to be the spirits of deceased men. Some of these were believed to be benevolent and to delight in the happiness of mankind, but they were oftener believed to be malevolent, and their principal interference in human affairs was to inflict misery of some kind. Hence the general sentiment towards them was fear, and the principal worship consisted in sacrifices, offerings, rites, and ceremonies to pacify them and induce them to let mankind alone—not to injure or trouble them. The votaries of this horrid superstition have no affection for the beings they worship, they only fear and dread them. They expect no favors or good from them. They only fear evil, as though they interfere in human affairs only to do evil. Sometimes they will torture themselves or inflict pain upon one another in the belief that their supposed deities are pleased with such sufferings. A religion with such supposed deities for its objects of worship contains material and will furnish occasion for every kind and degree of cruelty and wickedness, which the depraved and guilty heart of man can conceive, or which human nature can endure. And this religion with its dreaded divinities, its sacrifices of food and animals, its offerings of various kinds of food and spirituous liquors, its horrid cruelties and its self-inflicted tortures, continues still in some districts and among some tribes, who are reckoned to belong to the lower castes.

2. The next form of religion in India was Brahminism, or the religion of the Vedas and Purans, and commonly called Hinduism. The system was probably introduced 12 or 14 centuries before the Christian era, and became established and matured in the districts which compose the valley of the Ganges. From

these provinces, its first seat in India, it spread by degrees, incorporating in its progress in different directions many of the local deities with their legends, rites, etc., till it became the religion of the most populous and civilized parts of the country. This system, though varying much in different places, as might be expected from its many and conflicting sacred books, its almost innumerable deities, and its rites and ceremonies more than one man could ever learn or have time to perform, continues to be the religion of the great body of the people to the present time.

3. Budhism was the next form of religion. This appears to have been at first a schism in the brahminical system. There is much obscurity about its origin, but so far as can be ascertained, it appears to have originated in attempts to reform some pretended abuses in the prevailing religion, but it soon became a rival system. It appears certain that Budhism was awhile the established religion of several dynasties in central and northern India, and many monuments of it remain in the peninsula. Of the contests and controversies between Budhism and Brahminism, and by what means the former was expelled from nearly all India, we have little authentic information. It is still the religion of Nepaul and the south part of Ceylon, and it is the prevailing religion of the countries east from India, as Burma, Siam, and China. Its temples in India, now generally in ruins, or appropriated to the system which triumphed over it and expelled it from the country, show that its power was once great and had a strong hold on the feelings of its votaries.

From the compilation of the Code of Menu to the Mohammedan invasion was 2,000 years, so there was ample time for all the changes which the allusions and fragments of history and the fables of mythology suggest. The system of the Vedas and Purans (of which the Institutes of Menu form a part,) became early established in the valley of the Ganges, and there obtained its greatest development. We may suppose that this Code shows the state of civilization for a very considerable period in those provinces, while in the other parts of India the inhabitants were in every stage of civilization up to a state of barbarism. The religion and civilization which had thus become established in the central parts of India, supported and enforced as they were by a learned hierarchy and a military class, was gradually extended in different directions till they included nearly all India, especially the parts which were most fertile and populous.

The Hindu governments have always been despotic, and are described as having power to manage the affairs of the State as they pleased. The sacred character and supposed spiritual power of the brahmins must always have been a restraint upon the exercise of arbitrary power. The distinctions of caste also must have caused a peculiar kind of civilization, and it is remarkable that some of the ancient rajas and princes belonged to the general division or caste called Shudras. Such facts show that the Institutes of Menu, which assign all honor and power to the higher castes and only servitude and degradation to the Shudras, were not the laws of all India. Indeed, these are some of the indications which show that this celebrated Code was the work of men, who wrote it to show the form of government and society which they preferred and wished to be adopted and followed, and not a body or system of laws and usages actually in force. These Shudra princes or their families probably acquired their power before they embraced the religion of the Vedas and Purans. This extension of Hinduism increased the number of castes, and contributed to the confusion which now exists. The people of a new province or kingdom were formed more or less into distinct castes, but did not amalgamate or unite with those of other districts.

The state of civilization in India previous to the Mohammedan invasion, though very unequal in the different kingdoms into which the country was divided, was yet such as clearly to place the inhabitants among civilized nations. This is evident from the character of the Sanscrit language and many works in its literature. Among these works none have excited more attention and none deserve more consideration than the Institutes of Menu. This work has been generally supposed to have been written as early as the 9th or 10th century before the Christian era, and it contains a code of religious, civil, and criminal laws, all claiming to be of divine authority, and so regarded by the orthodox Hindus. The great object of these laws appears to be to exalt the brahminical caste, and they contain evidence of having been compiled by men of this caste and with an unscrupulous view to their own interest. Some have supposed that this Code was once the universal law of India. But there is not sufficient reason for believing this opinion. It is more reasonable to suppose that the compilers arranged these laws so as to show what in their opinion ought to be, or what they wished to be observed, than what had been or were being observed. Still this Code, if not at its origin, yet at an early period in its history, was received as of divine authority, and so exerted much influence among the people. But it was probably with this Code as it was with the Jewish laws of old, and as it has been in modern times with the doctrines of Mohammedanism and Christianity, that many who live in countries where these systems prevail, pay little or no regard to them; while many others who profess to believe them, yield obedience no farther than is convenient and agreeable.

Among the celebrated names in Indian mythology and history is Vikram and Vikramditya, and these names are applied at pleasure to the same individual. Several monarchs of this name are mentioned, but the one who established the commencement of his reign, as an era which still continues in use in central India, has been chiefly celebrated. He commenced his reign in Oujein, then called Awanti, 56 years before the Christian era. He was renowned for his virtues in peace and for his prowess in war. He encouraged learning and supported many learned men at his court, among whom was the celebrated poet Kalidas. Those who enjoyed the patronage of the monarch, celebrated his piety, liberality, and bravery in a manner which shows that if some actions and qualities ascribed to him were facts, yet much of what they said must be fiction. He is said himself to have worshipped the infinite and invisible God, but at the same time to have erected temples and endowed shrines of the deities which were generally worshipped by his subjects. This may have been all true concerning him, or it may have been said merely to praise him; as though his knowledge was so great and his mind so enlightened that he could worship without the use of any images, rites, etc., while yet he was so kind and liberal as to provide such aids for the use of those to whom for want of knowledge or mental capacity they were necessary.

In the Deckan a king by the name of Shalewahan reigned at Pytan on the Godavery, in the first century of the Christian era. The popular literature and tradition contain some marvellous and fabulous stories about his birth and early life. He made war upon Vikram and compelled him to withdraw from the Deckan. They then came to a mutual understanding that Vikram should reign over all the country lying north of the Nerbudda and that his era should be there used, and that Shalewahan should reign over all the country south of that river and that his era should there be used. These eras continue to be used according to this supposed agreement up to the present time.

It has been already remarked, that at the time of the Mohammedan invasion and at every previous period when we can get a view of the state of India, we see it divided into a number of separate and independent kingdoms. Thus in the extreme southern parts of the peninsula we see the kingdom of Pandion with Madura for its capital and using the Tamul language; then next to it, the kingdom of Carnata with Vejyanuggur for its capital and using the Carnarese language; then the kingdom of Telingana with Warangole for its capital and using the Telugu language; then north-east, the kingdom of Orissa with Cuttac for its capital and using the Oriya language; then in the Deckan, the kingdom of Marashtra with Pytan and the Deoghur for its capital and using the Mahratta language; then to the north-west, the kingdom of Gujerat with Anhalwara for its capital and using the Gujeratee language. In this way we might proceed all over India. Awanti (now Oujein) in Malwa, Gouri in Bengal, Palibothra, Magadi, Ayodhya (now Oude), Mithili, and Delhi, in the great valley of the Ganges were the ancient capitals of kingdoms. Sometimes one of these kingdoms was divided into two or three governments for awhile, and would then be united again. These kingdoms could generally show long genealogies of kings, often terminating to fables and mythology. The virtues and victories of their kings were chronicled in legends, celebrated in poetry, and sung in ballads, but they had no properly connected and arranged records of public events or authentic history of their kings or their kingdoms. It appears to be unnecessary, in view of the present state of India and the object of this work, to try to gather up or to arrange any further facts or opinions concerning these obscure kingdoms, whose political existence ceased some centuries ago, and which do not appear likely again ever to recover any political importance or any national existence. Some account of the sacred books of the Hindus, their deities, their literature, their religious rites and ceremonies, their customs, manners, etc., will be given in another part of this work.

CHAPTER II.

THE MOHAMMEDAN PERIOD.

For many centuries previous to the origin of the Mohammedan religion the inhabitants of Arabia and the southern parts of Persia had carried on a large trade with the western coast of India, and when the inhabitants of these countries embraced the Mohammedan religion and became imbued with its spirit, they would naturally endeavor to propagate it in those parts of India with which they were best acquainted, and had most intercourse. And so it was. In the time of the early Caliphs, expeditions were sent from Arabia and Persia to the western coast of India to propagate the new faith. The accounts of these are meagre, consisting of traditions gathered up by Mohammedan historians long afterwards. In the time of the Caliph Waleed, the governor of Bussora dispatched an army of 6,000 men to India under the command of Mohammed Causim. This army was well prepared with means for aggressive war, and the commander was determined to retain possession of the countries he might conquer, and to convert their inhabitants to the true faith. This army made its first descent at Dewal a seaport in Scinde, belonging to a Hindu prince, called by Mohammedan historians, Raja Dahir. Causim commenced his warfare by beseiging a large, fortified temple near the city. Being informed that a large flag flying at the top of the temple was regarded as its palladium by the superstitious inmates, Causim directed his engines to it and soon brought it down. The people seeing the flag fall were panic-struck, and soon surrendered. Causim issued orders that all the males should be circumcised, but on account of the resistance of the brahmins, or for some other reason, he became so much exasperated that he caused all the males over 17 years old to be put to death, and all under that age, as well as the women and children to be reduced to slavery.

Causim next attacked the town, which was soon taken, and much booty was obtained in it. One fifth part of the booty was reserved for the governor of Bussora or the Caliph, according to early Mohammedan usage, and the rest was divided among the captors. The submission of the country around Dewal soon followed, and Causim proceeded up the Indus to Schwan and other places, of which he took possession. This invasion from a foreign country, and the barbarous manner of forcing the inhabitants to embrace a new faith, aroused the native powers and the spirit of the people, and Causim found his further progress opposed by a large army under the Raja. Having been reinforced by 2,000 cavalry from Persia, and animated by that enthusiasm which so powerfully influenced the early Mohammedan conquerors, Causim resolved to maintain his ground, though attacked by an army of 50,000 men. The attack was commenced by the Raja, who in the style of that age in India, was mounted on a war-elephant. A fire-ball, thrown from the engines having struck the animal, he was so much frightened that he ran from the battle field, and plunged into the river. The army, supposing that the Raja had been killed, became dismayed and soon gave way on every side. And though the Raja returned to the field, yet he could not rally his flying troops. But he showed his own courage by continuing the battle till he fell among the slain.

This battle took place near Allore, the ancient capital of Scinde. The Raja's widow, or the widow of one of his sons, then in the city, furnished an instance of the courage and desperation which sometimes occur in the ancient history of India. "She collected the remains of the scattered army, put the city into a posture of defence, and maintained it against the attacks of the enemy until the failure of provisions rendered it impossible to hold out any longer. In this extremity her resolution did not desert her, and the garrison inflamed by her example determined to devote themselves along with her, after the manner of her tribe. The women and children were first sacrificed in flames of their own kindling; the men performed their ablutions, and then with solemn ceremonies took leave of each other and of the world; the gates were then thrown open, the men rushed out, sword in hand, and encountering their enemies, all perished to a man."

If this tragic scene exhibits the character and spirit of the Hindus, the following shows the savage barbarity of the Mohammedans: "Those of the garrison who did not share in this act of desperation, gained little by their prudence; the city was carried by assault; all the men in arms were slaughtered in the storm, and their families were reduced to bondage."

Causim continued the war till the dominions of Raja Dahir had submitted to his authority. These dominions included the country each side of the Indus, from its mouth to Multan, which is mentioned as one of the cities he conquered. This territory then included all Scinde and the southern part of the Punjab. These conquests were made in the spirit of the Mohammedan religion at that early period of its history. When the army approached any city, the inhabitants were summoned to embrace the Mohammedan faith, or to submit to such tribute as might be imposed upon them. If they refused such terms, the city was attacked, and if it did not capitulate upon some stipulated conditions, when taken, all the fighting men were killed and their families reduced to slavery. When cities resisted to the last extremity, the slaughter was often very great, and the misery of families was extreme. Traders, mechanics, etc., if they continued quiet, were not oppressed or injured beyond paying the tribute exacted, and enduring such evils as originated in the seige or storming of the city. When tribute was agreed to, either on the part of the prince or the people, they were allowed to live, so long as they paid the tribute, according to their own religion, and to such laws and usages as were conceded to them. The Mohammedans who invaded India, appear soon to have lost something of the stern and fanatical spirit which animated the first Mohammedan conquerors of Egypt, Syria, and Persia. Causim made treaties with several Hindu princes, and employed natives of the country in high situations under his government. He formed plans for greatly extending his conquests, and was preparing to carry them into effect when sudden reverses came upon him, and he was deprived of the command of the army. Mohammedan historians say he was put to death by the orders of the Caliph, upon some groundless charges made against him. Temin his successor had not the ability and enterprise required to lead the army to further conquests. The Mohammedan doctrines, and especially the rite of circumcision, were exceedingly odious to the Hindus, and they defended their religion and their country with great obstinacy. The Mohammedan army, in the course of a few years, became much reduced, and the Hindus uniting in a general insurrection expelled the invaders from India, and the country continued for several generations in their undisturbed possession.

The failure of the Mohammedans to extend their conquests and even to retain what they had acquired in India, so different from their progress and success at that time in other countries, arose from the state of India and the peculiar character and institutions of the Hindus. The country was subject to many independent princes, who must all be conquered in succession, and could only be subdued by carrying war into the successive territory of each one separately. The Hindu religion has so little connection with the state that the conquest of the country and the expulsion or extinction of dynasties would have but little direct influence upon the religion of the people. Their religion depends upon their hereditary priesthood and their sacred books and places, and this priesthood has nothing like a hierarchy, has no authoritative spiritual head. Again, the division of the people into different castes presents a great barrier to social intercourse and religious sympathy, and yet those of the same caste are more closely united together than any society or community which has ever existed in any other social state or religious system. These were obstacles to the progress of the Mohammedan religion, which it had never encountered in any other country. Further, the invasion was made from Persia, where the people had not the stern fanatical zeal for religion which distinguished the early proselytes and immediate successors of Mohammed, as they went from Arabia to spread their faith and reform the world. And as this zeal for the simple faith of their creed and their admiration of the austere manners of the prophet diminished, they gradually acquired a love of wealth, luxury, and splendor. They were glad to exchange the simple tent for the splendid palace, and the plain dress which their prophet wore for the gorgeous robes of courtiers and monarchs. And in order to attain these things they became willing to make treaties of alliance with idolaters, and the consequence of this course was that they were themselves expelled from the country.

The next Mohammedan invasion of India was from a different direction and was of a more permanent character. Persia was one of the first countries which the Mohammedans invaded and conquered. The inhabitants generally embraced the faith of the conquerors more from compulsion than from conviction of its truth, for in a few years they attempted to expel their conquerors and to reëstablish their former religion. Such people are not likely to have much zeal for spreading their new faith, and Mohammedanism made its way very slowly in the countries between Persia and India. In the year 977 of the Christian era, Subuctagee became the governor of the province of Candahar. He had a high character for military talents, and the army having selected him as their sovereign he assumed independence. He selected Ghizni for his capital and laid the foundation for one of the most powerful kingdoms then in the world. The Hindus, who had painful experience of the aggressive and intolerant spirit of the Mohammedans, looked with great anxiety upon this kingdom now established near their border, and several excursions of Afghans into their territories soon convinced them that their fears were not without reason. Provoked by these attacks, Jypal, Raja of Lahore, collected a large army and proceeded towards Ghizni either to invade Afghanistan, or to repel an expected invasion. As he and Subuctagee were preparing to engage in battle, a great tempest arose, which either from its violence or some circumstances connected with it, frightened and disheartened the Hindus so much that Jypal solicited peace, which he at length obtained by paying a large sum of money and surrendering 50 of his elephants. This treaty in some of its conditions, it is said he afterwards refused to fulfil, and also treated the ambassadors of Subuctagee with great insolence.

Such conduct greatly exasperated the Afghan sovereign, and assembling a large army he began his march towards India, while Jypal, who aware what the effect of his conduct would be, had formed an alliance with several princes in the northern parts of India, prepared to defend his territory. The Mohammedan historians, to whom we are chiefly indebted for information on the Mohammedan conquest of India, say that Jypal's army contained 100,000 cavalry and an almost incredible number of foot-soldiers. But such great numbers add little to the strength or efficiency of a half-disciplined army. They can seldom all be arranged so as to engage in battle. The disciplined force in whatever direction it moves, compels all to give way before it, and when disorder and confusion once commence, the greater the army the greater the carnage and slaughter. The fierce and warlike tribes of Afghanistan have seldom had reason to feel much respect for the armies of India, and they have often had reason to hold them in contempt. Subuctagee commenced the attack by a succession of charges by his best cavalry upon the centre of the Indian army, and as soon as he saw this part in disorder and giving way, he ordered an attack to be made upon their whole line. The Hindus soon gave way; a total rout ensued, and the fugitives were pursued with great carnage to the Indus. Subuctagee obtained great booty in the Hindu camp; he took possession of all the country west of the river and annexed it to his dominions.

Subuctagee died in 997, leaving the character of a wise prince and skilful general. As usual in the oriental kingdoms at that time, dissensions arose and civil war followed about the succession. His son Mahmoud had generally accompanied his father in his campaigns, and had displayed much military talent. His father had reposed great confidence in him, and he had generally been regarded as the heir to the throne. But he was in some of the western provinces at the time of his father's death, and a younger brother, Ishmael, succeeded in obtaining possession of his father's treasures, and in causing himself to be acknowledged the successor of his father's power. A war now ensued between the two brothers, which after exhibiting for some time the usual characteristics of intrigue and deceit in oriental armies and courts, was terminated by a severe battle, the taking of Ghizni, and the confinement of Ishmael for life. Mahmoud, now the undisputed sovereign of all his father's dominions, was occupied for some time in establishing order and strengthening his government. As soon as he had arranged his affairs so that they no longer required his personal attention, he began his preparations for invading India, a purpose he had long cherished if he should succeed his father. He had accompanied his father in his expedition to Multan and Lahore, and so had seen something and heard more of the wealth and glory of India. He had seen what armies the Hindu princes brought into the field. He knew the superior qualities of his Afghan troops, and believed that victory would follow his colors when unfurled in battle with the armies of the idolaters of Hindustan. He was at this time a very devout Mussulman, believing it was his duty to destroy all idols and temples for idol-worship, and to bring all idolaters to embrace Mohammedanism as the only true faith.

Mahmoud, with such means at command, such a purpose long and fondly cherished, and such views of his own faith and of idolatry, would soon cause his power to be felt in India. In 1001, the 4th year of his reign, he left Ghizni with a large force to invade those parts of India which were contiguous to his own dominions. Jypal, Raja of Lahore, was yet living and prepared to meet him with a large army. But Mahmoud defeated this army and took Jypal prisoner. He then took Betinda, which was the capital or one of the principal cities of Jypal, and contained his treasures. He then returned to Ghizni with a great amount of spoil. Jypal was set at liberty to govern his own dominions as a dependent and tributary prince or deputy of Mahmoud. This purpose, if it ever was his purpose, he did not carry into effect. On arriving in his capital he invested his son Anundpal with the government, caused a funeral pile to be prepared and funeral ceremonies to be performed, and then prostrating himself upon it he applied the fire with his own hand and perished in the flames.*

Mahmoud was now engaged for some time in wars with the princes and tribes north and west of Afghanistan, and so had not leisure to add to his conquests in India. He made a hurried expedition to Lahore, and also to Multan to adjust some matters requiring his personal attention, but he returned to Ghizni as soon as possible. So the Hindu princes had time to consider what a dangerous neighbor they had on their borders, and to concert measures among themselves for self-defence.† From what they knew of Mahmoud's warlike character, his hatred of idolatry, and his love of plunder, they had reason to expect he would repeat his invasion as soon as the state of his dominions would admit, and so they formed a strong confederacy to resist him as their common enemy. This confederacy included the Rajas of Lahore, Oujein, Gwalior, Kalinga, Kanouj, Delhi, and Ajmere. This large combination shows that the invasion of Mahmoud had caused great excitement in northern India. And this excitement was not without sufficient cause. Wars in India have generally been contests between princes for the governing power, and in no way affecting the interests of the great body of the people, who cared little about the issue, if they were only let alone. But the invasions and conquests of Mahmoud were of a very different character. They aimed at the subversion of the religion of the inhabitants as well as of the power of the princes, and all classes were roused to self-defence. "Even the Hindu women sold their jewels, melted down their golden ornaments, and sent their contributions from a distance to furnish resources for this holy war."

* "In those days it was a custom of the Hindus that whatever Raja was twice defeated by his enemies, should be by that disgrace rendered unfit for further command. Jypal, in compliance with this custom, having raised his son to the government, ordered a funeral pile to be prepared, upon which he sacrificed himself to his gods."

† Mahmoud's reign of 33 years was spent in continual war, enlarging his dominions or plundering idolaters, or suppressing insurrections. But we shall only give a sketch of those which had respect to India. We would remark, however, as showing his power and the customs and means of war in that age, that in a great battle near Balk, Mahmoud had 500 war-elephants, which spread around them terror and death and contributed much to gain the victory.

Mahmoud, as soon as the state of his dominions would allow of his leaving them for awhile, again invaded India with a large force. The confederated army, which had been prepared to resist his further advance, much exceeded his expectations. He selected his position, entrenched his camp, and resolved to watch some favorable opportunity to attack the hosts arrayed against him. A body of archers who were sent out to attack the Hindus, brought on a conflict in which the army of Mahmoud at first suffered severely, but the elephants of the Raja or general commanding the Indian army, becoming frightened, fled from the field, and the Hindus seeing their general had disappeared, and supposing he had been killed, relaxed their efforts and soon began to give way. Mahmoud observing their state sent out a large body of cavalry, which routed and dispersed them with great carnage. Resolved to make the utmost of the dismay thus produced, he pursued them in every direction, and so completely dispersed them that they did not rally or unite any more to resist him while on this expedition.

Thus relieved from apprehension of any attack or further resistance, Mahmoud proceeded to attack a fortified temple called Bheem or Bheemghur, in the territory of Nagracote. This temple being regarded as a sacred place as well as impregnable fortress, the neighboring princes and rich people had deposited in it a great amount of treasure, jewels, etc. According to Ferishta, "This temple contained a greater quantity of gold, silver, precious stones, and pearls than was ever collected in the royal treasury of any prince on earth." But the statements of Mohammedan historians concerning the amount of treasure found in some of the Hindu temples, must be greatly exaggerated. This temple was strongly fortified, but the garrison had been removed to swell the army just defeated and dispersed; only the priests and a few families remained, and they soon surrendered at discretion. All the treasures and whatever of value was found in the temple, were seized and became the property of the conquerors. From this place Mahmoud returned to Ghizni, and the next year he appointed a festival to celebrate his victories and conquests in India. A large plain was selected for the exhibition, and the festival continued for 3 days. The gold and precious stones were exhibited in a manner to excite the greatest admiration of the spectators and the highest ideas of their value, as well as of the riches of the country where they were obtained. His generals assisted in giving splendor to the festival. "Sumptuous banquets were provided for the spectators, alms were liberally distributed among the poor, and splendid presents were bestowed on persons distinguished for their rank, merits, or sanctity."

Such scenes were well fitted to prepare the minds of a people like the Afghans to make further invasions and yet greater conquests in India, and there can be no doubt that they were designed to produce this effect. Accordingly we find that apparently as often as the state of his dominions would allow of his absence, Mahmoud made expeditions into some parts of India. In 1017 he commenced his ninth expedition, in which the amount of forces he took with him, and the plans he intended to accomplish, exceeded all the preceding. Ferishta says that his army, when he left Ghizni, consisted of 100,000 horse, and 20,000 foot. His intention was to take the city of Kanouj, which is situated on the Ganges, 200 miles south-east from Delhi, and was then one of the most wealthy and populous cities in India. He took an unusual route, passing on the south side of Cashmere and the Himalaya mountains till he reached the Ganges, and then followed the river to Kanouj. He found the Raja quite unprepared, who surrendered at discretion. Mohammedan historians agree in saying that Mahmoud neither exacted any tribute nor obtained any plunder. They describe the city as being the most wealthy and splendid in India, and say that he left it uninjured, after tarrying only three days. All this may be true, but it is so different from his general character and his conduct towards other cities in India, and also from what might be expected from him and his army, and so different from their intentions and expectations when leaving Ghizni, and during their march of three months, that we feel inclined to doubt what the historians say, or to suppose that we do not understand the subject in some of its important connections and circumstances. Mahmoud proceeded to Muttra, taking and plundering several places on the way. Muttra, or Mathura, had long been a place of great sanctity, and the temples were large and splendid. He stopped there for 20 days, and plundered the temples and the city of all the wealth that could be found. This amount is described as being very great, many of the idols being large and of pure gold and silver, all which were seized and melted down. One idol, when melted, yielded 2,150 lbs. of pure gold, and the gold and silver obtained from all the idols were sufficient to load 100 camels. So say Ferishta and the Mohammedan historians.

But if Mahmoud found great plunder in some places, he encountered great resistance in others. One fort, called Mungee, resisted his attacks for 25 days. "And when the beseiged found the place no longer tenable, some rushed through the trenches upon the enemy and met that death which they no longer endeavored to avoid. Some threw themselves headlong from the walls, and were dashed to pieces, while others burnt themselves in their houses with their wives and children, so that not one of the garrison survived the fatal catastrophe."

At length Mahmoud, weary of destroying, or satisfied with plundering, returned with his army to Ghizni. "The plunder or spoils he had obtained, consisted of 23,000,000 drachms, 53,000 captives, 350 elephants, besides jewels, pearls, and precious stones, which could not be properly estimated. Nor was the private spoil less than that which came into the public treasury." A part of their plunder was expended in the erection of a splendid mosque, far exceeding any before seen in Afghanistan. He also founded a university, which had a large library and many learned men connected with it. His nobles also, who had seen the splendid buildings in Kanouj, Muttra, and other cities in India, erected large palaces, with parks around them, and Ghizni soon became one of the most splendid cities of that age.

Some years passed without any expedition being made into India, when Mahmoud heard that the Raja of Kanouj, with whom he had made some treaty, was involved in war with some of the neighboring princes. He hastened into India with a large force, but did not reach Kanouj in time to save the Raja from being defeated, his capital taken, and himself put to death. The princes who had united to effect his ruin, on hearing of the arrival of Mahmoud, retreated in different directions, and finding it impossible to gratify his feelings of revenge upon them, he hastened back to Ghizni.

Mahmoud gloried in being one of the great apostles of Mohammedanism, and a destroyer of idols and idolatry. He had caused a work to be written in which his great efforts for propagating the true faith and his zeal against idols and idolatry were celebrated. This book he sent to the Caliph. The Caliph was extremely pleased with the work, and "he appointed a festival day when it was read to all the people of Bagdad, and God was publicly praised for the spread of the true faith."

Still Mahmoud was not satisfied with the reputation he had acquired for his zeal and exertions in propagating the true faith, or his avarice was not satisfied with the spoils he had acquired in eleven different expeditions into India. He had heard of a celebrated temple called Somnat, which was situated in the south-west part of Gujerat on the sea-shore. This temple was strongly fortified and richly endowed. The revenues of 2,000 villages were appropriated for its support. From 200,000 to 300,000 people sometimes resorted there at the time of an eclipse. Princes and rich men in all western India often sent valuable presents to the temple. 2,000 brahmins, 500 dancing women (courtezans), and 300 musicians were attached to it. The idol was reported to be of pure gold and was so sacred that it was daily washed with water brought from the Ganges, a distance of nearly 1,000 miles. The brahmins and votaries reported and professed to believe that the success of the Mohammedans in plundering the temples and destroying the idols in the northern provinces of India, was because the people there had offended their gods and so had been abandoned to their enemies, but that neither Mahmoud nor any other Mohammedan would ever be able to obtain possession of Somnat; and so none of his worshippers had any reason to fear, for the god would repel all attacks, was able to destroy all his enemies in a moment, and that this power would be at once manifested, if any violence should be offered to his temple and his idol.

These reports stirred up the zeal of Mahmoud, and he resolved to make another expedition into India, which should exceed all he had yet made. He left Ghizni with a large army in September, 1024, and proceeded to Multan. From this city he had to cross a desert of more than 300 miles nearly destitute of water and forage. He caused 20,000 camels to be loaded with water and provisions, and enjoined on all his army and followers to provide for themselves as well as they could. He crossed the desert to Ajmere and proceeded to Somnat by way of Anhalwara, then the capital of Gujerat. His appearance was everywhere so sudden that neither the princes nor the people were prepared to make any resistance, and they generally fled from their towns and cities for safety, while he pressed forward to accomplish the great end of his expedition. At length Mahmoud came in sight of Somnat, which appeared like a great castle situated on a peninsula connected with the main land by a narrow isthmus. This isthmus was strongly fortified, and the walls were covered with men prepared to defend the place from sacrilege. As Mahmoud approached the place, a herald proclaimed to him and his army the danger of making any attack upon the temple, and warned them that if they should have the presumption and wickedness to show any disrespect to the god, he would instantly destroy them. Mahmoud had too much confidence in his own faith and too much contempt for the Hindu idols and deities to be deterred by such threats, and he made arrangements for attacking the temple the next day. His army was no less eager than himself, and as soon as it was sufficiently light, the archers commenced the attack upon the men on the walls. The courage which the assailants manifested and the great numbers that fell before their deadly aim, spread dismay amongst the Hindus. They assembled in the temple and prostrating themselves before the idol and imploring the god to assist them, they devoted themselves to death for his honor and the defence of his temple. In the spirit of desperation or rather of self-sacrifice, they seized their weapons and rushed to the walls. Some of the Mohammedans had got upon the wall, many others were ascending by ladders, and all were shouting "Allaho Acber," "God is great." The Hindus attacked them with such fury that all who had got upon the walls, were killed or thrust down, and those ascending were repelled. Ferishta says the attack was commenced early in the morning and was continued through the day till evening, when the Mohammedans retreated to their tents.

Ths next day Mahmoud ordered the attack to be made simultaneously the whole length of the walls, but the Hindus defended the place with great vigor, killing or thrusting down all who reached the top, so that the loss of the Mohammedans was greater than on the first day. On the third day Mahmoud was informed that a large army, the united forces of several princes who were anxious to protect their temple, was approaching to attack him. He arranged his army in order of battle, and marching to meet them, the two armies were soon engaged in conflict. While the battle was raging the Raja of Anhalwara arrived with a large force and joined the Hindus. This gave them fresh courage and disheartened the Mohammedans. Mahmoud seeing the dangerous state of himself and army, dismounted, and prostrating himself on the ground, implored God to interpose for the true faith and for the destruction of idolatry. He then mounted his horse, and exhorting all around him to fight for God valiantly and in the assured hope of victory, he called on them to follow him in the last and desperate attack upon the idolaters. By these means he inspired them with fresh courage, and raising a shout they renewed the battle with such impetuosity, that the Hindus soon gave way and fled, leaving 5,000 men dead on the field.

The men, who had defended the temple with so much valor and obstinacy, seeing no hope of relief lost all courage, and attempting no further defence, a large part of the people in the temple endeavored to escape in boats. But Mahmoud having learned what they were doing, ordered his men to seize all the boats they could find, and then to pursue and destroy the fugitives. He placed guards around the place, and with a few select companions proceeded to inspect the interior parts of the temple. They were struck with admiration at the grandeur of the structure. The roof or dome was supported by 56 great pillars curiously wrought and ornamented with precious stones. No external light was admitted, but the temple was illuminated by a great lamp in the centre, suspended from the roof by a chain of gold. The idol Somnat, which was 15 feet high, stood facing the entrance. Mahmoud, who gloried in his abhorrence and destruction of idolatry, was filled with indignation at the sight of this idol, and aiming a blow at the face with his iron mace, he struck off the nose. The brahmins of the temple apparently shocked at such daring wickedness and anxious for the honor of their god, threw themselves at his feet and offered an enormous ransom * if he would spare the idol. His friends who accompanied him, advised him to accept the sum offered, and allow the brahmins to retain their idol. But Mahmoud, exclaiming that he had always gloried in destroying idolatry, and wished to be known and remembered as "a breaker and not a seller of idols," repeated his blow upon the idol. Others then joined him, and the idol, which was hollow, soon bursting poured out a great quantity of diamonds, pearls, rubies, etc., which had been concealed in it, and would have been amply sufficient to pay the ransom offered by the brahmins. Besides the idol and the treasures contained in it, "there were in the temple some thousands of small images of gold and silver," and the amount of gold, jewels, and silver exceeded all he had acquired in his former expeditions into India.

Mahmoud remained at different places in Gujerat for considerable time, and was so much pleased with the climate and country that he thought of transferring his court to some place in that part of India, and making it his residence. His success in acquiring possession of Somnat and the great amount of treasure obtained, appear to have inspired him with a desire of further conquests. But his friends, who wished to return to Ghizni, united in dissuading him from undertaking such plans, and he relinquished them. Having inflicted what he thought was merited punishment upon the Hindu princes who had united in opposing him, he set out on his return home. On his way through the desert he and his army suffered exceedingly for want of water and provisions, and many died, but Mahmoud with his spoils succeeded in reaching Ghizni in safety. From this time till his decease he was occupied in expeditions into different parts of his extensive dominions to collect arrears of tribute, or to chastise some refractory vassals. A short time before his death, aware from his declining health that he could not long survive, he ordered all his gold, jewels, silver, etc., to be brought out and arranged before him. "And after surveying them for awhile he wept at the thought of seeing them no more,

* Ferishta says, "some crores of gold." A "crore of gold" would be nearly 5,000,000 dollars. Dow says "ten millions of gold." A crore is 10,000,000. Gibbon says the brahmins offered £10,000,000, or nearly $50,000,000.

and ordered them all to be carried back into the treasury. The next day he ordered a review of all his army, his elephants, camels, horses, and chariots, with which having feasted his eyes for some time from his travelling throne, he again burst into tears and retired in grief to his palace." He died at Ghizni in 1030 at the age of 63, of which he had reigned for 35 years.

Mahmoud was the most distinguished sovereign of the century in which he lived, and one of the most distinguished in all Mohammedan history. By some historians he has been extolled as the model of a perfect prince, and by others he has been described as a monster of avarice, injustice, and cruelty. Mohammedan historians, forming their opinions of his conduct and character according to their principles and prejudices, would give him a high place as a religious man and as a sovereign. But the inhabitants of India, who suffered so much from his avarice, his cruelty, and his fanaticism, would regard him as a man and monarch of unparalleled wickedness. He appears to have acted on the sentiment too common in Asiatic princes that it was right to treat as enemies and to plunder all who will not purchase peace upon such terms as may be dictated to them. He also appears to have acted upon the principle of some other early Mohammedan conquerors that it was right to make war upon all idolaters, to seize their property and sell them into slavery, if they did not at once embrace the faith of the Koran. He encouraged learning and founded a university at Ghizni. He invited several learned men to his court, and gave them liberal salaries. Among these was the celebrated Persian poet Ferdousi, whose work called *Shah Nameh* is so well known in oriental literature. Parts of this poem were recited to Mahmoud at different times, who expressed great admiration of the work, and gave liberal gifts to the author. But when finished after 30 years' labor upon it, the sum Mahmoud offered to give to the writer was so much less than he expected, that he refused to receive it, left the court of the monarch in disgust, and would never return. The edifices Mahmoud had seen in India made him anxious to increase the splendor of his own capital, and the mosques and palaces erected by him and his nobles made Ghizni at the time of his decease one of the most magnificent cities in the world.

Whatever may have been the character of his government over the countries professing his own faith, his expeditions into India, 12 in number and made at different times during his reign of 35 years, inflicted great miseries upon the inhabitants. Princes were defeated, dethroned, and in many cases put to death; cities were plundered and burnt; forts were seized and the garrisons massacred; the country was laid waste and so many of the inhabitants carried to Ghizni and sold into slavery, that sometimes the price of a man did not exceed one dollar. Mahmoud's zeal against idolatry was conspicuous in robbing and profaning temples, in destroying idols, and when intrinsically valuable in appropriating them to his own use, and in plundering their worshippers. But he showed little anxiety to convert them to his own faith, nor does it appear that the Mohammedan religion made any considerable progress in India in the way of conversions during his reign.

Mahmoud left two sons, Mohammed and Masoud. The former was designed by Mahmoud to be his successor, and soon after his death Mohammed was duly invested with authority, and generally acknowledged to be the sovereign. But Masoud, who was at that time in Ispahan, possessed the personal qualities which in the opinion of the Afghans better fitted him for exercising the supreme power. He had daring courage, a noble personal appearance, love of power, and great decision and energy of character. These qualities had always made him the favorite of the army, and plans were soon formed to invest him with the supreme authority. On his arrival at Ghizni the whole army declared themselves in his favor. Mohammed was seized; and his eyes were put out; he was placed in confinement, and Masoud ascended the throne in a few months after his father's death. The western provinces of his kingdom were in a very unsettled state, and he was occupied much of the time for several years in suppressing insurrections and repelling the invasions of the Tartar tribes. In 1039 he was defeated by the Turki chief, Togrul Beg, and finding himself no longer able to defend his dominions or to support his authority, he collected what force he could, and proceeded into India. Soon after crossing the Indus, a mutiny took place in his army, which finally resulted in deposing him, and declaring his brother

Mohammed to be Sultan. Mohammed was incapable of administering the government on account of his blindness, and so retaining only the name for himself he appointed his son Ahmed to be his deputy, who began his administration by putting Masoud to death.

The affairs of Ghizni continued for a long time in an unsettled state. The army was occupied in repelling the invasions of the Tartar tribes, and in suppressing insurrections in the western and central provinces of the empire. The provinces on the Indus continued in nominal subjection to Ghizni, while the Hindu princes of places further east, as Delhi, Kanouj, etc., gradually recovered courage and strengthened their power against any future invasions. The temples were rebuilt and new idols were consecrated in the place of those destroyed by Mahmoud. Encouraged by the distracted state of Ghizni, and anxious to expel the Mohammedans from India, some Hindu princes laid siege to Lahore, then the capital of the Mohammedan possessions east of the Indus. But they failed to accomplish their object. Lahore was vigorously defended, and the Hindus after beseiging it for some months, were compelled to leave it in the possession of their enemies.

The sovereigns of Ghizni, though unable for several successive reigns to extend their power in India, and frequently without the means of enforcing their authority in provinces nominally subject to them, did not relinquish their claim to their former conquests, nor their purpose of extending their dominions. The Hindu princes were all aware of this fondly cherished purpose, and had frequent presages that it would at some future time be carried into effect. Among the sovereigns of Ghizni was Sultan Ibrahim, who was a professed devotee. He spent much of his time in religious duties, as prayer, fasting, etc. He sent two splendid copies of the Koran, written by himself, as presents to the Caliph, who caused one of them to be deposited in the library of Mecca, and the other in the library of Medina. Mohammedan historians say that his government was as remarkable for its moderation and justice, as he was himself for his temperance and piety. As soon as he was quietly settled in his own dominions he despatched an army into India, which Ferishta says, "conquered many places which had not before been visited by the Mussulman arms." Some time afterwards he made another expedition into India, accompanying the army himself. He is said to have penetrated further into the country than any previous conqueror. He took several cities and fortified places, and returned to Ghizni with much plunder and a great number of captives.* He reigned 42 years, and he left 40 sons and 32 daughters. He was succeeded by his son Masoud, who sent a large army into India under one of his distinguished generals. "This army crossed the Ganges, and plundered many rich cities and temples of their wealth." He transferred his court from Ghizni to Lahore, and made this city his capital during a part of his reign. He was the first Mohammedan sovereign who fixed his capital in India.

In the early part of the 12th century a violent civil war raged in Ghizni, and for several days the city was plundered and the inhabitants were massacred. Ferishta says, "The noble city was given up to flame, slaughter, and devastation. The massacre continued for the space of 7 days, in which time pity seemed to have fled the earth, and the fiery spirits of demons to actuate the bodies of men." The splendid mosques and palaces erected by Mahmoud and his nobles and successors, were burnt and demolished. All were destroyed except the tombs of Mahmoud, Masoud, and Ibrahim. Thus, this city, which had been made so magnificent by the plunder of the cities and temples of India, became itself a scene of desolation, and never again recovered its former splendor. From this time Lahore became the capital as long as the descendants of Mahmoud retained their power.

THE HOUSE OF GHORI, A.D. 1160–1206.

This civil war resulted in the triumph of Alla ud Deen, a prince of the province of Ghor, and hence the dynasty which he commenced took the surname of Ghori. His family after some reverses succeeded in establishing their power in Ghizni. They exhibited the too common qualities of the princes of central Asia, courage, cruelty, treachery, and revenge. In A.D. 1176, Shahab ud Deen of this family made his first expedition into

* Ferishta says, "one hundred thousand."

India, and took Uch, then a considerable city at the junction of the rivers of the Punjab and the Indus. Two years after he made an expedition into Gujerat. He was here defeated and was compelled to return with much loss and in great distress. He made two attacks on Lahore and compelled the prince Khusru Malik to deliver up his son as a hostage for fulfilling the treaty then made. He next invaded Scinde and overran the country to the mouth of the Indus. Returning from Scinde he again made an attack upon Khusru Malik, apparently determined to subvert his power and take possession of his kingdom. Khusru defended his kingdom with unexpected vigor, and Shahab ud Deen resorted to treachery to accomplish his purpose. He pretended that in consequence of alarming intelligence from Ghizni he was anxious to proceed there immediately with his army, and wished first to make peace with Khusru. And to show how anxious he was for peace he unbound Khusru's son, who had continued with him as a hostage, and sent him to his father with the proposals. The aged king not suspecting any treachery, went out with a small force to meet his son thus unexpectedly sent to him. In the mean time Shahab ud Deen with a select body of cavalry interposed by an unfrequented way between Khusru and his capital. He then surrounded him and took him prisoner. Lahore made no further resistance. Khusru and his family were sent prisoners to Ghizni, where after a while they were all put to death. Shahab ud Deen took possession of all Khusru Malik's dominions, and had no Mohammedan rival or power to oppose him or to interfere with his purpose of conquest.

India was at this time divided into many small kingdoms, and apparently no way prepared to contend with an army of Afghans, Tartars, and other tribes of central Asia, whose profession was war, and who had passed much of their life with their weapons in their hands. The Hindus, too, had much painful experience of the superior skill, courage, and prowess of the Mohammedans. The effect of Mahmoud's expeditions and victories was that the Mohammedans went into battle *expecting* to conquer, and the Hindus engaged in conflict with the *expectation* of being defeated. The fanatical spirit of the Mohammedans, their avowed principle that it was their duty to propagate their faith in the use of all the means they had used, as the robbing and profaning of temples, the destruction of idols, and plundering and reducing to slavery all who resisted, all this was well known to the inhabitants of India. If the Mohammedans despised and abhorred the Hindus for their superstition and idolatry, these in turn dreaded and detested the former for their bigotry and intolerance, for the contempt they showed to all the rules of caste, and for the violent and sacrilegious manner in which they treated the most sacred persons, places, and things of the Hindu religion. If the Mohammedans believed that they were obeying the command of God, when compelling the Hindus to abandon idolatry and embrace the faith of their prophet, the Hindus were not less confident that they were themselves obeying their deities and securing their favor when defending their temples from being profaned, their idols from being destroyed, and themselves and their families from being polluted. The views of the Mohammedans in invading and conquering India, and of the Hindus in repelling such invasion and endeavoring to preserve their independence, involved motives and feelings of a very different character from those which are involved in the common wars of aggression and defence.

Shahab ud Deen's first battle was with the Rajas of Delhi and Ajmere, who had united their armies to resist him. Ferishta says the united army of these princes contained 200,000 men and 3,000 elephants. The battle was fought on the great plain a few miles from Panniput, where the fate of the empire of India has been several times decided. The Afghan armies consisted chiefly of cavalry, and their mode of fighting was to make successive charges at full speed upon the centre of their enemies, till they gave way and were thrown into confusion. The Hindu mode of fighting was to outflank their enemies and so inclose them on three sides. In this battle they succeeded by their superior numbers in nearly surrounding the Afghans. Shahab ud Deen fought with great valor till he was severely wounded, when he escaped with much difficulty, and his army fled. The Hindus pursued them with great slaughter for many miles. At Lahore Shahab ud Deen collected the remains of his army, and putting the city in a state of defence, proceeded to

Ghizni. Here he collected an army of Afghans, Tartars, and Turkish adventurers, who were ready to follow the fortunes of war under his command in India. The Raja of Delhi expecting he would return, had collected an immense army and proceeded to meet him. Shahab ud Deen found an opportunity of attacking the Hindu army unexpectedly with a part of his force in the night. The attack at first caused some confusion, but daylight soon appearing, order was restored, and the Hindus prepared to become the assailants. Having failed in his original design, Shahab ud Deen now retreated before them till they became disordered in pursuit, when suddenly turning "he attacked them at the head of 12,000 chosen horse in steel armor, and this prodigious army once shaken, like a great building tottered to its fall and was lost in its own ruins." The victory was complete, and the loss of the Hindus, among whom were several of their princes, was very great. After this battle Shahab ud Deen extended his conquests in India, taking and plundering Kanouj, Benares, Gwalior, Gujerat, and many other places and provinces. When encamped on the bank of the Indus, the state and circumstances of his tent were carefully observed by some Gakkars, whose friends he had caused to be put to death, and who were watching for an opportunity to take revenge. Twenty of these men swam over the river in the night, and entering his tent assassinated him when he was asleep. He had reigned 32 years. His conquests in India were greater than those of Mahmoud, and they were of a more permanent character. Mahmoud retained possession of only a small part of what he conquered and plundered. Shahab ud Deen annexed the provinces he conquered to his own dominions, and as far as possible retained possession of them. The treasures he accumulated were immense, requiring 4,000 camels to carry them. At the time of his decease nearly all India north of the Nerbudda, together with Bengal, Scinde, and Gujerat, had acknowledged his authority. He had no sons, and one of his nephews, Mahmoud Ghori, was proclaimed his successor. No opposition was made to this course, but it was soon obvious that he would not succeed to his uncle's power. Shahab ud Deen had educated several Turkish slaves, and then put them into responsible situations. At the time of his death, Cuttub ud Deen, one of these slaves, was governor of the provinces in the northern part of India, and another, Nasir ud Deen, was in charge of Multan and Scinde. These governors became virtually independent princes on Shahab ud Deen's death in A.D. 1206.

CUTTUB UD DEEN AND HIS SUCCESSORS—A.D. 1206–1288.

From the death of Shahab ud Deen the Mohammedan dominions in India became entirely separated from the countries west of the Indus, and so formed an independent kingdom. Cuttub ud Deen, the first independent sovereign, was originally a Turkish slave, and was purchased by Shahab ud Deen, who finding that he possessed good natural abilities and had been well educated, intrusted him with some important transactions. In these matters he exhibited so much capacity, moderation, and faithfulness that Shahab ud Deen intrusted him with the administration of the government when absent himself from his capital on political affairs at Ghizni, or pursuing his career of conquest in India. Cuttub ud Deen had been intrusted with the administration of Delhi and its dependent provinces for most of the time for several years previous to Shahab ud Deen's death, and soon after that event he was generally acknowledged to be sovereign, or emperor. He was respected for his ability, moderation, and justice, but unhappily for his subjects he lived only 4 years after his accession to the supreme power.

Cuttub ud Deen was succeeded by his son Aram, who soon showed that he had not capacity for administering such a government, and was removed to make room for his brother-in-law Altumsh, who had for some time been commander-in-chief of the army. Altumsh had the reputation of being the son of a Tartar chief, but being the favorite of his father he was envied by his brothers and sold to some travelling merchants, who carried him into Bochara and again sold him. He was remarkable for his beauty and his abilities, and having passed through various hands and lived in different places, he was at length purchased at Delhi by Cuttub ud Deen, and became a great favorite with his daughter. He was occupied for several years after his accession to power in suppressing insurrections in different parts of his dominions. The Hindus were ready to embrace any opportunity which occurred for expelling the Mohammedans, whose government and religion with the means they used to propagate it, were exceedingly odious. It was in the reign of Altumsh that Ghengis Khan with his Tartar hordes overran and laid waste Persia and other countries west of the Indus. Great anxiety was felt for several years in view of their probable invasion of India, and all eyes were turned to the west. But this scourge of so many nations did not extend his ravages east of the Indus. One of his chiefs crossed the river and laid siege to Multan, but failing in his attempts to take it, he proceeded into Scinde and then went into the countries west of the Indus. In this invasion the Tartars, or Moguls, as they were usually called, conducted with their accustomed cruelty and barbarity, ravaging the country, plundering the cities and seizing the inhabitants for slaves, if they could make any use of them, or obtain any price for them. At one time they massacred 10,000 prisoners to save the expense of keeping them rather than set them at liberty, when they would have gone into different parts of the country and found provisions for themselves.

Altumsh, as soon as he was relieved from apprehension of an invasion by the Moguls, resolved to extend his dominions in India, and he was thus engaged during the remaining years of his reign. At the time of his decease all the countries to the north of a line running from Surat to the mouth of the Ganges acknowledged the government of Delhi. The measure of obedience, however, differed much in different places, and at different times. In some provinces the old Hindu dynasties of sovereigns were soon annihilated, and in other places they were allowed to retain and exercise much of their former power in their own territory, upon condition of paying an annual tribute to the emperor. This tribute was always paid reluctantly, and was withheld when it was believed payment could not be enforced. The army of the emperor and his deputies or governors consisted chiefly of Mohammedans, who became the military class, but the great body of the inhabitants still continued to profess the Hindu religion, and to practice its rites and ceremonies openly so far as they could do it, without incurring persecution. The Hindus were so much attached to their superstitions, especially to their distinctions of caste, that they often chose to suffer death rather than embrace the Mohammedan faith. This passive resistance to Mohammedanism on the part of the inhabitants of India, concurred, with some other causes, to abate the zeal of the conquerors for its propagation. Some of them became apparently satisfied with the possession of the country and the professed obedience of the people, leaving conversion to be effected gradually by persuasion, and the aid and influence of the government in giving rewards and employment to proselytes. Still the course of the government varied according to the religious character of the respective conquerors and their subordinates, and the Hindus had the greatest dread of zealously religious rulers.

Near the close of his reign Altumsh received investiture from the Caliph of Bagdad. This was a great honor, and it came in the view of all Mohammedans from the highest authority. His zeal for Mohammedanism and hatred of idolatry, may have procured this honor for him; or it may have inspired him with zeal in propagating the faith of the Prophet. The historian says that in the ancient city of Oujein "Altumsh destroyed the magnificent and rich temple of Makal, which was formed upon the same plan with that of Somnat, had been building 300 years, and was surrounded by a wall 100 cubits high." In this city, also, he found an image of Vicramditya, formerly a celebrated Raja, from whom the people of that country still reckon their era. This image, with many others, some of stone and others of brass, "he ordered to be carried to Delhi, and broken to pieces at the door of the great mosque."

The celebrated column called Cuttub Minar, near Delhi, was commenced in the reign of Cuttub ud Deen, but was finished in the reign of Altumsh.* Near it is a mosque in an unfinished

* This pillar, or tower, is 242 feet high and 106 feet in circumference at the base. It has 4 balconies, each supported on large stone brackets, and surrounded with battlements of richly cut stone, to enable people to walk round the pillar with safety. The 1st balcony is at the height of 90 feet; the 2d at 140; the 3d at 180, and the 4th at 203 feet. Up to the 3d balcony the pillar is built of fine red sandstone. From the 3d balcony it is built chiefly of white marble, but "the summit is crowned with a majestic cupola of the fine red sandstone." From the base to the 1st balcony the exterior part is fluted into 27 divisions, alternately semicircular and angular. From the 1st to the 2d bal-

state, which for grandeur of design, and elegance of execution is said not to be exceeded by any in India. Several men, distinguished for learning, lived upon his bounty at his court, and by their presence and influence increased his fame. His reign continued for 26 years, and he is reckoned by the Mohammedan historians as a prince of great valor, prudence, and piety.

Some years previous to his death Altumsh appointed his son and intended successor, Feroze Shah, to high situations, that he might acquire experience and reputation, and so be prepared to succeed him. He was at Delhi when his father died. He immediately ascended the throne. The nobles swore allegiance and brought their presents to him. The poets celebrated his praises, and he gave presents to them. These congratulations and rejoicings were scarcely passed when he began to show how unworthy he was of the imperial dignity, by indulging in debauchery and profligacy, and by squandering the treasures his father had accumulated, on "courtezans, comedians, and musicians." The affairs of government were chiefly managed by his mother, who to gratify her envy or ambition caused many innocent persons to be put to death. The profligacy of the emperor and the abuse of power by his mother gave so great dissatisfaction that several attempts were made to dethrone him. One of these, in which the nobles put his sister, Sultana Rezia, upon the throne, was successful. The emperor was taken prisoner and kept in confinement until his death.

Sultana Rezia is remarkable among the rulers of India. Ferishta, the most reliable historian of that period, in describing her reign, says, "This princess was adorned with every qualification required in the ablest kings, and the strictest scrutineers

cony, the flutings are all semicircular; from the 2d to the 3d they are all angular; and from the 3d to the summit the surface is smooth. Around the 1st story are 5 horizontal belts containing sentences from the Koran, engraved in bold relief. In the 2d story are 4 such belts, and in the 3d there are 3. The ascent is by a spiral staircase within, containing 380 steps. From this staircase are passages into the balconies with windows at intervals for the admission of air and light. This pillar, generally reputed to be the finest in the world, has stood more than 600 years. The same emperor began to erect another pillar near this, but died before it was raised to the first balcony. Tradition says that he designed these pillars to be the minarets of a mosque of corresponding size and grandeur.

of her actions could find in her no fault but that she was a woman." Her education was such that she could read the Koran, and so ascertain for herself the principles of her faith. She evinced such a knowledge of business and talent for government, that her father Altumsh, when leaving Delhi to conduct the war in Malwa, appointed her to be regent in his absence. And when asked by his nobles why he appointed his daughter to such an office, instead of some one of his sons, he replied that she was more capable and trustworthy than any of them. The reputation she then acquired in her father's reign, procured her elevation to power when her brother was dethroned for his incapacity and profligacy. On being invested with the supreme power she changed her apparel, and assuming the imperial robes appeared daily on the throne, and transacted all the public business in the manner usual with the emperors.

Of the parties who united in dethroning Feroze Shah, one was opposed to investing Rezia with the supreme power, and collecting a large force, they proceeded to Delhi and defeated the first army that marched against them. The empress, however, proved herself quite equal to the exigency by sowing dissensions among the leaders, so that the confederacy was soon dissolved, and peace restored. The commander-in-chief of the army having died, several changes were soon made among the great officers of State. One of them, who was originally an Abyssinian slave, gave great offence to the other nobles, who formed a combination to depose her, as soon as they could find an opportunity to do it. The empress having ascertained their plan opposed them with great spirit. She marched against the governor of Lahore, who was one of the parties. He was disappointed in respect to aid from some of the confederates, and was compelled to throw himself upon her mercy. When on the way with her army to chastise another refractory noble, a mutiny occurred among her own forces, in which the Abyssinian favorite was killed, and she was herself seized and sent to the fort of Tiberhind. The nobles then assembled at Delhi, and declared Byram Shah, her brother, to be emperor. Alturia, to whose fort she was sent for custody, who was one of the first that rebelled against her, on becoming acquainted with her, was so much captivated with her beauty, her accomplishments, and her talents, that he offered to marry her, at the same time pledging himself to support her right to the throne against all his former friends and confederates. The marriage was soon celebrated, and by their united influence collecting a large force they proceeded to Delhi to assert and sustain her rights. A severe battle was fought near the city, in which the empress was defeated and fled to Tiberhind. In a short time she was able again to appear in the field, but she suffered another defeat. She and her husband were taken prisoners, and both were put to death. Thus died Sultana Rezia or Rezia Begum, who, considering the class of people to whom she belonged and the age in which she lived, appears to have been one of the most remarkable personages in the Mohammedan history of India. Her reign continued for three and a half years.

The nobles united in putting Byram Shah on the throne, but he soon showed that he was unfit for the dignity to which he had been promoted, and it became equally obvious that some of the nobles had united in raising him to this dignity merely to attain their private ends. Dissensions and intrigues, conspiracies and assassinations followed each other in quick succession. In the mean time news reached Delhi that the Moguls had invaded the Punjab and plundered Lahore. A general council of the State was called, and it was determined to send a large army to Lahore under the vizier. This man appears to have been talented, ambitious, and treacherous. While absent from Delhi with the army, by misrepresentations to the nobles concerning the emperor, he excited their disaffection towards him, and then by informing the emperor of their disaffection he excited his jealousy of them, and obtained from him an avowed intention of punishing them. The consequence was that the army returned to Delhi and besieged the emperor three months in his capital, when the city was taken, and he was first thrown into prison, and then put to death.

Alla ud Deen was the next emperor. He was raised to this dignity by those who had deposed his predecessor. If he excelled his predecessor in capacity, he was also more profligate, more addicted to low vice, more cruel and more oppressive. In his reign the Moguls made an invasion into Bengal through Tibet, but they were defeated and driven back. The next year they invaded Scinde, but on the approach of the emperor's army they retreated and soon left the country. The emperor at length became so unpopular that the nobles united in deposing him. He was then thrown into prison and there kept till he died.

Nasir ud Deen, a grandson of Altumsh, became the next emperor. For some years in the early part of his life he was kept in confinement by the reigning sovereign. He was afterwards released and intrusted with the government of Barage, where he was much respected for his moderation, wisdom, and love of justice. The Moguls had now obtained possession of the countries west of the Indus, and the government and people of India were in continual dread of them. No great invasion, however, was made by them during this reign. Nasir ud Deen's reign continued for 20 years. Misrule and anarchy had prevailed in some provinces of the empire during the two preceding reigns, and he was occupied for several years in restoring order and enforcing the payment of tribute. In accomplishing these objects he had some severe conflicts with some of the Mohammedan governors of provinces and with the Hindu princes. Among these the Rajpoots were conspicuous. The conflicts with them were severe and conducted with great barbarity on both sides. In one battle 10,000 Rajpoots were slain, and 90 chiefs were taken prisoners. The chiefs were all put to death, and all the soldiers, who were taken prisoners, were killed or condemned to perpetual slavery.

In this reign an ambassador came to Delhi from Haluku Khan, the grandson of the celebrated Ghengis Khan, and was received and entertained with royal magnificence.* Nasir ud Deen in his private life and habits was a dervish. His personal expenses

* The following extract from Ferishta will give some idea of the court of Delhi at that time: — "The vizier went out to meet the ambassador with 50,000 horse of Arabs, Agims, Turks, Khiljees, and Afghans; 200,000 infantry in arms; 2,000 choice elephants of war, and 3,000 carriages of fire-works. He drew up in order of battle, formed in columns of 20 deep, with the artillery and cavalry properly disposed. Having then exhibited some feats of horsemanship in mock battles and fully displayed his pomp, he conducted him into the royal palace. There the court was very splendid, every thing being set out in the most gorgeous and magnificent manner. All the omras, officers of state, judges, priests, and great men of the city were present, besides five princes of

he defrayed by making copies of the Koran and selling them. He had only one wife and no concubines. His food was of the simplest and plainest kind, and was all prepared by his wife. When she one day complained that she had burned her hand in baking the bread, and requested a female servant to assist her, he refused, saying that "he was only a trustee for the State, and that he was determined not to burden it with needless expenses." He was learned, and supported several learned men at his court. His government during the latter part of his reign was popular, and appears to deserve a high place among the early Mohammedan emperors in India. He left no children.

Ghias ud Deen Bulbun, commonly called by European historians Balin, succeeded to the vacant throne. He was vizier and had the chief administration of government in the preceding reign. There are different accounts of his origin. Ferishta says that his father was a Turkish chief, and had the command of 10,000 horse in the war in which his son was taken prisoner, and that the merchant who bought him on learning that he was a relation of the emperor, Altumsh, brought him to Delhi and presented him to the emperor, who in return gave the merchant a liberal reward. He took an active part in the intrigues and revolutions in Delhi till he obtained the office of vizier. He then conducted the affairs of the government in such a way that Nasir ud Deen for many years had little besides the name and title of royalty. In the reign of Altumsh he was one of a society of 40 Turkish slaves, who engaged to support one another, and on the emperor's death to divide the empire among themselves. But jealousies and dissensions prevented them from attempting it. Several of them however rose to fill high situations, and when Bulbun became emperor he began from feelings of jealousy or some unknown cause to remove them, and continued to do so till all perished by the sword or by poison. Having removed all who were members of this association, he was careful to appoint only men of respectable family connections to situations in his government. He excluded

Ayrac, Khorassan, and Maverulneer with their retinues who had taken protection at Delhi from the arms of Ghengis Khan, who a little before that time had overran the most part of Asia. Many Rajas of Hindustan, subject to the empire, were there and stood next to the throne."

Hindus from all situations of honor and responsibility. His proceedings appear to have had much of that capricious character so common in the despotic sovereigns of Asia.

He wished to acquire a character for liberality, and to have a splendid court. In this respect circumstances favored him. Of the sovereigns and princes who were expelled from their dominions by Ghengis Khan and his successors, or who fled from their ravages, more than 20 were living at one time in Delhi. The emperor gave them palaces for their residence, and pensions for their support. On all public occasions they all stood to the right and left of his throne, ranged in order according to their dignity. These sovereigns and princes brought with them from their respective countries many men distinguished for their learning and their knowledge of the arts and sciences. These philosophers, poets, and other learned men assembled every night in the palace of Khan Shedid, the heir apparent, where they had Ameer Chuseru a celebrated poet, for their president. When Bulbun went abroad, his body-guards consisted of 1,000 noble Turks in splendid armor and mounted on the finest Persian horses. The great nobles of the empire imitated the emperor as far as they could in pomp and display, and his court was then probably the most splendid in the world.*

* The following extract from Ferishta will give some idea of the court of Delhi at this time, or in A.D. 1265 :— "In the retinue of these princes were the most famous men for learning, war, arts, and sciences that Asia at that time produced. The court of Hindustan was therefore in the days of Bulbun reckoned the most polite and magnificent in the world. All the philosophers, poets, and divines formed a society every night at the house of Khan Shedid, the heir apparent of the empire, and Ameer Chuseru, the poet, presided at these meetings. Another society of musicians, dancers, mimics, players, buffoons, and story-tellers was constantly at the house of the emperor's second son, Kera Khan, who was given to pleasure and levity. The omras followed the example of their superiors, so that various societies and clubs were formed in every quarter of the city. The Sultan having a great passion for splendor and magnificence in his palaces, equipages, and liveries, he was imitated by the court.

"Such was the pomp and grandeur of the royal presence, that none could approach the throne without terror. The ceremonies of introduction were conducted with so much reverence and solemnity, and every thing disposed so as to strike awe and astonishment into the beholders. Nor was Bulbun less magnificent in his cavalcades. His stall elephants were caparisoned in purple and gold. His horseguards, consisting of 1,000 noble Turks in splendid armor,

Insurrections were made in several provinces in the early part of Bulbun's reign. In suppressing these, he acted with great vigor and energy. But he at the same time exhibited great and apparently unnecessary severity and cruelty. In Mewat he is said to have caused more than 100,000 persons to be put to death. In suppressing some disorders in Juanpore and Benares he caused many thousands of men, women, and children to be killed in one common massacre. The governor of Bengal having refused to send to the emperor any part of the plunder he had acquired in some war, and soon afterwards assuming the title of king, the emperor proceeded against him at the head of a large army. He was occupied in this expedition three years, and was successful in suppressing the rebellion. The army of the governor, or king as he called himself, was defeated, and the governor was himself killed as he was endeavoring to swim his horse over the river. The emperor's cruelty towards those who had taken any part, or who were taken prisoners in this rebellion, excited great displeasure at the court, and in the circle of his friends. They resolved to remonstrate against such unnecessary severity. But it was with great difficulty that the Cazees, the Mufties and the great and learned men of the court uniting in one petition, were able to induce the emperor to change his conduct. If this fact shows the cruel disposition of the emperor, it also shows the character of the court in a very favorable light, that should dare openly and publicly to express to an absolute and tyrannical despot, their views and feelings of his actions in a matter of this nature, and that they should succeed in inducing him to change his purpose.

Near the close of his reign the Moguls invaded the Punjab. The emperor's oldest son Mohammed defeated them in battle, but was himself killed in the pursuit. The emperor grieved much for the loss of this son, as he was much attached to him

were mounted upon the finest Persian steeds, with bridles of silver and saddles of rich embroidery; 500 chosen men in rich livery, with their drawn swords upon upon their shoulders, ran proclaiming his approach, and clearing the way before him. All the omras followed according to their rank with their various equipages and attendants. The monarch, in short, seldom went with less than 100,000 armed men, which he used to say was not to gratify any vanity in himself, but to exalt him in the eyes of the people."

and intended he should be his successor. He was now in his 80th year and soon sank under his afflictions and infirmities. His reign continued for 22 years.

Soon after the death of Bulbun his grandson Kei Kobad was raised to the throne. His father Bokarra Khan was yet living and was the governor of Bengal. In his personal appearance Kei Kobad was remarkably handsome, in his manners he was affable and agreeable, and in his disposition mild and amiable. His education had been conducted by able masters, and he excelled in a taste for literature; he had also much general knowledge and great expectations were formed of him. But their hopes were soon disappointed. When declared emperor he was only 18 years old, an age little suited to the temptations, trials, and intrigues of an eastern court. He soon yielded to temptation and gave himself up to pleasure. The vizier, Nizam ud Deen, with a view to secure the throne for himself, encouraged the young emperor in his vicious course. Nor was he in any way scrupulous in respect to the means he used. He managed to remove by death or disgrace all the ministers and servants of the emperor, who would not be subservient to his own promotion. As he had reason to believe that the Mogul and Persian chiefs in the employment of the emperor would continue to be faithful to their royal master, he endeavored by intrigue and treachery to procure their assassination, and he accomplished his purpose. This course of villainy for raising himself to the throne was interrupted by the approach of Bokarra Khan, the emperor's father, who had come from Bengal to visit his son. The vizier representing to the emperor that his father had come to deprive him of all his power, induced him to go out with a force to oppose his father. But as the two armies drew near each other, Bokarra Khan appealed so strongly to his son's feelings that the vizier was compelled to make arrangements for an interview between them. The vizier still endeavored to prevent the interview by requiring some humiliating ceremonies to be performed by the father. But Bokarra Khan submitted to them all. After performing all that was required of him, and bowing several times to his son who took no notice of him, the aged father burst into tears. The emperor seeing this, could no longer suppress his emotions, but leaving his throne hastened to meet his father, and the latter seeing his son approaching, rushed to meet him. They remained in each other's embraces, both weeping for some time. This sight produced a deep impression on the court, and all thoughts of war between the father and son were at end. Bokarra Khan remained at Delhi for some time. He was much affected in view of the habits, circumstances, and prospects of his son, but finding he could do nothing of any importance in reforming him or delivering him from the power of the vizier, and learning that the state of affairs in his own province required his presence, he returned to Bengal.

Kei Kobad continued his course of debauchery till his constitution becoming impaired he had an attack of palsy. This unexpected illness aroused him to reflection, and on reviewing his course of profligacy he saw reason for being much displeased with the vizier. He soon began to look upon the vizier as his greatest enemy, and he determined if possible to get rid of him. With this view he ordered him to proceed to the government of Multan. But the vizier, under various pretences, deferred leaving Delhi, and in the mean time he began to ply all his art at intrigue and treachery to remove Kei Kobad, and assume the supreme power himself. Some of the nobles, to whom he had become very odious, becoming acquainted with his plans, found means to remove him by poison, the not unfrequent end of an odious minister in oriental courts.

As Kei Kobad, from the bad state of his health, could not be expected to survive long, several parties began to form plans for assuming the supreme power, and then dividing the offices of government among themselves. After awhile the party commonly called the Khiljees gained the ascendency, not without much intrigue, treachery, and murder. Fearing they might lose the advantages they had thus secured, they resolved to put their chief upon the throne while they had the power to do it. So an assassin was employed to despatch Kei Kobad, and Jelal ud Deen, the head chief of the Khiljee tribe, ascended the throne and commenced a new dynasty, called the House of Khiljee; Kei Kobad was the last of the series of sovereigns called the Slave Emperors. They were ten in number and their average reign was a little more than 8 years each. Six of them were put to death, or were deposed and died in confinement.

THE HOUSE OF KHILJEE, A.D. 1288–1421.

Jelal ud Deen, of the tribe of Khiljee, was 70 years old when he assumed the imperial power. He had taken the leading part in the revolution which raised him to the supreme power. The late emperor was assassinated by his orders, and yet he affected great reluctance to fill the throne. The courtiers and people gave him but little credit for sincerity in these pretensions, as he kept the son of the late emperor in prison and put him to death as soon as he dared to do it. Some historians, however, deny his agency in this murder. Be this as it may, when he felt that his power was well established he became lenient in his proceedings, not only pardoning offences against himself but transgressions of the laws of the empire. He exhibited this disposition so far that people lost their respect for the laws, and all fear of his displeasure. Governors refused to pay their tribute, and neglected to enforce his laws in their provinces. When some of his ministers remonstrated with him for showing so much forbearance and advised him to follow the example of Bulbun, he replied that he could not live long and wished to die in peace. Yet when a large Mogul army * invaded his dominions he acted with great vigor, proceeding against them with his army and defeating them in a severe battle.

The most remarkable event in this reign was the execution of a celebrated dervish called Syud Molah. He had travelled over several countries and acquired a high reputation for piety before coming to India. He soon acquired great respect at Delhi, and expended so much money in charity that people all believed he had the power of transmuting other metals into gold. He gathered around him a great number of disciples by whom he was held in the highest estimation. Among these was Cazee Jelal ud Deen, an intriguing and ambitious man, who acquired much influence with Syud Molah. The Cazee persuaded the dervish that his disciples all believed God had sent him to Delhi

* Ferishta says that this army contained "ten tomans;" a toman consisted of 10,000 men.

to reform the people, to restore order in the kingdom, and propagate the religion of Mohammed, and that they were prepared to support him in any measures to accomplish the great ends of his mission. Whether the dervish was fanatical and ambitious enough to believe this or not, yet two men were hired to join the emperor's retinue as he was going to the mosque on Friday, and to assassinate him. The disciples were then to proclaim the dervish to be emperor. But one of the disciples not satisfied with the office assigned to him in the contemplated government, went to the emperor and disclosed the whole plan. The emperor ordered the dervish Syud Molah and Cazee Jelal ud Deen to be seized and brought before him. As they denied all knowledge of any such plan, he ordered a great fire to be prepared that they might be put to the trial of ordeal. The emperor and all his court went to see the trial. The dervish, the cazee, and the two assassins were then brought that they might walk through the fire and prove their innocence by coming out unhurt. When they had said their prayers and were just ready to go into the fire, the emperor ordered them to stop, and turning to his court he said, "the nature of fire is to burn, paying no respect to the righteous more than to the wicked. Besides, it is contrary to the Mohammedan law to practise this heathenish superstition." The emperor then ordered the cazee to Budayoon, the dervish to be kept in chains in a vault under the throne, and the two assassins to be put to death. As the dervish was being carried through the court, the emperor said to the Calenders, a class of religious mendicants, "behold the man who devised such evil against us. I leave him to you to be judged according to his deserts," and then proceeded to his palace. The court and all the multitude understood that the dervish was delivered up to them to do with him as they pleased. Neither the court nor the multitude were in a state of mind to show him mercy, and he was soon trampled to death by an elephant, a mode of execution often practised by the former governments in India. Many believed the dervish to be innocent, and that the accusation against him originated in envy. He protested his innocence to the last, and his last words to the emperor were, "be assured that my curse will lie heavy upon you and your posterity." Just as the dervish was put to death, "a black whirlwind arose which for the space of half an hour, changed day into night. No rain fell at Delhi that year, and a dreadful famine followed in which thousands perished of starvation. The emperor's oldest son became insane, the emperor himself died by the hands of assassins, and his family were excluded from the throne." These phenomena and calamities were regarded by the superstitious as evidence of the innocency of the dervish, and of the guilt of the emperor in putting him to death.

In the latter part of this reign, Alla ud Deen, a nephew of the emperor and one of the most remarkable men in the history of India, began to acquire notoriety. When governor of Kurrah he undertook to suppress some insurrections in the provinces south of Delhi. In this expedition he defeated the insurgents, took several forts, plundered the country, and obtained so much booty that he was able to send some of it to the emperor, and to increase his own army. The emperor was so much pleased with Alla ud Deen's success in this enterprise that he gave him large presents, and increased his government by annexing the province of Oude to Kurrah. Alla ud Deen having conciliated the good-will of the emperor and brought his own army into an efficient state, informed him that there were some Hindu princes of great wealth in the country south of Delhi, and if he could have permission he would reduce them to obedience, add their dominions to the empire, and send the wealth he might obtain from them to the royal treasury. The emperor was pleased with the proposal and assented to Alla ud Deen's undertaking the expedition, not expecting he would go beyond the valley of the Nerbudda. Alla ud Deen had a force of 8,000 chosen horse, and he resolved to invade the Deckan, which had hitherto remained undisturbed by the Mohammedans. He proceeded on his way by rapid marches to Ellichpoor, where he made a short stop to refresh his army. The better to conceal his purpose he gave out that he had left his uncle, the emperor, in disgust, and was going to offer his services to the Raja of Telingana. He left Ellichpoor in the night, and changing his course in two days reached Deoghur, the object of his expedition. This city (the modern Dowlutabad) was the capital of Ramdev, who was generally regarded by the Mohammedans as the sovereign of all the Deckan, though he was only the Raja of Maharashtra or of the Mahrattas. The arrival of Alla ud Deen was quite unexpected. The Raja was in the city but his wife and son had gone to a temple in the neighborhood. He collected what force he could and resisted Alla ud Deen's entrance into the city, but was defeated and compelled to retreat into the citadel. Alla ud Deen took possession of the city, plundered the inhabitants and tortured the merchants and bankers to make them disclose their treasures. He then gave out that he was only the vanguard of the imperial grand army, which would arrive soon. This declaration produced great consternation among all the Hindu princes of the Deckan. The Raja expecting a greater force would arrive, and having only a small quantity of provisions, was anxious to come to some terms. Negotiations were commenced and an agreement was nearly completed when the Raja's son arrived with a large army. Contrary to the advice of his father, he attacked Alla ud Deen but was defeated. Alla ud Deen now raised his demands. As the Raja was expecting large reinforcements would soon come to his relief, he hesitated awhile, but on learning that the provisions in the fort were nearly exhausted he agreed to pay a great sum of money,* jewels, etc., and also to cede the province of Ellichpoor to the empire of Delhi. Alla ud Deen having received the money, etc., raised the siege and commenced his return to Delhi, on the 25th day after taking the city. This expedition of Alla ud Deen, in which he marched 700 miles, the greater part of it through an unknown and unexplored country, attacked a powerful monarch, defeated his army, plundered his capital, obtained by treaty an immense amount of treasure and a cession of territory, and then returned in safety, evinced military talents of the highest order, though, in the language of the historian, "we can not but lament that a man formed for such great exploits, should not be actuated by better motives than rapine, violence, and a thirst of gain."

Alla ud Deen went on this expedition into the Deckan, without obtaining the consent of the emperor, and as nothing was

* This amount is thus stated by Ferishta:—"15,000 lbs. of pure gold, 175 lbs. of pearls, 50 lbs. of diamonds, rubies, emeralds, and sapphires; 25,000 lbs. of silver, 4,000 pieces of silk, and a long list of other precious commodities."

heard from him for considerable time, the emperor became very anxious. But when he heard that his nephew had conquered Deoghur and was on his return with a vast amount of treasure, he was much pleased and appeared to think only of seeing it all soon in the royal treasury. But some of his friends, who were well acquainted with Alla ud Deen, intimated that this daring and unauthorized invasion of the Deckan and the renown and plunder there acquired, might be only part of a plan not yet fully revealed. The emperor was at this time near Gwalior with his retinue. Not fully satisfied in respect to Alla ud Deen, the emperor assembled his council and inquired of them whether it was best to march to meet him, or to wait his arrival where they were, or return to Delhi. There was much difference of opinion in the council in respect to the best course to be pursued, and it was finally resolved to return to Delhi. Soon after the emperor reached Delhi a messenger brought him a letter from Alla ud Deen in which he acknowledged himself to be the servant of the emperor, that all the wealth he had acquired in his expedition into the Deckan was intended for the royal treasury, that wearied by their long journey, he wished to rest a few days at Kurrah, that he intended then to come and kiss the footstool of the royal throne, but as some enemies had made insinuations against him and his chiefs in their absence, they therefore requested a letter of grace from the emperor, assuring them of the royal favor and protection. The emperor was much rejoiced on receiving this letter. His suspicions were at once removed, and he ordered a letter full of assurances of kindness and good-will to be returned. In the mean time Alla ud Deen caused reports to be spread by emissaries in different places that the emperor was intending to put him to death for going on his expedition into the Deckan without the royal sanction, that he was extremely sorry for having incurred his majesty's displeasure, and that his grief had been insupportable. Letters to this effect were sent to his brother who was at court and showed them to the emperor, and all possible means were used to induce him to proceed to Kurrah to meet his humbled, penitent, affectionate, and half-distracted nephew. At length the emperor, anxious to secure the treasure brought from the Deckan as well as to see his nephew, left Delhi with a small retinue to meet him. On arriving at Kurrah, Alla ud Deen received the emperor with the greatest respect and affection, in the midst of which some assassins whom he had hired and placed near, upon a concerted signal rushing upon the emperor instantly killed him and then put to death all his attendants. His head was stuck upon a spear, and carried through the city and the camp. His reign had somewhat exceeded 7 years. He acted a leading part in the insurrection and revolution which raised him to the throne, and the then reigning emperor was assassinated by his orders. And after a reign of a few years he was removed in a similar manner, to make way for his ungrateful, cruel, and perfidious nephew.

Alla ud Deen at once assumed the imperial dignity, invested himself with all the insignia of royalty, and caused himself to be proclaimed emperor. He increased his army, conferred titles and rewards upon his friends, and liberally distributed the treasure he had acquired in the Deckan. Wherever he encamped he used to scatter among the multitude or throw to a distance pieces of gold to be scrambled for. By such means he endeavored to acquire notoriety and popularity.

The late emperor's widow at Delhi on hearing of his death caused her youngest son Ruckun ud Deen to be placed upon the throne, and endeavored to unite the family interest in his support. Alla ud Deen felt it was important to establish his power in the capital, and hastened to Delhi. Ruckun ud Deen, unable to meet his enemies in the field, fled with his friends and what treasures they could carry to Multan, where his older brother was governor. The inhabitants of Delhi, after their departure, regarding the cause of Alla ud Deen as now triumphant, joined him. He entered the city in triumph, ascended the throne, and ordered the current money to be struck in his name. He exhibited shows, made grand festivals, and by such means acquired popularity and praise among the fickle and inconsiderate multitude. The people of Delhi appear to have cared little who was emperor or by what means the power and dignity were acquired.* One of Alla ud Deen's first

* Ferishta says:—"He [the emperor] who ought to have been hooted with detestation, became the object of admiration to those who could not see the darkness of his deeds through the splendor of his magnificence."

measures was to get rid of all who could prefer any claim to the throne, and so to prevent any future disturbance from the late emperor's family. With this view he despatched a large army to Multan where two of the sons and many friends had taken refuge. After a siege of two months Multan surrendered, the sons and friends of the late emperor were taken prisoners, their eyes were put out, and soon afterwards they were put to death. All the ladies in the late emperor's harem and all his other children were also killed. But the emperor soon found there was danger from another source. News reached him that a large Mogul army had invaded his dominions, and "were carrying every thing before them with fire and sword." Alif Khan, the emperor's brother, and Zafar Khan were ordered to proceed against them with a large force. The armies encountered each other near Lahore, and the Moguls were defeated with the loss of 12,000 men and many of their chiefs. The Raja of Gujerat not having sent any tribute to Delhi for several years, the emperor sent his army to chastise him and enforce payment. "They laid waste the country with fire and sword, and having appointed rulers over the provinces, they returned to Delhi with prodigious treasure."

The Moguls though defeated and driven back, yet after two years again invaded India in greater force than ever. "Their army consisted of 200,000 horse, and they promised to themselves the entire conquest of Hindustan." There was no force in the provinces they invaded which was able to meet them in the field, and so they proceeded towards Delhi without opposition. On their approach the people of the country rushed into the city, and as no supplies could be procured, a dreadful famine soon commenced its ravages. In these circumstances the emperor called a council of his generals, and prepared his plan for attacking the Moguls. Ferishta says "the army which the emperor brought into the field consisted of 300,000 horse, 2,700 elephants, and foot without number," and that in the history of India no battle had taken place between two such armies, both commanded by generals of great ability and experience. The battle was very severe and the victory obstinately contested. But the Moguls were defeated, and their Prince, Kulugh Khan, collecting his shattered army, retreated till he crossed the Indus.

In A.D. 1306, Alla ud Deen sent a large force into the Deckan under Cafoor, to chastise Ramdev, who had neglected to send the annual tribute, and to extend his conquests. Ramdev submitted in time to preserve his kingdom. Cafoor then proceeded into Telingana, where he committed great ravages, took and plundered Warangole, the capital, and then compelled the Raja to pay a great sum of money and an annual tribute. The expeditions into the Deckan were found to be so successful and profitable that in a few years Cafoor was again sent there with a large army. At this time he penetrated into the kingdom of Canara, defeated Raja Bullal Dev and took him prisoner. Cafoor then plundered the capital and all the towns and temples he could find. If we are to believe the Mohammedan historians (and there are no others) who give the weight of the gold, the value of the plunder obtained in this expedition amounted to nearly $500,000,000. Even the common soldiers were so burdened with spoils that they could only carry the gold, leaving the silver behind them.

Alla ud Deen died in A.D. 1316, having reigned somewhat more than 20 years. He possessed great military talents, and the empire was greatly enlarged by his conquests. He acquired the throne by a course of intrigue, treachery, and violence, and his whole reign was a continuation of actions of a similar character. The Moguls invaded the empire several times during his reign. Some of these invasions were for plunder, but others were made with an intention to conquer the country, and then to keep possession of it. In two or three instances they reached Delhi, but Alla ud Deen succeeded in frustrating their purpose and driving them out of the country. Insurrections occasioned by his cruelty or the oppression of his governors, were frequently made in different parts of the empire. His first expedition into the Deckan and those subsequently made by his generals, appear to have been made more for the sake of acquiring plunder than for conquest. All his wars, whether repelling invasions, or suppressing insurrections, or for acquiring plunder, or for enlarging his dominions, were conducted with great barbarity and shocking cruelty. At one time and for no obvious cause, he ordered that all the Moguls or Persians in his employment should be dismissed. They were soon reduced to great distress, and some of them being detected in a conspiracy, he ordered them all, amounting to 15,000, to be massacred, and their families to be sold into slavery. He cared little or nothing about the Mohammedan religion, and it does not appear that he or his generals ever exhibited any zeal for its propagation, as a reason or motive for their conquests. Among the strange projects he at different times had in view, one was the formation and propagation of a new system of religion. He consulted his learned men on the subject and told them he would form a better system than Mohammedanism or any religion in the world. At one time he proposed to appoint a viceroy over the empire, and taking his army avow his purpose to conquer the whole world. He was so illiterate when he began his reign that he could neither write nor read, but he applied himself so assiduously to study that he was soon able to read and answer all communications addressed to him. From this time he encouraged learning, and several learned men were supported at his court. A conspiracy was once formed to dethrone him. He was attacked, cut down, and left for dead on the ground. The usurper proclaimed the emperor's death, ascended the throne, and ordered the usual ceremonies of inauguration to be performed. In the mean time Alla ud Deen revived, hastened to his army, and assuming the command, caused the usurper to be arrested and put to death. Having assembled his council, he requested them to give their opinions freely in respect to the causes of the unhappy state of the empire. One of the causes they mentioned, was intemperance. The emperor, who was intemperate himself, said he was satisfied this was one of the causes, and there should be a reform. "He published an edict against the use of wine and strong liquors upon pain of death. He himself set the example to his subjects, and emptied all the wine in his cellars into the street. In this course he was followed by all ranks of people, so that for some days the common sewers in Delhi flowed with wine." To prevent property and power from being accumulated in a few families, he issued orders that no marriage should take place among the nobility without a license from him. He also limited by law the quantity of land which any farmer could own, and the number of cattle which graziers could keep. He also attempted to enforce other impracticable laws, as fixed prices of grain and other commodities, the hours of labor for servants, etc.

The great amount of booty and treasure brought from plundered kingdoms and oppressed provinces to Delhi and there distributed and expended, gave to the city the appearance of great wealth and prosperity. "Palaces, mosques, universities, baths, forts, and all manner of public and private buildings seemed to rise as by the power of enchantment, neither did there in any age appear a greater concourse of learned men from all parts of the world; 45 men skilled in the sciences were professors in the University. There were distinguished professors and teachers in poetry, philosophy, medicine, divinity, astrology, music, morality, languages, and in all the fine arts then known in the world." *

* So says Ferishta. One would think it must have been as difficult to teach the precepts and principles of some of these sciences under the laws of the empire, and under the patronage of Alla ud Deen, as it now is to be a professor or teacher in some of the universities under the present despotic governments of Europe.

The following extract shows the character of the Sultan and of his learned men. It also shows the Mohammedan principles of government and the practice of the Sultan:—

"The Sultan one day said to Cazee Mogees ud Deen that he wished to know the law in some matters concerning the duty of sovereigns. As the Sultan had always shown a contempt for the cazees, and called them hypocrites and villains, ready to give any opinions to please those who would reward them, the cazee was much alarmed and replied, 'I fear from what your Majesty has requested that my last hour is come; if so and it be your Majesty's will, I am ready to die; and it will only be unnecessarily increasing my crime, if I must be punished for speaking the truth according to the word of God!' The Sultan inquired why he was so much agitated, and he replied, 'If I speak the truth and your Majesty is offended, it may cost me my life, and if I speak what is false and your Majesty should ascertain the truth, I may then be put to death for deceiving you.' The Sultan replied that he need not fear to answer his inquiries according to the clear and strict laws of the Koran. The Sultan then proposed several inquiries, of which the first was:—

"'From what class of Hindus is it lawful to exact obedience and tribute?' To which the cazee replied:—'It is lawful to exact obedience and tribute from all infidels, and they can only be considered as obedient who pay the poll-tax without demurring even should it be obtained by force; for according to the law of the Prophet it is written regarding infidels, "tax them to the extent they can pay, or utterly destroy them." The learned of the faith have also enjoined the followers of Islam to slay them or to convert them to the faith, a maxim conveyed in the words of the Prophet himself. The Imam Huneef, however,

In the latter part of his reign Alla ud Deen was in feeble health, and excessively irritable and jealous. He was chiefly under the influence of Malik Cafoor, a talented but very depraved man. Cafoor's plan was to remove as fast as possible every obstacle in the way of ascending the throne himself. By exciting the suspicions of the emperor he succeeded in persuading him to throw his two eldest sons and their mother into prison. He caused several men who were high in authority, and whose power and influence he had reason to dread, to be put to death. And it was generally believed that the emperor's death was hastened by poison given him by the same treacherous hand.

The day after the death of Alla ud Deen, Malik Cafoor assembled the nobles and produced a pretended will of the late emperor, by which his youngest son, only 7 years of age, was appointed his successor, and Cafoor was to be regent till the son should be of age. This son was then put upon the throne and Cafoor commenced his regency. One of his first acts was to put out the eyes of the late emperor's two oldest sons. He then caused the third son to be seized, and issued orders to put him to death. His conduct in these matters greatly shocked some of the nobles, and he soon met the fate he was so assiduously preparing for others. Mubarick, the third son, was then set at liberty and assumed the government for his brother, the young emperor. In a few months he found means to seize his brother, and having put out his eyes and sent him to Gwalior to be confined for life, he ascended the throne himself. One of his first acts after assuming the supreme power was to put those to death who had saved his life and elevated him to the throne. He invested some of his slaves with the highest offices in the government. He ordered all the prisoners in the jails and forts

subsequently considers, that the poll-tax or as heavy a tribute imposed upon them as they can bear, may be substituted for death, and he has accordingly forbidden that their blood be unnecessarily shed. So that it is commanded that the poll-tax and tribute should be exacted to the utmost farthing from them in order that the punishment may approximate as nearly as possible to death.' The Sultan smiling, remarked, 'You may perceive that without any aid from your learned books or consulting any cazee, I have always been practising of my own accord the principles of the Prophet.'" — *Gleig, Vol. I. p.* 128 – 131.

without any inquiry into their guilt or innocence, amounting to 17,000, to be set at liberty. His reign was little else than one continued series of outrages upon decency, justice, and morality. Much of the time he was in a state of intoxication, and his delight was in low and disgusting revelry and debauchery. In suppressing insurrections the most monstrous barbarity and cruelty were used in massacres and tortures. His brothers who had been previously blinded, were put to death without having given, so far as was known, any occasion for suspicion. All respectable people withdrew from the emperor and his court for their own preservation, as well as from disgust of the vices there practised. At length Khusru, one of the emperor's favorites, more depraved if possible than his master, formed a conspiracy to assassinate him and assume the government. In this plan he was successful, but soon after he ascended the throne another conspiracy was formed among the nobles, who associated to save the throne from further disgrace and the empire from total ruin. The usurper Khusru was defeated and put to death. On inquiry it was found that no member of the royal family was living—all had been put to death. The House of Khiljee had become extinct. In 33 years, 5 emperors had ascended the throne, and all had perished by assassination or poison.

THE HOUSE OF TOGHLUCK, A.D. 1321–1412.

Ghazi Khan was head of the conspiracy which deposed Khusru. When he entered Delhi he made a proclamation that he had engaged in the revolution for the good of the empire; that if any of the royal family remained, they should be brought forward and put upon the throne; and that if none remained, the people might elect any emperor they pleased, and he would abide by their choice. As none of the royal family remained, the nobles and magistrates presented him the keys of the city, and proclaimed him to be emperor. He assumed the name of Ghias ud Deen, though he is probably better known by the name of Toghluck and Toghluck Shah. The state of the empire required an able and energetic emperor, and such Ghias ud Deen soon showed he was. He reformed the internal administration, and placed a strong force on the north-western frontier, where the empire was threatened by an invasion from the Moguls. The affairs of the Deckan having fallen into disorder, he sent his son, Jonah Khan, there with a large force. Jonah Khan laid siege to Warangole, the capital of Telingana. The siege was protracted, and the hot season having commenced, great sickness prevailed in the Mohammedan army. In the mean time reports being circulated of a revolution at Delhi, the army became discouraged and it became necessary to raise the siege. When retreating towards Deoghur, Jonah Khan was pursued with great slaughter by the Hindus, and when he reached Delhi only 3,000 of his whole army remained. He again assembled a large force and proceeded into the Deckan. On his way to Warangole he besieged and took Beder. He then laid siege to Warangole and soon got possession of the city. The Raja and his family were made prisoners and carried to Delhi. The emperor having received many complaints of disturbance and oppression in the provinces of Bengal, appointed Jonah Khan his deputy in Delhi, and proceeded himself with a large army to Lucknow and Tirhoot, where he was occupied for some time in restoring order. On his return to Delhi, his son entertained him in a large pavilion built of wood and hastily erected for the purpose. When the entertainment was over and just as the emperor was leaving the place, the roof over him fell and killed him. By some persons his death was believed to be accidental, but the more general and probable opinion was that the pavilion had been erected and every part of it prepared to fall upon the emperor in the manner his death took place. His reign somewhat exceeded four years. The expectations formed concerning him when he ascended the throne were fully realized. He was among the best sovereigns of Delhi.

Jonah Khan immediately after his father's death assumed the supreme power and took the name of Mohammed, sometimes called Mohammed Toghluck. He commenced his reign with great liberality and magnificence. The streets were strewed with flowers, the houses were all ornamented, music was everywhere played, large presents were given to the nobles, and handfuls of gold and silver were scattered among the multitude. He was careful in observing the hours for worship, and ordered prayers to be read in all the mosques five times every day. Unlike his predecessors generally, he abstained from wine. He had been well educated in Persian and Arabic literature. He encouraged learning and gave salaries to learned men at his court. His actions, acquirements, and personal qualities were such as secured great respect, and gave his subjects the hope of a long and happy reign.

But it was not long before he began to exhibit a different character, and the prospect of his reign became dark and gloomy. A large Mogul force invaded the empire, and instead of repelling them, he gave them an enormous sum of money to leave the country, thus inviting them to return soon for the same purpose. He collected a vast army (Ferishta says 370,000) with the avowed purpose of conquering Persia. As he had not means to support them, they soon scattered over the empire, seizing whatever they required. Having heard of the wealth of China, he sent his nephew with an army of 100,000 men to conquer and plunder that country. The army was urged forward over mountains, rivers, and forests, suffering much from disease and want till they met a Chinese army. Here they encountered so many difficulties that nearly all the army perished, only a few returning to relate their disasters and their sufferings. He next resolved upon another way for relieving his wants. He caused some copper coins to be struck with his name upon them, and issued a decree that all such should pass for silver. In this way his debts were easily paid, but as these same coins were taken in payment for revenue, his financial difficulties were not diminished, while such measures destroyed all confidence in the credit of the government and caused confusion and bankruptcy among all classes, so that he was compelled to annul his decree and restore the former currency. At one time when his army had surrounded a large district in the manner of a grand hunt in India, he gave orders that the circle should close towards the centre, and that they should kill every human being found in it. This horrid barbarity was more than once repeated, and in one such instance, "there was a general massacre of the inhabitants of the great city of Kanouj." No wonder "the miseries of the country exceeded all power of description."

Among all this emperor's mad projects none probably caused more misery than his attempt to change the capital of his empire from Delhi to Deoghur, which he called Dowlutabad,* the name by which it is still known. When he proposed in his council that the capital of his empire should be changed to Deoghur, they recommended Oujein, as more centrally situated, but he was inflexible. So he issued orders that the inhabitants, men, women, and children, with all their effects and living creatures, should migrate to Dowlutabad, a distance of more than 700 miles. Delhi was left almost desolate. He took up his residence at Dowlutabad for 2 or 3 years, and then returned to Delhi, giving permission to the inhabitants to do the same. But so many perished from suffering, sickness, and famine, that but few of those who had removed from Delhi reached the city on their return.

In such a reign, insurrections, conspiracies, and revolts might naturally be expected. And such there were. Insurrections were suppressed, but not without much destruction of life, the plundering of cities, and the desolation of provinces. Conspiracies were detected and their object defeated, but not without the ruin of many individuals and their families. The governor of Bengal revolted and asserted his independence. The country on the Coromandel Coast followed the same example. The Rajas of Telingana and Carnata combined to recover their independence, and succeeded in expelling the Mohammedan armies and garrisons from their dominions. The emperor died at

* This city, now in ruins, is 8 miles from Aurungabad. The writer visited the ruins in 1834. The following is an extract from his private journal:—"The fort consists of an isolated mountain of a semi-oval shape, about 500 feet high. One third of the way from the base to the top the hill is scarped all around, and presents on every side a perpendicular cliff of about 150 feet high. At the base of this cliff, is a wide and deep ditch, excavated in the solid rock, and extending round all the circuit of the hill, which is not included in the walls of the city. The only way of ascending the hill is by a long, dark, and winding way from the city, and excavated through the rock. The entrance of this way is near the base of the mountain, and is surrounded by towers and walls for its defence. The fort, or mountain above the cliff, has cisterns for water, magazines for provisions, military stores, cannon, etc. The mountain is a mass of natural rock, and the labor of reducing it to its present shape must have been incalculable. This fort was formerly regarded as impregnable."

Tatta in Scinde, where he had proceeded to suppress an insurrection, in A.D. 1351, having reigned for 27 years. Of his character, one historian says, "he left the reputation of one of the most accomplished princes and most furious tyrants that ever adorned or disgraced human nature." Another says, "he appears to have labored with no contemptible abilities to be detested by God, and to be feared and abhorred by all men." Another speaks of his death as "delivering India from the dreadful scourge of his government." And another says, "he left a reputation as little to be envied as that of any sovereign who ever reigned in India."

Mohammed Toghluck having no son, recommended his nephew, Feroze Toghluck (sometimes called Feroze Shah), to his nobles to be made his successor. The army, soon after the death of the emperor, fell into much disorder. A plan was formed to seize the treasure, and a part of it was carried away by the Mogul mercenaries. In this perilous state of affairs the nobles united in requesting Feroze Toghluck immediately to assume the supreme power. To this request he assented, and was proclaimed emperor. He was then at Tatta in Scinde. Having settled the affairs of that province, he proceeded to Uch, where he heard that another person had been set up for emperor at Delhi. He entered into amicable negotiation with the party, and they submitted to Mohammed Toghluck, when he proceeded to Delhi and ascended the throne without any further opposition. The empire was in a state of great disorder, and the people were groaning under injustice and oppression.

To these evils he applied a steady and vigorous hand. "He limited the number of capital punishments, and put a stop to the use of torture and the practice of mutilation, which last prohibition was the more meritorious, as it was at variance with the Mohammedan laws. He abolished a great number of vexatious taxes and fees, put an end to all fluctuating and precarious imposts, and fixed the revenues in such a manner as to leave as little discretion as possible to the collectors, and to give precision and publicity to the demands of the State."* Such reforms display great energy and judgment. They were received with gratitude, and gave great satisfaction.

* Elphinstone, p. 357.

Scinde, Gujerat, and some other provinces were in a state of insurrection when he ascended the throne. In such places the authority of the emperor was soon established, and with less cruelty and barbarity than in previous reigns. Bengal, which revolted under a Mohammedan governor, and the Deckan, in which the Rajas of Telingana and Carnata united and expelled the Mohammedan garrisons in the preceding reign, continued to be nearly independent. They sent embassies with tribute or presents, thus acknowledging the superiority of the emperor, and were then permitted to manage their own affairs as they pleased. In the latter part of his reign the emperor made an expedition into Bengal. The reasons for this do not appear, as he did not subdue the country. Ferishta says, "About this time an embassy arrived with presents and new conditions of peace from Bengal, which the Sultan accepted, and soon after ratified the treaty. Bengal now became in a great measure independent of the empire, paying only a small acknowledgment annually by way of presents.* He exacted no other terms of the Deckan, so that these two great members were now kept from the government of Delhi."

The government of Mohammed Toghluck exhibited a striking contrast with that of his predecessors in some other respects. Instead of lavishing the revenues of the empire upon depraved and worthless favorites, he expended them upon public works of various kinds. Of these the following are enumerated:— 50 canals to promote agriculture by irrigation; 40 mosques; 30 colleges; 100 caravansarais; 30 reservoirs for irrigation; 100 hospitals; 100 public baths, and 150 bridges. For the permanent support of these he made assignments of land. If some of these should be the *estimated* number of the works of his reign, yet the ruins of the works, which were executed by this emperor and remain to the present time, show a zeal for the public good, a spirit of enterprise and an expenditure of revenue, which few sovereigns of any age or country ever exhibited. And these public works were made by a Mohammedan emperor in India nearly five centuries ago.

* "In the year 759, (A.D. 1353,) the Sultan of Bengal sent a number of elephants and other rich presents to Delhi, which were amply repaid in Arabian and Persian horses, jewels, and other rich curiosities."

Having reached the age of 87, Mohammed Toghluck's infirmities made him incapable of the requisite attention to the affairs of government, and the administration gradually fell into the hands of the vizier. This depraved man resolved to use his influence with the emperor and the power of his office with the army, in removing the oldest son, the heir apparent, so as to succeed the emperor at his death. The emperor and his son on becoming acquainted with the conspiracy, made an attempt to seize the vizier, but he escaped from Delhi. Mohammed Toghluck immediately resigned the government in favor of his son, who was proclaimed emperor by the title of Mohammed Shah. The new emperor soon showed himself to be unfit for administering the government. He dismissed some of the most approved public servants, and filled their places with depraved and worthless favorites. He neglected public affairs, and spent his time in revelry and debauchery. A conspiracy was formed for deposing him, and an insurrection ensued. In the struggle between the insurgents and the emperor and his party, "the city of Delhi became a horrid scene of slaughter and confusion. During the space of two days and two nights there was nothing but death in every street; friends and foes, victors and vanquished were jumbled together without any possibility of distinction." On the third day the insurgents carried out the old emperor and set him down in the streets. The young emperor's party, supposing this was done by the order of the old emperor, flocked to him and the insurgents, when the young emperor seeing himself almost deserted, fled from the city to the mountains of Simone. Both parties while surrounding the old emperor and in his presence, made peace with each other. A grandson named Toghluck Shah was then put upon the throne, soon after which Mohammed Toghluck died at the age of 90 years. He had reigned 38 years, which was a longer time than the reign of any previous Mohammedan emperor of Delhi.

Toghluck Shah was soon involved in quarrels with those who had raised him to the throne. He intrusted the affairs of the government to his ministers and servants, and spent his time in frivolity and revelry. A conspiracy was formed against him and he was assassinated when he had reigned only five months.

Abu Beckur Toghluck, another grandson of Mohammed

Toghluck, next succeeded to the throne. The man whom he appointed to be his vizier, was soon detected in a conspiracy to cut off the emperor and assume the supreme power. The emperor caused the vizier and many others connected with the conspiracy to be put to death. But though relieved from this enemy, he had to encounter another. Mohammed Shah who had fled from Delhi to the mountains of Simone, collected a large force, and proclaiming himself to be the emperor, he proceeded to Delhi. Abu Beckur defended his own claims to this dignity as well as he could, and the conflict was protracted for some time. At length the good fortune of Mohammed Shah prevailed. He ascended the throne. Abu Beckur fled and afterwards surrendered himself and was kept a prisoner for life. But Mohammed Shah survived this triumph but a short time. After his decease his son, Humayoon Khan, was proclaimed emperor by the title of Secunder Shah, but he died in 45 days after ascending the throne.

On the death of Secunder Shah there was much dissension among the nobles concerning the succession to the throne. At length it was determined that Mahmoud, a son of Mohammed Shah, should succeed, and though he was a child yet he was proclaimed emperor by the title of Mahmoud Shah. Some important changes were also made at the same time among the principal nobles. The youth of the emperor and the dissensions existing in the court encouraged revolt in the provinces. Muzzuffer Khan, the governor of Gujerat, began to assert his independence. The governors of Malwa and Candesh did the same. The vizier took up his residence at Juanpoor, assumed the title of King of the East, and began to act as an independent prince. A faction at Delhi set up another claimant to the throne, and civil war raged in the capital. It was when the empire presented this scene of anarchy and distraction, some provinces already independent, others in a state of insurrection, the central parts rent by faction, and the capital suffering all the miseries of a civil war, that reports came from the west, which were fitted to excite more alarm and anxiety than any thing which had occurred to India for several centuries.

TAMERLANE, A.D. 1398.

Tamerlane was the son of a Mogul or Tartar chief in a village near Samarcand. From the death of Ghengis Khan the central parts of Asia had been the scene of frequent insurrections and revolutions. In these scenes Tamerlane early engaged, and soon acquired a high character for military talents. Having become the generally acknowledged sovereign of his native country, he made an attack upon Persia, which was soon added to his dominions. He extended his power over Mesopotamia, and drove the Caliph from his throne in Bagdad. He returned to Samarcand, and then with an immense army directed his course towards India. He overcame all difficulties, whether the natural obstacles of the road, or the resistance of the inhabitants, or the want of provisions for his immense army. He crossed the Indus near Attock, and directed his course towards Delhi, plundering the cities and massacring the people, or taking them prisoners on the way. When he was near Delhi he ordered that all the prisoners in the camp, who had been taken since crossing the Indus and were over 15 years of age, should be put to death. Mohammedan historians say that the number massacred in obedience to this inhuman order amounted to 100,000. If we allow this number to be somewhat exaggerated, still the number was no doubt very great, and the barbarity and cruelty thus manifested are shocking. Mahmoud Shah marched out of the city with all the force he could command, and offered battle. But they fled on the first attack from the troops of Tamerlane, who for many years had closed every battle with a victory. The conqueror pursued them till they entered the gates of Delhi. The emperor made no further effort at defence, but fled to Gujerat. The nobles and distinguished men of the city then proffered submission to Tamerlane, and he promised them that if they would pay him a certain specified contribution, he would spare the city and protect the inhabitants. He then ordered himself to be proclaimed emperor of India in all the mosques of the city. He placed guards at all the gates that none might escape, and gave orders that the sum of money to be paid him, should be contributed according to the wealth and rank of the citizens. Complaints were soon made that some of the nobles and bankers refused to pay their portion, and he sent some troops into the city to assist the magistrates in making the collection. Tamerlane's troops had been accustomed to seize all they could get, and were unwilling to take only a part of the wealth of a city which they had been so long expecting to plunder. Plundering, confusion, and uproar soon commenced, and no authority either of the Mogul officers then in the city, or of the magistrates, could restrain it. Tamerlane was then in his camp, engaged in celebrating a grand festival for his success in having taken the city and been proclaimed emperor of India. And he continued this celebration for five days, while plundering and massacring raged in the city. Very many of the higher classes seeing how the women were ravished, and the men tortured to disclose their wealth which was all then seized, collected their families, killed their wives and daughters, set their houses on fire, and then seizing their weapons, and rushing into the streets in the spirit of desperation, fought till they were killed. The streets are said to have been filled with the slain, and a large part of the city was reduced to ashes.

Tamerlane remained at Delhi 15 days, and then unexpectedly to all, he began his return towards Persia. The day before his departure, "he offered up praises to God in the mosques for his success." The money, jewels, and other valuable things which he and his army obtained in India and carried away with them, were very great. Great numbers of men and women were dragged into slavery. He greatly admired the mosques and palaces of Delhi, and he carried away with him many architects, masons, and sculptors, with the intention of erecting similar edifices in Samarcand, his capital. On arriving at Panniput, he sent one of his generals to take Merut, but the force was not sufficient. Tamerlane then proceeded to Merut with all his army. The city and fort were defended with great obstinacy. But the Moguls having filled the ditch, scaled the walls and "put every soul within to the sword." Tamerlane then continued on his course towards his own country, "marking his way with fire and sword, and leaving anarchy, famine, and pestilence behind him." There is nothing said of his investing any one with authority, or making arrangements for any regular government in Delhi. He confirmed the governors who submitted to him in their respective provinces, and they engaged to govern in his name. These circumstances appear to indicate that he intended to return and assume the government, or send some one to govern in his name, but something unexpected prevented his doing so.*

The city of Delhi remained in a state of anarchy for some months after Tamerlane's departure. When it was seen that he had left India, several different parties endeavored to assume and exercise the supreme government. Some of these attempted to govern in the name of Tamerlane, and others in their own name. The governors of the different provinces asserted their independence and called themselves kings, so that only a small district around Delhi continued attached to the city and subject to its power. In the course of half a century there were 7 different emperors or men who assumed the title in Delhi. There was nothing in their character or actions, or in the state of the districts acknowledging their authority, which appears to be deserving of consideration or being mentioned.

Among the military chiefs at Delhi, who became conspicuous in this period of anarchy and misrule, was Beylol Lodi. The family had been military leaders of distinction for several generations. After long-continued intrigue and effort he became emperor in A.D. 1450. He was assisted in acquiring this dignity by the vizier of the preceding emperor, and as has often happened in oriental courts, his first exercise of this power was to remove him by whose aid he had acquired it. The early part of his reign was spent in struggling with factions and suppressing insurrections at Delhi. He was then engaged for many years in endeavoring to extend his power over some provinces, which had formerly belonged to the empire, but had become independent. In these wars he was generally successful, and at the close of his reign the kingdom of Delhi had become the most powerful of any in the northern part of India. His reign somewhat exceeded 38 years.

Secunder Lodi, a son of the late emperor, succeeded him at Delhi. His brothers, who were governors of different provinces for some years before their father's death, refused to acknowl-

* Elphinstone, p. 362.

edge his superiority. Secunder's claim to be acknowledged emperor over all the dominions of his father and his brothers' resistance to this claim, were the occasion of frequent conflicts and wars between them. In these wars Secunder was generally successful, and the provinces which were subject to his father acknowledged his authority. He then extended the empire by annexing some provinces in Bahar and Bundelcund. He was very bigoted in his attachment to Mohammedanism, and destroyed many temples and idols in the cities and provinces recovered from the Hindus. He even forbid them to resort to some of their sacred places on pilgrimage. A brahmin, in reply to a Mohammedan who had abused him for his worshipping idols, said, "All religions, if practised with equal sincerity, are equally acceptable to God." For this opinion the brahmin was called before a council of the Moolahs, who decided that he must either become a Mohammedan or be put to death. The brahmin showed that he was sincere in his religion by suffering death rather than change his faith. This emperor for some reason removed his court to Agra, which in the latter part of his reign became the capital of the empire. He was much esteemed by the Mohammedan part of his subjects, and is reckoned among their best emperors. His reign somewhat exceeded 28 years.

BABER, A.D. 1526.

Ibrahim Lodi succeeded the late emperor his father. His haughty manners and imperious temper made him unpopular. Some insurrections soon occurred, and the parties concerned in them were treated with great barbarity. The governor of Lahore revolted, and fearing the fate of some who had been put to death, applied to Baber, the Sultan of Cabul, for assistance. Baber, who had for some time been meditating the conquest of India, was glad to receive such an invitation. He soon appeared in India with his army, and as the conquest of the country was his object he proceeded towards Delhi. On arriving at Panniput he was informed that the emperor was approaching with an army of 100,000 men and 1,000 elephants. Baber's force, though much inferior in numbers, was yet greatly superior in discipline and valor. He had also himself great military talents and experience, and he possessed the entire confidence of his army. In the battle which decided the empire of India, the emperor's want of judgment was as conspicuous in his preparatory arrangements, as the want of discipline was in his army during the conflict and in the retreat. In this battle the emperor Ibrahim Lodi was killed, and his army was routed with great slaughter. Baber then proceeded forthwith to Delhi and Agra, and both cities surrendered without making any resistance. Though in possession of these imperial cities and proclaimed emperor, he was yet acknowledged by only a small part of what had formerly constituted the empire. The governors of the provinces were in no haste to acknowledge their allegiance to the new emperor. Many in his army disliking the oppressive and enervating heat of the Indian climate, became anxious to return to Cabul. As the dissatisfaction and murmuring on the subject increased, Baber assembled his officers in council and told them that having become the emperor of India, an object he had long had in view, he was determined to remain in the country, that all who wished to return to Cabul had his permission to do so, but in future he would tolerate no more murmuring on the subject. A few of his officers returned to Cabul, but the greater part, seeing the emperor's determination, resolved to unite their fortunes with his, and so remained in India. When this determination became known, the governors of some of the provinces who had been expecting that Baber, like Tamerlane, would soon leave India, took the prudent course of acknowledging allegiance to him. His son Humayoon, was also successful in reducing some provinces to obedience, so that in the course of a few months the empire included all the provinces which acknowledged allegiance to his predecessor.

But Baber soon found himself surrounded with new difficulties. The Rajpoot princes uniting with some Mohammedan nobles of the same family or clan with the late emperor, formed a powerful combination against him. In the first conflict with this confederated army a part of Baber's force was defeated with heavy loss. His army and his officers were much affected with this unexpected result. A celebrated astrologer arriving at this time from Cabul, predicted from the position of the planet Mars the certain defeat of the army in the approaching campaign. Many of Baber's army now began to desert, the force of his enemies increased, and his officers and friends became disheartened. He contemplated his circumstances and prospects with much anxiety. He tells us in his Memoirs that he repented of all his sins and implored pardon of God; he solemnly resolved that he would drink no more wine, which he acknowledges he had sometimes used to excess, and he caused his drinking vessels of gold and silver to be melted up and distributed in alms to the poor. He also made a vow to let his beard grow and remit the stamp-tax on all Mohammedans, if it should please God to give him the victory over his enemies. He then assembled his officers in council, and described their past exploits, their present dangers, and the glory which it was yet in their power to obtain. The assembly was greatly excited by this address;* all proclaimed their determination to support him, and swore on the Koran to conquer or die. Seeing the army in this state, Baber resolved to prosecute the war with vigor. His arrangement of his forces showed his great military talent and experience in war, and he soon obtained a decided victory in which several of the princes confederated against him were slain.

Soon after this victory Baber, in extending his conquests, laid siege to Chanderi, a strong fort belonging to the Rajpoots. When the garrison saw they could defend the place no longer, "they, according to their dreadful custom, murdered their wives and children in the following manner. They placed a sword in the hand of one of their chiefs, and he slew the unhappy victims, who one after another bent of their own accord before him; they even contended among themselves for the honor of being the first slain. The soldiers then threw turmeric powder over

* Baber closed his address to the council of his officers thus:—"The voice of glory is loud in my ear, and forbids me to disgrace my name by giving up what my arms have with so much difficulty acquired. But as death is at last unavoidable, let us rather meet him with honor face to face than shrink back to gain a few years of a miserable and ignominious existence, for what can we inherit but fame beyond the limits of the grave?" The whole assembly, as if inspired by one soul, cried at once, "War! war!"—*Ferishta*, vol. ii. p. 119.

their garments as on a day of festivity, and throwing loose their hair, issued forth with their swords and shields and sought that death which they all obtained. Not one was found alive in the fort when it was taken."

Baber survived the conquest of India only 5 years. He died at the age of 50. His body was carried to Cabul to be buried as he had directed. His tomb is still preserved, and the cemetery is "the great holiday resort of the people of the city." Few Asiatic sovereigns ever had so many good personal qualities and performed so many splendid actions to commend them while they lived, and to be held in esteem after they were dead. He was descended on the side of his father from Tamerlane, and on the part of his mother from Ghengis Khan, the two great Tartar conquerors of the middle ages. At an early age he succeeded his father who was the king of Indija and Ferghana, and he was soon involved in war with his uncles, who endeavored, by taking advantage of his youth, to deprive him of his paternal possessions. After many successes and reverses he was ejected from his hereditary dominions, but in his 23d year he became the sovereign of Cabul, where he reigned 22 years before he made his great invasion of India. He possessed the rare qualities for an Asiatic sovereign of living on familiar terms of social intercourse with his officers and friends, and yet of retaining great influence over them. He was incessantly occupied in wars and revolutions, and yet he found time to cultivate a taste for the fine arts, and Ferishta says, "he was a master in the arts of poetry, writing, and music." In Hindustan, while apparently occupied in suppressing insurrections and extending his power over provinces which for awhile refused allegiance to him, he was also forming plans for making aqueducts, reservoirs, canals, and caravanserais, and for introducing foreign fruits and other edibles, for the improvement of the country. His Memoirs,* in the Turki language, written by himself, are exceeded by very few works, ancient or modern. He also wrote many elegant poems in Persian, and a collection of compositions

* There is an English translation of this work, commenced by Dr. Leyden, and completed by Mr. W. Erskine. It gives a graphic and interesting account of the religion, customs, manners, etc., of the Mohammedans and Hindus of that age.

in Turki, which have always been regarded as works of uncommon merit in those languages.

In the last year of his life his conduct in one instance exhibited some peculiar traits of character, as well as the superstitious prejudices of the age. His oldest son Humayoon was for some time very sick, and when his physicians all gave over further efforts, saying he must die, Baber, in accordance with a generally received opinion among his people that it was possible to save the life of the sick man in such cases by devoting another life for him, resolved to devote his own life for his son. On declaring his purpose, his nobles and friends who had entire confidence in the efficacy of the means, endeavored to dissuade him by representing how important his own life was to his family and to the interests of the empire. But Baber had formed his purpose and continued unmoved, saying, that he was himself becoming old, his constitution was already broken and he could not live long, but his son was young, and if restored to health might rule over the empire for many years. When all the circumstances for the ceremony of devoting himself to save the life of his son had been performed, Baber walked three times round the bed of the dying man in the manner required. He then retired for prayer, and soon experienced such assurance that the substitution he had made had been accepted, that he exclaimed aloud, "I have borne it away, I have borne it away." These proceedings were deeply affecting to the father and the son, and to all who witnessed them or then heard of them, and the Mohammedan historians agree in saying that Humayoon began from that time to recover, and that Baber, who had been previously ill, became more unwell, and continued to fail till he died.

HUMAYOON, A.D. 1531.

Humayoon, Baber's oldest son, succeeded him in the empire of India. He had three other sons, Kamran, Hindal, and Mirza Askari. Kamran was governor of Cabul for some years before Baber's death, and Humayoon allowed him to continue in undisturbed possession. He even added Lahore to the territory of Cabul. The empire of Baber became thus practically divided into two governments. At the beginning of his reign

Humayoon had great confidence in astrology, and he fitted up halls for reception and business according to the supposed influence of the different planets on human affairs. Thus he had the hall of Mars for general and military matters, the hall of Mercury for his judges and matters of justice, etc. But the affairs of the empire soon became too urgent for him to pursue this course. The governors of several provinces were determined not to yield obedience until they were compelled to do it, and so he was soon involved in war with them. Among these Bahadur of Gujerat was conspicuous for his power and enterprise. Humayoon proceeded with a large force into Gujerat, but he had scarcely time to establish his power there before he had to hasten back to his own capital. Shere Khan, who had for some time been in possession of Bengal, proved a yet more formidable enemy. This prince had great military talents as well as unscrupulous ambition. Humayoon proceeded into Bengal with a large force, but a series of reverses compelled him to retreat and return to Agra. Again he assembled a large army and proceeded against the rebellious governor, who had now assumed the title of king. In this war the emperor suffered several defeats, and was twice near being drowned in the Ganges. Shere Khan improved the advantages he had gained, and pursuing Humayoon in his retreat towards Agra, at length compelled him to abandon his capital. Humayoon, seeing his affairs thus apparently desperate, fled with his family and what treasure he could carry to Scinde. While crossing the desert he and his followers suffered exceedingly, and in these distressed circumstances, in the desert, his son Acber, afterwards so celebrated in the history of India, was born. Humayoon continued in Scinde for three years, and seeing no prospect of retrieving his affairs, and becoming apprehensive for his own safety, he escaped to Persia.

In the mean time Shere Khan ascended the throne of Delhi, and was proclaimed emperor by the title of Shere Shah. The governors of some provinces refused allegiance, and a combination of the Rajpoot chiefs against him became so powerful that he had to proceed into their territories with an army of 80,000 men before he could enforce submission. When superintending the batteries at the siege of Kallinger he was so much injured by the explosion of a magazine that he survived only a few hours. He continued, though in a state of intense suffering, to direct the operations of the siege, and when intelligence was brought to him that the fort was taken, he exclaimed, "Thanks be to Almighty God," and these were his last words. He had been emperor for 5 years, and notwithstanding he was much occupied in reducing refractory governors to submission, he introduced many improvements, and left the empire in a flourishing state. One historian of India says that "Shere Shah made a high road extending for four months' journey from Bengal to the western Rohtas near the Indus, with caravanserais at every stage, and wells at every mile and a half; there was an imam and muezzin at every mosque, and provisions for the poor at every caravanserai, with attendants of proper castes for the Hindus as well as Mohammedans. This road was planted with rows of trees for shade, and in many places was in this state when the historian saw it, fifty two years after it was made." Shere Shah is generally described as a usurper by the Mahommedan historians, who were in the interest of the house of Tamerlane or Baber. But he was born in India, he was high in power when Baber crossed the Indus, and he united the forces of the country and expelled a foreign family who had been only fourteen years in power. He always sustained a good character when a provincial governor; he displayed great military talents in his wars with Humayoon, and when at the head of the empire he managed its affairs with wisdom, moderation, and success. He was buried at Sahseram in a mausoleum which he had prepared for himself. It is still a substantial stone structure, and "stands in the centre of an artificial piece of water a mile in circumference, which is faced by walls of stone with flights of steps descending to the water."

Shere Shah's eldest son, Adil Khan, was designed by his father to be his successor. But he had never exhibited abilities suitable for such a difficult situation, while Jelal Khan, his brother, had displayed good talents for government, and distinguished himself in the army in his father's wars. For these reasons the chiefs combined to promote Jelal Khan to the throne, who assumed the title of Selim Shah Soor. In this reign Shekh Allai, a man of great learning, zeal, and eloquence, attempted to introduce a new form of religion, which occasioned much trouble. Many soon embraced his sentiments. "They threw their property into a common stock and some even left their families and devoted themselves to the Shekh. Khowas Khan, a distinguished officer, was among his followers. At first the Shekh's fanaticism was inoffensive, but some of his followers went beyond all tolerable bounds. They thought it was their duty to interfere whenever they saw a man in any act of sin, and if he did not attend to their remonstrance, to put him to death. The civil government as well as the Moolahs thought it was high time to interpose. The Shekh was tried and condemned to death, but the emperor remitted his sentence and banished him to Hindia on the river Nerbudda. This only spread the infection of his doctrines; for he soon converted the governor and the garrison, and was making greater progress than ever when he was recalled to the capital. The emperor was importuned by the Moolahs to put him to death, and after many delays he ordered him to be whipped and then to be left to consider for a while whether he would recant his errors. The Shekh was suffering from an epidemic then prevailing, and was so reduced that he expired at the third lash." The Mohammedan religion has had far more reformers than is generally supposed, and its history furnishes, among these reformers, numerous instances of zeal, self-denial, sufferings, and even death for their faith.

On Selim's death, his son, Feroze Khan, then only 12 years of age, was proclaimed emperor, but in a few days he was assassinated by his uncle Mubariz, who assumed the office of emperor by the title of Mohammed Shah. He spent his time in revelry, and squandered the royal treasures in folly and dissipation. The emperor and his court were soon despised by all respectable people at the capital. The governors of the provinces treated the royal commands with neglect, and the empire was fast verging to a state of anarchy, when Humayoon, who had become ruler of Cabul, being aware of the distracted state of India, and invited by many of his former friends to return, resolved on an effort to recover his former throne.

Humayoon had been 9 years emperor of India when he was compelled to take refuge in Persia. Shah Tahmasp, who was then king of Persia, as soon as he heard of the arrival of Humayoon in his dominions, issued orders for him to be treated with all due respect. The governors of the provinces received him with great honor; all the wants of himself and his followers were supplied, and they were lodged in the royal palaces. But there were some circumstances of a painful and humiliating character. Humayoon was not allowed to approach the capital for some time, and several months passed before he was admitted to an interview with the Persian monarch. Soon after personal intercourse between them commenced, Humayoon was informed that if he continued in the kingdom and to enjoy the protection of a sovereign, he was expected to profess the Shiah principles of the Mohammedan faith. Humayoon at first declined, and insisted on having liberty of conscience, but Shah Tahmasp was inexorable, and Humayoon publicly professed to embrace the faith of the Shiahs, and united with them in religious worship. Several circumstances combined to make the situation of the exiled monarch painful and humiliating, and he resolved on making an attempt to obtain possession of Cabul, which had been a part of the dominions of his father, and was now nearly in a state of anarchy on account of the tyranny and unpopularity of his brothers. Shah Tahmasp furnished Humayoon with a large body of cavalry, and the latter was glad to leave Persia for a country of better hopes and prospects. Humayoon succeeded in obtaining possession of Cabul, and was its acknowledged ruler for several years before he resolved on recovering his former throne in India. His success in this last enterprise was in a great degree to be ascribed to the heroic conduct of his son Acber, who at that early age began to exhibit those talents, which subsequently distinguished him above all the Mohammedan sovereigns of India.

Humayoon did not live long to enjoy his restoration to power. In a few months after his return to Delhi, he met with an accident which soon caused his death. As he was descending the stairs from the terrace of his palace one evening, he heard the muezzin's call for prayers from the minaret. He sat down and repeated the creed. As he was rising, his staff slipped on the smooth marble stairs, and losing his balance he fell over the parapet to the ground. He was insensible when taken up, though he soon recovered his senses, yet he was so much injured that he died on the fourth day. His life consisted of a series of remarkable adventures, fortunate and unfortunate. His death occurred in the 50th year of his age, and in the 26th year from the time he commenced his reign. He was an exile from his capital for 16 years. Ferishta ascribes his misfortunes to his *virtues*, and says, "had he been less mild and religious, he would have been a more successful prince. Had he been a worse man, he would have been a greater monarch." His son Acber erected a noble mausoleum over his tomb.*

ACBER, A.D. 1556.

Acber was in his 14th year when he succeeded his father, and though uncommonly manly, vigorous, and intelligent for his age, yet he was not capable of administering a government which required great energy, prudence, and self-reliance in all its departments. Happily there was one man, who from his long connection with the late emperor, his experience in the affairs of government, and his having the confidence of the army and the nobles, was well qualified to become regent. This was Byram Khan, who was distinguished in the army before the expulsion of Humayoon from India, who was his companion in his exile in Persia, and who rendered important assistance in procuring his restoration to the empire. This man was now invested with the administration of the government, and there was soon occasion for all his prudence, experience, and energy. Encouraged by the youth of Acber and the unsettled state of the empire, several parties soon appeared in arms. But Byram Khan was everywhere victorious, and the

* This tomb or mausoleum is thus described by Bishop Heber:— "Humayoon's tomb is a noble building of granite inlaid with marble, and in a very chaste and simple style of Gothic architecture. It is surrounded by a large garden with terraces and fountains, all now gone to decay except one of the latter. The garden itself is surrounded by an embattled wall with towers, four gateways and a cloister within all the way round. In the centre of the square is a platform, about 20 feet high, and I should apprehend 200 feet square, supported also by cloisters, and ascended by four great flights of granite steps. Above rises the tomb, also a square, with a great dome of white marble in its centre."

government under his vigorous hand acquired respect, order, and stability. But though the regent's administration of public affairs was generally satisfactory, yet his haughty and overbearing manners and his abuse of power to gratify personal feelings, raised up many enemies in the court, who wished to see him removed or restrained. Acber, who was now becoming a man, was displeased with the arbitrary and irresponsible manner in which the regent had exercised his authority, and also with the spirit he had manifested towards him. He resolved to extricate himself if possible from the regent's control, and to assume the administration of the empire. His plan was wisely formed and successfully executed. When engaged on a hunting expedition, he suddenly left the regent and proceeded to Delhi, upon the pretended intelligence of the illness of his mother. On arriving in Delhi he issued a proclamation, informing all the government functionaries that he had assumed the administration of public affairs, and forbidding obedience to any orders not sanctioned by himself. The regent was taken with surprise, and aware that his own situation would soon be critical, he sent two of his most trusty friends to Delhi to effect a reconciliation with the emperor. But Acber refused to see them, and for some unexplained reason he soon put them in prison. Byram Khan now saw how ready all appeared to turn from the falling minister to the rising emperor. He devised various plans for retrieving his affairs, but pride, suspicion, and the unexpected popularity of the emperor prevented his carrying them into effect. He was eventually reconciled to the emperor, who treated him with respect, and allowed him a liberal pension for life. But when preparing to embark on a pilgrimage to Mecca, he was assassinated by an Afghan, whose father he had many years before killed in battle.

Acber was only 18 years old when he assumed the responsible administration of the affairs of the empire. But in his personal appearance, in his manners, and in his mind, he was uncommonly mature for his age. He had also much experience in the wars of his father's reign, and under the regency of Byram Khan he had enjoyed opportunities for becoming well acquainted with the state of the empire and the character of his subjects. He saw that the great body of his subjects were

Hindus, who notwithstanding all the means used for their conversion by their conquerors, still adhered to the religion of their forefathers, and if permitted to follow their own superstitions, they were disposed to live quietly and peacefully under the government of foreigners. Their conduct in this respect presented a striking contrast to the Mohammedans, who were constantly engaged in intrigues, insurrections, and attempts at revolution. This view of the character of the people comprising the great body of the empire, appears to have induced Acber to resolve upon a uniform mode of proceeding towards all classes of his subjects, and to promote persons to situations of honor and responsibility without regard to their nation or religious creed. This was a noble purpose, but the pride and jealousy of the Mohammedans and their contempt for the idolatrous Hindus made it expedient for the emperor to proceed cautiously in carrying his intention into effect.

Acber was occupied for several years in reducing some provincial governors to submission, who had maintained more or less independence from the invasion of Tamerlane. In these military expeditions he exhibited great ability and energy. His proceedings often evinced more daring than discretion, but he gradually succeeded in recovering to the empire the revolted provinces.

But Acber's reputation as a wise and politic prince, rests more upon the changes and improvements he made in the civil administration of the empire, than upon his military talents and success, great as these confessedly were. The revenues had been derived from a variety of taxes very unequally proportioned, oppressive to the people, and embarrassing the operations of the government. Most of these he annulled, and determined to substitute for them a larger and fixed tax on the land. For the purpose of ascertaining the quantity of productive land, he caused all the cultivated lands to be measured. Then he endeavored to ascertain from the quality of the soil the amount of produce from each *bega*, (a measure of about three fourths of an acre), and what proportion of this amount ought to be paid to the government; and then to determine the value of this proportion in money. This scheme was carried into effect under the care of able men, and produced a great change in the state of the country. When completed, this scheme exhibited an amount of general and particular information concerning the empire which was probably never before collected concerning any country in the world. The nominal revenue of the empire to be collected according to this scheme was diminished, but the amount actually realized was generally increased. The papers, comprehending the whole system of revenue with the emperor's instructions for carrying it into effect, have been preserved and translated into English.* They show the state of India as it was under one of its most enlightened sovereigns nearly three centuries ago.

The changes Acber introduced into the army, were also great and important. The Mohammedan armies in India consisted of a class of nobles called Omras, with a specified number of men under each class. For the support of these troops, the revenues of a certain district were assigned to each chief, which he generally leased for an annual sum to some Hindu banker. Each omra was required to support in a state ready for service the specified number of troops, who were all paid by him, as well as under his command. These omras were the nobles of the empire, and having the army so much under their command, they often stirred up insurrections and revolutions, and sometimes deposed and set up emperors. Acber changed the manner of their support, making them dependent directly upon the royal treasury. The pay of a trooper, if a Persian, or from any country west of the Indus, including his horse, was 25 rupees per month; if he was a native of India, 20 rupees per month. The pay of common soldiers varied from 3 to 6 rupees per month. A rupee is about 47 cents.

It was the custom of the emperors to leave their capital as soon as the rainy season had closed, and spend 7 or 8 months in their travelling cantonments. These were fitted up with regal splendor and resembled a large city more than a camp. They moved about from one province to another, as pleasure, or business, or health inclined them. They often went to Cashmere and spent the hot months in the delightful climate and beautiful scenery of that celebrated valley. The following is a description of Acber's cantonment:—"His camp equipage consisted of

* "Ayeeni Acberi," or Institutes of Acber, translated by Mr. W. Gladwin.

tents and portable houses in an inclosure formed by a high wall of canvas screens, and containing great halls for public receptions, apartments for feasting, galleries for exercise, and chambers for retirement; all framed of the most costly materials, and adapted to the most luxurious enjoyment. The inclosure was 1530 yards square. The tents and walls were of various colors and pattern within, but all red on the outside and covered with gilded globes and pinnacles, forming a sort of castle in the midst of the camp. The camp itself showed like a beautiful city of tents of many colors, disposed in streets without the least disorder, covering a space about 5 miles across, and affording a glorious spectacle when seen at once from a height." *

The following extract from the same author gives a view of Acber's splendor on particular occasions:—"The greatest displays of Acber's grandeur were at the vernal equinox and on his birthday. They lasted for several days, during which there was a general fair and many processions and other pompous shows. The emperor's usual place was in a rich tent in the midst of awnings to keep off the sun. At least 2 acres were thus spread with silk and gold carpets and hangings, as rich as velvet embroidered with gold, pearls, and precious stones could make them. The nobility had similar pavilions where they received visits from each other, and sometimes from the emperor. Dresses, jewels, horses, and elephants were bestowed upon the nobles. The emperor was weighed in golden scales against gold, silver, perfumes, and other substances in succession, which were distributed among the spectators. Almonds and other fruits of gold and silver, were scattered by the emperor's own hand, and eagerly caught by the courtiers. On the great day of each festival the emperor was seated on his throne in a noble palace, surrounded by his nobles wearing high heron plumes, and sparkling with diamonds like the firmament. Many hundred elephants passed before him in companies, all most richly adorned, and the leading elephant of each company with gold plates on his head and breast set with rubies and emeralds. Trains of caparisoned horses followed, and after them rhinoceroses, lions, tigers, panthers, hunting leopards, hounds, and

* Elphinstone, p. 481.

hawks, the whole concluding with an innumerable host of cavalry glittering with cloth of gold."

One of Acber's favorite residences was Futtypoor, which was abandoned soon after his death, 250 years ago. Bishop Heber visited it in 1826, and says that "the approach to the city is striking, being surrounded with a high stone wall with battlements, and round towers, that within he found marble palaces, serais, mosques, mausoleums, etc., some of them in ruins, some partially dilapidated, and some in a state of good preservation." The Bishop closes saying, "Futtypoor is one of the most interesting places I have seen in India."

These accounts give us a view of oriental courts and camps, and of the state of civilization in India at that time. Acber was yet more remarkable for his religious opinions and practices. In the early part of his life he showed the sincerity of his religious profession by going on pilgrimage to the tombs of reputed saints, and at one time he avowed his intention of going on pilgrimage to Mecca. But he afterwards became sceptical in respect to the Koran and avowed deistical sentiments. He had also several learned men at his court, who were originally Mohammedans, but became sceptical in their principles. Some of these learned men became well versed in Sanscrit literature, and translated some of the Hindu sacred books into the Persian language. Acber though he became sceptical in respect to the Koran, did not at once become indifferent to all religion. He showed a great desire to become acquainted with the different systems of faith in the world, and he sent letters to Goa for Roman Catholic priests to come to Agra. Accordingly 3 priests proceeded to Agra and remained there for considerable time. These missionaries held several public discussions with the muftis and brahmins before the emperor, each party stating and vindicating his own system. The Romish missionaries were much pleased with the emperor's apparent sincerity, and in their letters and journals expressed the hope that he would soon profess his faith in Christianity. But when his curiosity had been gratified, he became more indifferent to the subject, and becoming discouraged they returned to Goa.

Some years afterwards, Acber again wrote to Goa for missionaries and another deputation proceeded to Agra. Their reception and treatment were at first very gratifying. They had several conferences with the emperor, and also public discussions with the muftis and brahmins. But it was not long before they thought they saw reasons for believing that he had no sincere desire to embrace Christianity, and no higher motives than curiosity and amusement in the inquiries he made concerning its history, doctrines, rites, etc. So the missionaries returned to Goa. About four years after their return, Acber again wrote to Goa, "with so many promises and kind expressions that the governor could not refuse to gratify him a third time." This mission proceeded to Lahore where the emperor with his court was then residing. He received them with great respect and manifested so much sincerity in his inquiries, and gave such earnest attention to their statements and instructions, that they were encouraged to hope for his conversion to their church. But on further acquaintance with his principles and practices, especially when they saw the homage he paid to the sun, and the reverence which he encouraged the people to pay to himself, and which appeared to them to partake of religious homage, they became discouraged and requested permission to return to Goa.

The religion of Acber appears to have been deism, and such was the religion of his most intimate friends. He was fond of the society of learned men, and had many such from different countries and of different systems of religious faith residing at his court. It was his custom to assemble them all every Friday to discuss subjects of religion and philosophy. In these discussions he took great delight, and often took an active part in them. The Dabistan, a Persian work on the different systems of religion in Asia, contains specimens of the discussions in these assemblies. One of them (probably only an imaginary or pretended one, but showing what they generally were,) is a Dialogue between a brahmin, a Mohammedan, a Zoroastrian, a Jew, a Christian, and a philosopher, in which the professor and advocate of each religion states his system and the arguments for it. These dialogues or discussions were generally closed by some one, who in the character of a philosopher, avowed deistical sentiments, who recommended a system of religion founded on the light of nature, on reason and virtue, and whose opinions and arguments were supposed to have the approbation of the emperor. The Acber Nameh contains an account of a discussion of this nature. The parties were a Romish priest by the name of Redif, and a number of Mohammedan moolahs, and it was carried on before the emperor and a large assembly of learned men of different religions. In this debate the priest has the advantage in temper and argument. The debate or discussion was closed by the emperor, who reproved the moolahs for their angry temper and bigotry, and declared his own belief to be that God could be most acceptably worshipped by following our own reason and what we can learn concerning him from his works, and not by taking our creed from any of the pretended revelations. Such discussions show the sentiments of Acber, and also the state of religious parties at his court. The toleration and protection which all religious denominations enjoyed in Acber's reign increased his general popularity and the prosperity of the empire, though by pursuing this course, he gave great offence to devout and bigoted Mohammedans. But of the influence of this class he had no fear, and for their opinions he had no respect. Acber died in 1605. His reign was the longest, and he must be reckoned the greatest of all the Mohammedan sovereigns of India; and he was probably the most powerful monarch at that time in the world.*

JEHANGHEER, A.D. 1605.

Acber reigned for 51 years, and was succeeded by his son

* Acber was buried at Secundra, and his tomb or mausoleum is among the most remarkable structures in India. Bishop Heber calls it "magnificent," and says, "it is the most splendid building in its way which I had yet seen in India. It stands in an area of about 40 English acres, inclosed by an embattled wall with octagonal towers at the angles, surmounted by open pavilions, and 4 very noble gateways of red granite, the principal of which is inlaid with white marble, and has 4 high marble minarets. The space within is planted with trees, and divided into green alleys, leading to the central building, which is a sort of solid pyramid, surrounded externally with cloisters, galleries, and domes, diminishing gradually on ascending it, till it ends in a square platform of white marble, carved with a delicacy and beauty which do full justice to the material, and to the graceful form of Arabic characters which form its chief ornament. At the bottom of the building, in a small but very lofty vault, is the real tomb of this great monarch, plain and unadorned, but also of white marble." — *Heber's Journal*, Vol. I. p. 473.

Selim, who took the title of Jehangheer, (Conqueror or Agent of the World,) by which he is known as the emperor of India. He had been intemperate in the use of wine and opium in the reign of his father, and much apprehension was felt in view of what might be his conduct and character when he should become emperor. Though he did not wholly reform himself, yet he prohibited the use of wine, and made laws to regulate the use of opium; all transgressions of these rules were to be severely punished. He publicly professed his faith in the Koran, and complied with the usual forms of the Mohammedan religion, though he manifested no particular zeal in this cause. His oldest son, Khusru, had long been alienated in feeling from his father, and each looked upon the other with suspicion. A few months after his father's accession, Khusru secretly fled with a few of his friends to Delhi, and collecting what force he could, he proceeded to Lahore. He easily obtained possession of the city, but before he could take the fort, the force sent in pursuit of him by his father arrived. He arranged his own force, now consisting of 10,000 men, in order and attacked the royal army. He was defeated and fled in the direction of Cabul, but he was pursued, overtaken, and brought back to his father a prisoner. The emperor treated the partisans of Khusru at Lahore with great barbarity, causing 700 of them to be impaled in one row near the gate, and his son Khusru to be borne along the line on an elephant to witness their sufferings. Khusru was so much affected that he passed three days in tears, and groans, and fasting. He was kept in prison for some time, and was finally assassinated.

The most remarkable part of Jehangheer's life was his acquaintance and marriage with Noor Jehan, or Noor Mahal, as she called herself. This remarkable woman was descended from Persian parents, of a noble family, but in reduced circumstances. She was remarkable for her beauty, her accomplishments, and her abilities. Her life, previous to her marriage with Jehangheer, was such a series of actions, adventures, and events, as could only occur in oriental history. Her influence over the emperor must have been as great as the most ambitious of her sex could desire. "He took no step without consulting her, and on every affair in which she took an interest, her will was law."

Her father was made prime minister, and filled the place ably and honorably. Her two brothers were raised to high situations, and on the death of her father, one of them succeeded him. They were both men of distinguished talents, and "their modesty and their virtues reconciled all men to their sudden elevation." Previous to his marriage, the emperor had been intemperate, capricious, and cruel. Through her influence his habits and conduct were greatly improved, if not entirely reformed. "The ceremonies, manners, and usages of the court were remodelled by her; its splendor was increased by her arrangements, while its expenses were diminished by her management. The furniture of the palaces was greatly improved by her taste, and she introduced female dresses more becoming than any in previous use in India." "One of the accomplishments by which she captivated Jehangheer, is said to have been her facility in composing extemporary verses." In the civil war, in the latter part of Jehangheer's reign, on one occasion she put herself at the head of the army, "appearing in the howdah of a high elephant with a bow and quivers full of arrows in her hands." She was among the foremost in the battle, and the most furious assault was made upon her. Her elephant was surrounded with a crowd of Rajpoots, upon whom "she discharged four quivers of arrows with her own hand." But her guards were overpowered and cut down; balls and arrows fell thick round her howdah; three of her elephant-drivers were killed, and the noble animal having received a sabre-cut on his proboscis, rushing into the river, was carried a long way down the stream by the current, and with great difficulty reached the opposite shore, the empress continuing all the time upon him in her howdah.

This remarkable woman was concerned in all the affairs of government till the close of Jehangheer's reign, and she showed as much capacity for the intrigues of the court as she had courage in the dangers of the camp and the perils of the battle field. She survived the emperor nearly twenty years. She was treated with great respect, and had a princely allowance, living retired from the world, refraining from all scenes of amusement and gaiety, and wearing a dress of deep mourning. She was buried at Lahore, by the side of the emperor, in a tomb which she had prepared for herself.

The last years of Jehangheer's reign were extremely unhappy. His sons Khusru, Parviz, Khurrum, and Sheriar aimed at different times to secure the succession each for himself. The empress Noor Jehan exerted all her influence with the emperor, and engaged, with her characteristic ardor and ability, in all the intrigues of the court in these matters. Khurrum, who had been declared to be heir apparent and invested with the title of Shah Jehan, felt compelled afterwards to take extreme measures to secure his promised rights, and was for some time in a state of rebellion against his father. The emperor was himself, at one time, for several months a prisoner of Muhabut Khan, a distinguished military leader, who was compelled to use these measures to secure his own safety from a party excited against him by Noor Jehan. For several years the emperor had scarcely any fixed residence, living in his travelling palace, and continuing only a short time in one place. He died on a march from Cashmere to Lahore, A.D. 1627, in the 60th year of his age, and after a reign of 22 years.

Jehangheer's reign was distinguished by two English missions to his court. William Hawkins, captain of the ship *Hector*, was furnished with letters from James I. for the Emperor Jehangheer, to be used if the state of matters at Surat should make it expedient for him to proceed to the court. He experienced so many difficulties at Surat from the Mohammedan governor and the Portuguese, that he resolved to proceed to Agra. The governor of Surat was averse to this course, and Hawkins narrowly escaped assassination on the road. The emperor received him courteously, and having learned that Hawkins could speak the Turkish language, and that he could have direct communication with him, he invited him to come daily to the palace, where "his majesty held long discourses with him respecting different countries and various matters." The emperor made promises to redress the grievances of which Hawkins complained, and he instituted such measures to remove them that for a while the objects of the mission appeared likely to be soon accomplished. But after a while, through the influence of the Portuguese, the opposition of the prime minister, Abdul Hassan, and the prejudices and intrigues excited by the governor of Surat, matters began to resume their former course. Hawkins endeavored for a while to oppose this combined current against him, but at length seeing no prospect of accomplishing any thing further, he left Agra, after residing there two years and a half, and returned to Surat.

Sir Thomas Roe was at the head of the next mission. He arrived at Surat in September of 1615, and "landed in great pomp, with 80 men at arms." The emperor was then at Ajmere. Sir Thomas proceeded first to Burhanpoor, where he had a public interview with Prince Parviz, the emperor's second son, who was surrounded with oriental splendor, as the emperor's viceroy. The prince promised a private interview, but unluckily among the presents Sir Thomas gave the prince, were some bottles of wine, which the latter used so freely that he was not in a fit state for an interview till the time arrived for the ambassador to take his departure. On the way to Ajmere, Sir Thomas passed Chittore, concerning which he says, "above 100 temples, many lofty towers, and houses innumerable, were seen crowning the lofty rock on which it stands, but it was at this time entirely deserted." At Ajmere, the emperor received Sir Thomas at the durbur, or the place of public audience with great respect. Indeed, "he was assured that no other ambassador, either Turk or Persian, had ever obtained the like, and at the next interview he was allowed and ever after retained a place higher than that of all the other courtiers." He had several conferences with the emperor, and though opposed by all the influence of the governor of Surat as well as of the prime-minister and Prince Khurrum, (then Jehangheer's favorite son, and afterwards Shah Jehan,) yet he succeeded in obtaining a firman which, though not all that was desired, yet greatly facilitated the English trade with the sea-ports in the dominions of the empire. Sir Thomas Roe resided in India for some years, and gave so great satisfaction that the East India Company gave him an honorary seat in their committee of management, and an annuity for life.

SHAH JEHAN, A.D. 1627.

Of Jehangheer's sons, only two, Khurrum, or Shah Jehan, and Sheriar survived him. Many years before his death he had publicly acknowledged Khurrum to be heir to the throne, bestowing upon him at the same time the title of Shah Jehan,* by which he was afterwards generally known. He had also exhibited distinguished abilities, and rendered his father important assistance in suppressing some insurrections and administering the affairs of the empire. In the last years of his life, Jehangheer became somewhat alienated in feelings from Shah Jehan, and through the influence of Noor Jehan he appointed by his will Sheriar to be his successor. Asaph Khan, the prime-minister, had long been pledged to support the rights of Shah Jehan, and he took vigorous measures to secure his succession. Sheriar seized the royal treasure and gained over part of the army to his interest, but he was defeated in a battle near Lahore and taken prisoner. Shah Jehan, who was in the Deckan at the time of his father's death, hastened to Delhi, where by the vigorous coöperation of his friends he was acknowledged emperor and soon took formal possession of the throne. But the possession of present power did not satisfy him. His brother Sheriar, in accordance with his father's will had attempted to secure the throne for himself. In these attempts the other members of the family had united. But they had failed and all were now prisoners of State. Shah Jehan saw that the easiest way to secure himself and his family from all danger and anxiety from those who might in future prefer any natural or family claim to the throne, would be to remove all such persons out of the way. So he caused his brother Sheriar and all the descendants of his father to be put to death, and "there remained not a drop of the blood of Tamerlane in India, except what flowed in his own and his children's veins."

All fear of any revolts or other dangers being removed, Shah Jehan resolved to celebrate the commencement of his reign with great liberality and splendor. He bestowed great honors and rewards on the men, to whose influence and coöperation he owed his accession to power. He had always been fond of pomp and show, and he had now the means of gratifying his inclinations. He caused palaces to be erected in all the principal cities of the empire. He had an establishment of tents prepared for himself and household, which included as much space

* King of the World.

and would accommodate as many people as a small city. It was the practice for oriental sovereigns to cause themselves to be weighed against gold coins and jewels, and then to distribute such articles in charity or appropriate them to some sacred purpose in the superstitious belief that such offerings would avert calamities and secure success. In addition to such ceremonies and charities, the emperor caused vessels to be filled with gold coins, jewels, and precious stones, and then having been waved around him or poured over him, they were given to those around, or scattered among the crowd, or sent away as presents. The entire expense of this festival, including gifts of money, jewels, precious stones, rich dresses, arms, elephants, horses, palanquins, etc., according to Khafi Khan, exceeded $7,500,000.

Shah Jehan's jealousy and cruelty in putting his brother and all his nephews to death, did not annihilate all aspirants to the throne. Khan Jehan Lodi, who boasted of being descended from the former Afghan emperors, and who had held high military command under the late emperor, took the part of Sheriar, and so incurred the displeasure of Shah Jehan. A reconciliation between them took place, but Khan Jehan Lodi saw reasons for believing that the emperor was only waiting for an opportunity to degrade and disgrace him. So he left Agra with what force he could collect and proceeded into the Deckan, where he had formerly held high military command. The state of the Deckan soon became such that Shah Jehan found it necessary to proceed there with a large army. Khan Jehan Lodi was killed near Kalinger, but the war was continued in the Deckan for several years. The kingdom of Ahmednuggur was finally annexed to the empire, and the kings of Beejapoor and Golconda, acknowledged the sovereignty of the emperor of Delhi, and engaged to pay yearly tribute.

Having settled the affairs of the Deckan, Shah Jehan returned to Delhi and enjoyed some years of repose, when the state of Cabul became such that he resolved to assert the ancient claims of his family to it. This was the commencement of a long and arduous war, in which the emperor proceeded himself several several times to Cabul. But it was chiefly carried on by his sons Dara and Aurungzeb. Balk, Candahar, and Cabul were besieged and taken. But war with the Usbecks, the Persians, and Afghans was found to be very different work from what it was with the Hindus, or with the Mohammedans of India. And after 8 or 10 years spent in victories and defeats, in sieges and surrenders, the emperor withdrew all his force from that country, and no further attempts were made by the emperors of Delhi to extend their power over the countries west of the Indus.

Shah Jehan was apparently very fortunate in his family, which consisted of 4 sons and 3 daughters. His sons when young all gave evidence of good natural abilities, and acquired the education, manners, and accomplishments becoming their birth and expected stations in life. As good-will and harmony appeared to exist among them while under the care of their father and they all manifested great respect towards him, he appointed them to high and responsible situations in the government. Dara Sheko, who was the oldest and designed to be his successor in the empire, he retained with him to assist him in administering the affairs of the government. Shuja, his second son, was appointed viceroy of Bengal. Aurungzeb, the third son, was appointed viceroy of the Deckan; and Morad, the youngest son, was viceroy of Gujerat. These situations they filled honorably and ably. The office of viceroy in India is one of great honor, the man filling it representing the sovereign, and having the command of the army and of the revenue of the provinces under his government. While in these situations it became manifest that each of the sons had some intention of making an effort to secure the throne for himself on the death of their father. This intention might in part originate in a feeling of self-preservation as well as in a love of power. In the Mohammedan governments in India the oldest son was regarded as the natural heir of the throne, unless set aside by the reigning sovereign while living, or by his will at his decease. But neither the rights of primogeniture, nor the will of the sovereign were sufficient always to secure the succession. Other sons and other parties, if they saw any prospect of success by the use of any means, or power, or influence, or treachery, would not unfrequently make an effort to secure the throne, and then it became a struggle for life as well as power, among all engaged in it. Shah Jehan caused his own brothers and their sons to be put to death that he might thus be rid of all danger and anxiety of any rival or family claim to the throne. And what the sons had seen their father do to secure the undisputed succession for himself and family, each of them had reason to fear might be the fate of himself and family. So the choice before each of them was to secure the throne for himself, or to be put to death by the brother who should succeed in obtaining it; a horrid, but often true picture of the royal family in oriental governments.

While Shah Jehan was vigorously administering the affairs of the empire, and appeared likely so to continue for some years, and the distance of his sons, who were viceroys, from their father and also from each other was so great, there was no call or occasion for declaring or divulging their purpose in the event of his death, and so the affairs of government proceeded quietly at the capital and in the provinces. In A.D. 1657, the emperor was taken suddenly very ill, and for some time was thought by all to be near his end. Dara Sheko, who had been acknowledged to be heir apparent, and had been for some years assisting his father, at once assumed the administration of affairs in his father's name. He showed a jealous feeling towards his brothers, expelled their agents from the city, or put them under restraint, and endeavored to prevent any intelligence of the state of the emperor from being communicated to them. But his brothers had means of obtaining information which he could not control, and as soon as they heard of the state of the emperor, and how Dara was managing affairs in Agra, each of them began to carry into effect the purpose he had long cherished of securing the throne for himself and his family. Shuja in Bengal and Morad in Gujerat, each assumed the royal title, and collecting as large a force as they could command, began their march towards Agra. Aurungzeb acted with more caution. He did not assume the royal title, but collecting all the force he could, he proceeded to the northern frontier of his territory, there to watch the course of events, and be in circumstances to take advantage of them. In the mean time the emperor, contrary to all expectation, recovered his health and resumed the administration of the government. Shuja and Morad were ordered to return to their respective governments. Shuja affected not to believe the intelligence, treated the letters as forgeries, and continued his march. Suliman, the son of Dara, was sent against him with a large army, defeated him near Benares, and compelled him to return to Bengal.

In the mean time Aurungzeb wrote to Morad, encouraging him in the course he had begun, promising to assist him in securing the throne, and that as soon as he should see him established in the government, he would himself resign all power, and retiring from the cares of the world devote his remaining days to religious duties. Morad apparently reposed entire confidence in the professions of Aurungzeb, and the two princes uniting their forces near Oujein, defeated the imperial army sent against them under Jeswunt Sing. On the union of the two brothers, Aurungzeb took an oath to be faithful to the interests of Morad, and before and after the victory he publicly professed that his sole object was to aid his brother to secure the throne. His superior abilities enabled him to control matters according to his own views, and the victory over the imperial army was gained by his superior valor and experience in war.

This defeat of the royal army awakened the emperor and all the court to the formidable nature of the rebellion. A large force was stationed at the passes of the Chumbul to prevent Aurungzeb and Morad crossing the river. But Aurungzeb, having discovered an unknown and unguarded ford at some distance, left his camp standing to deceive his enemies, and soon surprised them by appearing with all his force in their rear. Shah Jehan now resolved to put himself at the head of his army and proceed to engage with his rebellious sons. But he was dissuaded from this course by the members of his family and other friends. Dara took charge of the royal army, containing all which could then be collected, and which consisted, according to Khafi Khan of "70,000 horse with innumerable elephants and guns." Bernier is of the opinion that the army contained "100,000 horse, 20,000 infantry, and 80 pieces of artillery." The two armies met at Samaghur, one day's journey from Agra. In this battle both armies fought with great obstinacy. Aurungzeb urged his elephant to places of the greatest danger, calling aloud to his troops, "God is with us, and we have no other refuge or retreat." The battle had raged long and was undecided, when a rocket struck Dara's elephant, and the animal became so unmanageable that he was compelled to leap off and mount a horse. His disappearance was soon observed by his army, and supposing he had been killed, they became alarmed, fell into disorder, and soon began to give way. Dara, finding it impossible to restore order or to rally his troops, was compelled to seek his own safety by flight. As soon as the battle was closed, Aurungzeb descended from his elephant, kneeled down in the presence of the whole army, and praised the Almighty for the victory he had granted them. He then went to Morad and congratulated him upon having secured the throne and empire.

Dara, on arriving at Agra, took his family and what treasure he could carry with him, and proceeded to Delhi. In three days after the battle, Aurungzeb and Morad proceeded to Agra, and took possession of the city without any resistance. As Morad was suffering from wounds received in the late battle, the sole command now devolved on Aurungzeb, who knew well how to turn every circumstance to his own advantage. He sent humble messages to his father, trying to assure him of his continued respect and affection, and justifying himself in the course he had pursued. His desire probably was to effect a reconciliation with his father, and then to carry on the government in his father's name, and assume the throne on his decease. But Shah Jehan could not forgive Aurungzeb for what he had done, and he continued inflexible in his attachment to Dara. When fully satisfied that he could make no arrangement of this nature with his father, Aurungzeb sent his own son Mohammed to take possession of the citadel, with strict orders to prevent all communication between the emperor and any one beyond its walls. The conduct of Aurungzeb and the other parties is thus described by Murray:—

"The confederate armies proceeded to Agra, where Morad being confined with his wounds, the entire command devolved upon Aurungzeb. His first care was to send an emissary to corrupt the troops of Suliman, in which he easily succeeded, or rather they corrupted themselves by following the usual Asiatic system of going over to the prosperous party. His next anxiety was to obtain possession of his father's person.

This was a measure both delicate and difficult, for the fortified palace in which Shah Jehan resided was capable of withstanding a long siege; which pressed by a parent against a son, a monarch so popular and highly respected, would have placed him in a very odious position. It was most desirable, therefore, to effect his purpose by stratagem; but he had to deal with one versant in all the wiles of policy and in all the forms of human deceit. Determining, however, to make the trial, he sent a messenger to the emperor, expressing deep regret at the situation in which he found himself, assuring him that he still retained all the affection of a son, and all the loyalty of a subject. Shah Jehan gave very small credit to these professions, yet he resolved to temporize, and sent his favorite daughter Jehanara to visit her brothers, and to ascertain how affairs really stood. She went first to Morad, who, knowing her to be entirely devoted to the interests of Dara, received her with very slender courtesy. The offended princess returned to her palanquin, and was hastening out of the camp, when she met Aurungzeb, who saluted her with the utmost kindness and respect, complained of her having held so little communication with him, and prevailed upon her to enter his tent. He then professed the deepest remorse for the conduct into which he had been hurried, and his anxiety by any means to make reparation. He even expressed a willingness to espouse the cause of Dara, were it not that it already appeared quite desperate. Jehanara was thus induced to lay open all the resources of that prince, and to name the chiefs who remained still attached to him, disclosing to her brother many most important secrets of which he afterwards fully availed himself. He then declared that he was entirely satisfied, and that in two days the emperor would see at his feet his repentant son.

"Jehanara, now hastened to her father with this joyful intelligence. But the monarch did not place full reliance on these professions, yet believing that Aurungzeb really intended to pay him a visit, he determined to take advantage of the opportunity to secure his person. He was not aware that he was playing the game with one who possessed skill superior to his own. Aurungzeb sent a humble message, representing that the guilty are always timid,—that being scarcely able to conceive how crimes such as his could be forgiven, he could in no way be reassured, unless his son Mohammed were allowed previously with a small guard to enter the palace. Shah Jehan was so bent on his object and so convinced of the sincerity with which the proposal was made, that he hesitated not to agree to it. The youth entered, and being cordially received, he stationed his party in a convenient situation. But his eager eye soon discovered a large body of troops occupying a very suspicious position. He went to the emperor and stated the apprehension to which this circumstance could not fail to give rise, observing that unless these men were removed, he must immediately inform his father, who would then probably renounce his intended visit. The old man, still credulous and determined to make every sacrifice rather than fail in his object, consented that the soldiers should quit the palace, thus rendering Mohammed and his party the real masters. Then indeed it was announced that Aurungzeb had mounted his horse and was approaching with his retinue. Shah Jehan seated himself on his throne in the highest exultation, expecting to see the complete accomplishment of his schemes and hopes. He soon learned, however, that Aurungzeb, instead of entering his presence, had gone to pay his devotions at the tomb of Acber. Considering this as a decided slight to himself, Shah Jehan indignantly inquired of Mohammed, "What means Aurungzeb by this behavior?" Mohammed deliberately replied, "My father never intended to visit the emperor." "Then why are you here?" inquired Shah Jehan. "To take charge of the citadel," replied Mohammed. Shah Jehan saw at once the abyss into which he had plunged himself, and burst into a torrent of invective and self-reproach, which induced his grandson to withdraw. On sober reflection, he sent again for the youth, and painting the miseries of his condition, he urged the most pressing entreaties that the prince would restore to him his liberty, promising in reward even the empire of India, which his influence with the army and the people would be sufficient to secure. Mohammed appeared to hesitate for a moment, but then hastening out of the apartment, turned a deaf ear to every subsequent solicitation." *

* History of India, p. 272, 273.

Shah Jehan lived for several years, but here his reign ended. From this time he was a mere prisoner of State. He had a princely allowance, and was treated with great respect, but he never again saw either of his sons, nor went outside of the walls of the citadel. He reigned 30 years. He was 67 years old when he was deposed, and 74 years old when he died.

The reign of Shah Jehan, when compared with his predecessors, was quiet, and the people generally were prosperous. The wars in the Deckan and Cabul, did not much disturb the general state of the empire. Previous to his accession to the throne, he had much experience in war, and had exhibited great military talents. And if he did not exhibit equal wisdom and ability in administering the affairs of the empire, still his government was generally satisfactory to the Hindus, and decidedly popular with the Mohammedans. The historians of that period describe the state of the empire as very flourishing, while some of them declare him to be the greatest and best of all the Mohammedan sovereigns of India. Khafi Khan, who is generally considered the best of the Mohammedan historians, is of the opinion that Acber excelled all the other emperors as conqueror and lawmaker, yet that no monarch in India ever excelled Shah Jehan in the general administration of all the departments of the government. Tavernier and Bernier, who had passed several years in India, and saw the state and circumstances of the inhabitants, describe the government as good, the country as prosperous, and the people as generally quiet and contented. In pomp and display, this emperor exceeded all his predecessors, and wherever he went, into the Deckan, or to Cabul, or to Cashmere, he appeared in the same splendor and magnificence. The royal pavilion, with all its different parts and appurtenances, was as large as a small city, and could accommodate many thousand people. Cashmere was his summer retreat. In the cool and delightful climate of that valley, the time was spent in feasts, dances, illuminations, excursions by land and water, hunting, and other sports and pleasures congenial with the climate, the seasons, and the scenery.

The public works of this reign are monuments of taste, skill, and enterprise. The royal cities of Delhi and Agra were greatly enlarged, and acquired their highest state of splendor.

The palaces, mosques, and baths were on a royal scale. The Jumma Musjid, or royal mosque, was a magnificent edifice and cost half a million of dollars. The gardens of Shalemar with their baths, fountains, statues, etc., now in ruins, were a mile in circumference, and are said to have cost more than four millions of dollars. The imperial palace, in which the emperor was confined for the last 7 years of his life, was large and magnificent. When the Mahrattas, in 1760, obtained possession of the city, their chief Sudashew Bhow caused the silver ceiling and ornaments of the audience hall to be taken and coined into money, and the value was nearly $800,000. No one of the emperor's works excited so much curiosity as his celebrated peacock throne. This curious work took its name from a part of it resembling the expanded tail of a peacock, the natural colors of which were imitated by sapphires, emeralds, rubies, etc., all wrought into it, and forming the chief ornament of a mass of diamonds, and other precious stones of surpassing brilliancy. Tavernier, who saw it and was himself by profession a jeweller, and so a competent judge in such matters, says that the common estimation of its cost exceeded £6,000,000, or nearly $30,000,000. This sum included the precious stones in it.

The mausoleum called Taj Mahal, erected by the emperor over the tomb of his favorite wife, exceeded all his buildings. It stands on the banks of the Jumna in a large park, which is beautifully situated and highly ornamented. Two elegant mosques stand, one on each side of the mausoleum, at a moderate distance. The edifice is built of white marble with a minaret at each corner, and a high dome, 70 feet in diameter, over the central part. In the middle, under the dome, is the tomb, which is inclosed by an open screen of marble inlaid by mosaics. "The walls," says Elphinstone, "are of white marble with borders of a running pattern of flowers in mosaics. The graceful flow, the harmonious colors, and above all the sparing use of the rich ornament with the mild lustre of the marble on which it is displayed, form the peculiar charm of the building, and distinguish it from any other in the world. The materials are lapis lazuli, jasper, heliotrope, or blood-stone, a sort of golden stone (not well understood) with chalcedony, and other agates, cornelians, jade, and various stones of the same description." "A single flower in the screen," says Veysey, "contains a hundred stones, each cut to the exact shape necessary, and highly polished." Tavernier (already referred to) who lived many years in India in the reign of Jehangheer, and who saw this edifice when it was commenced, and when it was completed, says that 20,000 men were employed upon it for 22 years, and that it cost 31,748,000 rupees, or nearly 15,000,000 dollars.

The construction of these works must have cost Jehangheer immense sums of money. The expenses of his wars in the Deckan, and of his frequent expeditions to Cabul, Candahar, and Balk must have been very great. His regular standing army of 200,000 men was maintained in an efficient state, and at the time he was deposed the royal treasury contained more than $100,000,000 of coined money, besides a great accumulation of uncoined gold and silver, and of jewels and precious stones.

Shah Jehan, whose reign commenced with the murder of all his brothers and their families, that he might obtain the throne and then be rid of all who might trouble him, passed the last 7 years of his life a prisoner in his own palace, deprived of all power by a son who had usurped the throne, and who to secure it for himself and his family had not only deposed and imprisoned his father, but had also put to death his 3 brothers and their families. What an exhibition of the lust of power in the conduct of this emperor in the early part of his reign, and again in the sufferings and circumstances of himself and his family in the latter years of his life!

AURUNGZEB, A.D. 1657.

Aurungzeb, having thus made his father a prisoner of State in his own palace, had next to dispose of his brother Morad. This unhappy and deluded prince was confidently expecting soon to be acknowledged emperor of India. Aurungzeb continued for awhile to deceive him with this expectation, pretending himself at the same time to be making preparations to embark on a pilgrimage to Mecca as soon as Morad should be safely seated on the throne. But in the mean time he was secretly using all the means in his power to prejudice the army and the public against his brother, and to attach all parties to his own interest. His proceedings were so much at variance with his professed intentions that the suspicions of Morad and his friends were at length excited. A plan was formed to assassinate Aurungzeb; but he became aware of his danger and escaped the snare laid for him. In turn he formed a scheme for getting Morad into his possession. This plan was successful. Morad was soon a prisoner in the power of his brother, and his friends could not ascertain in what place he was confined. Aurungzeb now took formal possession of the throne, and caused himself to be proclaimed emperor by the name or title of Aulumgheer, the Conqueror or Agent of the World. Among Mohammedans in India he is generally called and known by this title, but among all other classes of people he has been chiefly known by his previous name, and so he will continue to be called in this work.

Aurungzeb had now succeeded thus far in all his plans. He had deposed and imprisoned his father. He had deprived his brother Morad of all authority and power, and put him in close confinement. Dara had been defeated and fled to Lahore, and Shuja had been defeated and returned back into Bengal. But Aurungzeb had still much cause for anxiety. His treatment of his father, and his brother Morad, had excited much indignation against him. Shuja was in possession of Bengal and all its resources. Dara was collecting an army at Lahore, while his son, Suliman was at the head of a considerable force, on the way to join his father. Aurungzeb, having arranged his affairs at Delhi and Agra as well as he could, began to pursue Dara, who finding his force not sufficient to meet his brother in the field, fled from Lahore to Scinde. Aurungzeb pursued him to Multan, where on hearing that Shuja was on the way from Bengal to Agra with an army of 25,000 men, he abandoned the pursuit of Dara, and returned to his capital. Here he stopped only for a few days, and then marched to meet Shuja. The two brothers met near Allahabad and a severe battle was fought, in which Shuja was defeated with great loss of troops and all his cannon and his baggage. Aurungzeb, having despatched his son Mohammed, and Meer Jumla one of his principal generals, in pursuit of Shuja, returned to Agra.

But there was much to be done before Aurungzeb could quietly enjoy the throne he had acquired by such perfidy and iniquity. Dara had found friends in Gujerat. The governor, Nawaz Khan, regarded him as the rightful heir to the throne, and believing he would yet be able to obtain it, espoused his cause, and joined him with all his force. Thus Dara soon found himself at the head of an army of 25,000 men, and at once commenced his march towards Agra. Aurungzeb, who well understood how much in his circumstances depended upon despatch, hastened to meet Dara, and the two brothers, with their armies in hostile array, met near Jypoor. When the battle had raged furiously for some hours, and victory was yet undecided, Nawaz Khan was seen to fall, and this produced such a panic that the troops soon gave way, and fled in all directions. The unhappy Dara fled towards Gujerat. His fortunes now appeared desperate, and nearly all his pretended friends forsook him, though not without aggravating his distress by seizing and carrying away with them nearly all his treasure. He was for some time a fugitive in Gujerat, himself and family reduced to great distress. Finding neither sympathy nor safety in Gujerat, he resolved to proceed to Candahar. On the way he claimed the hospitality of Jehan Khan, a petty prince who had formerly been sentenced to death by Shah Jehan, and been pardoned by Dara's intercession for him. This prince at first received and entertained Dara in a kind and friendly manner, but instead of assisting him to proceed on the way to Candahar, he made him a prisoner, and delivered him into the hands of Aurungzeb's general, who soon arrived in pursuit of him. He was carried to Delhi, where he was conducted through the principal streets, miserably mounted, and meanly clothed. The feelings of the inhabitants, excited by this wanton cruelty, was compassion for the unfortunate sufferer, and indignation against his heartless brother. So strong were the feelings of the people in view of the sufferings of Dara and the base conduct of Jehan Khan, his ungrateful betrayer, that the latter was attacked with tiles and stones, and would have been killed in the streets, if he had not been rescued by the soldiers. Aurungzeb seeing the state of public feeling, resolved at once to remove Dara, and he was soon assassinated in prison. His dead body was publicly exhibited on an elephant, and his head was cut off and carried to the emperor, that there might be no doubt of his death in the city or in the army.

Aurungzeb was now apparently rid of all who could prefer any natural or family claim to the throne, except his brother Shuja, who was in possession of Bengal and Bahar. Against him the emperor soon sent his eldest son and acknowledged heir, Mohammed, and his most experienced general, Meer Jumla, with a large force. On their arriving near the camp of Shuja, some very remarkable occurrences took place. Previous to the illness and deposition of Shah Jehan, when all his sons were on friendly terms with each other, this prince Mohammed had been betrothed to a daughter of Shuja, to whom he had formed a strong attachment. This lady, in concert with her father, now addressed a letter to Mohammed; and their reference to his former pledges and promises and their appeal to his feelings, produced such an effect upon him, that he resolved to fulfil his marriage engagement, though it could be done only by forsaking the interest of his father and joining the party of Shuja. Perhaps he hoped in this way to effect a reconciliation between his father and uncle; or that the army would follow his example, and then the united force would enable them to restore peace to the empire. He embarked upon the Ganges, professedly on an excursion of pleasure, and proceeded to the camp of Shuja. This conduct of Mohammed produced a great sensation in the army, but Meer Jumla by his great energy and influence was able to preserve order, and the excitement soon subsided. Mohammed was received by his uncle with great honor, and his marriage with the daughter of Shuja was celebrated with great pomp and festivity. As soon as the season would admit, Mohammed put himself at the head of Shuja's army, and marched out in front of the army he had left, expecting some great movement among them in his favor; and when he saw the force he lately commanded approaching, he thought they were coming to join his standard. But their fierce attack soon showed their spirit and aims. Mohammed and Shuja exerted themselves to the utmost, but their force soon gave way and fled with great loss.

Soon after this defeat, Aurungzeb, who never scrupled at any means for accomplishing his purposes, wrote a letter to his son, which professed to be in answer to one from him, in which he referred to a plan for betraying Shuja into his power. This letter was designed to fall into the hands of Shuja, and matters were purposely so arranged that it should come into his hands without his suspecting any artifice to deceive him. The plan succeeded. Shuja was shocked at discovering the treachery, as he thought, of his son-in-law. It was in vain that Mohammed asserted his innocence and fidelity, and that he had written nothing whatever to his father since he abandoned his interest. Shuja's suspicions still continued, and Mohammed was told that he must at once depart from Bengal. The unhappy prince was now reduced to the greatest distress. He had now no resource but to throw himself upon the clemency of his father, and he had never been known to show clemency to any one who had once offended him, or of whom he was suspicious. Aurungzeb caused his son to be arrested and confined in Gwalior, the common prison for all persons supposed to be dangerous to the State. And here the unfortunate Mohammed remained in prison till his death. Sepher a son of Dara, Suliman a son of Shuja, and a son of Morad, were also confined in the same prison, and all were kept there for life, or were put to death. The affairs of Shuja became worse till he was compelled to escape with his family into Arracan, where they all soon perished.

The reign of Aurungzeb, though commenced with such cruelties and atrocities yet enjoyed more quiet than those of his predecessors generally, perhaps more than any of them. Under him the Mogul empire in India attained its greatest extent, including nearly all the peninsula, with Cabul on the west, and Assam on the east. In the 6th year of his reign, he had a severe and dangerous illness. While he was in this state, intrigue and faction were busy, and he had reason to fear the consequence to himself and his family. In these circumstances he exhibited great fortitude under his sufferings, and great energy and sagacity in the administration of his affairs. On his recovery, these factions and intrigues were soon suppressed by his prudence and vigilance. The interruptions of amicable relations between the court of India and Persia, and the threatened invasion of India by Shah Abbas, then King of Persia and the most powerful and warlike sovereign in Asia, for awhile caused Aurungzeb great uneasiness. He was naturally very suspicious, and he was apprehensive that in the event of such an invasion, the Persians who were numerous in India, would unite with the invaders. But it was not long before the death of Shah Abbas occurred, and the state of anarchy which ensued in Persia, relieved him from all anxiety from this source.

There was one insurrection at this time which showed the superstitious character of the Hindus and Mohammedans. An old Hindu woman in Marwar, having in some way acquired a high reputation for sanctity, collected around her a large number of faquers and other devotees, who assumed the form of an army and defeated some force sent against them. Exaggerated reports of these victories were circulated, and this fanatical host was soon increased to 20,000. This woman pretended to perform miracles, and that by the rites she practised and prescribed to her followers, they would become invulnerable to any kind of weapons or fire-arms. Several of the petty princes joined her party. They marched towards Agra, overcoming all resistance, and proclaiming Bistamia, (the name of this woman,) the Queen of India. Aurungzeb was surprised at this sudden outbreak, and he became alarmed on finding that his own army was becoming infected with this superstition. The means he used to suppress this insurrection, showed that he well understood the character of his army, and the spirit of the age. He caused selected sentences of the Koran, some written with his own hand, and all duly consecrated, to be applied to their weapons, and then to be put upon their standards, assuring them that these would prove an infallible protection against any magical rites and miraculous powers possessed by their enemies. Having thus inspired his army with confidence, he made an attack upon the fanatical hosts, and dispersed them with great slaughter.

The Rajpoot princes had at different times acknowledged the sovereignty of the emperors of Delhi, and paid them an annual tribute, but they retained the control of affairs in their own territories, and supported very considerable military forces. With these armies they often assisted the emperors, and perhaps as often they resisted them. Aurungzeb was a bigoted Mohammedan, and had a great abhorrence of idolatry. Some means he used to proselyte the Hindus, and some laws he enacted in favor of the Mohammedans gave great offence to the Rajpoots, and they united in self-defence. This had more the character of a religious war than any which had occurred under the Mogul dynasty. The combination at one time became very formidable, the Rajpoot army amounting to 70,000 men. Acber, the emperor's youngest son, joined them, and they proclaimed him emperor. Their intention was to depose Aurungzeb, and put Acber upon the throne. Aurungzeb was once very near falling into their hands. But he soon succeeded in effecting divisions among his enemies. Acber becoming discouraged, fled into the Deckan and joined the Mahrattas. The state of the Deckan now requiring Aurungzeb's immediate attention and all the military force he could collect, he offered such terms of peace to the Rajpoots, as they gladly accepted.

In the latter part of the reign of Shah Jehan, the Mahrattas under Shevajee began to act a conspicuous part in the affairs of western India. Shevajee was the son of Shahjee, a Mahratta chief, and he inherited a part of his father's possessions. He early conceived a strong aversion to the Mohammedan religion, and was more than ordinarily scrupulous in performing and sustaining the superstitions of the Hindus. When Aurungzeb was viceroy of the Deckan, Shevajee occasioned him much trouble. The natural features of the country, the character of the people where Shevajee began his course, and the declining and often distracted state of the kingdom of Beejapoor, were all favorable to his progress. Nor was he at all scrupulous in respect to the means he used to increase his power, or to replenish his treasury. Having obtained information concerning the immense wealth and defenceless state of Surat, then the great commercial emporium of western India, Shevajee took 4,000 horse, and proceeding rapidly by unfrequented ways came unexpectedly upon the city, plundered it for several days, obtained a great amount of booty, and returned to his own hill-fort among the Ghats. Aurungzeb sent a large force against him under experienced generals, who carried on war for several years with various success. An arrangement was at length made by which

Shevajee surrendered a part of his territory and was to have a high command in the emperor's army. He then proceeded to Delhi, where he was to be duly invested with the command. But Aurungzeb, regarding his enemy as now in his power, instead of fulfilling his part, first treated Shevajee with neglect, and then put him under restraint. The latter found means to escape, and after wandering about for nine months in the guise of a Hindu devotee, reached his friends in safety. From this time he was irreconcilably opposed to Aurungzeb, and to all Mohammedan power. In 1674, he assumed the title of Raja, and though illiterate (for he was never able to read or to write), yet his territory was well governed, and he was very popular among the Mahrattas. His power continued to increase, and his army at one time amounted to 30,000 cavalry, and 40,000 infantry. He died in A.D. 1680, in the 53d year of his age. His name and character have always been revered by the Mahrattas.

Aurungzeb became at length so much dissatisfied with the manner in which the wars in the Deckan were carried on, that he resolved to proceed there and superintend them himself. The kingdoms of Beejapoor and of Golconda, had acknowledged the sovereignty of the emperor of Delhi and paid annual tribute, but they still retained the management of their own internal affairs. Aurungzeb resolved entirely to subdue these kingdoms, as well as to conquer the Mahrattas. He first commenced war on Beejapoor, which had become much diminished by previous wars, and was then distracted by internal feuds. He besieged and took the city in 1683, and annexed the territory to the empire of Delhi. Beejapoor had been the capital of one of the Mohammedan kingdoms of the Deckan for 200 years. He then commenced war on the kingdom of Golconda, which was annexed to the empire in 1687. While engaged in this last-mentioned war, he became suspicious that his son Moazzim had some plan to depose him and seize the throne. He immediately caused his son to be arrested. It was in vain that his son asserted his innocence, and that all believed he was innocent. He was put into confinement, and was kept under more or less restraint for 7 years. Aurungzeb's youngest son Acber, who first joined the governor of Gujerat in an insurrection against his father and then fled to the Mahrattas, now fearful of falling into his father's hands, fled to Persia and never returned again to India.

Aurungzeb continued in the Deckan till his decease in 1706. His residence there exceeded 22 years. He did not select any city as his capital, but removed about from place to place. His encampment in extent and population resembled a large city. The royal pavilion was of great extent, and every thing connected with it was in a style of imperial magnificence.*

*"The display of power presented by Aurungzeb's marches and encampments in the Deckan, was grand and imposing to a degree which has seldom been surpassed. Besides foreigners, his cavalry, assembled from Cabul, Candahar, Multan, Lahore, Rajpootana, and the extended provinces of his vast empire, was the flower of his army and array of gigantic men and horses completely armed and accoutred, whom it might be imagined the more slender and light-armed natives of the Deckan could hardly venture to oppose. His infantry was numerous and was composed of musketeers, matchlock men, and archers, well equipped, besides bodies of hardy Boondelas and Mewattees, accustomed to predatory contests among the mountains, and better able to cope with the Mahratta Mawulees. To these were afterwards added many thousands of infantry raised in the Carnatic. There were several hundred cannon manned by natives of Hindustan, but directed by European gunners. A great number of miners were attached to the park of artillery with artisans of every description. A long train of war elephants was followed by a number of the same animals on the emperor's private establishment, employed to carry the ladies of his seraglio. Numerous led horses magnificently caparisoned, formed a stud for the emperor's riding. A menagerie accompanied the camp, from which the rarest animals in the world were frequently brought forth and exhibited by their keepers before the emperor and his court, while hawks, hounds, hunting tigers, trained elephants, and every accompaniment used for field sport, swelled the pomp of the prodigious retinue.

"The canvas walls which encompassed the royal tents, formed a circumference of 1,200 yards, and contained every description of apartment to be found in the most spacious palace. Halls of audience for public assemblies and private councils, with all the courts and cabinets attached to them, each hall magnificently adorned, and having in it a raised seat or throne for the emperor, surrounded with gilded pillars, with canopies of velvet richly fringed and superbly embroidered; separate tents as mosques and oratories; baths, and galleries for archery and gymnastic exercises; a seraglio as remarkable for luxury and privacy as that at Delhi; Persian carpets, damasks, and tapestries; European velvets, satins, and broadcloths; Chinese silks of every description, and muslins, and cloths of gold were used in the utmost profusion, and arranged for the greatest effect. Gilded balls and cupolas surmounted the tops of the royal tents, the outside of which and the canvas walls, were of a variety of lively colors disposed in a manner which heightened the general splendor. The entrance into the royal inclosure was through a spacious portal, flanked by two

12

The war with the Mahrattas continued all this time. Sumbhajee, the son and successor of Shevajee, was a depraved and profligate prince. "He put the widow of Shevajee to a painful and lingering death; he imprisoned her son Raja Ram. He threw the brahmin ministers who had been most active against him into prison, and he beheaded such of his other enemies as were not protected by the sanctity of their class." When in a state of intoxication and revelry, he was taken prisoner by Tokarnab Khan, one of the emperor's generals. Sumbhajee had imbibed his father's hatred of Mohammedans, and their religion. "To an invitation to become a Mussulman, he replied in language so insulting to the emperor and so impious towards the prophet, that an order was given for his immediate execution. His eyes were first destroyed with a hot iron, his tongue was cut out, and he was then beheaded." This barbarity increased the hatred of the Mahrattas towards Aurungzeb and the Mohammedan government, and the war on their part had much of a religious character. Unable to meet the emperor's forces in the open country, the Mahratta chiefs avoided coming to pitched battles, but kept up a harassing warfare, plundering the country around the royal encampment, cutting off convoys, attacking departments, etc. Aurungzeb obtained possession of nearly all the forts, and the grand army exhibited a striking contrast to any force the Mahratta chiefs could assemble. Still after 20 years of warfare, the emperor's army and power had decreased, and theirs had increased. Indeed, so

elegant pavilions, from which extended on each side rows of cannon, forming an avenue, at the extremity of which was an immense tent containing the great state drums and imperial band. A little further in front was the post of the grand guard on duty, commanded by a nobleman who mounted it daily. On the other side surrounding the great inclosure just mentioned, were separate tents for the emperor's armory, harness, etc., a tent for water kept cool with saltpetre, another for fruit, a third for sweetmeats, a fourth for betel, and so on, with numerous kitchens, stables, etc. Such luxury in a camp is scarcely to be conceived. And besides what has been described, *every tent had its exact duplicate,* which was sent on in advance to be prepared against the emperor's arrival. His march was a grand procession, and when he entered his pavilion, a salvo from 50 pieces of ordnance announced the event. In all places and circumstances he assumed and maintained every form and ceremony observed at the established residences of the imperial court." — *Calcutta Review.*

great had been the change, that it was becoming evident the emperor must bring hostilities to a close by making peace with the Mahrattas, or withdraw from the Deckan, leaving the country to their undisputed possession.

But this state of matters was brought to a close by the death of Aurungzeb, which took place near Ahmednugger, in 1706, in the 89th year of his age, and the 50th year from his assuming the imperial power — a long and eventful reign.* He made his way to the throne by deposing and imprisoning his father, and putting to death his three brothers and all their sons. And he was equally unscrupulous during all his life in respect to using means to preserve his power. He had no confidence in his own sons that they would not at any time treat him and each other, as he had treated his father Shah Jehan, and his brothers. And his sons, knowing as they did, by what means he acquired the throne, and seeing his suspicions of them, had neither confidence in him nor affection for him. His oldest son Mohammed joined his uncle and father-in-law Shuja, and fought against his own father, and when he afterwards again espoused his father's interest, he was put in prison and never again had his liberty. Acber, another son, joined the governor of Gujerat, in an insurrection against his own father, and when this failed, he fled to the Mahrattas, and ultimately to Persia, where he died.

* Historians differ in respect to his age and reign. One says "he died in the 89th year of his age, and in the 50th year of his reign." Another says, "In the 94th year of his age, and in the 49th year of his reign." Another says, "In the 93d year of his age, and in the 48th of his reign." And yet another says, "In the 93d year of his age, and in the 51st year of his reign."

Aurungzeb's body was buried at Roza, 16 miles from Aurungabad. Roza contains the mausoleums of many Mohammedan kings, princes, and nobles. When at this place in 1834, I inquired for the tomb of Aurungzeb, and expected to find a mausoleum corresponding to his dignity and fame. I was conducted to a grave covered with a well-wrought stone, and with a small frame of wood over it, but surrounded with several large and elegant mausoleums erected over graves. Great reverence was shown to the grave of Aurungzeb, and the moolahs in charge of the burial ground apparently thought more of it than of all the mausoleums of the place. I asked them why the great Aurungzeb had not a mausoleum corresponding to his rank and dignity, and they replied that the grave and the small wooden frame over it were prepared and had been preserved just as he directed before his death, as he wished thus to show to the world the end of all human greatness, pomp, and power.

Moazzim, another son, was in confinement for many years. Of his other sons he showed great suspicion, and they lived in constant dread of him.

In all the departments of government, in war as well as in peace, he exhibited great talents. Nor was his care limited to a general superintendence of the different departments. "He conducted every branch of his government in the most minute detail. He planned campaigns and issued instructions during their progress; drawings of forts were sent to him to fix on the points of attack. His letters embrace measures for keeping open the roads in the Afghan country, for quelling disturbances at Multan and Agra, and even for recovering Candahar; and at the same time there is scarcely a detachment marches, or a convoy moves in the Deckan without some orders from his own hand. The appointment of the lowest revenue officer of a district, or the selection of a clerk in an office, is not beneath his attention, and the conduct of all these functionaries is watched by means of spies and of prying inquiries from all comers, and they are constantly kept on the alert by admonitions founded upon such information."

In his personal habits, he was remarkable for an Asiatic sovereign of a great empire. He was plain and simple in his dress, abstemious in his food, refraining entirely from the use of spirits, indulging in no amusements or revelry, systematic in the employment of his time, and punctual in performing his religious duties. His zeal for the Mohammedan faith and the means he used to propagate it, made him unpopular and even odious among the Hindus, and excited prejudices which greatly impaired the stability of Mohammedan governments in India. He would employ the Hindus in no situation of honor or responsibility. The Mohammedan conquerors of India, in accordance with the general principles of their faith, imposed a capitation tax on the Hindus, thus discriminating between them and the believers. This tax was always odious among the Hindus, as taxes always must be which are founded upon a difference of faith. This odious tax was annulled by Acber, and was not exacted for more than a century. But it was re-imposed and exacted by Aurungzeb. He also forbid the use of liquors, gambling, and idolatrous processions. He fòrbid the public celebration of the Hindu festivals. In a few large cities the most celebrated temples were demolished, and mosques were erected in their places.* Many of his letters, on personal as well as public matters, have been preserved, and the life and reign of no Asiatic sovereign have been so fully described and are now so generally known. Mohammedan historians often speak of him as the greatest of all the emperors of India.

The following extract appears to give a just view of the character of Aurungzeb. "He was a man of a mild temper and cold heart; cautious, artful, and designing; a perfect master of dissimulation; acute and sagacious, though not extended in his views; and ever on the watch to gain friends and to propitiate enemies. To these less brilliant qualities he joined great courage and skill in military exercises; a handsome, though not athletic form; affable and gracious manners, and lively and agreeable conversation. He was so great a dissembler in other matters that he has been supposed to have been a hypocrite in religion. But although religion was a great instrument of his policy, he was beyond all doubt a sincere and bigoted Mussulman. He had been brought up by men of known sanctity, and had himself shown an early turn for devotion; he at one time professed the intention of renouncing the world and taking the habit of a fakir; and throughout his whole life he evinced a real attachment to his faith in many things indifferent to his interest, and in some most seriously opposed to it. His zeal was shown in his prayers, and reading the Koran, in pious discourses, in abstemiousness, (which he affected to carry so far as to subsist on the earnings of his manual labor,) in humility of deportment, patience under provocation, and resignation in misfortunes; but above all in earnest and constant endeavors to promote his own faith, and to discourage idolatry and infidelity. But neither religion nor morality stood for a moment in his way when they interfered with his ambition; and though full of scruples at other times, he would stick at no crime that was requisite for the gratification of that passion." †

* This Aurungzeb caused to be done in Benares and Mathura. The materials of the temples were used in building the mosques.

† Elphinstone, p. 521.

In reading the actions and contemplating the character of such men as Aurungzeb, we often wish to know how their conduct appeared to themselves, especially in such a review of life as they can take in their old age. The following extracts from his letters to his sons give a striking picture of his feelings in view of his past life and death then just before him. He says:—

"Old age is arrived; weakness subdues me, and strength has forsaken all my limbs. I came a stranger into this world, and a stranger I depart. I know nothing of myself, what I am, and for what I am destined. The instant which passed in power, has left only sorrow behind it. I have not been the guardian and protector of the empire. My valuable time has been passed vainly. I had a patron in my own dwelling (conscience), but his glorious light was unseen by my dim sight.—I brought nothing into this world, and except the infirmities of man, carry nothing out. I have a dread for my salvation, and with what torments I may be punished. Though I have strong reliance on the mercies and bounty of God, yet regarding my actions fear will not quit me; but when I am gone, reflection will not remain.—My back is bent with weakness, and my feet have lost the powers of motion. The breath which rose is gone, and left not even hope behind it. I have committed numerous crimes, and know not with what punishments I may be seized.—The guardianship of a people is the trust by God committed to my sons.—I resign you, your mother, and son, to God as I myself am going. The agonies of death come upon me fast.—Odiporee, your mother, was a partner in my illness, and wishes to accompany me in death; but every thing has its appointed time.—I am going. Whatever good or evil I have done, it was for you.—No one has seen the departing of his own soul, but I see that mine is departing."

Such were the feelings of this great emperor in review of a life containing probably a greater amount of deliberately perpetrated wickedness than was ever committed, more uninterrupted success in all his schemes, and prosperity in all his affairs, than was ever realized, more wealth and power than was ever possessed, and more grandeur and splendor than was ever enjoyed, by any other monarch or mortal in the history of the world.

THE SUCCESSORS OF AURUNGZEB.

Aurungzeb's love of power and his jealousy of his sons, did not allow of his investing any of them with much power while he was living. In a paper containing a kind of will, found under his pillow after his decease, he recommended that Moazzim should be recognized as emperor, and that he and Azim should divide the empire, the former having Delhi for his capital, with the northern and eastern provinces, and the latter having Agra for his capital, with the south-western and southern provinces including the Deckan, excepting the kingdoms of Beejapoor and Golconda, which were to belong to Cambuksh. As soon as Moazzim, who was in Cabul, heard of his father's death, he assumed the dignity of emperor, and the title of Bahadur Shah, though for some time before his father's death, he was known by the title of Shah Aulum. Azim who was in Malwa, hastened to the royal camp and was acknowledged emperor of India. The two brothers then proceeded towards Agra, with as large a force as each could collect. Some historians say that, as the two armies were approaching each other near Agra, Bahadur Shah wrote to his brother, proposing to divide the empire between them, and that Azim rejected the offer. The two armies soon came into conflict, when Azim was defeated and himself and his two sons were slain. Bahadur Shah then took formal possession of the throne, palace, etc. Cambuksh, who had taken possession of the kingdom of Beejapoor and Golconda, and acknowledged the sovereignty of Azim, refusing now to acknowledge Bahadur Shah, the latter marched into the Deckan, and in a battle near Hyderabad defeated his brother, who died of his wounds the same day. Bahadur Shah died in 1712, having reigned nearly 6 years. In the latter part of his reign he was involved in war with the Sikhs, then a religious sect and beginning to acquire importance in the northern parts of India. This war was conducted on both sides with great barbarity.

Bahadur Shah left four sons, who began to contend each for the throne soon after their father's death. Nor did this struggle cease till three of them had fallen, and the oldest was left in undisputed possession. Jehander Shah proved to be a weak-minded and profligate sovereign. One of his first acts was to put to death all the males of the royal family, whom he could get into his power. But there was one, Ferokshere, a son of his brother Azim Shah, then in Bengal and beyond his reach. Ferokshere and his friends, among whom were Abdoolla Khan, and Hoossen Ali, two brothers, who were then the governors of Bahar and Allahabad, knowing the emperor's purpose, and shocked at his cruelty and selfishness, collected a large army, and defeated the force which was sent against them. They then proceeded towards Agra. On arriving near the city, the emperor and his vizier met them with an army of 70,000 men. The emperor was defeated, and Ferokshere soon took possession of Agra. The emperor, the vizier, and many others were put to death, and Ferokshere ascended the throne in A.D. 1713. He appointed Abdoolla Khan his vizier, and Hoossen Ali his commander-in-chief, and the emperor was little else than a pageant in their hands while he lived. These brothers were Syuds or descendants of Mohammed.

The reign of this emperor continued for about 6 years. The empire was all the time in a very distracted state in the capital as well as the provinces. Intrigues in the court, assassinations in the palace, and insurrections and battles in the provinces, constitute the principal matters of his reign. This state of the empire encouraged the Sikhs to renew the war, which was carried on with greater barbarity, if possible, than before.* So

* The following extracts show the character of the parties and the spirit and manners of the age:—"The Sikhs under a new chief named Bandu, who had been bred a religious ascetic, and who combined a most sanguinary disposition with bold and daring counsels, broke from their retreat and overran the east of the Punjab, committing unheard of cruelties, wherever they directed their steps. The mosques were destroyed and the moolahs were butchered. The rage of the Sikhs was not restrained by any considerations of religion, or by any mercy for age and sex. Whole towns were massacred with wanton barbarity, and even the bodies of the dead were dug up and thrown out to the birds and beasts of prey."—The same horrors marked their route through the country eastward of the Sutledge and the Jumna, into which they penetrated as far as Seharanpoor. In their next excursion they ravaged the country as far as Lahore on the one side and of Delhi itself on the other. Such was the character of the Sikhs in their former wars. And they were not reformed by suffering punishment from

many of the Sikhs were put to death and otherwise perished in this war, that it was a long time before they appeared again upon the page of history. Ferokshere was put to death by order of Abdoolla Khan and Hoossen Ali, who then proclaimed a child, a great grandson of Aurungzeb, to be emperor, but he lived only five months. They then proclaimed another similar child to be emperor, but he lived only three months. They then placed a grandson of Bahadur Shah, then 17 years old on the throne, by the title of Mohammed Shah. This emperor was for a while a mere pageant of those who had placed him on the throne, but becoming impatient of their control, he united with others in a plan for removing them. Hoossen Ali was soon assassinated in his palanquin, and Abdoolla Khan was deposed and deprived of all power. The empire continued to be in a distracted state. The emperor was dissolute in his habits, and fickle in his purposes and plans. He was often at variance with his ministers, and they again were quarrelling among themselves. Nizam ul Mulk, who established the family and

the government, nor the principles of their own religion.—"Meanwhile the long continued dissensions among the Mohammedans afforded an opportunity to the Sikhs to recruit their strength. Bandu issued from his retreat, defeated the imperial troops and ravaged the country with greater fury than before. At length an army was sent against him, under an able chief named Abdusemed Khan. By him the Sikhs were beaten in repeated actions, and Bandu was at last made prisoner with a number of his men and some of his principal followers. Most of these persons were executed on the spot, but 740 were selected and sent with Bandu to Delhi. They were paraded through the streets on camels, dressed in black sheep skins with the wool outside, and were exposed to the execrations of the people, which it must be confessed they had well deserved. But their punishment exceeded the measure of their offences, even such as theirs. They were all beheaded on 7 successive days, and died with the utmost firmness, disdaining every offer to save their lives at the expense of their religion. Bandu was reserved for greater cruelties. He was exhibited in an iron cage, clad in a robe of cloth of gold and a scarlet turban. An executioner stood behind him with a drawn sword. Around him were the heads of his followers on pikes, and even a dead cat was stuck on a similar weapon to indicate the extirpation of every thing belonging to him. He was then given a dagger and ordered to stab his infant son, and on his refusing, the child was butchered before his eyes, and its heart thrown in his face. He was at last torn to pieces with hot pincers, and died with unshaken constancy, glorying in having been raised up by God to be a scourge to the iniquities and oppressions of the age." —*Elphinstone*, p. 607, 608.

power of the present Nizam of Hyderabad, and Sadat Khan, who established the family and power of the present Nabob of Oude or Lucknow, became prominent in the affairs of the empire at this time. The Mahrattas, though their chiefs were often at war among themselves, yet carried on an aggressive war most of the time on all sides, and appeared likely soon to become the predominant power in India.

While affairs were in this state in India, intelligence arrived from the west, which reminded the princes and the people of the former invasions of Tamerlane and Baber. Nadir Shah, the most conspicuous prince of Persia in the last century, commenced his military career as the head of a company of banditti. The increase of his followers soon gave him power, and his daring spirit produced an inclination to engage in the political affairs of Persia, then in an unsettled state. He was for some time engaged in war with the Turks, and then again with the Afghans. In all circumstances he displayed military talents of the highest order, and wherever he went, victory followed his standard. For some pretended offence he seized the king of Persia, put him under restraint, and governed the country in the king's name. Having restored order in the kingdom and become popular in the army, in the plain of Maghan he assembled a great council, which including the army under his command, was said to amount to 100,000 men, and he was there proclaimed king of Persia. He then put out the eyes of the late king Thamas or Tahmasp, so as to make him incapable of recovering his throne. Nadir Shah was himself of a restless spirit, and it was necessary to find employment for his army, and means to support them. The countries east of Persia were in an unsettled state, and he formed the purpose of adding Afghanistan to his dominions. While engaged in the siege of Candahar and Cabul, and subsequently in settling the affairs of these cities and their provinces, he sent several messages to Mohammed Shah then emperor of India, and he affected to be much displeased with the manner in which they were received, and with the answers returned to him. Some Persians or Afghans who had incurred his displeasure, having taken refuge at Delhi, Nadir Shah sent an ambassador to demand that they should be delivered up to him. The ambassador and his escort were murdered at Jellallabad. This excited his rage, and he was soon on the way to inflict vengeance, and his army committed shocking ravages on the inhabitants of the offending city. From Jellallabad he proceeded to Peshawur, and then to Lahore, without encountering any opposition to retard his progress. The emperor, his army, and the inhabitants of Delhi were astonished to hear that Nadir Shah with his victorious army had already passed the Indus, and so was within the borders of the empire. Historians differ much in respect to the number of Nadir Shah's army. By some it is put at 160,000 men, and by others at not more than half this number. From Lahore he proceeded on the way to Delhi. When the emperor became assured that the Persian army had entered India, he despatched against him all the force which could be collected. The two armies met and encountered a few marches from Delhi. The Indian army, hastily collected together, relaxed in discipline and without experience in war, were no match for the disciplined Persians, who were inured to war and led by the greatest hero of that age. The Indian army was easily routed, and the commander-in-chief was slain.

The emperor Mohammed Shah had no resource but submission or flight, and he chose the former. He sent his vizier Azof Khan to the Persian camp, and he soon repaired there himself. Some negotiations ensued, and Nadir Shah agreed to spare the city and leave India upon receiving a definite sum of money. But some of the emperor's courtiers and counsellors interfered, and the city with its emperor and nobles, and all its riches and inhabitants, was at the mercy of the conqueror. Mohammed Shah was compelled to join the Persian camp, and accompany Nadir Shah on his march towards Delhi. On arriving at the city, the gates were opened to admit the Persian army, and the two sovereigns took up their residence in the royal palace. Nadir Shah distributed his army in different parts of the city, and for two days strict order was observed. But the state of parties gave little promise of continued quiet and safety. The Persians were anxious to grasp the immense wealth now before them, as the reward of their long labors and sufferings, and the people of the city looking upon them as ruthless invaders and plunderers, were in the spirit of seizing their arms and falling upon them. In the evening of the third day a report was circulated that Nadir Shah had been killed. The inhabitants began at once to attack the Persians wherever any could be found, and before morning several hundred were killed. As soon as there was sufficient light in the morning, Nadir Shah mounted his horse and endeavored to suppress the tumult, but seeing many of the Persians murdered and being attacked himself, he despatched his troops over the city, with orders to make a general massacre of the inhabitants. The Persians were accustomed to such work, and "the slaughter raged from sunrise till the day was far advanced, and was attended with all the horrors that could be inspired by rapine, lust, and thirst of vengeance. The city was set on fire in several places, and was soon involved in one scene of destruction, blood, and terror." While this terrible carnage was going on, Nadir Shah sat alone in gloomy silence, no one daring to speak to him. At length, Mohammed Shah and some of his nobles ventured before him, and entreated him to stop the carnage. He immediately issued orders, and before night all was quiet. Historians differ much in respect to the number who perished in this dreadful massacre, some accounts making it not more than 30,000, and others as many as 120,000.

But the sufferings of the inhabitants were far from being at an end. Nadir Shah's object in invading India appears to have been to enrich himself and his army by plunder. To this work he now applied himself. He seized all the imperial treasure, gold and silver, coined and bullion, jewels, precious stones, and whatever was valuable, which could be converted into money or carried away. He then seized the money, etc., of the nobles, bankers, and merchants. Guards were placed at all the gates to prevent any thing being carried out of the city. People of all classes were tortured to deliver up their money, or to disclose where it was. Many died under the tortures thus inflicted, and many killed themselves rather than suffer the tortures, losses, and disgrace that awaited them. To these miseries were soon added famine (the Persians consuming the provisions found in the city and the inhabitants of the country afraid to come to the city,) and pestilence occasioned by the great number of the slain which remained unburied. It is scarcely possible to conceive of a city in a more deplorable state than Delhi was at this time.

Nadir Shah, having become satisfied that nothing further was to be obtained at Delhi, began to prepare for his departure. He required Mohammed Shah to cede to him all the provinces west of the Indus. He reinstated him on the throne of the empire. He arranged a marriage between one of his sons and a daughter of the emperor. He enjoined all the nobles to give implicit obedience to Mohammed Shah or to expect his future displeasure and vengeance, and having collected all his treasure and plunder he departed. His stay at Delhi was 37 days,* and the amount of treasure, jewels, and other property he carried away, has been generally estimated at 320,000,000 rupees, or $160,000,000.†

Nadir Shah lived 8 years after his return to Persia. He became so jealous and irritable, so excessively capricious and cruel, that no one of those around him felt he had any security for his own life for a single day. A conspiracy was formed to rid the world of a tyrant no longer endurable, and he was assassinated in his tent. Immediately after his death, Ahmed Shah Abdallee, one of his most experienced generals, and who commanded his Afghan troops, withdrew with the force under him to Candahar, and was there soon proclaimed king of Afghanistan. He was a skilful commander and had a large and well disciplined army. He was of a restless and ambitious spirit, and soon began to interfere in the affairs of India. Mohammed Shah died in 1748, after a reign of 30 years. He was succeeded by his son Ahmed Shah, who after reigning 6 years, was deposed and blinded by Ghazee ud Deen, who elevated one of the royal family by the title of Aulumgheer II. to the throne, and then obtained for himself the office of vizier. In the third year of this emperor's reign, Ahmed Shah Abdallee invaded India and plundered Delhi. The horrors of Nadir Shah's invasion were repeated, and "the city again became a scene of rapine, violence, and murder." Several other cities in the same part of India were plundered, and the inhabitants were treated with

* One account says that Nadir Shah remained at Delhi 58 days.

† The statements of historians differ much in respect to the amount of this wealth. The lowest sum I have seen is 320,000,000 rupees, and the largest is 1,250,000,000 rupees. The lowest estimate is a large sum, and the largest estimate appears to be incredible. A rupee is nearly half a dollar.

great barbarity. A violent sickness breaking out in his army, Ahmed Shah Abdallee was compelled to return to his own country.

The distracted state of affairs at Delhi and in the provinces around it, invited such people as the Mahrattas and the Afghans to plunder and conquests. The Mahrattas were now at the zenith of their power, and formed a plan of extending their conquest over all the northern parts of India. In pursuance of this plan, a large force proceeded into the central and northern provinces. Ahmed Shah Abdallee, who abhorred idolatry and all idolaters, had done much to destroy the Mogul empire, yet he was unwilling to see the Hindus extending their power over the true believers. So he again invaded India and defeated the Mahratta force under Duttajee Scindia, and again under Mulhar Row Holkar, in both instances with great slaughter. These defeats excited strong feeling among the Mahrattas, and arrangements were made to send as soon as possible, a much larger army into the northern provinces. This force, after various changes, became concentrated at Panniput, about 40 miles north-west from Delhi. The entire number there assembled, including the cavalry, infantry, and artillery, and all the adventurers and camp followers, are stated to have amounted to 300,000. Ahmed Shah Abdallee, who had been for some time encamped on the other side of Delhi, on learning the plans and movements of the Mahrattas, proceeded to the vicinity of Panniput and there encamped. His entire force is stated to have been 91,000 men. Of these 40,000 are said to have been Persians and Afghans, who had been inured to war all their lives, and the rest consisted of additions since he entered India.

The two armies remained encamped near each other for nearly three months. Each army endeavored to cut off the supplies and convoys of the other. In this work the Afghans had more success than the Mahrattas, who on account of their great numbers and crowded state, began to suffer from famine and pestilence. These sufferings soon became so great that the Mahratta leaders resolved to risk a general battle, and orders were issued to prepare for it. The celebrated battle of Panniput was fought in January of 1761. The Mahrattas were defeated with great slaughter. The pursuit was continued in every direction for 15 or 20 miles, the Afghans slaughtering the Mahrattas wherever found. The inhabitants of the country around Panniput, to whom the Mahrattas had become odious on account of their extortions and arrogance, united with the Afghans in the pursuit and slaughter of their common enemies. The whole number who perished in the battle and pursuit, was estimated at 200,000. "Never was there a defeat more complete, and never was there a calamity that diffused more consternation." It was expected that Ahmed Shah Abdallee would assume the empire of India. But for some reasons not known he made but little use of this victory for his own advantage. Having made, or rather approved of some arrangements at Delhi for its future government, he returned to his own country and never again interfered in the affairs of India.

The history of the Mohammedan empire in India may properly close here. The power and influence of him who was called emperor from this time were little beside the prestige of his name and titles, and the thought that possibly he or some one of his family might again recover their former power and greatness. The battle of Plassey, which laid the foundation of the English power in India, was fought in 1757, or 4 years before the great battle of Panniput. So the English were now becoming prominent actors on the great field of Indian history, and might be reckoned one of the powers among which the country was divided. Hyder Ali had now established his power in the southern part of the peninsula, having Seringapatam for his capital. The Nizam ul Mulk with Hyderabad for his capital, and the Mahrattas with Poona for their capital, had established their power in the Deckan. The Nabob of Oude and the Rajpoot princes were now virtually independent. The history of these different powers, Mohammedan and Hindu, will come into view, so far as the limits of this work will admit of an account of them, in the European history of India. From the battle of Plassey in 1757, or of Panniput in 1761, the English became the most important and the rising power in India.

The professed object of the Mohammedans in invading and conquering India, was the conversion of the inhabitants to the faith of their Prophet, and this object they openly avowed to the people of the country. But when their power had become established in the country, they lost much of their zeal for the propagation of their religion, and so long as the Hindus paid their tribute and their taxes, they were generally permitted quietly to practise their own superstitions. The Mohammedan emperors, princes, and nobles employed the Hindus in various ways, chiefly in matters of finance and revenue, in which they have always excelled. The Mohammedans would always have preferred men of their own faith, and would often reward with honors or employments, converts from Hinduism. The influence of the government in oriental countries is generally great, and considering the power and the spirit of the Mohammedan governments and people, and the character and circumstances of the great body of the Hindus, it might naturally be expected that great numbers of the latter would embrace the religion of their conquerors and rulers in the long course of the 7 or 8 centuries of their power. But the general opinion is that not more than one eighth or one tenth of the whole population have ever been Mohammedans, and probably one half of these are the descendants of those who were Mohammedans when they came into the country.

Should it appear strange how the Mohammedans, who have always formed so small a proportion of the population, could conquer and govern the country for so long a period, we must consider that the armies which invaded and conquered India, were large, that they were composed of men superior to the Hindus in physical strength, energy, and courage, that they were inured to war, and were in a state of high military discipline; that it was a sentiment of all the early Mohammedans that they ought not, and their determination that they would not, be subject to idolators, that they seized and appropriated the wealth and resources of the country to their own use without scruple, that they always formed the military class and composed nearly all the armed force of the empire, and that their armies were often reinforced by great numbers of daring and warlike adventurers from Arabia, Persia, and Central Asia.

It was mentioned that, in the anarchy consequent upon the invasion of India, and subversion of the empire of Delhi, by Tamerlane, some of the Mohammedan governors of the provinces asserted their independence, assumed regal titles, and began to exercise the functions of kings. In this way Bengal became a kingdom, and continued under its own sovereigns for two centuries. Kulburga, Ahmednuggur, Beejapoor, Beder, and Golconda, became the capitals of small Mohammedan kingdoms in the Deckan. So Gujerat, Candeish, and Scinde, became separate governments. Some of these provinces, or kingdoms as they were then called, maintained their independence for one, two, and even three centuries, but all at length became again subject to the emperor of Delhi, and provinces of the empire. The limits of this work does not allow of giving any particular description of these kings and their governments. Nor does it appear to be necessary, as in their general character and spirit they resembled the emperors of Delhi, though on a reduced scale. Their courts exhibited the intrigues, deceit, profligacy, assassinations, etc., so common in oriental governments. Some of these Mohammedan kings erected large palaces, mosques, and mausoleums, and some of the capitals of these former kingdoms are remarkable for splendid edifices, though now many of them are in ruins. There are such remains of former splendor at Beejapoor, Aurungabad, Ahmedabad, and other places.*

* The writer saw many such monuments and ruins in different places in India. The following are extracts from his notes on some ruins at Beejapoor. "The Jumma Musjid, or great mosque is a splendid edifice, 290 feet long, and 165 feet wide, and the two wings which project from the front corners are 210 feet long, and 45 feet wide. The roof consists of one large dome in the centre, and many smaller ones in rows, supported by pillars united at the top by arches. The *Kebla*, or principal place for prayer, contains many extracts from the Koran, beautifully carved in stone, and the letters covered with gold. This immense structure in its design and execution displays much genius and skill. It is built of stone or brick and lime, no wood appearing to be used in any part of it. This mosque was erected nearly 300 years ago, and is in a state of good preservation.

"The mausoleum of Sultan Mohammed is an immense pile, 240 feet square. The interior is one vast room, covered by a single dome. The tombs of the royal founder and his family are in the centre under the dome. At each corner of the mausoleum and contiguous to it, is a minaret, containing a spiral staircase ascending through 8 stories to the top, where a passage leads through the dome at its base. The inside view of the edifice at the base of the dome, appeared to be more sublime than at any other point.

"Some cannon here deserve a passing notice. One of these is of brass, and its weight is more than 40 tons. The diameter of the muzzle is 4 feet 8 inches,

Mr. Mill, in his History of British India, at the conclusion of the Mohammedan period, attempts to show at considerable length, that India must have gained much in civilization, humanity, etc., from the Mohammedan conquest and government of the country. The reasons he gives for this opinion are, that the Mohammedans were in many respects superior to the Hindus: — as, 1. In their classification and distribution of the people; 2. Their form of government; 3. Their laws; 4. The taxes; 5. Their religion; 6. Their manners; 7. Their literature.* Mr. Mill was never in India, and so could have had no personal acquaintance with the classes of people, or the governments he has described. In his accounts of the Hindus, their customs, manners, religion, etc., he shows in many places a strong prejudice against them, while he gives too favorable a view of the state and character of the Mohammedan population. If we admit that the Mohammedans who invaded India, were superior to the Hindus in all the respects he has mentioned, still it will not follow that they communicated these benefits to the inhabitants of the country. Had the Mohammedans embraced the religion they found in India, as the Goths and Vandals embraced the religion of the southern nations of Europe, which they conquered, or if the Hindus had become Mohammedans, as the inhabitants of Persia did, so as in either case to have formed a homogeneous population, then a superior state of civilization would probably have been the result. But no such union or amalgamation took place. The Mohammedans did not unite with the Hindus, and only a small portion of the Hindus, and those generally persons of low caste became Mohammedans. The two classes continued to be separate and distinct for generations and for centuries, with as little knowledge of

and the diameter of the calibre is nearly 30 inches. 'A cast-iron ball for this cannon would weigh 2,646 pounds.' This cannon was cast at Ahmednuggur in 1559. It was part of the spoils of war, taken by the king of Beejapoor in a battle near Purinda, and carried thence to Beejapoor. On one of the bastions of the fort is an iron cannon with a muzzle of 4 feet and 3 inches, and a calibre 21 inches. On a high mound or tower, nearly in the centre of the city, is an iron cannon, more than 30 feet long, with a calibre of 13 inches. These two last mentioned are made of bars of iron hooped round and welded so as to make a compact mass."

* History of British India, vol. 1, p. 625–648. 4to edition.

each other, as little respect for each other, and as little influence upon each other, as there could well be between different classes of people in such circumstances.

The Mohammedan invasions of India from A. D. 1000 to 1200, destroying idols, demolishing temples, plundering, massacring, and enslaving the inhabitants, produced incalculable evils and miseries. From A. D. 1200, or the establishment of the Mohammedan power in Delhi, to the invasion of Tamerlane in 1399, or to the invasion of Baber in 1526, the character and spirit of the Mohammedans and the oppressed and suffering state of the Hindus, who were then more than nine tenths of the population, do not exhibit a favorable view of the effects of the government. It is not easy to believe that the general state of India, the state and circumstances of more than nine tenths of the people, were in any way improved during this period by the Mohammedan government of the country. Nor was the state of the Hindu population much if any improved during the reigns of Baber and Humayoon. In the reigns of Acber, Jehangheer, Shah Jehan, and Aurungzeb, a period of 140 years, the Mohammedan power was extended and consolidated. And yet during this period there were often wars of a religious character, which were carried on, as such wars always are, with great barbarity and cruelty. Nor did such wars and the spirit engendered by them cease with the dissolution of the empire of Delhi, consequent upon the death of Aurungzeb. A strong spirit of fanaticism pervaded the government of Tippoo Sultan, of the Mahrattas, and of Ahmed Shah Abdallee, producing persecution and oppression, wars and revolutions. The Mohammedan courts, government agents, and armies may have had a higher state of civilization than any Hindu courts, agents, or armies, but they had little influence upon the state and circumstances of the Hindus, who were always the great body of the inhabitants, and who were often suffering in various ways from the proselyting efforts and haughty spirit of their rulers.

CHAPTER III.

THE EUROPEAN PERIOD.

DISCOVERIES AND CONQUESTS OF THE PORTUGUESE.

The 15th century is remarkable for great events, inventions, and discoveries. The invention of the art of printing and the capture of Constantinople united in producing the revival of letters among the nations of Europe, while their discovery of America and of the passage round Africa to the southern countries of Asia and its islands, spread out before them the world for conquest and commerce. In the early part of this century the Portuguese were far in advance of any other nation in maritime discovery. In 1413 they discovered the Islands of Madeira, and in 1454 they reached Senegal. In accordance with the spirit of the age, the propagation of Christianity was avowed as the leading object in prosecuting these discoveries. And to excite greater interest in such enterprises among his people, Prince Henry applied to the Pope, setting forth that the propagation of the Christian faith, the enlargement of the Holy See, and the salvation of the heathen in the countries discovered, had been and would continue to be his great object, and soliciting for his nation exclusive rights and privileges. Eugene IV. who then filled the Holy See, and who, as the vicegerent of Christ, professed to have power to dispose of all parts of the earth as he pleased, strongly commended the zeal of the king and his people, and issued a bull exhorting them to continue in the same glorious career, and granting them exclusive right to all the countries they should discover from Cape Non to the continent of India. This grant not only infused new ardor into the Portuguese nation, but as it was not supposed in that age that the Holy Father had exceeded his power, it prevented all the other nations of Europe from in any way interfering with the rights of the crown of Portugal to all the discoveries they might make.

In 1484 the Portuguese reached the coast of Congo, and

finding the coast there turned towards the east, supposed they must have nearly reached the southern limit of the continent. This hope induced John II. to send out three vessels under Bartholomew Diaz, an experienced and skilful officer, who encountered much tempestuous weather, and was carried so far into the Southern Ocean that in sailing back in search of land he reached the continent near its southern extremity. Diaz would gladly have prosecuted his voyage on the eastern side, but his officers and crew all insisted upon returning home, and he was obliged to yield to their wishes. The king, on hearing a description of their discovery, named the point of land the Cape of Good Hope, which it has ever since retained. Affairs of a more urgent nature occupied the time of John till his death in 1495. In the mean time maritime enterprise had received a new impulse from the discovery of America in 1492 by Columbus. Emanuel, who had succeeded John, now resolved to prosecute discovery with increasing ardor. He caused several vessels to be prepared in superior style, and intrusted the expedition to Vasco de Gama, a member of the royal household, and who had acquired a high reputation for nautical skill and enterprise. No previous expedition had excited so much interest and so high expectations. When all the preparations had been completed, Gama received his instructions from the king in open court, with a consecrated silk banner, and a letter to the mysterious Prester John, who it was supposed was then reigning somewhere in Southern Asia. Previous to embarking, all the officers assembled in the church and received the sacrament, and the priests and monks accompanied them to the ships, bearing wax tapers and chanting prayers. All the sailors went through the ceremonies of confession and absolution, as a suitable preparation for so uncertain and dangerous an expedition.

Gama sailed from Lisbon on the 8th of July, 1497, but as he stopped at several places on the coast they did not reach the southern extremity of the continent till November, and when they changed their course for India, they celebrated the event with religious services and great rejoicings, an event in modern discovery only exceeded by the discovery of America.

Gama then proceeded along the eastern coast, endeavoring where he could, to hold intercourse with the inhabitants and obtain all possible information concerning the countries and their inhabitants, till he reached Mozambique. Here they found another class of people, professing the Mohammedan religion, wearing turbans, and clothed in cotton, silk, and velvet. The Portuguese were now in high spirits, as they appeared to be approaching the rich and civilized nations of India, of whom they had heard such marvellous accounts. Their intercourse with the inhabitants at Mozambique was for some time of a friendly character, but the Mohammedans, on learning who the Portuguese were and their objects in coming to the East, became jealous of them, and were soon detected in plans for cutting them off. Having obtained a pilot, Gama proceeded to Mombas, where the people at first appeared very friendly, but soon became hostile and made repeated attempts to surprise his ships and cut their cables. From Mombas, Gama proceeded to Melinda, which is described as a well-built and beautiful city, surrounded by numerous gardens and forests of palm-trees. The king was a Mohammedan, who lived in regal splendor and invited Gama to visit him in his palace. But Gama, remembering the treachery manifested by the same class of people in the ports he had left, pretended that the king of Portugal had strictly forbidden him to go on shore, and proposed a meeting in boats. The king accepted this proposal, and he and Gama had an interview in this manner. He made many inquiries about the vessels and also about the king of Portugal, his army, the number of his ships of war, etc. When an image of Mary was exhibited to some Hindu merchants who were on board, they worshipped it with a readiness and veneration which greatly surprised the Portuguese. Probably this image was taken for an idol of some Hindu goddess, or their veneration may have originated in their superstitious reverence for any object of worship.

Having obtained a pilot who had often been to India, Gama left the coast of Africa and steered his course for Calicut. In 23 days they descried the mountains of India, and soon after reached Calicut, the place above all others which they wished to see. At this time the northern parts of India were subject to the Mohammedans, but the southern parts, or nearly all south of the Deckan, was subject to different Hindu sovereigns.

Among the latter, the king of Calicut, who had the title of Zamorin, or king of kings, was conspicuous. The commerce of the western coast of India with the Red Sea and the Persian Gulf, was chiefly in the hands of the Mohammedans who had originally come from those places, and of proselytes to their faith from the Hindus. Aware from his past experience of the treachery of this class of people, Gama first sent on shore his pilot and a criminal, who had been sentenced to death in Portugal, and brought out to be employed in cases of peculiar peril. On their return to the ship the next day, a man accompanied them, who said he was a native of Tunis, where he was acquainted with many Portuguese and had professed Christianity. He accosted Gama in a cordial manner, and expressed his feelings as being glad to see them in a country abounding in precious stones, spices, drugs, and all the most valuable articles of commerce. The Zamorin was at that time absent from Calicut, but was expected to return in a few days, when Gama was encouraged to expect a very friendly reception. In these circumstances many things conspired to excite the interest and wonder of the Portuguese. On one occasion a party of them being on shore, and being near a large pagoda which had somewhat the appearance of a church, they were invited into the vestibule, and supposing the images they saw around them might be those of the Apostles and saints, they began to prostrate themselves in adoration. One of them, however, more inquisitive or less superstitious than the rest, examined the figures more carefully, and observing that some of them were of hideous and monstrous forms, having 4 or 5 hands and arms, several faces, etc., he exclaimed, "If these are devils, then it is God whom I worship." An examination of the idols by the rest of the company soon brought their worship to a close.

The Zamorin received Gama with much oriental pomp, and for considerable time manifested a friendly disposition. But the Mohammedans, jealous of this interference with the trade which had been so long in their hands, and averse to all nations professing the Christian faith, soon succeeded in exciting prejudices against the Portuguese, and formed plans for effecting their ruin. They excited the superstitious fears of the Hindus by predicting approaching ruin, and declared Gama and all his company to be pirates, who subsisted by plundering and destroying ships and cities wherever they had been, and who would continue to pursue the same course wherever they went. Gama was once kept in arrest as a prisoner for some time, and soon after he was released, Diaz and another of his officers were put into confinement. He at length effected their release by seizing a considerable number of natives and detaining them till his own men were restored. He then left Calicut, forcibly carrying with him several of the men whom he had arrested. These he intended to take with him to Portugal, so that they might return with the next expedition and inform their countrymen of the power and glory of the Portuguese nation. This conduct in Gama was impolitic as well as unjust, and excited great indignation against the Portuguese wherever it became known to the people of India. In four months he reached the coast of Africa at Magadoxo, and passing the Cape of Good Hope, he reached Lisbon in August, having been absent 2 years and 2 months. Of the 108 mariners he took with him, only 55 returned to their native land. On reaching Lisbon, Gama and his men went to the same church in which religious ceremonies were performed previous to their embarkation, and they spent 8 days in ceremonies, services, and the worship of Mary. He then made his public entrance into Lisbon with great pomp; the king bestowed upon him a title of nobility and liberal rewards for his services.

The return of Gama and the accounts he gave of his voyage and of the wonders he had seen, produced a strong excitement through all Portugal. A fleet of 13 ships and carrying 1,200 men, was prepared with all possible despatch. This expedition was intrusted to Alvarez Cabral, a man every way qualified for such an important enterprise. The conversion of the nations discovered, was not forgotten, and so 8 Franciscan friars accompanied the expedition, who were instructed, if we are to believe De Barros, "to carry fire and sword into every nation who would not listen to their preaching." This armament sailed in March of 1500, and on their way to the Cape of Good Hope, proceeded so far to the west that they discovered the coast of Brazil, which subsequently became the most important of all the Portuguese foreign possessions. When near the Cape of

Good Hope, he was involved for nearly two months in very stormy weather; he lost several of his ships, and had only 3 with him when he passed round the Cape. He followed the coast of Africa, like his predecessor, till he reached Melinda, and then proceeded directly to Calicut. He restored the captives carried away by his predecessor, who were well clothed, and gave a wonderful account of what they had seen in Europe. After some delay and trouble in arranging preliminaries, Cabral obtained an interview with the Zamorin, who received him in apparently a friendly manner, and gave the Portuguese permission to establish a factory in Calicut. Thus far all appeared to be promising, but the Mohammedans soon began in various ways to oppose them and to embarrass their operations. Cabral after suffering their annoyance for some time, seized one of their ships richly laden with spices, and transferred its cargo to his own ships. The Mohammedans made their complaints to the Zamorin, representing that the Portuguese had now shown themselves in their true character of robbers and pirates. The Zamorin either gave, or was understood to give, permission to seek redress in any way they might choose. Collecting some force they made an attack upon the factory so suddenly, that there was barely time to close the gates against them. Correa, who was in charge, arranged his men on the roof to make the best defence they could, but while his force consisted of only 70 men, their assailants consisted of several thousands. A part of the wall was battered down, the assailants entered the factory, put 50 of the Portuguese to death, and the rest leaped into the sea and swam to their boats.

Cabral, not appreciating the provocation he had given, was very indignant at this loss of the factory and so many of his men, and hearing that the Zamorin was participating in the plunder, he resolved to make retaliation and reprisals. He seized 10 Mohammedan ships, and having transferred their cargoes to his own vessels, arranged them in order for greater effect on the people, and set them on fire. At the same time he opened a cannonade on the city, which set it on fire in several places. All further amicable intercourse with the king and people at Calicut was at an end, and Cabral sailed for Cochin. Here he had an audience with the prince, who received him in a friendly manner. This prince was a vassal of the Zamorin of Calicut, and being then involved in some difficulties with his sovereign, was probably for this reason more ready to cultivate the acquaintance of the Portuguese. Cabral here succeeded in completing his cargoes, and returned to Lisbon. But of the 13 ships he took with him only 6 returned; all the rest were lost.

The accounts which Cabral and his company gave of their adventures, and of the countries and nations they had seen, produced a strong sensation through the kingdom. Revenge for supposed injuries, desire of conquest and of foreign possessions, zeal for propagating the Christian faith, and the hope of gain by a profitable commerce, all conspired to enlist the feelings of the nation. The Pope, too, had conferred on Portugal the dominion of all the eastern countries which her fleets might discover, and so the king thought it was right for him to take possession, peaceably if he could, and if not, then by conquest, and then it was his duty to convert the inhabitants to the Romish faith. The king assumed the lofty title of "Lord of the Navigation, Conquest, and Commerce of Ethiopia, Arabia, Persia, and India." The most vigorous measures were taken to prepare a force that would be able to subdue any opposing power, and a fleet of 15 ships soon sailed from Lisbon, under the command of Vasco de Gama. A part of this fleet was designed to blockade the Red Sea so effectually as to stop all the trade carried on by the Mohammedans between its ports and India. The Mohammedans had so uniformly manifested an unfriendly spirit towards the Portuguese, and been apparently the exciting cause of their troubles in so many different places, that Gama appears to have resolved to treat them everywhere as enemies. The general prejudice which then pervaded the nation against all who professed this faith, had probably also some influence on Gama and all under him. He had an opportunity of soon showing this spirit, for on approaching the coast of India, he seized a large Mohammedan vessel, and having taken out all that was valuable, he shut up the crew in the hold and set the ship on fire. Lafiteau says that 300 persons thus perished, among whom were many pilgrims on their way to Mecca. On arriving at Calicut, and failing to obtain such redress as he demanded, Gama collected 50 natives from ships he had seized, and holding an hour-glass in his hand told the messenger that unless his demands were satisfied before all the sand should run out, he would cause all these men to be put to death. And no answer having been received within the time specified, the 50 men were put to death. He also mutilated several natives who were then on board his ships by cutting off a hand or foot, and then sending them ashore. One account says he treated 50 fishermen in this way. He then bombarded the city for some time, causing great destruction of life and property. Gama then proceeded to Cochin, where he was received in a friendly manner. It was not long before a brahmin of venerable age and appearance, and very plausible and insinuating in his address, arrived at Cochin, with a message from the Zamorin to Cabral. The brahmin, having understood that the Portuguese were anxious to convert the people of India to their own faith, began by making some inquiries about Christianity, for which he professed to have great admiration, and was only wishing for some further instruction before he would publicly embrace it. He then assured Gama that the Zamorin was very sorry for all that had occurred at Calicut, that he was willing to make any redress for the injuries which had been suffered, and to renew friendly relations and amicable intercourse with the Portuguese. By these means Gama was induced to return to Calicut, but instead of having an audience with the Zamorin as he expected, he found his ship surrounded with 36 war proas, filled with armed men, who already considered him as their prisoner. Perceiving his danger, he cut the cable of his ship, and the wind being in his favor he succeeded in extricating his ship from her perilous state and returned to Cochin. He then cruised about for some time, took and plundered several ships with valuable cargoes, and having stationed part of his squadron at the entrance of the Red Sea to intercept the trade of the Mohammedans, he returned to Portugal.

As soon as the Zamorin heard that Gama and his fleet had gone, he prepared to chastise the king of Cochin who was his vassal, for receiving and treating the Portuguese in so friendly a manner, and for assisting them in procuring cargoes, provisions, etc. He assembled a large army, and proceeding to Cochin, demanded that the Portuguese in charge of the factory Gama had established there, should be delivered up to him, and that the king should engage to have no more intercourse or connection with any of the Portuguese nation. The king of Cochin was determined to preserve the alliance he had formed, and defended his city with much gallantry. But he was overpowered by the superior force of the Zamorin, and with the agents of the factory and some of his friends he was compelled to take refuge on the island of Vipeen. This island was then one of the sacred places on the coast and was easily defended. The king, his allies and friends, continued here, though reduced to great distress, till they were relieved by the arrival of some ships from Portugal. The Zamorin seeing the Portuguese had returned, soon evacuated the city and returned to Calicut, and the king of Cochin, aided by the Portuguese, soon recovered his capital, and was reinstated in his dominions. Albuquerque, who had the charge of the Portuguese fleet, went to Calicut and opened negotiations for peace and commerce with the Zamorin, but the exorbitant demands of the Portuguese, and the losses, injuries, and wrongs which the Zamorin and his subjects had suffered, did not admit of any permanent and satisfactory adjustment. So Albuquerque left a few hundred men at Cochin under Duarte Pacheco, to guard the capital of his ally, and returned to Europe.

The Zamorin now resolved to make another attempt to chastise his refractory vassal, and to prevent the Portuguese from acquiring any secure hold in the country. He collected his nobles and his allies, and many Mohammedans viewing their interests as largely involved in the issue, engaged in the war. The army amounted to 50,000 men, and the vessels to 160. Two Italian adventurers, who had come to India by way of the Red Sea, undertook to cast cannon, and introduce into the Zamorin's army the latest improvements of European warfare. The force collected was so large and the preparations by land and sea were so formidable, that the affairs of the king of Cochin appeared desperate to his friends generally as well as to his enemies. In these feelings the king participated, and intimated to the Portuguese commander that resistance would be quite useless, and the choice before them was unconditional submission or death. To his surprise he found Pacheco, instead of being discouraged, was confident that if the forces of the king would do their part, he could repel the vast army then surrounding them. The king was so much pleased with the spirit which Pacheco showed, that he intrusted to him the entire management of the war. Pacheco made a judicious arrangement of the forces under his command, and securing for himself every advantage which the state of the city and their circumstances admitted, he awaited the onset of the enemy. The attack was made on the sea and land. The forces of the king as soon as they saw the vast army approaching, glittering with armor and loudly shouting, were seized with a panic and fled for safety. But the Portuguese repelled the attack with such coolness and valor, and poured upon their enemies such a destructive fire that they were finally beaten and retreated. Attacks were afterwards made several times in which the Portuguese suffered the loss of several brave men, but the loss of the Zamorin was fearfully great. His army becoming disheartened, and sickness raging in his camp, he gave up all hope of success and returned to Calicut.

This war, though of so short duration, probably exerted more influence than any other in the history of European warfare in India. Indeed, it may be regarded as having laid the foundation of European empire in southern Asia. It was now manifest that the vast armies which oriental sovereigns bring into the field, can effect little in the way of conquest or defence, when opposed to men of cool valor, thorough discipline, and under the command of brave and experienced officers. This opinion encouraged the Portuguese, and afterwards the English, Dutch, and French, in their spirit of conquest and daring adventure, though it sometimes led small bodies of Europeans to put themselves in circumstances of great peril, and in some instances, probably, of certain destruction.

In 1505, the king of Portugal sent a large fleet under Francisco Almeida, on whom he conferred the title of viceroy of India. From this time the Portuguese had generally a large fleet in the Indian seas, and they became the terror of all places on the coast, and of all ships on the seas which had sufficient wealth to be a temptation to their avarice. The Sultan of Egypt, who derived a large revenue from the trade between his dominions and India, and whose ships the Portuguese had often plundered, sent a large fleet to protect his trade and to inflict merited revenge for the injuries which his subjects and others of his faith had suffered. The Egyptian flotilla found a squadron of the Portuguese fleet near Choul, about 30 miles south from Bombay. The two fleets here engaged in conflict, which was continued for several days, and resulted in the defeat of the Portuguese and the death of their commander, who was a son of Almeida. The viceroy resolved to avenge the death of his son, and destroy the Egyptian fleet, or compel the ships to return to the Red Sea. He had prepared a fleet of 19 ships and was nearly ready to sail, when Albuquerque arrived from Portugal with a large reinforcement, and showed a commission appointing himself viceroy. Almeida was indignant at being thus superseded in power at such a time, and having learned that his officers would support him in refusing obedience in such peculiar circumstances, he told Albuquerque that he was determined to continue in the command of the fleet till he had avenged the death of his son and destroyed the Egyptian fleet, or driven them all from the Indian seas. Albuquerque remonstrated, but all was in vain, for he had no means to enforce obedience, and so Almeida sailed on his expedition. While on his way, learning that Dabool, a place of large trade on the coast, had espoused the cause of the Egyptians, he made a furious attack upon it, and got possession of the fort and the city. He first gave up the whole place to plunder and massacre, and then set the city on fire. "The streets streamed with blood, the fire raged furiously, and in a few hours there remained of this magnificent city only a pile of smoking wood and ashes. The shipping in the harbor was also consumed." * Almeida then

* The Jesuit Lafiteau describing the capture of Dabool says, "The Portuguese spared neither age nor sex. The wife of the Governor himself could not purchase his life with the offer of all her riches. The insolent conquerors fell with such savage fury upon the miserable inhabitants that they took pleasure in tearing children from the bosom of their mothers and dashing their brains out against the walls; so that their cruelty has passed into a proverb in Hindustan, the Hindus in their imprecations being accustomed to say, '*May the wrath of the Feringhis fall upon thee, as it fell upon Dabool.*" When at length they were glutted with murder, they thought of nothing but satiating their avarice, and

proceeded to the Gulf of Cambay in search of the Egyptian fleet, and found it near the island of Diu. The Portuguese attacked the Egyptians, sunk or seized all the large ships and obtained great booty. Almeida compelled the Egyptian admiral to deliver up all the European prisoners, and he then set sail for Cochin. When near Cannanore, he ordered a general massacre of all the prisoners on board his ships. Such wanton cruelty excited great dread of Portuguese power, and the abhorrence of men who appeared to delight in murder and massacre.

On returning to Cochin, Almeida reluctantly resigned his power into the hands of Albuquerque, and soon after sailed for Portugal. When passing along the southern coast of Africa, he went ashore with some of his men, who becoming involved in a quarrel with the natives, he interfered and received a wound which soon proved mortal. Albuquerque now duly invested with the power of viceroy, proceeded to carry into effect the plans of conquest he had formed. He failed in an attack on Calicut, where in a severe conflict "he was so stunned by repeated blows, that he remained for some time apparently dead, but his followers carried him off; he revived and slowly recovered." In 1510 he took Goa. The prince to whom it belonged, made vigorous attempts to recover it and expel the Portuguese, but after much severe fighting and great loss on both sides, Albuquerque retained possession of the place. He erected strong fortifications, and made it the capital of all the Portuguese dominions in the Indian seas. He next took Malacca, then a place of large trade with the eastern archipelago. His attempts to take Aden failed, but he succeeded in obtaining possession of Ormuz, then the chief emporium of commerce in the Persian Gulf.

Albuquerque greatly enlarged the power of the Portuguese in India, and his government has always been regarded as the most successful and brilliant period in their eastern history. Succeeding viceroys were animated by a similar spirit, and were

Almeida, before he could get them away, was obliged to set fire to the town and thus put the finishing stroke to the destruction of all that had escaped the hands of the rapacious soldiery."

almost constantly engaged in some warlike enterprise. No one of the European nations interfered with the Portuguese for a century after they commenced their conquests in the East, and so they had only the native powers to contend with. These wars were often carried on with great cruelty and barbarity. The Portuguese were superior to the native powers in the construction and management of their ships. They were also superior in the quality of their guns and other materials of war, and they had more skill in using them. It was their custom to seize and plunder all ships trading without a license from them, and if any city or town refused to allow them such privileges as they demanded, or to carry on trade with them on such terms as they dictated, they attacked and plundered all such places as far as they could. In 1500, "they attacked Calicut, then the most commercial city on the Malabar coast, seized the ships of the king, burnt many richly laden in the harbor, and made slaves of the crews." In 1502, "they again attacked Calicut, burning the palace and many houses, and seized several ships, with rich cargoes, in the harbor." In 1505 "they again attacked the city and reduced a large part of it to ashes. They also took Cranganore and burned it. The king of Quiloa refusing to pay them tribute, they seized and plundered the town. In 1507 they took Mombas by storm, and made slaves of the inhabitants. They also burnt down and destroyed the shipping in the harbor." In 1507, "they took Muscat, and committed great ravages on the towns upon the coast of Africa, plundering and burning all places where the chiefs refused to become tributary." In 1508, "Brena was plundered and burnt, and great cruelties were inflicted upon the inhabitants." In 1509, "Calicut was again attacked, and was taken, plundered, and burnt." In 1510, "Goa was attacked and taken by the Portuguese, but being soon after recovered by its native sovereign, was again seized, and the whole garrison put to the sword." In the same year they also "plundered and destroyed Zanzibar." In 1511, "they took Malacca by storm, and plundered the city." In 1512, "they seized and plundered Surat." In 1516, "Zeyla was taken and burnt by them." In 1526 and 1527, "they plundered and destroyed Doofar and Massowa, and plundered and burnt Mangalore, Porcia, and Chitwa." In 1530, they again "burnt

Surat and several villages," and the next year they "destroyed Gogo, Pate, Mangarole, and most of the other towns on the coast of Gujerat."

Such instances show the spirit and manner in which the Portuguese carried on their wars of aggression, which were continued through the government of several successive viceroys. In 1536, a powerful combination was formed against the Portuguese. The kings of Cambay and Gujerat raised an army of more than 20,000 men, and the Sultan of Egypt sent 70 galleys, containing 8,000 Turkish soldiers and a powerful train of artillery from Suez. The chief place of conflict was Diu, then in the possession of the Portuguese. At one time the affairs of the Portuguese appeared to be desperate, but they defended themselves with such valor, perseverance, and skill, that the combination failed to accomplish their purpose, and Diu remained in the possession of the Portuguese. In 1570, a yet more powerful combination was formed against them by the Zamorin of Calicut, Adil Shah, king of Beejapoor, and Nizam Murtezza, king of Ahmednuggur. At this time Goa was the principal place of attack, and the united force collected against it was estimated to exceed 100,000 men. This siege of Goa is one of the most memorable in the annals of European warfare in India. After a siege of nearly 2 years and great loss on both sides, the siege was abandoned, and the native powers returned to their own capitals. The Portuguese at one time possessed Sofala, Mozambique, and Mombas on the eastern coast of Africa; Aden and Muscat in Arabia; Ormuz and Bussora in the Persian Gulf; Diu, Damaun, Basseen, Salsette, Bombay, Choul, Dabool, Goa, Onore, Barcelore, Mangalore, Cannanore, Cranganore, Calicut, Cochin, and Quilon on the western coast of India. On the eastern coast they had Negapatam, St. Thome, and Mausalapatam, and they had several places in Bengal; they had also a considerable part of Ceylon. These possessions were all subject in civil and military matters to the viceroy, who lived at Goa. The archbishop of Goa was over them in all ecclesiastical affairs.

In 1580, Portugal was annexed to the crown of Spain, and the two crowns continued united till 1640. During this time the Spanish possessions in America chiefly engaged the attention of the government, and the possessions acquired by the Portuguese in the East were neglected. From this time the power of Portugal in the East declined, and she gradually lost most of her possessions, some to the Dutch, who took Cochin, Ceylon, and Nagapatam, and some to the native powers. The Portuguese dominions in the East are now limited to a few places of small population and no political importance, and a Portuguese ship is now seldom seen in the Indian seas.

Near the close of the 16th century, Holland took its place among the nations of Europe, and soon acquired the first rank as a maritime power. They first attempted to proceed to the East Indies by the Arctic Ocean, but after making three unsuccessful efforts, a fleet of several ships proceeded round the Cape of Good Hope in 1576. The Dutch were soon engaged largely in eastern trade, and contended with the Portuguese for supremacy in the Indian seas. This was the first interference which the Portuguese experienced from any European power, and the eastern nations then saw the only two Christian nations of whom they had any knowledge, engaged in violent war with each other. The ships of each nation seized and plundered those of the other, wherever they could be found. The conflict was chiefly in the islands and places east and south-east from India, where the Dutch soon gained the ascendency and still have large possessions. They also took Ceylon, Cochin, Negapatam, and some other places from the Portuguese in India.

COMMERCE AND CONQUESTS OF THE ENGLISH.

The first attempts of English navigators to reach India were made through the Arctic Ocean, by Sir Hugh Willoughby, Frobisher, and others. In 1577, Sir Francis Drake commenced his voyage round the world, passing through the Straits of Magellan and returning by the Cape of Good Hope. While on the western coast of South America, he made prizes of several richly laden Spanish ships, and brought home with him great wealth. His success produced great excitement, and a strong spirit for discovery and foreign commerce. Queen Elizabeth visited him on board his ship, and conferred upon him the honor of knighthood.

In 1583, some enterprising travellers and merchants proceeded to India by way of Aleppo, Bagdad, and Ormuz. Among the places they visited, were Goa, Beejapoor, Golconda, Burhanpoor, Agra, Benares, Serampore, Malacca, and Ceylon. The description they gave of the productions, wealth, and commerce of the countries they visited, excited strong desire for opening communication with them. In 1591, three ships sailed for India round the Cape of Good Hope. So many of the crews became sickly on this voyage that one ship returned home with the invalids. Another ship disappeared soon after passing the Cape of Good Hope, and was never again heard of, and the other having seized several rich prizes, and traded in different places with varied success, returned home after an absence of more than three years. In 1599, Queen Elizabeth sent Sir John Mildenhall on an embassy to the emperor of India, the Great Mogul, as he was called. But he died in Persia, on his way home, and it does not appear that any important advantages were secured by his embassy.

The nation had now obtained so much knowledge of eastern countries, there was so much demand for the manufactures and productions of those countries, and they saw the Portuguese and Dutch obtaining so much advantage from commerce with them, that in the early part of 1600, an association was formed in London for carrying on direct trade with India, and on the 13th of December, A. D. 1600, this association obtained an Act of incorporation, under the title of "The Governor and Company of Merchants of London, trading to the East Indies." The company was to be under the management of a governor and 24 committee-men, all to be chosen annually. The rights and privileges of the Act were to continue for 15 years, but if the monopoly should be found to be injurious to the public welfare, then upon two years' notice, it might become annulled. Such was the origin of the East India Company.

Such was the confidence in the newly formed company, that the subscriptions to the capital soon amounted to more than £75,000, and in a few months they despatched 5 ships under the command of Captain Lancaster, who some years before had made a voyage to the East Indies. He proceeded to Sumatra, Java, and some other places, but he found the articles he required so scarce and costly, that "he became apprehensive of incurring loss, and what he seems to have dreaded still more, the disgrace of returning home without a cargo. From this anxiety he was relieved by meeting a Portuguese vessel of 900 tons, of which he made a prize, and found it so richly laden with calicoes and other valuable goods, that he not only occupied all his tonnage, but could have filled more ships, if he had had them."

For several years, the business of the company consisted of a series of separate adventures, in which each subscriber shared in the profits on the final adjustment, in proportion to the sum he had paid. In 1612, it was resolved to have a permanent or fixed capital on the principle of a joint-stock company for four years, and the sum of £418,691 was subscribed to it. This change gave more stability, regularity, and responsibility to their proceedings. Their trade was embarrassed by the opposition of the Portuguese and Dutch, and in 1615, Sir Thomas Roe was sent as ambassador to the Grand Mogul. He remained in India several years, and obtained some important advantages for the company.

In 1617, the period of four years having expired, a fresh subscription for four years more was opened, and such was the desire to participate in it that £1,629,040 were subscribed. The subscribers "consisted of 15 dukes and earls; 82 knights, including 2 judges; all the king's council, and 5 privy-councillors; 13 countesses and ladies; 26 doctors of divinity and physic; 18 widows and virgins; 313 merchants and 214 tradesmen; 212 without titles; 13 merchant-strangers, and 36 whose occupations were unknown, making in all 954." These facts show that the trade with India had taken strong hold of the feelings of the nation. The affairs of the company were sometimes prosperous, and sometimes embarrassed, varying with the state of the nation, and their success or losses in their conflicts with the Portuguese and Dutch in the East Indies. When England was at war with either of these nations, each party endeavored to seize the other's ships engaged in the Indian trade, as such ships had generally very rich cargoes. And when there was no war between these nations, yet if it was easier and cheaper to obtain cargoes by seizing ships already laden than to purchase such commodities, little scruple was felt about seizing and plundering such ships. The Portuguese, the

Spanish, the Dutch, and the English, who were engaged in the Indian trade, were generally at war with each other when east of the Cape of Good Hope, though the nations in Europe were in a state of peace.

The first territory acquired by the Company in India, was Madras, which was obtained in 1640, by treaty with a native prince. The Company erected a fort there, and called it St. George, the town retaining its original name. In 1667, this place was incorporated by a royal charter. In 1668, the island of Bombay, which was included in the dowry Charles I. had received by his marriage with the Infanta of Portugal in 1662, was ceded by him to the East India Company, and in 1687, was constituted the chief seat of the British government in India.

The charter of the Company was from time to time renewed and altered, as experience suggested and the exigencies of its affairs appeared to require. In 1661, the Company's governor and council in any of the factories, were empowered to exercise civil and criminal jurisdiction according to the laws of England. Also to export warlike stores, and to make peace and war with any princes in the limits of their trade, not being Christians. In 1670, the Company employed 30 ships with from 60 to 100 men each. Their affairs were subject to great fluctuations, and in 1665 their stock in the market was 70 per cent. In 1676 it rose to 245 per cent., and in 1685 it was sold for 500 per cent. Soon after this the capital was increased, and in 1702, it amounted to £2,000,000, and they had factories in more than 60 different places. A factory was originally a house of agency for the sale and purchase of goods. Some of these in the progress of trade had become very large establishments, and often contained a great amount of money and valuable property. Such were generally fortified to secure them against the Portuguese and Dutch, and also against native princes in times of anarchy and civil war. These fortified factories were often the scenes of severe conflict, sometimes taken and plundered, and at other times successfully defended. In 1664, when Shevajee, the founder of the Mahratta empire, attacked Surat and plundered the city, the agents of the Company defended their factory with so much valor, that much as he wished to get possession of it, he did not succeed.

The factories or commercial establishments of the European companies often contained property of great value. In oriental cities, the police is generally inefficient and frequently very corrupt. The countries are often distracted by civil wars, when the parties become more intent upon enriching themselves by plunder than upon bringing war to a conclusion. In such cities every rich man was obliged to regard his house as his castle, and have some means for defending it. In such circumstances the reasons for Europeans fortifying their factories are obvious, but the native princes in permitting this to be done, supposed nothing would be done beyond what was necessary for self-defence. They never supposed that these places of trade would become strong forts to resist their power, involve them in war, subvert their governments, and bring their countries into subjection to foreign princes. In these respects history shows how much they were disappointed.

It was in Bengal, where the business of the Company became most extended, that they first attempted to acquire and establish political and military power. The agents there complained to the Directors of the Company of the injuries and losses they had suffered from the native powers, and expressed their firm belief that the only way of obtaining any redress for the past and security for the future, was by being put into circumstances to defend themselves, and to assert and maintain their rights. In consequence of these complaints and representations, the Directors sent 10 armed ships, carrying from 12 to 70 guns each, and 6 companies of soldiers. It was expected this military force would be largely increased by companies or regiments of native soldiers, commonly called sepoys, and ready to fight for any power which will pay them. The plan was to take Chittagong, fortify it, and then make it the centre of their military operations. The expedition appears to have been badly managed. The fleet arrived in the Ganges at different times, and did not act in concert. They made an attack on Hoogley and were repulsed. Their factories at Patna and Cossimbazar were taken and plundered. The Nabob assembled all his army and made an attack upon them. There was much severe fighting, and the Nabob's forces were repulsed in several assaults. The English defended themselves on the island of Injellee, which they siezed and fortified, while they took and plundered Balasore, and burnt 40 ships in the harbor. The next year a treaty was made with the Nabob, and the English were allowed to return to their former factories. But through the indiscretion and rashness of some of the agents, hostilities were soon renewed, and all the business of the Company in Bengal was suspended.

Aurungzeb, the last of the great Mogul sovereigns, was then in power. He was much exasperated with these proceedings, and also with the measures of Sir John Child in Bombay and other places subject to him. The emperor resolved to expel the English from his dominions, and issued orders for a general attack upon their factories and other possessions. Surat and several other factories were taken, and Bombay was besieged. Thus threatened and straitened, "the English stooped to the most abject submissions," and at length succeeded in obtaining a cessation of hostilities.

At this time the Directors and many proprietors of the Company carefully reviewed its history, and examined its state and prospects. And the result was a determination to acquire territorial possessions in India as well as to carry on trade in the country. For pursuing this course they had the example and experience of the Portuguese and Dutch, whose territorial possessions in India and places east from it were large, and who were supposed to realize great advantages from them. They had also learned by experience the inefficiency of the native armies, when opposed to the cool valor and disciplined skill of European troops. In 1689, the Directors sent the following instructions to their governors and councils in India. "The increase of our revenue is the subject of our care as much as our trade; it is that must maintain our force, when twenty accidents may interrupt our trade; it is that must make us a nation in India. Without that we are but as a great number of interlopers, united by his Majesty's royal charter, fit only to trade where no body of power thinks it their interest to prevent us; and upon this account it is that the wise Dutch in all their general advices which we have seen, write ten paragraphs concerning government, their civil and military policy, warfare, and the increase of their revenue, for one paragraph they write concerning trade."

This was a new object to be realized, an object not contemplated in the original plan of the Company, and not avowed till nearly a century after the Company was formed. The introduction and steady prosecution of this principle of policy has resulted in the conquest of India, so that England now governs as large and perhaps larger population there than was ever subject to any Hindu or Mohammedan sovereign in that country.

The charter was regarded by the directors and proprietors of the Company as exclusive, and securing to them a monopoly of all trade to places east from the Cape of Good Hope. It was always difficult, and often found to be impossible, to enforce this monopoly, and as this trade was very profitable, many adventurers engaged in it. These men were called *interlopers*, and occasioned the Company much trouble, as they reduced the profits of the trade, and interfered with the treaties with native powers. The governors and agents were instructed to seize all such ships, and to treat all who were found in them as pirates. Many such ships were seized, and the manner in which their officers and crews were treated, furnished ground for great complaint against the Company.

They had also other difficulties to contend with. In 1618, James I. granted letters patent for an East India Company for Scotland. This was generally regarded as an infringement of the right of the original Company, and it was some time and not without much trouble and loss that matters were restored to a satisfactory state. In 1635, Charles I. granted a royal license to Sir William Coureen and others to trade to the East Indies. This was regarded as an infringement of the chartered rights of the Company, and it was some years before matters were adjusted.

In 1698, some merchants in London obtained a charter as "the English Company trading to the East Indies," the other or old association being called the London Company. These two Companies were rivals for several years. Great animosity raged between them, each being apparently as intent on injuring the other, as it was upon seeking its own advantage. In 1708, the two Companies were united. The Company formed in 1698, had loaned to the English government £2,000,000, and when the two were united, they loaned £1,200,000 more, making £3,200,000. This sum shows that their resources must have been great.*

HISTORY OF BENGAL TILL 1800.

The British settlements in Bengal, were commenced subsequently to those on the coast of Coromandel, and in western India. In 1698, the English purchased a few small villages on the Hoogley, where Calcutta now is, and there established a factory. Changes often took place in the ruling princes, and complaints of unjust demands and unreasonable exactions were sometimes made, but the trade here and at some other places in Bengal, was carried on with little interruption for more than 50 years. On the death of Aliverdi Khan in 1756, Suraja Dowla, his grandson, became Nabob. This prince was ignorant and licentious, cruel and avaricious. Previous to the death of Aliverdi Khan, on several occasions he manifested much dislike of the English. As Calcutta was exposed to be attacked and plundered by the French, the English began to erect or repair some fortifications around it. Suraja Dowla was greatly offended at their doing this, saying it showed a distrust of his power to protect them, or an intention to rebel against him. He began his march with a large force from Rajmahal towards Calcutta. On his way he made the English agents at Cossimbazar prisoners, and plundered the factory.

The English in Calcutta, on hearing that Suraja Dowla was on the way with a large army and had plundered Cossimbazar, resolved to defend the place. He arrived sooner than he was expected, and commenced a furious attack upon them. It was soon apparent that the fort could not be long defended. The women, children, and some of the men (among whom were the

* Complaints were made that the original Company obtained votes and favors by distributing large sums of money in Parliament. The House of Commons resolved to inquire into the ground of these charges, and ordered their books to be examined. The charges were found to be fully sustained. "It appeared that it had been the practice and even the habit of the Company to give bribes to men in power, that previous to the revolution their annual expenses under that head had scarcely ever exceeded £1,200; that since the revolution, it had greatly increased, and that in the year 1693, it amounted to nearly £90,000," or nearly 450,000 dollars.

governor and 2 members of the council), found safety on board the ships, which went down the river. The men, 146 in number, remained. There appears to have been indiscretion, indecision, and mismanagement among those who went away in the ships, or in those who remained behind, or among all parties, Suraja Dowla soon obtained possession of the place, and expressed great indignation that they should attempt to defend it against him, the ruler of the country. The number of men who became prisoners was 146. The confinement and sufferings of these persons is a remarkable part of the history of the English in India. It occurred in June, the hottest part of the year in Calcutta, and the weather was unusually warm and sultry for the season. The following is the most particular account of this horrid affair which I have seen. "The place fixed on for their confinement, was the common dungeon of the fortress, called the *black hole*. It consisted of a space 18 feet square, with only 2 small windows, barred with iron, opening into the close veranda, and scarcely admitting a breath of air. Into this narrow receptacle, the whole of the officers and soldiers, 146 in number, were compelled to enter, and on their venturing to remonstrate, the commander ordered every one who should hesitate to be instantly cut down. Thus were they forcibly thrust into this fearful dungeon, into which the whole number could with difficulty be squeezed, and the door was then fast barred from without. Their first impression on finding themselves thus immured, was the utter impossibility of surviving one night, and the necessity of extricating themselves at whatever cost. The jemadars, or Indian guards, were walking before the window, and Mr. Holwell, seeing one who bore on his face a more than usual expression of humanity, adjured him to procure for them a room in which they could breathe, assuring him in the morning of a reward of 1,000 rupees. The man went away, but returned saying it was impossible. Thinking the offer had been too low, the prisoners tendered 2,000 rupees. The man again went and returned, saying the Nabob was asleep and no one durst awake him; the lives of 146 men being nothing in comparison to disturbing for a moment the slumbers of a tyrant. Mr. Holwell has described in detail the horrors of that dreadful night, which are scarcely paralleled in the annals of human misery. Every moment added to their distress. All attempts to obtain relief by a change of posture from the painful pressure to which it gave rise, only aggravated their sufferings. The air soon became pestilential, producing at every moment a feeling of suffocation; and while the perspiration flowed in streams, they were tormented with the most burning thirst. Unfortunately, as the stations near the windows were decidedly the best, the most dreadful struggles were made to reach them. Many of the prisoners being foreign soldiers, and now released from all subordination, made the most frightful efforts, and the sufferers as they grew weaker, were in some instances squeezed or actually trampled to death. Loud cries being raised of "water," the humane jemadar pushed through the bars several skins filled with that liquid, but this produced only an increase of calamity, owing to the very violent endeavors made to obtain it. The sepoys without found only a savage sport in witnessing these contests, and even brought lights to the window in order to view them to greater advantage. About 11 o'clock the prisoners began to die fast; six of Mr. Holwell's intimate friends sank at his feet, and were trodden upon by the survivors. Of those still alive, a great portion were raving or delirious; some uttered the most incoherent prayers, and others the most frightful blasphemies. They endeavored by furious invectives to induce the guards to fire into the prison and to end their miseries, but without effect. When day dawned, the few who had not expired, were most of them either raving or insensible. In this last state was the governor himself when, about 6 o'clock, Suraja awoke and inquired for him. On learning the events of the night, he merely sent to ascertain if the English chief yet lived, and being informed there were appearances as if he might recover, gave orders to open the fatal door. At that time, of the 146 who had been inclosed, there breathed only 23." *

The news of the surrender of Calcutta, and the dreadful sufferings of the prisoners, produced intense excitement at Madras, and it was at once resolved to despatch all the forces, naval and military, which could be spared, to Bengal as soon as possible; the naval under the command of Admiral Watson, and the military under Col. Clive. The whole force of the expedition

* Murray, p. 361 and 362.

consisted of 900 Europeans, and 1,500 sepoys. On arriving at Fulda, they found the few English that had escaped from Calcutta before it was surrendered. It was determined to proceed at once to attack Calcutta, which was recovered soon, and with but little loss. The property of the East India Company was found entire, having been reserved for the Nabob, but private houses had been plundered. The English then took Hoogley, in which considerable plunder was obtained. The Nabob was then at Moorshedabad, his capital, but on hearing that the English had arrived, he assembled his army and began his march towards Calcutta. Some efforts at negotiation were made on the way, but these proving ineffectual, and the Nabob having now surrounded Calcutta, Clive resolved to attack his army. In this attack the English were successful, though their loss was very heavy in proportion to the number engaged. A treaty was then made, by which the English were permitted to fortify Calcutta, to carry on trade and enjoy the same rights and privileges as before. The Nabob then returned to Moorshedabad.

Intelligence having arrived that war had commenced between England and France, Clive and Watson united in making an attack upon the French settlement of Changanore upon the river Hoogley. The garrison, consisting of 500 Europeans and 700 sepoys, became prisoners of war, and a great quantity of ammunition and military stores was obtained. But this attack upon the French, who had not interfered in the war between the English and the Nabob, and who were regarded by the Nabob as under his protection, much exasperated him. And it was not unreasonable for him to be thus dissatisfied, regarding as he did, both parties as foreigners permitted to reside in his dominions for purposes of trade. When he heard what the English were preparing to do, he sent them peremptory orders to let the French alone, and he put his army in motion to protect Changanore, but the place was compelled to surrender before his army could render any aid. Just at that time the Nabob received the alarming news that Ahmed Shah Abdallee had taken Delhi, and was preparing to extend his conquests over all parts of India, which had formerly composed the Mogul empire. In these circumstances, while he protected the remaining French factories, he thought it prudent not to involve himself again in war with the English.

But the fickle disposition of the Nabob, his hatred of the English, his corrupt ministers and evil counsellors, and the daring, ambitious, and unscrupulous character of Clive, already flushed with success, all these gave little prospect of continued peace. A plan was soon formed to dethrone the Nabob, and in his place to set up Meer Jaffer, who was paymaster-general of the army, and supported himself a very considerable military force. "In manufacturing the terms of the confederacy," says Mill, "the grand concern of the English appeared to be money; and the situation of Jaffer Khan and the manners and customs of the country made him ready to promise whatever they desired." The amount which he stipulated to pay to the agents of the East India Company for their assistance and influence in procuring for him the office and dignity of Nabob, is stated by Mill to be £1,238,575, or about $6,000,000. This sum was distributed among the agents of the Company then in Bengal, each one apparently securing for himself as large a share as possible.

The suspicions of the Nabob in respect to Meer Jaffer, for some reasons, became excited, and to remove them the latter made the strongest assurances of innocence and faithfulness, and even took an oath of fidelity on the Koran. This allayed the fears of his royal master, but made no change in his own purpose. Clive, in accordance with the plan which had been formed, mustered his force of 3,100 men, of whom only 950 were English, with 10 pieces of cannon, at Chandernagore, and commenced his march towards Plassey, where the Nabob was then encamped with his army, estimated at 35,000 infantry, 15,000 cavalry, and a large train of artillery.* A part of this force was under the command of Meer Jaffer, who had lately bound himself by the most solemn oaths to be faithful to his royal master, and also promised to join the English and ruin his master as soon as he could safely do so. The battle of Plassey, the most celebrated and important in its consequences of any in the English history of India, was fought on the 23d

* Another account says 50,000 infantry, 18,000 cavalry, and 40 pieces of artillery.

of June, 1757. The battle was commenced by the Nabob, about 8 o'clock in the morning, and for some hours it was only a distant cannonade. As soon as Meer Jaffer perceived it was safe to do so, he began to move the force under his command to join the English. Clive, perceiving this movement, ordered his force to attack the other part of the Nabob's army. These soon gave way, and the rout became general. The loss on the part of the English was only 20 Europeans killed and wounded, 16 sepoys killed, and 36 wounded. The Nabob fled, escorted by a body of cavalry. He was pursued, and soon reduced to a state of great distress. He disguised himself, and endeavored to escape to Patna, but was discovered, brought back, treated with great indignity, and assassinated in his own palace.

The next day after the battle Meer Jaffer was proclaimed Nabob, and on the 26th (3 days after the battle) the Bengal treasury was examined. The contents were found to be much less than was expected; not sufficient to pay the stipulated amount to be given to the different English parties. Still the amount realized, either according to previous stipulation or in the way of presents was large. Clive acknowledged that he secured $800,000 for himself.* Meer Jaffer soon found himself surrounded with difficulties. He had come under pecuniary obligations to the English, to whom he was indebted for his elevation, far beyond what he had any means to pay, and the distracted state of the country did not allow of his realizing so much revenue as he expected. He was also annoyed that the English, on learning that the treasury contained so much less than was expected when the stipulated sums were agreed upon, were not satisfied with what they then got, but insisted upon the whole being in some way realized and paid to them. He thought they had been abundantly remunerated for all they had done to raise him to power, and he was so much vexed with their importunate demands, while his own troops were almost in a state of mutiny on account of their large arrears of payment, that he declared to some of his friends, "that if a French force would come into the province he would assist them, unless

* "Clive acknowledged to have secured £160,000, while to each member of council there fell £24,000." —*Murray*, p. 373.

the English would release him from all their claims of money, territory, and exemptions." The means he used to replenish his treasury made him unpopular, and he had reason to fear assassination or some conspiracy to destroy him.

In 1758, a commission arrived from the East India Company in London remodelling the government in Bengal. Instead of one man being governor all the time, the office was to be filled by 4 men in rotation for 3 months each. Clive was much dissatisfied that no place was assigned to him in the new establishment, and his name was not even mentioned in the commission. The reason of this probably was that he was supposed to have returned to Madras. But he wished to continue in Bengal, and supposed the importance of his services and his own desires would be regarded by the Directors. When the government was being remodelled according to the commission, the 10 men who were to form the council, including the 4 of them who were to fill the office of governor in rotation, invited Clive to take the place of President. With this invitation he says "he hesitated not one moment to comply." When the Court of Directors learned that he still continued in Bengal, and previous to receiving these proceedings of the Council, they sent another despatch to Bengal, appointing "him to be the chief and presiding member."

Bengal, though it had become virtually independent, yet continued nominally a dependency upon the Great Mogul at Delhi, and the Nabob was nominally his deputy. As Meer Jaffer was a usurper and had neither been appointed to the place nor confirmed in the office he had assumed, the office of Nabob was regarded at Delhi as vacant, and the emperor appointed his oldest son to be Subadar or Nabob of Bengal, Bahar, and Orissa, and several native princes were inclined to unite in placing him in power in those provinces. In these circumstances Meer Jaffer solicited the aid of Clive, who, accompanied by Meer Jaffer's son, Meeran, with such force as could be spared, proceeded to Patna. On arriving at Patna, they found the native princes had withdrawn their promised aid, and the son of the emperor of Delhi and the legal Nabob of Bengal, Bahar and Orissa was in such straitened circumstances that he was glad to obtain from Clive a small sum of money for his subsistence, and then withdraw from the province. For this important service he procured for Clive the rank of an omra of the empire, and bestowed upon him the whole of the revenue or rent which the East India Company were bound to pay for the territory which they held around Calcutta. This territory is frequently called in Indian history "Clive's Jaghire," and the revenue amounted to the large sum of $ 150,000 annually. In the early part of 1760, Clive resigned his office in the government and embarked for Europe.

When Lord Clive resigned his office in the government, his influence and other causes procured the place for Mr. Vansittart, then at Madras. The state of affairs in Bengal was distracted and discouraging. Meer Jaffer had become unpopular among all classes of people. He was indolent, voluptuous, extravagant, and tyrannical. There was no reason to expect any reformation in him, nor any improvement in the government of the country, while the power continued in his hands.* He owed his elevation to the office of Nabob to the English, and it was only through their aid that he had been able to retain his place. But he had not paid, and was unwilling to pay the debts he had incurred to them, while he was evidently quite alienated from them in feeling, and endeavored to avoid intercourse with them. In these circumstances, the state of the country and the course to be pursued were subjects of much consideration in the council at Calcutta, and it was resolved to invest Meer Cossim, a son-in-law of Meer Jaffer, with the power, if not with the office of Nabob. Meer Cossim became a party to the arrangement, and Meer Jaffer, though very reluctant for a while, yet finally resigned his office and removed to Calcutta.

There were other elements in bringing about this change in

* "The situation of Meer Jaffer was deplorable from the first. With an exhausted treasury, an exhausted country, and vast engagements to discharge, he was urged to the severest exertions; while the profusion with which he wasted his treasure upon his own person and some unworthy favorites, was ill calculated to soothe the wretched people under the privations to which they were reduced. The cruelties of which he and Meeran, his son, were guilty, made them objects of general detestation; the negligence, disorder, and weakness of their government, exposed them to contempt; and their troops, always mutinous from the length of their arrears, threatened them every moment with fatal extremities."

the government, which caused many violent discussions and dissensions in the council of the East India Company in Calcutta. "The vast sums," says Mill, "obtained by a few individuals who had the principal management of the former revolution, when Meer Jaffer trod down Suraja Dowla, his master, were held in vivid remembrance, and the persuasion that similar advantages of which every man burned for a share, were now meditated by the select committee, excited the keenest emotions of envy and jealousy." *

Meer Cossim, aware of his circumstances and of what was expected from him, made great exertions to meet his pecuniary engagements, and was soon relieved from the most pressing claims. But a new difficulty soon appeared. The emperor of Delhi, who had never relinquished his claims over Bengal, again manifested a determination to assert and enforce his rights, and there were some indications that the French would espouse his cause. This gave Meer Cossim great uneasiness, and he proceeded to Patna to meet the emperor, who was then in that city. The emperor invested Meer Cossim in due form with the office of Nabob over Bengal, Bahar, and Orissa, and the latter engaged to pay 24,000,000 rupees (nearly $12,000,000) annually as the tribute of those provinces. Meer Cossim was now free from all anxiety on this source.

But new difficulties now claimed his attention. The inland trade in India was at that time much embarrassed by local exactions and transit duties. The governors of provinces and the petty princes of small districts, required duties to be paid on all goods passing through their territories. The agents of the Company claimed an exemption from these duties on the ground that the emperor had given a firman that no such duties should be required for goods of the Company when being carried under the Company's seal from one place or factory to another within the country. Had this privilege or right been restricted, as was intended, and as it ought to have been, to the *bona fide* goods of the Company, probably no serious difficulty would have occurred. But some of the agents of the Company were engaged largely in trade on their own account, and they

* Mill, vol. 2, p. 219, 4to.

misused this privilege of the Company for their own advantage. And not only so, but native traders under the protection of these agents, or in partnership with them, managed to obtain the same advantage for themselves. "Of the council, a great proportion was deriving vast emoluments from these abuses." By such means the revenue suffered much, and all regular and lawful trade was depressed and injured. Complaints of these things were so loud, and the abuses were shown to be so many and so great, that Mr. Vansittart made an agreement with the Nabob that the Company's agents and the country traders should pay equally the same duties. This just and judicious arrangement was annulled by a majority of the council after the Nabob had began to carry it into effect, and so matters were again in confusion. The Nabob then resolved as an extreme and final measure to abolish all the inland duties which had occasioned so much trouble, and so he put the English and the native traders upon an equality. But "of this the English unreasonably and loudly complained, because it left no distinction between them and his own." *

Complaints of mutual injuries continued to increase till the excitement resulted in a state of open warfare. The English again invested Meer Jaffer with the office and dignity of Nabob, who readily promised whatever they desired. They then sent a force against Meer Cossim, who was defeated at Geriah. They then besieged and took Monghir, which Meer Cossim had made his capital and fortified. Meer Cossim was greatly enraged, and declared that if the English force should advance upon Patna, he would cause all the garrison who had been taken prisoners in that city to be put to death. As soon as the English force approached Patna he fulfilled his threat. "The whole garrison of Patna, consisting of 50 gentlemen and 100 soldiers, were put to death with the single exception of Mr. Fullerton,

* "The conduct of the Company's servants upon this occasion furnishes one of the most remarkable instances upon record of the power of interest to extinguish all sense of justice and even of shame. They had hitherto insisted, contrary to all right and all precedent, that the government of the country should exempt their goods from duty. They now insisted that it should impose duties upon the goods of all other traders, and accused it as guilty of a breach of peace towards the English nation because it proposed to remit them."—*Mill.*

who was spared on account of his medical skill." This is called in history, "the Patna massacre." Patna was soon besieged and taken. Meer Cossim fled to Oude and found refuge with the Nabob, or vizier as he is often called. The emperor of Delhi was then with the Nabob. These three, namely, the Emperor, Meer Cossim, and the Nabob of Oude, united their forces and attacked the British army then encamped near Patna. They were repulsed and retreated to Oude, but the English were not in circumstances to pursue them. A spirit of insubordination now broke out in the English army, and for a while threatened the worst results. Sir Hector Munroe, having assumed the command, acted with great firmness in this exigency. In one battalion that mutinied, 24 of the ringleaders were executed—blown from cannon—and order was generally restored through the army. As soon as the rainy season was past, Sir Hector marched to attack the Nabob, and defeated him near Buxar, on the Soane. A great quantity of military stores and 130 pieces of artillery were taken. The emperor of Delhi now found an opportunity of withdrawing from the Nabob, and he went over with the corps personally attached to him, to the English army. The Nabob in connection with a body of Mahrattas under Mulhar Row Holkar and Ghazee ud Deen, made another effort to retrieve his affairs, but his army was dispersed almost as soon as attacked. When the army reached Benares, the Nabob of Oude offered as conditions of peace, to pay $1,250,000 for the expenses of the war, $1,250,000 to the army, and $400,000 to the commander-in-chief. But he refused to deliver up certain persons under his protection, and whom the English demanded. A treaty was then made with the emperor, in which he authorized the English to obtain possession of the dominions of Bulwant Sing, Raja of Benares, and they engaged to put him in possession of the dominions of the Nabob of Oude, and he was to reimburse to them all the expenses which this service might oblige them to incur.* In this campaign victory had become so common to the English forces, and defeat to the native armies, that each party appeared to look forward to such a result. Wherever the English army went, they conquered.

* This part of the treaty was strongly disapproved by the Court of Directors, and so was not carried into effect.

Whatever fort or city they attacked, they soon got possession of it. They were now masters of the great central plain of India, and the emperor of Delhi, the Grand Mogul, if not their prisoner, was under their protection, and in their camp.

In the mean time important events were taking place in Calcutta. "Meer Jaffer had died, partly it would seem of vexation at not having been able to meet the enormous pecuniary demands of the English rulers." His son, Nujeem ud Dowla, a youth 20 years old, had been invested by the council with the office of Nabob. But little power was reposed in his hands. The Court of Directors and the English nation had become much dissatisfied with the state of affairs in India, and having lost confidence in the agents of the Company, they were decided in the opinion that great and important changes were urgently required. In these circumstances after much inquiry and deliberation the Directors appointed Lord Clive (he had been raised to the peerage) to be governor and commander-in-chief of their civil and military establishments in Bengal. At the same time they passed stringent laws forbidding their servants to engage in future in any kind of private trade, and also forbidding them to receive presents from any natives, whether princes or common people.

Lord Clive arrived at Calcutta, in May of 1765, and proceeded at once to organize the government on the new form sanctioned by the Court of Directors. His despatches to that body describe the country as in a state of misrule bordering upon anarchy, and of great oppression. He describes the agents of the Company, as negligent of their public duties, and intent only upon enriching themselves. And the history of Bengal for several years shows that private ends and personal gains had much influence in making peace and war, and in setting up and then deposing native princes. Many servants or agents of the Company accumulated large fortunes by obtaining presents or donations or bribes for their silence, or influence, or exertions in these changes and revolutions.

Before the close of the year Clive returned to Calcutta, and resumed his seat as president of the select committee. He left India for England early in 1768, so that his second residence in India was less than two years. His government had much vigor, but while rigorously enforcing the laws and orders of the Directors of the Company upon the junior servants, he and the select committee engaged largely in private trade and speculation, thus violating those very laws which were designed for them as well as others; "and this course was continued in defiance of more than one positive prohibition. At length, however, orders arrived so peremptory and so decisive, that they could no longer be disregarded." Some of Clive's measures were very unpopular. In the army a conspiracy was formed, embracing a large portion of the European officers, and the English power in India was seldom if ever in greater danger, than it was for a while from this source. Several officers, including some of high rank, were dismissed, and order and discipline were again restored. The Nabob Nujeem ud Dowla died and was succeeded by his brother Syeff ud Dowla. The office or situation of Nabob formerly of so much power and dignity, had now become, and from this time continued to be, a mere pageant, as the civil and military government of the provinces was in the hands of the English. After the Court of Directors had peremptorily forbidden any person in their employment in India to receive presents from any class of natives, a sum of money was given or left to Clive by Meer Jaffer, as a present or legacy. It appears to have been the former under the latter name. His right to receive this in the existing circumstances was much discussed, and he finally made it over to the East India Company to constitute a fund for the relief of certain persons connected with the Indian army. He also appropriated a yet further sum received from the succeeding Nabob to the same purpose. These two sums, with the interest which had accumulated upon them, when paid into the Company's treasury in 1770, amounted to $600,000, and constitute what is well known in Indian history as Lord Clive's Fund.

The proceedings of the East India Company now began to excite much attention in Parliament, and through the kingdom. They presented the remarkable fact of a company of merchants originally associated in London for purposes of trade, acquiring a territory larger than the united kingdom, maintaining a large army, making war and peace with independent nations, and setting up and deposing at their pleasure, independent sovereigns and princes. The large fortunes accumulated in India gave extravagant ideas of the wealth of the country. The price of the stock of the Company on exchange, rose to 263 per cent., and the court of proprietors voted a dividend of 12 per cent. The feelings of the English nation were much excited. Parliament interfered and passed an act limiting the dividend to 10 per cent. for a certain time, and requiring the Company to pay $2,000,000 annually into the public treasury for their chartered privileges. This Act was afterwards somewhat modified, and the period prolonged. The time had now come for some important changes in the government of India, and there were many earnest debates in Parliament, and in the Court of Directors in respect to the changes required, and how far the affairs of the Company in India should be put under the control of commissioners or officers appointed by the crown. At length three men, namely, Messrs. Vansittart, Scrafton, and Ford, who had formerly been in the employment of the Company in India, were appointed commissioners or supervisors, and sailed from London for Calcutta, but neither the ship nor any one on board was heard of after sailing.

In 1772, a select committee was appointed in the House of Commons to inquire into the affairs of the East India Company. Their affairs were now so much involved that they applied to Parliament for a large loan and obtained it. Important changes were now made in the constitution of the Company. A proprietor of stock must own £1,000 to have one vote; one who owned £3,000, could have 2 votes; one who owned £6,000, could have 3 votes, and one who owned £10,000, or more, could have 4 votes. A governor was to be appointed over Bengal with a yearly salary of £25,000, and 4 councillors with £8,000 each. A superior court of judicature was to be established in Calcutta, consisting of a chief justice with a yearly salary of £8,000, and 3 other judges with £6,000 each.

The following resolutions, which were passed by the House of Commons, show how the proceedings of the Company were regarded by that body.

"1. That all acquisitions made under the military force or treaty with foreign princes, do of right belong to the State.

"2. That to appropriate acquisitions so made to the private emolument of persons intrusted with any civil or military power of the State, is illegal.

"3. That very great sums of money and other valuable property have been acquired in Bengal, from princes and others of that country, by persons intrusted with the civil and military powers of the State, by means of such powers, which sums of money and valuable property have been appropriated to the private use of such persons."

These resolutions, though violently opposed by the Court of Directors and their partisans, were yet passed by a large majority. They involved important principles, which if enforced, would put an end to usages and practices by which many large fortunes had been accumulated, and great oppression had been exercised in India. We now come to a period of Indian history, which excited more interest and acquired more notoriety than any period before or since that time.

Warren Hastings,* who had acquired so much notoriety in the history of India, and in the proceedings of Parliament, was the first governor-general of India. The members of council were General Clavering, Col. Monson, Mr. Barwell, and Mr. Francis, who could not be removed within the time (5 years) for which they had been appointed, except by the king upon representation of the Court of Directors. The salaries of the men thus placed over the affairs and interests of the East India Company in India, will show something of the spirit of the Company. Mr. Hastings's salary was £25,000, or nearly $125,000 yearly, General Clavering, who was commander-in-chief, had £16,000, or $80,000, and the other 3 members of council had £8,000, or $40,000 each.

The state of India was very distracted when Mr. Hastings assumed the administration of affairs, and vigorous measures were required to restore order and system. One of the meas-

*Mr. Hastings was the son of a clergyman of the Church of England. He went to India in the service of the East India Company in 1749, being then in his 17th year. He filled various situations in different places in Bengal, till he returned to England in 1765. In 1768, he was appointed by the Court of Directors a member of council at Madras, where he remained till he proceeded, in 1772, to Calcutta, to become governor-general of India, a situation of greater honor, power, and responsibility, than had ever been conferred on any European in that country. For instance, his salary was £25,000, or $125,000 yearly. This has been the salary of the governor-general of India for more than 80 years past.

ures adopted at this time has often been the subject of severe and just animadversion. It was a change in the tenure of the land to obtain a greater amount of taxes. It is thus described by the best authorities. "There was not a field in Bengal, Bahar, or Orissa, which was not the property of some owner, and these owners were in nine cases out of ten, the occupants and cultivators. And yet it was resolved to divide all the land in these provinces into small districts, and then sell them to the highest bidder, to the man who would pay the government the highest tax or rent for them. The specified period was for 5 years, but it was generally expected it would then be made permanent. This act has rarely been equalled in point of iniquity under any government in ancient or in modern times. The justice of a law which went to dispossess such proprietors of their right in order that their rulers might enjoy a greater amount of land-tax, need not be discussed. The measure was as arbitrary as it was cruel."—"It was an innovation by which the whole property of the country, and along with it the administration of justice were placed upon a new foundation. It was a change far greater than if all the existing tenures of land in England, whether temporary or perpetual, were all at once abolished, and new tenures of a very different description, new possessors in many instances, and a new administration of justice were introduced." The changes involved in this measure were many and great, and instead of producing order and system, the result was disorder and confusion as well as complaining and suffering. But however wanting the government might be in moral principle and sympathy with the native population, it was not deficient in efficiency, energy, and perseverance, and so its obnoxious measures were enforced, though, as was soon apparent, without realizing the expected advantages.

For no part of his administration has Mr. Hastings been more censured than for the part he performed in what is called the Rohilla war. The Nabob of Oude was very anxious to add to his dominions the territory belonging to the Rohilla chiefs, called Rohilcund. But as they were brave and had a well disciplined army, he was not able to wrest it from them in war. The English had at this time a large and efficient military force, which was not in active service. The Nabob offered to pay for the aid of this force to subdue the Rohillas; all the expenses of the war, and also 40 lacks of rupees (about $2,000,-000), to be paid into the Company's treasury. In this way the expenses of this part of the army would be paid while thus employed, and also a large sum of money be obtained for other purposes. On these conditions Mr. Hastings supplied the Nabob with the force he required. War was made upon the Rohillas; they were defeated in battle; their country laid waste and plundered with a barbarity and cruelty seldom known even in Indian warfare, till "every one who bore the name of Rohilla, was either put to death, or sought safety by flight."

The affairs of the emperor also came under the consideration of Mr. Hastings while at Benares. When the emperor gave the *dewany* of Bengal, Bahar, and Orissa to the English, it was stipulated that he should receive 26 lacks of rupees ($1,300,-000) as his tribute. But his putting himself into the power of the Mahrattas to be placed by them on the throne of his ancestors at Delhi, was made the occasion of withholding from him the stipulated tribute; and not only so but "his districts of Allahabad and Corah, which the English occupied on the pretext of possessing them for him, were dishonestly sold to the vizier (the Nabob of Oude) for the sum of 50 lacks of rupees ($2,500,-000). Thus was the honor of the country coolly bartered away for gold, and two of the grossest acts of injustice committed that had yet blotted the annals of British authority in the East."

The new constitution framed by Parliament for the East India Company was to go into operation in August, 1774. The government consisted of Mr. Hastings, who was governor-general, and Mr. Barwell member of council, both in India when appointed, and of General Clavering who was commander-in-chief, with a seat in council, and Colonel Monson and Mr. Francis, members of council, from England. It was soon manifest that there was not likely to be harmony in their opinions and proceedings. The members who lately arrived from England, instituted inquiry into some proceedings which were commenced before their arrival, and were yet in an unfinished state. Mr. Hastings resisted such inquiry and refused to give the information they demanded, while he strenuously opposed some measures which they proposed. The council was generally divided in opinion, Mr. Barwell concurring with Mr. Hastings, and the other three members opposing him. Among the matters that came before them, were charges against Mr. Hastings for obtaining large sums of money from princes and others for his official influence and favors, and then appropriating them to his own use. He denied the right of the council to inquire into such matters, but a majority of them believed that to investigate such charges when properly brought before them was clearly within the province of their duty. These dissensions were sometimes so violent, that Mr. Hastings would declare the council dissolved, quit the chair and go out. The majority would then vote the first member into the chair and continue the proceedings. Raja Nuncomar, a native of high rank and great influence, offered to produce proof of such charges before the council to a great amount. But Mr. Hastings and his friends caused him to be prosecuted for forgery, and he was condemned and executed. These proceedings produced the most intense excitement, and was regarded in India and in England as the most exceptionable and atrocious act of his whole administration.*

In 1776, Colonel Monson, one of the members of the council, died, and from this time Mr. Hastings, by having the privilege of the casting vote, had the direction of the government, though debates and dissensions were as violent as they previously had been. Matters of revenue and changes in the laws and modes for the administration of justice, were almost constantly under the consideration of the council, but the difficulties which beset these subjects were so many, and the difference of opinions and plans was so great, that but little progress was made or improvement effected. The Directors in several instances severely censured Mr. Hastings' proceedings, and he in return treated their

* The author of the History of the British Empire in India, remarks as follows, concerning these proceedings: "To the eternal disgrace of all concerned, a man who was not legally amenable to the court that tried him, who committed the offence before English law was established in India, according to the usages of whose native courts forgery is not a capital crime, and against whom the evidence was far from conclusive, that man in defiance of the respect due to the feelings of the whole native population, suffered death by the hands of the executioner. There is not among all the acts of Mr. Hastings' administration, one which has left so deep a stain upon his memory as this."

opinions and instructions with little respect; in some instances he deliberately disobeyed them.* The opposition between Mr. Hastings and Mr. Francis became at length so personal and bitter that it resulted in a duel, in which the latter was wounded. Soon after this he embarked for Europe.

In 1781, Mr. Hastings made a visit to Benares, Oude, and some other places in the upper provinces. He was invested by the council with the full power of the government, and the means he used while at these places to extort large sums of money from the Raja of Benares, the Nabob of Oude, and the two Begums (Princesses) were much censured, and they were among the charges brought against him after his return to England. By these means, (among which several innocent persons were severely tortured, to compel them to surrender treasure, or give information where it could be found,) he obtained for himself or for the East India Company, several millions of dollars. At Benares, Mr. Hastings arrested the Raja and imprisoned him in his own house under a military guard. The government of the Raja, as well as of his father before him, had given the people uncommon justice and protection. So his people were prosperous, his government was popular, and himself and family much respected. When the circumstances of the Raja and the treatment he was suffering became known, the people rushed together in great numbers, overpowered the guard and set the Raja at liberty. Mr. Hastings was for a while in much danger, being a prisoner and surrounded by an enraged population. But he found means to escape. "He secretly quitted the city after it became dark," and fled to Chunar, a strong fort then in possession of the English. Here he remained till he had collected a force sufficiently large to enable him to return to Benares, and put down all opposition.

When Mr. Hastings entered upon his duties as governor-general, a majority of the council was opposed to his policy, and so he could but very imperfectly carry out his plans. But in about 2 years Colonel Monson, one member of the council died, and Mr. Hastings then, by the casting vote, had the government generally in his own hands. Mr. Wheeler who succeeded Colonel

* The Court of Directors in one despatch to Mr. Hastings, say, "We have read with astonishment, your formal resolution to suspend our orders," etc.

Monson in council, was also opposed to Mr. Hastings' policy, but as General Clavering then died, the power still continued in Mr. Hastings' hands. After Mr. Francis' return to Europe (wounded in a duel with Mr. Hastings), he appears to have devised and carried into effect whatever plans he pleased in the name and with the full power of the East India Company in India.

Mr. Hastings resigned the government early in 1785 after an administration of more than 12 years. Some measures of his administration and the part he had personally performed in them, had excited much attention in England, and been often referred to in Parliament. He had authorized agents and numerous friends to take his part, and to maintain his cause in Parliament and in the English journals, but the dethroned princes and suffering people of India had neither agents in England to write, nor representatives in Parliament to speak, for them. This subject was taken up with greater earnestness after Mr. Hastings' arrival in England, and brief as our sketch of Indian history must be, it must yet contain some notice of Mr. Hastings' celebrated trial for maladministration while he was governor-general in India.

The impeachment of Mr. Hastings was a measure of the House of Commons. The articles were prepared and the prosecution was managed by a committee, of whom the celebrated Edmund Burke was chairman. The impeachment was before the House of Lords, as the high court of judicature of the kingdom. Long preparations were made, and the trial commenced in February of 1788. "So great was the interest which these proceedings against Mr. Hastings had excited, that persons of the highest rank assembled to witness the scene.* The opening address was made by Mr. Burke, and occupied 4 days. The trial, partly from its novelty and for want of precedents and usages to guide the proceedings, and partly from the difficulty of procuring evidence which was known to exist but was concealed and withheld as much as possible, and also from the rejection of evidence of different kinds on account of lega.

* "The Queen, the Prince of Wales, and 3 of the royal princesses were in the gallery. The Prince of Wales and 3 of the royal dukes with their trains followed the Chancellor."

technicalities and formalities, proceeded slowly. The Directors of the East India Company, though they had often severely censured Mr. Hastings, and strongly condemned the very actions set forth in the charges against him, yet now apparently regarding their own character as involved in the trial of their governor-general, had a large interest in procuring his acquittal, and exerted all their influence in his favor. The trial was adjourned from time to time, partly on account of the peculiar difficulties which embarrassed and delayed the proceedings, and partly because other and urgent matters claimed the attention of Parliament. Thus year after year passed away. Mr. Hastings, his counsel, and his friends complained of this delay, but it was shown that this delay had been chiefly caused by them, and not by the managers of the prosecution. It was apparent, also, that this delay and the complaints of Mr. Hastings and his friends were exerting a strong influence on public sympathy in his favor, and against the managers of the prosecution, so that he and not they had an interest in prolonging it. The trial was extended, notwithstanding all the managers could do to hasten it forward, from February in 1788 to April in 1795, a period of more than 7 years, and it occupied the House of Lords for 145 days. The verdict of the court was given on the 23d of April, and Mr. Hastings was acquitted by a majority of the judges on all the charges preferred against him.

The East India Company's charter, unless renewed, was to expire in 1783. This circumstance and the excitement produced by the proceedings of Mr. Hastings in India, necessarily brought the affairs of the Company in England and in India before Parliament. The proceedings of the supreme court in Calcutta having caused great dissatisfaction to both Europeans and natives, an act was passed, defining its powers and province. This act was one of much importance to all classes of the people. Several plans and schemes were discussed for the better government of India. Mr. Dundas, chairman of a select committee in the House of Commons, on Indian affairs, prepared a bill, but a change of the ministry then occurring, he dropped the subject. Mr. Fox, then in power, proposed his plan for governing India, but it was lost in the House of Lords. Mr. Pitt having succeeded to power, brought forward his plan.

The principal feature of this bill or of the change introduced by it, was the creation of a Board of Control, to consist of 6 members of the Privy Council, of whom the Chancellor of the Exchequer and one of the Secretaries of State were to be two, and the senior of the other four was to be the President of the Board. This was essentially making a new Secretary of State for India, with a committee or council under him. The Board of Control thus became a part of the ministry for the time being, and this bill made them to a great extent the controlling and governing power over India. The bill specified what powers belonged to this Board, and also what powers and privileges still remained in the hands of the Directors and Proprietors. This bill made some important changes in the form and constitution of the East India Company, and it has been continued to the present time.

The Court of Directors had appointed Lord Macartney, who was then governor of Madras, to succeed Mr. Hastings as governor-general in Bengal. But as Mr. Hastings wished to leave Bengal sooner than was expected, and Lord Macartney had not arrived, he resigned his office into the hands of the senior member of council, Mr. Macpherson. Lord Macartney soon after proceeded to Calcutta, but the state of his health was such that he did not assume the office of governor-general. After remaining a few days he sailed for England.

The first governor-general appointed under the new constitution was Lord Cornwallis,* who arrived in Calcutta and assumed the reins of government in September of 1786. The first object which claimed his attention, was the state of the Nabob of Oude. Mr. Hastings' proceedings at Oude formed a prominent part of the charges preferred against him at his trial. As soon as the Nabob heard of the arrival of Lord Cornwallis in India, he proposed to come himself to Calcutta, and if not allowed to do so, he begged that he might send his minister. Lord Cornwallis investigated the affairs of the Nabob, and Mill says, "it appeared that for during the 9 preceding years the Nabob had paid to the Company under different titles at

* The same who had recently acted so conspicuous a part in the war between the United States and England, and surrendered the British army at Yorktown.

the rate of 8,400,000 rupees (nearly $4,200,000) per annum, though by the treaty of 1775 he had bound himself to the annual payment of only 3,121,000 rupees, and by the treaty of 1781 to that of 3,420,000 rupees. It was agreed that 5,000,000 rupees should be the annual payment of the Nabob, and that this sum should embrace every possible claim. The governor-general declared that this was sufficient to indemnify the Company for all the expense which it was necessary for them to incur in consequence of their connection with the Nabob. In other words, he declared that for the 9 preceding years unjustifiable extortion to the amount of 3,400,000 rupees annually had been practised on that dependent prince."

The administration of Lord Cornwallis in Bengal, was chiefly remarkable for some measures connected with the revenue. In India, from the earliest authentic history, the sovereigns obtained their revenue chiefly from the produce of the land. And in the early and more rude state of society, the sovereigns took their part in kind. The cultivator was the owner of the land; he could alienate it, or it could be taken and sold by a legal process for his debts, and it descended to his heirs. But whoever had possession of it, he was bound to pay the proportion claimed by the government, and if he failed to do this, government could enforce its claim by taking possession of the land and vesting it in others. The proportion claimed by the government varied in different provinces, and according to the different kinds of soil and produce. It has generally varied from one half to one fourth. In the provinces of Bengal, Bahar, and Orissa, the committee on Indian affairs assumed or determined that two fifths was the proportion of the produce for the cultivators, and three fifths for the government. And as the Mohammedan government in these provinces, instead of taking their proportion of the produce in kind, had for some time required its estimated value in money, the committee determined that the same course should be pursued. If the case of the cultivators was hard when they were required to give three fifths of their produce to the government, it became yet harder when they were required to pay the government the estimated value of the three fifths in money.

The native government for realizing the revenue, had caused

the country to be divided into districts, and appointed a collec tor over each district. The collectors, commonly called Zemindars, received a certain percentage, generally one tenth of the amount collected. They were merely the agents of government, with no right in the soil, but as they were seldom removed so long as they gave satisfaction, and the office frequently continued in the same family two or three generations, it came often to be regarded as a kind of hereditary property. There is a strong feeling in India to make every thing hereditary. If a man holds any situation till he dies, his family will always feel that they have a claim to the same place.

It has already been stated that in the administration of Mr. Hastings, the land was divided into districts, and sold to the highest bidder for 5 years. The purchasers were generally the collectors of the taxes or rents, and they made the purchases with the expectation that at the close of 5 years, some further settlement would be made. But as the English government had not fixed on any system, the collectors generally continued in charge on such terms as could be agreed upon with the government. But all parties were in a dissatisfied state. Lord Cornwallis appears to have had strong aristocratical prejudices, and believed the country could be best governed and improved by creating a landed aristocracy. So the Zemindars, who were all natives of the country, were declared to be the landlords, or proprietors of their respective districts, upon condition of paying to the government annually a certain specified amount of taxes or rents, and the cultivators were all declared to be the tenants of the Zemindars. Thus in provinces containing a population of 30,000,000 of people, the cultivators of the land, in whose possession it had been for many generations, and whose right to it had never been questioned, were made the tenants of landlords (the Zemindars) who had previously no right whatever in the soil by inheritance, occupation, or purchase. It was intended at first, that this arrangement or settlement should continue for only 10 years, and then be made permanent, if approved by the Court of Directors, and the results should be such as were anticipated. But Lord Cornwallis, after some delay, resolved to make this settlement permanent, and so it was made.

This was the greatest change yet made by any English administration in India. Indeed, so great a change was probably never made in the state of any country by the mere enactment and operation of law. And probably no change ever produced more unhappy consequences — unhappy to the East India Company in its effects upon their revenue, and the improvement of the country; unhappy upon the Zemindars, many of whom became involved and insolvent; and yet more unhappy upon the cultivators, who were oppressed and impoverished, and, to a fearful extent, ruined. Such is the general testimony and opinion of numerous writers upon this settlement. The author of the Rise and Progress of the British Power in India, whose principal aim appears to have been to seek, in all the proceedings of the East India Company, and of their governors and agents, for what he could praise, and for circumstances and reasons to excuse what he could not commend, says, "this attempt to create a landed aristocracy out of the hereditary contract agency in managing the land revenue, was attended by a vast subversion of individual property and the loss of a considerable portion of revenue to the State, without securing that relief to the cultivator of the soil which formed one of the principal objects contemplated on the introduction of the system." * And Sir H. Strachey, who was for many years one of the Company's magistrates in Bengal, declared, "that an almost universal destruction had overtaken the Zemindars, and that if any survived, they were reduced to the same condition and placed at an equal distance from their masters (the English), as the lowest ryots (cultivators)." Another historian of British India says: "It is impossible to read the accounts given, by the Company's most intelligent agents, of the state of the country, and of the causes of its moral decline, without receiving a full conviction that with the best intentions in the world, Lord Cornwallis, by his financial changes brought more injury upon British India, than had been brought by all his predecessors put together." †

A reform in the courts of law, or rather the introduction and establishment of a judicial system was not less required

* Auber, vol. 2, p. 83. † Gleig, vol. 3, p. 132.

than changes in the revenue. The revenue concerned the government; the administration of justice concerned all classes of people. The country was divided into districts, and a series of courts, with appeals from the lower to the higher, was arranged. Europeans connected with the army were of course subject to military laws. Europeans in the other departments of government, and those unconnected with the government, were amenable to the Supreme Court in Calcutta. In respect to the native population generally, where both parties were Hindus, the matters in question were to be decided in accordance with Hindu laws, as defined and interpreted by the Hindu law-officers of the courts. So where both parties were Mohammedans, the decision was to be in accordance with the established principles of Mohammedan law. And where the parties were of different creeds, then the law of the defendant was to govern the decision. In the application of these general principles, much must have remained for the discretionary consideration and decision of the magistrates.

The great mistake in framing this system, and one which greatly embarrassed its operations, was the introduction of tedious and technical forms in conformity with English courts and usages. Here, as in the matters of revenue, the governor-general, though a man of great ability, and with the best intentions, appears to have been misled by his admiration of every thing English, and by his not being sufficiently acquainted with the character, the history, and the habits of the native population, to see that such a system was not suited to them. So in the administration of justice among the people as well as of revenue for the government, Lord Cornwallis's measures, instead of producing the good effects which were expected from them, became the cause of great, complicated, and long continued evils. These two measures, one concerning the land revenue, and the other concerning the judiciary, were the greatest errors ever made by the English in their government of India.

In October, of 1793, Lord Cornwallis embarked for England, having been governor-general for 5 years. The East India Company gave him an annuity of £5,000 for 20 years, to commence from the time he quitted India, and to be continued to his family in the event of his death. His salary had been £25,000 annually, while in office.

Sir John Shore, subsequently Lord Teignmouth, then became governor-general, and held the office till 1798. He had previously been many years in India, and so had much experience in the affairs of government. His administration gave general satisfaction in India as well as in England.

HISTORY OF MADRAS TILL 1800.

Madras is the oldest of the English possessions in India. It was obtained by the East India Company in 1640, from a native prince, who had then some possessions on the Coromandel Coast. The territory acquired, consisted of only a few square miles. The English here erected a fort and called it St. George. The village or town has retained its original name Madras, or Madraspatam, the town of Madras. It was soon made the seat of the East India Company's government and agency on that coast, and has ever since retained its preëminence, having increased from a native village to a city of half a million of inhabitants.

With the close of the 17th century the difficulties of the East India Company in England terminated, and with the 18th century a new era commenced. The two rival companies which had so long contended for the trade of India, had become united in one corporation to manage their affairs under legislative sanction. Their charter gave them the exclusive right to the trade with all places east of the Cape of Good Hope, and power to seize and punish any of their nation, who should interfere with it. They had civil and criminal jurisdiction in the courts they had established. They had resolved to extend their power and to increase their revenue by acquiring territorial possessions. They had determined that "independence was to be established in India;" and to become "a nation in India." And what was of great importance, they had all the experience acquired by the management of their extensive and complicated affairs, for more than a century. They knew the character, the power, and the weakness of the native princes and governments, and by observation, social intercourse, and transactions of business, they had become well acquainted with the character, circumstances, and habits of all classes of the native population.

Arrangements were made in London for managing the affairs of the Company in a manner far superior to any that had before existed. The proprietors assembled in due form for business, were called "the Court of Proprietors," and to take a part in the proceedings of this body, a proprietor must own £500 of stock. The proprietors chose 24 of their body to be a committee of management; these were called the Directors, and when assembled for business, "the Court of Directors." But no one could become a Director, who did not possess £2,000 of stock.

In India the Company had 3 presidencies, namely, Calcutta, Madras, and Bombay. A presidency consisted of a president or governor, and council, all appointed by the Directors in London. Subordinate to these presidencies, were 80 factories scattered in all the considerable seaports and cities in India and other parts of southern Asia. Some of these factories were strongly fortified and garrisoned.

For some years little of historical interest occurred in the affairs of the English in India. In 1715, a physician by the name of Hamilton, who accompanied an embassy to Delhi, cured the emperor of a disease which had baffled the native physicians. For this service the emperor gave liberal presents to Hamilton; he also gave 3 villages near Madras, and 37 villages near Calcutta, to the East India Company. He also gave permission for their agents to transport their goods through his dominions to some places without paying duty. The trade of the Company was generally prosperous. In 1717, they paid dividends of 10 per cent. upon a capital of £3,194,030, and this appears to have been the rate of dividend for 10 or 12 years.

In 1721, Indian calicoes were so much used in England that they were considered "a great detriment and obstruction to the woollen and silk manufactures of the kingdom, and occasioned several riots and tumults among the weavers in London," in consequence of which Parliament passed an act, which "prohibited the wear of Indian printed calicoes under a penalty of £5 for each offence on the wearer, and £20 on the seller." This was rather a singular way of protecting domestic manufactures.

The Company had great difficulty in obtaining a renewal of

their charter in 1730. Among the means used for effecting this was the reduction of the interest upon the sums they had loaned to the English government from 5 to 4 per cent., and also the payment of a bonus of £200,000 to the public service. The charter thus renewed was to continue till 1766, and if not then renewed, the 3 years' notice required would extend the period till 1769. In 1744, when the English nation was engaged in an expensive war, the Company offered to loan to the government £1,000,000 upon 3 per cent. interest, provided their exclusive privileges should be extended to 1780, or with the 3 years' notice to 1783. On these conditions a new act to extend the charter was passed. The object of this measure on the part of the Company appears to have been to allay complaints in the public mind, and conciliate the good-will of the government; for the same act in order to enable them to make this loan to the government authorized them to borrow the same amount upon their bonds.

The Company now became involved in war on a larger scale, more severe in its character, and more perilous to their interests than ever before.

The French did not engage in trade to the East Indies until nearly half a century after the English East India Company had been formed. Their first endeavors were to form a settlement on Madagascar, but this island does not yield any commodities in sufficient quantity for any considerable exportation to any European market. The inhabitants are ferocious and warlike, and very unlike in their habits and character to the people of the southern parts of Asia and its islands. The French, after much harassing warfare and suffering, were compelled to leave Madagascar, and the survivors chiefly settled in Mauritius and Bourbon. The French East India Company then turned their attention to India, and established several factories in different places. Among these Pondicherry held the first place. It was fortified; its trade much increased, and its state was prosperous. The French eastern possessions at this time constituted two presidencies; namely, Mauritius which included Bourbon, and Pondicherry which included the factories in India.

In 1744, England and France, which had for some time been engaged in war on opposite sides as auxiliaries, came to mutual declarations of war with each other. This war soon extended to their possessions in all parts of the world. In 1746, Labourdonnais, a man of great talent and energy, who had previously been governor of Mauritius, and was well acquainted with the state of India, collected a small fleet and attacked Madras. This city was the first place acquired by the English in India, and had been the capital of their possessions on the Coromandel Coast for more than 100 years. The territory was small, extending about 5 miles along the shore and 1 mile inland. The population was estimated at 250,000. The English amounted to only 300, of whom 200 were soldiers belonging to the garrison. The city was bombarded for 5 days, during which a few persons were killed, and 2 or 3 houses demolished. The people fearing an assault, became anxious for capitulation, and the city was surrendered, Labourdonnais promising that it should be restored again after a stipulated period and for a fixed ransom. The inhabitants were protected and all private property respected, but the French took possession of the warehouses and magazines of the East India Company, and appropriated them to their own use. Having thus taken the capital of all the English possessions on the Coromandel Coast, Labourdonnais returned to Pondicherry without the loss of a single man. But here he found to his surprise that his gallant conduct, instead of being appreciated and approved as he expected, was severely censured. Dupleix, then governor of Pondicherry, an aspiring and ambitious man, apparently jealous of his fame and influence, opposed him in all his plans and treated him with so much contumely that, unable any longer to endure it, he sailed for France. There too, the misrepresentations of Dupleix had preceded him. One of Dupleix's brothers was a director in the French East India Company, and had much influence. Labourdonnais was thrown into the Bastile, where he remained in confinement for 3 years, and died soon after he was released.

It was never Dupleix's intention to fulfil the terms of the capitulation made by Labourdonnais to restore Madras again to the English, and the Nabob of Arcot, becoming fully satisfied of this, and exasperated by his deceitful and faithless conduct, espoused the part of the English and sent an army of 10,000 men under his son to take Madras from the French. The garrison at that time consisted of about 1,200 Europeans, who encountered the Nabob's army, astonished them with the rapidity and destructive fire of their artillery, routed them and gained a decided victory. A century before this battle was fought, the Portuguese had shown on several occasions the superiority of a small body of Europeans with their cool valor and disciplined skill in the time of conflict over the numerous, disorderly, and undisciplined armies which the princes of India bring into the field. But these victories of the Portuguese had apparently been forgotten, and the English and French, not having yet learned their own superiority from experience, were accustomed to look upon the emperors of India as mighty monarchs, and their armies as brave and formidable. This spell was again dissipated, and the consequent estimation of the native armies opened before both nations, scenes of future conquest and power scarcely yet thought of. The opinion which they now began to form of their own power, soon led to very important results in their wars with the native governments.

Dupleix, who was now in charge of the French interests in India, was a man of great ambition, energy, and talent. He had previously filled several important situations with much credit to himself and advantage to the public interests. He now formed plans of conquest and power for himself and his nation not inferior to those of any of the great conquerors, who in different ages have invaded India. Possessing an ample private fortune as well as the liberal salary of an Indian governor, he adopted the style of living and frequently the costume of an oriental prince, and the government house in Pondicherry, in its ceremonies, pomp, and gorgeous splendor resembled the palace and court of a Nabob or Emperor. The first step Dupleix took in pursuing his scheme was to retain the advantage already acquired over the English, and proceed to expel them from all their possessions on the Coromandel Coast. Accordingly he sent orders to the officer in charge of Madras to declare publicly that the treaty of restoration for a ransom had been annulled, and to take possession of all magazines and all articles of property, except the clothes which people wore, the furniture of their houses, and the jewels of their women. These orders were carried into effect with great severity. The English governor and the most respectable men were carried prisoners to Pondicherry.

Dupleix next laid siege to the fort of St. David, which was 12 miles south of Pondicherry. The fort was small but strongly fortified, and the territory connected with it, was larger than the territory of Madras. He had but just commenced the siege, when the army of the Nabob of Arcot, appeared in sight to assist the English. The French force retreated, but not without some loss. Great efforts were made to gain over the Nabob to the French interests, and he was at last induced to join them. The siege of St. David was revived and prosecuted with vigor, but without the expected success, and Dupleix was compelled to abandon it. In 1748, a fleet of 9 ships of the royal navy, and 11 ships of the East India Company with 1,400 men arrived, which added to those already in India, made the largest European force ever in the country. The English were now in a state to commence offensive operations, and they resolved to besiege Pondicherry, the chief seat of the French power in India. They were now in high spirits expecting soon to see Pondicherry taken, and the French power humbled, if not annihilated. The siege was commenced, but was badly managed, the rainy season began, sickness broke out in the camp, and the English were obliged to abandon the place, a measure not more painful to them than joyful to the French. Soon after the siege was raised, and before offensive operations could be again commenced, news arrived from Europe that peace had been made between England and France, one condition of which was that Madras should be restored to the English. This restoration put each nation in possession of the same places and territories in India, which they had when the war commenced. Such was the result of several years of hard fighting and great expenditure of treasure and of life. No events of any importance occurred during the war in the other presidencies. In Bengal the viceroy of the emperor forbid the English and French to carry on any hostilities with each other in his dominions, and the French had no possessions in the Bombay presidency.

The peace between England and France produced a cessation of hostilities between the English and French in India, and left each party in possession of the territories they possessed previous to the war. But both parties were left in circumstances unfavorable to continued peace. While the war was in progress, they had received large reinforcements from Europe, and they had now a much larger force than was necessary for defence in a time of peace. This force must return to Europe, or live on reduced pay, or find some employment in the country. They had learned their superiority over the native armies in valor and discipline. Personal and official intercourse with the native princes and courts had disclosed their weakness, fickleness, duplicity, and corruption. And there were among the English and the French many restless, ambitious, and aspiring men, who were anxious for opportunities to achieve great things for themselves, for their party, and for their nation. Such men were unwilling to return to Europe, or to remain idle in India.

In these circumstances it is easy to see that peace was not likely to be of long continuance, and that if hostilities should again commence, they would be managed on a larger scale, and in a different manner, and would involve other parties and have greater ultimate objects in view than ever before. The English were the first to disturb the general tranquillity by taking part in the affairs of Tanjore, a small Hindu principality, about 200 miles nearly south from Madras. Sahujee, the Raja of Tanjore, had been expelled from his throne, and he applied to the English to reinstate him, promising to give them the fort and district of Devacotta. Their first attempt to obtain possession of the fort was a failure. The second attempt was successful. The second attack was led by Lieut. Clive, who afterwards became so conspicuous in the affairs of India. A treaty was soon made with the reigning Raja of Tanjore, who ceded the fort and district to the English, and they abandoned the cause of Sahujee.

In the mean time Dupliex was concerting plans to procure for the French the ascendency in the southern parts of India. At this time the principal Mohammedan princes in the southern parts of the peninsula, were the Nizam of Hyderabad, sometimes called the Subadar of the Deckan, and the Nabob of Arcot, sometimes called the Nabob of the Carnatic. These persons were originally subordinate to the emperor of Delhi, but in the state of anarchy which ensued upon the invasion of India by

Nadir Shah, they had become gradually independent. Nazir Jung was now Nizam, but the office or throne was claimed by another member of the family, called Murzapha Jung. Anwur ud Deen was now Nabob, but the place was claimed by a man called Chunda Sahib. Dupliex, having become acquainted with the state of parties in these native governments, saw that he might act an important part among them, and perhaps raise the French power to a state of supremacy over them all. Murzapha Jung and Chunda Sahib, having united their influence and forces to prosecute their claims, assembled an army and approached the Carnatic. The native princes had become aware of the superior valor and discipline of European troops, and were anxious to obtain the assistance of Dupliex; and he saw that by espousing their cause, he might obtain the highest advantage for himself and his nation. So he promised them assistance, and sent a considerable force under M. de Auteuil to their aid. The forces being united, they marched to attack Anwur ud Deen, who was then at Amboor, 50 miles west from Arcot. The first and second assaults were repulsed, but the third was successful. Anwur was killed, his eldest son was taken prisoner, and his second son, Mohammed Ali, with the remains of his army, fled to Trichinopoly, of which fort he was governor. Murzapha Jung, and Chunda Sahib, then proceeded to Arcot, and afterwards to Pondicherry, where Dupliex entertained them in oriental magnificence, and received from Chunda Sahib the cession of 81 villages in that province. They next went to Tanjore, and demanded a large sum of money, as arrears of tribute due to the Nabob of Arcot, or the Carnatic. While thus engaged, they heard that Nazir Jung was on his march with a very large force to attack them. They were much disconcerted at this news, and breaking up their camp, returned to Pondicherry. The state of matters now called forth the talent of Dupliex for engaging in Indian politics. He exerted all his art and persuasion to encourage them; he lent them £50,000 (nearly $250,000), saying he would let them have more if they required it, and he increased the French forces to 2,000. Still he was fearful of the power of Nazir Jung, whose army was described as amounting to 300,000 men, and so he endeavored to negotiate a second treaty with him. The English had also engaged in secret negotiation for some time with Nizam ul Mulk and Nazir Jung, endeavoring to prejudice them against the French, and secure favor for themselves. They had assisted Mohammed Ali, by sending some small aid to Tanjore and to Trichinopoly. When they were informed of Nazir Jung's approach with a large army, Major Lawrence proceeded to join him with 600 men. Some difficulties about this time occurred in the French force, and 13 officers resigned in one day. Their commander, D'Auteuil, becoming embarrassed and discouraged, returned with his division of the force to Pondicherry. Murzapha Jung and Chunda Sahib now lost all confidence in their army. The former surrendered and was cast into prison, and the latter took refuge in Pondicherry.

Thus frustrated in his plans and calculations, Dupliex had recourse to other expedients. In his negotiations with Nazir Jung, he had learned that some Afghan chiefs, who had the command of some regiments of their countrymen in his army, had conspired to dethrone him. He opened a communication with these conspirators, and engaged to assist them in carrying their plan into effect. D'Auteuil, leaving Pondicherry, attacked Nazir Jung's camp in the night, and made great slaughter, when, supposing no enemy near, they were quite unprepared. The French also took Mausalapatam, the principal seaport on that coast. Major Lawrence, who commanded the English force, becoming dissatisfied with the Nizam's conduct, withdrew from his army, and so left an open field for the French. D'Auteuil now sent a force to take Gingee, a mountain fort, strongly fortified and celebrated in Indian history, and they seized it in the night with but little loss. Nazir Jung, who had been spending his time at Arcot in his favorite sport of hunting, and in the harem, was now roused to action and took the field, but unable for some time to accomplish any thing decisive, and wishing to return to the Deckan, he opened negotiations with the French. Dupliex prolonged this negotiation, and kept up his friendly communication with the dissatisfied Afghan chiefs, till their plans for dethroning the Nizam were matured. At length they informed the French commander in Gingee of their concerted plans. He proceeded at once to attack the camp of the Nizam in the night, and in the confusion that followed, the Nizam was killed by one of the Afghan chiefs. Murzapha Jung, who had remained in confinement since he surrendered himself, was now brought out and proclaimed to be the Nizam, or Subadar of the Deckan.

By this sudden revolution Murzapha Jung, instead of being a prisoner of State, became the sovereign of a territory at that time larger in population than England or France. The treasure of Nazir Jung, of which he acquired possession, exceeded $12,000,000. This change in the subaship, or government, greatly increased the French influence. Murzapha Jung visited Pondicherry, where he was received with great pomp and installed on the throne of the Deckan, and Dupleix in return was created governor and collector in all the districts on the river Kistna, a territory larger than France. Murzapha Jung ceded several districts to France in perpetuity, and paid Dupleix $250,000 for the expenses of the war. But he soon found his new situation to be surrounded with difficulties. The Afghan chiefs made heavy demands for the part they had performed in raising him to power. Dupleix exerted his influence for some satisfactory adjustment of these claims, but without effect, and Murzapha Jung left Pondicherry for the Deckan, accompanied by M. Bussy with a body of French troops. After a few days' march, the dissatisfaction of the Afghan chiefs resulted in an open revolt, in which Murzapha Jung was killed. Sulabat Jung, a brother of Murzapha Jung, was now proclaimed and installed Subadar. He promised the French to fulfil the engagements made by his predecessor, and the army proceeded on the way to the Deckan.

The apathy and indifference with which the English contemplated these proceedings, appear not less surprising than the remarkable success of the French. They were at length roused to make some efforts to retrieve their circumstances. They made an attack upon Madura, but were repulsed. They were defeated at Valiconda, and retreating on the approach of the enemy at Utatoor and at Pitchonda, took refuge in Trichinopoly, where they were soon besieged by the united forces of Chunda Sahib and the French. This sad state of the English was further increased by an unhappy contention among their officers. While their affairs were in this discouraging state, a new actor appeared on the stage. Mr. Robert Clive, afterwards so celebrated in the history of India, arrived at Madras in 1748, in the capacity of a writer of the East India Company. When the promised restoration of Madras was violated, he escaped to fort St. David in the dress of a Mohammedan. When the siege of Trichinopoly was undertaken, he was permitted to enter the army as an ensign. Here, on several other occasions, he exhibited great intrepidity and knowledge of military tactics. When the expeditions for which he joined the army were finished, he returned to Madras to his own department of the government. But when he saw the distracted and discouraging state of the English affairs, he again joined the army, and having obtained a force of 500 men, of whom only 200 were Europeans, he made an attack on Arcot the Nabob's capital. The Nabob's troops, seeing the approach of this force, evacuated the place without making any resistance. It was not long before a detachment of 4,000 or 5,000 men arriving from Trichinopoly, he was besieged in the fort he had taken. He repelled their attacks with great vigor and ability during a siege of 50 days, when the enemy becoming discouraged, raised the siege and withdrew from the place. He pursued them for some distance, and having gained some advantages over them and taken several small forts, he returned to Madras.

The siege of Trichinopoly was still continued. But very considerable reinforcements now arrived from England. Mohammed Ali succeeded in obtaining aid from the Raja of Mysore, who sent a force of 20,000 men. The Raja of Tanjore was also induced to send a force of 5,000 men. In these circumstances the English resolved to attack the French in their camp, but the French seeing the force arranged to attack them, abandoned Trichinopoly and took possession of Seringham, an island in the river Coleroon. This place was soon attacked with vigor, and unable to make any further defence and suffering for provisions, Chunda Sahib surrendered to the Raja of Tanjore, and the French surrendered to the English. The Raja of Tanjore gave Chunda Sahib a promise of protection, but he was soon put to death.

The state and prospects of the English were now encouraging beyond any former period, and those of the French in turn were uncertain and discouraging. But Dupleix was not to be easily disheartened, and began to form plans yet more extensive. M. Bussy, his agent, having placed Sulabat Jung on the throne of the Deckan, proceeded with him to Golconda and Aurungabad, when the Subadar entered upon his government with great parade and pomp. But he found a rival in Ghazee ud Deen, another son of Nizam ul Mulk, and Sulabat Jung soon saw that he must rely upon the French to sustain him in the office, which through their aid he had acquired. So he retained his power under the direction of M. Bussy. In the Carnatic, Dupleix resolved if possible to restore the ascendency of the French by taking the advantage of the fickleness and weakness, the fortunes and misfortunes of the native princes. He had learned much of the native character, and he turned this experience to great advantage. While the English were yet rejoicing in the success of their arms and allies in raising the siege of Trichinopoly, they were surprised to learn that the Nabob, Mohammed Ali, had promised to cede this city and the territory around it to the Raja of Mysore, as the reward of the assistance he had given. He admitted that he had made the promise, but refused to fulfil it. Much negotiation followed, and the matter was professedly adjusted, but strong dissatisfaction was still cherished and certain soon to manifest itself.

The next measure of the English was the reduction of Gingee, which was garrisoned by the French, and was the strongest fort in the Carnatic. A force supposed to be sufficient to take the fort was sent for this purpose, but it was defeated, and so the expedition failed. Dupleix also seized a company of Swiss who were in the English service and on the way to Madras. The French, elated with their success in different places, reinforced their victorious army with as much force as they could send into the field. Major Lawrence made his arrangements to encounter the French force as soon as possible. His force consisted of 400 Europeans, and 1,700 sepoys in the service of the English, and 4,000 sepoys belonging to the Nabob, and 9 pieces of cannon. The French force consisted of 450 Europeans, 1,500 sepoys, and 500 cavalry. They met and fought at Bahoor. The English were victorious, but the eagerness of the Nabob's troops to plunder the French camp, prevented the English from realizing the full advantages of the victory. The rainy season now setting in, compelled both parties to withdraw their armies from the field.

In the mean time the siege of Trichinopoly was pressed by Nundraj, the commander of the Mysore troops. He, as well as the Raja of Tanjore and some Mahratta chiefs, then in the Carnatic with considerable force, were ready to join the English or the French, according as one or the other of these parties from time to time appeared to have the ascendency. A treaty having been negotiated between Nundraj the commander of the Mysore troops, and Dupleix, the latter sent a French force to assist in pressing the siege of Trichinopoly. The garrison was also soon after reinforced by a body of English troops. This siege is one of the most memorable in the history of Indian warfare, and continued for a year and a half.

While these transactions were taking place in the Carnatic, M. Bussy was active in promoting the French interest in the Deckan. His influence in the councils of Sulabat Jung was felt to be humiliating to the great men at court, and excited their united opposition against him. They took the advantage of his temporary absence to diminish his influence, and to embarrass his position. His troops did not receive their pay according to the terms of their service, and they were separated into detachments and stationed in different places. But on his return he soon collected them together. There was then fear of an invasion by the Mahrattas, which would make the assistance he could render in such case very important. This probable want of his aid, added to the injury it was in his power to do them, enabled him to take higher ground and exert more power than he had ever done before. He insisted that those who had shown themselves to be his enemies, should be excluded from the council, and to make up the arrears of pay and to prevent any such delay or delinquency in future, he obtained the cession of a large extent of territory in the Carnatic. This territory, added to the districts which the French previously possessed, gave them more than 600 miles of sea-coast, and an annual revenue of $4,500,000. The revenue of all the possessions acquired by the English during this long and arduous struggle, did not exceed $500,000 annually.

The English and the French East India Companies, dissatisfied with the expenses of these wars in India, and unable to approve of the proceedings of their agents, urged them to adjust their mutual difficulties. With a view to such a settlement they commenced examining and comparing their respective titles to the territories they claimed. It was soon found that no progress could be made in bringing their difficulties to a satisfactory conclusion in this way, as each party declared the titles, papers, etc., produced by the other to be forged. Other proposals and offers were made, but nothing satisfactory to either party could be done.

This severe and long-continued contention between the English and French in India, occasioned earnest discussion between their respective governments in Europe. There was more dissatisfaction in France concerning what the agents of their East India Company were doing, than in England concerning what their Company's agents had done. Large reinforcements were also preparing in London to proceed to India. In these circumstances it was agreed between the two governments that Commissioners should be appointed to investigate all the matters of difference, and make an adjustment of them upon such principles of equity as would be mutually satisfactory. On the part of the French Company, M. Godheu was appointed Commissioner, with power civil and military over all the French possessions in India, and on the part of the English Company, Mr. Sanders, their governor or president in council in Madras, was appointed. M. Godheu arrived at Pondicherry in 1754, and superseded Dupleix. An armistice of 3 months was agreed upon, and before the close of the year a provisional treaty, subject to the ratification of their respective companies, was signed by the Commissioners. In this treaty the places and territories which each party was to retain, were specified. Each party engaged to withdraw from all interference in the affairs of the native princes, and never again to interfere in any wars or dissensions that might occur among them. All hostilities were to cease, and the possessions of each party to remain as they were, till the decision of the respective companies in Europe should be known.

Dupleix, as might be supposed, was exceedingly dissatisfied

with the appointment of these Commissioners, reflecting as it did upon his conduct, and arresting his schemes for extending the French power in India. On the arrival of M. Godheu, he resigned all power into his hands. He delivered up his accounts with the French Company, and showed that he had paid for the expenses of the war, £400,000, nearly $2,000,000, out of his own private fortune. In October 1754, he embarked for Europe. On his arriving in France, the French East India Company declared that in much of what he had done in India, he had acted without any orders from them, and often contrary to their avowed principles and known purposes. They refused to reimburse any part of what he had expended from his own property on their account. He appealed to the French government, but they refused to interfere further, than "by granting him letters of protection against any prosecution which might be raised by his creditors." He published a statement of his services and the treatment he had received in return, which excited much attention and sympathy, and his case was generally regarded as one of great hardship and injustice.

This treaty was regarded by all parties as favorable to the English interests,* and as the French East India Company had manifested a strong desire for peace in proposing to refer matters of difference to a commission, and also in the adjustment of such matters in the treaty, there appeared to be reasons for hoping that the agents of the respective Companies would now quietly pursue the objects for which they had professedly gone to India. Such was the prospect when the commissioners Sanders and Godheu, soon after the conclusion of the treaty, embarked for Europe. But such expectations were of short continuance. The English soon began to interfere in the affairs of the Nabob of the Carnatic, and sent a force to assist him in reducing the districts of Madura and Tinnevelly to submission. The French exclaimed against these proceedings as a violation of the treaty just made. And when they saw that their remonstrances were disregarded, they began to follow the example of

* "By this treaty, every thing for which they had been contending was gained by the English; every advantage of which they had come into possession was given up by the French."—*Mill.*

the English, and sent a body of troops against the Raja of Terrore. Each party soon appeared as intent and as unscrupulous in endeavoring to secure every possible advantage, as they were before the treaty was made. Thus matters soon became as much involved and hostilities again were as severe, as they had been before the treaty was ratified. Whatever might be the state of England and France towards each other, war appeared likely to be continued between the two nations in India, as long as they should be able to support it.

Such was the state of matters in India, when war commenced between England and France in 1756. The French, now better informed in respect to the state of India, resolved to acquire and then maintain their ascendency there, and with this view despatched a large force under the command of Count Lally, an officer who had distinguished himself on several occasions by great intrepidity and valor. The day Lally arrived at Pondicherry, he despatched a force to take St. Davids, then the strongest and most important of the English possessions on that coast. The whole besieging force at St. Davids consisted of 2,500 Europeans, exclusive of officers, and about as many sepoys. The garrison consisted of 800 Europeans and 1,600 sepoys. The siege was urged on with great vigor, and in 5 weeks the fort was compelled to surrender. The garrison became prisoners of war, and the fortifications were all demolished. He then sent a detachment against Devacotta, which the garrison immediately abandoned. He then returned with his army to Pondicherry in triumph, and caused *Te Deum* to be celebrated. Elated with his success, Lally resolved to follow up his plan, and to expel all the English from the country without delay. But he was much embarrassed for want of funds, and he resolved to enforce some old claims against the Raja of Tanjore, who was reported to possess much hoarded wealth. So he proceeded to Tanjore and laid siege to the fort. But before he was able to get possession of it, news was brought that an English fleet had arrived on the coast, when in accordance with the advice of a council of war, he raised the siege. He next proceeded to take Arcot, and several smaller forts, where his wants were partially supplied. He next made arrangements to lay siege to Madras, where he arrived in January of 1758, with an army of 3,500 Europeans, and 4,000 natives. The garrison consisted of 1,758 Europeans, and 2,220 natives. When the siege had continued for 2 months, an English fleet arrived with a large reinforcement. Lally then raised the siege and returned to Pondicherry. The French army suffered much, while carrying on the siege, for want of provisions and other things. For the first 5 weeks, the officers and soldiers received only half-pay, and for the last 3 weeks they received no pay. For some time they were nearly in a state of mutiny, and ready to desert, or to go over to the English.

When the French were compelled to raise the siege of Madras, and every way embarrassed for want of funds, the English thought the time favorable for them to regain what they had lost, and to extend their power and influence. "But they also found their operations cramped by the narrowness of their funds," and so could not improve the advantages before them. And considering the spirit that animated both parties, it was well for the native princes and for the general peace of the country, that both the English and the French had not the means to gratify their desires, and prosecute their ambitious schemes of power and conquest. Each party was earnestly engaged with such resources as they could command in extending or defending their possessions, and both were waiting anxiously for expected aid from Europe.

The reinforcement from England having arrived at Madras, the English were now in circumstances to enter upon more active operations. They were under the command of Sir Eyre Coote, who subsequently acquired much celebrity in Indian warfare. After many marches and manœuvres, the chief force of the two armies met at Wandewash. Accounts differ in respect to the amount of their force. The most probable account says that the English force consisted of 1,900 Europeans, 2,100 sepoys, and 125 native cavalry; and that the French consisted of 2,250 Europeans, and 1,300 sepoys. In this battle the French were defeated, and suffered great loss. This victory decided the supremacy of the English power over the French in India. The English continued their course of success by taking some smaller forts and extending their power over the Carnatic, till Pondicherry was the only place on the coast which remained in the hands of the French.

The English, having received several large reinforcements, and the French not having received any for a long time, Sir Eyre Coote made arrangements for besieging Pondicherry. In September, the place was closely besieged, and all supplies were cut off. In January, the garrison being no longer in a position to offer any effectual resistance, and much straitened for provisions, the city was surrendered to Sir Eyre Coote. The garrison then consisted of 2,072 Europeans. In the fort were 500 pieces of cannon, 100 mortars and howitzers, and a great quantity of ammunition and military stores.

Thus fell Pondicherry, which had long been the capital of the French possessions in India. Their few remaining forts soon surrendered, and in a few months nothing was left to them of the territories, which only a few years before had extended for 600 miles on the sea-coast, and yielded a yearly revenue of $4,500,000.

Three days after the surrender of Pondicherry, Lally sailed for Europe. He had been in bad health for some time. He was worn out with vexation and anxiety, and exhausted with exertion and fatigue. The latter part of his life in India had been one continual series of disappointments, losses, and misfortunes. And yet greater trials and sufferings awaited him on his arrival in France. Public feeling had become much exasperated by the loss of possessions, and of national character in India. The idea of a great Indian empire, as set forth in the aspirations and plans of Labourdonnais, Dupliex, and Lally, had been too fondly cherished to be given up without feelings of strong indignation and revenge against some party, and circumstances now directed the chief force of this excitement against the late governor-general. Conscious of having used his best exertions for the honor of his country, and the interest of the French East India Company, Lally vindicated himself with energy, and imprudently accused Bussy and some others, who in return retaliated, by charges against him. "These charges were vague and frivolous, and nothing whatsoever was proved against him, except that his conduct did not come up to the very perfection of prudence and wisdom, and that he did display the greatest ardor in the service, the greatest disinterestedness, fidelity, and perseverance, with no common share of military talent and mental resources." And yet he was thrown into the Bastile, and a sentence of death was procured against him. Conscious of his innocence, he was confidently expecting an honorable acquittal, and when the sentence of death was read to him in the prison, he exclaimed with astonishment, "Is this the reward of 45 years' service?" and attempted to kill himself with a pair of compasses with which he had been sketching the coast of Coromandel. He was carried to the place of execution in a common cart, and a gag was forced into his mouth, lest he should address the people.

The struggle between the English and the French for ascendency in India, closed with the fall of Pondicherry. Labourdonnais, Dupliex, Bussy, and Lally were men of great ambition and great ability. Their views and plans extended to the creation of a great empire in India, subject to France;—such an empire as we now see subject to England, though it appears not then to have been thought of by any of the English governors, officers, or agents, who carried on these wars with the French. Dupliex for some time adopted the dress and manners, the style and pomp of an oriental Nabob. To him has been ascribed the origin and successful experiment of enlisting native regiments under European officers, training them in European discipline, and so making them efficient for permanent service;—a practice which the English soon began to imitate, and which is yet the system of their army in India. Had the French government and their East India Company supported their interest in India as vigorously and liberally as the English government and East India Company supported their interests, the French apparently might have sustained the ascendency which they at one time possessed, might have expelled the English from India; the ambitious aspirations and schemes of Labourdonnais, Dupliex, and Lally might then have been realized, and all India now be as subject to France, as it is to England.

These wars between the English and the French in India, though they occupy no prominent place in general history, and even in the history of the country appear small when compared with the great armies engaged, and the great battles fought in the wars between the English and Hyder Ali, Tippoo Sultan, the Mahrattas, the Afghans, and the Sikhs, yet when considered in their consequences, were the most important wars in the European history of the country. These wars, though limited to the Carnatic, were yet in reality a severe and long-continued struggle for ascendency, and for the government of India. The issue of these wars was to be no other than whether the English or the French should be the governing power of the country, whether India should become a dependency of England, or of France. Such was the view of Labourdonnais, Dupliex, and Lally, and had the French power in India been supported by their own country, they might have kept the ascendency they had acquired and for some time held, and they might have expelled the English from the country. But France failed to support her cause in India, and censured and punished, even with imprisonment and death, the distinguished men who had done their utmost to support her cause and extend her power, while England supported her cause with great vigor, supplying money, men, and all the materials of war, and rewarding those who distinguished themselves in her service (as Clive, Hastings, Cornwallis, and others), with wealth and honors. And the consequences of this different course of policy were, the French were expelled, their power annihilated, and India has long been included in the foreign possessions of England.

In view of this whole subject, we cannot but feel some satisfaction in looking at the result. Had the French succeeded in their object of becoming the controlling power of India, there is reason to believe they would have pursued a course of conquest in ways and by means at least as unscrupulous as the English have used. The French have never succeeded so well as the English in governing their foreign possessions, and there is reason to believe that the state of India has been better under the government of England than it would have been under the government of France. Had France become the governing power of India, the religion of the European population in it would have been Roman Catholic, and if we may judge from the French policy in their foreign possessions, no other form of religion would be tolerated; or if tolerated, they would allow no means to be used for propagating any other form of Christianity, and so all the inhabitants would be shut up to receive the Roman Catholic faith, or to continue in their present religious state of ignorance, superstition, bigotry, and idolatry. There is reason, therefore, in contemplating the present religious state and prospects of India, for thankfulness to Him who rules among the nations, and disposes of countries and kingdoms according to his pleasure, that this country with its vast population has come under the government of England, rather than of France or any other European nation.

The overthrow of the French power in the Carnatic, left the English in the possession of paramount influence in that part of India. The Nabob was the generally acknowledged sovereign of the country, but he owed his elevation to the English, and he had no means of successfully resisting any demands which they might make upon him. Previous to the taking of Pondicherry, he had offered to pay certain sums towards the expenses of the war, if certain advantages in return were conceded to him, and he pretended to believe that his offers had been accepted. But it was not so understood by the English. After much negotiation, and after being assisted by them in exacting large sums of money from some native princes in his territories, he engaged to pay them 50 lacks of rupees, ($2,500,000). But the English wanted something besides money for expenses already incurred. It was important in their view to reduce his power of troubling them in future, and they wanted the means of supporting a much larger military force than they now had. So they demanded, and he was compelled to cede to them 4 districts. The governor of Madura had paid no tribute for several years, and in the distracted state of the country, was gradually acquiring independence. On his refusing to pay the amount demanded of him, the Nabob and the English united their forces in attacking him. He defended his territory and fortress with great ability, and the war unexpectedly cost a great amount of treasure and of life. And at last it was only by treachery that they obtained possession of his person and terminated the struggle.

The war between the English and the French closed in India with the surrender of Pondicherry, but it was some time before it ceased between France and England. In the treaty of peace between the two nations in 1763, it was agreed that each nation should restore to the other the possessions acquired in India during the war, while France renounced all right to any conquests she had made there in the war. So by this treaty France recovered some of her former possessions on the Coromandel Coast, but these were small when compared with those which remained in the possession of England.

But the Carnatic was not to enjoy any long repose. In 1761, Nizam Ali found means to imprison his brother Sulabat Jung, then Subadar of the Deckan, and assumed the office and dignity. After keeping his brother in prison for 2 years, he caused him to be put to death. In 1765, he collected a large army and marching into the Carnatic, plundered and laid waste the country. The Nabob and the English united their forces and proceeded to meet him. But he had no wish to risk an engagement, and so retreated hastily into the Deckan. This invasion and the means by which Nizam Ali had acquired his power, clearly showed his character, and were calculated to make the English watchful about his future course. Just at that time Lord Clive called at Madras on his way from England to Bengal. On learning the state of affairs at Madras and in the provinces which then constituted the Madras presidency, he resolved to use the emperor of Delhi, then in a state of dependence upon the English, to increase their power and territory. So he obtained two firmans from the emperor, one ceding the provinces called the Northern Circars to the English, and the other appointing Mohammed Ali to be Nabob of the Carnatic. The English proceeded to take possession of the newly acquired provinces. Nizam Ali was greatly offended at these proceedings, and declaring that the Northern Circars were a part of his own territory, and that the Nabob owed fealty to him and not to the emperor, he began to make great preparations to attack the Nabob and the English. The governor and council at Madras were alarmed at the prospect of such a war in the exhausted state of their treasury, and opened negotiations with Nizam Ali. A treaty of peace was made, in which the English engaged to pay a large annual tribute to the Subadar for the Circars, and to assist him with troops in the event of a war. This treaty was severely censured by the Court of Directors, especially the engagement to assist the Subadar, as this was likely to involve them with other native powers. And it was when assisting the

Subadar, in accordance with this treaty, that the English first came in conflict with Hyder Ali, the most powerful enemy they ever encountered in their wars in India.

Hyder Ali, who acquired so much notoriety in the history of India, was descended from ancestors who came from the northern provinces, and settled in Mysore. He passed his youth in destitute circumstances, and having enjoyed no advantages of education he was never able to read or to write. On entering the army at the age of 27, he soon distinguished himself in various ways, and became the captain of an organized company of freebooters, who were authorized to rob and plunder in any provinces of the enemy upon condition of paying to their prince, a certain part of what they realized. In this way he became rich, and acquired a high character for the daring valor and ability with which he managed and achieved whatever he undertook. Such qualities in the armies of India soon attract attention, and when animated by an ambitious and aspiring spirit, secure rapid promotion. In a few years Hyder had the command of 10,000 men, and stood high in the confidence of the Raja of Mysore. It became evident that he was determined to acquire as much influence, rank, and power as he could, and that he would have no scruples in respect to using any means for accomplishing his purpose. At that time the Raja of Mysore was young and effeminate, and the affairs of the kingdom were managed by two brothers, Devraj and Nundraj. The former soon died, and the latter being profligate and unpopular, Hyder managed to obtain the command of the army. By a long course of intrigue, duplicity, treachery, and treason, such as compose a large part of the history of eastern courts and princes, Hyder became the sovereign of Mysore, only allowing to the Raja an annual sum for his personal and family expenses.

The ambitious and restless spirit of Hyder could not long remain quiet, and he soon began to enlarge his dominions by conquest, and replenish his treasury with plunder. In Bednore, the plunder he obtained, was estimated at £12,000,000, or nearly $60,000,000. The Mahrattas, then the terror of all India, made a sudden invasion into Mysore, defeated Hyder, and could only be turned back by a cession of territory, and the payment of a large sum of money. Still Hyder continued his attacks on the

19 *

princes around Mysore. Among these was the Zamorin of Calicut, so distinguished in the early wars of the Portuguese in India. This prince, rather than endure the disgrace and sufferings that awaited him from Hyder, set fire to his house and perished in the flames.

The ambitious spirit of Hyder and the success of his plans, excited the larger powers of southern India, and a confederacy of the Mahrattas, the Nizam, and the English was formed against him. The Mahrattas arrived on the confines of Mysore two months before the other confederates. Hyder endeavored to prevent their further advance "by causing all the grain to be buried, the wells to be poisoned, the forage to be consumed, and the cattle to be driven away." These means did not prevent their progress, and finding they would soon penetrate the heart of his dominions, he resolved if possible to separate them from the confederacy, and sent a messenger to negotiate a treaty. In this attempt he was successful, and the Mahrattas agreed, for a certain sum of money ($6,750,000), to return to the Deckan. In the mean time the Nizam and the English force under Col. Smith, had entered Mysore. It was soon apparent that the Nizam was not cordial in his feelings towards the English, and some events which occurred about this time increased his disaffection. Hyder becoming aware of the feelings of the Nizam, commenced a secret correspondence with him which soon resulted in a treaty of union against the English. The Nizam, when remonstrated with for such conduct, consented to Colonel Smith's quietly retreating towards Madras before he should be molested. The forces of the Nizam and Hyder, when united to attack the retreating English, consisted of 43,000 horse and 28,000 foot, while Colonel Smith had only 6,000 infantry and 1,000 cavalry. They had also the advantage of an accurate knowledge of the country, and of the coöperation of the inhabitants for want of which Colonel Smith suffered much. Still he was able to repel all their attacks, and to their astonishment he found means to sustain his force and continue his retreat, notwithstanding all their efforts to reduce him to straits and compel him to surrender. The Nizam seeing this unexpected state of affairs, and hearing that his own dominions were invaded by an English force from Bengal, entered into a treaty with the English and withdrew to his own territory. The hostile parties now were the English and Hyder, and the war was prosecuted with vigor on both sides, the English generally acting on the defensive for 2 years, when "a treaty was concluded in April, 1769, on the condition of placing the possessions of both parties with scarcely an exception on the same footing as before the war." This confederacy of the English with the Mahrattas and the Nizam against Hyder cost a great amount of treasure and life for which they gained nothing, while Hyder was left at the close of the war more powerful than he was when it commenced.

One reason which induced Hyder to desire peace with the English, was some apprehension of another invasion by the Mahrattas. Nor was this apprehension without cause, for they soon entered his dominions in much larger force than before, and under able commanders. Hyder's efforts to impede their progress and to resist them in the open field proved unavailing, and they proceeded to besiege his capital, Seringapatam. But the Mahrattas had not skill sufficient for such a strong fortress, and soon became weary of carrying it on. Hyder was gradually collecting his strength against them, and at length after gaining some advantages over them, he offered such terms of peace that the Mahrattas were glad to accept them and return to their own country. Hyder thus relieved, continued to enlarge his dominions by subduing and plundering the petty native princes with the usual barbarity and cruelty of Indian warfare. The manner in which the fort of Chittledroog was defended, shows the fearful and debasing superstition of the Hindus. On the highest part of the fort they had erected a temple to Karlee or Doorga, the Hindu goddess of destruction, and they believed that so long as the goddess was propitiated, the place could not be taken. At fixed times the goddess was worshipped with solemn rites (that is, these rites were performed before her image), and then a bugle was blown and the garrison rushed forth, shouting the names of the goddess to procure human heads to be suspended before her image, and thus propitiate her. These attacks were made with so much fury, frenzy, and success, that if such bloody offerings could have preserved the place, it would have been secure. When this fort was taken, 2,000 human heads, all which had been offered to Karlee, were piled up before her temple.

Hyder was now advanced in years, supposed to be nearly 80. He had long been intemperate in his habits, and as might be expected, had become capricious, irritable, and self-willed. He had for some years been becoming more prejudiced towards the English, and had endeavored to form a treaty with the Mahrattas to expel the hated foreigners from India. The war between England and France, consequent upon the war between the North American colonies (now the United States) and England having commenced, the English proceeded at once to take all the French possessions in India. This gave offence to Hyder, who was inclined to the French interests. It was at this time that Schwartz, the Danish missionary, was sent by the governor and council of Madras, on a mission to Seringapatam. Hyder, who was previously acquainted with his character, received him kindly, and on his return intrusted to him a letter containing a list of the wrongs he had suffered from the English, and added, "I have not yet taken my revenge." In June, 1780, Hyder mustered his forces at Seringapatam, consisting of 23,000 horse, 53,000 foot of various kinds, 2,000 rocketmen, 5,000 pioneers, and about 400 Europeans. He caused prayers to be offered in all the mosques, and religious ceremonies in all the Hindu temples, for the success of his expedition. He then proceeded into the Carnatic, plundered the inhabitants and laid waste the country.* This attack found the Madras government quite unpre-

* The following is Mr. Burke's graphic description of this invasion, and gives a striking view of the barbarities of wars in India, when carried on by the native princes.

"When at length Hyder found that he had to do with men who would sign no convention, whom no treaty and no signature could bind, and who were the determined enemies of human intercourse itself, he determined to make the country possessed by these incorrigible and predestined criminals a memorable example to mankind. He resolved, in the gloomy recesses of a mind capable of such things, to leave the whole Carnatic an everlasting monument of vengeance, and to put perpetual desolation as a barrier between him and those against whom the faith which holds the moral elements of the world together, was no protection. He became at length so confident of his force and so collected in his might, that he made no secret whatever of his dreadful resolution. Having terminated his disputes with every enemy and every rival, who buried their mutual animosities in their common hatred against the creditors of the Nabob of Arcot, he drew from every quarter whatever a savage ferocity could add to his new rudiments in the art of destruction, and compounding all the materials

pared. Embarrassed for want of money and distracted in council, they made no well-arranged and effectual resistance to Hyder's career of conquest and devastation, till Sir Eyre Coote arrived from Bengal with considerable force and treasure, to take the command. No officer then in India enjoyed so high a reputation, or had so much experience of Indian warfare, as Sir Eyre Coote, and his presence and arrangements soon inspired the army with new courage. Hyder was soon compelled to raise the siege of several places. As the country had been laid waste, the English suffered much for want of provisions, and also for means to remove their military stores, etc., with them. After much desultory and harassing warfare, Sir Eyre Coote defeated Hyder in two or three partial engagements, and the war began to assume a less discouraging aspect. But there were other difficulties besides the war. The depredations of Hyder, and the large military forces spread over the Carnatic, had destroyed or consumed the crops, and a severe famine in several provinces was the consequence. In no place was this famine so dreadful as at Madras, where many thousands died

of fury, havoc, and desolation into one black cloud, he hung for a while on the declivities of the mountains. While the authors of all these evils were idly and stupidly gazing on this menacing meteor, which blackened all their horizon, it suddenly burst and poured down the whole of its contents upon the plains of the Carnatic. Then ensued a scene of woe the like of which no eye had seen, no heart conceived, and which no tongue can adequately describe. All the horrors of war before known or heard of, were mercy compared with this new havoc. A storm of universal fire blasted every field, consumed every house, and destroyed every temple. The miserable inhabitants, flying from the flaming villages, in part were slaughtered; others without regard to sex or age, to the respect of rank or the sacredness of function, parents torn from children, and husbands from their wives enveloped in a whirlwind of cavalry, amid the goading spears of drivers and the trampling of pursuing horses, were swept into captivity in an unknown and hostile land. Those who were able to evade this tempest, fled to the walled cities; but escaping from fire, sword, and exile, they fell into the jaws of famine. For 18 months without intermission this destruction raged from the gates of Madras to the walls of Tanjore. And so completely did these masters in their art, Hyder and his ferocious son, absolve themselves from their impious vow that when the British armies traversed as they did the Carnatic, for hundreds of miles in all directions through the whole line of their march, they did not see a man, or a woman, or a child, or a four-footed beast of any description. One dead universal silence reigned over the whole region."

of starvation. Sir Eyre Coote now became too feeble to superintend the affairs and direct the operations of the army, and returned to Calcutta. This was a severe stroke to the English, but its force was somewhat mitigated by the death of Hyder. The death of the heads of both parties suspended active operations for some time. Hyder's son Tippoo, who had already distinguished himself for his military talents, succeeded his father and urged on the war with vigor. The government of Bombay attacked the dominions of Tippoo on the Malabar Coast, with so much vigor and success that he withdrew from the Carnatic to the western provinces, where his presence was more needed. The war between England and France still continued, and a French fleet more than once left a considerable force on the coast which joined the army of Tippoo. These greatly strengthened him and discouraged the English, when to their great joy they heard that peace had been made between France and England. Negotiations were opened with Tippoo, but peace was not obtained for more than a year, and then "it was on the general condition of a mutual restitution of conquests."

Tippoo, often called in the history of India Tippoo Sultan, was ambitious, intriguing, superstitious, and cruel. Hyder professed the Mohammedan faith, as his forefathers for many generations had done, but he was tolerant towards Christians and Hindus, and not disposed to molest them while quietly following their own religion. Tippoo was as earnest and as unscrupulous in propagating the faith of Mohammed, as he was in enlarging his dominions. In the western provinces of his dominions were many Roman Catholics, who had been converted from heathenism by the Portuguese and other Romish missionaries. He collected these together to the number of 60,000,* compelled them to be circumcised, and then distributed them in his army and his garrisons. In the province of Coorg, he compelled 70,000 Hindus to submit to the same rite, and profess the faith of Mohammed.

Tippoo's restless spirit and growing power soon attracted the attention of the Mahrattas, who formed an alliance with the Nizam, and uniting their forces, they invaded his dominions.

* Abbe Dubois, who was then in Mysore.

But they found a far more formidable enemy than they expected, and after suffering some reverses, they made peace with him, and returned to their own territories. The successful issue of this war greatly increased the fame of Tippoo. He was now at liberty to extend his dominions, and to propagate the Mohammedan faith. His father had conquered the country lying between the Ghat mountains and the sea, and Tippoo now resolved to convert the inhabitants to his own religion, declaring that "they were all born in adultery, and more shameless in their connections than the beasts of the forests." They, on the other hand, had a great abhorrence of the Mohammedan religion, and many of them fled from their country rather than submit to circumcision and eat beef. He carried on this war of proselytism till he boasted that he had destroyed 3,000 temples with all their idols. In extending his dominions, he made an attack upon the kingdom of Travancore, which was in the extreme southern part of the peninsula. The ruler of this province had some time before entered into a treaty, offensive and defensive, with the English, and by this attack, Tippoo incurred their displeasure. In his first attack upon the fortified posts of Travancore, Tippoo was repulsed with great loss. He was near being taken prisoner, and lost his weapons, seals, etc. Chagrined at being thus repulsed by an enemy he despised, Tippoo was greatly enraged, and collecting all his forces, prosecuted the war with great vigor and barbarity, and soon overrun the whole province.

The Marquis Cornwallis, at this time the governor-general of India, on hearing of this attack of Tippoo upon Travancore, resolved to commence hostilities as soon as possible, and with this view he formed an alliance with the Nizam and the Mahrattas against the Sultan. The command of the English force was intrusted to General Medows. The campaign was commenced in June, 1790. Dindigul, Paulgaut, and several other forts were taken, and the English force penetrated far into Mysore, but the disasters and reverses, originating chiefly in the severity of the monsoon and in ignorance of the country, soon compelled them to retreat with much loss. In the mean time, Tippoo, with a large body of cavalry, invaded the Carnatic, laying waste the country, or levying extreme contributions upon the inhabitants. He also proceeded to Pondicherry, and attempted to form an alliance with the French. The governor-general, becoming dissatisfied with the manner in which the war was carried on, resolved to take the command himself. He arrived at Madras early in 1791, and having made the requisite arrangements proceeded by rapid marches to Bangalore, which was strongly fortified and contained the Sultan's harem and treasury. These Tippoo found means to remove before the English could invest the place. The governor-general, having taken Bangalore, resolved to proceed with as little delay as possible to attack Seringapatam, the Sultan's capital. When the English force reached Seringapatam, Tippoo, who had in vain endeavored to arrest their progress, resolved to hazard a general battle. The English were victorious, but the country around having been laid waste and all means of support destroyed or removed, they were soon in so great want of provisions and in such a sickly state, that Cornwallis was compelled to retreat to Bangalore, leaving behind him much of his baggage and the battering train which he had prepared to besiege Seringapatam.

Cornwallis remained at Bangalore for some time, making arrangements again to proceed to Seringapatam. All the resources of the English power in all parts of India, were now brought into requisition. The Nizam's force of 15,000 cavalry, and Purseram Bhow with a yet larger force of Mahrattas had arrived, but all these were so deficient in weapons and discipline that they added but little to the strength of the army. When the preparations for proceeding to Seringapatam were completed, the force under the command of Cornwallis amounted to 30,000. If to these the forces of the Nizam and of the Mahrattas are added, the invading army will appear to be large. On arriving in sight of Seringapatam the army of Tippoo, estimated at 45,000 infantry and 5,000 cavalry, was seen encamped near it. Arrangements were made to attack this force in the night. The loss of Tippoo was great, and the state of his capital and the position of the English force soon became such that he earnestly sued for peace. After some days of negotiation a treaty was made in which Tippoo agreed to cede about half of his dominions, to pay a large sum of money ($16,500,000), and deliver up two of his sons as hostages. The conditions of this treaty were fulfilled on the part of the Sultan in due time, and his sons returned to him. For several years he was engaged chiefly in attending to the internal affairs of his own kingdom, a longer period of peace than had been known in the peninsula for a long time.

In 1798, the Earl of Mornington, subsequently the Marquis of Wellesley, became governor-general of India. He was instructed, when appointed to this responsible situation, "not to engage if possible in hostilities with any native power, and yet he waged deadly war with every one of them." Soon after reaching India, he learned that Tippoo had negotiated a treaty with the governor of Mauritius, in which it was stipulated that a large French force should be sent to India to assist Tippoo in regaining his lost dominions. As Tippoo was deceived by a French adventurer who induced him to send an embassy to Mauritius, and the governor had no authority to make any such treaty, nor power to carry it into effect, the whole affair showed the disposition of Tippoo more than any cause of danger to the English power in India. But the governor-general regarded this conduct as "a public, unqualified, and unambiguous declaration of war," and his decided opinion was, that "an immediate attack should be made upon Tippoo Sultan." It was also believed, if not fully proved, that Tippoo had endeavored to excite the Mahrattas and the Nizam against the English, and that he had also sent an embassy to Zeman Shah, the ruler of Cabul, then contemplating an invasion of India. In these circumstances, the governor-general resolved to deprive Tippoo of those means and resources which made him so formidable an enemy to the English power in India. Some correspondence of a peculiar character and with mutually unsatisfactory results, was carried on for a while between the governor-general and the Sultan. In the mean time a large force under General Harris, was prepared at Madras to proceed to Mysore, and there coöperate with another force from Bombay under General Stuart. The Sultan fully aware of the force and plans of his enemies, endeavored first to encounter the army on the way from Bombay, and a severe battle was fought in which he claimed the victory, though his loss was much greater than that of the English.

The main army (the force from Madras) reached Seringapatam in April of 1799. For some time the Sultan had been discouraged,* and having been disappointed by several movements of the English force, he at last resolved to take refuge in the city and defend it to the last extremity. The siege was urged forward with all possible vigor, and all attempts at negotiation having failed, the place was attacked on the 4th of May, and the English became masters, though not without suffering severe loss and committing dreadful carnage of the Mysore troops and inhabitants. The Sultan's body was found among the slain, and all his family were made prisoners. The treasures of the Sultan, amounting to nearly $5,000,000, became the prize of the conquerors.

With the fall of Seringapatam all resistance ceased, and the war closed. The English took possession of the kingdom, gave pensions to the members of the royal family, allotted some districts to the Mahrattas and to the Nizam, took the sea-coasts and some other districts for themselves, and placed a descendant of the original Hindu sovereigns over several internal districts under the title of the Raja of Mysore. This descendant was a child only 5 years old, and as the English retained all the essential powers of government in their own hands, he and his party had little but the name and pageantry of rank and dignity. Still the change from the state of poverty in which the family had lived for some years to the honor conferred upon them, was great, and conciliated the native population to other important changes now to be introduced. The war with Tippoo was the last great struggle of the English for ascendency in the southern part of the peninsula. The remaining native princes had not sufficient power to make much resistance, if disposed, and they generally submitted to such terms as were dictated to them.

The Nizam became now more than ever fearful of the power of the Mahrattas, and a treaty was made between him and the governor-general, in which he ceded to the English all the territory which he had lately acquired from the Mysore kingdom,

* "He assembled his principal officers in council, and closed his address, saying, 'We have arrived at our last stage, what is your determination?' 'To die along with you,' was the universal reply. All were deeply affected, and some could not refrain from weeping."

yielding $3,000,000 annually, and they in return engaged to support a certain specified force in his dominions, and to defend him from all aggressions from the Mahrattas or others. This subsidiary force the English were at liberty to use as they might have occasion in the event of any war. In such case he also bound himself to assist them with his own troops.

HISTORY OF BOMBAY TILL 1800.

In 1662, Charles II. married the Infanta Catharine of Portugal, and obtained the island of Bombay as part of her dowry. The king of England claimed Salsette as a dependency of Bombay, but the king of Portugal refused to allow the claims. In 1668, Charles ceded Bombay to the East India Company, and they soon removed their chief agency on the western coast of India from Surat to Bombay. The island was easily defended, and its excellent harbor made it important as a naval station. It was once besieged by the admiral of the Mogul fleet, but the island has never been taken by any hostile power since it first became an English possession. Salsette and Bassein continued in the possession of the Portuguese till 1739, when they were taken by the Mahrattas, who had possession of the coast opposite to Bombay for several hundred miles. This native power first became prominent in the history of India in the reign of Aurungzeb. When the Mogul empire fell into a state of anarchy on the death of this emperor, the Mahrattas, who for some years had been struggling for independence, commenced an aggressive warfare on all sides, and soon became the most formidable native power in India. For half a century they were united in one government under Sevajee, their first prince and his descendants. They then separated under different chiefs, who divided the original and acquired territories among them. Each of these chiefs was independent in the affairs of his own territory, and made war and peace with those around him as he pleased. But they still continued united under one nominal head, and though often at war among themselves yet like the Greek republics of old, they were ready to join their forces as often as there was any occasion for doing so against a common enemy.

One of these Mahratta chiefs, Conajee Angria, had possession of the Concan, the territory between the Ghats and the sea south from Bombay, and had nominally the rank of admiral. As his situation was unfavorable for carrying on any aggressive warfare on land, he commenced plundering such ships as he could seize. He had a fleet of ships built for this purpose, and he plundered the vessels of all nations without distinction. These ships, if attacked by any force too powerful for them, would run into some of the creeks or harbors on the coast, where they were protected by his forts. He took several vessels with rich cargoes, and became so powerful that in 1754, he took and plundered a squadron of 3 Dutch ships, one of 50 guns, one of 36 guns, and one of 18 guns. Such depredations could no longer be endured, and the government of Bombay resolved to put a stop to them. Conajee Angria was at this time at variance with the other Mahratta powers, and so when Commodore James proceeded to blockade his forts by sea, a Mahratta force proceeded from the Deckan to besiege them by land, and in this way 2 or 3 of his forts were reduced. The next year Admiral Watson and Colonel Clive, (afterwards Lord Clive,) having arrived at Bombay, a more powerful expedition proceeded against Conajee Angria. Admiral Watson took command of the ships, and Colonel Clive of the land forces. They succeeded in taking Gheriah, his principal fort, with a large amount of treasure, naval and military stores, and other property of various kinds. This property, which was of great value, became prize-money and was divided among the captors.

The aggressive warfare carried on by the different Mahratta chiefs upon all the native powers not belonging to their confederacy, greatly enlarged their dominions. In 1760, the revenue paid by the people, was estimated at $45,000,000, though it was supposed that not more than $35,000,000 entered the treasury so as to be available for any of the purposes of the government. Their army, collected at the great and disastrous battle of Panniput, consisted of 55,000 cavalry in regular pay, 15,000 irregular horse, 15,000 infantry, and an efficient body of artillery with 200 guns. Their revenue, their army, and their military character, made them the first native power in India.

In 1772, Madu Row, the Peishwa and nominal head of the Mahratta empire, died without leaving any issue, and he was succeeded by Narayan Row, a younger brother, who was soon after assassinated. After his death, two parties contended for the succession. Ragoba, who was uncle to the late Peishwa, and one of the claimants to be the acknowledged head of the Mahratta empire, made application to the government of Bombay for assistance. The Court of Directors had long been anxious to obtain the islands of Salsette and Bassein, and had instructed their governor in Bombay to obtain them in any lawful and proper way. The government of Bombay, now made a treaty with Ragoba, who ceded Salsette, Bassein, and some possessions of the Mahrattas in Gujerat to the English, in consideration of receiving certain assistance to enable him to obtain the office of Peishwa. And having heard that the Portuguese government in Goa was preparing to make an effort for recovering these islands, the government of Bombay at once took possession of them. The governor-general and supreme council in Bengal now interfered, and expressing their strong disapprobation of the proceedings of the government of Bombay, sent an embassy from Calcutta to Poona. And soon after this, despatches from the Court of Directors were received by the Bombay government, in which they approved of the treaty made with Ragoba. It was finally compromised that the English should retain Salsette, and the Mahrattas should have Bassein.

But this peace was of short duration. Neither the government of Bombay, nor of Calcutta, nor the Court of Directors, were satisfied with the terms on which matters had been adjusted. The state of parties among the Mahrattas was continually changing, and a man named St. Lubin having arrived at Poona in the pretended character of an ambassador from France, great anxiety began to be felt by the English, on account of supposed French influence among the Mahrattas. These circumstances soon led to a renewal of hostilities, and it was resolved that a force should proceed from Bengal to Poona, there to meet one which was to proceed from Bombay. The force from Bombay amounting to about 4,000 men, proceeded into the Deckan, and on reaching Tullagaum, 18 miles from Poona, they found an army of 50,000 men to oppose their further progress. Some skirmishing took place, and the English feeling unable to contend with such a force, formed the purpose to return to Bombay. No sooner had they commenced their retreat, than furious attacks were made upon their rear, and 300 men and 15 English officers were soon killed. They had now no resource but negotiation, which resulted in an agreement called the Convention of Wurgaum, and they were permitted to return quietly to Bombay, thus terminating the most unhappy expedition hitherto in the history of British India.

The army which was proceeding from Bengal into the Deckan under Gen. Goddard, met with some unexpected difficulties and delays, and on hearing that the force which was to proceed from Bombay to coöperate with them had returned back, Gen. Goddard proceeded into Gujerat. Here he took Ahmedabad and several other large places, and surprised and routed the united forces of Scindia and Holkar, two Mahratta chiefs. He then proceeded to lay siege to Bassein, which surrendered before the close of the year. Hostilities having commenced between Hyder Ali and the English in the southern part of India, it became important to bring the war with the Mahrattas to a close as soon as possible. In these circumstances, General Goddard resolved to proceed into the Deckan with his army. He marched as far as the Bhore Ghat, about 50 miles east from Bombay, but finding greater difficulties and more discouraging circumstances than he expected, he returned to Bombay, though not without suffering considerable loss from attacks on his rear. But in some other parts of the Mahratta country, the English were eminently successful. Major Popham, with a force of 2,400, proceeded from Bengal into the territory of Scindia, and took the fort of Lahar after a severe struggle. He then resolved upon the yet more adventurous enterprise of attempting to take Gwalior, one of the strongest forts in India. This fort is erected on the top of a mountain of rock, and is supposed to be inaccessible on all sides. It had always been regarded in wars among the native powers as impregnable, and at this time it had a garrison of 1,000 men. Major Popham, after carefully inspecting the fort, resolved to make an attempt to seize it by escalade. The attempt was made in the night on a part where no danger was apprehended. The garrison surrendered with but little resistance, and in the morning the English flag was waving over the fort. The daring nature and success of this attack produced a deep impression upon the native mind. It was thought best to follow up the success, and accordingly General Carnac proceeded with a yet larger force into the dominions of Scindia, where he was joined by Major Popham. General Carnac suffered much for want of provisions, and was obliged to retire from Seronge, but near Mehidpoor he made an attack on the army of Scindia, and dispersed them with great loss of troops and baggage. These victories produced a state of feeling favorable to peace on the part of the Mahrattas, and the English were also desirous of it, as all their resources were required for the war with Hyder Ali. After much negotiation with the different Mahratta chiefs, a general peace with all the confederacy was made, which is generally known in Indian history as the treaty of Salbye. By this treaty, Ragoba renounced all claim to the dignity of Peishwa; he was to receive from the Mahratta government a fixed sum annually for his support, and was allowed to choose his own place of residence.

HISTORY OF INDIA FROM 1800–1850.

At the commencement of the present century, the British power had become paramount in India. In the southern part of the peninsula were several native princes more or less independent, but no one of them, and no combination that could be formed among them, would be equal in power and resources to the English government in Madras. In the Deckan, and Central India, were two of the largest remaining native powers, namely, the Nizam, and the Mahrattas. And the former of these, whose capital was Hyderabad, had entered into a treaty with the English, by which he ceded to them territory (all he had obtained in the partition of the kingdom of Mysore), yielding $3,000,000 annually, and they in return engaged to support a large subsidiary force * in his dominions, and "to defend them from every aggression." By the same treaty he had also engaged "neither to make war, nor so much as to negotiate by his own

* Such subsidiary forces consisted partly of Europeans and partly of native troops, but all were under the control of European officers, and the whole force was to be under the control of the English government, or of their agents in the native government where this force was stationed.

authority, but to refer all disputes between himself and other States to the English, and be guided by their decision; also to allow the subsidiary force in his service, to be employed by them in all their wars, and in such cases to increase the subsidiary force by 6,000 horse, and 9,000 foot from his own army. But it was stipulated that "the Nizam was to remain absolute in respect to his own family and subjects, and the English were on no pretext to disturb his authority." All the superior officers also of his own army were to be English, and were to be approved by their Resident or minister at his court. It must be obvious that, however oppressive such a government might be to its own subjects, it was never likely to endanger the stability of the British power in the country. A part of the kingdom of Mysore was offered to the Mahrattas upon condition of their entering into a similar treaty for a subsidiary force to be supported in a similar manner and for similar purposes in their territory. But the offer of such a force was not accepted. The Peishwa, the nominal head of this confederacy, lived at Poona, 100 miles from Bombay, and so Poona was generally regarded as the capital of the Mahratta empire. But the different chiefs had each his own capital. Ragojee Bhonsla had Nagpore, Scindia had Gwalior, Holkar had Indore, and Damojee Guickwar had Baroda, for their respective capitals. These chiefs were often at variance, and sometimes in open war with each other, while each of them made war and peace with other powers, and governed his own territory and extended his own dominion as he pleased. Confederated and yet separated as they were, their political importance and influence were less in the general affairs of India than the same population, territory, and revenue would have been under one united and consolidated government.

The titular emperor of Delhi had become a dependant upon Scindia, one of the Mahratta chiefs, and he lived in the palace and capital of his illustrious ancestors, more like a prisoner than like an Indian prince. Scindia made all the use of having a nominal emperor of Hindustan in his power, which he possibly could for his own aggrandizement. In the central and northern parts of India were several States and princes, as the Rajpoots, the Jats, the Sikhs, the Scindeans, etc. Of these princes, some were in alliance with the English and tributary to them; some were tributary to the Mahratta chiefs, and some had preserved or acquired their independence. No one of these, Scindia perhaps excepted, was looked on as sufficiently powerful to involve the country in war, were they so disposed, nor had any one of them the means of long resisting the power of the English, should they become involved in war with them.

The city of Surat was the great emporium of foreign commerce in India, when Europeans discovered the passage round the Cape of Good Hope. It was the seat of important and extensive manufactures, and the capital of a populous, commercial, and manufacturing country. It was easy of communication with Arabia and Persia, and shared largely in the trade of India with Europe and the western countries of Asia through the Red Sea and the Persian Gulf. The population was estimated in 1790 at 800,000, but probably this estimate was too large. It was also the port from which Mohammedans generally embarked on their pilgrimage to Mecca, and so it was regarded on this account as a place of great importance. One of the earliest and largest trading factories of the East India Company was established in this city, and several agreements and treaties, varying according to circumstances and exigencies, had been made with the Nabob. This prince was originally a deputy of the emperor of Delhi, but the office had become hereditary, and its powers were often exercised, in the distracted state of the empire, with little reference or respect to the emperor's wishes. The relations between the English and the Nabob had long been in an unsatisfactory state. Frequent attempts had been made to define and adjust them, but with little success. Early in 1800, the governor-general transmitted to the governor of Bombay, the form of an agreement or treaty to be carried into effect with the Nabob. This agreement the Nabob for some time refused, but at length seeing the English preparing to carry it into effect by force, he signed it, and thus "resigned his government, civil and military, with all its emoluments, powers, and privileges, to the East India Company, and the Company agreed to pay to the Nabob and his heirs one lack of rupees ($50,000) annually, etc." By this transaction, which is styled in the History of British India, "the Nabob of Surat deposed," Surat was added to the English possessions.

Mention has often been made of the Raja of Tanjore in the Carnatic. This was one of the Hindu States, which though tributary to the Nabob of the Carnatic, and a party in some of the treaties between this prince and the English, yet preserved much of its independence under its Hindu sovereigns. In 1786, Toolajee, the Raja of Tanjore, died, and was succeeded by his son Ameer Sing. This prince, at different times, caused much uneasiness and anxiety to the Madras government. In 1798, the claims of another son, Surfojee, were brought forward. The English espoused his cause and removed Ameer Sing from the throne. But Surfojee, who was entirely dependent on the English, instead of succeeding to the power and dignity of Raja, signed an agreement by which he resigned all the powers of government to the English, and in return was to receive an annual pension for the support of himself and family. The same historian, describing this transaction, styles it, "the Raja of Tanjore deposed."

More than half a century had passed since the first treaty was made between the English and the Nabob of the Carnatic. During this period, 4 or 5 Nabobs in succession had filled the office. Several treaties or agreements, varying with the circumstances and exigencies of the parties, had been made at different times. Each party had often complained of the other, but dissatisfaction appears never to have proceeded to open hostilities. In pursuing the course of policy towards the native governments which the governor-general had adopted, the state of this prince and his relations came under consideration. The relations between him and the English had long been in many respects very unsatisfactory, and all attempts to remodel and readjust them had failed. The territory subject to the Nabob, was badly governed, and there appeared no reason to look for any reform in his administration. He was incumbered with debts, and there appeared to be no reasons for expecting any improvement in his finances. The governor-general resolved to effect a transfer of all the rights and powers of government, civil and military, to the English, reserving or allowing to the Nabob, what might appear to be necessary to support him and his family in becoming style and dignity. Omdut ul Omrah, who was then Nabob, was sick, and not expected long to survive; so it was thought expedient to defer the "dethronement" till after his decease. He died in July, 1801. As his son, Ali Hoosun, who was appointed in the will of the late Nabob to succeed him, refused to sign the treaty prescribed to him by the governor-general, Azeem ul Dowla, a nephew of the late Nabob was selected, and on his promising to sign the treaty which had been prepared, he was acknowledged by the English to be the Nabob, and installed into the office in the usual manner. From this time this office became a mere pageant, as the Nabob, by the treaty then signed, delivered over all the powers of government in perpetuity to the English, and totally and forever renounced them for himself and his family. This treaty between him and the English was just what the latter wished it to be. The allowance or pensions given to him and his family from the revenues of the territories he thus ceded away, were liberal, and have been continued. Ali Hoosun and his friends protested against these proceedings, and transmitted a memorial concerning them to England, but they obtained no redress. The historian before referred to, describes these proceedings under the title of "the Nabob of Arcot deposed."

No native power had given the English more trouble than their ally, the Nabob of Oude. Treaties and agreements with him had been made and changed, till the parties could not agree what had been annulled and superseded, and what continued to be still in force, while all were dissatisfied with the state of matters as they were. Negotiations were commenced and attempts at definition and explanation were made, and all these were carried on for a long time in the hope of bringing the relations between the English and the Nabob into a more satisfactory state. But in these negotiations little progress was made, and there was but little prospect of any mutually satisfactory result. At length the governor-general proposed or more properly *dictated* a treaty, and prepared at once to enforce it with such a power that any effectual resistance on the part of the Nabob was impossible, and any further delay or reluctance would be unavailing. So this treaty was signed by the Nabob, and by it he ceded to the English more than half his territory, relinquishing in their favor all right and control over it. The revenue of this ceded territory was nearly $7,000,000 annually. The Nabob also engaged to govern his remaining territory in such a manner, or according to such regulations and counsels and to produce such results, as would give the English discretionary authority or permission to interfere in his administration at any time they might think it expedient to do so.

Nearly west from Oude was the province of Furruckabad. The government of this province was at this time in the hands of a regent, the Nabob having died some time before, and his son and heir being yet a minor, the affairs of this province had become somewhat complicated with the State of Oude, and there had also for some years been a treaty of alliance with the English. These matters in connection with the affairs of Oude, and in carrying out the policy of the governor-general, now came under consideration, and as the young Nabob was just becoming of age it was a favorable time for introducing any change. To the governor-general it appeared to be expedient that the province of Furruckabad, should also be added to the English possessions, and so the young Nabob, instead of succeeding to the office and dignity of his ancestors, was required to sign a treaty by which he ceded all his territory with all his rights and control over it to the English, only to receive in return from them out its revenues a pension for the support of himself and family.

When the kingdom of Mysore was to be disposed of, after the fall of Seringapatam and the death of Tippoo, several districts were offered to the Mahrattas, upon condition that they would then cede these to the English in return for the support of a subsidiary force to be stationed at some place in the Mahratta territory, in a manner similar to the arrangement then made with the Nizam. Such subsidiary forces consisted partly of European and partly of native troops. But all the officers were European, and the force was to be under the control of the English government, or their agents. This offer the Mahrattas then refused. But the agent of the English at the court in Poona, was instructed to intimate to the Peishwa and the Mahratta chiefs, that such an arrangement would at any time be taken into consideration, if they should wish for it. The Mahrattas were generally engaged in warfare: sometimes they were united against a common enemy, sometimes each chief was carrying on war to enlarge his own dominions, and sometimes they were fighting among themselves. In 1803, some dissensions having occurred between Scindia and Holkar, a severe battle was fought near Indore, in which the latter was defeated with great slaughter, loss of guns, etc. He collected his scattered forces and proceeded with all possible despatch to Poona. Here Scindia and the Peishwa united their forces to oppose him, but they were both defeated "in one of the most obstinate battles recorded in the annals of Indian warfare." When the Peishwa saw that the war between Scindia and Holkar was likely to be transferred to Poona, he intimated his wish to the English agent for some arrangement for obtaining the aid of a subsidiary force for his protection. The approaching difficulties and dangers made him yet more anxious, and the day after the battle, in accordance with an arrangement made with the English agent, he proceeded to Severndroog, a fort in the Concan south from Bombay on the sea-shore, from which he went in a vessel provided for him to Bassein. The English agent proceeded from Poona to that place, and the celebrated treaty of Bassein was made there. By this treaty the Peishwa ceded to the English a territory yielding $1,250,000 annually, and they agreed to support a subsidiary force of 6,000 men in his dominions. They also engaged to reëstablish him in his full rights as the acknowledged head of the Mahratta confederacy. This treaty declared the friends and enemies of either of the contracting parties to be the friends and enemies of both, and it provided for the joint exertions of both to defend the rights or redress the wrongs of either, or of their respective dependants and allies. The document is of great length, containing 19 different articles.

This treaty laid the foundation for what has been called "the greatest war which England ever waged in India, and which was destined completely to establish her supremacy over that country."

It was the wish of Scindia and Holkar each to obtain possession of the person of the Peishwa, and then use his name and authority to increase his power and influence. The Peishwa was aware of their desire, and might have thrown himself upon either of them. But he knew he should be only a prisoner of State, to be used by the party for their own advantage. And so he chose rather to enter into treaty with the English, who engaged to restore him to be again the head of the Mahratta confederacy. For some time it appeared quite uncertain what course the Mahratta chiefs would pursue on hearing of the treaty of alliance between the English and the Peishwa. Scindia retreated after the battle at Poona towards his own dominions, and encamped near Burhanpoor. Holkar remained at Poona and endeavored to invest another member of the Peishwa's family with the office and dignity of Peishwa. The governor-general made arrangements to carry on the war with vigor, if the chiefs separately, or in combination, should resist the restoration of the Peishwa, or any other provisions of the treaty.

In accordance with this intention, Sir Arthur Wellesley, (who was brother to the governor-general, and subsequently became the Duke of Wellington,) was ordered to take the command of a large force which had assembled at Hurryghur, and to proceed towards Poona. Col. Stevenson was ordered to proceed from Hyderabad with the subsidiary force at that place and the Nizam's contingent force, and to join Sir A. Wellesley. The two forces met at Akloos, and when united constituted an army of 27,000 men. Lord Lake was commanded to proceed with a large force from Bengal and invade the northern parts of the dominions of Scindia. A force was to proceed from Madras, and to invade the southern parts of the dominions of Ragojee Bhonsla, the Mahratta chief or Raja of Berar. And a force was to be sent from Bombay to invade the territory of the Mahrattas in Gujerat. It was expected that these simultaneous invasions of the territories of the different chiefs would prevent any continued coöperation or union of their forces.

It was necessary that Sir. A. Wellesley should proceed to Poona to prepare the way for the restoration of the Peishwa. As he approached the city, Holkar with his force withdrew, and no resistance was made to his taking possession of the place. The Peishwa, who had remained at Bassein, was then escorted to Poona by a force of 4,000 Bombay troops under Col. Murray, and he was duly installed in office again. Efforts were now made to induce the Mahratta chiefs to acquiesce in this new state of matters, and also to become reconciled with each other. With this view several months were spent in fruitless negotiation, when it became evident that some of them were determined to try the issues of war. Scindia and Ragojee Bhonsla (often called the Raja of Berar or Nagpore), united their forces for this purpose, and proceeded into the territory of the Nizam. Sir A. Wellesley then marched from Poona to meet them. On his way he took possession of the town and fort of Ahmednuggur, which had been in the possession of Scindia. A plan was concerted between Sir A. Wellesley and Col. Stevenson to attack the army of Scindia and Ragojee Bhonsla on the 24th of September, at Bokerdun, where they were supposed to be encamped. But on the 23d, Sir A. Wellesley unexpectedly found them near Assaye. Their united army consisted of 38,000 cavalry, 18,000 infantry, and 100 guns. The battle here fought is one of the most remarkable in the history of British India. The English were victorious, but the loss was very heavy, "the killed and wounded amounting to more than one third part of the force engaged." The influence of this victory on all parties was great. The force under the command of Col. Stevenson arrived the day after the battle and pursued the retreating enemy. In the course of a few weeks the battle of Argaum was fought, in which Scindia was again defeated, and the forts of Asseerghur and Gawulghur were taken. In the mean time the war was carried on vigorously in other parts of the Mahratta territories. Lord Lake proceeding from Bengal with a large force, invaded the northern parts of Scindia's dominions. The following graphic account of his operations in this expedition is from Murray's History of British India:—

"Meantime, the central regions of Hindustan were the theatre of events equally memorable. Scindia's force there consisted almost exclusively of the large corps formed on the European model by De Boigne, who having returned to France, was succeeded by Perron. These troops were considered very formidable, consisting of 16,000 or 17,000 regular infantry, from 15,000 to 20,000 cavalry, a large body of irregulars, and a well appointed train of artillery. Lord Lake having been informed of the failure of the negotiation with their master, moved from Cawnpore on the 17th of August, 1803; on the 28th he passed the frontier, and the next day he found the whole of Perron's horse in a strong position near Coel, a town in the Doab. He presently led his troops to the attack; when the native army, deemed so efficient and well equipped after a short random fire, retreated with such rapidity that the English could not overtake them. The next object was the fort of Allighur, the main depot of the enemy. It was a very strong place, surrounded with a good glacis, and a broad and deep ditch always filled with water. It would have been unassailable, had the entrance been confined to a draw-bridge; but a terrace had been imprudently formed for that purpose, over which Lord Lake concluded his troops might force their passage. Colonel Monson, who had led the storming party, soon penetrated across the mound and over the breastwork, but the wall was so strongly guarded by spearmen that he could not attempt an escalade. A twelve pounder was brought forward to burst open the gate, but before it could be pointed the soldiers remained exposed to a most galling fire, which severely wounded and disabled their leader himself. Major McLeod succeeded to the command, and after the first gate had been forced open, pushed his way through a long and intricate passage and two successive gateways to a fourth, against which, however, the gun was employed without effect. The situation of the assailants would now have been serious, had not the Major succeeded in forcing the wicket, and thus opening an entrance to his countrymen, who soon became masters of the place.

"It being understood that Perron was discontented with the service of Scindia, Lord Lake was authorized to make large offers on condition of his coming over to the English and bringing his troops with him. In fact, a letter was received from him on the 7th of September, requesting to be allowed to repair with his family, servants, and property in safety to Lucknow, but without expressing any disposition to detach his army from their allegiance. His request was readily granted, and he afterwards stated his desertion to have been occasioned by the appointment of another officer to supersede him in command.

"After the capture of Allighur, Lord Lake marched directly upon Delhi, the imperial capital, and the residence of him who still enjoyed the rank and title of Great Mogul. He had advanced within view of its walls, when he discovered the army organized under French command, and drawn up in a strong position to defend its approaches. Though he had only 4,500 men against 19,000, yet he determined to give battle without delay. But as the enemy could not without difficulty and some loss, have been dislodged from their present ground, he used a feigned retreat as a stratagem to draw them from it. This delicate manœuvre was executed by the British troops in the most perfect order, and the enemy imagining the flight real, quit their intrenchments and eagerly pursued. But no sooner were they fully drawn forth on the plain than Lord Lake faced about, and in a single charge drove them from the field with loss of 3,000 in killed and wounded, as well as their whole train of artillery.

"The British general now entered Delhi without resistance. He immediately requested and obtained an audience of the emperor, with whom a secret communication had previously been opened. He beheld this unfortunate descendant of a long line of illustrious princes 'seated under a small tattered canopy, the remnant of his former state, his person emaciated by indigence and infirmities, and his countenance disfigured with the loss of his eyes and marked with extreme old age and settled melancholy.'

"The conquerors now marched upon Agra the rival capital, which still possessed the advantage of being defended by a strong fort, and occupied by a large body of troops. Anarchy, however, prevailed in the garrison, and the officers being chiefly of English extraction had become objects of suspicion and thrown into confinement. At the same time 7 battalions of Scindia's army having been denied admittance lest they should claim a share of the riches it contained, still kept their post in the city and the principal mosque. It was considered necessary to begin by dislodging them, which was effected, though not without an obstinate resistance, and the soldiers to the amount of 2,500 immediately transferred their services to the victors. The Mahratta leaders meanwhile resolved to propose a treaty of surrender, but as the time for its ratification approached they suddenly recommenced firing. The trenches were forthwith opened, and a breach being effected on the 17th of October, 1803, the enemy capitulated the same evening, stipulating only for the safety of their persons and their private property. The treasure found there, amounting to no less than £280,000 ($1,400,000), was divided among the troops as prize-money.

"There remained still in the field a corps composed of troops detached from the Deckan, reinforced by fugitives from the different armies. Lord Lake hastened in pursuit of this force, and considering it only as a collection of runaways, deserted by their officers, little apprehended that he was about to encounter the most obstinate resistance he had sustained during the whole campaign. This body, consisting of 9,000 foot, 5,000 horse, and a numerous train of artillery, were rapidly retreating, when on the 1st of November he overtook them with his cavalry alone, and determined by an immediate attack to prevent their escape. The enemy, however, having their motions concealed by a cloud of dust, speedily threw themselves into an advantageous position, which they strengthened by cutting the embankment of a reservoir in front. The dragoons were led on and had gained some advantages, when they suffered so severely from the fire of a number of well-served guns, that it was judged necessary to withdraw them and wait till the infantry could come up. That force accordingly advanced, but the 76th regiment and a few companies of sepoys having arrived earlier than the others, were exposed to so destructive a fire that the general deemed it the wisest as well as safest plan to lead singly to the charge, 'this handful of heroes.' They accordingly carried all before them though with severe loss, and when the Mahratta cavalry attempted to break their thinned ranks, the British horse triumphantly repelled the charge. The remainder of the foot soon appeared, and after a desperate stand the enemy for the most part were either destroyed or made prisoners. In short by this brilliant success the entire army, formed and disciplined for Scindia by French officers, and considered the finest possessed by any native power, was completely annihilated." *

In addition to these brilliant achievements on the part of the English, the force despatched from Bombay into the Mahratta territories in Gujerat, took Broach and some other places; the force from Madras invaded the territory of Ragojee Bhonsla and took possession of Cuttack, and another force under Colonel Powell were not less successful in Bundelcund. Thus

* Murray's History of British India, p. 531–534.

attacked on every side and defeated in every engagement, their armies dispersed and their forts taken, the Mahratta chiefs had recourse to negotiation. Ragojee Bhonsla, Raja of Nagpore, withdrew from Scindia and made a separate peace. In a few weeks a treaty was also made with Scindia. Both princes made large cessions to the English, by which as well as by the severe defeats they had suffered, their power was much crippled and their resources reduced. This war brought into the field large forces on both sides. The force in the employment of the East India Company, and under the command of British officers in this war exceeded 50,000, while the forces opposed to them were much more numerous.

Holkar at one time appeared inclined to join the other chiefs in this war, but the success of the English in the battles of Assaye and Argaum induced him to preserve neutral ground. When peace had been made with Scindia and the Raja of Nagpore, it became necessary to adjust the unsettled state of matters with Holkar. Negotiations were commenced, but learning that he could not make peace on any terms consistent with some schemes he had formed, he resolved to engage in hostilities with the English. His army had been much increased by military adventurers and deserters, and now amounted to 75,000 men, who were supported and kept together in a great measure by levying contributions and plunder obtained in predatory excursions. When Lord Lake proceeded to attack him he retreated in great haste and confusion. Soon afterwards, he made an attack upon General Monson, whose retreat, losses, misfortunes, and sufferings form one of the most painful chapters in the history of modern warfare in India. This war was carried on for some time with varying success. The English forces took possession of Indore, Holkar's capital, and of nearly all his dominions, but he continued to support his large army by plundering and levying contributions wherever any thing could be obtained. The neighboring princes sometimes encouraged and assisted him, and they sometimes opposed him. He had become reckless of all faith, character, and consequences, and there appeared to be no way of bringing the war to a close, but for the English to appropriate to themselves or distribute among other princes all his territories, and utterly disperse his army and annihilate his military power.

While the war was carried on in this manner, other important events occurred. The governor-general, previous to the commencement of the war with Holkar, had intimated to the Court of Directors his intention to resign the government and return to Europe, as soon as the war with Scindia and Ragojee Bhonsla could be brought to a close. His course in India had been brilliant and successful, but it had produced much dissatisfaction in England. His plans for enlarging the English possessions and consolidating their power in India, had been carried into effect with much ability and success, but the Ministry and the Court of Directors could not see sufficient reason for all these wars, while they were alarmed at the enormous expenditure incurred in carrying them on. They were decided in the opinion that a pacific course of policy should be pursued, and they fixed on the Marquis Cornwallis (the same who had formerly been the governor-general) to govern India according to their views. He arrived at Calcutta in July, 1805, and at once assumed the government. He was instructed to pursue a different course of policy from his predecessor, and to procure peace on almost any terms. He remained a few weeks in Calcutta, and then left for the upper provinces, where urgent and important matters required his personal attention and examination. On his way he became ill and on reaching Ghazepore he died on the 5th of October. Previous to leaving Calcutta he had commenced negotiations with Holkar to bring the war to a close. He also declared that his course of policy would be to secure and to preserve peace as far as possible with all the native powers, and leave them to adjust their quarrels and carry on their wars among themselves.*

* "The vast scheme of conquest and subsidiary alliance by which Marquis Wellesley had studied to place this great eastern empire under British control, had excited in England a very deep sensation. The public were to a certain degree dazzled with its splendid success; yet a numerous body of politicians exclaimed that this course was contrary to all true principles of policy — that it formed an interminable principle of war — that the East India Company in seating themselves upon the throne of the Mogul, and endeavoring to effect the conquest of all Hindustan, had entirely relinquished the basis on which they had uniformly professed to act. The contest with Holkar breaking out with so formidable an aspect after all the others had closed, gave rise to painful feelings as to the endless duration of Indian hostility. The Directors of the Company,

By the death of Marquis Cornwallis Sir George Barlow, the senior member of the supreme council, became governor-general. He pursued the measures which had been commenced by his predecessor. A new treaty was made with Scindia, who had become much dissatisfied with some parts of the last treaty, or rather with the manner in which those parts had been interpreted and the matters referred to in them had been carried into effect. As Holkar refused to consider any reasonable terms of peace, and continued his reckless course of war and plunder, no way or expedient remained but to deprive him of his power. For this purpose Lord Lake pursued him from place to place, depriving him of his plunder and not allowing him time to levy contributions, and dispersing his followers till at length he was reduced to such straits that he sent his agents with an application for peace to the English camp. A treaty was soon made and signed on terms far more favorable to Holkar than he expected, knowing as he did how his conduct had been regarded by the former governor-general, and what purposes were at one time formed concerning him and his possessions.

In 1806, a mutiny took place in the army at Nellore near Madras, which caused great anxiety for a while in India and in England. The military force of the East India Company consists partly of Europeans and partly of natives; the former are called soldiers, and the latter are commonly called sepoys, the word in the native language for soldier. The European portion of the army has seldom exceeded one fourth, and often not more than one sixth or one eighth part of it. The sepoys are voluntarily enlisted, formed into regiments, and disciplined and commanded by English officers. There had been no interference with their superstitious prejudices or national customs. In

strongly influenced by public opinion, and struck by the enormous expenditure in which the campaign had already involved them, determined to change entirely the system on which their affairs were conducted. Accordingly in the place of the Marquis Wellesley, who, with or without reason, had acquired the reputation of a war-governor, they substituted the Marquis Cornwallis. His instructions were to proceed on principles every way opposite to those of his predecessor, —to conclude peace almost at any price,—to form a defensive line beyond which English interference was not to extend, and to allow the native powers to treat and to fight with each other as if situated at the extremity of the globe."—*Murray's History of British India*, p. 543.

1806, some change was made in their cap or turban, which at first excited some disaffection and resulted in a few cases of military discipline at Nellore, near Madras. The excitement apparently soon subsided and no further trouble was apprehended, when the native force suddenly attacked the Europeans, consisting of their officers and 2 companies of soldiers. The attack was unexpected and was made in the night. All the Europeans, consisting of 14 officers and 100 soldiers, were massacred. The insurgents then took possession of the fort and town, and prepared to defend them. In a few hours this meeting and massacre became known at Arcot. The force stationed at this place proceeded as soon as possible to Nellore. The insurgents defended themselves with great obstinacy; 350 of them were killed and 500 were taken prisoners before the mutiny was suppressed and order restored.

This mutiny produced a great sensation through all India, especially as there were indications of disaffection at Hyderabad, Bangalore, and several other places. Alarming and unfounded rumors and reports of intended mutinies and massacres were circulated among the Europeans, and endeavors were apparently made to excite prejudice and apprehension among the native population in respect to some intentions of the English government, and what they were preparing to do with the people of the country.* It was a time of intense anxiety, and led to a careful inquiry into the state, circumstances, feelings, etc. of the native troops. There were no more mutinies; the excitement gradually subsided, and general confidence was restored. What punishment should be inflicted on the insurgents, and what should be done in respect to the innovation which had occasioned this mutiny, were grave questions. Differences of opinion on these matters and proceedings growing out of them, led to the recall and dismission of Lord William Bentinck, then governor of Madras, and of Sir John Cradock, the commander-in-chief. Ultimately a few of the most guilty suffered death,

* "At Hyderabad it was currently reported that the Europeans were about to make a human sacrifice in the person of a native, that 100 bodies without heads were lying along the banks of Moose river; that the Europeans had built a church which it required 100 heads to sanctify, and that they designed to massacre all the natives except those who should put the sign of the cross on the doors of their dwellings."

but the greater part of the insurgents escaped with but little punishment.

Sir George Barlow was succeeded in the office of governor-general by Lord Minto, who arrived in Calcutta, July, 1807. The pacific course of policy commenced by Marquis Cornwallis, was pursued for several years, and the English were not involved in war with any of the large native powers. Among the remaining petty princes were always some of a restless and intriguing spirit, and who were reckless and faithless in respect to observing the treaties they had formed with the English and with each other. Of this kind was the Raja of Travancore. This prince intrusted the management of his affairs wholly to his dewan or first minister, who was a profligate, deceitful, and depraved brahmin. The subsidy, which the Raja was bound by his treaty to pay annually to the English, not having been paid for 2 or 3 years, Colonel Macaulay, the English agent at the Raja's court, made a demand for it. This gave offence to the dewan, and he began in various ways to oppose the English government. A concerted attack was made on Colonel M. in the night, and he narrowly escaped with life. A ship arriving at Allepie with a surgeon and 33 soldiers on board, they were induced by falsehoods and treachery to go on shore, when they were all seized and barbarously murdered. The Raja then began openly to prepare for war, and endeavored to excite the Raja of Cochin, and the Zamorin of Calicut to do the same. A force was sent from Madras into Travancore, which after much harassing warfare and taking several forts, compelled the Raja to fulfil his treaty. The dewan being rejected from his office, and having become obnoxious to all classes of people for his atrocious conduct, fled to the temple of Bhagawady and committed suicide.

The Sikhs had been for some time the increasing power in the north-west part of India. Runjeet Singh, afterwards so celebrated in Indian history, had become their principal chief. "This extraordinary person had afforded some ground for apprehension, but a negotiation conducted by Mr. Metcalf,* assisted by a military force, ended in a conclusion of a treaty by which

* Subsequently Lord Metcalf, and for some years governor-general of Canada.

the British government engaged not to interfere with the territories or subjects of the Sikh chief north of the Sutlege, he on his part binding himself not to maintain within his territories on the left bank of that river more troops than might be necessary for carrying on the ordinary functions of government, and to abstain from encroaching on the rights of the chiefs in that vicinity." This transaction shows the extended power of the English at that time in India. They were at war with the Raja of Travancore, in the extreme southern part of the peninsula, because he had delayed to pay them the annual subsidy stipulated in their treaty with him. And they were making a treaty with the sovereign of Lahore concerning matters in the extreme northern part of India. Not more than one fourth part of India was probably at this time under the direct control of the English, yet there was not a petty prince between these extreme points, nearly 2,000 miles apart, with whom they had not treaties, and treaties too, which from their complicated nature and the defects and infirmities of the native character, were likely to furnish occasion for interference, and then for war, and a state of yet greater dependence or entire subjugation. And the possessions of the English were so situated and scattered that there was no place over this great extent of country, which could not easily and speedily be reached by a military force.

Wars between France and England always affected more or less the state of political and commercial matters in India. At such times the islands of Mauritius and Bourbon, became the places of rendezvous for French cruisers, which made prizes of the English ships engaged in the India and China trade, to an immense amount. The losses sustained in this way by the Insurance Companies in Bengal alone, amounted in a few years to $15,000,000. These losses at length roused the English nation, and a determination was made to take possession of these islands. The armament for effecting this was chiefly prepared and sent from India. The islands were taken in 1809 and 1810. Mauritius still continues to be an English possession, but Bourbon was united to France in 1814. Holland having become a part of the French empire under Napoleon, her foreign possessions of course became subject to France. England was now engaged in war with France, and it was determined to take these eastern possessions. For this purpose a large armament was fitted out in India, and the governor-general accompanied it. This expedition was successful in taking Java, and the other possessions in the eastern archipelago, which had formerly belonged to the Dutch. Thus the East India Company not only extended their own power over India, but added other foreign possessions to England. The naval force of the Company was also vigorously and successfully employed in suppressing piracy in the eastern seas.

Lord Minto, though pacific in his general policy, was yet vigilant in providing for English interests in India. He made a treaty with the Ameers of Scinde, by which those chiefs bound themselves not to permit any Frenchman to reside in their territories. He sent an ambassador to Cabul, who made a treaty with the Afghan sovereign, who engaged not to permit any French or Persian force to pass through his dominions to India, and not to allow any Frenchman to reside in his territory. He also sent an ambassador to Persia, and a treaty was made by which the king of Persia engaged to resist the passage of any European force through his dominions towards India, and the English in return engaged to assist Persia, if invaded from Europe. In consequence of this treaty, the French political agents then in Persia, were compelled to quit the country, and the French influence in Persia was checked, and for a while nearly destroyed. Such transactions show that whatever might be said or thought of the East India Company in Europe and in America, yet that in the southern countries of Asia, they had become an acknowledged nation, and that their power and influence were not inferior to the greatest monarchs known in the history of those countries.

In 1813, Lord Minto resigned the office of governor-general of India, which he had held for 6 years, and returned to England. He survived his arrival only a few weeks. In the same year the renewal of the East India Company's charter, which was soon to expire, came under the consideration of Parliament, and occupied their attention for several months. The result was that the charter, with some important changes, was renewed for 20 years. Among these changes were the following:— The Company had hitherto enjoyed a monopoly of all the trade between England and all places east of the Cape of Good Hope. The trade between England and India was now to be open for all, but the trade with China was to continue to be a monopoly of the Company. An ecclesiastical establishment, consisting of a bishop and 3 archdeacons, was created to superintend the chaplains employed in India. Missionary operations and all proper means for the conversion of the native population to Christianity, were also to be tolerated.

The Earl of Moira, generally known by his subsequent title of the Marquis of Hastings, became governor-general of India in 1814. He found that some difficulties with the Nepaul government, which commenced in the time of his predecessors, still remained unsettled, and required his immediate attention. Commissioners on the part of both governments were appointed to examine the matters in dispute, but they made no progress towards any final adjustment, and both parties became more dissatisfied. The Nepaulese at length refused all further negotiation, and invaded the territory belonging to the English, plundering the villages, and murdering many of the inhabitants. War having now become inevitable, the governor-general resolved to prosecute it with vigor, and with the view of bringing it to a conclusion as soon as possible, arrangements were made to invade Nepaul simultaneously in four different places, and 30,000 men took the field. But the war was commenced without due preparation, and it proved to be more harassing than any war in which the English had been engaged in India. The officers found it impossible to obtain correct information concerning the country of Nepaul. They were deceived by those who pretended to inform them, and their ignorance and mistakes on this account were the cause of frequent embarrassments and disasters. The seasons were very inclement, and the troops suffered much from sickness and for want of provisions. The country was everywhere unfavorable for military operations, especially for transporting guns and military stores, while the points of attack were so far apart that they could not coöperate or assist each other. The Goorkas were found to be a brave, as well as treacherous people, and they fought with unexpected obstinacy. The war continued for nearly 2 years, and it makes a painful chapter in the history of British warfare in India. But the resources of the English were every way so much greater than their enemies, that the latter became gradually reduced, and a treaty of peace was negotiated. This war and the treaty by which it was concluded, became the subject of much discussion and censure in India and in England.*

Wars among the native princes and powers in India, have been generally to a great extent supported by exactions and plunder. Whatever the officer, or the sepoy, or the camp-follower wanted, if he could find it among the people of the country, he at once appropriated it to his own use. Wars were sometimes commenced and carried on for this purpose. When this was the object, some order and system were generally observed. The prince or commander would make the exactions from princes or commanders like himself, and then leave those under him to oppress and plunder as they pleased. Or the leaders would require a certain proportion of the exaction and plunder to be given to them, and leave the rest to be distributed among their followers according to some rules. No nation in India was ever more imbued with this spirit of war, or carried on such wars to a greater extent than the Mahrattas. When the treaties made with Scindia, Holkar, and the other Mahratta chiefs, compelled them to cease from their wars and to reduce their armies, great numbers of people who had been accustomed to this kind of life and to find their support in this way, were thrown out of employment. Many such persons associated themselves under leaders to resume their former habits. They then fixed their residence in the dominions of some native prince, perhaps they obtained from him a cession or grant of some district, and made their predatory excursions into places beyond his territory. Many such marauders lived in the dominions of Scindia and Holkar, and were protected by them. Remonstrances were made by the governor-general to those princes, but no regard was paid to them. Indeed, there were strong reasons for believing that these princes encouraged such associations, if not sharing in their plunder, yet granting them protection upon condition that they did not commit any outrage in their dominions. They probably thought that in the event of

* Thornton's History of British India, vol. 4, pages 251–346.

war, such leaders and their followers would become useful auxiliaries. These robbers always made their predatory excursions on horses, and they were called Pindarrees.* The depredations committed by them soon became so great that the governor-general saw it was necessary to suppress them.

The Mahratta chiefs so long accustomed to war and its consequent excitement and changes, were becoming impatient of the restraints imposed upon them by their late treaties with the governor-general, and Bajee Row Peishwa, who owed his restoration to be the nominal head of the Mahratta confederacy entirely to the interposition and power of the English, began a course of intrigue and treachery, which showed that he had no regard to the treaty he had made, while he continued to carry on his duplicity, though solemnly denying it in a manner and to an extent which showed that no confidence could be placed in his veracity. In these circumstances it became necessary to have further means for enforcing the treaty. So a large addition was made to the subsidiary force in the dominions of the Peishwa, and he was required to cede territory sufficient for its support, to the English. This subsidiary force furnished the garrisons for several of the best forts in his dominions. This

* I have often heard people in India describe the appearance of the Pindarrees, and what they suffered, and saw others suffer from them. The following, I have no doubt, is a true account of them:—"The Pindarrees were nothing more than robbers, elevated by their number into armies, and their boast was, not that they were able to encounter disciplined troops, but that they could elude them. If overtaken or surprised, the point of honor was who should flee the most swiftly. No barrier arrested them. They penetrated the closest chain of military posts, finding a way even between the divisions of an army drawn up to oppose them. They desolated countries, going out and returning home by different routes. Their aim was, not to take permanent possession of a district, but to sweep away all that was in it. Obliged to pass with a celerity almost preternatural, and to employ expeditious modes of exacting treasure, they inflicted the most merciless torments to compel owners to yield up their concealed hoards. Redhot irons were applied to the soles of the feet, oil was thrown on the clothes and inflamed, the head was tied into a bag filled with hot ashes, pepper, etc., which was then shaken. Women were subjected to yet worse treatment, and often died from abuse in the hands of their captors. The intervals of time between these expeditions for plunder, were spent in idleness, gambling, drunkenness, and debauchery." The climate in a large part of India is so warm that snow is unknown, and frost seldom if ever seen. Such a country is favorable for people of habits and pursuits like the Pindarrees.

subsidiary force and the forts, as usual in such cases, were under the control of the English agent at the Peishwa's court in Poona. This new arrangement or treaty, though signed by the Peishwa, yet only made him more impatient of the restraints imposed by it, and more reluctant to observe its conditions. It was becoming evident that this impatience with his circumstances and the intrigues which in violation of the express conditions of the treaty he was carrying on with the other Mahratta chiefs, would erelong result in open war.

In the mean time the Marquis of Hastings, at this time governor-general, resolved to suppress the Pindarrees, who had become the terror of all central India. These mounted freebooters were associated under different chiefs, some of whom had 200 or 300, and others had 8,000, or 10,000 followers, and if united they would amount to 35,000, all mounted and armed. Their refuge and residence were chiefly in the dominions of Scindia and Holkar, who not only refused to use any means to suppress or expel them, but secretly encouraged and protected them in the hope of their aid in the event of a war with the English, which appeared to be approaching. For the purpose of breaking up and dispersing these hordes, it was resolved to invade the territories they occupied on four different sides at the same time, and 34,000 troops were so employed. The policy of the Pindarrees was never to fight, but always to flee and avoid their enemies, plundering and ravaging at the same time wherever they went. War with such an enemy was expensive, harassing, and discouraging. The Pindarrees were dispersed in smaller companies more widely than ever, so that the country was not relieved from their ravages, nor was there any prospect of peace.

In these circumstances some more efficient measures were evidently required to obtain any peace for the country, or any security of life and property for the inhabitants. It was apparent also that these measures must be formed and undertaken in view of the probability of a general war with all the Mahratta people. The Marquis of Hastings had much experience in military matters, and prepared the plan of a campaign whose avowed object was the suppression of the Pindarrees, but which also provided for a possible, and in his view probable, war with all the Mahratta powers. His plan was comprehensive, and the force employed in it was obviously far beyond what was required to extinguish the association of freebooters in central India. A part of this force proceeded from Bombay into the Mahratta territories; a part did the same from Madras, and a part from Bengal. The entire force occupied in this war, and under the English control, amounted to 81,000 infantry, and 33,000 cavalry. The avowed object of this great force was to suppress the Pindarrees, but those who understood what was going on in the Mahratta courts, had no doubt there would be other work for these armies before they could all return to their respective quarters. And such expectations were not disappointed, for it was not long before the Peishwa made a sudden attack upon the English subsidiary force at Poona. The Raja of Berar did the same at Nagpore. Holkar commenced war with the English. Scindia was only kept in subjection by a large force stationed near his capital, while a force from Bombay restrained the Guickwar in Gujerat, from commencing open hostilities. These attacks were successfully repelled, but further battles and sieges, flights and pursuits followed. The war upon, rather than with the Pindarrees, was at the same time carried on, and for a while nearly all the Mahratta territory appeared to be occupied by troops, and in a state of warfare. In these outbreaks and conflicts, the English were generally victorious, and the native powers soon saw that submission or ruin was before them. The Peishwa, after being a fugitive from his capital and fleeing before an English force for several months, made a treaty in which he renounced all his possessions, rights, etc., to the English, and promised, upon condition of receiving a stipulated allowance for life, to fix his residence in Bengal, outside the Mahratta territories. Scindia, Holkar, the Raja of Nagpore, and the Guickwar of Gujerat, entered into new treaties, which by reducing their power and admitting subsidiary forces into their dominions, or increasing the forces previously stationed there, contained new guarantees against engaging in any further wars, or again disturbing the general peace. The Pindarrees, wherever they could be found, were attacked and dispersed, and as associated bodies they were annihilated. And the native princes, in whose dominions they formerly found refuge and protection, entered into treaties to refrain themselves and to restrain their subjects and all in their territories from such predatory warfare. By this war the English obtained a large accession of territory, and what was of more importance to the general welfare of the country, they suppressed and extinguished that horrible predatory warfare which had been spreading for several years, and which appeared likely, if not put down by strong force, soon to spread confusion, anarchy, and devastation into all parts of India.

The Marquis of Hastings continued in the government of India for 3 years after the close of the Mahratta war. He was a nobleman of high character, and had exhibited distinguished talents in war and in Parliament before going to India.* His government was generally popular in India and satisfactory to the Court of Directors of the East India Company. He did not attempt to introduce the revenue and judiciary systems of Bengal into the territories acquired during his government. These new possessions were intrusted to the superintendence and management of able and experienced men, who with the sanction of the government, introduced such changes as the state and character of the people appeared to require. The consequence has been that these districts have been governed in a manner far more satisfactory to the people, and furnishing better security for the protection of life and property than the early possessions of Bengal. The Marquis of Hastings left India in January, 1823, having been governor-general for 9 years, a longer period than any governor-general since Warren Hastings.

Mr. George Canning, so well known in the parliamentary and political history of England, was appointed governor-general in succession to the Marquis of Hastings. But previous to embarking for India, the death of Lord Londonderry caused some changes in the ministry, and Mr. Canning became the foreign secretary. Lord Amherst was then appointed governor-general, and arrived in Calcutta in August, 1823. The country was

* The Marquis of Hastings was in the war in the United States, which resulted in their separation from Great Britain. His title was then Lord Rawdon. He was at the battle of Bunker Hill, and commanded the British army at the battle of Eutaw Springs, where the American forces were commanded by General Greene.

then generally in a state of peace, enjoying as much of quiet and repose as could reasonably be expected in a population so large, so heterogeneous in their character, and so recently brought under the British government. But it was not long before there were clear indications that there must soon be a conflict with a new power, the Burmese.

Burma, or the Burmese empire, is not generally considered a part of India, but some account of the Burmese war deserves a place in any historical sketch of British India, as it resulted in an increase of the empire which England has acquired in the southern countries of Asia. The Burmese empire was formed by a union of several States, which had some time previously a separate national existence. As might be expected of an oriental nation thus suddenly exalted, the Burmese were conceited and arrogant, and as their country bordered on India it appeared likely that difficulties would arise which would furnish occasion for the interference of the British government.

In 1794, a class of people called Mugs, and who had for some reason become obnoxious to the Burmese government, fled in great numbers into the English territory near Chittagong. A Burmese prince with a force of 5,000 men without any intimation, invaded the district belonging to the English, where he took up a position and began to fortify it, while an army of 20,000 encamped near the border. General Erskine proceeded with considerable force from Calcutta to Chittagong, where the difficulty was finally adjusted without any fighting, and the Burmese returned into their own territory. But the invasion and the negotiation exhibited the spirit of the Burmese. The governor-general wishing to insure future amicable intercourse and to obtain more information of a people and country with which the English might at any time be brought into conflict, despatched Colonel Symes on an embassy to Ava, the Burmese capital. This embassy was apparently successful, and for a while all was quiet. But in a few years great numbers of the same class of people, again fled for protection into the English territories, and caused fresh troubles on the frontiers. Colonel Symes was again sent to Ava, and matters were adjusted. In all these transactions the Burmese exhibited an overbearing and arrogant spirit, which did not promise long peace. In 1818, when in the midst of the Mahratta war, the governor-general received a letter from the king of Burma, in which he claimed Chittagong, Dacca, Moorshedabad, and Cossimbazar, as provinces which at some former period had belonged to the kingdom of Arracan, and he demanded that they should be surrendered to him. The governor-general returned a suitable answer to this letter, which was never noticed by the Burmese. Had the Mahratta war continued, it was then believed that the Burmese would soon have invaded the eastern provinces of Bengal. In 1820, '21, '22, and '23, they committed many outrages upon persons in the employment or under the protection of the English government. Some of these persons were plundered, some were killed, and some were taken prisoners and kept in confinement. The English in repelling these attacks killed a considerable number of the Burmese. Thus a state of actual war existed, though there had been no declaration of war on either side.

Early in 1824, the English government communicated a statement or declaration of these matters to the government of Ava, and in a few weeks they received a reply in which the claim formerly made to several British provinces was renewed; some injuries suffered from the English were alleged, and it was declared, that as the Burmese governors and officers had full power to act in all such affairs, no further communication should be made to the Burmese sovereign, "the lord of the seas and the earth," till all the matters in question should be finally settled. It was now evident that nothing further could be obtained by negotiation, and the British prepared to prosecute the war with vigor. A small force was despatched against Assam. They had great difficulties in passing through the districts, not from any enemies, but from thick jungles, ravines, etc. They at length reached the place and took possession of it without any opposition. The principal force was despatched from Calcutta and Madras against the maritime possessions of the Burmese. Sir Archibald Campbell was appointed to the chief command, and the forces, when united on the Burmese coast, exceeded 11,000. They reached Rangoon in May, 1824. The Burmese forces, or the inhabitants, fired a few guns and then fled. When the English forces entered the town they found it deserted, and before night the English colors were flying on the Burmese staff.

On the approach of the fleet, all the foreigners in the city were seized and confined. As soon as the British were in possession of the place, one of the prisoners, (Dr. Judson, of the American Baptist Mission,) was sent to the officer in command to inquire what terms would be granted, the inquiry being accompanied by an intimation that the lives of the foreigners depended upon the answer that should be returned. The answer was that it was too late to inquire about terms, that the prisoners must be given up, that any injury to them would be punished, and that their persons and private property should be respected. The messengers said they would consult those who sent them and then bring an answer. But on returning to consult them, they had removed to another place, and could not be found. Three of the prisoners had been left behind; the others had been hurried away. "Great fears were entertained for their safety. Those fears were happily relieved on the morning after the occupation of the town, the missing persons being discovered by some reconnoitring parties, before whom the guards placed over them had fled."* The city, or town of Rangoon, was supposed to entertain 50,000 inhabitants, but all had fled, and "not a native of any age or sex was to be seen." In a few days, some individuals returned, but they came as spies to observe the conduct of the invaders. The rainy season soon commenced, and the rains were very heavy. The English, supposing, as they were going to a large city, a seaport surrounded with a populous and cultivated country, that provisions would be easily procurable, were not prepared for such circumstances as now surrounded them. They began to suffer for want of provisions, while fever and dysentery were very severe. It was soon apparent that the war had been commenced at an unfavorable season of the year, and without due preparation. The force was compelled to remain shut up in Rangoon for some time, only making now and then short excursions into the vicinity and capturing the Burmese military posts, which were generally only stockades recently erected. The English force also suffered much inconvenience and loss for want of more knowledge of the country around them.

* Thornton, vol. 5, p. 21, 22.

Near the close of the rainy season, an expedition under Col. Godwin, was despatched against Marteban, which succeeded in taking the place. A large number of guns and a great quantity of military stores were found in it, the loss of which must have been severely felt by the Burmese. An expedition under Col. Miles was sent to the Tennasserim coast, which took possession of Tavoy and Mergui. Some reverses which resulted in the defeat and dispersion of the British force on the frontier, encouraged the Burmese to undertake more aggressive operations. In December, a large army approached Rangoon, and began to throw up intrenchments in front of the British army. These were soon attacked, and the men occupying them were dispersed. The Burmese then endeavored to burn the English ships by sending fire rafts down the river.* On the 5th and 7th of December, vigorous attacks were made upon the Burmese army which had encamped near Rangoon, and they were defeated and routed with great loss. After some time the army again returned and made arrangements for burning the town, and at the same time attacking the English force. The town was set on fire in several places and half of it reduced to ashes, but for some unknown reasons no attack on the English force was then made. A few days after the conflagration, the English force made an attack upon the Burmese army, estimated at more than 20,000, and took possession of their intrenchments and stockades. The same day also more than 40 Burmese war-boats were taken. The Burmese now retired from Rangoon, and Sir A. Campbell prepared to carry the war into the enemy's country, and if possible to reach Prome. A part of the force

* "These fire rafts were ingeniously contrived and formidably constructed, made wholly of bamboos firmly wrought together, between every 2 or 3 rows of which a line of earthen jars of considerable size, filled with petroleum or earth-oil and cotton were secured. Other inflammable ingredients were also distributed in different parts of the rafts, and the almost unextinguishable fierceness of the flames proceeding from them can scarcely be imagined. Many of them were more than 100 feet in length, and were divided into many pieces attached to each other by means of long hinges, so arranged that when they caught upon the cable or bow of any ship, the force of the current should carry the ends of the raft completely round her, and envelope her in flames from the deck to her top-mast-head, with scarce a possibility of being extricated from immediate destruction."

embarked in boats to proceed on the Irrawaddy, and the rest began their march on the land. On their way the two forces united in taking the strong fort of Donobew. When this fort was invested, "the garrison made a sortie with a considerable force, and 17 war elephants fully caparisoned, and bearing on their capacious bodies armed men." On arriving at Prome, the place was found to be deserted. In this city the army found comfortable accommodations, and remained for several months in consequence of the setting in of the rains.

So much difficulty had been experienced in making any impression on the Burmese government by these operations, that it was resolved to send a large force into Arracan. For this purpose an army of 11,000 men under Gen. Morrison was collected in Chittagong, and a large armed flotilla was attached to it. A part of the force embarked in the flotilla, and the rest proceeded by land. The army reached the city of Arracan, and on the 29th of March, made an attack on the place. A considerable Burmese force was collected there, but their efforts in defending the place availed but little, as Gen. Morrison succeeded by changing his mode of attack in taking the city without much loss. The Burmese, on the loss of the capital, abandoned all their positions in Arracan. Thus far this expedition had been successful, but greater trials were yet before them. It was found impossible to proceed over the mountains to effect a junction with the force on the Irrawaddy, and the rainy season which now commenced, proved to be very unhealthy, bringing with it fever and dysentery, the same diseases which were so mortal at Rangoon in the previous rainy season. Sickness became almost universal, and the mortality became so great that it was thought expedient to withdraw the greater part of the army from the province, only a small force remaining in some places not so unfavorable to health.

The rainy season having passed away, Sir. A. Campbell was preparing for more aggressive operations, when proposals for negotiations were received from the Burmese. Several weeks were spent in conferences on the subject. But all was without any satisfactory result, and both parties prepared to renew hostilities. A large Burmese army soon approached Prome, throwing up intrenchments and stockades in their peculiar manner, as they advanced towards the British lines. On the 30th of November, and the 2d and 5th of December, attacks in which the land force and the flotilla coöperated, were made upon different parts of the Burmese army, and resulted in the British obtaining possession of all the positions of their enemies, and dispersing them in every direction. The British army now advanced further into the Burmese country, but they suffered much from sickness and want of provisions. The country exhibited on every side the shocking evils of barbarian war.* Nevertheless the army continued to advance, stopping now and then to take some fort or stockade, or to attack some Burmese force, or to consider some unsatisfactory proposals for peace. A treaty was once agreed upon by the negotiating parties, but the Burmese government would not ratify it, and so hostilities were continued. As Sir A. Campbell was approaching the capital, he was informed that a new sovereign had acceded to power, and the treaty some time previously made was soon ratified. By this treaty the Burmese sovereign made large cessions of territory to the English, and paid 2 crore of rupees, ($10,000,000,) towards the expenses of the war.

In the central part of India lived a tribe called the Jauts. Their chief had the title of Raja, and was often called the Raja of Bhurtpore, the principal city in his dominions, and situated about 40 miles nearly west from Agra. In 1823, the Raja died without issue, and was succeeded by one of his brothers, whose claim and dignity were duly recognized by the English government. Doorjun Singh, the son of another brother, now formed a plan of succeeding himself to the throne, should it again become vacant. In 1825, the Raja died, leaving one son, then in his 6th year. Soon after the Raja's death, Doorjun Singh, having gained a part of the army to his cause, made an attack upon the fort, killed some of the family and took others (among whom was the young Raja) prisoners. The state of matters soon became complicated, and as the English had made a treaty with the deceased Raja, by which the succession had been guaranteed to his son, they felt it their duty now to interfere. Much effort was made to adjust the difficulties and reconcile the parties to each

* Snodgrass' Journal, p. 253–260; also, Thornton, vol. 5, p. 73.

other, but without any success. In the mean time a quarrel arose between Doorjun Singh and his brother, 'Madu Singh, and soon each attacked the other with all the military force he could command. Matters continued in a state of civil war for some time, when the resort of military and lawless adventurers to Bhurtpore, and the spirit manifested towards the English power became such, that means for suppressing them were deemed necessary. As Doorjun Singh was determined to support his pretensions, and the fort of Bhurtpore was known to be very strong, and generally believed by the natives to be impregnable, it was resolved that a large force should proceed against it. Accordingly an army of 25,000 men, with 200 pieces of artillery, arrived at Bhurtpore, in December of 1825, and invested the place. Mines were sunk under the bastions, and when these exploded, the besieging army rushed in and took possession of the fort. The young Raja was soon duly established in power, and the usurper, Doorjun Singh, was taken prisoner and sent to Allahabad. As a former attempt by Lord Lake to take Bhurtpore failed, the natives regarded the place as impregnable, and believed the English would never be able to obtain possession of it. This belief excited great interest in this war, and the fall of the fort in so short a time after it was invested, (only 37 days,) and on the first assault, produced a profound impression throughout the country, and increased the confidence of all classes of people in the resources and power of the English government. A large amount of treasure was found in Bhurtpore, which became prize money of the conquerors.

The taking of Bhurtpore was the last great act in the administration of Lord Amherst. The next year the Raja of Kolapore, one of the Mahratta princes and a man of profligate character, became involved in some difficulties with the government of Bombay, and it became necessary to despatch a force against him. On the arrival of this force at his capital, the difficulties were adjusted by negotiation without any fighting. In 1824, Singapore, Malacca, and the Dutch possessions were obtained from the king of Holland, by negotiation. New treaties were made with several of the native princes. Such treaties were generally made on the occasion of some new prince succeeding to power, or some change in the dynasty, or some family or political troubles which were referred to the English government for adjustment, or which were of such a nature that the government thought their interference was required. Such treaties were generally more and more in favor of the English government; they were generally such as the English demanded or dictated, and showed that the scattered fragments of the native powers were becoming fewer and weaker.

In 1827, Lord William Bentinck became governor-general of India. The country was generally in a state of peace. Some pretended reformers among the Mohammedans caused much trouble at Baraset in Bengal, which at length assumed so much the appearance of a religious war among the different classes of Mohammedans and Hindus that it became necessary to send an armed force against them. In an attack upon them 50 were killed, 350 were taken prisoners, and the rest were dispersed. Several petty princes occasioned trouble, and required, as the English thought, the interposition of their power to adjust their difficulties. Among these were the Raja of Queda, and the chief of Nanning in the Malay peninsula. These chiefs came into connection with the English by their acquisition of Malacca.

In 1834, the Raja of Coorg occasioned much trouble. Coorg was a small native State on the west side of the peninsula, having the Ghats for its western border. This country had been but little explored by Europeans, and was so rough and mountainous that it was almost impassable. The British forces attempted to penetrate the country from different directions, but they found it fortified by numerous stockades which the inhabitants defended with great bravery. The war was of a very harassing nature and continued for some time. The capital of the district was at length taken, and the Raja surrendered himself a prisoner. His territory was annexed to the British dominions. A pension was assigned to him and he fixed his residence at Bangalore. Little sympathy was felt with the Raja for the loss of power which he had so much abused. "The occupation of Coorg opened to the conquerors a vast body of evidence relating to the crimes of its former sovereign, evidence of numerous murders, some secret, some public, some the offspring of revenge, and some the results of a barbarous policy. Women not less than those of the sterner sex, and children as well as adults, were numbered among the victims of his cruelty. Of the royal family, not a single male, except the guilty Raja, survived." * The money found in the treasury of the Raja became the property of the conquerors, and $600,000 of prize money were distributed among the officers and soldiers.

Scindia, the most powerful of the Mahratta chiefs, dying without issue, the supreme power was seized by his widow, who in accordance with native usage adopted a son to succeed her husband. A violent quarrel between her and this adopted son occurred, which occasioned for some time a state of anarchy and civil war. A compromise was at length made, the widow receiving a fixed pension and the adopted son assuming the government.

The Raja of Joudpore, one of the Rajpoot States, having refused to pay the stipulated tribute to the English for 2 or 3 years, and in some other respects having manifested a hostile disposition, an army of 10,000 men was sent to reduce him to obedience. After much prevarication and delay he submitted just in time to prevent being deposed. Jeypore, another of the Rajpoot States, was the scene of more tragical events. The British subsidiary force having interposed in some quarrels in the native court, several officers were attacked, and 2 of them were killed. The persons ultimately found to be guilty of instigating this attack, were sentenced to be put to death, but the sentence was commuted into exile and imprisonment. In 1835, a great sensation was produced through India by the assassination of Mr. Frazer, the agent of the governor-general at Delhi. The murderer was discovered, when it was ascertained that in perpetrating this atrocious act he was the hired agent of the Nabob of Ferozepore, and was acting under his instructions. This murder was for considerable time involved in great mystery. The manner and means by which the principal and his agent were at length discovered, proved to be guilty, and the determination of the English government to inflict upon the guilty parties, the extreme sentence of the law, excited great attention in India. The Nabob and his agent were both pub-

* Thornton, vol. 5, p. 212.

licly executed at Delhi. The murder, the means by which the guilt of the parties was ascertained, and the manner in which they suffered the extreme penalty of the law, produced a strong moral impression on all classes of the native population. Such proceedings of the English government and of their courts have had great influence in consolidating their power.

There was no war with any large native power in the administration of Lord William Bentinck. The expenses of the government, especially in the military department, had become very large under his predecessors, and he was much occupied in making reductions of various kinds. These changes excited great discontent and murmuring in the army. But being himself a military officer of high character and having the confidence of the Court of Directors, he was able to carry his plans of reform into effect. He prohibited the practice of Suttee, or of a widow burning herself with the body of her deceased husband. He also passed a law designed to secure to converts to Christianity their personal and property rights against the intolerant rules and usages of caste, and he is generally reckoned among the best governors-general India has ever had. In 1835, his health failed, and he returned to England.

The East India Company's charter which had been renewed in 1813, was to expire by limitation in 1833. In anticipation of its approach, large committees were appointed in both houses of Parliament in 1830, to make inquiry into the affairs of the Company, and into all matters connected with the state of India, the views and circumstances of the inhabitants, etc. The affairs of the Company were investigated with great care and labor. The proceedings of these committees were long and particular, and their reports* furnished occasion for much discussion and long debates in Parliament. The result was a renewal of the charter and its continuance, with some important changes, for another 20 years. Among the changes made were the following: — The monopoly of the trade between England and China was to cease. The commercial character of the Company was also to cease. All the property of the Company

* These reports, and the other papers concerning the East India Company, then printed and laid before Parliament, made 14,000 closely printed pages of large 4to.

was to be surrendered to the crown in return for an annuity of £630,000, redeemable after 40 years, at the rate of £100 for every £5. 5s. of this annuity. This sum of £630,000, or a dividend of 10 1-2 per cent. upon the capital, was to be charged to and paid from the territorial revenues of India, and the crown (or England) became responsible for all the debts and obligations of the Company. In closing the commercial business of the Company, £2,000,000 of the assets were to be invested as a guaranty fund for the future redemption of the capital or stock of the Company. And as the proprietors could receive only a fixed dividend, whatever might remain from the commercial assets after satisfying the claims of all persons employed in this department, was to be appropriated to the objects and purposes still under the Company, as the payment of debts, current expenses, etc. The government of India was to continue in the hands of the Company for 20 years. The ecclesiastical establishment was enlarged. Under the previous charter it consisted of a bishop in Bengal, and an archdeacon in each of the minor presidencies. The bishop in Bengal was made metropolitan by this charter, while Madras and Bombay were to have each a suffragan bishop.

Lord William Bentinck left India in 1835, and as no successor had arrived, the government devolved upon Sir Charles Metcalf, the senior member of council. His administration was chiefly remarkable for removing some restrictions which had hitherto existed on the press in India. This change caused much discussion in India and in England. Many apprehended that to allow every individual to publish what he pleased, subject only to such penalties for abusing this liberty as existed in England, would soon be productive of great evils, and that it would soon be necessary to reimpose the former restrictions, or something equivalent to them. But the press, though used as freely by different classes of the native population in the discussion of political, religious, and all other matters in their respective languages, as it is by the European population in the English language, has continued to be free, and none of the evils which were anticipated, have resulted from it. Thus making the press free, showed much liberality in the government, and its continuance so long to be free, without any unhappy consequences resulting from it, is a strong testimony to the general wisdom of the administration of the government through all the changes of this period.

Lord Auckland became governor-general in 1836. For some time after his arrival in India, nothing remarkable occurred. In 1837, the Nabob of Oude, a weak-minded and profligate prince, died, and as usual in oriental courts, a quarrel ensued for the succession. On one occasion he had acknowledged two lads to be his sons, but the common belief then was that he had done this at the instigation of certain parties. He afterwards acknowledged that he had done so, and that he had no children. In these circumstances the governor-general resolved to support an uncle of the late Nabob, who, according to Mohammedan usage, was the legal heir. The friends of one of the pretended sons united in supporting his claim, and for a while the palace and the city were the scene of violent dissensions and tumults. The party which was supported by the English prevailed, as might have been foreseen, and the other party was compelled to withdraw from the Nabob's territory. All these changes strengthened, and they generally enlarged the English power and influence among all classes of people.

A yet more troublesome difficulty soon occurred; the case of the Raja of Sattara. In the settlement of the affairs of the Deckan at the close of the last Mahratta war one of the family of Shevajee, the founder of the Mahratta empire, who had long been in confinement, was set at liberty and placed over a small territory with Sattara for its capital. This prince, naturally of a restless and intriguing disposition, was accused in 1836, of being engaged in carrying on secret correspondence with other native powers, and also of some other acts in violation of his engagements to the English authority, with a view to excite prejudice against them to whom he was indebted for his freedom and elevation to power. Inquiries into these matters were carried on for 2 or 3 years, and became the subject of much correspondence and discussion in India and in England. The result was that he was deposed and removed to Benares. A generous pension was allowed for his support, and his younger brother was put in his place. The question of his restoration continued to be agitated in the Court of Directors for several years, by his friends and a well paid agency. The Mahratta people generally appeared to feel much interest in the proceedings and the result. Their sympathies were with the Raja, and their desire was for his restoration to power. The Raja and his brother, who was put on the throne, both died some 4 or 5 years ago, and as they had no male offspring, the English took possession of the kingdom of Sattara, and annexed it to their own territory.

All the great invasions of India, previous to Europeans proceeding round the Cape of Good Hope, were from the northwest. Thence Alexander the Great, Mahmoud, Tamerlane, Baber, and Nadir Shah entered the country. The English soon after commencing their course of conquest and possession in India, became apprehensive of danger from the north-west, and before the close of the last century Zemaun Shah, the sovereign of Cabul, occasioned them much uneasiness. In the early part of the present century the English government in India, made several treaties with the rulers of Persia and Afghanistan, with a view to secure India from invasion by the French; and after the fall of Napoleon, means were used to strengthen Persia against Russia for the security of India. In the course of a few years a war occurred between Persia and Russia and the latter obtained a large accession of territory from the former, and so extended her southern border towards India. She also acquired a paramount influence at the court of Persia, and under that influence, Persia laid claim to several provinces of Afghanistan, and proceeded to enforce that claim by making war upon Herat. If Persia should succeed in establishing her power over these provinces, and so extend her border thus far towards India, then being under the influence of Russia, and even holding her national existence by the sufferance of Russia, this extension of the Persian border would be in effect the extension of the Russian border towards India. The government of India becoming aware of the influence at work in Persia, and in the country between Persia and India, sent Sir A. Burnes on a mission of observation and inquiry into Afghanistan. He reported that at Cabul, he found a duly accredited Russian agent, forming treaties with the Afghan chiefs, and encouraging them in an aggressive warfare towards India, by promises of aid from Russia. Sir A. Burnes' communications to his government concerning the state of political parties and plans in Afghanistan, excited great attention in India, while at the same time the communications of the British Ambassador in Persia concerning Russian agency and intrigue in that country, to the Ministry in England, excited great attention there. The result of much correspondence and consideration was a determination to establish a counteracting British influence in Afghanistan, and as Dost Mohammed, then the ruler of Cabul, had declined the interest and friendship of the English, it was resolved to reëstablish Shah Shuja, a former sovereign of that country, who had been expelled by Dost Mohammed, and for some years had been living under English protection in India.

In accordance with this determination a treaty was made with Shah Shuja, and he was assisted to raise a force to take possession of his former kingdom, while a yet larger English force under Sir Henry Fane was to accompany him.* Treaties were also made with Runjeet Singh, the ruler of the Sikhs, and between him and Shah Shuja. By this treaty Runjeet Singh engaged to invade Afghanistan, by way of Peshawur, while Shah Shuja and the army that accompanied him, invaded it by way of Candahar and Ghizni. It was intended the two forces should meet at Cabul. The army which was to proceed by way of Candahar, amounted to 25,250 men. The army which was to proceed by way of Peshawur amounted to 10,800 men. The large army arrived at Candahar without encountering any resistance, but they suffered much on the march for want of provisions and water. At Candahar the ancient capital of Afghanistan, "Shah Shuja was crowned with every circumstance of pomp and external honor." From Candahar they proceeded to Ghizni, reputed to be the strongest fort in Afghanistan, and supplied with a large garrison under a son of Dost Mohammed. In the vicinity of the fort was also a large Afghan force prepared to embarrass them, if they should besiege it, and to resist their further progress. The fort was found to be much larger and apparently stronger than was expected. Despatch was of great importance, and as one of the gates was accessible,

* Sir Henry Fane soon resigned the command to Sir John Keane, who had the chief command in the early part of the Afghan war, and who became Lord Keane.

a resolution was formed to blow it open, if possible, with powder. For this purpose bags of powder containing 900 lbs. were placed at this gate in the night, and a train was prepared to fire it. At the time expected, just after dawn, the powder exploded and "shattered the gate entirely to pieces." The storming party immediately rushed in and soon had possession of the fort. The loss of Ghizni, on which Dost Mohammed had placed great dependence, disconcerted his plans, and through one of his brothers he opened negotiations with the English, but on learning that the first condition of any treaty would be for him to surrender all his power and possessions, and go to reside in some part of the English territories in India, he refused compliance and retreated into the northern part of his dominions. The army proceeded from Ghizni to Cabul, and took possession of the fort and town. In a few weeks the force that had proceeded by way of Peshawur and Jellallabad reached Cabul, and the two armies united. The greater part of Afghanistan appeared now quietly to submit to the government of Shah Shuja. Some petty chiefs in the remote districts had not tendered their submission, but no reason appeared for anxiety on account of their power, or of any combination likely to be formed among them. Dost Mohammed was at liberty and had refused to surrender his power and possessions, but as his artillery had been taken and his army dispersed, it was not supposed he had power remaining to occasion much trouble.

The conquest of Afghanistan having been thus apparently achieved and Shah Shuja acknowledged as its sovereign, the English army began to prepare to return to India. There were still some indications that the obedience generally manifested to Shah Shuja was more from fear than from loyalty, and unhappily he and his sons did not pursue a course calculated to procure respect and confidence. So it was resolved that a very considerable force should remain in Afghanistan to secure the sovereign in power, and for any other purposes that might occur in those changing countries. A part of the Bombay army on its return attacked and took Kelat, which belonged to Mekrab Khan, an Afghan chief, who had manifested a hostile spirit to the English, and committed some depredations upon the baggage of their army on its march to Candahar. It was afterwards retaken by the Afghans, and recovered by the English. It was the scene of much hard fighting. The tribe of Murrees and the tribe of Ghilzies, by their refractory spirit and plundering habits, occasioned the army great trouble, and required extreme measures to suppress them.

In the mean time, Dost Mohammed, having obtained aid from the Usbeck tribes and collected a very considerable force, recommenced hostilities to recover what he could of his former possessions. He was joined by several Afghan chiefs, and his force increased to 10,000. He made several attempts to retrieve his affairs, but finding that his force was leaving him, and that he could place little reliance upon his followers, he resolved to surrender himself at discretion to the British authority at Cabul. He and his family (all who had surrendered) were removed to India, and a generous sum was allowed them for their support.

It was supposed that the surrender and removal of Dost Mohammed would restore quiet, and reconcile the people to the government of Shah Shuja. But it was not so. A spirit of disaffection was evidently increasing in the country. Many harassing conflicts took place, and Gen. Sale was forced to abandon his position, and with great effort and difficulty succeeded in retreating into Jellallabad, and there defending himself. In November of 1841, Sir A. Burnes, who had his quarters in the town of Cabul at some distance from the English cantonments, was suddenly attacked, and with his brother and 2 other English officers, was assassinated, and the house in which he lived was set on fire. Several other officers were attacked the same day. The insurrection thus commenced soon spread over the country. The English force in Cabul consisted of 5,500 men under Gen. Elphinstone, who was in feeble health, and greatly wanting in the energy and decision requisite for such an emergency. The English camp was soon surrounded with an infuriated army. In a few days this force got possession of the English commissariat, which was soon plundered. The state of the army now daily became more distressing. Various plans were proposed, considered, and rejected. Attacks upon them were made, repelled, and renewed. The English forces daily became weaker and more discouraged, and the assailing forces became more numerous and furious. Negotiations were opened, but no terms could be agreed upon, and war was renewed with fury. At length some terms were mutually agreed upon between Sir W. Macnaghten, the English Envoy and several Afghan chiefs, but before these were ratified, the Envoy was invited to a conference with some of the chiefs, and there assassinated. The state of the English became now, if possible, still more distressing, and the purpose was formed to retreat to Jellallabad, 100 miles nearly east on the way towards India. "The army, though the loss had been considerable in the late harassing warfare, still consisted of 690 Europeans, 2,840 native infantry, and 970 cavalry, in all 4,500 fighting men. There were besides, 12,000 camp-followers, who rendered the preservation of any order almost impossible." They commenced their march on the 6th of January, 1842. The weather was cold, and the snow was deep. On the 9th, the ladies with their husbands, (all the latter who chose,) placed themselves under the protection of Akbar Khan, a son of Dost Mohammed, and remained behind. The retreat or rather flight of the army continued, the infuriated Afghans pursuing, plundering, and massacring them. Many of them went over to the enemy. Some were taken prisoners, but more were killed, or perished through fatigue, hunger, and cold. Only one, Dr. Brydon, reached Jellallabad to communicate the tragic intelligence of what had taken place at Cabul and on the retreat. Of this retreat, the History of British India says:—"The captives were about 70; an unknown proportion of the native troops and followers had gone over to the enemy, but by far the greater part of the 16,500 who left the cantonment at Cabul, had miserably perished. This retreat may be considered without a parallel, if not in the extent, at least in the completeness, of its calamity."

This insurrection extended through all parts of Afghanistan. The fort of Ghizni was attacked and surrendered. Candahar was attacked by a large force, but they were repelled by Gen. Nott, then in charge. Several attacks were made upon Jellallabad, but they were repelled. The Afghans having assembled in large force at Jellallabad, an attack was made upon them by the garrisons, and they were routed with great slaughter. The news of these disasters, and of the circumstances of the force still remaining in Afghanistan, produced a great sensation in India among the European and native population. The English army had never before suffered such reverses in the East. The government took vigorous measures to sustain its power, to relieve the scattered forces, and obtain the prisoners yet in Afghanistan, as soon as the season would admit of any advance into that country. With this view Gen. England proceeded from Scinde with 4,000 men, and a large supply of funds and stores to reinforce Candahar, but the Afghans attacked him with so much vigor on the way, that he was compelled to halt in the fort of Quetta, where he was besieged, and could not advance till a large force came to his aid. A large force proceeded from Peshawur, under Gen. Pollock, and succeeded in reaching Jellallabad.

Some proceedings in England in respect to the war in Afghanistan, and the continued occupation of that country, added to the disasters and reverses which had taken place, induced Lord Auckland, the governor-general, to resign, and Lord Ellenborough, his successor, arrived in Calcutta, in February, 1842. The course now to be pursued in respect to the continuance of the war and the occupation of Afghanistan, became the subject of much consideration and correspondence. Shah Shuja, who had been restored as the sovereign of the country by the power of the English, had from his first return to his country, disappointed the expectations which had been formed of him. One of his sons, Suftur Jung, joined the Afghans in their insurrection against the English, and there were reasons for believing that this course had his father's concurrence. When Shah Shuja was endeavoring to put himself at the head of one party, he was attacked by another party and put to death. Akbar Khan, the son of Dost Mohammed, and principal agent in the insurrection there, became the acknowledged head of the Afghan nation. So the purpose of the English to restore Shah Shuja and his family to their former place and power, and by their means establish a permanent English influence in the countries north-west from India, had utterly failed. Runjeet Singh, the head of the Sikhs and sovereign of Lahore, who was a party to the treaty with Shah Shuja, for invading Afghanistan, had died, and his kingdom was almost in a state of anarchy. The Sikhs were now too much occupied with their own internal affairs to become a party in any further measures or plans concerning Afghanistan.

In these circumstances it was resolved to recover the prisoners remaining in Afghanistan, and then withdraw all the forces and leave the chiefs and people to establish what government they pleased. Negotiations for an exchange of prisoners, including Dost Mohammed, were commenced, but no terms could be agreed upon. In August, 1842, General Pollock left Jellallabad for Cabul. There was much skirmishing and some hard fighting with the enemy at different places on the march, but the English army reached Cabul on the 14th of September. A part of the army at Candahar returned under General England to Scinde, and the rest under General Nott proceeded to Cabul. He had several conflicts with the Afghan chiefs on the way, but arrived at Cabul safely and joined General Pollock. The prisoners, 70 in number, among whom were a number of English ladies, were still in the hands of the Afghans. Various plans and schemes were formed, and negotiations on the part of the prisoners and the officers with the different chiefs were commenced, and before the close of the month all were recovered. The Afghan chiefs now all went to the north beyond the reach of the English force, so after taking and destroying a few forts in the vicinity of Cabul, the army returned to India. Dost Mohammed and other Afghan prisoners were set at liberty, and returned to their own country, and the Afghans were left to establish any form of government over themselves, and make any treaties with other nations which they pleased.

Russia, when called on for some explanation concerning her agency in Afghanistan, denied having had any such agency there as was ascribed to her. But while Count Nesselrode made such declarations to the English cabinet, Count Simonich (the Russian ambassador in Persia) and his agents continued to pursue their course unchanged. There was much difference between the declarations of the Russian government, and the actions of her agents in the countries between India and Russia, and perhaps the English were more alarmed for the safety of their possessions in India, than there was occasion. Be this as it may, yet all are agreed that no war in which the English have ever been engaged in the East, appears to have been managed with so little ability, foresight, and discretion, and none have been so unsatisfactory in respect to any substantial and permanent results. The loss of life, European and native, was very great. The expenses were enormous, and all defrayed from the revenues of India. And the losses and miseries inflicted on Afghanistan were probably far greater than all endured by the English and the people of India.

The disasters, losses, sufferings, and expenses in the Afghan war and its unsatisfactory results, produced a more earnest desire for continued peace than had existed in India for many years. But this desire was not to be realized. Mention has been made of the Ameers of Scinde, a country lying each side of the river Indus for several hundred miles from its mouth. Treaties were made, or rather some old treaties were renewed and modified, with these chiefs by Sir John Keane on his way with the army from Bombay to Afghanistan in 1839. The state of Scinde was far from being quiet during the Afghan war, and some matters which then occurred became the subject of inquiry and complaint soon after the war had closed. The country of Scinde was divided between several chiefs, who were confederated and yet partly independent, who were profligate and at variance with each other. The disasters and misfortunes which the English suffered in Afghanistan and the generally known unsatisfactory result of that expedition, destroyed for a while much of the *prestige* of English valor and success in war. Negotiations for the explanation or removal of the difficulties with the Ameers became complicated, and at length resulted in open hostilities. Several battles soon took place between the Ameers and Sir Charles Napier, who had then command of the English forces in Scinde. The character and result of these battles were similar to what we have generally seen in warfare between Europeans and natives of India. The Scindeans, though personally brave, yet being under unskilful leaders, were easily defeated by forces who had been carefully trained in European discipline, and were commanded by officers who had become experienced in the most approved tactics of modern warfare. The armies of the chiefs were defeated and dispersed, their treasures were seized, their cities and forts taken, and the greater part of their territories annexed to the English possessions in

India. There was much severe controversy in the journals and many pamphlets were published in India and in England, in censure and in vindication of this war, of the measures and policy in which it originated, of the manner in which it was carried on, and the results produced by it, involving the character and relative position of the Ameers, and the state, climate, revenue, resources, etc. of the country and its respective provinces.* Some facts and figures are certain. It was well known that the Ameers had a large amount of treasure, which in the event of a war would become prize-money and the property of the captors, The portion of this prize-money which Sir Charles Napier obtained for his share was $350,000. By the conquest of the country he became the governor and commander-in-chief of the military forces in it, the salary of which was first £10,000, and then £15,000, or nearly $50,000, and $75,000 yearly.† Scinde has been permanently annexed to the British dominions in India.

The disturbed state of affairs in another native territory soon claimed consideration. Scindia, the most powerful of the Mahratta princes since the close of the last Mahratta war, died in 1843, without leaving any issue or appointing any one to succeed him. His widow with the concurrence of the family and friends, adopted a son, and he was duly installed. But he was a child, only 8 years old, and so it became necessary to appoint some regent during the prince's minority. A regent was appointed, but he soon found a combination against him too powerful to be controlled. Some connected with the army joined this combination, and soon the court and the army were near a state of anarchy. The subsidiary treaty between the English and the deceased prince bound the former to secure the succession to the throne to the legal heir of the latter, and matters soon came to such a state as required them to interpose for the young prince. So a large force under Sir Hugh Gough, then commander-in-chief, accompanied by Lord Ellenborough, the governor-general, proceeded from Agra towards Gwalior, the capital of the territory of Scindia. Several efforts to effect a settlement of the difficulties were made, but they were unsuc-

* Thornton's History of British India, vol. 6, p. 395–466.

† Annals of India, p. 17.

cessful. A large part of the Mahratta army took the part of the insurgents, and it was not till after two severely contested battles that the insurgents would listen to any terms of submission. When peace was restored, "the Raja was installed with great ceremony at Gwalior in presence of the governor-general, the commander-in-chief, and an immense assemblage of native chiefs."

When appointed governor-general, Lord Ellenborough's instructions were, to pursue, as far as was possibly consistent with the honor and interest of the East India Company and of India, a pacific course of policy. But instead of this he had manifested and encouraged a military spirit beyond any of his predecessors for many years. "This spirit frequently led him to the neglect of his civil duties and the internal government of India, which was his principal business as governor-general. His whole course of procedure was erratic and opposed to the definite policy by which the Court of Directors had sought to avert a continued system of aggression on the surrounding native States, and to consolidate the vast possessions over which their rule was only very partially and imperfectly extended." The Directors at length became so much dissatisfied with his conduct that, in the exercise of a right reserved to them in the charter, and without consulting the Ministry, they voted his recall. This proceeding of the Directors of the East India Company caused much surprise and discussion, and, on the part of the governor-general's friends, much censure. But no power could reverse it, and public opinion in England and in India soon approved of the measure. By this act the Directors evinced great decision, and showed themselves to be the true friends of India.

Sir Henry Hardinge, subsequently Lord Hardinge, was appointed the next governor-general in May, 1844, and proceeded immediately to assume the duties of his office. The death of Runjeet Singh, the head of the Sikhs and sovereign of Lahore, has been mentioned. He was the most distinguished native prince of India in this century. He had built up his kingdom for himself, and it was generally expected that it would fall to pieces on his demise. Kurruck Singh, one of his sons, succeeded him, and was duly installed in power. He soon removed his father's prime minister Dhian Singh, and appointed another in his place. The ex-minister soon found means to destroy the new favorite. He then put Kurruck Singh under restraint, and placed all the power nominally in the hands of Kurruck Singh's son, Now Nihal, the power being really reserved in his own hands. But it was only a few weeks before the father and son both died, whether by sickness or violence, is not known. The affairs of the Punjab then fell into much confusion. The profligate and reckless character of some of the chiefs, who came in for a share of power and plunder, gave no assurance that they would restrain themselves or their followers to their territories, and so a large English force was concentrated near the Sikh territory on the opposite side of the river. This warlike demonstration, though designed only for defence, yet being evidently collected in view of the Sikhs, was perhaps more fitted in their state of feeling to provoke an attack than deter them from it. The Sikh soldiers or sepoys were brave, conceited, and impulsive, and those who were acquainted with their history and national character, did not expect war would be long delayed. Nor was this expectation to be disappointed. In December, 1845, a party of Sikhs crossed the Sutlege and carried off 50 camels, and distributed the plunder in their own camp. In a few days some further depredations were committed, and it was apparent from various circumstances that they were preparing to invade the English territory with a large force. The Sikhs constructed a bridge of boats over the Sutlege, and in the course of a few days a large force with their guns, etc. passed over. The first battle was fought at Moodkee, 20 miles from Ferozepore. The English force under Lord Gough amounted to 11,000, and the Sikhs were somewhat more numerous. The Sikhs made the attack and were repulsed with severe loss of men, and 17 of their guns were taken. The English loss was also severe, among whom were Sir Robert Sale and Sir John McCaskill, officers who had greatly distinguished themselves in the Afghan war.

The Sikhs continued to pass the river till the force collected in the English territory was variously estimated at from 40,000 to 60,000, with 150 pieces of artillery. The force of the English there assembled did not exceed 18 or 20,000. On the 21st and 22d of December, further battles were fought at Ferozepore, in which the English remained masters of the ground and of 73 pieces of the Sikh artillery. The loss of the English force was severe, amounting in killed and wounded to one seventh part of the force in the field. They also suffered severely for want of provisions and from the extreme cold. They were also embarrassed for want of ammunition. The unprepared and ill-furnished state of the army was the occasion of severe censure. Severe and bloody battles were soon fought at Aliwal and Sabraon. In the last-mentioned battle the loss of the Sikhs exceeded 8,000 men. These losses and reverses at length inclined the Sikhs to propose negotiations which resulted in peace, the Sikhs ceding a large part of their country to the English, and paying them $7,500,000 towards the expenses of the war.

These defeats, disasters, and humiliating terms of submission, were supposed to have broken the spirits of the Sikhs, and laid the foundation for peace with them for some years at least. Such was the general expectation, and Lord Hardinge on returning to England, "declared that all danger of insurrection or disturbance in the Punjab was at an end." But the warlike and independent spirit of the Sikhs was overawed, not subdued. It was only suppressed for a while, again to appear in the spirit of desperation and fanaticism. Several of the chiefs had still preserved some independence, with very considerable military force and pecuniary resources. And a great many, who had formerly been soldiers in the regular army, their regiments being now disbanded, were without any employment suited to their taste and habits, and having no means of support, were anxious to resume their former mode of life. Some devotees and fanatics encouraged this spirit by assuring them of divine aid, favor, and success. Only a rallying point and leader were wanting to bring many such persons together, and then to mature purposes and plans. The first exhibition of this feeling took place at Multan. This city was celebrated in the ancient history of India for its strength, and it was generally the capital of some independent prince, or the residence of a royal governor. It was for some time subject to the sovereigns of Afghanistan, but in 1813, Runjeet Singh obtained possession of it, and annexed it to his dominions. In the arrangement and settlement of the Sikh States consequent upon the peace, Sirdar Khan Singh had been appointed governor of Multan, and Messrs. Agnew and Anderson were sent by the British agent at Lahore to install the governor into office. On reaching Multan, the former governor, Moolraj, surrendered the fort, etc. into their hands, but on the next day a sudden attack was made upon them and both were assassinated. It was supposed for some time that this outrage was to be ascribed to the Sikh soldiers, many of whom were known to cherish feelings of revenge towards all English officers. But it was not long before various circumstances led to "the discovery of a conspiracy of the most alarming character at Lahore, having for its object the massacre of all the British officers, the expulsion of all the English troops from the Punjab, and a revolution in the Sikh government." The English had now another Sikh war before them, and arrangements were made to meet the exigency as fast as possible. The first attack on Multan failed, the fort being stronger and more vigorously defended than was expected. At the second attack "the besieging army, including the allies, contained 32,000 men and 150 pieces of ordnance, nearly half of which was of the largest calibre." The city and fort were defended with great obstinacy, but were at length compelled to yield, and the citadel was occupied by an English garrison.

In the mean time the standard of war was raised in several places in the Sikh territories. Great numbers gathered around them, and the country exhibited the bustle of preparation for war. Dost Mohammed, who had again become the sovereign of Afghanistan, becoming aware of what was going on in the Punjab, came to the Indus with a force of 30,000 men, and crossing the river, took possession of Attock, apparently prepared to secure any advantages for himself which the course of events might place within his reach. Arrangements were made to collect a large English force at Lahore, and commence offensive operations under Lord Gough, then commander-in-chief. This army amounted to 24,000 men, and Lord Gough assumed the command in November, 1848. January 5th, the English camp was at Janiki, one day's march from the Sikh camp, which was on the other side of the river Chenaub. The Sikh army was estimated to contain 30,000 men. On the 11th the English marched in the direction of the Sikh encampment, and in the afternoon a severe battle, commonly called "the battle of Chillianwalla," was fought. "Darkness put an end to the engagement, leaving the British in possession of the field of battle. But their loss was terrible. Nearly 100 officers were killed or wounded; 2,269 troops, including nearly 1,000 European soldiers were disabled or left dead on the field."

In a few days after this battle, the force which had been engaged in the siege of Multan, reached the camp of the commander-in-chief. This was a large and timely reinforcement to his army, and enabled him again to commence aggressive operations. The next engagement is called "the battle of Gujerat," from a village of that name near which it was fought. The Sikhs were defeated in this battle, and "nearly all their guns, ammunition, camp equipage, and baggage were captured." This battle decided the campaign, and in a few days 13 Sikh chiefs, and 16,000 men voluntarily surrendered, the chiefs surrendering their swords, and the men their arms. A proclamation was issued that the war must continue till the Afghans either surrendered, or returned to their own country. Accordingly Gen. Gilbert, with a sufficient force, immediately proceeded to attack them, but found, on approaching Attock, that they were already crossing the Indus. He pursued them as far as to Peshawur on the way to Afghanistan, without overtaking them, and then he returned.

This second Sikh war having closed, the governor-general issued a proclamation annexing the Punjab to the British dominions in India. A Board, or Committee of Commissioners, of able and experienced men were appointed to assume the administration of the country till all the matters in it and connected with it, should be prepared to be put under the general system of government, which is now observed in the other territories in India, which are subject to the English.

We now close this sketch of the European History of India, with the last great events of the year 1850, just two centuries and a half from the origin of the East India Company.

REMARKS ON THE BRITISH CONQUEST OF INDIA.

At the close of this sketch of the origin and progress of the British power in India, it will not be irrelevant to make some remarks upon the particular qualities or circumstances which have enabled England to conquer and govern a country 10 times her size, containing a population 5 times as large, and situated at so great a distance. The first thing is

1. Superiority in the science and practice of war. In all the nations of Europe, military colleges are established, and men of the highest qualifications are supported in them. War, in all its branches, as fortification, gunnery, fencing, attack, and defence, has long been taught as science, and to no subject have the highest powers and faculties of the mind been applied with more assiduity and energy. Able works are published on all these subjects, and opinions, principles, and inventions are subjected to the test of experiment. Military operations are carefully analyzed. If successful, the causes of that success are ascertained; and if unsuccessful, the causes are searched out and understood. No native government in India has ever founded or supported any military or naval schools to prepare for the military or naval professions. The command of armies is generally intrusted to favorites, almost sure to be unfit persons, or to those who have some experience and been fortunate in such matters, whether the result of competency or chance. But those who may have acquired some experience and skill, having had no previous education in scientific principles to guide them, must be very inferior to what they would have been, could they have had the advantages of a suitable scientific edution at first.

Officers in the armies of the native princes of India have not the means and advantages of improvement which European officers have. They have no books on the subjects of their profession, and few if any histories of wars and battles which they can examine. Nor do they learn so much of each other in social and professional intercourse. In times of trouble and difficulty, councils of war are seldom if ever called or known. In oriental armies, all power is generally vested in one com-

commander, and all confidence is placed in him. If he is killed, and it becomes known, this generally decides the battle. There is none to take his place, none in whom they have confidence. All are panic-struck, and confusion and flight ensue. I have often heard the natives of India express their surprise at the difference between European and Indian armies in this respect. In European armies or regiments, if the commander is killed or wounded, another officer at once assumes the command, and then another and another if need be, and the battle still goes on, and all continue fighting as if no officer had fallen.

The difference between European soldiers and native sepoys, is scarcely less than between the respective officers. The natives become good soldiers, when formed into regiments and instructed in the discipline of European armies. But effective discipline was little known in the armies of India, when the English commenced their conquests there. The strength of armies was supposed to be in their number. The superiority of European armies on account of their discipline, was obvious in the conflicts of the Portuguese, the French and the Dutch, with the natives of India. Such conflicts were like those of the Greeks with the Persians, or the Romans with the barbarians, or the Spaniards with the Mexicans.

The European armies also as much excelled the armies of India in the superiority of their weapons, as their cannon, their muskets, pistols, and swords, as they did in their discipline. Indeed, we may say the same of all the material of war, as powder, balls, bombs, etc.

The superiority of the natives of Europe to those of India, and all the southern countries of Asia in all matters of war, became obvious as soon as they came into conflict with each other. When the European nations began to acquire territory and to evince a spirit for conquest, some of the Indian princes attempted to introduce European weapons and discipline into their armies, and with this view employed such persons as they could obtain. For this purpose many Europeans, chiefly French, were employed by Hyder Ali and his son Tippoo, by the Nizam, by Scindia, and by Runjeet Singh. Such officers were sometimes promoted to high command, and the most severe wars and battles the English have had with the native powers of India, were with armies into which European discipline had been more or less introduced. Aware of the obstacles and difficulties which they might encounter from this source, it became a principle with the English at an early period of their history in India to effect the removal as far as possible of all such officers from the armies of the native powers, and to prevent any Europeans—except such as they should themselves approve—being employed by any native powers. Articles to this effect generally made a part of their treaties with native princes. Future conquest was in this way made easy.

2. The government and constitution of the East India Company, though complicated and often slow and cumbersome in its operation, is yet well adapted for acquiring and governing such a country as India. The governments of Calcutta, Madras, and Bombay have generally consisted each of a governor and commander-in-chief, (who has always the rank of general in the English army,) sent from England, and two councillors who have long been in the employment of the East India Company in India. The governor in Calcutta is called the governor-general, and the government in Calcutta can assume power over the governments in Madras and Bombay, should any emergency occur. The governments in India are subject to the Directors of the Company, and these are subject to the Ministry, and the Ministry to Parliament; thus constituting a connection of control, responsibility, and restraint beyond the government of any country in the world. And not only have the Directors of the Company always had respect to ascertained and competent qualifications in the appointments of their agency, but when any one in their employment has exhibited decided incompetency, or did not follow their instructions and regulations to their satisfaction, he was dismissed or displaced, and some other one appointed. The Directors have shown great energy, decision, and independence in the exercise of their powers and rights in the government of India, and among those who have been displaced and dismissed by them, are councillors and governors, generals and governors-general. In 1844, the Directors of the Company in the exercise of reserved rights and without consulting the Ministry, recalled Lord Ellenborough, then governor-general, because his administration was not in their view for the

good of India, and though this exercise of their authority at first excited great surprise and incurred for a while much censure, yet when all the facts and circumstances became known, public opinion generally approved of what they had done.

Now if we compare the government and agency of the East India Company with the emperors, kings, and princes of India, who are absolute and despotic, arbitrary and often uneducated,* generally controlled by their minister or vizier, and other profligate favorites, and surrounded with their corrupt and venal courts, we shall at once see that the English would have great advantages over the natives in all matters of war and diplomacy, and that the natural and almost necessary result of hostile or official intercourse between them would be conquest, success, and exaltation on the part of the former, and defeat, submission, and degradation on the other.

3. The position of the first places which the English acquired in India, gave them great advantages in their wars with the native powers, and also for governing the country. Calcutta, Madras, and Bombay soon became large seaports, always open for communication with each other, as well as with every part of the sea-coast of India, and with Europe and all the world. No native government in India has ever had sufficient naval power to contend with the English, or to blockade any of their seaports. These cities became the seats of government, and they had such facilities for sending military forces to different parts of India, as no native power ever possessed. Thus in their wars with Hyder Ali,† and Tippoo Sultan, military forces proceeded from Madras to invade their dominions on the east side, and at the same time from Bombay to invade them on the west side. So in the Mahratta wars, forces proceeded into the Mahratta territories simultaneously from Calcutta, Madras, and Bombay. Thus these cities, all under one government, possessed great advantages for carrying on war in all parts of India, and these advantages have been well improved.

The English having at all times the command of the sea,

* Shevajee, Hyder Ali, and Runjeet Singh, who were among the most powerful princes of India, could never write or read.

† So Hyder Ali said, "It is not what I can see of the English power that I dread, but it is what I cannot see that I fear."

could send troops and military stores to any places on the sea-coast where they might be required, or from which they could be best transported to the scenes of war in the interior. In this way all their power in India could soon be concentrated upon any particular spot. The native princes, unable to comprehend the extent and sources of the English power, or to appreciate the celerity of their movements, were often surprised to find their territories invaded where they were not expecting it, and then to see their plans frustrated, their armies defeated, and their forts captured. And if their attack on any place failed, their ships were at hand to furnish escape for the army; and if the forces in any place were no longer necessary, the ships could at once transport them to places where they were required. The armies of Bengal, of Madras and the peninsula, and of Bombay, were available for any exigency in almost any part of India, and in a manner and to an extent previously unknown and unthought of in Indian warfare. And the great advantages the English have obtained from having the command of the sea in their eastern wars, have not been limited to India. The sable armies of India under English officers and English colors have been seen in Egypt, in Arabia, in Persia, in Mauritius, in Ceylon, in Burma, in Java, in Singapore, and in China. And in the revolutions and convulsions and changes yet to take place in the southern countries of Asia, even to the Pacific ocean, the native armies of India may be expected to be seen fighting under the banners of England, governed by English mind, supported by the revenues of India and the southern countries of Asia, and extending the English possessions till they shall include all places which may appear to be worth obtaining, or when acquired to be worth keeping.

4. The state of India when the English commenced their conquests and from that time must also be considered. The great Mogul empire of Delhi fell to pieces soon after the death of Aurungzeb in 1706. At that time the English possessions in India, consisted of only a few small forts or rather fortified factories on the sea-shore. It was not till the struggle between the English and the French for ascendency commenced in the Carnatic, in 1744, that the East India Company became one of the political powers in India. The English never had any war with the Mogul emperors, but only with the comparatively petty

princes and powers who, upon the breaking up of that great empire, succeeded in establishing, or were struggling to establish, their independence in some of its provinces. Thus India had become divided into a large number of small governments, and no inconsiderable part of it was often in a state of anarchy and revolution. The English conquest of India was effected gradually, and not only by employing the native soldiers or sepoys to subject their country to foreigners, but often by joining one native power when at war with another, and thus taking the advantage of their dissensions to bring them under foreign dominion.

The peculiar character of the inhabitants of India must be considered. It has already been mentioned that the East India Company found no difficulty in forming regiments of native soldiers, instructing them in European discipline, and then employing them as they had occasion. The Indian armies have always been ready to follow and to fight for those who would pay them most. No love of tribe or nation or country, has prevented them from seeking each one his own interests, so long as there was no interference with their customs and superstitions. So also in all other kinds of employment. The English have always been able to procure the best native talent in every place and in every kind of business, for diplomacy and all kinds of agency for which they might have occasion. It might be naturally and reasonably expected that such men as the East India Company appointed for their governors and agents with such native assistance as they could always procure, would exceed the native princes, ignorant, inexperienced, and profligate as these often were, and surrounded with depraved favorites and corrupt courts. It was as natural that the English governors and their agents in such circumstances, should exceed the native powers and their agency in diplomacy and all the affairs of government, as it was that the English officers with their disciplined forces should be superior to the native armies in the battle-field. And not only have the English always been able to procure the best native agency by paying liberally for it, but they have also been able to protect all such agents from any dreaded consequences of their conduct from the displeasure of their countrymen, by furnishing them with places of refuge and of residence in their own territories. Calcutta, Madras, Bombay, and some other cities have always furnished places of residence where natives of all classes could live in safety, ease, and luxury, under the protection of the government, when their subserviency to the interests of the East India Company had made them odious to their countrymen, and they could no longer live securely under the government of their own princes.

5. Resources. The capital of the East India Company was increased at different times, according to exigencies and the profits of business. Since 1793, the capital has been nominally £6,000,000.* The amount, however, which has been actually paid into the treasury of the Company for the stock is £7,784,000, some of the last additions having been subscribed at a high premium. From 1793 to 1833, private trade was permitted between England and India, but it was subject to many restrictions. The trade between England and China continued to be a monopoly till 1833. Previous to 1833, the resources of the Company consisted of the profits of their trade, and the revenues realized in various ways in India. In 1833, the Company ceased to be a trading corporation; commerce between England and India and China became free, and since that time their revenues have all been derived from India. The resources of the Company, consisting of the profits of their trade and the revenues derived from India, have probably exceeded for nearly a century past, the resources of any native power in India. And if these revenues of the Company at any time were not sufficient for the expensive wars in which they were engaged, they found no difficulty in obtaining money in the way of loans in England, and from their countrymen in India, to any extent they required, while the native powers seldom had any credit in financial matters among their own subjects, or in any other part of the country. A few facts will show the resources of the English.

In 1800, the revenue of the Company was $37,972,685.

* This sum does not show the value of their capital. For many years before the late renewal of their charter, the stock fluctuated from 250 to 300 per cent. Since the renewal of their charter, it has been from 225 to 250 per cent. So their capital, though nominally £6,000,000, has been really in value from £15,000,000 to £18,000,000.

Their cash and property on hand for sale, in India, China, and England was $50,155,000, and the amount of their debt was $62,921,830. In 1810, the revenue was $82,321,800. Their cash and property on hand for sale was estimated at $113,-707,710; and their debts had increased to $194,383,940. Every decade shows an increase of territory, of revenue, and of debt. In 1850, the gross revenue of India, all realized in that country, is stated to exceed £27,000,000 or about $135,000,000, and their debt in England and India is stated to exceed £50,000,000 or $250,000,000. As the Company was deprived of their exclusive trade with China in 1833, the amount of their disposable property had much diminished. But the Directors declared that the amount of money in the hands of their numerous agents, and the value of their ships, forts, munitions of war, public buildings, etc., were equal in value to the aggregate of their debts; so that if Parliament refusing to prolong the charter, should take possession of India for the crown, the public property of all the different kinds which the English nation would acquire, would be equal in value to the amount of the debts of the Company which they must by the terms of the charter assume. These facts and figures show that the resources of the East India Company in their nature, amount, and facility of realization and application, have been greatly superior to any native government, or to any combination of the native powers with which the English have come in conflict, for nearly a century past.

6. Compensation for services. The salaries of Europeans in all high situations in the East India Company's employment are large and sufficient to command the first rate of qualifications in every department of the government in India. The salary of the governor-general since 1773 has been £25,000 ($125,000) yearly while his contingent or extra charges have often exceeded this sum.* The commander-in-chief of the army has a salary of £18,000. The members of the supreme council in Bengal have £9,600 each. The chief justice has £8,000, and the puisne judges £6,000 each. The governors of Madras and Bombay have £12,000 each. The members of the council have

* In 1850, the governor-general's extra expenses amounted to £45,000.

£6,000 each. The chief justice in each place has £6,000, and the puisne judges £5,000 each. These sums show that the salaries which the Company gives, are sufficient to procure the first rate of qualifications, if money can procure them. True, the salaries mentioned belong to high situations, but the remuneration of all who obtain their appointments from the Court of Directors, amounting in the different departments called the "Civil, the Clerical, the Medical, the Military, and the Naval Services," to 9 or 10,000 commissions, is large. No governments in the world give such salaries to their functionaries as the East India Company gives to its agents and servants. These salaries are sufficient to engage the first and most efficient talent in England, and the East India Company has been fortunate in having had many distinguished men in its employment.

7. The English government in India has gained much by pursuing a liberal policy towards native princes in allowing them pensions and annuities, when in the course of political changes they had become reduced in their circumstances or involved in their affairs. In some instances these annuities have been given in consideration of their relinquishing certain rights and claims, though perhaps not in circumstances to enforce them, and so what was given them was a matter of discretion and not of necessity. For instance, the affairs of some prince have become involved and complicated, and it appears uncertain what will be the result. The agents of the East India Company offer, if he will resign his affairs into their hands, to give him and perhaps his family in perpetuity a large annuity with a secure retreat for life, and he at once prefers the certain annuity with a life of ease and luxury to the course of uncertainty and danger, and perhaps of disgrace and poverty. In some instances native princes have surrendered themselves and their families without any stipulations, trusting entirely to the generosity of the English to do what might appear to them to be proper and right. In the early part of the British history in India, their governments in that country and the Court of Directors in England manifested a very generous spirit in the provision they made for the embarrassed, reduced, and dependent native princes and their families, and their acts of this character had much effect in extending their influence and power.

The East India Company by its original charter in 1600, had a monopoly of all the trade between England, and the countries and islands of southern Asia. And the Company retained this monopoly with some modifications, introduced from time to time as the charter was renewed, for nearly 200 years in respect to India, and for 233 years in respect to China. It is very remarkable that, in such a commercial and manufacturing nation as the English, a company of merchants should retain for so long a time the monopoly of so large a part of the trade of the country. Their retaining this right so long was to be ascribed in part to their great wealth, and the power and influence they were able to exert in the councils of the nation. Previous to the Reform Bill in 1830, the Company were able always to have a large representation of their number and interest in Parliament. They also at different times paid to the English government previous to 1812, (as their accounts show,) in consideration of their monopoly and protection the large sum of £5,135,319 or more than 25,000,000 dollars. The proprietors and agents of the Company were also continually bringing much wealth into the country which contributed to increase the national resources. The English government or the ministry appear often to have been willing to devolve the complicated affairs of India upon a body of men, who would be responsible for its proper government to Parliament, and who could be at any time called on to give an account of their proceedings. It was also seen that the Company was frequently engaged in successful wars, and was acquiring large possessions which would ultimately belong to the English nation, and was doing all this, too, without adding to their taxes or to their debts.* And for these reasons, though they have not all the same comparative force as they formerly

* The East India Company has added India to the British foreign possessions and made India pay for the conquest of itself, and the expenses of this conquest have to a considerable extent been paid to England. "Our wars in India," says Dr. Wilson, "though attended with loss of life, as all wars are, *have not cost our nation a single farthing*, but have been defrayed from the revenues or credit of that country itself. Even when they have been waged in different provinces of the land, large advantages of a pecuniary kind have accrued to our nation." The numerous European officers and agents employed in these wars and conquests were English. All were well paid, and many of them by salaries and other means acquired princely fortunes.

had, the same Company still retain possession of India, and their charter has been lately extended till 1874.

In 1793, the dividend of the East India Company was fixed by Parliament at 10½ per cent., and it has still been continued at that rate. For nearly a century previous to that period the dividend had fluctuated from 5 to 12 per cent., and upon an average was about 8 per cent. This is not a high rate when it is considered that a part of it was subscribed at the rate of 200 per cent.; another part of it at 174 per cent., and another part of it at 155 per cent., so that for the nominal capital of £6,000,000, there was actually paid into the Company's treasury £7,780,000. But the advantages which the proprietors derive from stock, is not limited to their dividends. Through the Directors they elect, they have always managed to share among them a large part of the patronage or appointments to situations in the government of India.

In considering the course of policy pursued by the English, which has resulted in their acquiring in India one of the largest empires ever known, there appears much less to censure in the Directors and controlling power of the East India Company in England than in their agents in India. Increase of territory has not generally been the desire of the proprietors or Directors of the Company, and in accordance with this view have been the general spirit and often the positive character of their instructions to their agents in India. But many of these agents have been of a different spirit; especially has this been true of many in the army. Various causes have united to produce and keep alive this war-spirit. The spirit of an army is generally restive and aggressive. In war the wages of officers and soldiers are much increased. Promotion is more rapid. Honors are more abundant and more easily procured. Large spoils under the name of prize-money, have often been taken and distributed among the officers and soldiers. The conquest of a new territory generally creates a large number of lucrative and honorable situations, some of which must be filled for a while at least by military men. And even when wars were apparently commenced without sufficient reasons, yet if conducted to a successful termination, the actors would calculate to be commended, honored, and well rewarded. In these circumstances wars have been sometimes commenced not only without authority from the superior powers in England, but in opposition to their known spirit and general instructions. Indeed, their first intelligence concerning some of the Indian wars, was that hostilities had been commenced under the pretence that the case was too urgent to admit of delay for obtaining advice, and then there was no alternative but to carry it on. And then it became necessary for them to vindicate or exculpate their agents, in order to sustain their own position and interests before the English nation.

The governors and other agents of the East India Company in India, have often unexpectedly found themselves in circumstances of great difficulty and perplexity. The native governments, Mohammedan as well as Hindu, have always been despotic in their form, and their princes have often been ignorant, weak-minded and capricious, unacquainted with international laws and usages, and under the influence of unworthy, depraved, and faithless favorites. The history of Asiatic courts generally consists of purposes, plans, and actions of treachery, intrigue, duplicity, and venality. Some princes cannot control the agents for whose acts according to the laws of nations they are responsible, and again they will refuse to fulfil the engagements of their fully accredited agents. Revolutions and sudden changes often occur in oriental governments, and the party which comes into power will refuse to abide by the engagements of the previous government. Attacks upon the English and invasions of their territory, have been sometimes made, not only without any previous declaration of war, but while making, up to the last possible day, the strongest assurances of friendship, peace, and good-will. A knowledge of the Indian character, of the rulers and the inhabitants, and of the circumstances in which the English have often been placed, is necessary in order to a just appreciation of many things in their history. If some agents have been commended and rewarded when they ought to have been censured and punished, others have been censured when acting from the best intentions, and doing as well as they possibly could in their circumstances.

PART III.

THE GOVERNMENT OF INDIA.

THE EAST INDIA COMPANY.

The East India Company, now the rulers of India, is an association of merchants and capitalists incorporated in London in 1600, and continued by successive renewals of their charter with such modifications as experience suggested down to the present time. The capital which constitutes the basis of this Company is £6,000,000,* which is divided in transferrable shares. The number of proprietors varies as the stock may be more or less divided at different times. The proprietors when assembled in due form and order for business, is called the "Court of Proprietors." In these meetings a proprietor of £500 is permitted to speak but not to vote. A proprietor of £1,000 has one vote; a proprietor of £3,000 has 2 votes; a proprietor of £6,000 has 3 votes, and a proprietor of £10,000 or more has 4 votes. The number of proprietors generally exceeds 3,000, but as none can vote unless they have £1,000 or more of stock and have owned their stock for one year, the voters seldom exceed 2,000 and are often much less. Matters of a pecuniary nature are sometimes considered and transacted at these meetings, but their chief business is to elect their Committee of management who are called Directors, and to receive the dividends upon their stock. The rate of dividend is fixed by Parliament at 10½ per cent. The price of the stock in the market for many years previous to the late renewal of the charter, varied from 250 to 300 per cent. Since the late renewal of the

* Some of the last additions to this sum were subscribed for or the shares were sold at an advanced rate, and the whole amount of money paid into the Company's treasury is £7,780,000. The price of this stock for many years previous to the late renewal of the charter, fluctuated from 250 to 300 per cent. If 275 is taken as the average price, the value of the stock, or, in other words, the capital of the Company exceeded 80,000,000 dollars.

charter the stock appears to have varied from 225 to 250 per cent. The value of this stock depends in part upon the patronage, or power of appointing to situations, in the government of India, which the proprietors are able to secure through the agency of the Directors they elect. At the late renewal of the charter this patronage was somewhat diminished and variously modified, and these changes have reduced the value of the stock. The present charter is to continue till 1874.

The committee of management, or Directors, as fixed by the renewed charter, are 18 in number; of these 12 are elected by the proprietors, and 6 are appointed by the Crown or the Ministry. These latter must have resided 10 years or more in India. One third of the Directors go out of office every second year, but may be reëlected or reappointed. The Directors have £500 salary each, and their chairman and deputy chairman have £1,000 each. A proprietor to be eligible for Director must own £2,000 of stock. The Directors when convened in due form and order for business, is called the "Court of Directors of the East India Company." The office of Director has generally been valued far more for the power and patronage they enjoy, than for the salary they receive. This power and patronage, though diminished by the changes made in the charter when lately renewed, is still large and very valuable, enabling the Directors to secure for their families and for their friends many honorable and lucrative situations in India.

The affairs of such an empire as the English possessions in India now form, are not entirely subject to the East India Company. In the latter part of the last century, great complaints were made of the governors and other agents of the Company in India, and an inquiry into these matters in Parliament resulted in the creation of a body called "The Board of Commissioners for controlling the affairs of India," which has been continued to the present time. This body is a department of the English government, and is commonly called the "Board of Control for India." It consists of 6 members, of whom the first is called President of the Board of Control, but he might more properly be called the Secretary of State for India, and he is always one of the Ministry. This Board generally includes 2 or 3 other members of the Ministry, and all must be members of the Privy Council. This Board, having a general superintendence of the affairs of India, makes the ministry responsible for its government, and so brings India under the control and protection of Parliament.

The appointments to the most important and lucrative situations in India, are divided between the Board of Control, that is, the Ministry, and the Directors of the Company. The former appoint the Judges of the Royal Courts in Calcutta, Madras, and Bombay, the Bishops, and the officers of the royal troops serving in India. The latter appoint the governor-general and the other governors, but they must have the approbation of the ministry. They also have the appointment of the members of the councils. Previous to the late changes in the charter of the Company, the Directors had the appointment of nearly all situations in the government of India, but their patronage has been recently much diminished.

For nearly a century previous to the recent changes in the government of India, there was a governor-general and council in Bengal, a governor and council in Madras, and a governor and council in Bombay. The changes made or contemplated in the renewed charter are said to be: — The office of governor-general and the governments of Madras and of Bombay are to continue, a deputy governor to be appointed in Bengal, another in Northern India, and perhaps another in Scinde.

The office of governor-general is one of great honor, power, responsibility, and emolument. It is the highest office under the British Sovereign, and is probably the highest delegated power and honor in the world. The governor-general and the other governors have the most experienced and able men in India associated with them for councillors, secretaries, etc. The salary of the governor-general is £25,000 annually, and his extra expenses, which are charged to the account of India, not unfrequently amount to a larger sum. In 1850, these "extra expenses" amounted to £45,000. He resides in any place, or moves about the country wherever his presence or his power appears to be required. The members of his council have each £9,600 annually. The governors of Madras and Bombay have each £12,000 annually, and the members of their councils £6,000 each.

The number of persons employed in the government is very large. They are divided in 5 classes or departments, namely, "the Civil, the Clerical, the Medical, the Military, and the Naval Services." These all obtain their appointments in England. The "Civil Service," or department, is the first in honor and in emoluments. The East India Company has a college at Haileybury in England for the education of men for this department.* All who are admitted into this college are expected, at the close of their education, to proceed to India, to be there employed in the government. In India, they are under the control of the governors and councils. Their rank, office, and salary depend partly upon their supposed qualifications, and partly upon seniority in the service. They become governors, ambassadors, councillors, secretaries, judges, collectors of the revenue, financiers, etc. The number in this department in all India, is stated to be generally about 800. Their emoluments are large, especially of those who have been for considerable time in the country.† One printed statement says the average salary of this

* The East India Company, so long as it retained only its commercial character, could easily obtain suitably qualified agents in England. But when the Company began its career of conquest, and had foreign possessions to govern, agents of different qualifications became necessary. Men were required who were competent to be governors, ambassadors, legislators, etc., and who should also be well acquainted with the character, languages, and customs of the people, among whom they were to fill these responsible situations. The Marquis of Wellesley, then governor-general of India, perceiving the wants of the Indian government, in 1800 commenced an institution in Calcutta, called the College of Fort William, for the education of men for government employment. In this college, Dr. C. Buchanan, well known for his "Christian Researches in Asia," and other works, was vice-provost, and Dr. W. Carey, equally well known for his missionary labors, was one of the professors. This college did not meet the views of the Directors in England, and so in a few years it was abolished, and the college in Haileybury was established. This college has always been a favorite institution of the Company, and it has furnished many eminent men. Previous to the recent changes in the charter, admission into this college was in the power of the Directors and the Board of Control, but now admission for the number annually required is open to general competition, on such examinations as are prescribed. It is expected this change will produce important results in the government of India.

† "On first reaching India, a civilian is allowed about £30 per month, till, having passed the necessary examination in one or more of the oriental languages, (which must be within 12 months after his arrival,) he is attached to the service, the emoluments of which vary from £500 to about £10,000 per annum. The members of council receive £9,600 each per annum in Bengal, and £6,000 per annum in Madras and Bombay. Civil servants must have 3 years actual

class is £1,750 each. Another statement says it exceeds £2,000 each; and another says it is £2,250 each. The first statement appears to be the average of the fixed salaries of the whole class in India. The next appears to be the average of the fixed salaries in Bengal, where they are higher than in the other Presidencies; and the last appears to be the average sum which each actually receives, and which consists of the salary and sundry "extra allowances," which vary with their situation and duties, and generally amount to a very considerable sum, in addition to the fixed salary.

residence in India, to hold a situation of over £1,500 per annum, 9 years' residence to hold a situation of over £3,000 per annum, and 12 years' residence to hold a situation of over £4,000 per annum. No civil servant can receive a greater salary than £5,220 per annum, unless he be a governor or member of council."

The following statement from a late number of the Calcutta Review, shows the salaries of different situations in Bengal. The salaries are put down in rupees, which are the currency of India. A rupee is commonly reckoned at 2 shillings sterling, or nearly half a dollar, so that half of these sums will be nearly the amount of the salaries in dollars.

" Governor-General of India		250,000	rupees.
Chief Justice		83,347	"
2 Puisne Judges, each		62,510	"
4 Members of Council, each		96,320	"
5 Judges of Suddur Diwany Adawlut, average each		52,200	"
2 Members of Suddur Board of Revenue, do.		52,200	"
3 Members of Customs, Salt, and Opium, average each		52,200	"
4 Political situations, average each		50,000	"
4 Secretaries to government, do.		52,200	"
2 Opium agents, do.		42,000	"
9 Revenue Commissioners, average each		38,000	"
30 Judges, average each		30,000	"
45 Collectors and Magistrates, salaries from		38,000	"
	to	28,000	"
	and	12,000	"
9 Miscellaneous appointments, varying from		28,000	"
	to	15,000	"
22 Additional Collectors, Joint Magistrates, and Deputy Collectors, from		12,000	"
	to	8,400	"
2 Secretaries of Boards, each		30,000	"
1 Register		30,000	"
35 Assistants, at from		6,600	"
	to	5,000."	"

The Clerical Service, or the ecclesiastical establishment of India, consists of 3 bishops (one in Calcutta, one in Madras, and one in Bombay), and 120 chaplains of the Church of England; and 6 chaplains of the Church of Scotland, namely, 2 in Calcutta, 2 in Madras, and 2 in Bombay.* The bishops are appointed by the Queen or her Ministry. The bishop of Calcutta (who has the rank of metropolitan) has a salary of £5,000 annually, with large allowance for residence, for the expenses of visitations, etc., and a pension of £1,200 annually after filling his office a certain number of years. The bishops of Madras and Bombay have £2,500 each annually, with allowances for diocesan expenses, and retiring pensions of £800 annually. The chaplains are divided in 2 classes, seniors and juniors, or chaplains and assistant chaplains, and they have salaries varying partly according to seniority, and partly according to the place and duties assigned to them, from 2,500 to 6 or 7,000 dollars. They also receive fees for particular services, and after performing duty in India for a certain number of years they have pensions for life.† The ecclesiastical establishment originated, and has been continued, with special reference to the European, and nominally Christian population in the employment of the government, but other Europeans and Indo-Britons not connected with the government share in the attention and labors of the chaplains, as there may be occasion. Henry Martyn, whose Memoirs have been so much read in America, Daniel Corrie, who was the bishop of Madras at the time of his decease, and a few others engaged actively in missionary labors, but the chaplains generally have not done so, nor is it expected of them.

The Medical Service or department contains generally about 800 regularly educated and legally qualified European physicians. They are divided into 3 or 4 classes, according to seniority. Their salaries vary according to seniority, rank, and duty assigned to them from $1,500 to $10,000 annually. They also have liberal pensions after completing certain periods of service.‡

* This was the state of the ecclesiastical establishment in the latest accounts I have seen. Some changes were expected to follow the renewal of the charter.

† The pensions of chaplains are:—"After an actual residence in India of 15 years, £292 per annum; after 10 years, if unable on account of ill-health to reside any longer in India, £173 per annum; and after 7 years, £128 per annum."

‡ The pensions of surgeons are:—"After 17 years' actual residence and

Some account of the Military Service will be given under the head of the army.

Bombay is the principal seat of the naval force of the East India Company. It consists of a number of sailing ships and steam vessels, and performs important service for the government in transporting the army, and in protecting the general interests of commerce, not only of India, but of the eastern seas, which are often infested with pirates. In salaries, pensions, etc.,* it is supposed to be upon an equality with the military service.

ADMINISTRATION OF JUSTICE.

In each of the cities of Calcutta, Madras, and Bombay, is a Supreme Court called the Queen's Court, which has jurisdiction over the incorporated city in each place, and in certain specified cases over all the presidency. The court in Calcutta consists of a chief justice, with a salary of £8,000, and of 2 puisne justices, with salaries of £6,000 each. In Madras and Bombay the court consists of a chief justice with salaries of £6,000 each, and a puisne justice, with salaries of £5,000 each. All these judges have large pensions for life after filling their office for a specified time in India. In criminal cases the trial is by jury, but not in civil cases. The natives are eligible to be grand and petty jurors, and Europeans, Parsees, Mohammedans, and Hindus may often be seen intermingled in the same jury seats and boxes. In these courts, fees as well as salaries are very high; and the expenses of law-proceedings are heavy, and often ruinous to the parties. Still the natives generally have much confidence in the integrity and uprightness of the judges.

Agents of the English government called Residents always live in or near the capitals of the large native princes. They are expected to keep their government well informed concerning the state of affairs in the territory of the prince, and to transact any matters of business that may occur between the governments. The duties of these agents vary according to the relations of the

service, £200 per annum; after 21 years, £250; after 25 years, £300; after 29 years, £365; after 32 years, £500; and after 35 years, £700 per annum."

* "Every officer who has actually served 22 years or upwards in the Indian navy, is permitted to retire from the service with the following pay:—A captain, £360 yearly; a commander, £290; lieutenant, £190; purser, £190."

princes to the English government. Sometimes their power is greater than the princes, and they become more like the governors of the territory and guardians of the prince and his family than the representatives of another government. These agents fill situations of much honor and responsibility. They have princely salaries, and have often lived in oriental magnificence.

For the collection and management of the revenue and other public matters, and for the administration of justice among the native population, the territory of each presidency is divided into districts. In each district are two classes of European agents; one class has charge of the collection of the taxes, the management of the revenue, public works, etc., and they are generally called collectors. Each district has a principal collector, who has several assistants under him. The revenue is generally collected by the native agents and then transferred to the Europeans, who examine accounts, hear complaints, etc. Each district has a series of courts of 3 or 4 orders. In the lower courts the magistrates are natives, and in the higher courts they are Europeans. The lawyers or barristers in these courts are generally natives, who are admitted to practice in due form. Many of the native magistrates and lawyers are well-educated and respectable men, and their official and social position gives them much influence. Trials by jury have not been introduced in these courts. The manner of proceeding resembles the English courts more than the former Mohammedan and Hindu courts. All the proceedings are in the native languages. The intention is that the proceedings should be in the language of the parties whose matters are under consideration. The general rule in these courts has been to administer Mohammedan law among the Mohammedans, as it is contained in their standard works and declared by their jurists; and the principles of Hindu law among the Hindus, as it is contained in their own works. It must be obvious, from the different forms and kinds of government existing in India previous to the country's becoming subject to the English, as well as from the mixed and heterogeneous character of its inhabitants, that the satisfactory administration of justice among them, must be a work of great difficulty, and very much must depend upon the discretion and conscience of the magistrates. The people are very litigious, and in none of the departments of the government, does their moral character appear more unfavorable than in these courts. Deception, bribery, and perjury are of frequent occurrence. The want of a code of civil and criminal laws adapted to all parts of India and to all classes of its population, has long been felt and acknowledged. To supply this want many efforts have been made, and great expenses have been incurred. But such a uniform code of laws is yet a desideratum.

THE ARMY.

The army of the East India Company consists of two parts, namely, the European and the Native. The former consists of two classes, commonly designated the Queen's troops, and the Company's European troops. The Queen's troops consist of a certain number of regiments of the regular army of England, but employed in India and paid by the East India Company, according to such terms as are agreed upon with the English government. This force, according to the latest accounts, contained 29,480, officers and soldiers included. These regiments have the same general character as the British regular army in their other foreign possessions. The Company's European troops consist of regiments raised in England for employment in India, and they do not materially differ from the troops of the regular army. They amount generally to about 20,000, officers included. So the whole European force in India amounts to about 50,000 men.

The native army at the latest accounts amounted to almost 250,000 men. To these are to be added the contingent troops in the native States, which have European officers, and are subject to the Company in the time of war. This force is somewhat scattered in the territories of different native princes, but is estimated to exceed in the aggregate 30,000. So the whole military force under the control of the English in India considerably exceeds 300,000. This army consists of engineers, artillery, cavalry, and infantry, all under English officers, and kept in a highly efficient state.

The whole number of European officers in India, including those who are in charge of the contingent and subsidized forces in the territories of the native princes, was lately estimated at 8,000. These are all subject directly or indirectly to the English governments in the country.

The East India Company has a military college at Addiscombe, a few miles south from London, which was originated and is sustained with special reference to the education of officers for the engineer and artillery departments of their army in India. Previous to the late changes in the Company's charter the Court of Directors had the patronage of this college. Admission into it is now open to competition upon such examinations as are prescribed and approved.

The salaries of officers in the army, though less than in some other departments of the public service, are liberal. According to an official statement of the salaries of the officers of all ranks, and in all the different departments of the army in India, (reckoning the rupee at two shillings sterling, or half a dollar,) the salaries in the European and native infantry will be as follows: a colonel, $7,680 yearly; lieut.-colonel, $5,520; major, $3,810; captain, $2,226; lieutenant, $1,344; ensign, $1,080. These are the salaries in garrisons and cantonments. When in the field, their salaries are more. The salaries of the other departments, as engineers, artillery, and cavalry, are generally higher. These sums show the lowest rate of fixed salaries. "Many officers have staff situations or are employed on special duty, or hold places in the civil service, or have 2 or 3 situations in the army. Such situations and offices are very numerous and are highly paid. By these various means the emoluments which many of the officers realize, are 25, often 50, and not unfrequently 100 per cent. more than their fixed salaries."

The terms upon which officers can resign the service and receive pensions are also very liberal.* They generally obtain their commissions at ages varying from 18 to 22, and generally at 40 or 45 years of age, they can obtain a pension which will

* "All officers who have served in the Indian army for 25 years, including 3 years for furlough, or 22 years' continual service, may retire on the full pay of their rank for life. Officers may also retire on the following pensions without reference to rank, if they have served for the undermentioned periods, including a furlough, namely, after 23 years, £191 per annum; after 27 years, £292; after 31 years, £365; after 35 years, £456 per annum."

yield a comfortable support for life, to say nothing of what they may have accumulated from their salaries. If any prefer to continue in the army for promotion and increase of pay, they can do so, and the Indian army contains many officers, 50 and 60, and more years old. An officer does not generally acquire the rank of major before 20 and often 25 years of service.

The pay of soldiers and non-commissioned officers is small, but it is such that with their rations, etc., they can generally live comfortably. They are all enlisted for a certain period of service, and those who live to see the close of that period, can then have pensions for life, and return to England. But many of them prefer remaining in the army.

It was in the great struggle between the English and the French for ascendency in the south part of India, that the latter are said to have first brought into the field a battalion of native troops, armed and disciplined in the European manner, and commanded by European officers. This was at the siege of Cuddalore in 1746, and so great was the success of the experiment that before the close of the year, the English commenced the nucleus of their native army, which has been continued to the present time, and now contains 250,000 men. Important changes have at different times been made in the constitution of this army, but its essential features have always been the same; namely, native soldiers,* armed, dressed, and disciplined after the European manner, and commanded by English officers. There is a set of native officers in each regiment, generally of as many different ranks as exist among the English officers. But the pay of these officers is small, and the highest rank, the reward generally of 30 or 40 years' service, is much lower than the English ensign who has just joined the regiment. In respect to caste, which has so much influence in religious and social intercourse among the Hindus, the English have shown some indulgence in the army, to the superstitions and prejudices of the natives, and these in turn have yielded somewhat to the wishes of their masters and to the exigency of their own circumstances. The more important rules of caste pertaining to eating, drinking, and intermarriage, are carefully observed in the army.

* Called generally *sepoys*, the native name of soldiers, to distinguish them from the Europeans.

These usages are also regarded in free social intercourse, but give way to more important matters when on duty and under the immediate inspection and order of their superiors.* When on duty their dress is nearly the same in appearance, though much inferior in quality, to the English soldiers. When not on duty, they wear the ordinary native dress of their caste or class.

The pay of the native army varies in different parts of the country, and also in different departments, the cavalry and artillery receiving more than the infantry. The wages of a sepoy in the infantry does not often exceed 3 or 4 dollars per month. A subadar, or captain, a rank not often acquired before 25 or 30 years' service, receives about 18 or 20 dollars per month; and a subadar major, a rank not attained till 30 or 40 years' service, receives rather more than one dollar a day.† The sepoys have generally families,‡ and after a certain number of years, or when incapable of further service, they receive pensions for life. The system of pensions is much thought of, and has great influence in the native army. Each sepoy hopes to live till he can return to his native village, or some eligible place, with an income for life for his past services. In oriental countries there is generally a strong desire to be employed in the service of the government, and the English have no difficulty in forming regiments and obtaining recruits for the army. The regiments are generally raised and recruited in one part of the country, and then employed in another, and they do not often remain more than 3 years in the same place. Thus separated from their own people, from their own nation it may be said in respect to most of them, and often removed from place to place, they become dependent directly upon the government, are a distinct commu-

* "Off duty, the Brahmin and Rajpoot will not come into contact with the Shudra, far less will he touch the Pariar or eat of food they have cooked; but on duty they rub shoulders freely one with another, and fight side by side."

† "Only a small part of the sepoys, probably not more than 1 in 20 or 25 ever become officers, and the highest native officer's rank, the result of 30 or 40 years' service, is lower than the English ensign the day he joins the regiment. And the pay of the highest native officer is not more than one third, and often not more than one fourth as much as the lowest English officer."

‡ "Of the 250,000 men composing the native army, there are not probably 10,000 unmarried."

nity by themselves, form few connections and have little sympathy in common with the great body of the inhabitants. To enlist regiments in Germany and then employ them in Spain, or in Holland and then employ them in Italy, or in France and then employ them in Russia, would resemble the course generally pursued by the English in managing their native army in India. The natives of Europe do not differ more from each other in language, religion, customs, and manners, than the people of the different parts of India differ from each other. The sepoys and lowest class of officers in the army of the East India Company are better paid, and including the system of pensions, are better supported than in the armies of the native princes, while in dress, arms, and discipline, they are far superior to any other military forces in the southern countries of Asia.

The native army of the East India Company is not an inviting field of service or enterprise for the higher and wealthy classes of the native population,* and it must always consist of the lower and middling classes — not *castes*, for poverty often compels men of high caste to enter the army. The officers in the regular armies of Europe and America generally consist of men from the middling and higher classes, the gentry and nobility not excepted. What would the American, or the English, or the French army soon become, if constituted like the native army of the East India Company, in which all must enter the army as private soldiers, and then serve for some years

* "No native gentleman ever thinks of putting on the uniform of the regular army. It would be marvellous if he did, for length of service furnishes and has long furnished the only claim for promotion, and it takes from 20 to 30 years to earn the epaulets of a subadar." — "The pay of a sepoy is about five pence half-penny a day, out of which he is obliged to find his linen and the materials for keeping his arms and accoutrements in order. It takes him on an average from 5 to 7 years to become a naik, or corporal, about 10 more to reach the grade of havildar, or serjeant, and 20, or it may be 30 in all, to earn his first commission, when his pay is raised to 1s. 4d. (32 cents) per day. In his turn he becomes a subadar, or captain, with pay at the rate of half a crown per diem; and finally if he live, and his constitution does not fail altogether, he may become subadar major with 5s. a day. The average age of the native subalterns in the East India Company's service has been taken at 45, of the captains at 55, and of the subadar majors (the highest rank) at 65, or from that to 70 years of age."

before they can attain the rank of corporal, and then all promotion from this step must be in the way of seniority? And then if each regiment must have over it another set of officers, all foreigners, 22 in number,* the lowest of whom, a young man 18 or 20 years old, without any experience in military affairs, is yet higher in honor and authority, and receives 3 times larger salary than the highest native officer? Must it not be evident that an army thus originated, constituted, and managed, can never be a desirable service for any wealthy, well educated, and public spirited native man? And that however efficient such an army may be for war, and however ready to fight for those who pay them, in their own favorite phrase, "whose salt they eat," yet they can have little of those noble sentiments and patriotic feelings, which constitute the main strength and reliable principles of the armies of Europe and America.

The wars which the English have carried on in India have been but little known to the world, when compared with their wars in America and in Europe. Yet these wars have often been on a great scale, and their history shows many hard fought and bloody battles. In the great battle of Waterloo, the English loss was 1 in 6 of the force engaged. The following is the English loss in some of the battles in their wars in India:—

In the battle of	Assaye,	in 1803,	the English loss was	1 in 3	of their force engaged.
" "	Dieg,	" 1804,	" "	1 in 4½	" "
" "	Mehidpoor,	" 1817,	" "	1 in 6	" "
" "	Seetabaldy,	" 1817,	" "	1 in 4½	" "
" "	Coregaum,	" 1818,	" "	1 in 3½	" "
" "	Maharajpoor,	" 1845,	" "	1 in 6	" "
" "	Sutlege,	" 1846,	" "	1 in 5	" "
" "	Chillianwalla,	" 1848,	" "	1 in 7	" "

These battles were all fought with different native princes of the country, who generally led on their own armies, and the above figures show a fearful amount of loss on the part of the English. If the loss on the other side was greater, as it generally was, yet such figures show that India has not been brought to its present state of subjection without repeated and severe struggles to preserve its independence of foreign control, while

* "The complement of European officers for a native regiment is 1 Colonel, 1 Lieut.-Colonel, 1 Major, 5 Captains, 8 Lieutenants, 5 Ensigns, and 1 Surgeon."

the large military force which England finds it necessary still to support in a highly efficient state, shows that all the inhabitants are not satisfied with the government exercised over them.

REVENUE.

The amount of the gross revenue of the East India Company in the latest accounts I have seen, were as follows: — Land revenue, £15,178,676. Excise, etc., £1,088,254. Opium, £4,562,-586. Salt, £3,289,214. Customs, £946,561. Stamps, fees, and fines, £593,982. Tobacco, £115,000. Post-Office, mint, etc., £1,979,041. In all, £27,753,314. It is stated that when the various deductions for the expenses of the collection, the management of the different items, etc. were all made, this sum was reduced to £23,067,920, which was the amount actually paid into the treasury and available for the purposes of government.

The principal source of revenue in India from remote antiquity has been the tax or rent on the land. It was so when the country was divided into several different kingdoms, and the Hindus lived under their own sovereigns. It was so when the country became subject to the Mohammedans, and the original Hindu kingdoms became provinces of the empire of Delhi, and it has continued to be so since the country became subject to the English. In some territories it has been called a tax, and in others it has been called a rent, the government being regarded as the proprietor, and the occupants as only tenants. This tax or rent has varied in different parts of India, and sometimes in the same territory according to the pretended exigencies of the government and the supposed improvements made in the land. In some places it has been one half of the produce, or of the supposed value of it; and in others it has been one third, one fourth, one fifth, etc. The general opinion and practice have been that the occupants might dispose of their right in the soil, whatever this might be, and that the government might increase the tax or rent at pleasure, the occupants of the land for the time being, having no assurance or security against any increase, and no means of redress when it was exacted from them. And when the produce of the land would no longer pay the tax or the rent, and for the expense of cultivation, then it might be abandoned or changed into pasture when the tax would be of another kind, or according to another rate.

The course which was pursued in Bengal, and the unhappy consequences to all classes have been mentioned.* In other parts of the country the general practice of the English has been, as district after district came under their government, to continue the system of revenue previously in force till there should appear to be sufficient reasons for making changes, and these have generally been introduced with care and discretion. I am not aware that they have increased the land-tax or rent in any part of India, while in some districts it has been diminished. In some districts the lands have all been measured, and the tax has been fixed for a long period, as 15 or 20 years, during which there is to be no increase. This system gives the owner the advantage of any improvements he can make. It has thus far given much satisfaction to the cultivators, and great advantages are expected to accrue from it. The land-tax in India has generally been very high, and presses heavily upon the agricultural population. This tax has always produced more than half and sometimes as much as three fifths of the entire revenue of the government.

In the accounts given, the amount of revenue realized from opium is the next highest, though generally the revenue from salt has been the second. But they have often been nearly alike. This branch of the revenue was scarcely known under the native princes. It early became a monopoly of the East India Company, and is more fluctuating than any other item. In all the territories subject to the English in India, the cultivation, manufacture, and trade in opium, is a strict monopoly of the government. It can be cultivated and sold freely in the territories of the native princes, but as they have no sea-coast, it must be transported through the English territory before it can be exported, and for this transportation a large transit duty is exacted. The foreign trade in opium is carried on chiefly in Calcutta and Bombay. The export from Calcutta in some years has exceeded 40,000 chests of about 140 lbs. each. The export from Bombay has generally been about half as large as from

* Pages 195–197.

Calcutta. It is exported by English and native merchants in English ships to countries east from India, chiefly to Canton and other ports of China. The Chinese laws do not permit opium to be produced in the empire, and they forbid its importation and use under heavy penalties. The English traders and vessels appear to have paid little or no regard to the Chinese laws on this subject since the commencement of this century. The vessels and crews engaged in the traffic were armed, and the Chinese government found it impossible to sustain their laws prohibiting the introduction of opium. This illegal traffic inflicted great injuries for many years on China, and at length led to the war between England and China, which was properly designated in Parliament "the Opium War." The Chinese laws all remain unchanged, but they durst not enforce them for fear of becoming again involved in war with England.

The opium produced in India and what is exported to China, is chiefly used for its exhilarating and stupefying effects. It is the worst kind of intoxication. It is an expensive vice, and ruinous to body and mind. The habit is easily acquired, and then it is incorrigible, at least such is the general opinion. The agency of the East India Company and the English government in the production and traffic of opium, and in "the opium war," have been the subject of much severe but deserved censure in India and England. This subject has occupied a prominent place in the journals of India, England, and America. I know of nothing in the history of modern commerce, unless it is the slave-trade, more exceptionable in its moral character, and the manner in which it is carried on.*

The manufacture and traffic in salt is also a monopoly of the government and yields a large item in the revenue. It has been increased at different times, and as it enters largely into the consumption of all classes of people, the tax is regarded as burdensome and oppressive.

The customs, which are the principal source of revenue in the United States, and one of the principal sources generally in civ-

* Merchants Magazine, vol. 23, pp. 28, and 146. Also a work on "The Opium Trade, including a sketch of its History, Extent, and Effects, as carried on in India and China," by Nathan Allen, M. D.

ilized countries, produces only one twenty-fifth or thirtieth part of the revenue in India. The amount of revenue collected by the government is not large when compared with the number of the people, but when compared with the means of the classes who pay a large part of it, the taxes are heavy, and the agricultural population are generally poor, depressed in spirits, and in embarrassed circumstances.

The East India Company, soon after beginning to acquire territory in India, began to contract debts, which were increased by the frequent wars in which they were engaged. In 1800, their debt amounted to £12,584,366; and their revenue amounted to £9,742,947. In 1825, the debt had increased to £34,429,682; and the revenue was £20,750,183. In 1850, the debt had increased to £50,847,564; and the revenue was £27,-753,314. When the charter was renewed in 1853, about half the debt was in loans at 5 per cent., and half at 4 per cent. The interest is all payable in India, but much of the debt is owed in England. Soon after the charter was renewed, the Company began to pay off the 5 per cents. or exchange them for 4 per cents. at the option of the creditors, and in the course of a few months all the loans on 5 per cent. amounting to about half the debt were paid, or converted into loans at 4 per cent. So great a change effected in a few months shows that the East India Company must have great pecuniary resources, and that the public must have entire confidence in the stability of the English government in India.

It should be mentioned that the Company in order to carry on their complicated operations of governing so large an empire, find it necessary to have a large amount of money in their treasuries and in the hands of their numerous agents. For many years past it is said that this amount has been from £10,000,000 to £15,000,000. The aggregate amount of their property of various kinds, as money, ships, public buildings, munitions of war, etc., has been estimated to be of more value than their debts.

The largest item in the expenses of the government is for the army, which has generally varied from one half to three fifths of the whole expenditure. Another large item is the expenses of the Company in England. These expenses consist of dividends on the stock of the Company,* the interest on bonds or debts due in England, pensions of retired officers, etc. For some years past the expenses of the Company in England have exceeded £3,000,000, and they appear likely soon to exceed £4,000,000.

This large sum (from $15,000,000 to $20,000,000) India pays annually to England. A part of it has generally been remitted from India in the way of payments or advances to merchants, on the security of goods shipped to England, to be repaid on their arrival or sale, but the greater part is obtained in England for orders given by the Directors of the Company on their treasuries in India. This is a large sum for a poor country to pay annually to a rich one for such purposes.†

But the sum transmitted from India to England on account of the East India Company is not all that England derives from India. It has been already shown that many persons in England obtain appointments to situations in the government of India, where they receive large salaries. The amount of property accumulated in this way and remitted to England while in these situations, or when closing their period of employment and returning to England, is very large. Many English merchants and adventurers also proceed to India and there establish themselves in trade and other kinds of business, for which

* The capital is £6,000,000, and the rate of dividend is fixed by Parliament at 10 1-2 per cent. So the annual dividend on the stock of the Company is £630,000. This capital is redeemable at the close of its charter in 1874, at the rate of £5. 5s. for £100, and provision has been made for its redemption in a fund created out of the commercial assets of the Company at the close of their monopoly of the China trade in 1833. This fund, called the "Guarantee Fund," then consisted of £2,000,000 and is expected to become sufficient by accumulation to redeem the capital of the Company, so that at the close of the charter, the Company may take the accumulated fund for their capital, and Parliament assume the possession and government of the empire which the Company has acquired.

† Professor H. H. Wilson, who was formerly many years in India in the employment of the East India Company, and is now Professor of the Sanscrit language and literature in Oxford University, says, "This transfer of so much of the revenue of India to England is an exhausting drain upon the resources of the country, the issue of which is replaced by no reflux; it is an extraction of the lifeblood from the veins of national industry, which no subsequent introduction of nourishment is furnished to restore."

the laws in India and commercial regulations between India and England are more favorable than for persons from other nations. The profits of these various kinds of business are often large, and such men almost invariably return to England with their "fortunes" in a few years. In these various ways, namely, on account of the East India Company, private accumulations from salaries, and the profits of business, the amount of money or property transmitted from India to England, is variously estimated at from £6,500,000 to £8,000,000 yearly.* Thus, though the national or general government of England receives nothing directly from India, yet the wealth of the nation receives a large annual increase in the property which many thousand individuals in various ways realize from that country.

EDUCATION.

The government educational institutions are under the superintendence of a Board or Council of Education in each Presidency. These institutions are of different kinds. A few of them were established at an early period of the English power in India for particular classes of people, as the Madrissa, in Calcutta, for the Mohammedans, and the Sanscrit colleges in Calcutta, Benares, and Poona, for the brahmins. These institutions have not produced the results which were expected, and they will probably soon be made places of general education, either open for all classes, or will include all branches of learning. Some changes of this character have recently been made in them. The colleges and high schools established by the government within a few years past have generally two departments, namely, the English and Native, or Indian. In the former, the English language with its science and literature is taught, and in the latter, the vernacular language of the district, with the Sanscrit, or the Persian, or the Arabic languages and literature, at the option of the scholars. The professors and teachers in all these institutions are appointed and paid by the govern-

* Dr. J. Wilson, who lived many years in India, after describing these different matters says, that from them "about £8,000,000 sterling annually accrue to Great Britain."

ment. Some of the scholars are required to pay a small fee for entrance or for tuition, and some of them while pursuing particular branches of science and literature, receive some allowance from the government for their support. The number of these institutions in all the different parts of India has become large, and is likely to be increased.

There is probably nothing in which the nations of Europe more excel those in Asia than in the knowledge and practice of medicine and surgery. In India, these noble departments of science have always been much mixed up with superstition, imposition, and quackery, which have often caused great misery, and not unfrequently the loss of health and of life. To remove these evils and to enable the native population to realize the benefits to be derived from the present improved state of medical and surgical knowledge, the English government has established Medical Colleges in Calcutta, Madras, and Bombay. These institutions are under the instruction of able and experienced English professors, generally selected from the surgeons in the service of the government. The instruction in all the departments is nearly or quite gratuitous, and the students who enter them belong to respectable classes of people. In these institutions the peculiar diseases of India, the physical constitutions and habits of the different classes of the inhabitants, the medical skill, so far as there is any, among the *hakims* or native doctors, and the whole materia medica of the country, are made the subjects of careful and thorough inquiry and examination. These medical colleges will raise up and prepare well-qualified physicians for India, which she has never yet had, and so will prove of great advantage to all classes of people. A new era of medical science has commenced in India.

The government supports a large number of vernacular schools in the scattered villages. The education in these schools is in the common branches of learning, corresponding to the common free schools in the United States. They are generally under superintendents connected with the Councils of Education, and the magistrates of the respective districts.

The sums appropriated by the government for education have been much increased within a few years, and now amount to nearly $500,000 annually. It is expected large additions will be made to the educational institutions under the renewed charter.

Much dissatisfaction has been expressed by some people with the government system of education. The expenses of this system are defrayed from taxes collected from the native population, who consist of Hindus, Mohammedans, Parsees, and other classes of various religious sentiments. The Hindus are polytheists and idolaters. The Mohammedans believe in only one God, and abhor all idolatry. The Parsees, Jainas, etc., have each a different creed. These different classes of people would naturally feel unwilling to be taxed for the support of schools in which their religion was declared to be false, and some system which they abhor, was declared to be true, and the duty of all to practise it. It was also supposed that people would be unwilling to send their children to schools, in which such principles and doctrines concerning their religion made a part of the course of education. The government, in view of these facts and circumstances, resolved to exclude from their course of education all religion, except those moral precepts and general principles in which all classes would concur — thus making the course literary, scientific, and moral, but not religious. The books used in the schools were to contain and the instructors employed were to inculcate nothing directly opposed to Christianity, or to Hinduism, or to Mohammedanism, or to the religion of any considerable body of the native population. Such have been the general principles of the government system of education.

This neutral or common ground generally occupied by the government has given occasion for dissatisfaction on the part of a portion of the Christian community, saying that the government being professedly Christian in its principles, ought not thus practically to ignore its own faith, where it can exhibit and inculcate the truth upon its subjects. But it is not easy to see how the government could pursue any other course than has been pursued, consistently with its professed principles of non-interference with the religion of the native population. And further, it has been the wish of the government to pursue a course which would excite an interest among the native population, and secure their coöperation in carrying forward the cause of general education, and also to prepare and publish elementary, literary, and scientific works, which would be acceptable and useful. And these objects the government could only hope to accomplish by occupying this neutral ground.

But the government course of education, though it contains nothing which is peculiar to any particular system of religion, or which is of a controversial character, yet is exerting a strong influence on the native mind, and is producing important results in their religious opinions. This is in part the effect of the knowledge they acquire, thus removing their stupidity and ignorance, and communicating power to think, compare, reason, and judge on religious subjects; and in part from the principles and facts of modern astronomy, history, geography, etc., being utterly at variance with the declarations and doctrines of the Hindu Shasters, so that no person who believes in the former (and all educated people must believe them), can retain any confidence in the latter. The natural consequence of this course of education is to produce a spirit of scepticism in respect to all religion. It destroys all confidence in Hinduism, and does not supply its place with any other religion. This consequence is now seen in the religious or rather irreligious views of a proportion of the young men, who have been educated in European science and literature, in the government institutions. They are generally strongly opposed to Christianity, and often ridicule its most sacred and solemn truths. They openly avow their sceptical and deistical sentiments, but they have hitherto generally conformed to the popular superstitions so far as to avoid persecution, retain their social position, and to secure and enjoy their property-rights. Many of them, however, are very uneasy in their present state, and would gladly seize any opportunity to emancipate themselves from the shackles of caste and the various forms of superstition, which they clearly see have exerted such an unhappy influence on the state of their country and the character of their nation, but which they have not yet decision of purpose and energy of mind sufficient to renounce. But the sure and steady progress of knowledge in the native community, the increase of those who are embracing similar opinions, increasing independence of mind and self-reliance, and above all, the light which Christianity is shedding over the country —

these causes will erelong produce such a state of feeling and thinking in the educated classes that they will unite in breaking the bondage of the most degrading superstition, which apostate and erring men ever conceived, or human nature ever endured.

The government councils of education in the different presidencies, include among their objects, the preparation and publication of suitable books in the vernacular languages for education and general reading. They have done much in the way of preparing and publishing dictionaries, grammars, and such like works, which without their aid could not have been published. They also encourage translations and original works upon certain specified subjects of science and literature. They have also always evinced a readiness liberally to reward the authors of works of merit on any subject, which would be of advantage to the native population. In these ways a very considerable number of valuable works have been produced in the different vernacular languages within a few years past, and if this course is continued, India will soon have a valuable indigenous literature.

From these facts and remarks it must be obvious that the course which the government is pursuing in the cause of education in India, is destroying the confidence of the people in their own systems of religion, and introducing speculative scepticism and deism. Motives of worldly policy may lead most of the present generation of educated young men through life to show some deference and respect to notions, rites, and ceremonies, which they regard as false, unmeaning, and superstitious. Should these views pervade the masses of the native population, they may be expected to develop their genuine spirit in very painful consequences. How far Christianity will in the mean time acquire so much power as to hold such evil principles under restraint and prevent their full development, remains to be seen. Certainly the present state and prospects of the native population of India, as affected by the course of education we have been contemplating, present strong reasons for Christians to use all the means they can to supply such erring men with the holy Scriptures and a Christian literature, that through the Divine blessing they may be freed from the mazes of scepticism and the darkness of deism, and embrace the truth.

Since the preceding was written I have seen a despatch from the Court of Directors to their governors and agents in India, on the subject of education. They have taken up the cause with earnestness and appear determined to redeem the pledges and to fulfil the promises which were made at the late renewal of their charter. Their plan is to establish a university at the seat of each Presidency, namely, in Calcutta, Madras, and Bombay, and then in other large cities, if there should be sufficient encouragement. These universities are to have each a chancellor, vice-chancellor, and fellows, who are to constitute the senate or controlling power. "The offices of chancellor and vice-chancellor are to be filled by persons of high station, who have shown an interest in the cause of education. The senate may include natives of India of all religious persuasions, who have the confidence of the native communities." The Directors have taken the London University as the model of their universities in India, only making such changes as appear to be necessary to adapt them to the state of the country. Of these universities, the colleges supported by the government, and missionary high schools and seminaries if they have sufficient literary and scientific character, may become "affiliated institutions, in which students, after being matriculated in the universities, may pursue their course of study till required to repair to the university for the final examination for their degrees." The Directors say:—

"The examinations for degrees will not include any subjects connected with religious belief, and the affiliated institutions may be under the management of every variety of religious persuasion. As in England, various institutions in immediate connection with the Church of England, the Presbyterian College at Caermarthen, the Roman Catholic College at Oscutt, the Wesleyan College at Sheffield, the Baptist College at Bristol, and the Countess of Huntington's College at Cheshunt, are among the institutions from which the London University is empowered to receive subjects for degrees. So in India, institutions conducted by all denominations of Christians, Hindus, Mohammedans, Parsees, Sikhs, Budhists, Jainas, or any other religious persuasions may be affiliated to the universities, if they are found to afford the requisite course of study, and can be depended upon for the certificates of conduct which will be required."

The number of vernacular schools is also to be largely increased, and special efforts are to be made to increase the qualifications of the teachers and to improve the manner of instructing, by the establishment of normal schools in different parts of the country. The Directors also declare their intention to grant aid to private and missionary schools without in any way interfering with the religious instruction communicated in such schools, if they only impart a good secular education, this latter being the object of the government in all its educational operations. Schools which receive grants from the government for support, will be inspected by the school inspectors, but "they are to take no notice whatever of the religious doctrines which may be taught in any school, the duty of the inspectors being confined to ascertaining whether the secular knowledge conveyed is such as to entitle it to consideration in the distribution of the sum which will be applied to grants in aid."

The Directors refer to female education in a manner which must surprise the old orthodox Hindus, but which will be gratifying to many of their sons and daughters. The Directors say: —

"The importance of female education in India cannot be overrated, and we have observed with pleasure the evidence which is now afforded of an increased desire on the part of many of the natives of India to give a good education to their daughters. By this means a far greater proportional impulse is imparted to the educational and moral tone of the people than by the education of men. We have already observed that schools for females are included among those to which grants in aid may be given, and we cannot refrain from expressing our cordial sympathy with the efforts which are being made in this direction. Our Governor-General in Council has declared in a communication to the government of Bengal that the government ought to give to native female education in India its frank and cordial support; in this we heartily concur, and especially approve of the bestowal of marks of honor upon such native gentlemen as Bahadur Magaubhai Kurrumchund, who devoted 20,000 rupees ($10,000) to the foundation of two native female schools in Ahmedabad, as by such means our desire for the promotion of female education became generally known."

When the first American missionaries arrived in India, female education among the Hindus was unknown, and all their principles and all their prejudices were decided and strong against it. They declared that such education never had been, never should be, and never could be. The missionaries of different societies and denominations showed by their persevering efforts that native female education was practicable, and the females who were educated, showed that it was desirable. The educated and wealthy young men were soon able to appreciate its advantages, and began to wish that their sisters and the girls to whom they had been betrothed by their parents, might be educated. In Calcutta, Madras, and Bombay, the cause was taken up, and Europeans and natives united in supporting and encouraging it. And now we see the Court of the Directors, of the East India Company, the supreme government of India, including female schools in the system of education which is to receive their patronage, giving it their cordial support, and recommending it in the strongest way they can, to all the native population.

The course of policy which the government will pursue in respect to religion in their educational operations, is thus described: —

"Considerable misapprehension appears to exist as to our views with respect to religious instruction in the government institutions. Those institutions were founded for the benefit of the whole population of India, and in order to effect their object, it was and is indispensable that the education conveyed in them should be exclusively secular. The Bible is, as we understand, placed in the libraries of the colleges and schools, and the pupils are able freely to consult it. This is as it should be; and moreover we have no desire to prevent or to discourage any explanations, which the pupils may of their own free will ask from their masters upon the subject of the Christian religion, provided that such information be given out of school hours. Such instruction being entirely voluntary on both sides, it is necessary in order to prevent the slightest suspicion of an intention on our part, to make use of the influence of government for the purpose of proselytism, that no notice shall be taken of it in their periodical visits."

The Directors also say that education, as certified by examinations and degrees, will be regarded as an important qualification and recommendation for employment in the service of the government of India, and that other qualifications and claims being equal, the best educated man will always be preferred. If this rule is carefully followed in the government service, it will have great influence in promoting the cause of education.

While the government adheres to its established policy not in any way to interfere with the religion of the native population, the Christian character of missionary seminaries and the religious principles taught in them, are to be no objection to their becoming "affiliated institutions of the Universities." This places missionary educational institutions upon the same ground as the colleges established and supported by the government. And further, the vernacular schools, male and female, which are established and supported by missionary societies, are placed upon the same ground as other schools for receiving "grants in aid" towards their support from the government. It remains to be seen how far missionary societies will be able to secure advantages from this system. The objection sometimes formerly made, that the government not only ignored Christianity, but purposely excluded it from all parts of its system of education, can no longer be made; for it is placed upon the same basis for government patronage and public favor as Hinduism and Mohammedanism, though the revenues are nearly all paid by people professing these latter forms of religion, and sincerely attached to them. An educational system more favorable to the promotion of science and literature and to the propagation of Christianity cannot reasonably be expected from a government, which has a due respect for the rights, and principles, and property of its subjects.

If these plans and purposes of the Directors should be fully carried into effect by the governors and other agents of the Company, it will commence a new era, not only in the cause of education, but in the government of the country.

PUBLIC WORKS.

The land-tax, or rent, as it has often been called, has always formed the principal item of revenue in India. And as this varied with the estimated productiveness of the land, it has been for the interest of the government to make land as productive as possible. It was also for the interest of rulers to increase the resources, population, and power of their respective kingdoms, as they had often to defend their dominions and their subjects against the encroachments of their unscrupulous neighbors. The circumstances and opinions of the people of India have always been such as to call the attention of their governments to such matters. The people have always been too ignorant to devise any public works, and too poor to execute them by private means or united capital. They regard all such matters as the proper work of the government, which alone has the ability to execute them, and will derive the principal advantage from them.

The ancient Hindu sovereigns, in accordance with such views of their own interests, and of the circumstances and expectations of their subjects, constructed roads and bridges to facilitate travel and traffic, and made canals and embankments to irrigate lands for cultivation. The remains and the ruins of many such works are found in different parts of the country. It was lately stated in one of the Indian journals, that in the Madras presidency alone, there are 43,000 works for irrigation in a state of repair, and more than 10,000 out of repair, all which were constructed before the English obtained possession of the country. These works greatly increased the fertility and resources of the country, and the wealth and happiness of the people. They furnish means for carrying on cultivation in times of drought, and so prevent sufferings in seasons of scarcity and famine, which are frequent on account of the failure of the rains in some parts of India.

Many noble public works were also constructed in the northern parts of India. Previous to the Mohammedan invasion, roads were constructed by the Hindu Rajas between large cities with wells of water and caravanserais at convenient distances.

The Mohammedans, who have been often described as semi-barbarians and oppressors, constructed many noble public works. Feroze Toghluk, who was emperor of Delhi from A. D. 1351 to 1388, though engaged in frequent wars, yet found time and means to devise and execute numerous public works for the benefit of his subjects. The following is a list for the maintenance of which lands were assigned, namely: — "50 dams across rivers to promote irrigation; 40 mosques, 30 colleges, 100 caravanserais, 30 reservoirs for irrigation, 100 hospitals, 100 public baths, and 150 bridges." *

Of Acber it is said that "he constructed a series of canal-works of greater extent and utility than any previously in existence." The canal commonly ascribed to Ali Merdan Khan, probably because it was constructed under his superintendence, but at the expense of the emperor Shah Jehan, was yet more extensive and completed in a superior manner. The eastern Jumna or Doab canal, a large work, was also made in the reign of the same emperor. These canals were channels of traffic, supplied water for cultivating large tracts of land, and furnished water for all the common purposes of life in the cities through or near which they were carried. In the anarchy which ensued upon the dissolution of the great Mogul government, consequent upon the death of Aurungzeb, many of these works for want of repair and preservation, became of little use.

With such examples of the former governments before them and the remains and ruins of such works around them, it does appear strange that the English should possess these territories for more than half a century, and have done so little in the way of public works. And it does not appear strange that the native

* Concerning this list, which is taken from Ferishta, Elphinstone remarks: — "The round numbers, as well as the amount of some of the items suggest doubts of the accuracy of the list, but the works of Feroze, that still remain, afford sufficient evidence of the magnitude of his undertakings. The most considerable of these is not specified in the list. It is a canal from the point in the Jumna, where it leaves the mountains by Carral to Hanse, and to Hissar. It reaches to the river Gagar, and in former times was again connected with the Sutlege, the nearest of the rivers of the Punjab. It seems to have been intended for irrigation, but as it has been disused perhaps since the death of Feroze, we can only judge of it by the part of it restored by the British government, which takes in the whole beyond Hissar, a distance of 200 miles."

population, while suffering the consequences of these works being out of repair and comparatively of little use, should complain of the English government over India; that the country was governed and its revenues expended too much for the interest of themselves, the rulers, and too little for the good of the people, their subjects. A few years ago this subject of internal improvement was taken up by the government, and if the plans formed, the promises made, and the pledges given, are all carried into effect, they will produce a new era in India. A few good roads have been made, and more are in the process of construction. If these are continued till the large cities and towns are united with each other and then with the seaports, they will be of great advantage to the country.

In the great valley of the Ganges, much progress has been made within a few years in repairing and improving the old canals and in constructing new ones. The entire length of the great canal and its branches is 445 miles, and the amount of land irrigated by it exceeds 1,000 square miles. The population obtaining their subsistence from this land, is estimated at 300,000, and the revenue collected from the irrigated land exceeds $450,000 annually, "nearly all of which is attributed to the use of the canal." This canal answers other important purposes besides irrigation. The amount of tolls collected on the traffic upon it and the rents for water-power to work machinery, are large. There are several other canals in the same great valley. The aggregate length of all these canals is 765 miles. The amount which the English government has expended in repairing and constructing them, exceeds 7,500,000 dollars, and the revenue from navigation, irrigation, water-power, etc., is estimated to vary from 1,500,000 to 2,000,000 dollars annually. These results are not less beneficial to the people than profitable to the government, and as there are yet large tracts of land, which can be brought into a state of new or improved cultivation by the same means, it is expected that internal improvements will be carried on vigorously for some years to come.

The government of India was much censured for some years in England, as well as in India, for not undertaking, and not sufficiently encouraging the construction of railroads. Great difficulties were anticipated from the rainy seasons, and from the mountains in some districts, and the alluvial nature of the soil in others, where the railroads were most needed. After much delay, companies were formed and several railroads were projected. One of these railroads commences at Madras, and runs westward to Bangalore, where it is expected one branch will proceed to the western coast of the peninsula, and another proceed north into the Deckan, probably there to communicate with one leading to Bombay, and another to Calcutta. One is to commence at Calcutta and proceed to Delhi, and another is to commence at Bombay and proceed to Delhi, and there form a junction with the one from Calcutta. From Delhi it is to be extended to Lahore in the Punjab. These railroads are now in the process of construction, and I saw cars running on one of them before I left India. A large part of the capital for constructing these railroads is subscribed in England. The conditions are such that capital to any amount required can be readily obtained on the fixed dividend or interest of 4, 4½, and 5 per cent., which is guaranteed for 20 years, by the East India Company. When these railroads are completed, they will form the grandest system of internal improvement ever yet accomplished in any country. And they will produce greater results than have yet been seen produced by the introduction and extension of railroads in any part of the world.

The electric telegraph has been introduced into India, and the large cities of Calcutta, Madras, and Bombay, can communicate simultaneously with each other, and with the large cities in the northern parts of India as far as Attock on the Indus.

India once supplied Europe and America with cotton goods, but her manufactures have been ruined by the use of machinery in England. She is capable of producing cotton enough to supply all Europe, but her cotton districts are far from her seaports, and the means of transportation are slow, difficult, and expensive. She has mines of coal of unknown extent, but they have hitherto been of little use for want of means to transport the coal to the seaports and other places where it has been required, and she has been to a great extent dependent upon England for coal for her steam-ships and her machinery. India has valuable iron mines, (the writer once heard a distinguished geologist who had been inspecting them say, they contained iron enough to supply the world,) and yet nearly all the iron used in the country is procured from Europe, because the iron mines are in one province, and the coal is in another, and there have been no means for bringing them together. Among her great population are several millions, who are often suffering for want of employment, and who are ready to work in agriculture, or mining, or manufactures, for less wages than are known in any country in Europe or America. When the railroads now in the process of construction shall be completed, the people will require only the additional aid of machinery to change her cotton into cloth, and again supply Europe with manufactured goods. Her mines of coal, iron, etc., hitherto almost worthless and useless, will become of incalculable value and utility. The amount of sugar, indigo, grain, etc., produced, will be greatly increased, and the natural resources of the country will be developed.

England has yet made no adequate return to India for the immense wealth she has drawn from it. Let some of this wealth be invested in the public works now in progress and projected. Let the excessive salaries of the English government agents and officers be reduced to a proper standard, and the savings be expended on internal improvements.* Let the sur-

* The Court of Directors previous to the last renewal of the charter, in 1853, had the patronage of the government of India chiefly in their hands, and they had also the determining of the salaries which the men they appointed should have. They appointed the members of their families and their friends, and the salaries, though fixed by the Directors, were yet all paid out of the revenues of India, and whatever these salaries, or the expenses of India were, no Director of the company or proprietor of the stock contributed any part towards them, or received any less himself on account of them. These facts will account in part for the high salaries in their employment, salaries generally quite beyond the value of any services rendered to India, or any qualifications required for the duties to be performed. This must be evident from the estimated value of these appointments. The Directors were forbidden by severe penalties to receive any pecuniary consideration for their patronage, but it was still very valuable, as they could bestow it upon the members of their own families and friends, or upon those who elected them. It was said by the best authorities on Indian affairs, that a commission in the Civil Service, when the fortunate possessor embarked for India, was worth from £4,000 to £5,000, and that a commission in the army was generally worth from £1,000 to £1,200. Recent changes in the charter have put the appointments in the most highly paid departments of the gov

plus and suffering population of India be employed under European direction and superintendence. Let the system of education recently promulgated by the government be fully carried into effect. Let the laws for securing equal religious liberty and protection to all classes of people be faithfully administered. Let the means and facilities now enjoyed for diffusing religious knowledge, be continued — and then the English conquest and government of India will prove as advantageous to the latter as it has hitherto been profitable to the former.

GOVERNMENT CONNECTION WITH IDOLATRY.

Much has been said and written concerning the connection of the English in India with the Hindu and Mohammedan religions, and the Indian governments have been often and severely censured for their support and patronage of idolatry, superstition, and false religion. The origin and nature of this connection and supposed patronage of idolatry and superstition require some explanation.

For many centuries Brahminism was the religion of the governments and of the great body of the inhabitants of India. During this long period many temples were erected and endowed. In some instances temples were erected by individuals, who then endowed them or procured endowments for them from the government. In some places temples were erected and endowed by the government by appropriating a part of the revenue of the district for a while to religious purposes. The permanent endowments generally consisted of the taxes or rents of certain lands, often of villages or districts in whole or in part, for keeping the temples in repair and supporting the prescribed rites and ceremonies of worship daily and on holidays. These endowments were made in form something like a deed,* describing the tem-

ernment of India (namely, the Civil Service, and the Engineers and Artillery of the Military Service) upon the competition of public examinations for admission into the college of Haileybury and the military academy at Addiscombe. There is therefore now reason to expect that the expenses of the European agency in India will be reduced, and the saving thus effected be expended on internal improvements. Such a change as this would soon produce great effects in developing the resources of the country, and in improving the state and circumstances of the inhabitants.

* These deeds are generally called *sunnuds*. I have seen many of them.

ple, and the lands and property given to it, and then appointing a certain family or families and their descendants to be the agents or trustees, to have the charge of the temple and its endowments, and to carry into effect the purposes for which the latter were made. Thus these families became the trustees of the temple, and so long as they performed their part, the use or income of the endowments belonged to them. These endowments were often of far more value than the services required in return for them. Indeed, one object in giving them often was to provide for the liberal and permanent support of the individuals and families, to whose management they were intrusted. Thus important and valuable personal and property rights became involved in these endowments. And if there should ever be any failure on the part of the trustees or agents to support these temples and the prescribed worship in them, then the inhabitants of the village, district, or city, for whose use and supposed benefit these temples were erected and endowed, could complain to the government, and it became the duty of the government to inquire into the matter and to cause the duties for which the endowments were made, to be performed.

Another class of endowments consisted of annual or stated payments of money from the taxes or revenue of a district to certain temples in it. These payments were made at first by the orders or formal acts of the government, and if paid for a few years in succession, they were considered to be of the nature of a permanent endowment. Though the government did not generally give any *sunnud* or deed to secure its payment in future, yet the brahmins connected with the temple, and the inhabitants of the village, district, or city, always expected it would be continued so long as they did nothing to forfeit it. Such payments were made to the brahmins who had the charge of the temple, and were to be expended for certain specified purposes. These purposes or objects generally were to keep the

They are generally engraved on plates of brass or copper, and are often many hundred years old. Translations and descriptions of several such plates are to be found in the Asiatic Researches, and in the Journal of the Royal Asiatic Society. They generally close with imprecations of the displeasure of the gods upon any government or individual, who shall ever in any way interfere with the endowments or prevent their object from being carried into effect.

temples in a state of repair, and for the celebration of festivals and holidays — works in which the people joined, and so obtained some equivalent for the money they paid for the expenses.

Another class of endowments consisted in a certain sum of money, or a certain proportion of the taxes collected in each village, being expended for religious purposes in the village, generally for keeping the temples in a state of repair, and for illuminations and ceremonies on particular occasions. This in many places became an established usage, and was regarded as a government regulation or law.

There were some circumstances of a peculiar character connected with some of these temples and sacred places. The Mohammedans had established their power in India several centuries before any part of it became subject to the English. Their professed object in conquering the country was to destroy idolatry and to convert the inhabitants to Islamism. The first conquerors were accustomed to demolish the Hindu temples, pollute their sacred places, and break their idols in pieces. But after a while their successors became more tolerant and imposed taxes on temples and pilgrims, endeavoring in this way to discourage idolatry by making it expensive and difficult, and also to obtain means for erecting mosques near the temples, and for other purposes of revenue.

And sometimes when a temple had acquired a high character and the resort of people to it had become great, the brahmins, who had the charge of it, exacted a tax from all the pilgrims for their own support and to keep the temple in repair, and pay the expenses of illuminations, festivals, etc. In some instances also Hindu princes imposed a tax upon temples, or upon pilgrims resorting to them, for purposes of revenue. Taxes of this kind were collected at Gya, Allahabad, Juggunath, Tripetty, and many other places by the Mohammedans or the Hindus, as either power happened to be in the possession of the shrines. The presents and offerings made to the deities at the great festivals were often very valuable. These according to general usage, became the property of the officiating brahmins, but disputes concerning their comparative rights, not unfrequently made it necessary for the government agents to interfere and adjust matters between them.

In the progress of their conquest the English acquired possession of the provinces containing these celebrated temples and sacred places, and so succeeded to the powers and rights of the previous governments. They did not impose any new taxes on pilgrims at these temples and sacred places; they only collected such as the previous governments had established and long collected. The amount of these taxes varied with the rank and caste of the worshippers, the shrines where they wished to worship, the ceremonies they wished to perform, the number of days they wished to be admitted, etc. These taxes, usages, and ceremonies were adjusted by the artful brahmins, who shared in the revenues and collections of the temples, so as to exact as much as possible from the deluded pilgrims.*

What has been said about the Hindu temples, might be applied to the mosques, in respect to their origin and the management of their endowments. I am not aware that any taxes were imposed upon them or exacted from any persons resorting to them.

Such was the state of the temples and mosques in India, when the English acquired possession of the country. The English then became the governing power, but the people all retained their religion, their language, their customs, etc., unchanged. The English in accordance with usage among civilized nations in such cases, acknowledged the laws and acts of the previous governments, especially in matters involving civil and personal rights and privileges. For instance, if any foreign nation should conquer the United States, such conquest and possession of the country would not deprive any person or party of their property, nor any church or college of its endowments, or its chartered rights and privileges. So the conquest of India by the English, did not deprive the temples and mosques of their

* These pilgrim taxes at Tripetty in one year, amounted to $110,000 more than the expenses of the temple. They were nearly as large at Gya, and also at Pruyag, and very considerable sums were collected at some other temples. These taxes are now said to be relinquished, or the management of the temples to be intrusted to the natives, so that the East India Company has no direct relation to them, has no management of them, and derives no benefit from them. The amount which the East India Company realized by taxes at these temples, from the time they came under their control and management, till they relinquished them, exceeded £2,000,000 or nearly $10,000,000.

endowments, nor exonerate the men intrusted with the management of these endowments from their obligation to use them for the objects for which they were originally given. The English government and its agents thought it their duty to enable the brahmins in charge of such endowments to collect their revenues and rents, and then to compel them to expend such income, or so much of it as might be required, for the purposes for which the endowments were originally made, and to which they had been for centuries appropriated and expended. In some places the native governments having long been in a feeble and distracted state, the temples were neglected and out of repair, not because the people had changed their religion or become indifferent to it, but because the brahmins either could not collect the income of the endowments, or had appropriated it to their own use. In such cases the English agents thought it their duty as the governing and administrative power, to enforce the rights of the brahmins to the endowments, and then their obligations to the temples and the people. In carrying out this policy it not unfrequently became necessary for the English magistrates to consider and decide disputes and quarrels between different persons and parties claiming a right to the management of the temples and their endowments, and in some cases the magistrates assumed the control and management of such endowments and the temples and mosques connected with them, and made the arrangements for celebrating their festivals. Thus the English magistrates became apparently the superintendents and managers of these temples and mosques, repairing them, appointing priests to officiate in them, fixing and paying their salaries, paying for illuminations, festivities, ceremonies, etc. These expenses were ostensibly paid out of the endowments of the temples. But it was said, and probably with some truth, that the expenses sometimes exceeded the income of the endowments, and that the deficiency was supplied from the government treasury, while in other cases the expenses for the temples were less than the income of the endowments, and that the surplus was then paid into the government treasury. Thus in some districts the government was supporting idolatry by payments directly from its treasury, and in other places it was realizing a revenue from the endowments of the temples. And in all such cases this policy of the government in supporting Hinduism and Mohammedanism exhibited the appearance of approving and sanctioning those systems as true, and their observance as for the benefit of their votaries. Many felt, and not without some reason, that so long as the English government should pursue this course, little good could be expected from any means or efforts to introduce Christianity, or to promote civilization, or even any reformation of morals and manners.

In respect to the other kind of endowments, namely, the annual payments of money to temples, and allowing a part of the revenue or taxes of villages to religious purposes, the English, in assuming the government of the country, generally continued the practice of the native governments that preceded them. The people who paid the taxes, regarded themselves as having a right from long and established usage to these payments for religious purposes. The English government, or the governors in India never gave any pledges, nor made any engagement or treaty to support Hinduism nor Mohammedanism; yet they were expected, both by the native princes and people, to respect the established laws and acts of the previous native governments. And when they had once begun the course of policy which has been mentioned, then to change it, to refuse such aid and support when the people, on their part, had given no occasion for any such change, appeared to them to be arbitrary and oppressive.

In this way the English government in India became involved in the control, management, and support of heathenism and Mohammedanism. This course of policy was commenced, as successive districts and territories became subject to them, by their governors and agents, in the exercise of the discretionary power intrusted to them. And this course was carried on for some years before the Christian public and proprietors of India stock in England became aware of its nature and extent. The speeches, debates, discussions, and despatches on this subject, (especially concerning the temple of Juggunath,) are generally known. It was not so easy for the governments in India to change their policy and dissolve all connection with the temples and mosques and their endowments, as was generally supposed. The Court of Directors were unwilling to take avowed and decisive measures, while some of their agents in India were disposed to favor and support Hinduism and Mohammedanism to an extent quite inconsistent with any due preference for Christianity. When this policy of the government and state of matters in India became known in England, it excited strong dissatisfaction. Earnest and able discussions took place among the proprietors of India stock, the Directors of the Company, and the Board of Control. Memorials and petitions from churches and missionary and other religious societies, were sent to Parliament, requesting its interference to prevent the continuance of what appeared to be a recommendation and approbation of Hinduism and Mohammedanism, and which could not be otherwise than a great obstacle to the introduction and progress of Christianity. The subject was in various ways kept before the Christian public for some years, and it became obvious that, whatever might be the opinion of the Directors and some of their agents in India, they would be compelled to yield to the authority of public opinion. In these discussions and debates, Mr. J. Poynder, and Mr. C. Grant, (subsequently Lord Glenelg,) took a very active part, and performed services for Christianity and benevolence, which will long be remembered.

Peremptory inquiries and instructions were at length sent out to India, and the results showed that the government had a more intimate and extensive connection with the religions of the country than had been supposed. It was found that in the presidency of Madras alone, the government had under its care and patronage 8,292 Hindu temples, and that the sums paid to them annually, amounted to $400,000. It was also found that the fund which had accumulated from the excess of the endowments above the expenses of these temples, amounted to $600,000 in the government treasury. The result of much inquiry, correspondence, and discussion, was that $400,000 of this accumulated fund should be given to promote education, and the remaining $200,000 to various benevolent and charitable objects; and that the temples and mosques, with all their endowments, should be intrusted to the management of committees of the inhabitants, where these places of worship are situated. These arrangements have in most places been carried into effect, and there is no reason to doubt that those who began this work of reform, will carry it on till the English government in India shall be entirely unconnected with the religion of its native subjects.

NATIVE PRINCES.

The native princes yet remaining in India, are of two classes, namely, those who receive pensions or annuities for themselves and their families, in consideration of their former power and possessions, or of their loss and misfortunes; and those who still retain some territory and power.

Oriental princes have always been fond of pageantry, and of indulging in habits of capricious extravagance. These tastes and habits have generally made their personal and family expenses very large. The pensions and annuities given by the East India Company to these fallen princes, have commonly been on a princely scale, but not unfrequently united with some conditions of a humiliating nature, though regarded by the English as necessary for the public safety, or for the stability of their own power. Some of these conditions are as follow:—Some are required to reside in certain specified cities or districts, and not to go out of them. They are not permitted to have any personal intercourse nor correspondence with other pensioned princes, nor with any princes still retaining power and territory in India or out of India. They are not permitted to have any personal intercourse or correspondence with any European, except the English agents of the government. In short, these fallen and deposed princes, though retaining their titles, and living in pageantry and luxury, are yet kept in circumstances which are painful and humiliating. Among these pensioners upon the East India Company, are the titular Emperor of Delhi the Great Mogul, the Nabobs of Bengal and the Carnatic, the Rajas of Burdwan, Benares, Tanjore, and Malabar, the families of the late Peishwa, and of Tippoo Sultan, and many others. The amount of pensions and annuities given to persons and families of this class and character, amount to about $7,000,000 annually. These are generally continued to their descendants, but as such families often become extinct, and some of them forfeit their claims by improper conduct, the number of pensioners and the amount paid on their account, are yearly diminishing. The very liberal manner in which the English in India have provided for this class of people, has contributed much to facilitate their conquest of the country, and to consolidate their power.

The native princes and nobles, who yet retain some power and territory, are numerous. They are to be found in nearly all parts of the country, and their territories vary from a few villages to provinces containing several millions of inhabitants. These scattered remains of former kingdoms and governments, were lately estimated to contain nearly one third of the population of India, or 50,000,000 of people, and rather more than one third of the whole territory of India. Some of these princes retain but little power, their territories being chiefly managed by English agents, while others are nearly independent in their own dominions. But none of them are permitted to hold any political intercourse with each other, nor with any nation or power out of India. Their relations to the East India Company, now the paramount power in the country, vary according to treaties and agreements made at different times. Their armies, so far as they are permitted to keep any, are commonly more or less under the command of English officers, and a certain amount of English force is generally stationed in their territories. An accredited English agent generally resides in or near their capital. In this way their policy and the state of their territory are always well known to the English, who have the means of restraining or deposing them, should there at any time appear to be reasons for doing it. The courts of these princes have the usual amount of intrigue, treachery, feuds, and profligacy found in oriental governments. Hence there is frequent occasion for the interference of the English agents, and such interference generally results in loss to the native princes, and the increase of the English power.

Formerly it was the opinion of the leading English statesmen in India, that these scattered remains of the former sovereigns and princes increased the stability of the English, and so were to be perpetuated. But for some years past, it has been the policy of the English governors and agents to annex all such territories to their own dominions, as soon as the failure of male descendants, or political disturbances, or misgovernment, should furnish occasion or excuse for doing it. Formerly it was an established usage or law among Hindus and Mohammedans, that if any prince had not any male issue, he could adopt a son, and if such adoption was made in the prescribed form and accompanied by certain religious rites, then such a son became the legal heir of the honors, titles, and possessions of the family. In this way the dynasties of the native princes were perpetuated. The English formerly allowed the native princes dependent upon them, to transmit their power and perpetuate their family honors and possessions by adoption. But for some years past they have generally refused to allow this right, and when princes and noble families have become extinct in the direct male line, they have annexed their possessions to their own dominions. In this way, within a few years past, the English have taken possession of the dominions of several deceased princes, as of the late Raja of Berar, estimated to contain 4,000,000 of inhabitants, of the late Raja of Sattara, estimated to contain 1,000,000, and some others. The remaining princes and their families have reason also to expect the loss of their honors, possessions, and wealth, whenever male heirs in the direct line shall fail. This change of policy in the English, of annexing and absorbing the territories of the native princes, instead of sustaining, protecting, and perpetuating them, which they formerly did, and to which these princes and their families have claimed a right, has produced strong excitement in India, and called forth earnest memorials, appeals, and protests. These princes and their families must contemplate this course of policy and the consequent prospect before them, with feelings of deep anxiety. And many others have similar feelings, who have looked upon these princes and their possessions as remaining witnesses of their former nationality, and who have cherished some vague hope that they might in some way recover their former power and dignity. But when they see these dynasties annihilated, or the representatives of them reduced to the state of the common people, and no native powers remaining to raise a banner, and no territory on which it could be raised and which could be made a basis for any political organization, their hopes of any future national government vanish, and they feel an increasing sense of their conquered, humbled, and dependent state. There are far more and stronger feelings of this nature among the middling and higher classes of both Hindus and Mohammedans, than Europeans generally suppose. It is not likely there will be any change in the present policy, which has been deliberately adopted in India and in England. The prospect is that all the territories now in the power of the native princes, will be gradually brought under the direct government of the English, and that the descendants and representatives of the emperors, kings, nabobs, and nobles of India, will decrease in number and power, until they eventually become extinct, or their posterity, if any remain, will have no social or civil distinction among the common people.

In a former part of this work some account was given of the power and splendor of the emperors of Delhi. This family, descended from Genghis Khan and Tamerlane, the great conquerors of the middle ages and occupying the throne of Delhi through a line of powerful sovereigns, (the most powerful then in the world,) must be viewed with peculiar feelings while they continue to be numbered among the princes of India. In 1803, Lord Lake took Delhi, which had for some years been in the possession of Scindia, one of the Mahratta chiefs. The emperor (or Grand Mogul as the title of the dynasty was for some centuries called) and his family then came under the protection of the English. When Lord Lake first saw him, "he was seated under a small tattered canopy, the remnant of his former state, his person emaciated by indigence and infirmities, and his countenance disfigured by the loss of his eyes, and marked with extreme old age and settled melancholy." Since that time the emperor has lived under the protection of the English, who settled upon him and his family an annuity, first of 10, then increased to 12, and subsequently to 15 lacks of rupees,* with as many of the palaces and other royal buildings of his ancestors as they have occasion to use, and more (as their state shows) than they keep in repair. The following account given by Bishop Heber of his interview with the emperor in 1826, shows

* Bishop Heber's Journal, vol. 2, p. 311. A rupee is nearly half a dollar, and a lack is 100,000; so the annuity or pension of the emperor was 500,000, then increased to 600,000, and subsequently to 750,000 dollars yearly.

the pageantry and ceremony observed in the court of a fallen and dependent prince in India.

"The 31st of December was fixed for my presentation to the emperor, which was appointed for half past eight in the morning. Lushington and Captain Wade also chose to take the same opportunity. At eight I went accompanied by Mr. Elliot with nearly the same formalities as at Lucknow, except that we were on elephants instead of in palanquins, and that the procession was perhaps less splendid and the beggars both less numerous, and far less vociferous and importunate. We were received with presented arms by the troops of the palace, drawn up within the barbican, and proceeded still on our elephants, through the noblest gateway and vestibule I ever saw. It consists not merely of a splendid gothic arch in the centre of the gate-tower, but after that of a long vaulted aisle like that of a gothic cathedral, with a small open octagonal court in its centre, all of granite, and finely carved with inscriptions from the Koran and with flowers. This ended in a ruinous and exceedingly dirty stable yard! where we were received by Captain Grant, as the Mogul's officer on guard, and by a number of elderly men with large gold-headed canes, the usual ensign of office here, and one of which Mr. Elliot also carried. We were now told to dismount and proceed on foot, a task which the late rain made inconvenient to my gown and cassock and thin shoes, and during which we were pestered by a fresh swarm of miserable beggars, the wives and children of the table servants. After this we passed another richly carved, but ruinous and dirty gateway, where our guides withdrawing a canvas screen, called out in a sort of harsh chant, "Lo, the Ornament of the World! Lo, the Asylum of the Nations! King of Kings! The Emperor Shah Acber! Just, fortunate, victorious!" We saw in fact a very handsome and striking court with low but richly ornamented buildings. Opposite to us was a beautiful open pavilion of white marble, richly carved, flanked by rose-bushes and fountains, and some tapestry and striped curtains hanging in festoons about it, within which was a crowd of people and the poor old descendant of Tamerlane seated in the midst of them. Mr. Elliot here bowed three times very low, in which we followed his example. This ceremony was repeated twice as we advanced up the steps of the pavilion, the heralds each time repeating the same expressions about their master's greatness. We then stood in a row on the right hand of the throne, which is a sort of marble bedstead richly ornamented with gilding, and raised two or three steps. Mr. Elliot then stepped forward, and with joined hands in the usual eastern way announced in a low voice to the emperor who I was. I then advanced, bowed three times and offered a nuzzur of 51 gold mohurs* in an embroidered purse, laid on my handkerchief in the way practised by the Baboos (native gentlemen) of Calcutta. This was received and laid on one side, and I remained standing for a few minutes while the usual court questions about my health, my travels, when I left Calcutta, etc., were asked. I had thus an opportunity of seeing the old gentleman more plainly. He has a pale, thin, but handsome face, with an aquiline nose and a long white beard. His complexion is little if at all darker than that of a European. His hands are fair and delicate, and he had some valuable looking rings upon them. His hands and face were all that I saw of him, for the morning being cold, he was so wrapped up in shawls that he reminded me extremely of the Druid's head on a Welsh half-penny. I then stepped back to my former place, and returned again with 5 more gold mohurs to make my offering to the heir apparent, who stood at his father's left hand, the right being occupied by the resident, (i. e. Mr. Elliot, the agent of the East India Company). Next, my two companions were introduced with nearly the same forms, except that their offerings were less and that the emperor did not speak to them.

"The emperor then beckoned to me to come forward, and Mr. Elliot told me to take off my hat, which till now remained on my head, on which the emperor tied a flimsy turban of brocade round my head with his own hands, for which however I paid 4 gold mohurs more. We were then directed to retire to receive our 'Khelats' (honorary dresses), which the bounty of the 'Asylum of the World' had provided for us. I was accordingly taken into a small private room adjoining the Zennana, where I found a handsome flowered caftan edged with fur, and

* Nuzzur is a present; a mohur is a gold coin worth 15 rupees, or nearly 7 1-2 dollars.

a pair of common looking shawls, which my servants who had the delight of witnessing all this fine show, put on instead of my gown, my cassock remaining as before. In this strange dress I had to walk back again, having my name announced by the criers, as 'Bahadur, Boozoony, Dowlutmund,' etc., to the presence (the emperor), where I found my two companions, who had not been honored by a private dressing-room, but had their Khelats put on them in the gateway of the court. They were, I apprehend, still queerer figures than I was, having their hats wrapped with scarfs of flowered gauze, and a strange garment of gauze, tinsel, and faded ribbons flung over their shoulders above their coats. I now again came forward and offered my third present to the emperor, being a copy of the Arabic Bible and the Hindustanee Common Prayer, handsomely bound in blue velvet laced with gold, and wrapped up in a piece of brocade. He then motioned to me to stoop and he put a string of pearls round my neck, and two glittering but not costly ornaments in the front of my turban, for which I again offered 5 gold mohurs. It was lastly announced that a horse was waiting for my acceptance, at which fresh instance of imperial munificence, the heralds again made a proclamation of largesse, and I again paid 5 gold mohurs. It ended by my taking leave with three times three salams, making up I think the sum of about threescore, and I retired with Mr. Elliot to my dressing-room, whence I sent to her Majesty (the *Queen*, as she is generally called, though the Empress would be the ancient and more proper title) a present of 5 gold mohurs more, and then the emperor's chobdars came eagerly up to know when they should come to receive their bukshish (presents).

"It must not be supposed that this interchange of civilities was very expensive, either to his Majesty or me. All the presents which he gave, the horse included, though really the handsomest which had been seen at the court of Delhi for many years, and though the old gentleman evidently intended to be extremely civil, were not worth much more than 300 rupees, so that he and his family gained at least 800 rupees by the morning's work, besides what he received from my two companions, which was all clear gain, since the Khelats which they got in return were only fit for May-day, and made, I fancy, from the cast off finery of the Begums (princesses). On the other hand, since the East India Company have wisely ordered that all the presents given by native princes to Europeans, should be disposed of on the government account, they have liberally at the same time taken on themselves the expense of paying the usual money nuzzurs made by public men on these occasions. In consequence none of my offerings were at my own charge, except the professional and private one of the two books, with which as they were unexpected, the Emperor, as I was told, was very much pleased.

"While in the small apartment where I got rid of my shining garments, I was struck with its beautiful ornaments. It was entirely lined with white marble, inlaid with flowers and leaves of green serpentine, lapis lazuli, and blue and red porphyry; the flowers were of the best Italian style of workmanship, and evidently the labor of an artist of that country. All, however, was desolate, dirty, and forlorn.

"After putting on my usual dress, we waited a little, till word was brought us that the 'King of Kings,' 'Shah-in-Shah,' had retired to his Zennana; we then went to the hall of audience which I had previously seen but imperfectly, from the crowd of people and the necessity of attending to the forms which I had to go through. It is a very beautiful hall of white marble, open on one side to the court of the palace, and on the other to a large garden. Its pillars and arches are exquisitely carved, and ornamented with gilt and inlaid flowers, and inscriptions in the most elaborate Persian character. Round the frieze is the motto, recorded, I believe, in Lalla Rookh,

> 'If there be an Elysium on earth,
> It is this, it is this.'

The marble floor, where not covered by carpets, is all inlaid in the same beautiful manner, with the little dressing-room I had visited.

"The gardens, which we next visited, are not large, but in their way must once have been extremely rich and beautiful. A channel of white marble for water, with little fountain pipes of the same material, carved like roses, is carried here and there among these parterres, and at the end of the terrace is a beautiful octagonal pavilion, also of marble, lined with the same Mosaic flowers as in the room which I first saw, with a marble fountain in the centre and a beautiful bath in a recess on one of its sides. We were then taken to the private mosque of the palace, an elegant little building also of white marble, and exquisitely carved. We went last to the 'Dewanee aum,' or hall of public audience, which is in the outer court, and where on certain occasions the Great Mogul sat in state, to receive the compliments or petitions of his subjects. This is also a splendid pavilion of marble, not unlike the other hall of audience in form, but considerably larger and open on three sides only; on the fourth is a blank wall, covered with the same Mosaic work of flowers and leaves, as I have described, and in the centre a throne, raised about 10 feet from the ground, with a small platform of marble in front, where the vizier used to stand to hand up petitions to his Majesty." *

REMARKS ON THE GOVERNMENT OF INDIA.

The professed policy of the East India Company in their government over their Indian subjects, whether Christians or Jews or Mohammedans or Hindus, has been neutrality in all matters of a religious character. It was also a part of their policy to govern each class of people, according to their previous laws, and not in any way to interfere with their religious principles, rites, or usages. The laws and usages of some classes are very intolerant, and utterly inconsistent with any equitable religious toleration and protection. The laws of the Mohammedan and Hindus do not respect the rights of conscience, nor of private judgment in religious matters. If a Mohammedan should renounce his religion, their laws enjoin persecution even unto death. And if a Hindu should renounce his ancestral faith, he is declared to be an *outcaste*, and then, according to Hindu laws, loses all his marital, parental, social, and civil rights. He is to be expelled from his house and his home, be disowned by his family and his friends, and be deprived of every thing which in their view makes life desirable, we may almost say, which leaves it endurable.

* Heber's Journal, vol. 2, p. 297–304.

Here we see that the English in India were placed in peculiar circumstances. If they administered the government according to the previously existing laws, and any Hindu or Mohammedan in accordance with the dictates of his conscience, should change his religion, then he must suffer severe persecution, the government enforcing the intolerant and persecuting laws of these different religious systems, or quietly allowing the people to enforce them. And if the government should change these laws, with a view to secure full religious toleration and protection to such as should apostatize from their ancestral faith, then nineteen twentieths of the people would complain that the English had begun to interfere with their religion, and would soon be compelling them to renounce it. It has often been loudly and industriously proclaimed, and by many believed, though without any evidence, that the English in taking possession of the country either by treaty with the former princes, or by promises and pledges to the inhabitants, had solemnly engaged to make no changes whatever in their religion, or the laws and usages connected with it. Some English persons, high in authority, as well as many natives, affected to believe that any change in the religious laws, or interference with their superstitions, would be the signal for insurrection through all India, and not unlikely would soon terminate in the expulsion of all Europeans from the country. Such declarations were frequently and confidently made in speeches, journals, and pamphlets.

None of the Hindu superstitions have excited more horror than the rite of Suttee, and we cannot well conceive of any thing which called more urgently for the interference of the government. And yet Bengal, the part of India in which this horrid rite was the most frequent, and where 700 or 800 women were every year burnt alive with the dead bodies of their deceased husbands, had been subject to the English more than 75 years before they forbid this horrid and inhuman custom. And though no insurrection resulted from the prohibition, yet the native mind was strongly excited, public meetings were called, resolutions were passed, and memorials numerously signed were sent to the Governor-General against the law designed to put an end to this horrid rite. And when it was seen that no means that could be used in India, would avail any thing, a large sum of money was subscribed, and an English barrister, well known in Calcutta, was sent to England to implore the interposition of the Parliament to annul the law of the Indian government forbidding Suttees. This effort showed the disposition of the native population in respect to any legislative changes in their religious customs.

The conquest and government of India by England, a country situated at such a distance, not one tenth of its size, and containing not more than one fifth of its population, form one of the most remarkable chapters in the history of the world. No nation but the English ever had the moral and intellectual power and the pecuniary means of accomplishing such a work, and in no country but India could such a work be done. England, by the conquest and government of India, has greatly increased her wealth and power. And what has been the effect upon India? On this subject there are different opinions, as all know who have read the proceedings in Parliament and the English journals, as often as the merits of the East India Company's government has come under consideration. In some respects, the change of India's having become subject to England, is of advantage. There is now general religious toleration and protection for all classes of people who live in the English territories, a state of freedom or liberty which never existed, and which could scarcely be expected ever to exist, certainly not for a long time to come, under any native government, Mohammedan or Hindu. This is certainly a great change, and cannot but prove of great advantage in various ways to the country. Again there is more security to life and property, better laws and better administration of justice under the English government, than there was generally, perhaps better than there ever was, under the native governments. The country is preserved in a state of more quietness in respect to internal difficulties and agitations and to external wars, than it was when under a number of separate and independent native governments, or than when nearly all India was subject, as it once was, to the emperors of Delhi.

In the early history of the East India Company, many ample fortunes were soon acquired in India. Salaries, mercantile adventures, monopolies, presents from native princes for political influence, and bribes for judicial favor, all contributed to enrich the fortune-seekers in India. The East India Company also often paid large sums of money from the revenues of India to persons and parties for which the public in England and in India could see no sufficient reasons. Near the close of the last century various laws and regulations were passed by Parliament and the Directors of the Company, restraining the official conduct of the agents, and defining their privileges, rights, and duties. These laws reduced the affairs of India to system and order, and exacted responsibility from those who administered them. Since the commencement of this century, there has seldom been any good reason for complaint of the abuse of power or confidence in the European agents of the government. Large fortunes are now often accumulated in India, but they are the avails of salaries which are large in the service of the government, or of legitimate mercantile pursuits in which the English, from their superior knowledge of business and foreign commercial connections, have many advantages over the natives.

The lower and middle classes (if there can be said to be any middle class in India), are better satisfied with the English government than the higher classes. The former are better protected than they were under the native governments, while they are as well rewarded for their labor. Formerly, all places of honor and emoluments were in the hands of the higher classes of natives, but now, all the power and the high situations are in the hands of the English and are filled by them. The fixed salaries and emoluments of office generally, under the native governments were not large, often not so large as some natives now obtain in the service of the English government, but the honor and the number of persons employed were much greater. Many were employed merely to furnish them with the means of support, and to secure their good-will and influence. But the policy of the English is to employ no more natives than are necessary to do their work, while the order and system they have introduced into all the departments of the government, enable them to accomplish the same work with far less help. The salary of an English secretary of the government, or a judge, or a collector of the revenue, is often sufficient to support 100 native families in respectable style, and this sum, under native governments, would be distributed among many families and support them comfortably and respectably, who now for want of employment are often in very straitened circumstances.*

But while many of the higher classes, who formerly found employment and support in connection with their governments, and who feel from their caste, or social position or family connections that they still have a claim for similar favor from the present English government, are dissatisfied because this claim is not realized, there is a portion of the higher class who are more satisfied with the present state of matters and the course of the government. This class consists of the wealthy merchants, bankers, and those who live upon invested and accumulated property. These classes are better protected in their property and all their rights than they would be under any native government. These classes of people live in the large cities, chiefly in Calcutta, Madras, Bombay, and their suburbs. The native governments were often very oppressive to these classes of people, not unfrequently exacting heavy and arbitrary contributions of money, and sometimes seizing and confiscating all their property for some merely pretended reason. No such arbitrary oppression and violence have ever been suffered under the English government in India, and none are feared. This is is a kind of protection, which those can appreciate who enjoy it, and as these classes are generally wealthy and intelligent, their opinions and influence do much to strengthen the English government in the country. Still these classes regard the expenses of the government, especially of the European agency, as much too high, and urgently requiring reduction. They also complain, and not without good reasons for it, that the English government has done but little to develop the natural resources of the country. Yet as they enjoy protection and security of life and property, and as the taxes bear more heavily upon the agricultural than upon the commercial and wealthy population, few of this class of persons would wish to change the English for any native government.

There has long been much dissatisfaction among the mercan-

* See pages 300–304. Also Pamphlets on Indian Reform, No. 1 to 6.

tile and manufacturing classes in England with the government of India for consulting their personal interests, and expending the revenues in high salaries, instead of making internal improvements to develop the resources of the country, and so increasing its commerce with England. When the renewal of the East India Company's charter was coming under the consideration of Parliament in 1853, an Association called the "India Reform Society," was formed, which by pamphlets, speeches, etc., endeavored to effect great and important changes in the government of India. Some of these pamphlets contain a list of the Association, among whom are the names of 36 members of Parliament, and several of them among the most prominent members of that august body. The charter was renewed with some organic changes in its constitution, and many promises respecting education, canals, railroads, and irrigation were made; whether these promises will be fulfilled and the expectations thus excited will be realized, remains to be seen.

The question is often asked in this country, — How long will India continue to be subject to England? To this inquiry no answer can be given. The native kings and princes of India having been subdued — some dynasties annihilated and all prostrated — the withdrawal of the English power would leave the country in a state of anarchy. But England has yet made no adequate return for the immense wealth she has drawn from India, and it remains to be seen whether she will ever make any such return. At each renewal of the charter of the East India Company, (as in 1813, 1833, and 1853,) some changes were made in it, which were expected to have an important influence on the well-being of the country. At such times pledges were given and promises were made, but complaints soon followed that the former were not redeemed, and the latter were not fulfilled. Still considerable progress or improvement in the government has been made, and there is now reason for expecting that this progress will be greater during the period of the present charter (which is to continue till 1874), than all that has been hitherto made since the English obtained possession of the country. These changes, if made, will greatly strengthen the connection between the two countries. As no English colonies have been or are likely to be formed in India, there can be no people there of European origin, who will desire a separation from England. For the mixed classes, partly of European and partly of native origin, are not likely to be sufficiently numerous to be of any considerable political weight and importance, and what influence they have, will be in favor of the English government. The army though consisting chiefly of natives, yet is not likely to prove unfaithful, if constituted of the same classes which now compose it, and treated in future as they have hitherto been. The difference in language, religion, and caste will long be an obstacle to any organization or coöperation among the native population against the English government. The native kings, princes, and nobility are diminishing in number and power, and there will soon be none of them remaining to raise the standard of war, or to make his territory the rallying ground for conflict or for attack. There will be no party which will have the pecuniary means or the confidence of their own people enough to originate and sustain any efficient and permanent opposition. The diffusion of knowledge and the progress of Christianity will not produce those changes in the character of the inhabitants, at least not for a long time, which some people confidently expect. Considering all these facts and circumstances, and that England may be expected to be as determined in using all her possible policy and power to retain India in permanent subjection, as she formerly was to sustain her power over her North American colonies, now the United States — considering all these things, it appears probable that India will be subject to England for some generations yet to come.

The question is also sometimes asked, — Where will be the limit of British conquest and power in the East? The answer to this inquiry is yet more in the future — more in the future providence of God — than the previous one. A century ago, the English possessions in India consisted of only five or six forts for the protection of their trade, and a few square miles of territory around them. Now, they are masters of the country; their territory contains 100,000,000 inhabitants, and they control indirectly, but effectually, 50,000,000 more, who live upon the scattered fragments of the kingdoms of the former sovereigns of the country. Nor is the English power limited to India properly so called. They have acquired a large part of what was formerly the Burmese empire. And yet further east they have Singapore, Penang, Malacca, and Hongkong, which are surrounded with nations and tribes who are likely soon and often to furnish occasions for the English to interfere to secure their own rights, or to preserve the balance of power among their neighbors, as is said of their interference in the present war between the Turks and Russians. Looking at the history of the British power in the southern countries of Asia, and to the present state and prospects of those nations, we believe their power has not yet there reached its limits. In 1852, they engaged in a second war with the Burmese, in the course of which the Governor-General, unable to effect a satisfactory treaty with the Court of Ava, took possession of Pegu, and by proclamation annexed it to the British possessions with such declarations as were expected to bring the war to a close, by inducing the Burmese to cease from further hostilities, if they wished to preserve their national existence. This proclamation, with the reasons for it and the policy that dictated it, was the subject of numerous articles in the English papers of India. These articles doubtless indicated the general sentiment of the English in that country, which was that the annexation of Pegu was only one step in their progress eastward, and that extension of territory, by conquest or annexation or treaty, would continue till the Pacific had become their eastern boundary, — that their reaching that boundary was merely a question of time, depending upon the policy of their governors, and the revolutions and changes which were taking place in the intermediate countries. The *Friend of India*, which has always been supposed to indicate the English sentiment in India more than any other paper in the country, in its remarks concerning the proclamation annexing Pegu, said, — "Every one out of England is now ready to acknowledge that the whole of Asia from the Indus to the sea of Ochotsk, is destined to become the patrimony of that race which the Normans thought six centuries ago they had finally crushed, but which now stands at the head of European civilization. We are placed, it is said, by the mysterious design of Providence in command of Asia, and the people of England must not lay the flattering unction to their souls that they can escape the responsibility of this lofty and important position by simply denouncing the means by which England has attained it." Whether England is thus to include among her foreign possessions "the whole of Asia from the Indus to the sea of Ochotsk," comprehending India, China, and all the intermediate countries, and containing more than half of the human race, remains to be seen. But the present state of England and her achievements in India, indicate that she possesses the pecuniary and physical means thus to extend her possessions, and also the moral and intellectual power then to govern them. And it does not now appear so improbable that before the close of this century her power will extend over all these countries and nations, as it appeared at the beginning of this century that her power would by this time reach its present limits.

In the mean time another great power is beginning to take an active part in the politics of Asia. The Afghan war of 1838–42, the most severe and unhappy war in which the English were ever engaged in India, originated in Russian influence and intrigues in central Asia. The results of this policy not corresponding to her expectations, Russia withdrew her agency from the scene, but as was then believed and has since become evident, only to renew it in more favorable circumstances. The war in which Russia, Turkey, France, and England, are now engaged, originated in the aggressive attack made by Russia upon Turkey. But no one can doubt that other motives than the defence of Turkey have induced England to engage in this conflict. England wishes to check the aggressive spirit of Russia, as it is likely to affect her possessions in southern Asia. Papers recently from India, contain accounts of Russian agency, pecuniary and political, again at work in central Asia. And the same papers contain accounts of her interference in the affairs of China, of her having obtained a large territory from its northern part, and it appears not unlikely she will take the advantage of the present distracted state of that empire to extend her power over a considerable part of it. It now appears likely that at no distant day, the greater part of Asia will be divided between Russia and England, each power extending its border till they meet, and no one can now say where this will be, or what Asiatic nations will receive their laws from London, and what nations will receive them from St. Petersburg.

PART IV.

THE EUROPEAN POPULATION.

The different classes of people in the employment of the government of India, have been somewhat brought into view in the different parts of this work. And these classes, including the army and navy, comprise the great body of Europeans in India. The European population, unconnected in any way with the government, is comparatively small. They live chiefly in the cities of Calcutta, Madras, Bombay, and their suburbs, and are merchants, agents, and manufacturers. A few, who are sugar and indigo planters, live in the rural districts. It is not easy to form any estimate of their number. Sir John Malcolm in 1826 said:—"The total number of English in India, not in the public service, has been computed at 3,000, of which 2,000 are given to Bengal, 500 to Madras, and 500 to Bombay. The calculation is probably beyond the actual numbers, including even those in the shipping of the country."* The territory subject to the English in India has been much increased since 1826, and the European population, unconnected with the government, has probably increased in a yet faster ratio. Should we suppose this European population has doubled since 1826, so as to have become 6,000 or more, it is still very small for so great a country, and compared with the vast native population, estimated at 150,000,000.

Should the small number of the European population unconnected with the government in India appear strange, it must be considered in explanation that the exclusive powers and privileges of the English East India Company from its origin in 1600 till comparatively a recent period in its history, enabled its managers and agents to exclude their countrymen from settling permanently or residing temporarily in any part of their terri-

* Malcolm's Political History of India, vol. 2, p. 246.

tories. They early resolved to allow no Europeans, except their own agents, to reside in any part of their possessions. They were strongly opposed to forming European colonies, or to permitting any to be formed in India. And in this policy they professed to have the good of their countrymen in view, as well as their own interests. They referred to the state of the colonies of the Portuguese and Dutch on the western and eastern coast of Africa, and in the southern countries and islands of Asia, as a warning to the English nation to pursue a different course. And as the English nation acquired more knowledge of the state and character of the people of India, and more experience of the influence of a tropical climate upon the European constitution, there was less disposition to form colonies in the East, and more concurrence in the policy of the East India Company.

The restrictions which formerly existed against Europeans settling in India, have been gradually much modified if not entirely removed, but there are natural causes, now better understood than formerly, which prevent emigration from England to India. The climate of India, though not so unhealthy as is generally supposed in this country, must yet always be sickly and enervating to Europeans. The climate of that country generally is so hot that the European constitution cannot endure out-door labor, nor indeed physical labor of any kind, so much as is necessary for the ordinary avocations of life, including all classes of people. If the European constitution is subjected to ordinary manual labor, and exposed to the enervating influence of the climate in India, it will suffer a certain and sure deterioration. Though this effect may be slow and gradual, yet it is an ascertained and settled fact.

Further, the price of labor of all kinds in India, is so low that Europeans can never hold any competition with the natives in any kind of work which the latter can perform. And they can perform all kinds of agricultural and common labor, and if they have not the skill of Europeans in some of the mechanical arts, still they understand and can practise all such arts as well as the state of the country, and the taste, the habits, the wants, and circumstances of the inhabitants require. The price of common labor varies in different parts of India from 6 to 10 cents per day, the laborers finding their own food. And for such wages they will work as many hours daily, as hired laborers work in this country. And laborers at this low rate are abundant. Mechanics have higher wages in proportion to common laborers, than in the United States. Still their wages everywhere in that country are very low.

Now it must be obvious that Europeans, who are acquainted with the nature of the climate of India and with the state of labor there, will never emigrate to that country to follow any kind of occupation, which the people there understand and can perform. So it has been, and so it will continue to be; and so there is not now, nor is it likely there ever will be in India any self-perpetuating community of English or European population engaged in private business, using their vernacular language, and preserving their own religion, customs, and manners.* The introduction of railroads, the establishment of manufactures, the extension of education, and the spread of Christianity, will occasion some increase of European agency for the management of such kinds of business. But such agency will not materially affect the state and circumstances of the European population, who will continue in future to sustain the same political and social relations to the inhabitants which they have hitherto sustained.

The Europeans in India, though so small a part of the population of the country, yet possess much wealth and have great influence. Their wealth does not consist so much of property (though many of them are rich), as of large and fixed salaries with retiring pensions and annuities. Their influence consists in their high political situations, which give them the distribution of wealth and power in the appointment to numerous and important places in the government service. There has been a gradual and steady improvement in the moral character of the European population of India since the commencement of the present century; and if many still yield to the unhappy influence that surrounds them and act unworthy of the Christian name and of their nation, there are many others who are examples of all that is lovely in human nature and excellent in the

* See Appendix, A.

Christian profession. Among no people of any country can be found more hospitality, more kindness and sympathy, and more liberality. At Calcutta, Madras, Bombay, and some other places, are Bible, Missionary, Educational, Book, Tract, Temperance, and other religious and benevolent Societies, which are liberally supported, and which exhibit evidence to the native population, of the principles, views, purposes, etc., of the European inhabitants. In 1852, it was ascertained that the donations and subscriptions from the European population for the support of the different missions and the societies immediately connected with them, in the previous year amounted to £33,500 or more than $160,000. This was certainly a noble testimony to the interest they felt for the conversion of the native population to Christianity.

For the European population the government supports an Ecclesiastical Establishment, consisting of 3 bishops and 120 chaplains of the Church of England, and 6 chaplains of the Church of Scotland.* The number of chaplains bears a larger proportion to the European population, than the number of ministers bears to the population in the United States. But the European population in India is so scattered, often only a few families living in the same place, that many can have the instructions of a chaplain only a part of the time, and some of the small civil and military stations are seldom visited by any chaplain. This want has been in part supplied by the missionaries of different societies, who have felt it their duty when they found professing Christians living without the preaching and ordinances of the gospel, to devote some time to them. At many of the missionary stations religious services are performed in the English language, once or twice every week, and with a view to such services Europeans have often contributed liberally for the erection of mission churches. Religious services are sustained in English in more than 70 mission chapels. The congregations then consist of Europeans, Indo-Britons, and a few natives who have acquired the English language. These labors of missionaries have been much blessed, and have contributed to produce the present improved state of moral char-

* See page 303.

acter and active piety among the European population of India.

In Calcutta, Madras, and Bombay, and a few other cities, are voluntary Christian societies of Europeans and Indo-Britons who have provided their houses of worship and support their ministers. These societies are often of different religious principles from the chaplains. Some of them are Independents, some are Presbyterians, some are Baptists, some are Methodists, etc. These churches are generally in close connection with missions of their own denominations; indeed, they have generally had their origin in connection with the missionary cause. Thus they are to be included among the results of the missionary enterprise, and they are now exerting a strong influence in promoting this cause.

THE INDO-BRITONS.

These are a class of people who occupy an intermediate place between the European and native population. They are the offspring of European fathers and native mothers, and their descendants. They have been known by different names as Half-caste, Eurasians, Anglo-Indians, and Indo-Britons. This last-mentioned name is the one now in general use, and appears likely to be perpetuated. Their fathers were of different ranks, as civilians, officers, soldiers, etc., and their mothers belonged to different classes of the native population. I have known some instances of such persons, whose mothers were Mohammedans, being educated in that faith, and becoming mingled with the Mohammedan population. Instances have been more frequent, where their mothers were Roman Catholics, of their being educated in that religion, and mingling with that class of the native population. But they have generally been brought up in the Protestant religion, and been educated in the English language and in English habits. They regard themselves as forming a branch of the European population of the country. They have the advantage of Europeans in being acquainted with the vernacular languages, and in having constitutions more adapted to the climate of the country, but they are generally deficient in education and energy of character. Some among them have acquired wealth, influence, and respectability. It would be difficult to form any estimate of their number. They have shared largely in the instructions of missionaries, as they have often been in circumstances deserving special sympathy and attention. Many of them are respectable in character and social position, and some are usefully employed in the missionary work. Many of them are in the employment of the government. They are also merchants, agents, shop-keepers, clerks, etc. The result of many inquiries lately made concerning them by the Committees of Parliament on the state of India, when the renewal of the East India Company's charter was under consideration, did not exhibit them in respect to numbers, increase, character, and influence, and the prospect of their ever acting any prominent part in the affairs of the country, in so favorable a light as was expected.

PART V.

THE NATIVE POPULATION.

THE FIRST RELIGION OF INDIA.

The religion of the first inhabitants of India consisted in the worship of local deities, some supposed to be benevolent, and some malevolent. They were originally supposed to be spirits of deceased persons, who still retaining the feelings they had when alive, haunted the places of their former residence, and gratified the feelings they still retained, or the feelings excited by what they heard and saw. They were believed to have the power of assisting their friends and of injuring their enemies. Thus able to interfere at pleasure in human affairs, they became objects of great anxiety. Rude images and symbols of them were set up in particular places, sometimes in small rudely constructed temples and under green trees, and prayers and offerings were made to them. The worship of them partook more of fear and dread of evil, than of hope and expectation of good from them. To these beings the people ascribed accidents, misfortunes, afflictions, and diseases, and so they resorted to various means to propitiate them, and to secure their favor. They gave offerings of food, and made sacrifices of fowls and animals. They sometimes offered human victims in sacrifice, and parents in the fear of losing all their children in times of sickness, would sometimes devote one of them to some of the malevolent demons. And people would sometimes inflict tortures upon themselves, in the hope of appeasing these malevolent beings, or of exciting their compassion.

The authority for these opinions and rites, appears to have depended on traditions and local usages; for if they had any sacred books, none have come down to the present time, and none are mentioned in history. There was no hereditary priesthood, but there were persons who, pretending to witchcraft, sorcery, and necromancy, acquired great influence in religious matters. These persons professed to have intercourse and influence with these supposed deities and demons, and they generally officiated in religious rites, especially on important occasions. The Bheels of Central India, the Coolees of Gujerat, the Goands of Berar, the Santals of Orissa, and the Shanars, and other tribes in the peninsula, are apparently the remains of these ancient inhabitants, and they retain among them many of their opinions and rites, the same as their ancestors had 3,000 years ago. The religion of these classes has but little affinity with the system commonly called brahminism. Among some of them the brahmins have never been acknowledged in their religious character, and have never become the officiating priests. And in many districts where brahminism is the commonly received system of religion, the places of worship and pilgrimage, the deities, rites, and ceremonies, are of a mixed character, clearly showing that the brahminical system in its progress, incorporated with itself many of the previously established local superstitions.

When any of these local deities were found to have a strong hold on the feelings of the people, they were declared or assumed to belong to the almost infinite number of the Hindu gods, and supplemental sections were added to some chapter in the Purans containing the popular legends concerning them, and thus authorizing their worship. Thus, as brahminism enlarged its borders and increased its votaries, it also increased the names and number of its recognized deities. And the system was well adapted to increase in this way, as the sacred books do not contain the names of a thousandth part of their gods, any one of whom, if he has revealed himself, becomes a proper object of worship. It is in part owing to this mixed origin, that brahminism is so different in its usages and ceremonies in different districts in India.

The first inhabitants of India, in their religious state and character, much resembled the aborigines of America and Africa, and the ancient inhabitants of Europe in a similar state of civilization. Their gods were local deities, originally the supposed spirits of deceased persons haunting the abodes of their former residence, still retaining the feelings they formerly had, or experiencing in view of what they might see, similar feelings to what they would have had, if still living, and having power, more or less, to gratify these feelings. In all their worship, their prayers, their offerings, their sacrifices and rites, superstitious fear and dread appear to have been the principal motives of the people, and hypocrisy and fanaticism appear to have formed the character of those who professed to be spiritual guides, and who officiated in their religious rites.

BRAHMINISM — THE VEDAS.

There are no means of ascertaining at what period the system of religion, commonly called Brahminism, was introduced into India. It appears to have been the religion of a nation or people who invaded the country from the north-west, and established their government along the banks of the Jumna and the Ganges, as early as 1300 or 1400 years before the commencement of the Christian era. The books containing their religion at that time, are called the Vedas. Of these there are commonly reckoned 4, namely, the Rig, the Yajur, the Sama, and the Artharva. The Hindus believe that these books (the language of them) came directly from the mouth of Brahm, or the infinite Spirit, and that they were infallibly preserved by tradition till put into the state in which they now are. Their present order and arrangement are ascribed to a sage of great celebrity, called Vyas, and sometimes Ved-Vyas, on account of this work. An analysis of their contents shows that they were compiled by different men, and at different times. There are no means of ascertaining when this compilation was made, but it is the general opinion of orientalists who have investigated this subject with great care, that they were put into their present state 1300 or 1400 years before the Christian era. They are written in the ancient style of the Sanscrit language, differing so much from the later or common Sanscrit, that only a small part of the educated brahmins can read them intelligibly. Each Veda consists of two parts; the first part is called the Sanhita, and consists of prayers, hymns, invocations, rites, ceremonies, etc., to be used in offering oblations, and performing sacrifices.* These prayers and hymns in the same Veda often differ but little from each other. And the same hymns with but little variation are found in the different Vedas. The second part is called Brahmana, and treats of the first cause, of the creation of the world and its inhabitants, moral precepts, religious duties, rewards, punishments, festivals, purifications, castes, ceremonies at births, deaths, etc.

These books have always been held in great veneration. In the early age of India, it was a part of the prescribed duty of the three highest castes to read the Vedas, but the fourth or lowest caste, including the great body of the people, were not allowed to read them, or to possess them, or to hear them read. If a shudra should read them, or hear them read, or

* The following is a translation of the first hymn of the Rig Veda. It was designed to be used in offering sacrifices to Agni, the god who presides over fire, and who manifests himself by it. Agni is also one of the names of fire, which, in the mystical and pantheistical notion of the Hindus, is sometimes worshipped, as the symbol of the god; so that in their worship the god and the element appear to be confounded together.

"I praise Agni, (the god of fire,) the high-priest of the sacrifice, the all resplendent, the conductor of the sacrificial rites, the chanter of the invocation hymns, and the chief holder of the precious gifts (that reward the sacrificers).

"Agni, when praised by the sages of ancient times, assembled the gods, and now when praised by us the modern sages, he will assemble them to our sacrifice.

"By means of Agni, the sacrificer obtains without fail, daily increasing wealth, and the fame connected with an army of heroes.

"O Agni, whenever a sacrifice proves fortunate, it is because thou art there to be the guardian on every side; also thou goest on high to convey it to the gods.

"Agni is the chanter of the invocation hymns, and the director of the sacrifice; he is faithful and possesses all possible renown; himself a god, let him now accompany the gods.

"O Agni, whatever benefits thou conferrest on the offerer, these will turn to thy own advantage; of this be assured, O god of fire.

"O Agni, daily, yea day and night, do we approach thee with reverential awe, prostrating ourselves in thy presence.

"We approach thee who flamest over the sacrifices, the preserver of truth, the grand illuminator, and who growest great in thy own sacred recess by our offerings.

"Cherish us, O Agni, as a father doth his children, and be with us to keep us in safety."

should commit any part of them to memory, or perform any rite or ceremony contained in them, the king or magistrate was directed immediately to put such a man to death. In modern times the brahmins have been the depositaries of these sacred books. And so faithful were they to their trust and so cautious in their conduct, that it was not without great difficulty and much expense, Europeans could procure them. But copies of them are now to be found in public libraries in India and Europe, and translations are in the course of being made and published under the patronage of the East India Company.

There is a class of works called Upanishads, which contain extracts of certain portions of the Vedas, and commentaries upon the doctrines of theology contained in them. Of these extracts and treatises, there are said to be 52. Some of them are short. They are designed to exhibit, explain, and defend the doctrines of the Vedas. There is also a class of works called Upa-Vedas, which are supplementary to the Vedas. There are 4 of them. They treat of diseases and medicines, of music as an aid to devotion, of the use of arms and other implements of war, and of the mechanical arts. There is yet another class called the Vedangas, that is, members of or supplements to the Vedas. These treat of their pronunciation, the manner in which they should be read, etc.

There are also 6 works called Durshans, each professing to contain a system of theological philosophy. The doctrines, definitions, explanations, etc., of these professed systems, partly from their abstruse nature, their technical phraseology and the manner in which the subjects are treated, are very obscure and difficult to understand. They show how active the Hindu mind was at that early age in such philosophical speculations. But they are of as little consequence now as the speculations of the schoolmen of the middle ages would be to us at the present time.

There are several ancient works which profess to explain the meaning of the Vedas. Some of these are ascribed to Vyas, the reputed compiler of the Vedas. One of these works is called the Vedant Sar, which is said "to contain an abstract and quintessence of all the Vedas brought together." The Brahm

Sutras or Aphorisms, and the Bhagawat Gita are also ascribed to the same writer.

THE INSTITUTES OF MENU.

This name is given to a code of religious and civil laws, and makes a part of the Hindu Scriptures.* The general opinion of orientalists is that it was compiled about 9 or 10 centuries before the Christian era, which would be soon after the reign of Solomon. This work contains a long and obscure account of the creation of the world, the origin and laws of the different castes, the laws which kings are to observe in administering the affairs of their governments and carrying on war, penalties and penances for offences, rewards and punishments after death, etc. These Institutes give us the best account we have of the civil, social, and religious state and character of the nations of India at the time they were compiled. And as such a work is in part a compilation of previously existing usages and laws, these give us a view of the people for considerable time previous to the compilation's being made.

As these laws profess to be of divine origin, kings had no authority to change them; their duty was to administer their governments according to them. There was to be no toleration of any neglect or violation of these laws by any class of people. In these respects they resembled the laws given by Moses and contained in the Old Testament. In no nation were ever civil and religious matters more closely united than among the Hindus. All the rules concerning caste were to be fundamental laws of the country, and kings were to govern according to them and to enforce them. Brahmins were the expounders and interpreters of these laws, and kings and all invested with authority were to carry these laws into effect. If this system of civil and religious laws, including the regulations concerning the different castes (and these regulations were regarded as of the highest importance) contained in these Institutes, were carried into effect according to their spirit and intention, it is not easy to conceive of any despotism more absolute and unhappy in its consequences. And such probably the ancient governments of India

* Sir William Jones made an English translation of this work.

were. Such the governments in heathen nations have generally been.

THE PURANS.

There are 18 works of this class which are generally known by different names, as the Bhagawat Puran, the Vishnu Puran, the Padma Puran, etc. They all belong to the Hindu Scriptures. They are popularly ascribed to Vyas, and were formerly regarded as of early origin in the history of India. But the general opinion of orientalists now is that most, if not all of them, were written since the commencement of the Christian era. They are generally written in the form of dialogues between disciples and their religious teachers, the latter supposed to be some deity, or god in human form, or some inspired sage. They treat of the creation, preservation, destruction, and renovation of the universe, of the genealogy of the gods, of chronology according to their fabulous system, of rites, ceremonies, legends, etc. Some of them were written to exalt some particular one of the gods, and to set forth his good qualities and his marvellous actions. There is much of repetition in them, and much that is contradictory, absurd, and to all but Hindus, utterly incredible. The idea of using any reason and criticism in judging of the contents of their sacred books, or of comparing different professedly inspired works, or different parts of the same work, with each other so as to ascertain their consistency or otherwise, appears never to occur to the Hindus so long as they believe in their own religious system.

There is also a class of works called the Upa-Purans, commonly reckoned 18 in number. They are supplementary to the Purans, containing such matter as the writers thought had been omitted.

The Ramayan, and the Mahabharat are not generally classed with the Purans, but may be reckoned among the Hindu sacred books. Of the former name are two works, one of which is ascribed to Vyas, the reputed compiler of the Vedas. Whatever he wrote, has been believed to be inspired, and so this work may be classed with the Hindu Scriptures. The other work was written by Valmiki, and is more common and better known.

Of this work it is often said, and perhaps it is the general opinion of the Hindus, that it was all written before the events and actions described in it took place, and that when these occurred, every thing was found on comparison to have occurred exactly as they had been previously written. This opinion involves the highest degree of inspiration, and so would confirm the truth of every thing in it. The subject of the Ramayan is the life, actions, etc., of Rama or Ramchundra, king of Ayodya, and believed to be one of the incarnations of Vishnu.

The Mahabharat is also ascribed to Vyas, the compiler of the Vedas. The principal subject is the life, actions, etc., of Krishna, one of the incarnations of Vishnu. These works were written before the Purans, and evidently furnished much of the materials of which they are composed. The Bhagawat Gita, sometimes called in India the 5th Veda, and which has excited so much attention in Europe, is an episode of one of the chapters of this work. This part is regarded as possessing the highest degree of inspiration, the author or speaker being no other than Krishna, an incarnation of Vishnu, or of Vishnu himself incarnate in the person of Krishna. It teaches and illustrates Vedantism or pantheism.

THE SUPREME BEING.

The Vedas say in repeated texts that "There is in truth but one Deity, the supreme Spirit, the Lord of the universe, and whose work is the universe." A brahmin who was learned in the Vedas gave the following view of the Deity, as his character is described in these works:—"Perfect truth, perfect happiness, without equal, immortal, absolute unity; whom neither speech can describe nor mind comprehend; all-pervading, all-transcending; delighted with his own boundless intelligence, not limited by time or space; without feet, moving swiftly; without hands grasping all worlds; without eyes, all-surveying; without ears, all-hearing; without any intelligent guide, understanding all; without cause, the first of all causes; all-ruling, all-powerful; the creator, the preserver, and the transformer of all things; such is the Great One." This Being the Hindus call Brahm. 'A distinguished writer on the history, religion, etc. of the Hindus, and long a resident in India, says, "The primary doctrine of the Vedas is the unity of God." The same author, referring to the Institutes of Menu, says, "The doctrine of Monotheism prevails throughout the Institutes, and it is declared towards the close, that of all duties the principal is to obtain from the Upanishads the knowledge of one supreme God."

The meaning of such language appears to be plain and explicit, and we should naturally expect that this asserted unity of God would pervade all their religious views, and that he alone would be the object of their homage and worship. But it is necessary before we can understand the religious principles and practices of the Hindus, to see what other doctrines their sacred books contain. And here we find that it is said in the account they give of the creation, that the eternal and infinite Spirit, or Brahm first created the god Brahma, and "he created an assemblage of inferior deities with divine attributes and pure souls, and a number of genii exquisitely delicate." These deities are declared to be worthy to be adored, and their favor and protection are to be sought and procured by prayers and offerings. Some of these deities are described as presiding over the elements and intrusted with the performance of certain parts in the government of the world. Agni is the god of fire, Pavun is god of the wind, Warun is the god of water, Indra is god of the skies, Yama is god and judge of the dead, etc. Prayers, praises, oblations, and sacrifices are to be offered to these deities. Indeed, no inconsiderable part of the Vedas consists of prayers, praises, rites, and ceremonies to be used in oblations and sacrifices to these gods. The Institutes of Menu, which are regarded as of divine authority, in the account they give of the creation, mention the names of many deities who are declared to be "lords of created beings, eminent in holiness, and who are to be adored and worshipped." Thus, though according to the Hindu sacred books, there is only one self-existent, eternal, and unchangeable Deity, yet they also teach that he or Brahma by his power, "created an immense assemblage of inferior deities with divine attributes," that these deities are intrusted with power in the government of the world, that they can interfere whenever they please in human affairs, and so are to be feared, praised, propitiated, and worshipped. The number of these deities is almost infinite.

In the early history of the Hindu religion and in their oldest sacred books nothing is said of idolatry. Images are mentioned as worthy to be reverenced, but whether these were images of their deities or of their ancestors, is uncertain; probably they were the latter. But an ignorant and superstitious people like the Hindus, with such a system of polytheism, were not likely long to retain and practise only the spiritual worship of such deities. It was easy and natural for them to conceive, form, and use some material and visible objects as the likeness or symbols or representatives of their deities. And we find that such things, as objects or pretended aids in worship, were soon introduced and in common use among them.

These deities, and the supposed incarnations of them, are believed to have the control of human affairs, and to have the power of conferring any favors which can be enjoyed, and of inflicting any evils which can be endured in this life. So they are the objects of religious homage and worship. Their favor is desired, and means are used to obtain it; their displeasure is dreaded, and means are used to avert it. But the Hindus have yet stronger reasons for worshipping these inferior deities, for their shastras further teach that the supreme and self-existent Spirit feels no interest and takes no part in the affairs of mankind. Kapila declares the true doctrine of the Vedas to be that "the Supreme Spirit has nothing to do with creatures, nor they with him." He is described as existing in a state of serene repose or quiescence, quite indifferent to every thing exterior to himself; sometimes he is described as unconcious of every thing whatever, like persons in a state of sleep, and in this state he will continue till the end of the world — all the affairs of the created universe being superintended and managed in the mean time by the inferior deities he has created. So, as the infinite and self-existent Spirit takes no interest in human affairs, all worship or fear of him, all prayers or praise or gratitude or love to him, are vain and useless. To him no temple is ever consecrated, no worship is ever offered. The Hindu sacred books contain declarations concerning the Supreme Being and their learned men often use expressions concerning him, which would naturally be understood by one not acquainted with their philosophy and their religious system, to exclude all other deities and make him the only object of adoration. And Europeans have sometimes been surprised on further acquaintance, to learn how much they had mistaken some of the first principles and usual practices of Brahminism. But the meaning intended by such expressions is quite consistent in the opinion of the Hindus with their whole system of polytheism, and with the worship paid to its numerous deities. By such expressions they do not mean the unity of the infinite Spirit to the exclusion of other gods, any more than to the exclusion of men. They mean that he alone is the self-existing God, primarily the Creator of all things, and into whom all created beings and things, spiritual and material, will hereafter be absorbed, so that as he alone existed at first, so he alone will exist at the close of this dispensation or *kalpa*.

Thus, though expressing views of the Unity of God, which have often appeared to Europeans to be inconsistent with the worship of any other deity, the Hindus have a system of polytheism containing gods more numerous, multiform, monstrous, and immoral, than any other nation ancient or modern. The number of these deities is declared to be 330,000,000, and any one of these deities may be worshipped. Some of these have great power, and others are comparatively small and feeble. Some are male and others are female. Some are parents and others are children. Some have a form in which they generally appear — a kind of natural form — and yet they can assume any form they please, and become visible or invisible as may best suit their purpose or convenience. Strange and monstrous forms are common among them. Some have eyes on different parts of their bodies. Some have faces on all sides of the head. Some have four, and others have many more hands. And as though these variations, distortions, and perversions of the human form were not enough, some of the Hindu deities have forms partly human and partly animal, and some are entirely in the animal form.

Brahminism has yet another form — it is not only monotheistic and polytheistic, but it is also pantheistic. And this is generally the system of the learned, and the primary doctrine of the Vedantas. They say that the supreme Spirit and the universe are one and the same — that he does not exist separate from the creation, nor is the creation separate from him. The universe is only an expansion of the Deity, and the expansion of the Deity produces the universe. So with mind and so with matter. There is no mind or spirit in the world which is really separate from the infinite Spirit. Nothing but this Spirit exists in the universe, and all which appears to be material, actual, and substantial, is such only in appearance and not in reality — it is all illusion. It is only the endlessly varied energetic operations of the all-pervading infinite Spirit, the all-pervading and animating principle or agent in the world. He alone has any real existence, and he produces by his immediate and direct agency, all the phenomena in the universe. There is no such thing as substance or matter, and all that appears to be such, is only the infinitely varied and diversified operation of the self-existing and all-pervading Cause. The advocates of this system say that it is owing to the ignorance, dulness, and darkness of the human mind, or to the qualities which produce this state in human beings, that men think they are separate, distinct, and individual beings, and have the power of voluntary action and moral responsibility, that if men could in any way acquire sufficient knowledge, discernment, purity, and light, they would at once lose all consciousness of individual existence, and their spirits be absorbed into union with the infinite Spirit.

The following extracts show these sentiments: — "Bramh, (the infinite Spirit) and individuated spirit are one." — "That which pervading all the members of any body, is the cause of life or motion, is called individuated spirit; that which pervades the whole universe giving life or motion to all, is one. That which pervades the members of the body, and that which pervades the universe, imparting motion to all, are one. So Bramh and all individuated spirits are one. All life is the Creator or Bramh; he is the soul of all creatures. All spirits are one, not two, and the distinctions I, thou, he, etc., are all artificial, existing only for present purposes. The universe is only an expansion of the divine substance. The human spirit like the divine, is eternal and uncreate. The highest object of religious meditation is to discover that the worshipper is himself God, or a part of God, and the ultimate reward of such discovery is absorption into the Deity. As soon as a man can fully realize that God is every thing and every thing is only a part of

God, he will no longer retain any conscious existence—his spirit or what he thought was his spirit, will be united with or absorbed into the infinite Spirit from whom he emanated."

MINOR DEITIES.

In the accounts given of the creation of the world it is said that the supreme Spirit Bramh created, or rather by his authority the god Brahma created, among other beings "an assemblage of inferior deities with divine attributes and pure souls, and a number of genii exquisitely delicate." It is said that the number of these deities is "immense," and they are declared to be "lords of other created beings, to be eminent in holiness and to be adored and worshipped." They are also declared "to have control over human affairs, and to interfere with them whenever they please." The world where these deities reside, is Meru or Sumeru, a mountain supposed to be north from India. This mountain is said in the Purans to be 600,000 miles high. Its form is like an inverted cone, being 128,000 miles in circumference at the base, and twice as much, namely, 256,000 miles, at the top. Here the principal gods, as Brahma, Vishnu, Sheva, Indra, etc., have each their separate places of residence where they live with their wives and children. Some of these places are described as being gorgeous and splendid, abounding with every thing which can contribute to their gratification. They have palaces, gardens, servants, musicians, courtesans, etc. These gods and goddesses are often engaged in domestic quarrels and in disputes and contests about their comparative rank, power, etc. They are described as having a natural and generally preserved form and appearance, but they have power to assume any form, to become invisible, and to proceed to any place at their pleasure. They can descend to the earth at any time, assume any shape or appearance, and manifest themselves to any human being whenever they please.

Among these deities Brahma, Vishnu, and Sheva hold the highest place in the Purans and in the general opinion of the Hindus. They are sometimes called the Hindu triad. Brahma is often called the creator, Vishnu the preserver, and Sheva the destroyer, of the world. Some account of them will be given.

BRAHMA.

The creation of the world is generally ascribed to Brahma. The Ayeeni Acberry says there were 16 different accounts among the Hindus of the creation of the world. Some of these accounts are long, obscure, contradictory, and much of them unintelligible. The more commonly received opinion is that Brahma first created the waters, then the earth, then a great number of inferior deities, good and bad genii, etc. Then he created the brahmins, who came from his mouth; the kshatryas, who were produced from his arms; the vaishyas from his thighs, and the shudras from his feet. These constituted the four primitive castes.

Brahma is described as of a bright yellow or golden color, with four faces and four hands, dressed in shining garments, and riding upon a bird resembling a swan. In one hand he holds a portion of the Vedas, in one he holds a vessel of water, one is raised as bestowing a blessing, and the fourth as offering some gift. No temples are ever dedicated to him, and he is never worshipped alone or separate from the other gods. The brahmins sometimes make prayers to him, and perform some ceremonies in his name. It appears strange that this god, who is declared to have created the universe, and who is always mentioned first in enumerating the deities, should receive no worship from the great body of the people, and have no temple dedicated to him. The reason of this neglect and dishonor is stated in the Purans to be that in some matters, which involved the honor and veracity of Vishnu and Sheva, Brahma not only told what he knew was false, but hired two witnesses to confirm what he said. The gods, on knowing this iniquity, deprived him by their curse, of all homage and worship. Sheva was so angry (the falsehood was concerning him,) that he cut off one of Brahma's heads. Before this he had five, but since then he has had only four heads.*

These are not all which is said in the Purans concerning Brahma. When spirituous liquors were first made, all the gods,

* Some accounts ascribe Sheva's cutting off one of Brahma's heads to another and yet more disreputable cause.

genii, etc., used them, and often to intoxication. One day Brahma having become intoxicated, made an attempt upon the virtue of his own daughter. In one of the Purans, it is said that he lived in a state of incest with his daughter for 100 years.

The residence or heaven of Brahma on Sumeru, is said in the Mahabharat to be 800 miles long and 400 miles broad. His reputed son Narad, when inquired of concerning the place, declared he could not describe it in 200 years, and that it contained in a superior style all that is in the heavens of the other gods, and that whatever of beauty, splendor, and glory exists in all the creation of Brahma on the earth, may be seen there in its highest perfection.

VISHNU.

This god has acquired the character of the preserver of the world. He is commonly described in the form of a dark, or blue or black man with four arms, holding in one hand a war-club, in another a conch-shell, in another a weapon called chuckra, and in the fourth a water-lily. The vehicle on which he rides, is a creature partly human and partly bird. This god is chiefly worshipped in the form of the supposed incarnations, which he at different times assumed for the preservation of the world.

The incarnations of this god called *Awatars*, form so prominent a part in the Hindu system, that their probable origin and nature appear to deserve some consideration. Some have supposed that Brahminism is indebted to Christianity for this peculiarity in its system, or at least for the suggestion of it. But the incarnation of the Hindu gods were all so different in their nature and object from any thing contained in the Christian system, that it does not appear necessary nor reasonable to suppose that they ever had any connection whatever. The account of these incarnations are contained in the Purans, which are chiefly made up of poems and traditions. The early poetry of the Hindus was of a very fanciful and extravagant character. The Hindus have always been exceedingly credulous, ready to believe almost any thing however strange, improbable, and unreasonable. This spirit is apparent in their accounts of the creation of the world, of astronomy, geography, etc. The conduct and character of their heroes must be such as to excite wonder and admiration. The circumstances of their birth, the actions of their life, and the manner of their death must all be marvellous. Descriptions and representations of this character were suited to the general taste, pleased the national vanity, and flattered the pride of kings and princes, on whose patronage the poets were dependent.

The Romans were accustomed to deify their heroes and emperors after their death, and to set up their images in their temples, and then include their names among their deities. The Hindus proceeded still further. In the Satya, the Treta, and the Dwapar yugas or ages, the gods are described as often assuming the human form and associating familiarly with men for a while, and then suddenly appearing in their superhuman character. Contemplating the fanciful and marvellous actions ascribed by the poets to their heroes, the Hindus instead of understanding these feats and exploits as the fictions and flatteries of the writers, assumed them to be true, and then as such actions altogether exceeded human power, they declared the actors must be deities in human form, or incarnations of some of the gods. And when this had been assumed, and was believed in respect to one instance, it was easy and natural to extend this mode of understanding the marvellous parts of their early history, all comprehended as it was in the works of their poets. In this way the legends of heroic poetry came to be taken for the facts of history, and the character of the personages were elevated to be deities in some assumed form, called *awatars*, or incarnations, in order to account for their being able to accomplish the wonderful things ascribed to them.

And this manner of understanding the Hindu legends and traditions was not limited to things performed by human agency. There were legends and traditions of strange events and actions, in which other agents were concerned. Some of these were also declared to be true, and to be effected by divine interposition. The mystical notions of pantheism, that the Deity is the all-pervading and animating spirit of the universe, that the spirit of man is only a modified existence of the infinite Spirit united with matter in the human form, and after death to exist in the form of brutes, reptiles, fish, and of vegetables and minerals—these notions of the Deity made it easy for the Hindus to believe almost any marvellous legend or fiction, and ascribe the agency to the interposition of some of the gods. Hence some of the *Awatars* occurred in the form of animals, and one in the form of a fish, and in such incarnations or manifestations the Hindus saw nothing inconsistent with the attributes, or derogatory to the character of their deities.

The first incarnation of Vishnu is called Matsa Awatar,* when he is reputed to have assumed the form of a fish and recovered the Vedas, which a demon had purloined and concealed in the sea.

The second incarnation is called Vuraha Awatar. "A monster-demon delighted in afflicting the earth, and at last rolled it into a shapeless mass and plunged down with it into the abyss. Vishnu seeing this assumed the form of a boar which soon became of immense size, his voice was like thunder and shook the universe. He plunged into the ocean, found the earth at the bottom, and bringing it up on his tusks, restored it to its former shape and state."

The third incarnation is called the Kurma-Awatar in which Vishnu assumed the form of a tortoise. The circumstances connected with this awatar, the object to be accomplished by it and the different kinds of agency connected with it, are more unreasonable and absurd, if possible, than the awatars already mentioned.

The fourth incarnation is called the Nursu Awatar, and in its nature and object has more the appearance of possibility. A wicked and unbelieving man was persecuting his son and threatening to kill him for his faith in Vishnu and for worshipping him. After much angry disputation the father asked his son, in contempt and derision of the pretended power and omnipresence of Vishnu, if the god was in a certain pillar then before them, at the same time giving the pillar a kick. At that instant the pillar parted and the god became manifest in the shape of a man

* The fish-incarnation.

with the head and paws of a lion. He instantly seized the blasphemer and destroyed him. He then disappeared and the pillar resumed its former shape.

The fifth incarnation is called the Waman Awatar. This awatar consisted in Vishnu's assuming the form of a dwarf-brahmin to deceive and destroy a king who was giving great trouble to the Hindu gods.

The sixth incarnation was the Awatar of Pursuram, a brahmin-warrior, who in a great war between the brahmins and the kshatryas overcame, and as some say, annihilated the latter, or the military caste.

The seventh incarnation was the Awatar of Rama or Ramchundra, the celebrated king of Ayodhya, whose life, misfortunes, and exploits form the subject of the celebrated epic poem called the Ramayan. According to this work, Rama was the son of Dushurath, king of Ayodhya, the modern Oude. He was married early in life to Seeta, a daughter of the king of Mithili. Some domestic troubles, occasioned by the intrigues of his mother-in-law, compelled him and Seeta to retire into a forest. While in this seclusion, Rawun, king of Singul-Dwip or Ceylon, is said to have carried away Seeta to his own capital. Rama then collecting a large force and assisted by allies in the Deckan, proceeded towards Ceylon, and building a causeway across the strait of the sea, invaded the island, defeated and killed Rawun, recovered his wife and returned to Ayodhya. But Rama's troubles were not yet at an end. Having by his imprudent conduct caused the death of his brother Luxuman, who had shared with him in all his dangers and his success, he was in so much distress of mind that he threw himself into a river, and was reunited to the Deity. The allies who joined Rama in the Deckan, and assisted him in this expedition, are described as a class of monkeys under the command of a leader called Hunnuman. He is described as Rama's principal military leader, and as possessing superhuman qualities of body and mind. He is declared to be an incarnation of one of the gods. His image in the form of a monkey is very common in temples, and perhaps there is no god more worshipped through the Deckan.

Krishna is generally reckoned the eighth incarnation. But many say that Balarama, a celebrated military hero, was the eighth, and that "Krishna was greater than and distinct from all the awatars, which had only a portion of the divinity in them, while he was the very person of Vishnu himself in a human form."

The ninth incarnation took place in the person of Budh, who was a teacher of a false religion. It is said that Vishnu assumed this form for the purpose of deceiving the enemies of the gods! Budh is regarded as an incarnation of Vishnu, and yet the doctrines he taught are declared to be heretical, and those who believe and practise them are declared to be deserving persecution. The origin and object of this incarnation, the circumstances that accompanied it and the consequences that followed it, are among the most marvellous things of Hindu mythology or theology.

"The tenth awatar" says Sir W. Jones, "we are told is yet to come, and is expected to appear mounted on a white horse with a scimetar blazing like a comet to mow down all the incorrigible and impenitent."

The life of Krishna is the principal subject of the great poem called Mahabharat. As no one of the Hindu gods is more worshipped than Krishna, and as he is declared "to be not an incarnation of Vishnu but to be Vishnu himself," and also to be the "eternal and self-existing Creator of the universe," it is proper to give some further notice of him. He was the son of Vasudeva and Devaki, and of the royal family of Kousa. Circumstances are narrated concerning his birth, which decency will not permit here to be mentioned. His infancy and childhood were remarkable for mischievous pranks and actions, which would be marvellous, if they were not incredible, puerile, and foolish. When he grew up to manhood he manifested his superhuman powers chiefly in amorous, wanton, and licentious intercourse with the women of the district where he then lived. The Hindus say, "as he was divine, he was not subject to the moral laws binding on human beings, and so it was lawful for him to do what he pleased among the women. And in regard to their husbands, they could have no right which tended to the exclusion of any god. So the women could do what they pleased, irrespective of any moral obligation to their husbands or their families."

At a more advanced age he engaged in the feuds among the families with which he was connected. He acted a conspicuous part in the great war between the Yadus and the Pandus, in which his feats and prowess contributed largely to the success and final triumph of the latter. After a long course of adventures he put to death most or all his own offspring, and was shot by an arrow. Of his wives, eight immolated themselves with his dead body upon the funeral pile.

"Krishna," says Elphinstone in his History of India, "is the greatest favorite with the Hindus of all their divinities. Of the sectaries who revere Vishnu to the exclusion of other gods, one sect almost confine their worship to Rama; but though composed of an important class, as including many of the ascetics and some of the boldest speculators in religious inquiry, its numbers and popularity bear no proportion to another division of the vaishna sect, which is attached to the worship of Krishna. This comprises all the opulent and luxurious, almost all the women, and a very large proportion of all ranks of Indian society. The greater part of these votaries of Khrisna maintain that he is not an incarnation of Vishnu, but Vishnu himself, and likewise the eternal and self-existing Creator of the universe." This statement refers more to Bengal than to India generally. Ward says, "six parts out of ten of the whole Hindu population of Bengal are supposed to be the disciples of this god." He is called by different names, and images of him used in his worship correspond to his supposed appearance at different periods of his life. Anquetil Du Perron says, "The whole history of Krishna is a tissue of Greek and Roman obscenities, which among the fanatics of all descriptions conceal the most abominable enormities." Buchanan, in his work on Mysore, speaking of a temple of Vishnu which he saw, says, "The rath, or chariot, belonging to it is very large and richly carved. The figures upon it representing the amours of that god, in the form of Krishna, are the most indecent I have ever seen." When in India I saw chariots or cars of this god, which were covered or ornamented with imagery as obscene as could be conceived. On these cars images of the god are placed on festival-days and they are then surrounded by immense crowds of people who worship them. I saw in one celebrated temple a great number of stone statues, in one part of it a long series of them, representing the amours of Krishna, which were of the most obscene character, which if exhibited or offered for sale, as statues, or pictures, or engravings, or in any form, or described in any language in this country, would subject the exhibiter or seller to severe but merited punishment from the laws. And yet such representations make a part of the Hindu religion, as publicly exhibited and celebrated. To reasoning and arguments about the worship of such gods the Hindus reply, " They were not men but gods, and so were not subject to moral laws as we are. They could do as they pleased. Actions which would be sinful in us were not sinful in them, for being subject to no law they could do what they pleased without doing any wrong or committing any sin."

The residence or heaven of Vishnu is Vykunt, and is situated on mount Sumeru. According to the Purans it is 85,000 miles in circumference and is chiefly of gold. The edifices in it are of jewels and precious stones. There are numerous pools of water containing lilies and other flowers of every variety of form and color. There are gardens with flowers of surpassing beauty, fragrance, etc. There Vishnu and Luxumee appear shining like the sun. Before and around them the inferior deities, the musicians, and various orders and classes of heavenly beings gaze on their dazzling and divine forms, and chant their praises. Into this heaven the votaries of Vishnu of every class say they hope to be admitted and to enjoy its pleasures till the merit of their actions shall be exhausted. They must then return to the earth, here to assume another birth.

SHEVA.

Sheva, often called the destroyer, has the third place in the order of the Hindu deities. This god is described in several different ways. In one form he has five faces, three eyes, and four hands. In another form he has one head, three eyes, inflamed by his intemperate habits, two hands, with a horn in one and a drum in the other, is riding upon a bull, and his body is covered with ashes. But he is commonly worshipped by a symbol with the figure of a bull (his favorite vehicle) looking at it. The origin of the worship of this thing as the symbol of Sheva is contained in the Purans, but it is too indecent to be translated, or the account to be narrated in the English language, and so it must be omitted. Sheva is described as having the appearance of a religous mendicant, intemperate in his habits, filthy in his person, every way disgusting and contemptible, except perhaps in the occasional manifestation of ungovernable temper and terrible power. When he was about to be married to Parwuttee, her mother and the neighbors cried out, "Ah! ah! ah! this image of gold, this most beautiful damsel, the greatest beauty in the three worlds, to be given in marriage to such a fellow— an old fellow with three eyes, without teeth, clothed in a tiger's skin, covered with ashes, encircled with snakes, wearing a necklace of human bones, with a human skull in his hands, with filthy hair twisted round his head, who chews and smokes intoxicating drugs, has inflamed eyes, rides naked on a bull, and often behaves like a madman." The Skand Puran makes Sheva describe himself thus: "Parwuttee must be very foolish to practise so severe a penance to obtain me, a wandering mendicant, who gets a rag from the dung-hill to clothe his nakedness, rides an ox, carries in his hand an axe and a young deer; who wanders here and there like a madman, dancing with demons in solitary places where corpses are burnt; who adorns himself with garlands made of snakes and heads of dead men, and rubbing ashes on his body goes about begging with a skull in his hand."

But this is not his *necessary* form, for he can at any time assume any form he pleases. But this is the form and the course of conduct, in which he most delights. Among the many strange things in the Hindu superstition there is nothing more strange than that a being of such conduct and character should ever become an object of religious worship.

There is much contradiction in the Purans in respect to the comparative rank and honor of Brahma, Vishnu, and Sheva. A sage called Attencin, becoming convinced that he ought to worship only one deity, thus addressed them:—"O you three Lords, know that I recognize only one God; inform me therefore, which of you is the true divinity that I may address to him alone my vows and adorations." The three gods, Brahma, Vishnu, and Sheva becoming manifest to him, replied:—"Learn, O devotee, that there is no real distinction between us; what to you appears such is only by semblance; the single Being appears under three forms, by the acts of creation, preservation, and destruction, but he is ONE."

Some of the Purans appear to have been written to exalt Vishnu, and others were written to exalt Sheva. The votaries of each claim the highest honors and attributes for their favorite deity, and each party can adduce the authority of the Purans for their opinions. By the votaries of Vishnu he is declared to be the Supreme God and the Creator of the universe,* and that Sheva and all the other gods are inferior and subordinate to him. The votaries of Sheva, calling him Maha Deva or the Great God, set up the same claims for him and depreciate Vishnu and all the other gods. These disputes and quarrels have sometimes been so violent as to require the interference of the government.

OTHER HINDU DEITIES.

It is not necessary to give any further particular accounts of the Hindu deities. Their number is almost infinite. Some of them are gods and some are goddesses. In their conduct there is little for imitation, and in their character nothing for admiration, and seldom any thing to procure respect. The same deities are called in different districts by different names, and worshipped by different rites and ceremonies. Probably some of them were the deities and demons worshipped by the rude tribes before they embraced the religion now generally called Brahminism. Some are monsters in form. Gunesh who is much worshipped, has an elephant's head on a human body. Hunnuman who is also much worshipped, is believed to have been an incarnation of one of their gods in the form of a monkey. Some of them are believed to be malevolent and to delight in cruelty, torture, and bloody-offerings. They all show how low human nature can sink in its conceptions of deity, and how debasing has been the religion of India for some thousand years past.

* One account of the creation of the world says that at the close of a kalpa, Vishnu was sleeping on the waters of the deluge, and a lotus, or water-lily, grew up from his navel. From this flower sprung Brahma, who in the form of Narayan proceeded to create the world, etc. I have often seen pictures and engravings thus representing Brahma springing from Vishnu. The votaries of Vishnu declare that he was really the Creator; they call him so and say that Brahma in all he did in creating the world was only the agent of Vishnu.

DEMONOLATRY.

The Hindus are very superstitious in respect to spiritual beings, who are supposed to have the power and the disposition to interfere in human affairs. Accidents, misfortunes, and afflictions are often ascribed to the malevolent agency of such beings. So also are insanity, epilepsy, sudden attacks of illness, and extreme sickness. To appease such beings and to avert their displeasure, deprecatory prayers are addressed to them, and offerings of food are made in places where they are supposed to resort. Almost every town and village contain places which are believed to be haunted by evil spirits and are carefully avoided, or if it is necessary to pass by them or to go to them, some prayer is offered or ceremony is performed to appease the evil spirit. Houses are often believed to be haunted and so stand empty till they fall to ruin. In such cases the evil being is generally supposed to be the spirit of some deceased person who formerly lived there.

The question whether magic originated in Egypt,* or in India, will probably forever remain undetermined. But a belief in magic, sorcery, and witchcraft has long existed among all classes of people in India. And for this belief they have high authority, for the Artharva Veda contains principles and doctrines of magic, and ways and means of practising it. Some people are supposed to be acquainted with these mysterious rites, mystical formulas, and secret incantations, and to have power over spiritual beings, who can thus be controlled and even compelled to be submissive and subservient. By these means evil spirits can be restrained and ejected. It is a common opinion that people who are skilled in magic and sorcery can by such means inflict evils, sickness, and even death upon their enemies. It is natural that persons supposed to be possessed of such power, should be much dreaded. Many of the annoyances, troubles, and afflictions of life are ascribed to witches, and there are few towns or villages without persons suspected or accused of such arts and powers. Jugglers, in India rather a numerous class, are believed

* Gen. 41: 8. Exo. 7: 11, 22. 8: 18, 19. 9: 11.

to have acquired their knowledge and skill by intercourse with evil spirits, and to perform their tricks and feats by the assistance of such beings.

There is also among them another kind of superstition. It is what they believe to be possession, or inspiration by some deity or demon. Instances of this state are very common among some classes and in certain districts. Sometimes this influence is experienced unexpectedly, and sometimes it is obtained by prayers, ceremonies, etc. It generally occurs when people are engaged in some kind of religious duties. It is sometimes partial, and sometimes complete. When complete, the individual is not supposed to have any control over his bodily actions, or mental faculties, and when he speaks it is believed to be the deity or demon speaking with his organs. At the festivals of some of the gods, generally some local deity or demon, the people go to his temple, or set up his image in some place, and perfuming it with incense, and celebrating his praise and worship with a kind of music used only on such occasions, some of them bow down before the image and invoke the deity or demon to come into them and take possession of them. Of those who thus engage in this worship, some are generally soon in the state they desire, and begin to appear like insane persons. The others then take possession of these persons, carefully observe what they say, make inquiry concerning matters they wish to know, implore the protection and blessing of the deity or demon in them, etc. This state generally continues only for a few hours. In most cases the possession or inspiration ceases soon after the worship and music cease.

I knew some persons who are sceptical in respect to the truth of such possessions and inspiration, but the people generally appeared to have entire confidence in the reality of such things. The Scriptures contain numerous instances of the possession of persons by evil spirits or demons in the time of our Saviour and the Apostles,* and there is no intimation and no reason to believe that they were peculiar or limited to that age or those nations. The Scriptures assure us that the devil

* Matt. 8: 16. 9: 34. 10: 1. Mark 1: 34. 3: 11. 16: 17. Luke 4: 41. 8: 2. 9: 1. Acts 5: 16. 8: 7. 16: 18. 19: 12–16.

has access to the minds of men, and if people renounce the true God, worship other deities and demons, invoke them to enter into them, and then carefully observe the operations of their own minds to perceive the expected and desired influence, is it unreasonable to believe that such persons may really experience what they seek and desire? that they do really become possessed, or inspired by the devil or some of his demons, and that these beings have had a greater and more direct agency in originating and perpetuating idolatry and the various systems of superstition and false religion, which exist in the world, than is generally believed? And may not those who wrote the books containing these false religions, have had assistance, or *inspiration* much beyond what is generally ascribed to them?

IDOLS.

Idols are made of various materials, as gold, silver, brass, stone, (black and white marble,) wood, clay, baked and dried, etc. They are of different materials and sizes, as may suit the means and convenience of the worshippers. They are intended to be in the form of the deities in whose worship they are to be used — to have the same shape the gods are described as having in their respective heavens. So some of the idols have several heads, many arms and hands, and eyes on different parts of them. These idols are made by any persons who have sufficient ingenuity and mechanical skill, as goldsmiths, sculptors, carpenters, potters, etc. These images are not regarded as fit to be worshipped till they have been consecrated. The consecration of the idol of a common village temple or of those kept in dwelling-houses, is performed by one or two brahmins without much ceremony. But the consecrating of large temples and the idols in them is celebrated with much ceremony, and great congregations of people assemble to join in them. The most learned brahmins are employed, and the rites are sometimes repeated and prolonged for several days. Among the rites are bathing the idols in milk, burning incense before them, invoking the god to take up his residence in them, etc. Bands of music are employed to extol the praises of the god, and when the image becomes, by the rites of consecration, a fit object to be worshipped, then all the people present begin to worship it.

In large temples and in sacred places idols are kept with great care, and no person of low caste is allowed to touch them, nor even enter the inclosure or yard surrounding them. They are often bathed in water from the Ganges or some other sacred place, and sometimes costly clothes and jewels are put upon them. Idols in common temples are kept with less care. These as well as idols set up in gardens, in fields, and in groves, are often exposed to any treatment that people may show them, but fear of being discovered and dread of the displeasure of the god generally preserve such idols and places from contempt and profanation.

TEMPLES.

The temples of India are of almost every size and form. They are not built to accommodate assemblies of people like churches, as there is no social prayer, nor praise, nor hearing instruction in their worship. The first and chief purpose of erecting a temple is to have a suitable place to contain the idol, the object to be worshipped. The space inclosed in the temples is generally large enough to allow the priest who has the charge of the idol, to walk around it. Sometimes the idol is placed near the wall opposite to the door. People of all classes except the lowest, go into many of the village temples scattered over the country, but only the brahmins are allowed to enter the largest temples and those which claim peculiar sanctity. At such places the other castes are allowed to come only to the door. In some temples the distance to which different castes are allowed to approach towards the idol is fixed in view of their supposed respective purity. Some of the temples have walls, and even several walls, one within another, surrounding them like the temple in Jerusalem. Some of these temples have more the appearance of forts than of places of worship, and in the former unsettled state of the country, they were often made places of refuge and defence. Temples of this character are now most frequently found in the southern parts of India.*

* The temple of Seringham, on an island in the river Coleroon, near Trichinopoly, is one of the largest in India. "It is composed of 7 square inclosures,

Many large and fortified temples were taken and destroyed by the Mohammedans in northern India in their early wars with the Hindus. Temples are generally of brick and stone, and are more substantially built than the dwelling-houses. Temples are often found in a state of good preservation among the ruins and rubbish of deserted villages and cities. In this way the Hindus show their respect for religion.

The temples have generally been erected by individuals. Sometimes the members of a family have united to erect one, and in some instances they have been erected by the native governments. Many temples have endowments. In the western part of India, a part of the revenue of the village is often appropriated to keeping one or more of the temples in repair, to lighting them and performing ceremonies in them on particular holidays. Wealthy individuals or families generally endow the temples they build. These endowments often consist of the rents of lands, sometimes of the whole or part of the rent of villages which belonged to the builders. Sometimes the builder and the people of the village or district would obtain an endowment from the government. In such cases whether the endowments are from individuals or from the government, the care of the temple is intrusted to some brahmin or brahmins and their families in succession, who are to receive the income of the endowments and in return are to keep the temple in repair, and to perform certain specified rites and services in it. It was regarded as the duty of the government to enforce the terms of such endowments. The brahmins and their successors were required to perform the duty for which the endowments were made, and were enabled to realize the income. Some such endowments were made several centuries ago and a large number of families are supported by them.

These endowed temples have sometimes a band of music

one within another, the walls of which are 25 feet high and 4 feet thick. These inclosures are 350 feet distant from one another, and each has 4 large gates with a high tower, which are placed one in the middle of each side of the inclosure, and opposite to the four cardinal points. The outward wall is nearly 4 miles in circumference, and its gateway to the south is ornamented with pillars, several of which are single stones 33 feet high, and nearly 5 feet in diameter, and those which form the roof are still larger." This temple has endowments to the amount of more than 20,000 dollars annually.

attached to them, who attend on festival days, and who also every morning at sunrise and again at sunset celebrate the praises of their god. I have seen many such temples, and in one instance the brahmins in charge wished to decorate me with flowers, and thus honoring me at the temple, then to accompany me with their band of music some distance on my way. This was on the Coromandel Coast, where I could but imperfectly use the language of the people, and it was some time before I could make them understand why I declined the honor they intended to show me.

Princes and wealthy people often have private temples in their gardens and parks. People often have a place in their houses, in which the idols they worship are placed. This place is sometimes a small room or closet or niche in the wall, in which several idols are placed. Sometimes a brahmin is employed to perform the daily rites of the idols, and sometimes some one of the household * will do it. The idols are often bathed, incense is burned, flowers and articles of food are offered, the worshipper joins his hands and bows his head or prostrates himself, repeats prayers, etc.

The worship, rites, etc., at some of these temples are such as might be expected from the character of their deities. The following is an extract from the author's journal written while at Jejury in 1833.

"Here is a celebrated temple of Khundoba, who is believed to be an incarnation of Sheva. His incarnation, it is believed, took place in this vicinity, and after accomplishing the object for which it was assumed, the god ascended to heaven from the top of a hill in front of the village. Hence this place became the principal seat of his worship. A work on India published some years ago contains the following description of this temple. 'It is built of fine stone, is situated on a high hill in a beautiful country, and has a very majestic appearance. Attached to it is an establishment of dancing girls amounting to 250 in number. This temple is very rich, £6,000 being annually expended on account of the idol, who has horses and elephants kept for him, and with his spouse is daily bathed in rose and Ganges water, although the latter is brought from a distance of more than

* See Judges, 17: 5, 12, 13.

1,000 miles.' Since this description was written the temple has apparently suffered somewhat in its revenues and popularity. The rites of idolatry, however, are still performed here with much parade and pomp. The 'dancing girls' are females who have been dedicated to the god, generally by their parents, though sometimes children have been purchased for this purpose. This dedication is made professedly in the fulfilment of vows, though the true reason sometimes is the inability of the parents to form marriage connections for their daughters. On arriving at a certain age the unhappy girl is brought to the temple, and in a prescribed form is dedicated and presented as an offering to the god. The customary ceremony of marriage is then performed between her and the idol, and this is the only marriage state she ever enters. This dedication to the god with the succeeding ceremony of marriage to the idol, is only an introduction to a life of prostitution, which is begun and followed without fear of sin or sense of shame on the part of the unhappy woman or of her connections; her dedication to the god, instead of requiring holiness of heart and life, becoming a reason why she may follow such a course without incurring infamy or guilt. A few of these women are employed in the temple, where they assist in performing the rites and ceremonies of worship, and as many as can find means of support, live in the village near the temple. But the greater part of them are scattered in the large villages and cities through the country and visit the idol only at the festivals. The number of this unhappy class who are thus introduced, we may say forced, into this course of prostitution and wretchedness for life without any choice or agency on their part is very large, and they spread around a pernicious influence."

There are other temples similar in the character of their deities and the conduct of their votaries. Thus some people can be as wicked as they please, and yet be serving their gods. But in these practices the Hindus are not worse than ancient heathen nations: not worse than the Canaanites who were driven out of their country, or destroyed by the Hebrews; and not worse than the ancient Greeks and Romans. The gods of the Hindus are not worse than Bacchus, Venus, and Laverna, or than Moloch, Baal-peor, and Astarte. History shows that heathenism, in its deities, its practices, and its influence, has been essentially the same in all ages and in all nations.

CAVE-TEMPLES.

The excavated rock-temples in the western part of the Deckan and in the Concan are the most remarkable and wonderful monuments of superstition in India, or in any country of the world. These temples are excavated in solid rock, and so are subterranean. Some of them are Budhist, some are Brahminical, and some of them contain the symbols and images of both these systems. The most remarkable of these are the temples of Elephanta and Kennery, near Bombay, and of Karlee, Adjunta, and Elora, in the Deckan.

The Elephanta temples are on an island a few miles east from Bombay, across the harbor. They are excavated in the rock of a hill 300 or 400 feet high, and about half-way up its ascent. The principal temple is 130 feet long, 123 feet wide, and 15 feet high. The roof, or ceiling, is flat, and supported by rows of pillars, which as well as the images, are a part of the natural rock of the hill. Most of these pillars are now fallen or mutilated. Tradition among the inhabitants says that the Mohammedans or the Portuguese placed cannon at the entrance of the temple and battered down the pillars and images as far as they could. The images, which were once numerous and some of them very large, are nearly all now in a mutilated and decayed state. But the principal figure of the temple, the image of the god to whom the temple was apparently dedicated, still remains nearly entire, though somewhat decayed. It consists of a gigantic bust with three faces at the end opposite to the principal entrance. This figure is richly ornamented, and shows a style of sculpture superior to what is generally seen in such temples. There are apartments communicating with the sides of this temple with images and symbols of the Hindu deities, descriptive of scenes and events in their sacred history, and shrines for performing the rites and ceremonies of their worship. The images, symbols, and shrines, in this temple, are brahminical. There is no inscription in it, and no mention is made of it in any Hindu work. So there are no means of ascertaining when it was made, or when or why it was abandoned. The general opinion of Europeans who have examined this temple is, that it was made subsequent to the Christian era, and some believe it was made as late as the 9th or 10th century.

The Kennery temples are in the island of Salsette, about 25 miles north from Bombay. They consist of two large, and a great number of small excavations. They are all apparently of Budhist origin and construction, and appear once to have formed a large monastic establishment. Probably this was a large Budhist theological seminary at the time when our Saviour was on the earth. There are some inscriptions on the walls in some ancient character, which have occasioned much speculation among orientalists. There is no well-authenticated history of these caves; and when they were made, how long they were used, and why they were abandoned, will probably always be unknown.

The Karlee temple is near the road from Bombay to Poona. It is a large and beautiful excavation about 130 feet long and 40 feet wide, with a high-arched roof. Like the Kennery temple, it is of Budhist origin and has two rows of pillars terminating in a semicircle. The temple and imagery are well preserved, and altogether form one of the most beautiful temples I saw in India. There are several smaller excavations near the temple, but they are in a dilapidated state, or were never finished.

The Adjunta temples are near a village of this name, situated 40 miles north-east from Aurungabad. These temples are excavated in the rocks on the side of a deep ravine. They are numerous; 25 had been examined when I left India, and it is said that others have been since discovered. One of these temples is 100 feet long and 40 feet wide. On each side is a row of large pillars, 12 feet high, and converging at the end opposite to the entrance so as to form a semicircle. The roof between these pillars and the walls is flat, but between the pillars it is arched, and at the end it is semicircular. This temple contains many images, and has also many figures painted upon the walls. There is one excavation which is 80 feet square, with a flat roof, or ceiling, supported by 28 pillars. In the sides of this excavation are many small cells, apparently designed for dormitories. There are two temples each 64 feet long and 62 feet wide. The roof of each is flat, and is supported with 20 pillars. These temples contain images and paintings on the walls. These temples are of Budhist origin and worship.

The Elora temples, so called from a village of this name near them, are 16 miles north-west from Aurungabad. These temples, in number, size, and magnificence, exceed any works which idolatry or superstition has made in India. One of these temples called Kylas, or the paradise of Sheva, is a temple formed of a single rock, which is an integral part of the mountain, in an excavated court 247 feet long and 150 feet wide. The walls of this court are the rock in which the excavation is made, and they vary in height from 50 to 100 feet. In these walls are many excavated rooms, halls, and galleries, some of them of two stories. In the centre of this court is the grand temple, 142 feet long, 60 feet wide, and 90 feet high to the apex. In this temple is one large room with 16 pillars to support the superincumbent mass of rock. There are also many small rooms and shrines. The outside of this temple is entirely covered with sculptured figures, representing actions and events described in the Purans. This temple, with its rooms, halls, galleries, shrines, images, and courts, consists of the original rock of the mountain, reduced to their present state and form internally and externally, by excavation and sculpture. The genius, skill, and labor, exhibited in its design and execution, place it among the most remarkable works of any age or nation.

Near Kylas is a temple which has three stories, or rather the excavation consists of three large temples, one above the other. The lower temple is 117 feet long, 42 feet wide, and 12 feet high, with a large recess for the principal image. The second temple is 114 feet long, 66 feet wide, and 12 feet high, with a recess, and the third temple is 110 feet long, 66 feet wide, and 12 feet high, with a recess. Near this is an excavation which contains two large temples, one above the other. The lower temple is 103 feet long, 46 feet wide, and 14 feet high, and the upper one is apparently of the same size. There are many other large temples excavated in the mountain, either of which, if alone, would excite admiration, but as in a city of palaces, one, which would be an ornament and honor to any common city, excites but little attention where it is, so here a temple excavated in solid rock as large as our largest churches, being only one of many similar to it, excites little surprise or admiration.

There are also excavated rock-temples at Juneer, Nasseek,

Badami, and other places, but they are not equal in size and magnificence to those at Elora. There are no means of ascertaining at what time these wonderful works were made. Some of them are Budhistical, some are Brahminical, and some show a mixture of both systems. The Budhist temples appear to be more ancient than the Brahminical, and in the temples of a mixed character, the images and symbols of the latter appear to have been ingrafted upon those of the former. The apotheosis of Budh is generally supposed to have taken place in the 6th century before Christ, and about 250 years B. C. a powerful prince by the name of Asoka, whose capital was Magadi, was very zealous in propagating, and generous in supporting Budhism. A long and severe controversy was carried on between the rival systems, which resulted in the triumph of the brahmins and their votaries, and the expulsion of the Budhists from India and their taking refuge in Ceylon. The oldest Budhist temples, it is believed, were made before the Christian era, and some of them were probably made after that epoch. The brahminical temples were probably made in the early centuries of the Christian era.

The Budhist temples would naturally be abandoned when the votaries of that system were driven out of India, unless the brahmins should convert them to their own use. But we know not what should cause the brahmins and their votaries to abandon these temples, the works of so much labor, and which could be used to so much effect in supporting their system of idolatry and superstition. Some have supposed that the Mohammedans profaned these temples, and so forcibly interfered with the Hindus using them. But the Mohammedans did not take possession of the western provinces of India till near the close of the 13th century, and I am not aware that there is any mention of their profaning or injuring these temples in any Hindu or Mohammedan history. Some have supposed that the Portuguese, who obtained possession of Bombay and Salsette early in the 16th century, profaned and mutilated some of these temples, and there is some such tradition among the natives. But had this been done, it is very improbable that the Portuguese historians of that age should not have mentioned it.

These works were made long before the discovery of gunpowder, and the labor of executing them appears to be incalculable and incredible. They show the power of false religion and superstition over former generations of the inhabitants of India. Whether the labor of executing these works was performed voluntarily from the strong and enduring feelings of superstition, or in reluctant obedience to despotic power, or for wages from the treasuries of kings, (for none but kings could pay for such things,) we know not, and apparently the world will never know.

Some of these excavated temples were monastic establishments and so would be places for religious education as well as for devotion. In India such education would include the whole circle of philosophy, science, and literature. Among the Budhists, celibacy is an essential qualification for the priesthood, and much of the labor of making these excavations may have been performed by those who occupied them, or expected to become their inmates.

In the present state of these temples, abandoned and partly filled with rubbish, the images mutilated and the paintings defaced, it is not easy to see how they must have appeared when the system of superstition to which they were dedicated, was in its glory, and when brahmins and budhists ministered at these shrines, and appeared to be the companions as well as the priests of these deities. In these vast halls and gloomy recesses, secluded from the light, (for there is evidence of curtains and screens having been once used,) surrounded by gigantic images of the gods and paintings of sacred scenes, all arranged and managed so as to produce the most striking effect, the pretended mysteries and the solemn rites and imposing ceremonies of polytheism and idolatry were performed. And we cannot conceive of any circumstances fitted more powerfully to affect the minds of an ignorant and superstitious people like the Hindus.

In view of the influence which these temples must have exerted in supporting and perpetuating idolatry and superstition, we cannot regret seeing them in the state in which they now are. Indeed, so far from feelings of regret, we have reasons for gratitude and thankfulness to God that in the course of his providence, by means unknown to us, these idols have been broken, the rites and ceremonies once performed here are forgotten, and that these palaces of the powers of darkness have become desolate and forsaken.

SACRED PLACES.

Sacred places are very numerous in India. The fame of some of them, as Juggunath, Benares, Hurdwar, Dwarka, Nasseek, extend through all the country, and people go from the extreme parts of India on pilgrimage to them. These places are celebrated for the manifestation of some god, or some other remarkable events mentioned in their sacred books, and great merit is believed to be acquired by making pilgrimage to them, and there performing religious rites and ceremonies. It is believed that people who die at some of these places, obtain emancipation from future birth and sufferings, and so devotees and rich men often go there to end their days. There are hundreds of sacred places of less notoriety scattered all over the country, to which people in the districts resort on pilgrimage. These pilgrimages are generally festivals, and continue often for 2 or 3 days. A part of the time is spent in religious rites, a part often in transacting business, a part in hearing the Purans read, seeing shows, etc. At some of the large temples the idols are placed on large cars and drawn round the temple. The people have then an opportunity of worshipping the gods and of manifesting their homage by drawing the cars. The brahmins who have the charge of such temples, contrive many ways to extort money from all classes of the pilgrims. Thieving, robbing, lewdness, and all kinds and forms of villany and wickedness are rife at such places. Many lose all their means, and then have to beg their way home. The sufferings endured and the superstition manifested on such pilgrimages are very great.* Travelling in India is slow, and in the hot and the rainy months is unhealthy, and great numbers die of cholera, smallpox, and other diseases at the places of pilgrimage, and in going and returning.

* I have often seen persons proceeding on pilgrimage, who measured the distance by prostrating themselves on the ground, repeating every time the name of the god, or of the place to which they were going. Such labor, fatigue, and suffering are believed to be peculiarly pleasing to the god and to secure his favor. Such pilgrimages are generally made in the performance of vows.

Devotees who have become weary of life and are without any social or domestic connections to bind them to their fellow-creatures, sometimes go to such places with the purpose of sacrificing themselves. Some pilgrims, who are reduced to distress by sickness or the death of friends, form the same purpose. And some persons of a superstitious spirit, becoming excited almost to a state of frenzy by what they see and hear, suddenly resolve to devote themselves to the deity there worshipped. In view of such circumstances, it does not appear strange that some persons should throw themselves under the ponderous car of Juggunath, or leap into the most holy places of the Ganges, expecting to go immediately to the heaven of the god to whom they sacrifice themselves. Shocking as such instances of self-immolation are, yet to those acquainted with the character of the Hindus and the nature of their religious system, such acts are only the natural result of their idolatry and superstition. Such acts of self-destruction are less frequent now than formerly, partly because there is less enthusiasm and fanaticism among the Hindus, and partly because the English government has enacted laws inflicting punishment upon any who shall aid or coöperate in such acts of self-destruction, and in some places such self-immolation cannot be performed without religious rites and ceremonies, which require the aid and coöperation of other persons.

PRIESTS AND SPIRITUAL GUIDES.

The brahmins form the hereditary priesthood in India. None but brahmins can teach and explain the Vedas, and according to the Vedas they alone can properly perform any religious rites. And any brahmin who has sufficient knowledge of the prescribed formularies, can perform the rites required. But many of the brahmins do not possess this knowledge, and so are not competent to perform the rites of their religion in the manner required. And further, in some parts of the country the right and duty of performing all the religious rites and ceremonies in a particular village or district was assigned by the native governments to a particular family and its descendants. In such cases the individual or families claim the right of performing all the religious ceremonies, and of receiving the remuneration for them in their respective village or district. The governments, native and European, protect them in these rights, and if any other brahmin should perform any such rites in such village or district, he is liable to prosecution and penalty. The temples also are always under the care of particular individuals or families, who manage the endowments, if there are any, and appropriate to their own use the offerings made to the god.

In some instances the officiating priests in the temples are not brahmins, but belong to some of the numerous castes into which the shudras have become divided. This arrangement, so different from the precepts of the Vedas and the prerogative of the brahmins, probably had its origin in a period anterior to the brahminical system's being received in these districts. It is probably a relic of the superstition of the primitive or aboriginal tribes. Brahminism, in its gradual progress, incorporated into its pantheon the local deities or demons, and had continued to tolerate usages and customs, which it has not power to extinguish or to reform. I saw many temples of this kind in India. Some of them are large and well endowed. Brahmins seldom worship in such temples, and learned brahmins generally look upon them and all connected with them with feelings of contempt.

Men of different castes often set themselves up for religious teachers, principally in the way of using and teaching mystical words and phrases, fortune-telling, etc. Such men often acquire great influence among people of their own caste. They are commonly called *Gurus*, and their followers often worship them, saying, "they are to us instead of God." They are supposed to acquire great influence with the gods. Their favor and blessing are earnestly desired, and their displeasure and curse are exceedingly dreaded. They often select particular favorites among their followers, pretend to impart to them special instructions, and so prepare them to become their successors in spiritual power and influence. These fanatics and impostors have sometimes given the governments, Hindu, Mohammedan, and English, great trouble, and it has been necessary to employ military force to restrain and to subdue them.

SACRED DAYS.

The number of sacred days in the Hindu religion is very large. Among these are the days of the new and full moon, and also certain days in its increase and in its decrease. Their name for Sunday, as with us, is derived from the Sun, and this is regarded as more sacred than any other day of the week. Nearly every month has some great holiday. Some of them continue for only one day, and others continue for 2 or 3 and more days. These are observed in honor of some god or mythological event. Business is generally suspended, and people spend their time in religious rites, visiting, amusements, etc. On some of these days, the rites and revelry, and the songs and amusements are of a very exceptionable character, and exert an unhappy influence upon the moral state of the people. One of these called Holee, which usually takes place in March, resembles the Saturnalia of the Greeks and Romans, and continues for several days. The amusements in which the men engage, the songs they sing, and the scenes which are witnessed in the streets at these times, are so exceedingly indecent and obscene that the native women avoid being seen in the streets or in their houses.

The Hindus are also very superstitious in respect to lucky and unlucky days. Their almanacs are chiefly valued for the information they are supposed to contain on these subjects. The large and small concerns of life are managed in a full belief of such lucky and unlucky days, and the trouble, loss of time, and difficulties which such a belief occasions, are among the burdens which the Hindus suffer from their religious system.

WORSHIP, RITES, ETC.

The Hindus can scarcely be said ever to worship the self-existing and eternal Spirit. Some say it is impossible to worship him, as it transcends our capacities in our present state, and that he does not take any cognizance of worship, and not having commanded it, so he will not regard it. Others have a more natural and common sense opinion on this subject and talk more reasonably, but their opinions have little influence upon their conduct. Temples are never without idols, and people if they wish to worship, always procure an idol or get to one, if possible. But when this is impracticable, they call upon their gods by repeating their names, offering short petitions, making vows, etc., and they believe that the gods hear them. Mental and spiritual worship is thus sometimes practised among them, but only when no access can be had to idols. One way of worship is for the worshipper to stand before the idol, fix his eyes upon it, join his hands, and bowing his head, repeat the name of the god, adding perhaps a short petition. Another way is to perambulate the idol, bowing to it as often as the worshipper comes before it. Another way is to prostrate the body on the ground before the idol. Garlands of flowers are often put upon idols, and offerings of flowers, fruit, sweetmeats, jewels, money, etc., are put before them. All such offerings, unless designed to be placed upon the idols, belong to the priests, who have the charge of the idols, and are appropriated to their own use. In some instances the idols on certain festival days are removed from the temples, placed on large cars, and drawn round their temples.

The rites and duties prescribed for the brahmins, if all were performed, would require a large part of the time. They consist of repeating the names of the different gods, reading the sacred books, ablutions intermixed with many ceremonies, repeating the Gayutree * and other mystic verses, at the same time keeping the head and body in various positions, etc. Few brahmins now perform the whole routine of daily ceremonies, and many perform only a small part of them. The other castes also have their daily rites, though compared with those of the brahmins, they are few in number and easily performed. But the Hindu religion is emphatically one of ceremonies. Religious

* Gayutree is the name of a holy and mystical sentence, or text, in the Vedas which brahmins repeat in performing their rites. It is variously translated, as: — "Let us meditate on the adorable light of the divine ruler; may he direct our intellects." "We meditate on that adorable light of the resplendent sun; may it direct our intellects." "We meditate upon the superexcellent light of the resplendent sun; let him direct our intellects." "We meditate upon the glorious sun; may he illuminate our minds." They must look at the sun, if visible, when repeating the words, and when the natural eyes gaze at the sun the mind should be fixed upon the Supreme Being, to whom the prayer as some pretend is really addressed.

rites are enjoined to be performed at birth, or rather before birth, and at all the personal and relative changes in life. Nor do these cease with life. As death approaches, the dying person, if near the Ganges, is hurried to the banks of the river, where a part of the rites is to fill his mouth with water, all which must aggravate his sufferings if it does not hasten his death. If not living near the Ganges, the dying person must be removed so as to die upon the ground. The Hindus generally burn their dead, though some who have not means to meet the expense of burning, and some devotees and lower classes, bury their dead or throw them into rivers. The burning or burial is generally performed in a few hours after death. The eldest son or nearest relation performs the funeral ceremony. There are few rites at death or the funeral, but for some days all who are nearly related to the deceased, are regarded as in a state of ceremonial impurity. When this time has passed, the near relatives assemble, generally on the bank of some river or tank, and numerous ceremonies called *Shradh* are performed in honor and for the supposed benefit of the deceased. In some parts of India the number of people, friends, brahmins, and devotees, who assemble at a *Shradh* is very great, and as all expect presents or charity, the expense is large.

It is usual to perform a monthly *Shradh* for the first year after the death of a parent, and once or more in every year a *Shradh* is performed for all their ancestors. These rites are believed to be very meritorious, as well as to give great pleasure to their ancestors, and so great importance is attached to performing them.

Many of the Hindu rites about touching dead bodies, physical impurity in men and women, persons diseased with the leprosy, etc., resemble the laws of the Jews contained in the Pentateuch. The laws of purification are also similar, as continuing separate for a certain time, then bathing, etc.

Numerous atonements and penalties are prescribed in the shastras. The actions for which many of these are required, are of a very frivolous character. Some of these atonements and penalties are very severe, and others are very light, when compared with the nature of the offences. Some of these penalties consist in presents of land, money, cows, etc., to brahmins, and in performing menial services for them; some consist in mutilating and branding certain parts of the body, in self-torture, in fastings, sitting or standing in painful positions, etc. These penalties appear from their inequality, cruelty, and indecency, evidently to have had their origin in a barbarous age, and among a very superstitious people. They are regarded as of divine origin, but it is scarcely credible that they should ever have been recognized as the laws of any country, or as making a part of any system of religion.

SACRIFICES AND OFFERINGS.

There is abundant evidence from the early records of the Hindus, that human sacrifices were sometimes offered. In this practice they resembled other ancient heathen nations. The Institutes of Menu say, "The sacrifice of a bull, of a man, and of a horse in the Kalee yug (the present age), must be avoided." There have been instances in modern times in which some fanatics and devotees have secretly devoted human beings to destruction, to appease Kalee or some of their malevolent deities. But such sacrifices do not now make a part of the Hindu religion, as publicly professed and practised.

The sacrifice of a horse is described at much length, in the Purans. This sacrifice could only be offered by kings and princes, and it is not known that any one has attempted to offer it for some centuries past. Sacrifices are now seldom offered according to the Hindu ritual, which is very prolix and expensive. Buffaloes, sheep, goats, and fowls are offered at some places on certain festivals, chiefly by the middling and lower classes, and with few rites. Sacrifices of this kind are sometimes offered when cholera or other epidemics prevail, to appease the malevolent deity, who is supposed to cause the disease. At such times the blood of the animal sacrificed is sometimes sprinkled in the streets and places where the disease most prevails. The frenzy that pervades people at such times, the rites they perform and the means they use, in the hope of stopping the disease, or appeasing the malevolent deities which are believed to be killing their friends, are very shocking, and appear truly diabolical. They remind one of what the Apostle says: "The things which the Gentiles sacrifice, they sacrifice to devils and not to God." *

Burnt-offerings called *hom*, consisting of clarified butter, boiled rice, honey, and other substances, are often made. Drink offerings called *turpun*, are made at the time of bathing, by taking up water in the hand, or a small vessel, and pouring it out, repeating at the same time the name of the god, or demon, or ancestor, to whom it is offered. This is a very common rite.

Meditation (*dhan*) is an important part of worship. The worshipper must assume a particular attitude, carefully adjusting his feet, hands, eyes, etc. He is then to meditate upon the god he wishes to worship, calling to mind his form, acts, etc. Or believing his own soul to be only a part of the supreme Spirit, or that his own thoughts, etc., are all the operations of the supreme Spirit pervading his body and all the universe, he endeavors by introspection to contemplate the Deity in the actings of his own mind. This kind of worship is believed to be very meritorious, and some devotees are believed in this way to acquire great knowledge of divine things. The gods are said often to have revealed themselves to people when thus engaged in meditation.

Repeating the name of some one of the gods is a very common mode of worship. To assist in this exercise a string of beads, pearls, or berries is prepared, containing 50 or 100, or some known number. The worshipper by removing one of these each time he repeats the name, is enabled easily to reckon his prayers and know when he has completed the intended number of repetitions. Some people spend hours in this practice. In view of this practice and the belief in which it originates, we see the propriety of what our Saviour said to his disciples, "When ye pray, use not vain repetitions as the heathens do; for they think they shall be heard for their much speaking." †

The Hindus seldom have any prayers in which a whole assembly, or any considerable number of worshippers unite. Generally each one prays by himself, and the object of his prayer is known only to himself. Hymns in praise of the different gods are not uncommon; they are sung, or played on rude

* 1 Cor. 10: 20. † Matt. 6: 7.

instruments by devotees and travelling minstrels, but they are seldom if ever used by congregations, or any considerable number of persons assembled for worship.

Vows to different gods are very frequently made, and if the contingency upon which they rest becomes fact, they are generally performed. The Hindus are superstitious on the subject of fulfilling their vows. Vows not fulfilled, are believed to incur the displeasure of the gods, and to involve those who disregard them in ruin. Temples are often erected and repaired, pilgrimages to sacred places, costly offerings to the gods, and gifts to the brahmins, are often made in consequence of vows.*

Fasting, gifts to brahmins, the building of caravanserais, roads, tanks, etc., for the public good, are declared to be works of merit, and much money is often expended in this way. They think much of a man's name being incorporated with such works in public opinion.

The hearing of the Purans read and explained, is declared to be very meritorious. Many brahmins obtain their livelihood by reading and explaining these sacred works. For this purpose people assemble in the yard of a temple or some private house, when some man will read and explain some work in course, occupying about an hour for several successive days. A certain compensation is generally promised at the beginning, and if the reader or lecturer finishes the course and gives satisfaction, he will obtain some addition to it at the close. These meetings diffuse much information concerning their gods and heroes, and their actions. I have often been surprised at the information of people on these subjects, who unable themselves to read, have

* Parents sometimes devote one or more of their children to some deity by vows. For instance, the children in some family are perhaps sick of cholera, and appear likely to die. The parents in their anxiety make a vow to some god, that if all the children recover, they will devote one child to him. The child thus devoted is generally a girl. When the time arrives for fulfilling the vow, she is taken by her parents to the temple, and is married by the priest to the idol of the god. This ceremony is an introduction to a life of prostitution under the name of being devoted to the god. The number of such women in some districts is large. Some of them live at the temple, assist in the ceremonies, etc., and others go wherever they please, but all are devoted to a life of prostitution.

acquired all their knowledge at such public and social meetings.

Some of the Hindu deities are malevolent, or if this is not their general character they are described as often indulging in envious, angry, morose, and malevolent feelings, and some of them in intemperance and licentiousness resemble Bacchus and Venus among the Greek and Roman deities. This diversity of conduct and character in the Hindu deities, furnishes excuses and reasons for any persons, who may wish to indulge in intemperance and licentiousness; for they can indulge in any kind of wickedness and yet be imitating some of their deities. Still, as such conduct would be opposed to all general opinions of propriety and morality, it becomes necessary, if personal and social respectability are to be preserved, to indulge in such practices secretly. And there are meetings and associations for such conduct under the name and profession of religion. These assemblies consist of men and women who meet in the night and indulge in licentiousness, intermixed with religious rites and ceremonies. At these meetings all distinctions of caste, and all sentiments of morality, propriety, and decency, are laid aside; forbidden things are freely eaten and drunken, passions are indulged and actions are performed without any sense of shame, scruples of conscience or fear of consequences, which show the depravity of human nature in union with the degrading influences of superstition and heathenism. Instead of describing such practices and rites it is better to apply to them the language which the Apostle used when speaking of the heathen nations in ancient times—"It is a shame even to speak of those things which are done of them in secret."*

ASCETICISM, ASCETICS, AND DEVOTEES.

This state or course of life originated in the doctrine that the soul is incorporated with matter, and that the great work of life is for the soul to obtain emancipation from this matter, and reunion with the supreme Deity. This end, it is supposed, may be attained by mortifying and subduing all those appetites and

* Eph. 5: 12.

passions which are believed to have their seat in matter, or in the body. The Institutes of Menu, a work written 10 or 12 centuries before the Christian era, contains the following directions to brahmins:—"When the father of a family perceives his muscles become flaccid and his hair grey, and sees the child of his child, let him then seek refuge in a forest. Abandoning all food eaten in towns, and all his household utensils, let him repair to the lonely wood, committing the care of his wife to his sons, or accompanied by her if she choose to attend him. Let him take up his consecrated fire, and all his domestic implements of making oblations to it, and departing from the town to the forest, let him dwell in it with complete power over his organs of sense and action. With many sorts of pure food, such as holy sages used to eat, with green herbs, roots, and fruit, let him perform the five great sacraments, introducing them with due ceremonies. Let him wear a black antelope's hide, or a vesture of bark; let him bathe morning and evening; let him suffer the hairs of his head, his beard, and his nails to grow continually. From such food as he may eat, let him to the utmost of his power make offerings and give alms; and with presents of water, roots, and fruit, let him honor those who may visit his hermitage. Let him be constantly engaged in reading the Vedas, patient of all extremities, universally benevolent, with a mind intent on the Supreme Being, a perpetual giver, but no receiver of gifts, with tender affection for all animated bodies. Let him slide backwards and forwards on the ground, or let him stand a whole day on tiptoe, or let him continue in motion rising and sitting alternately; but at sunrise, noon, and sunset, let him go to the water and bathe. In the hot season let him sit exposed to five fires, four blazing around him with the sun above; in the rainy season let him stand uncovered without even a mantle, and where the clouds pour down the heaviest showers; in the cold season let him wear a humid vesture, and let him increase by degrees the austerity of his devotion. Then, having reposited his holy fires as the law directs in his mind, let him live without external fire, without a mansion, wholly silent, feeding on roots and fruits. Or he may bring food from a town, having received it in a basket of leaves, in his naked hand, or in a potsherd, and then let him swallow eight mouthfuls. A brahmin becoming void of sorrow and fear, and having shuffled off his body by any of those modes which great sages have practised, rises to exaltation in the divine essence."

Such is the mode prescribed by the highest authority for obtaining complete and final beatitude. These directions may have been followed in the early and purer ages of the Hindu religion, but they are now seldom if ever regarded by the class referred to, namely, fathers of families, whose muscles have become flaccid, their hair grey, and who have seen their children's children. The ascetics of the present age generally become such early in life, choosing this course as an easy and respectable way of procuring a livelihood. They are originally of all castes, and are divided into different classes or orders, as the gosavees, sunyasees, vyragees, etc. Few of them are learned and some cannot even read. Some classes marry and have families. Others live a single life. These generally roam about the country, stopping only a few days in one place. They generally live in the temples, which are always open to them. They assemble in large numbers in places of pilgrimage. Some pass their lives in visiting the holy places, begging their support on the way. They go nearly destitute of clothing, their hair, beard, and nails are long, their bodies are almost naked and covered with ashes, and their whole appearance is hideous and disgusting. Their professed work is to subdue their appetites and passions, and to spend their time in religious rites and in meditation on divine things. But instead of this course, their time is spent in idle talk, in smoking and chewing intoxicating and narcotic substances, and in sleep. They are exceedingly irritable and impudent, have a ready use of abusive language, and have generally the character of being licentious. The Hindus generally appear to have but little respect for them, and often show contempt for their religious profession and character. But they have superstitious fears of incurring their displeasure and of their abusive language, while their maledictions and execrations are much dreaded. People generally have some superstitious notion and apprehension that the curses of such devotees cause or forebode evil. Some devotees inflict upon themselves tortures of various kinds, as lying on spikes, holding their limbs in one position till they become incapable of moving them, etc. I have often seen and conversed with such persons. I believe these tortures are seldom inflicted on account of any consciousness of guilt, or to atone for any offence, and seldom, if ever, with a view of acquiring merit. I believe these classes of men become ascetics and devotees, because it appears to be an easy and respectable way of obtaining a livelihood, and that they inflict these pains and tortures upon themselves to obtain respect, money, etc. The number of brahmins and different classes of devotees, who subsist by begging in India, is very large, and their support and the various evils resulting from these classes are among the burdens which the inhabitants of that oppressed and unhappy country have to endure. Some of the more enlightened Hindus would be glad to see these classes of people compelled to labor in some way for their support; they would approve of the government's using some measures of this kind. But such is not yet the feeling of the great body of the people. There appears to be no remedy but a more generally diffused and enlightened public sentiment for the numerous evils which have for so many centuries afflicted the inhabitants of this unhappy country. The darkness will continue to brood over it till the Sun of Righteousness shall arise and dispel its gloom by his cheerful beams.

THE FUTURE STATE.

The Hindu sacred books describe several different degrees or states of happiness for mankind after death. Of these the highest state is called *Mooktee*, and consists of union with the Deity, or absorption into the infinite Spirit. This state is the result or reward of attaining divine knowledge. As soon as any man acquires a perfect knowledge of Bramh, it overcomes or extinguishes all sin within him, and its influence upon him; he disregards all work, however meritorious in general opinion, and emancipated from all worldly desires and bodily passions his spirit becomes united with Bramh, or is absorbed into him, "as a drop of water when it falls into the ocean." He loses all personal identity. He is no longer, and never will again be, a conscious and separate being, and so is not subject to any further transmigration or change. And yet this is the highest state to which brahminism aspires, or holds out to its votaries, and the means of attaining this state are so exceedingly difficult that only a very small proportion strive for it, and they live and die in the utmost uncertainty of it.

The next state is for those who earnestly sought this divine wisdom, this perfect knowledge of Bramh, but died before attaining it. Such persons after death are taken to the peculiar residence of Bramh to dwell near him. They are there endowed with great capacity for enjoyment, can exercise some superhuman powers, and "can assume many bodies or only one, as a lamp can nourish more than one wick." But as they are not yet prepared to become united with Bramh, another birth at some future time will be necessary. The general belief is that after a period proportioned to the moral character they have acquired, they will descend to the earth and have another birth in the brahminical caste, or in very favorable circumstances for perfecting their knowledge of Bramh, the work which was interrupted by death.

The 3rd and 4th states of happiness are in the heaven or abode of the gods called *Swurg*. Some few persons who in this life have performed works of extraordinary merit, after death proceed to *Swurg* and reside there till the close of the present kalpa, when *Swurg* and all its residents, whether gods or saints, will be annihilated. Those whose works in this life have a less degree of merit, will only reside in *Swurg* till such merit has been exhausted, and must then return to the earth to assume another birth. The Shastras say that Yama, one of the gods, is the judge of mankind after death. His court is on the south-east side of the earth. He has an assistant whose name is Chitragupt, and he has also many messengers who conduct souls when they leave the body to his court for judgment. Those who have performed works of merit in life, are conducted along excellent roads to Yama's court. Heavenly courtesans are now and then seen singing and dancing, and are heard chanting the praises of other gods. Showers of flowers fall from heaven. Near the road are houses containing cool water and excellent food. There are pools of water covered with lilies, and trees diffusing fragrance and giving shade. The gods are seen moving about on horses and elephants with splendid canopies over them. Or they are in palanquins and chariots with attendants waiting upon them and singing their praises. Some of them appear so beautiful and dazzling by the glory issuing from them, that they can scarcely be contemplated. Yama receives the virtuous with much kindness and respect. He gives them excellent food and says, "Your works have been very meritorious; you have been wise, and for the merit of your deeds you shall ascend to great happiness. He who performs such meritorious works is my father, my brother, my friend."

The place where such are to enjoy the rewards of their meritorious conduct, is the paradise or heaven of the gods on mount Meru or Sumeru. On this mount which, in shape like an inverted cone, is believed to be 600,000 miles high, 128,000 miles in circumference at the base, and 256,000 miles at the top, the most prominent of the gods have each their separate place of residence or heaven. These places are described in the Purans in truly oriental style, and correspond to other parts of the Hindu religion. They are inhabited by the gods and goddesses and by many other beings, as musicians, courtesans, etc. These places are described as abounding with means and facilities for all kinds of amusements and sensual pleasures. Quarrels, intrigues, gambling, drinking, revelry, lewdness, etc., are among their occupations, pursuits, and pleasures. Persons who have acquired merit, or the merit of whose works exceeded their demerit in life, are admitted according to its degree to these different places and pleasures, and when the merit of their actions is exhausted, they must return to the earth again there to assume another birth.

A far different state awaits the wicked after death. They have to travel 688,000 miles to the court of Yama. In some places the road consists of stones, mud, and sand, burning hot. Showers of sharp instruments, burning cinders, and scalding water fall upon them. They fall into concealed wells, grope their way through darkness, and meet tigers and other dreaded animals. They proceed naked, their hair disordered, their lips and throats parched with thirst. They are covered with blood, they weep, wail, and shriek with pain and horror. They are hurried along, sometimes dragged, manacled, and unmercifully beaten by the messengers of Yama. At length they arrive at the court of Yama, whose appearance is terrible, his height is

240 miles, the hairs of his body are as long as a palm-tree, his voice is as loud as thunder, his eyes send out flames of fire, the noise of his breathing is like a roaring tempest, etc. His conduct towards them corresponds to his terrible appearance. Inquiry is made respecting their actions, etc., in life, and they are then driven from his court to suffer each his merited punishment in the different hells. — No wonder that the Hindus have a great dread of death.

Much is said in the Shastras of the future punishment of the wicked. One Puran says there are 100,000 different places or hells, in which punishments of different kinds and in different degrees are inflicted. Some of these hells are described: — One is a hell of utter darkness; another of utter darkness and horrid animals; another of burning oil; another of burning metal; in another the wicked are continually eaten by worms and other reptiles; in another they are tormented by redhot instruments and weapons applied to different parts of the body, etc. The punishments which are inflicted for particular crimes, as murder, adultery, stealing, perjury, etc., are described, and more horrible punishments cannot be conceived. For instance, "He who disregards the Vedas and brahmins is to be punished in a hell of burning metal for 3,500,000 years." "The brahmin, brahminee, brahmacharee, vaishna, or king, who drinks spirits, shall be thrown into pans of liquid fire."

It is not uncommon to see Hindu lecturers with long pieces of cloth upon which are delineated in glowing colors, the pleasures to be enjoyed in the different heavens as the reward of virtuous actions, and the punishments to be inflicted in the different hells for particular crimes. The preacher delivers a lecture on the future state of the good and of the bad, unrolling these cloths and illustrating his statements and enforcing his exhortations by exhibiting and explaining these delineations. Such lectures are interesting to the people and produce a strong effect on their feelings.

THE TRANSMIGRATION OF SOULS.

Metempsychosis, or the transmigration of souls, is a prominent doctrine of the Hindu religion. The Shastras teach that the spirits of all mankind were among the things which were created several millions of years ago, and that they have ever since existed in some state or place in the universe. So the spirit of every human being has been in existence for several millions of years. But in what state, or where he has existed, what good or evil he has done, what happiness he has enjoyed, or what misery he has endured, no one knows, for no remembrance of any previous existence ever remains from one birth to another. After death and the judgment, the reward of the good actions having been enjoyed, and the punishment of the bad actions having been endured, — or, as some say, the excess of the good above the bad having been enjoyed, or the excess of the evil above the good having been suffered, as the character of each person may be, — the spirit returns again to the earth for a new birth.* Some of the Purans say, and such appears to be the general opinion, that each spirit must go through a great number of births, (some say 8,400,000,) before it again assumes a human form. During this long period it may exist in minerals and vegetables, (for the Hindus believe these substances are *sentient* beings,) or in insects, or reptiles, or fishes, or fowls, or animals, till the cycle shall be completed for it again to assume or enter a human form.

The sacred books inform us what some of these births will be. "Sinners of the first degree, having passed through terrible rigors of torture in hell for a very long period, are then condemned to the following births: — The slayer of a brahmin must enter, according to the circumstances of his crime, the body of a dog, a boar, an ass, a camel, a bull, a goat, a sheep, a stag, or a bird. A brahmin who has drunk spirituous liquor, shall exist in the form of a worm, or an insect, or a moth, or a fly feeding on ordure, or a ravenous animal. If a man steal corn, he shall be born a rat. If he steal milk, he shall exist in the form of a crow. If a man censures his spiritual guide, he shall be born

* Some Purans say that each spirit after hearing its sentence from Yama, wanders about the earth an ærial being or ghost for one year, and then takes a body suited to his future condition, whether he is to ascend into the heavens to the gods, or to suffer in hell, or to enter at once into another body. But we are not to look for consistency in works which contain so much that is unreasonable, absurd, and utterly incredible.

an ass; if he defame him, he shall be born a dog; if he use his things without leave, he shall be born a worm. If a man violates the bed of his natural or spiritual father, he shall migrate a hundred times into forms of grass, or of shrubs, or creeping and twining plants, of vultures, and of tigers, and other carnivorous animals. If a man steal the gold of a priest, he shall pass a thousand times into the bodies of spiders, of reptiles, and snakes, of crocodiles, and other monsters living in the water, or of demons living on blood." "As far as vital souls, addicted to sensuality, indulge themselves in forbidden pleasures, even to the same degree shall the acuteness of their senses be raised in their future bodies, that they may endure analogous pains. They shall first have sensations of agony as in *tanusra*, or utter darkness, and in other places of horror. Multifarious tortures await them; they shall be mangled by ravens and owls; they shall swallow cakes boiling hot; they shall walk over burning sands, and shall feel the pangs of being baked like the vessel of a potter. They shall assume the form of beasts and reptiles, continually miserable, and suffer alternate afflictions from extremities of cold and of heat, surrounded with terrors of various kinds. More than once shall they lie in different wombs, and after agonizing births be condemned to severe captivity, and to servile attendance on creatures like themselves. Then shall follow separations from kindred and friends; forced residence with the wicked; painful gains and ruinous losses of wealth; friendships hardly acquired, and at length changed into enmities. Old age without resource, diseases attended with anguish, pangs of innumerable sorts, and lastly unconquerable death." One chapter in Menu, contains 266 specifications of crimes, penances, and expiations, but more instances of what the Hindus expect and dread in the future state need not be given.

This doctrine of previous and future births, appears to have been devised or assumed to account for the different state and circumstances in which people are born, for the perverse disposition some persons appear naturally to possess, for the prosperity, success, and happiness some bad men enjoy, and for the misfortunes, losses, and afflictions of some good men.* The only

* Menu says, "Men are born stupid, dumb, blind, deaf, and deformed, to be despised by the good, according to the various actions they have performed.

way they saw of reconciling these things with the justice of God and his providence over the human family, was in the supposition or belief that the causes of these things were laid in some former state of existence, and that the consequences of others would be realized in some state after death. This opinion has in various ways an unhappy influence upon the conduct and character of the Hindus. The actions of the former states or births, are believed to determine the events of the present state of existence, and so this life is the destiny of the past, — is fixed beyond human control, or divine interference. This opinion is a kind of fatalism, and in some respects, of the worst kind, because while it regards things as existing and events as occurring necessarily, it makes them the consequence of actions in a previous state. If any are born blind or deformed, or become blind, or diseased, or are afflicted in any way, or suffer losses and calamities, these things are ascribed to sins committed in some former state, and this opinion that such persons are only suffering the merited consequences of their own bad conduct diminishes, if it does not destroy sympathy with and pity towards them in their afflictions. I have heard Hindus of reputed sanctity speak thus to persons suffering from blindness, leprosy, etc. And such opinions and sayings are not limited to afflictions, misfortunes, and losses, which come in the course of divine providence. These opinions are often expressed concerning wicked conduct and its punishment, that such sinful actions and the punishments to be suffered for them, are only the necessary conse-

Penance must therefore invariably be performed to make expiation, since they who have not expiated their sins, will again spring to birth with disgraceful marks."

This opinion existed in India as early as the reign of Solomon in Jerusalem, and it was taught by Pythagoras, in Greece, some centuries before the Christian era. So it must have become well known to the Jews, and probably suggested to the disciples the inquiry they made of our Saviour on seeing a man who was blind from his birth, namely, "Master, who did sin, this man, or his parents, that he was born blind? Jesus answered, Neither hath this man sinned, nor his parents, but that the works of God might be made manifest in him." John 9 : 1–3. That is, this man's natural blindness, or his being born blind was not owing to any sin which he or his parents had committed. The disciples must have referred to the man's having committed sin in some previous state, and so as a punishment for it he was *born* blind.

quence of former sinful actions. Such opinions are regarded as an excuse for sins in the feelings of those who commit them, and in the view of others concerning them. So also in respect to prosperity. If any one is seen to have remarkable success in any kind of business, it is ascribed to the merit of actions performed in a previous birth. Such is the common sentiment.

Such opinions have a natural tendency to prevent all gratitude and thankfulness to any divine being for any favors or blessings. They also prevent any sense of guilt and penitence for sin, as well as feelings of shame when suffering punishment for sinful actions. They invest the affairs of this life with a kind of fatality, and produce feelings of indifference and despondency. And what can be a more gloomy and degrading view of the future world than the prospect of passing through millions of births of different kinds of animals, or of any kind of animals, and after attaining one human birth to pursue the same cycle again? And this is the prospect and the hope that brahminism presents to its votaries.*

* The Hindus show their faith in this doctrine of the transmigration of souls by their works. The early European travellers in India mention seeing in Surat and Broach, institutions for the relief and support of old animals, as horses, cows, etc. These institutions, with the decline of the commerce and manufactures of those cities also declined, and not unlikely they have become extinct. But Bombay, which has succeeded those cities in the commerce of western India, contains a similar monument of the faith and piety of the same class of the people. Motechund Amichund, a wealthy merchant, commenced an institution similar to those above mentioned, by giving a large and valuable piece of land with buildings upon it for this purpose. His family and a large circle of friends engaged heartily in the cause. Large accommodations and conveniences were provided. The superintendence of the institution was assumed by a committee of management, and it has been in vigorous operation for many years. Horses and cattle of all kinds which have become old or maimed and are of no further use, sheep, goats, dogs, etc., are admitted, and well supported. Some of these are removed from time to time to a branch institution in the country, where the expense of supporting them is less than it is in the city. I often visited this institution, generally in company with friends who were strangers in the city and wished to see it, and having become acquainted with some persons connected with it, I several times made inquiries concerning the expenses and was told that they varied from 50 to 100 dollars per day, a sum which did not appear large in view of the extent of the institution and the number of creatures supported in it.

SUTTEE.

Suttee is the name given to the act of a woman immolating herself upon the funeral pile with the body of her deceased husband. This practice was of very early origin. It is mentioned in the Vedas and other sacred books.* If not positively commanded, it is yet strongly recommended. The highest rewards are promised to those who thus sacrifice themselves, and their sacred history contains examples which exhibit it as the highest virtue. Krishna is believed to be the most complete incarnation of Vishnu, and they worship him more than all the other incarnations. And of Krishna's numerous wives, eight burnt themselves upon the funeral pile.

Thus recommended it is not strange that Suttees should be frequent among a people who practise polygamy, and where widowhood is a state of disgrace; and it is not strange that no

* The Rig Veda says: — " O fire, let the women with bodies anointed with butter, eyes covered with collyrium, and void of tears, enter thee, that they may not be separated from their husbands, but may be in union with excellent husbands, and be sinless, and jewels among women." The following are extracts from other sacred books, and writers of high authority: — " The woman who ascends the funeral pile with her husband will remain as many years with him in heaven as there are hairs on the human body. — The woman who expires on the funeral pile with her husband, purifies the family of her father, her mother, and her husband. — Should the husband have been guilty of killing a brahmin, or of murdering his friend, his widow by burning herself with him, purifies him from sin. — There is no virtue greater than a virtuous woman's burning herself with her husband. — No greater duty is known for a virtuous woman than to burn herself with the body of her deceased husband. — As long as a woman in her successive transmigrations shall decline burning herself like a faithful wife in the same fire with her deceased lord, so long shall she not be exempted from springing again into life in the body of some female animal. — It is proper for a woman, after her husband's death, to burn herself in the fire with his corpse; and every woman who thus burns herself shall remain in paradise with her husband three croses and fifty lacs (35,000,000) of years. — If the wife be within one day's journey of the place where the husband died, and intimate her wish to burn with him, the burning of his corpse shall be delayed till her arrival. — If the husband be out of the country when he dies, let the virtuous wife take his slippers, or any thing else which belongs to his dress, and binding them upon her breast, enter a separate fire." Numerous passages like these might be given.

Hindu government ever interfered, so far as is known, to prevent it. Indeed, so far from this, the practice was chiefly among kings, princes, brahmins, and the wealthy. The emperor Acber made a law forbidding this practice in the 15th century. I am not certain whether any other Mohammedan emperors or princes ever interfered with it. The rite appears to have been practised more or less in all parts of India, when they became known to Europeans. The practice was more frequent in Bengal and the districts on the Ganges, than in other parts of the country. No records of such acts were ever preserved by any Hindu or Mohammedan government, nor do any native authors contain any estimate of the number who thus immolated themselves. Dr. Carey appears to have been the first who made efforts to ascertain the extent of this practice in Bengal, and he found that the number of widows who perished in this way, within 30 miles of Calcutta, in 1803, was 438. In 1817 the number of cases officially reported to the magistrate in Bengal, was 706. In 1818 the number was 839, thus making 1,545 in 2 years. The number which took place in Bengal from 1815–1826, or for 12 years, as officially reported to the English magistrates, was 7,154. This number includes only those which took place in Bengal. There was no means of ascertaining the whole number of cases in the country. Mr. W. Ward estimated them at 3,000 annually.

The first interference of the English government with this practice was in 1813, when a law was enacted, forbidding its taking place without the consent of the local magistrate, who was required to ascertain whether it was entirely voluntary on the part of the woman, and that no improper means had been used to induce her to decide on such an act. If the magistrate on inquiry became satisfied that the purpose was voluntarily formed, and that no improper means had been used to persuade or induce her to make such a choice, he was then to give his consent. If any Suttee took place without the consent of the magistrate, those who assisted in it were punishable, and no woman could burn herself with the prescribed formalities and ceremonies without the aid of brahmins to assist her and perform some of the ceremonies for her. Such continued to be the law and practice for 16 years. Probably this law did not much, if any, diminish the number of Suttees, while it gave the consent and apparent approbation of the government to every one that did take place in territories where this law was in force.

In 1829, Lord William Bentinck, then governor-general of India, enacted a law declaring all assistance, aid, or participation in any act of Suttee, to be murder, and punishable as such. This law was at first applicable only to Bengal, but it was soon extended over all the territories subject to the East India Company. And from that time as often as new treaties were made or old treaties renewed with any of the native princes, the English governors and agents have endeavored to make the abolition of Suttees one of the articles and conditions of such treaties. It has been found much easier to carry this principle into effect in their regulations, arrangements and agreements, with the native princes than was expected. Thus this horrid practice, after continuing for more than 3,000 years, has ceased in nearly if not quite all India. Still watchfulness is required in many places to prevent it. Only a fear of punishment deters many from encouraging it, and the practice would soon be revived again in many places, if the native princes, the brahmins, and others of high caste, were not fearful of the consequences of violating the treaties and laws which forbid it.

The first interference of the English government with Suttee by the law of 1813, did not excite much attention among the native population. But it was far otherwise with the law of 1829. This law soon excited feelings of strong opposition. Happily the native community in Calcutta were divided upon the subject. The celebrated Ram Mohun Roy and some others were in favor of abolishing Suttees, and used their influence to support the measures of the government. But the great body of the brahmins and other castes clamored against it, as an interference with their religion. They called public meetings, appealed to their countrymen in their journals, and subscribing a large sum of money they sent an agent to England to procure the repeal of the law. But their efforts were unavailing, and the excitement soon passed away.

The rite or practice of Suttee is one of the darkest features of the Hindu religion. It probably commenced as early as the origin of the Vedas, that is 14 or 15 centuries before the Christian era, and continued till stopped in the manner already mentioned a few years ago, thus continuing through a period of more than 3,000 years. Such a practice must be shocking in any country, but some customs in India made it peculiarly so there. One of these customs is the early age at which females are generally married, often when they are not more than 7 or 8 years old, and among the brahmins it must be before they are 11 years old, though they do not live with their husbands till they arrive at a state of puberty. Many of these married girls become widows before they arrive at adult age, and among the Suttees were many such girls and young women. The custom of polygamy also often made this custom of Suttee peculiarly shocking. At the death of a prince, or a kuleen brahmin, or a wealthy man who had many wives, several of them were often burned with his dead body. Instances are recorded of 5, 10, 15, 25, and even more, who thus sacrificed themselves. It is said of Krishna, the most celebrated and the most worshipped of all the incarnations of Vishnu, that 8 of his wives immolated themselves upon his funeral pile. What an example did this supposed deity and his family present! The scenes which such funerals as have often occurred since the present century commenced, and as some people yet living have seen, must have been shocking beyond description. And such sacrifices are highly commended, if not positively commanded in the sacred books of the Hindus, and they are declared to be the holiest and most meritorious deeds that can be performed.

SUICIDE, MURDER, AND HUMAN SACRIFICES.

Brahminism, in its polytheism and mythology, its gods, goddesses, and demons, furnishes a warrant and example for every kind of enormity, iniquity, and fanaticism. Some of the cruel and unnatural usages of the Hindus originated in their religion, and some which originated in depravity, through the influence of superstition, soon assumed a religious character. Other usages originated in pride, lust, and avarice; yet men will always as far as possible conceal the true nature of their vices, and cause their iniquity to assume the appearance of piety. And unhappily some of the Hindu deities are of such a character that men may commit almost every kind of wickedness, and in this very conduct refer to the example and claim the protection of some of these deities.

Among the sacred places in the eastern part of India is Saugor, which is near the mouth of the Ganges. The people of that district were in the habit of making vows in times of sickness and distress to devote a child or children to some deity, and these vows were fulfilled by placing the children on the shore, or throwing them into the water, where they were soon devoured by crocodiles and sharks. At times of pilgrimage to Saugor these murders were frequent, and 23 such cases were perpetrated there in one month in 1801. The cases amounted to 39 in the course of the year. The next year the Marquis of Wellesley, then governor-general, passed a law "declaring this practice to be murder punishable with death." The law was promulgated, and a police force was stationed on the place. This measure entirely prevented the practice, and in a few years the people showed no desire to continue it. Dr. Buchanan, who was then living in Bengal, says: — "It is impossible to calculate the number of human lives which have been saved by this humane law of Marquis Wellesley."

The Hindus were accustomed to commit suicide in their sacred places in the belief that having removed their sins by performing rites and ceremonies, if they should die there and at that time, they would attain to higher happiness than if they should live longer and then die in some other place. Allahabad was one of these sacred places. An English officer saw 16 women drown themselves there at once, and Dr. B. saw 12 men drown themselves in a similar manner in one day.* To effect this self-destruction in the prescribed way it was necessary to have brahmins to perform the required rites and ceremonies, and also to have the aid of men with boats in order to reach the particular place in the river, where the act of drowning was so meritorious. These shocking practices were suppressed by making it a crime

* "Each woman had her brahmin who accompanied her in a boat to the holy place in the river. A large earthen vessel was then slung over each shoulder; she descended over the side of the boat into the water, and was held up by the brahmin till she had filled the vessels from the river, when he let go his hold and she sunk to the bottom."

accessory to murder, to assist any one to perform the preparatory rites, or to reach the place in the river for drowning themselves. This law made self-destruction, in the manner required by the shastras, impossible.

The Hindu sacred books in many places encourage self-immolation, and describe such acts as devotion of the highest kind, and most acceptable to the deities. Formerly such acts were of frequent occurrence in different sacred places. The manner of self-destruction varied according to the usage of the place and the character of the deity to be propitiated. Sometimes it was by drowning, sometimes by leaping from the top of the temple, or some tree or precipice, sometimes the devotee would prostrate himself before the idol and calling upon the god kill himself with some weapon, and sometimes he would throw himself under the wheels of the car of the god, and be crushed to death.

The English government has endeavored in many ways to prevent such acts. But no government can entirely prevent them, any more than governments in America can prevent suicide. If men or women have deliberately determined to devote themselves to some deity by self-immolation, they will find some way of accomplishing their purpose. When the ponderous car of Juggunath or of any other god is moving along, drawn by hundreds of deluded worshippers and surrounded by thousands of gazing and shouting spectators, if any man should suddenly throw himself under the wheels (as men sometimes do), no power or means can save him from death, any more than if the car was a locomotive engine going at its ordinary speed on a railway.

Infanticide has been one of the barbarous and unnatural customs of India from an early period of its history. This crime has been common among the rude tribes of the Goands and Khonds in Berar and Orissa, among the middling and educated classes in the valley of the Ganges, and among the Jahrejas and Rajpoots, the ancient nobility of the country, in the north-west provinces. The rude and uncivilized tribes have murdered their female children at birth to get rid of the care and trouble of bringing them up, and the middling and higher classes have done the same from inability to form suitable marriage connections for them when grown up. The English governors and agents in India have done all they could to suppress this shocking custom. They have made it a crime, and inflicted merited punishment for it in all the territories subject to them. To the rude tribes which are but partially subject to their government, they have promised rewards and used such other means as appeared most likely to be effectual. With the Jahrejas and Rajpoots they have tried to put a stop to infanticide, as they did to Suttees, by treaties, agreements, personal influence, etc. These means have had considerable influence in diminishing the practice, and all classes now know how the English governors and agents regard this custom, and not knowing what the consequence may be, they are more secret in what they do. No doubt the lives of thousands of infants have been preserved by these means. But it appears from some late accounts that the practice is still continued in some districts and among some tribes to a shocking extent. The English will no doubt continue to use their power and influence in this work of humanity and with some success. But I believe the only effectual and final remedy for this unnatural practice is to be found in the humanizing and enlightening influence of Christianity, in refining the domestic relations, in cultivating the natural instincts and the duties of parents and children, in understanding the moral relations of all the human family to each other, in fully believing the immortality of every human soul and the responsibility of all mankind to God as their Creator, Preserver, and final Judge.

Self-torture of various kinds enters largely into the Hindú notions of religion. Some profess to renounce the world, its comforts and its cares, and live a life of voluntary, self-inflicted suffering in the hope of attaining absorption into the infinite Spirit, at death, and so escaping any future birth. Others in the hope of deliverance in some time of distress, or of obtaining some worldly good they are seeking, make vows to some god or goddess to inflict torture upon themselves. These tortures are of various kinds, but among them there is none more frequent or more unreasonable than what is called in English *hook-swinging*. This kind of torture is practised in different parts of India, and in the fulfilment of vows made to different gods and goddesses.* I am not aware that the government has interfered with these kinds of torture further than to forbid their being practised in certain public places. And the government has done the same in respect to some other shocking and disgusting kinds of torture, which some persons at certain times inflict upon themselves. People are often injured and sometimes die under these tortures, and probably the government will soon declare it to be a crime and punishable for any person to assist another in any such practices. They must then cease.

The history of *Thuggism* shows the dark features of the Hindu character, and how their religious system can cover and sanction the most extreme depravity and wickedness. The Thugs are men who associate together to murder persons, generally travellers, for their property. Their invariable practice was first to murder, then to conceal the body, and then to take possession of the property. The murder is always committed by strangling. For this work of death they are prepared by long and careful training, and are then initiated into it with many religious rites and ceremonies. They worship the goddess Karlee, and believe they are under her special protection. They invoke her aid to assist them to commit murder; they use only instruments and weapons which have been consecrated to her, and they devote to her a part of the property they obtain. They believe the rules and principles of their business to be of divine origin, that this work of murder and plunder is their proper business, that the signs and omens they observe are indications of the will of their goddess, and that so long as they observe these signs and omens, and so obey her, they are sure of

* There are two ways of practising or suffering this torture. One is when a pole 20 or 25 feet long is set upright, one end in the ground and upon the other end another and generally much longer pole is placed transversely, and so adjusted that it can be turned round. One end of the transverse pole is then brought down and two or three hooks are then inserted through the back of the victim and fastened to the pole. The end of the pole is then raised as high as it can be, and is swung round, often for some time, with the person or victim suspended by the hooks fastened to the elevated end of it. The other way is when the upright pole or post has its lower end placed upon the axle of a cart, which is then drawn round the temple, the victim suspended aloft as before described. I saw several persons (one of them was a woman) undergo this torture of swinging on hooks, and I might often have seen it, had I wished.

having her favor and protection, and have nothing to fear. They live in different parts of the country, but easily become known to each other by secret signs. They associate in companies varying from a few individuals to a hundred or more. They are sometimes engaged for months in one enterprise, and in pursuing it will travel several hundred miles from their residence. When their company is large, they often separate into small parties, and the better to carry on their nefarious work, some of them assume the character and appearance of merchants, some profess to be pilgrims, some to be common travellers, some to be masters, and others to be their servants, etc.

The English did not become aware of the existence of the Thugs till about the beginning of this century, and several years passed away before they knew enough about them, and had sufficient possession of the country to enable them to engage in any measures to detect and punish them. A commission of well-qualified agents was at length appointed, and a course of investigation was prescribed for them. This course of inquiry was pursued for several years, and was carried into all parts of the country. They were found to be far more numerous than was expected, and the result disclosed an amount of wickedness mingled with superstition and cruelty, probably never before known in the history of the world. In ten years, 1,562 Thugs were arrested, imprisoned, and tried; 328 were sentenced to death, 1,000 to transportation, 97 to limited periods of imprisonment, and from 25 security was required; making 1,450 convicted of participation in murder. Of the others who were arrested, 21 were acquitted, 11 escaped, 31 died before trial, and 49 were admitted evidence for the prosecution. As most of these persons had been engaged for years, some of them for 40 or 50 years, in committing murder and robbery, no calculation could be made of the number of victims who had suffered death at their hands. By these means the Thugs, as a class, have been broken up and dispersed. But they are far from being annihilated, and it will be necessary for the government to exercise great vigilance for many years to prevent their resuming their former atrocious business under the protection of their yet more atrocious deity — the goddess Karlee.

It has been stated that the system called Brahminism was not the first religion of India, and that in some parts of the country it has exerted but little influence. There are tribes whose religion has but little affinity with Brahminism, as found in its sacred books, its rites, and usages. Among these tribes the brahmins have never become the officiating priests nor the religious teachers, and so there is reason to suppose their religion has continued essentially unchanged for more than 2,000 years. For a long time these tribes, often living in the territories of the native princes, or occupying the thinly settled and less frequented parts of the country, avoiding intercourse with strangers, and reserved in communicating any information concerning their peculiar customs and manners, were little known to Europeans. Some tribes of this character occupy a district called Goomsur, in the northern part of the Madras territory, contiguous to Orissa, and have been commonly called Khonds. In 1836 one of the agents of the English government ascertained that human sacrifices were sometimes offered among these tribes, and in 1837 a missionary from Orissa having become acquainted with their religion, published some account of these sacrifices, in the Calcutta Christian Observer, which excited so much attention that the government appointed commissioners to visit the district and inquire into the state and usages of the inhabitants. The result of these inquiries and researches was published, and showed that what was said long ago, is still true — "that the dark parts of the earth are full of the habitations of cruelty." *

It was found that these tribes had a very gross system of polytheism. Their principal deity was called the "earth-goddess." They had also a sun-god, a moon-god, a war-god, a god of hunting, a god of births, a god of the smallpox, a god of rain, and many other gods. But the centre of this system and the principal object of worship was the earth-goddess, and the chief part of this worship consisted in human sacrifices. This goddess was believed to order the seasons, to send the rains, to cause the seed of all kinds when put into the earth, to germinate and grow, to preserve people in health, or to afflict them with disease, and to make their gardens and fields fruitful. She has

* Psalm 74: 20.

no fixed bodily form, but can assume any form at her pleasure. They make no image and erect no temple for her. Sacrifices of men and animals are offered to her. Human sacrifices are private and public. The former are to be offered when any particular signs of her displeasure are discovered. The latter are performed for the common good, but every man's land must receive some portion of the flesh and blood of a victim at seed-time, and when the crops are gathered. Should there be any uncommon sickness among man or animals, a human sacrifice must be offered. And the same thing must be done if the *Abbaya* (priest) or his family are sick, or his crops fail, as such affliction and loss are regarded as an indication of the displeasure of the goddess against all the people connected with him.

These tribes were very averse to disclosing their religious practices and rites, and it was impossible to ascertain to what extent human sacrifices had been offered among them. It was found however that "in a small section of the country 300 or 400 human beings were annually sacrificed." The English government soon succeeded in rescuing several hundred persons from this horrid death. On one occasion 124 victims, all destined to be sacrificed, were delivered up to the government agents.

The printed reports of these agents contain particular accounts of the manner in which these horrid sacrifices were performed, not secretly but publicly, the whole tribe assembling together to witness the proceedings, and as far as possible take part in them. The agents have been pursuing their humane work for several years with encouraging success. Great numbers of destined victims have been rescued from a horrid death, and at the latest accounts there appeared reason for hoping that few if any more victims would be sacrificed.

The Hindu religion is thus graphically described by Mr. T. B. Macauley, the historian, who lived several years in India:— "Through the whole Hindu Pantheon, you will look in vain for any thing resembling those beautiful and majestic forms which stood in the shrines of ancient Greece. All is hideous, grotesque, and ignoble. As this superstition is of all superstitions the most irrational, and of all superstitions the most inelegant, so is it of all superstitions the most immoral. Emblems of vice are objects of public worship. Acts of vice are acts of public worship. The courtesans are as much a part of the establishment of the temple, as much ministers of the god as the priests. Crimes against life and crimes against property are not only permitted, but enjoined by this odious theology. But for our interference, human victims would still be offered to the Ganges, and the widow would still be laid on the pile by the corpse of her husband and be burned alive by her own children. It is by the command and under the special protection of one of the most powerful goddesses that the *Thugs* join themselves to the unsuspecting traveller, make friends with him, slip the noose round his neck, plunge their knives into his eyes, hide him in the earth, and divide his money and baggage. I have read many examinations of the *Thugs*, and I particularly remember an altercation which took place between two of those wretches in the presence of an English officer. One *Thug* reproached the other for having been so irreligious as to spare the life of a traveller when the omens indicated that their patroness required a victim. 'How could you let him go? How can you expect the goddess to protect us if we disobey her commands? That is one of your north-country heresies.'"

The Hon. M. Elphinstone, who lived many years in India, thus closes his description of the Hindu deities and their rites and ceremonies:—"Such is the outline of the Hindu religion. To give a conception of its details, it would be necessary to relate some of the innumerable legends of which their mythology is composed; the churning of the ocean by the gods and the asuras for the purpose of procuring the nectar of immortality, and the subsequent stratagem by which the gods defrauded their coadjutors of the prize obtained; the descent of the Ganges from heaven on the invocation of a saint; its falling with violence on the head of Sheva, wandering for years amidst his matted locks, and tumbling at last in a mighty stream upon the earth with all its train of fishes, snakes, turtles, and crocodiles; the production of Gunesh without any father by the intense desires of his mother Devi; his temporary slaughter by Sheva who cut off his head and afterwards replaced it with that of an elephant, the first that came to hand in the emergency;—such narratives with the quarrels of the gods, their occasional loves and jealousies; their wars with men and demons; their defeats, flights, and captivity; their penances and austerities for the accomplishment of their wishes; their speaking weapons; the numerous forms they have assumed, and the delusions with which they have deceived the senses of those whom they wished to injure;—all this would be necessary to show fully the religious opinions of India, but would occupy a space for which the value of the matter would be a very inadequate compensation.

"It may be sufficient to observe that the general character of these legends is extravagance and incongruity. The Greek gods were formed like men with greatly increased powers and faculties, and acted as men would do, if so circumstanced, but with a dignity and energy suited to their nearer approach to perfection. The Hindu gods, on the other hand, though endued with human passions, have always something monstrous in their appearance, and wild and capricious in their conduct. They are of various colors, red, yellow, and blue; some have many heads and some have many hands. They are often angry without a cause, and reconciled without a motive. The same deity is sometimes powerful enough to destroy his enemies with a glance or to subdue them with a wish; and at other times is obliged to assemble numerous armies to accomplish his purpose, and is very near failing after all.

"The powers of the three great gods are coequal, yet are exercised with so little harmony, that in one of their disputes, Sheva cut off one of Brahma's heads. Neither is there any regular subordination of the other gods to the three or to each other. Indra, who is called the king of heaven and has been compared to Jupiter, has no authority over any of the rest. These and more incongruities arise in part from the desire of different sects to extol their favorite deity. But as the Purans are all of authority, it is impossible to separate legends founded on those writings from the general belief of all classes. With all this there is something in the gigantic scale of the Hindu gods, the original character of their sentiments and actions, and the peculiar forms in which they are clothed, and the splendor with which they are surrounded, that does not fail to make an impression upon the imagination.

"The most singular anomaly in the Hindu religion is the power of sacrifices and religious austerities. Through them a religious ascetic can inflict the severest calamities even upon a deity by his curse; and the most wicked and most impious of mankind may acquire such an ascendency over the gods as to render them the passive instruments of his ambition, and even force them to submit their heaven and themselves to his sovereignty. Indra, on being cursed by a brahmin, was hurled from his own heaven and compelled to animate the body of a cat. Even Yama, the terrible judge of the dead, is said in a legend, to have been cursed for an act done in that capacity, and obliged to undergo a transmigration into the person of a slave.

"The danger of all the gods from the sacrifices of one king, appeared in the fifth incarnation of Vishnu. Another king actually conquered the three worlds and forced the gods, except the three chief ones, to fly and conceal themselves under the shapes of different animals, while a third went still further, and compelled the god to worship him.

"These are a few out of numerous instances of a similar nature, all doubtless invented to show the virtue of ritual observances, and thus increase the consequence and the profits of the brahmins. But these are rather the traditions of former days, than the opinions by which men are now actuated in relation to the Divinity. The same objects which were formerly to be extorted by sacrifices and austerities, are now to be won by faith. The followers of this new principle look with scarcely less disguised contempt on the Vedas and all the devotional exercises there enjoyed. As no religion ever entirely discards morality, they still inculcate purity of life and innocence, if not virtue, but the sole *essential* is dependence upon the particular god of the sect of the individual teacher. Implicit faith and reliance on him make up for all deficiencies in other respects, while no attention to the forms of religion or to the rules of morality is of the slightest avail without this all-important sentiment.

"It is an uncommon though not an exclusive feature in the Hindu religion, that the gods enjoy only a limited existence. At the end of a cycle of prodigious duration, the universe ceases to exist; the triad and all the others, lose their being, and the great first Cause remains alone in infinite space. After the lapse of ages his power is again exerted, and the whole creation, with all its divine and human inhabitants, rises once more into existence.

"It only remains to say a few words on the belief of the Hindus relating to a future state. Their peculiar doctrine, as is well known, is transmigration; but they believe that between their different stages of existence, they will, according to their merits, enjoy thousands of years of happiness in some of their heavens, or suffer torments of similar duration in some of their still more numerous hells. Hope, however, seems to be denied to none. The most wicked man, after being purged of his crimes by ages of suffering, and by repeated transmigrations, may ascend in the scale of being until he may enter into heaven, and even attain the highest reward of all good, which is, incorporation in the essence of God."

Bishop Heber, who was some years in India and died there, says, "It is necessary to see idolatry, to be fully sensible of its mischievous effects upon the human mind. But of all idolatries which I have ever read or heard of, the religion of the Hindus really appears to me to be the worst, both in the degrading notions which it gives of the Deity; in the endless round of its burdensome ceremonies, which occupy the time and distract the thoughts without either instructing, or interesting its votaries; in the filthy acts of uncleanness and cruelty, not only permitted but enjoined and inseparably interwoven with these ceremonies; in the systems of castes, a system which tends more than any thing else the devil has yet invented to destroy the feelings of general benevolence, and to make nine tenths of mankind the hopeless slaves of the remainder; and in the total absence of any popular system of morals, or any single lesson which the people at large ever hear, to live virtuously and do good to each other. I do not say, indeed, that there are not some scattered lessons of this kind to be found in their ancient books, but those books are not accessible to the people at large, nor are these last permitted to read them; and in general, all the sins that a shudra is taught to fear, are killing a cow, offending a brahmin, or neglecting one of the many frivolous rites by which their deities are supposed to be conciliated."

LANGUAGES, LITERATURE, AND EDUCATION.

The sacred books of the Hindus and all their ancient literature are in Sanscrit. This language has not been vernacular in India for several centuries past. But at some early period it must have been vernacular in the territory along the Ganges, and was probably understood in the north-west provinces. The Vedas are written in Sanscrit, and the Institutes of Menu (written in the same language) inculcate the daily reading of these works as one of the duties of the brahmins, the kshatryas, and the vaishyas, three of the four original Hindu castes. We cannot reasonably suppose that this duty would have been inculcated, unless these classes of people understood the language of the Vedas, and they could not all understand it unless it was their vernacular language.

Sanscrit became the depository of the brahminical system of religion, and of all the ancient Hindu literature, and it continued to be understood and written by the learned, as the Latin was in Europe, long after it had ceased to be vernacular with any class of people. The Sanscrit is a highly polished language. Sir William Jones says:— "It is a language of wonderful structure, more perfect than the Greek, more copious than the Latin, and more exquisitely refined than either." Halhed says:— "As a language it is very copious and nervous, and far exceeds the Greek and Arabic in the regularity of its etymology." Chezey calls it "the celebrated dialect, perhaps spoken by the gods of Homer; if not, worthy to be so." Professor H. H. Wilson, professor of Sanscrit in Oxford University, says: "The music of Sanscrit composition must ever be inadequately expressed by any other tongue." Similar opinions have also been expressed by Adelung, Talboys, Bournouff, Bopp, and other distinguished orientalists.

The Sanscrit language has not been vernacular in any part of India for some centuries past, and there are no means of ascertaining at what period it ceased to be used. It has continued to be studied, and some knowledge of it has always been regarded as necessary for the character of a well-educated brahmin. Not only are all their sacred books written in Sanscrit, but established usage, if no higher authority, has made it necessary that all the rites and ceremonies of the Hindu religion should be performed in this language, just as the ritual and services of the Roman Catholic Church are to be performed in Latin. So no brahmin can be qualified or competent, without some knowledge of the Sanscrit language, to perform the duties of a priest for his own nation.

The Sanscrit language has been the repository from which nearly all the theological, scientific, and technical words and terms in the vernacular languages have been taken. And as these languages become cultivated, and new works of science and literature are produced in them, the new terms required in such works will be obtained as far as possible, from the Sanscrit. So this language, containing as it already does, and furnishing as it will in future, the most important words and terms in the vernacular languages, will long if not always, make an important and interesting part of a liberal education over all India.

The Sanscrit language contains a large amount of literature, and great expectations were once entertained in Europe concerning its supposed value. This literature has been examined so far as is necessary to ascertain its character and value, and the expectations once cherished have not been realized. The literature includes grammars, dictionaries, and works on many different subjects, but all are of but little practical value. Indeed, it is an interesting fact in the history of India that it should have an ancient language so highly polished and containing so much literature, and yet of so little practical use. Many Sanscrit works have been printed in India and in Europe, and translations of them have been made and published in the English, the French, and the German languages. It was lately said in an article on Sanscrit literature, and the attention bestowed upon it in Germany, that there are at least two thousand men in that country who understand the Sanscrit language.

There is no prospect of this language ever again coming into vernacular use, any more than there is that the Latin will again become a vernacular language in Europe. But the connection of Sanscrit with the vernacular languages of India, and the estimation in which a knowledge of it is held, will probably always make it a branch of education in the universities and colleges of the country, and some knowledge of it will be deemed essential to a well-educated Hindu.*

The general opinion has been that the vernacular languages of India are to considerable extent derived from the Sanscrit and founded upon it, that the latter sustains to them a relation somewhat similar to what the Latin sustains to the modern languages of Europe. Some orientalists have been of the opinion that some of the southern languages of the peninsula were original and independent languages, but that the languages of the northern and central parts were derived from the Sanscrit. But the more reasonable opinion appears to be that the present vernacular languages of India were the languages of the aboriginal inhabitants previous to the introduction of the brahminical system of religion. The sacred books of this system were in the Sanscrit, and many of its rites and ceremonies must be performed in this language. And as this system of religion, with its distinctions of caste, etc., spread over the country, carrying with it and diffusing around it a higher kind of civilization, many religious terms and other words of Sanscrit became incorporated in the vernacular languages. Thus it appears to be more reasonable to believe that the vernacular languages of India, instead of being derived from the Sanscrit and founded upon it, existed there before the Sanscrit was introduced, and that this language was superinduced upon them. Thus in the spread of the brahminical religion and the progress of civilization, many of its words, technical terms, and peculiar phrases, became incorporated with the languages previously in use.

The general opinion concerning the social state and religious character of the original inhabitants of India, and also how the brahminical system of religion was introduced, have been mentioned. The primitive inhabitants must have had a vernacular language or languages, and it is in accordance with what is known of the aboriginal tribes of America and Africa, to suppose that these languages in India were numerous and distinct. How far they were cultivated, and whether all of them were written, and what literature they had, is now unknown. The brahminical system was the religion of a nation who came from the

* Appendix B.

west, or north-west, and for considerable time occupied the north-west provinces, and the country along the Ganges. Sanscrit was the vernacular language of this nation, or these tribes,* then consisting of the brahmins, or hereditary priesthood, the kshatryas, or military class, and the vaishyas, or mercantile class. The shudras, if there was then any such class, were in a state of servitude. This invading nation, as they extended their conquests and their religion, appear to have included the people of the country in the fourth class, if there was previously any such class among them, and perhaps the fourth class was originated to include only the conquered aborigines. In the great valley of the Ganges, the brahminical system became matured, and the early and most celebrated works of Sanscrit literature were there produced. Probably its vernacular use was limited to these districts, and even there it may have been confined to the higher classes.† In the course of time the brahmins succeeded in becoming the depositories of the Vedas, and the kshatryas, and vaishyas lost their relative position in the scale of caste.‡ Such a change would increase the power of the brahmins, and yet more restrict the use of the Sanscrit language, while it would also increase the use, and elevate the character of the vernacular languages. The brahmins, with their peculiar and generally acknowledged claims of caste, forming a numerous, learned, and united priesthood, the sole depositories and expounders of their sacred books, and alone qualified to perform any part of their mystical and complicated ritual, possessed such means and motives to propagate their

* This appears from the Institutes of Menu, making it the duty of these three classes daily to study the Vedas, which were in the Sanscrit language.

† Some of the Hindu dramas furnish evidence that the knowledge and use of the Sanscrit language was thus limited. These dramas were written to be performed before the courts of the kings and princes; all the parts spoken by the learned are in Sanscrit, but when servants and persons of low caste are introduced, they perform their parts in the vernacular language, each class thus using the language which was appropriate to the character they represented.

‡ Some of the Purans say these castes were annihilated in a war in which Pursuram, a brahmin, was the hero. It appears more probable that they were degraded from their social or caste position in some revolution in which he acted a conspicuous part. Pursuram is considered one of the incarnations of Vishnu.

system as no other body of men ever had. And as their system of religion and castes became extended, carrying its new doctrines, rites, and usages with it, new words and terms would become necessary in the vernacular languages, and these would naturally be taken or transferred from the books containing the religion which the people had embraced. The progressive civilization of the people would make it necessary to enrich their languages with new words and phrases, and these would naturally be taken from the language and literature of the people with whom they were most in connection, and from whom they chiefly received and were still receiving their civilization. It is easy to see how in these ways the vernacular languages have got many Sanscrit words and phrases, and yet not be derived from, nor founded upon, that language. It appears probable that some and perhaps all the present vernacular languages of India, were in use there when the Sanscrit was carried into that country, and that the Sanscrit words, terms, and phrases they now have, were received in connection with their religion, civilization, philosophy, etc., in the same manner that barbarous nations have always borrowed largely from the languages of those nations by whom they have been Christianized and civilized.

There has been some difference of opinion in respect to the number of languages now in use, as what some orientalists reckon different languages, others call only dialects, and believe will not be perpetuated as distinct languages. The following appear to differ from each other enough to be called distinct languages, namely, the Tamul, the Canarese, the Teloogoo, the Mahratta, the Oriya or Orissa, the Bengalee, the Hindui, the Gujerattee, the Scinde, the Punjaubee, and the Hindustanee. This may appear a large number of languages to be in use in one country. But it must be remembered that India is as large in extent, and contains nearly as large a population as all Europe south of Russia and the Baltic Sea. Could we contemplate India as it was for 1000 or 1500 years previous to the Mohammedan invasion, we should see an assemblage of 10 or 12 different and independent nations, each with its own government, laws, language, literature, etc. The Mohammedans gradually extended their power over these nations till nearly all India was subject to the emperors of Delhi. The native dynasties were extinguished, and the kingdoms became provinces of an empire under governors or deputies. In this way the political state and relations of the country were entirely changed. India, instead of exhibiting an assemblage of separate nations, each with its own king, laws, etc., became an empire under one political head, and divided into provinces under governors.

But though the political state of the country and the relations of the people had become changed, yet they still lived in the same territories, used the same languages and customs, and to a great extent they retained the same religion as they had when they were independent nations, and such continued to be their state while subject to the emperors of Delhi. And in these respects there was little change when the English power was extended over the country. The territories within which any language is now used, shows with very little variation the limits of its ancient kingdom. Thus the territory in which the Tamul language is vernacular, shows the limits of the ancient Tamul kingdom. So the territories or districts in which the Canarese language, the Teloogoo language, etc., are vernacular, show the limits of their ancient kingdoms respectively. And the territories in which, and the population by which these different languages are used, are nearly or quite as large on an average, as the kingdoms and population of Europe are, when compared with the number of languages there used.

The Tamul is more refined and polished, and it contains more literature than any other vernacular language in India. The ancient kings of this nation appear to have encouraged learning and learned men at their court, and these men wrote their works in the Tamul language. Learned men of the same age at the other native courts and over India generally, wrote their works in Sanscrit, as the learned men of Europe, in the middle ages, wrote in Latin. The other vernacular languages contain but little literature of native origin. What they have, consists of fragments of history, translations of some Sanscrit works, songs, almanacs, etc. The English government in carrying out its system of education, has encouraged the preparation of original works and translations in the vernacular languages, and many valuable books have been printed within a few years past. The Education, Missionary, and Book Societies, are also doing much to create a useful vernacular literature. The works which have been prepared and printed in the languages of India within 25 or 30 years past, are more in number and value than all which had ever been written and printed in them previous to that time.

Nearly all these languages have different alphabets. Some of these alphabets are capable by their single and double letters of expressing a great variety of sounds, making the language soft and musical. But some of them are harsh and guttural. Efforts have been made to substitute the use of Roman letters in all the vernacular languages, and so have only one instead of 8 or 10 different alphabets. Some books in Bengal were printed in this way. But this innovation, though it had zealous advocates for a while, did not meet with much favor; and for obvious reasons — the sounds of many letters and words, proper names as well as other words, cannot be properly, scarcely intelligibly, expressed by the Roman letters, at least not by any sounds which these have, in the English or any modern language.

The number of different languages in India occasions more difficulty to Europeans than to the native population. The latter experience no more inconvenience from these than the inhabitants of Europe do from the number and difference of languages there used. In India the languages of districts bordering on each other are easily acquired by the inhabitants so far as they have occasion to use them. In the cities where 2 or 3 languages are used, people who use the same language generally live in one part of the city, and their social intercourse is among themselves. And men of general business easily acquire as much knowledge of each language as they require. Europeans travelling or often changing their place of residence in India, have found so much difficulty from these different languages that the importance of making some one of these supersede the others and become the common language of the country, has several times been urged upon the public and upon the government. But this course would not be found to be practicable, nor would the anticipated effect be realized.

The native princes, Mohammedan and Hindu, often gave salaries and pensions to men of reputed learning and piety.

By such means they secured the influence of these men and their friends. Such men in return for the favors they received, were expected to celebrate the virtues and actions of their sovereigns. But the princes of India did little or nothing for the education of the common people. Education in reading, writing, etc., was regarded generally as a qualification for business, like the mechanical trades of carpentry, masonry, etc. Those who aimed to be employed in the service of the government, or to become merchants or shopkeepers, endeavored to obtain the education required for the work in view. And some education was generally regarded as essential to the personal respectability and influence of the brahmins. So schools supported by fees were frequent in the cities, towns, and large villages. These schools were seldom well managed, and the education acquired in them was often very imperfect, barely enough to transact the ordinary business of keeping accounts. But the great body of the people had no education. Till recently education was scarcely known among women, and of the men in some districts perhaps 1 in 5 could read, but in other districts not 1 in 20 could read. And so long as there were no papers or journals or books of any interest or utility to read, there was but little motive for taking the trouble or being at the expense of learning.

The native population now use the press with vigor and enterprise. The number of papers and journals printed in the vernacular languages in the different parts of India is now large. These papers are often badly managed, and yet worse supported; still they awaken the native mind and diffuse some useful information. The native presses also issue books of all kinds, which appear likely to sell so as to secure remuneration. Such papers and books make people feel the importance of education, and are contributing to promote it. These causes in connection with the course the English government is now pursuing, and the numerous mission schools and educational institutions, open a brighter prospect for India.

COMMERCE.

The commerce of India, both external and internal, is large. It is carried on with China, and the other countries and islands east and south-east from India, on a large scale. This trade is chiefly in the hands of the merchants of India. The vessels have, generally, European officers and native crews. The two principal articles of export to China are cotton and opium. The countries bordering on the Indus, the Persian Gulf, the Euphrates, and the eastern coast of Africa, also carry on a large trade with India. Calcutta, Madras, and Bombay, are the principal ports of the foreign trade. There is also much trade at the numerous smaller ports on the eastern and western coast of the peninsula. The trade between India and Europe is chiefly carried on round the Cape of Good Hope. There has been much speculation and calculation about ways and means for carrying on the trade between India and Europe by the Rea Sea, Egypt, and the Mediterranean Sea, and for a few years past small quantities of valuable goods have been transmitted by that way in the steam-ships which carry the mails. Whether any canal between the Red and the Mediterranean Seas across the isthmus of Suez, or any railroad between the same seas via Cairo, will hereafter restore the trade of the southern countries of Asia with Europe and the western countries of Asia to its former channel, remains to be seen. It appears to be the opinion of those who have given most consideration to this subject, that even if the Red Sea and the Mediterranean Sea should be united by a canal or railroad, still the greatest part of the trade between the southern countries of Asia and the western countries of Europe will always be carried on round the Cape of Good Hope.

The internal trade of India is large, but it is not so great as might naturally be expected, considering the variety of its climate, soil, and productions. The streams do not afford so many facilities for trade as might naturally be expected in so large a country. The rivers of the peninsula in the rainy season are much swollen and their currents are rapid, and in the dry season they are shallow, and have many sand-banks in their course and at their mouths. These obstacles make the rivers of the peninsula and also the Taptee and the Nerbudda of little use for commerce. The Ganges, the Brahmaputra, and the Indus are noble rivers, but navigation upon them is much impeded by inundations, currents, changes in their channels, and sand-banks.

There are steamboats on the rivers, but the results expected from them have not been yet realized. The railroads now in the course of construction and projected, when they are completed, will open an immense internal trade between the different and distant provinces of the country, and form a new era in its commerce.

For some years past there has been a well-regulated system of steam-navigation between the large seaports in the southern countries of Asia. One line of steamships runs between Suez and Calcutta, stopping at Galle and Madras. At Aden this line communicates with one running to Bombay, and at Galle it communicates with a line running between Bombay and Singapore, Canton, and other eastern ports. And at Singapore this last mentioned line communicates with one running from that port via Batavia to Australia. All these lines are under the patronage of the British government. The steamships are of the first class, and carry the mails, passengers, and merchandise. Such were these lines of steamships when I left India, and if the system has been altered, it has probably been in the way of enlargement. This system of steam navigation has much increased the trade of India, and is infusing new life and spirit into eastern commerce.

The places of commerce have much changed since it began to be carried on round the Cape of Good Hope. Calcutta, Madras, and Bombay, had no distinction under the native governments, and had only a few thousand inhabitants when the English acquired possession of them. Now each of them contains half a million of inhabitants, and in commerce as well as in population they rank in the first class of cities in the world. Surat, Cambay, Calicut, Hooghly, Dacca, and other cities which were once the seats of large commerce, have much declined and ceased to be places of foreign trade. The great imperial and royal cities of India, as Delhi, Agra, Oude, etc., had never much foreign trade. Their population, wealth, and splendor originated in their being the capitals of empires and kingdoms. And when they ceased to be the capitals of emperors, kings, and princes, they declined, and have now become chiefly remarkable for their ruins.

Accounts are kept in rupees, annas, and pies; 12 pies make

an anna, and 16 annas make a rupee, which is a silver coin nearly equal in value to half a dollar. The currency consists of bank-notes, silver, and copper. Only the banks established by the government issue bank-notes. The silver coins consist of rupees and parts, and the copper coins are parts of annas. Gold is not now a legal currency, and there is but little in circulation. The government has a large mint in Calcutta, and another in Bombay. There are Insurance Societies in the large cities, and also banks which do large business in loans, discounts, and exchange. These kinds of business are well understood by the native merchants. Indeed, exchange appears to have been in operation in India long before it was used in Europe. Many of the native bankers and merchants are intelligent, enterprising, and wealthy, and they often furnish a large part of the capital of the English merchants.

The foreign commerce is chiefly in Calcutta, Madras, and Bombay. The trade for the last year of which I have seen the accounts, was:—Imports at Calcutta, $26,415,850; at Madras, $4,530,020; at Bombay, $20,553,565. Of these $37,594,800 were from England. The exports in the same year were: from Calcutta, $50,740,190; from Madras, $8,364,440; from Bombay, $20,553,565. Of these, $35,132,350 were to England.

AGRICULTURE.

The agriculture of India, though it has been so long ranked among civilized countries, is in a very rude state. There has probably been very little change in the implements of labor or the mode of cultivation for 2,000 years past. The implements used are few in number, and their construction is extremely rude. The ploughs and harrows in general use would scarcely be recognized in this country, as designed for such a use. The cultivators understand very well the different kinds of soil, and for what kind of grain each soil is best adapted. Manures are but little employed in general cultivation, but are used in some places for horticulture and for sugar-cane and tobacco. As manure is seldom used for grain, and the ground is not in other respects well prepared, the crops are generally light, and the same kinds of grain are commonly repeated till the produce will not pay the tax, the seed, and the labor, and then it is abandoned for some years. Cultivated in this imperfect way, several acres in India do not produce more than one acre in America. The cultivated lands of each village are generally situated together. They are not separated from the pasture-lands by any wall or fence, and the cattle and sheep graze under the care of boys, who restrain them from injuring the crops of grain. The fields belonging to different owners are not separated from each other by any wall, fence, or hedge, but only by posts or marks at the different corners. Indeed, walls or fences, or hedges of any kind are seldom seen in India, except around villages, houses, and gardens.

Rice is much cultivated, and in some districts is the principal article of food. It is prepared for food in various ways, in some of which it becomes better than I have seen it in any other country. In other districts wheat, millet, and other cereal grains are cultivated. The inhabitants depend chiefly on the produce of the gardens and fields for subsistence. The brahmins and some other classes never eat any kind of meat, and the great body of the people using it sparingly.

Indigo is produced in large quantities, and India supplies Europe and America with this article. The districts in which it is most cultivated, are chiefly in Bengal. English capital is largely employed in its cultivation. The labor of the cultivation and the manufacture is performed by the natives, but the work is superintended by Europeans. Under their care and skill the quality of the article has been much improved, and the quantity has been greatly increased. The plant grows to the height of 3 or 4 feet, with a hard and woody stem of a gray color about the root, green in the middle, and reddish in hue towards the top. It is divided into a variety of knotty stalks with small sprigs terminating with about 8 pair of leaves each, of an oval shape, thick and of a dark green on the under-side. It is in these leaves that the coloring matter forming the dye is chiefly found, and it is obtained by macerating, beating, and washing them, and afterwards passing the highly colored liquor into boilers, where it is subjected to a certain degree of evaporation, and eventually run off into moulds, pressed free from moisture and dried ready for the market. An ordinary plantation comprises

4,000 acres of land, which may yield on an average 1,000 maunds of 82 lbs each.

The poppy is largely cultivated. The cultivation of the poppy and the manufacture of opium is a monopoly of the government in all places subject to the East India Company. The poppy is a delicate plant requiring good soil and much care in its cultivation. The cultivation of the poppy and the manufacture of opium from it are under the superintendence of government agents, and all that is produced belongs to the government, the cultivators being paid for their labor at fixed rates. This cultivation is carried on only in the valley of the Ganges, and the opium is chiefly disposed of by monthly auction sales in Calcutta. The cost to the government is generally from 125 to 150 dollars per chest of 140 lbs., and the price realized by sale is generally from 450 to 500 dollars per chest. It is nearly all exported to China, and other places east from India. Opium is also largely cultivated in some districts in Malwa, which are subject to some native princes. In these places the East India Company does not interfere with its cultivation. But as these districts have no sea-coast, the opium in order to be exported must be carried to some seaport through the territory belonging to the East India Company, and for this transit a heavy tax is exacted. Much of this opium is brought to Bombay, and is exported to China and other places east from India. The revenue realized from the monopoly in Bengal, and from the transit-tax in Bombay, is large. In the revenue accounts for 1852, which are the last I have seen, it amounted to £4,562,586, or more than $18,000,000.

Sugar-cane has been cultivated in India from the earliest periods of history. It was probably the "sweet cane" mentioned by Moses, and its product was "honey made by the hands of men," mentioned by Herodotus. Sugar is made for domestic use over a large part of India, and it is exported in large quantities from some districts, chiefly from Bengal, to foreign countries. The climate and soil of a large part of India are well adapted for its cultivation, and there is land in abundance suited to its growth. But skill is required to improve its quality, and capital might extend its cultivation to an indefinite extent.

Cotton is indigenous in India, and is mentioned in the Vedas, and in the Institutes of Menu, the earliest works of Indian origin. Herodotus also speaking of India says, "The wild trees of that country bear fleeces as their fruit, surpassing those of sheep in beauty and excellence, and the Indians use cloth made from those trees." For some centuries a large part of the cotton produced in India was manufactured into cloths, and then exported to Europe and the western countries of Asia. But since the invention of machinery and its application to the manufacture of cloths in Europe, most of the cotton of India, beyond what was required for home consumption, has been exported in its raw state to England and China. The great demand for cotton in England for her manufacturing interests, the large supplies procured from America, the comparatively small quantity and inferior quality of the cotton received from India, and the strong desire of the English people generally to obtain their supplies from their own possessions, have induced the East India Company to make great efforts to increase the quantity and improve the quality of this article in India. With this view, some 20 or 25 years ago, they procured large quantities of cotton-seed and some saw-gins from the United States, and sent them to India — the former to be distributed over the country, and the latter to be worked, and also to be for samples for making others, if these should succeed well. As these means did not produce the results which had been expected, the East India Company engaged a number of men from the United States, who were well acquainted with the cultivation of cotton in their respective localities, to proceed to India with the view of improving the cultivation of cotton in that country. Accordingly some 12 or 15 such men from Mississippi and other Southern States, proceeded to India at different times within 20 years past. They were to carry on their operations in different parts of the country; some of them in the districts under the government of Bengal, some in the districts under the government of Madras, and some of them in districts subject to the government of Bombay. They examined the different kinds of cotton produced, the modes of cultivation, cleaning, and packing, the different kinds of soil, etc. In some places they made suggestions and gave instructions to the native cultivators, and in other districts they superintended experimental farms and plantations, where the American mode of cultivation and cleaning could be fully introduced, and the native cultivators become acquainted with it. Most of these men, becoming discouraged with the unexpected obstacles and difficulties which beset them, or dissatisfied with the government agents in connection with whom they had to carry on their various operations, soon returned to America. A few of them remained for several years, but I am not aware that there is any one of them at the present time in India. Great expectations in England and in India were entertained of these experiments, and great dissatisfaction was expressed at the result. The quantity of cotton produced was little, if any, increased, nor did it appear that there had been any general, or would be much permanent improvement in the quality. In both these respects, expectations were disappointed. The enterprise and experiment were generally considered to be a failure. Different causes were assigned by the men employed, by the government agents, by the merchants in India, and by the manufacturers and public in England.

Whether any further means will be used to improve the cultivation of cotton in India by procuring seed and gins, and superintending knowledge and skill from America, remains to be seen. There is no reason to doubt that the quantity of cotton produced in India would soon be increased to several times its present yearly average, if the quality could only be improved so as to obtain a higher price. And it is the opinion of many competent judges that the quality of the different species might be greatly improved by better cultivation of the plant, and more careful cleaning and packing, adapting all to the climate, seasons, etc. It is certain that the finest fabrics used in Europe for several centuries were made of the cotton of India, and that some of the finest fabrics now manufactured in the world, as the Dacca muslins, and some others, are still made in India, and made of the cotton of India, and without the aid of machinery, a manner in which such fabrics could not be made in any country in Europe. And if the cotton for such fine fabrics was formerly produced in India, and is still produced there in a few places, where there is sufficient demand to pay for its cultivation, the manufacturers of England are confident that, as India formerly supplied Europe with such fine fabrics manufactured from her own cotton, so she could be made to supply England now with cotton adapted to all kinds of her manufactures. There is much dissatisfaction in England with the East India Company on this subject, and this was one thing urged lately against renewing and prolonging the Company's chartered rights for another period of 20 years.

The area of land in India which is suited to the cultivation of cotton, is 3 or 4 times as large as has been at any time used for cotton in the United States. Labor in those districts is abundant and cheap, not exceeding from 6 to 9 cents per day, and often cheaper than this, and the laborers generally finding their own food. And yet the cotton England has obtained from India for 20 years past, has been upon an average only one eighth part of what she has obtained in the mean time from the United States. The average price of Indian cotton in the English market, on account of its generally inferior quality, is only two thirds the price of American cotton. This difference in the price will make the value of all the cotton which England procures annually from India only one twelfth part of the value of what she procures from America.

India suffers much from drought. Seldom a year passes without the rains failing, and consequently the crops failing in some part of the country. In such cases the poverty of the people and the want of facilities for procuring grain from other places, occasions great distress. Not unfrequently nearly all the inhabitants are compelled to leave their homes, go into other places and appeal to the charity and compassion of the people to save them from starvation. Roads and railways for transportation would much diminish these evils. Means for cultivating ground by irrigation, would also greatly diminish them. In this way in many districts, the amount of the crops might be greatly increased, and in some places 2 or even 3 crops in succession be procured in a year. Formerly the native governments were awake to the importance of works of this kind, and some rivers and plains are lined with works for irrigation.*

* "In 14 districts in the eastern part of the Madras territory the public accounts show that there are upwards of 43,000 works for irrigation in repair, besides more than 10,000 out of repair, all of which were constructed before

Some large works of this kind have been constructed by the East India Company in the provinces on the Ganges and its branches, and the outlay has in all cases yielded a large return.* There are still millions of acres in different parts of India, now of little use and value, but which might in this way be brought to a highly productive state, and made to yield a large return for the expenses incurred upon them. Public works of this character would be profitable to the government by increasing the revenue. While in the process of construction they would furnish employment and means of support to many thousands of the inhabitants, and by increasing the productiveness of their lands would be of great permanent advantage to the cultivators. And unless the government undertakes such works and completes them, they can never be made.†

The agricultural population are generally very poor, and pass through life, depressed in spirits, and embarrassed in their circumstances. The appearance of their villages, their houses, furniture, personal appearance, lands, cattle, implements of husbandry, and conversation with each other, are all indicative of a state of depression and poverty. They are generally involved in debt, and it appears to them to be entirely beyond their means or power to improve their circumstances, or in any way ameliorate their condition. They have only the prospect of being able to obtain a scanty, coarse, and hard-earned subsistence while they live, and then to leave their families to the same state, or what they call their fate.

the English had possession of the country. The annual revenue from these lands is £1,500,000, or nearly 7,500,000 dollars."

* The aggregate length of these canals is 765 miles, and the expense of making them has been 7,500,000 dollars. The revenue of the government from navigation and irrigation, chiefly from the latter, is variously estimated at from 1,500,000 to 2,000,000 dollars annually, a result so gratifying that works of a similar character, for which there is much need, will probably soon be undertaken. These works, as well as the large railways, now in the course of construction, will produce great results in developing the resources of the country, and will be enduring monuments of British enterprise and skill.

† "In India, government is really the landlord, and the occupiers of the land are for the most part miserably poor, and generally in arrears to the government for their rents, or for money borrowed to pay them. Irrigation can only be conducted on a large scale, and therefore the expense of it, where-ever it is adequately performed, must be defrayed by the government."

Such has been hitherto the state and prospect of the great body of the people of India for many years past. The measures of the government fixing the rent or tax on the land in some districts for a certain period, as 15 or 20 years, and so giving the occupants the advantage of any improvements they can make, has been regarded by them as a great favor, and should be extended wherever they do not come in conflict with intermediate parties or previous revenue settlements.* If the works for irrigation, and the roads and railways for transportation, which have been projected, are carried on vigorously, and completed during the present period of the East India Company's charter, thus first furnishing employment to great numbers of the people, and then opening the way for industry and enterprise to develop the natural resources of the different parts of the country, it will constitute a new and important era in the history of India.

MANUFACTURES.

India and the other countries of southern Asia supplied Europe and the western parts of Asia with cotton and silk manufactures for many centuries. The traffic of the English and other East India Companies for two centuries was chiefly in articles of this kind, and such would apparently have continued to be the course of trade to the present time, if new causes had not occurred to interrupt it. The invention of machinery and its application to the various purposes of manufactures, have made great changes in the commerce between Europe and the southern countries in Asia. Fine fabrics of cotton goods to a great amount are now annually sent from England to India, and the manufacture of such articles in India has nearly ceased. The coarser kinds of cotton goods for domestic use are still made there in large quantities, but even in these articles manual labor holds very unequal competition with machinery. This change in the manufactures of India has been a great injury in those districts where the inhabitants were formerly largely engaged in such labor. High or moderate protective duties would have greatly diminished these evils, but

* For the revenue settlement of Bengal, see pages 188 and 196–198.

unhappily for India the power to regulate all the commerce between the two countries has been in the Parliament of England and in the East India Company, and the commerce between England and those parts of India subject to the English (which now includes nearly all India and all the seaports) has been managed on terms for the benefit of the manufactures of England, and much to the injury of the manufacturing interests of India. Villages, towns, and cities, which formerly subsisted by their manufactures and were in a flourishing state, are now becoming dilapidated, and falling to decay and ruin. The population in some such places I have seen, exhibit the appearance of extreme poverty, and they know not what to do for means of support, nor where to go for employment. A late governor-general of India, in a communication to the Directors of the East India Company, says: "Some years ago the East India Company annually received of the produce of the looms of India to the amount of 6,000,000 to 8,000,000 pieces of cotton goods. The amount gradually fell, and has now ceased altogether. English goods made by machinery has now superseded the produce of India. Cotton piece goods, for ages the staple manufacture of India, seem forever lost. *And the present suffering to numerous classes in India is scarcely to be paralleled in the history of commerce.*"

The use of machinery for any kind of manufactures is yet scarcely known in India. The inhabitants use the same kind of spinning wheels, looms, etc., which their ancestors had centuries ago. Very few among them have any capital to construct and apply machinery to manufacturing purposes, and the few who have means have not sufficient confidence in the success of such works to engage in them. The regulations of the government and some other causes have prevented Europeans from engaging much in such enterprises. And even if these difficulties were all removed, the want of motive power has been a great obstacle to the use of machinery. The rivers of India, owing to the peculiar seasons, in very few places furnish any permanent and reliable water power, and the coal-deposits are situated so far from the districts which have the raw material and the population for manufactures, and are so inaccessible for want of roads, canals, and railways, that steam power has been available only to a small extent for manufacturing purposes. Should the railroads which have been projected, be constructed and become available for the transmission of cotton, coal, etc., and the needful facilities and securities for establishing cotton manufactories in suitable localities be obtained, the abundance and cheapness of the raw material, and the low price of labor * and provisions may yet again make India a great manufacturing country. Her inhabitants may again be able to make their cotton into cloth not only sufficient for their own use, but to supply England and other countries, as they formerly did for many centuries, with fine fabrics, and at a cheaper rate than those nations can manufacture them.

Silk goods are made in considerable quantities for domestic use and also for exportation. The woollen goods manufactured in India are coarse, as the wool produced in the country is too coarse to be capable of being made into fine cloths. Cashmere shawls, known in all parts of the world, are still made in large quantity in Cashmere and other parts of northern India. At one time 30,000 looms were engaged in the Lahore districts in the manufacture of these shawls. Not more than 12,000 or 15,000 looms are now thus engaged. These shawls are much worn by native princes, nobles, and wealthy men. The material is the hair of a goat, which is said to thrive best in Cashmere. The implements used in agriculture and in the mechanic arts are generally made in the country. Cables, ropes, and cordage, are made of coir and different kinds of hemp. Good household furniture, carriages, etc., are made in all places where there is sufficient demand to encourage such work. All classes of people are excessively fond of jewelry, and their ornaments, which are of many different kinds, of gold, silver, and precious stones, are generally made by the native goldsmiths. The skill displayed in such work generally exceeds what Europeans expect to find in India, and they are yet more surprised to see so ingenious and good

* Wages in India seldom exceed 6 cents for a woman, and 9 cents for a man per day at common labor. Over a large part of the country wages are less than these sums. And the laborers, whether men or women, generally find their own food. There are millions of persons in India who would be glad to obtain work at these prices.

articles produced by the aid of so few and such rude implements. What was said about the manufacture of cotton cloths, is equally true concerning metals. There is abundance of iron ore, and of very rich quality, in different parts of India, but no fuel, procurable where it is, to smelt it, and no power to move machinery for manufacturing it into the various articles for which it is used. Could the difficulties in the way of using these natural riches of the country be removed, India might again become as much distinguished among nations for her resources, her manufactures, her wealth, and her power, as she was in ancient times.

ARCHITECTURE.

The most remarkable structures of Hindu and Mohammedan origin still remaining, are temples, mosques, and palaces, many of them now in a dilapidated state. The temples are generally of a heavy and sombre appearance, more resembling the Egyptian than the Greek or Roman architecture. Some are entirely of hewn stone, but they are generally of brick, or stone and lime, and are stuccoed. As the temples are designed for the accommodation of the idol, and not of an assembly of worshippers, they are generally small in circumference, but are often high and surrounded with a wall, sometimes 2 or 3 walls, inclosing a considerable area of ground. The outside of the temples are frequently covered with figures descriptive of the Hindu mythology. The Hindu palaces in their construction, decorations, and the durability of materials, appear to have been inferior to those of monarchs of the same age among the nations of western Asia.

The Mohammedans introduced a new era of architecture into India. Their structures are distinguished by the frequent use of the arch and of the dome; if these were previously known in India, they were seldom if ever used. The Mohammedan emperors and their nobles came to India from or through Persia. There was much intercourse between their courts and the Mohammedan monarchs in western Asia, and they had sometimes, if not generally, Greek and Italian, or Roman artists and architects in their employment. With such aid and abundant means it would naturally be expected that they would erect structures worthy of their age, their religion, and their name. And so they did; for their palaces, their mosques, their mausoleums, and their private dwellings, will long continue to be monuments of their magnificence, their zeal for their faith, their wealth and taste, and their respect for their dead, or desire of remembrance when dead.

The seats of English power in India, as Calcutta, Madras, and Bombay, contain many fine buildings, both public and private. Of the latter, many belong to wealthy natives. These are often well furnished, and being surrounded by beautiful gardens, are delightful residences. In all places occupied by the English as permanent civil or military stations, are some good houses, which from their adaptation to the climate (which is so warm over a large part of the country that fire is never required in houses for comfort), are more comfortable than strangers on first arriving in India suppose.

The houses of the wealthy and middle classes of the native population, excepting a small portion in the cities which have grown up under English influence, are generally badly constructed, inconvenient, and dark. In some parts of the country the houses and all their appurtenances are surrounded with a high wall, which has only one entrance and conceals all inclosed within it from view. Such cities and villages have a very gloomy appearance. This mode of building is designed to secure protection from robbers, etc. The houses of the lower classes are generally wretched, with little room, or convenience, or comfort. They often consist of bamboo-walls, thatched roofs, and earth floors. In other districts the walls are of stone and earth, with thatched or badly tiled roofs and floors of earth. They often consist of only one or two rooms with little convenience of letting in the light or letting out the smoke; while the furniture is so scant that the place appears more as though it was deserted than occupied.

Vessels of all kinds and classes are built in Bombay, Calcutta, Cochin, and some other places. The forests on the western coast of the peninsula, and on the eastern coast of the Bay of Bengal contain excellent timber for ships. The expense of building ships in India is much greater than in Europe or America, but they are far more durable. Ships of war and ships for commerce of the largest size have been built in the dock-yard in Bombay. The work in some cases was entirely performed by the natives. These ships are said to be equal in their materials and workmanship to any that belong to the royal navy or to the commercial marine, equal to any that carry the British flag. Steam-ships have also been built in Bombay, but the heavy machinery used in them was brought from Europe.

MUSIC.

Music appears to have been formerly reduced to scientific principles, and to have been more cultivated in India, than it now is. The native martial music, so far as they had any, has been changed with the government of the country and discipline of the army for European music, as the drum, fife, etc. Their religion furnishes but little occasion for the use of music. A few large temples have a company of musicians, who play a while nights and mornings. Operas are unknown, and theatrical amusements are of a meagre character. Marriages are almost the only occasions when usage requires musical performance and entertainments. The Hindus have many different kinds of instruments, as drums, trumpets, horns, cymbals, hautboys, fiddles, etc., but the musicians are generally men of low caste, who have little skill and less taste. A company of musicians at marriages commonly consists of 6 or 8, and sometimes of as many as 15 or 20 performers. The larger the company, the greater the noise and apparently the confusion of sounds. Singing is one of the accomplishments of women of loose morals, and some such have acquired much celebrity for their musical talents. The singing and dancing of this class of persons are the favorite amusements of the wealthy and at the courts of the native princes. The writers of popular songs have sometimes acquired much celebrity by their skill and taste in singing them. People when at work in company often beguile the time by singing, one singing a couplet and the rest adding a chorus. These songs have little meaning in them and are often very obscene. Still the Hindus have a natural fondness for music.

Singing has been introduced into the worship of the assemblies of native Christians. The hymns are in the native languages, but they are generally adapted to European tunes. This part of worship is performed with much propriety. The native Christians also show their fondness for music by often singing these hymns by themselves, in their families and in their social meetings.

PAINTING AND SCULPTURE.

The Hindus appear never to have excelled in painting. In this art they are inferior to the Chinese and to the Persians. Some of their colors are durable, as may be seen on the walls of some of the cave-temples of Adjunta, probably made in the 5th or 6th century. The walls of their temples often contain paintings of their gods, heroes, battles, etc., as described in their sacred books, so that the worshippers see on all sides illustrations of their sacred history and objects of adoration. The walls of private houses often contain similar paintings. I once saw a large royal palace, reported to have cost nearly $1,000,000, in which the walls of the rooms and halls were covered with paintings of the incarnations of Vishnu and other actions and events contained in the Purans. The paintings of this character have much influence in communicating a knowledge of their popular superstitions. This art is made subservient to what they believe to be truth and piety. Some years ago missionaries began to insert cuts and illustrations more frequently in religious and educational books, and the native taste was soon manifested by their increased estimation of such works and demand for them. The native press has since commenced the same course, and by such means greatly increased the sale and circulation of their publications. But in painting portraits, natural scenery, etc., the Hindus are inferior to the Chinese.

More attention appears to have been paid to sculpture than to painting. The cave-temples contain statues in great numbers and variety, some single and others in large groups. These figures are generally a part of the rock in which the excavations are made, and some of them are of colossal size. Many of these figures and groups are bold and spirited in their design, but they do not exhibit the human form in good proportions, nor are its parts well developed. Such statuary appears much better at a distance and in their partially lighted temples than on near inspection. Marble idols for their temples and for worship in their houses are common among the wealthy. In works of this kind the Hindus are far inferior to the Greeks and Romans, or to the modern nations of Europe. Their skill however is still sufficient to entitle them to a place in the rank of civilized nations.

ASTRONOMY.

There is much obscurity in the early history of astronomy in India. Their system, so far as any has come down to the present time, has been examined by some of the ablest astronomers and mathematicians of Europe, as Bailly, Playfair, Maskelyne, and Bentley, and there was much difference among them respecting various things in it. The general opinion now is, that though all the pretensions of Hindu astronomy cannot be allowed, yet that in astronomical science, they were once in advance of any other nation, and that the Greeks were indebted to India for much of their knowledge on this subject. The names of the Hindu astronomers, the time when they lived, and the places where their observations were made, cannot be certainly ascertained; only their works, and these not in any regular system or connected order, have come down to the present time. The modern astronomers in India know how to use these tables and rules in making their almanacs and calculating eclipses, but they are ignorant of the principles upon which these tables and rules are made. They generally say that these tables are the work of men who were divinely assisted to make them, and I have often heard the common people say that the original authors of such tables and rules must have been inspired, for how could they, unless inspired, have made tables by which the astronomers can foretell such future events as eclipses.

These ancient astronomical works show that the writers had correct views of the solar system. But the mythological opinions, for system it cannot be called, have continued to be the popular creed to the present time. The popular notion of eclipses is, that a great monster, called Ketu, then attempts to seize and destroy the sun or moon, and so at the time of an eclipse, the people fast and pray that the sun or moon, as the case may be, may not be destroyed. Sometimes they implore Ketu to forbear and spare the sun or the moon, and sometimes they beseech the gods to interpose and save them. The brahmins and the Hindus generally fast on days when an eclipse is expected, till it has passed over; they then perform the prescribed religious ceremonies and eat. If it is an eclipse of the sun, and is to be nearly or quite total, its beginning and progress is observed by many with much anxiety. All business is suspended. Some engage in prayers to the gods to interpose and preserve the sun; some implore the demon, who is believed to be making an attack upon the sun, to desist; and some give alms to the poor, supposed then to be peculiarly meritorious. There are men in different parts of the country who understand the astronomical tables and rules enough to make almanacs. These almanacs contain notices of the solar and lunar eclipses to be expected in the coming year. These notices generally vary some from the exact time, but as such eclipses are not observed for any practical purposes, and people have very indefinite notions of accuracy in time, the errors and differences generally pass unobserved. Changes and all phenomena in the heavenly bodies are much intermixed with superstitious notions on astrology, and the almanacs of the Indian astronomers are chiefly valued for the supposed information they contain concerning lucky and unlucky days, signs, etc. The superstition of the people in these matters is excessive, and notions of this character govern them in the greater part of the important transactions of life. The opinion of the astrologer is an important element in forming a marriage contract, and then in fixing upon the time for the ceremonies, in determining to make a voyage, journey, etc., and then in setting out upon it. So strong are the superstitious feelings of many concerning the supposed influence of the stars on human affairs, and that some days are lucky, and others again are unlucky, that no arguments or promises would induce them to deviate from the course which these stars, signs, etc., indicate as the way of safety, prosperity, and happiness. The evils and inconvenience of these superstitions and prejudices are among the things that press heavily upon the people of India.

MEDICINE.

Works on diseases and their remedies show that at some former period, much attention was given to these subjects. Works of this character were translated into the Arabic language, and the Arabian writers acknowledge their obligation to India. Inoculation for the smallpox was practised in India long before it was known in Europe. Venesection, lithotomy, and couching for cataract, were understood and practised. The list of Indian medicines includes many of mineral as well as of vegetable origin, and their chemical preparation was as well understood as in any country at that time. The giving and taking of medicines are often mixed with superstitious usages and foolish notions, which are regarded as essential to their efficacy. Their imperfect knowledge of anatomy does not admit of their becoming skilful in surgery. The practice of medicine is generally confined to the same families for successive generations, the father communicating to his sons his knowledge and his skill, his books, and as far as possible, his reputation. There appear never to have been any ancient schools of medicine which acquired celebrity, nor does the art of healing appear to have in any way received the patronage of native governments. Poets who could celebrate the praises of their benefactors, and brahmins and devotees, whose support, on account of their religious character, was deemed a work of merit, and obtained for their benefactors the reputation of piety as well as of liberality, were the objects of royal bounty. But those who were sick or injured by accidents, must seek for medical knowledge and surgical skill where they could find them.

The English government supports surgeons in the army, in the native as well as the European regiments. The care which the English government shows for the health of their native troops, and the treatment these receive when sick, so different from what is seen and experienced in the armies of the native princes, have greatly strengthened the power of the English in India. The European surgeons in charge of the native regiments have generally some native assistants under their care, who acquire considerable knowledge of diseases and the European manner of treating them. These men on leaving the army, and sometimes perhaps while in connection with it, practise medicine among the native population in the cities and large towns. And defective as the knowledge and skill of this class are when compared with the regularly educated physicians of Europe and America, they are yet far superior to the common native doctors. There are large hospitals in Calcutta, Madras, and Bombay, and in other large cities, and generally at the civil stations, where medical advice and medicines are given gratuitously to the poor and suffering. The English have done much to introduce and extend vaccine inoculation. The government also furnishes medicine and sometimes medical attendance for a while in places where cholera prevails. Medical institutions have been recently established by the English government in Calcutta, Madras, and Bombay. They have well-qualified professors, and it is expected that native men will become prepared in them to practise medicine among their countrymen, and so India, in the course of time, will have a qualified medical profession, for want of which she has so long suffered.

The oriental nations generally acknowledge the superiority of Europeans in medical science and skill. The readiness, and frequently the anxiety they manifest when ill, to put themselves under the care of European physicians, even when they have no more knowledge of the party than that he is an acknowledged physician among his countrymen, is surprising. This is true of the princes as well as of the common people, and European physicians, by their medical skill, with the emperors, kings, and princes, have often been able to perform important services for the English interests in India. In Calcutta, Madras, Bombay, and perhaps a few other cities, some European physicians have had profitable practice among the higher classes of the native population.

MARRIAGE.

Agreements and arrangements concerning marriage in India are made by parents for their children. They feel it as much a part of their duty to effect the marriage of their children, as they do to support them when young, and to educate them. Such has been the custom of the country for many centuries. One reason they assign for this custom is, that if their children should grow up unmarried, they might form unsuitable connections to the sorrow and dishonor of their friends, and to their own unhappiness. Another reason assigned is, that if allowed to grow up unmarried, they perhaps would not form any marriage connection, but would live idly and lewdly and become profligate. The marriage relation is also supposed to be necessary to preserve the moral character of their daughters. A long and intimate acquaintance with many people of different classes, and the spirit that generally pervades the native population, satisfied me that these opinions of the consequences of parents allowing their children to grow up unmarried, and then to form what connections they pleased or none at all, have more of prudence, wisdom, and consideration in their favor than they at first sight appear to have. Unhappy as such early marriages often must be, yet I am not certain but in India, where society is so corrupt, employment so difficult to procure, temptations to licentiousness so great, and the means of supporting families so hard to be realized, greater evils would result from parents allowing their children to grow up unmarried, and then to marry as they please or not marry at all. No doubt families, if the marriage connection between the parents was formed at mature age and from their free choice, would generally be happier, yet very many men, if they grew up unmarried, would never enter the marriage state, and it appears not unlikely that the social and moral state of people would be worse than it now is. Could polygamy be abolished and widows among all classes have the same right of again entering the married state that men have, so that widowers could marry women of their own age, and not be compelled, as they now are, to marry young girls and even children, it would probably be as well for the present custom of parents arranging and settling and completing the marriage of their children to continue until the people have become better educated, and a better moral spirit shall pervade all classes of the inhabitants.

The higher classes generally marry their children at an earlier age than the middle and lower classes. Boys are generally married at ages varying from 7 or 8 to 12 or 15 years, and girls at an earlier age. Among the brahmins, if any girl remains unmarried until she is 11 years old, the family is suspended from caste. The marriage of children, sons as well as daughters, is regarded as a matter of great importance. All classes are very superstitious in respect to lucky and unlucky days for this ceremony. The astrologer is called to show his knowledge of the future, and the stars and other powers,* supposed to have influence over human affairs, are consulted. If these opinions and indications should all be favorable, the marriage covenant between the parents of the children is made, and a propitious time for the ceremony is selected. The friends of both parties are invited to be present. The gatherings at such times are generally large, and continue for 2 or 3 days, and sometimes for a week. The marriage ceremonies are performed by some brahmin, in the presence of the assembly. These ceremonies are numerous, tedious, and mystical, and being in the Sanscrit language are utterly unintelligible; for even if the people understood the language (and not one in a thousand does understand it) he hurries through it so fast and speaks so low that none know what he says. Indeed, much of what he says consists of mystical words and phrases, which he repeats by rote, often understanding as little of them himself as those do who hear him. Yet all these ceremonies are believed to be of great importance. The expenses for ornaments, religious ceremonies, feasting, music, processions, illuminations, presents to friends, etc., are large. The rich expend money very freely on such occasions,

*I once became ill when on a missionary tour, and had to stop a while in the verandah of a temple. While there I was much troubled by people coming to consult the god about a marriage then under consideration. The way they proceeded was first to worship the idol, and then taking two flowers put them in water and pressed one of them on the right and the other on the left breast or cheek of the idol. The idol was of stone, somewhat resembling the human form, and having been recently besmeared with *shandur* (red lead and oil mixed), the flowers would adhere to it so long as they continued to be wet. The people having thus applied the flowers, would then stand before the idol and pray thus:—"O god, if this marriage now under consideration will be happy, then cause the flower on thy right breast or cheek to fall first; and if it will be unhappy, then cause the flower on thy left breast or cheek to fall first." They would then all stand anxiously waiting to see the result. They tried the experiment, or rather in this way consulted the god, several times, and were prepared to act in accordance with what they believed to be his revealed will. Similar ways of consulting the gods in important matters are often practised.

and the lower classes often incur debts which are a burden upon them for years.

When the marriage ceremonies are over, the bridegroom and the bride return to their respective homes, each living with their parents, and occasionally interchanging visits till they arrive at a state of puberty. Some further ceremonies are then performed, and the parties begin to live together.

One unhappy consequence of the early age at which marriages take place in India is, that one of the parties not unfrequently dies before they have lived together. A widower, whatever his age may be, and to whatever caste he may belong, can marry again. But a widow of the brahminical caste, whether she has ever lived with her husband or not, is not allowed again to enter the married state. She is not allowed to wear her hair, or any ornaments, or to be present at marriages or any other festive occasions. Thus excluded from the marriage state and disgraced in social life, her circumstances, especially if she has not sons to protect her, are very humiliating, and her situation becomes extremely painful. This state often leads openly or secretly to a life of vice and prostitution. It was this view of the painful prospect before them in life that formerly induced so many widows of this caste voluntarily to perish with the bodies of their deceased husbands on the funeral pile. There is some prejudice among some of the other high castes against widows marrying again, and in some places and circles such marriages seldom occur, but I am not aware that it is prohibited to any caste except the brahmins. Among the great body of the Hindus, widows as well as widowers can marry again. The statement sometimes made that widows in India cannot again enter the married state, is true only of the high castes. The marriage of widows is not prohibited by the shastras to more than one tenth part of the people. Among nine tenths of the people widows can marry again and again, if they please. The ceremonies of the second marriage of women are different from those of the first marriage. They are shorter, more simple, and less expensive. The marriage of widows, especially of such as have children, is not so frequent as it is in Christian countries. But among the Mohammedans and the great body of Hindus, there is no law or usage depriving widows of the privilege and the right of again entering the marriage state. Indeed, considering how early females are married, generally when mere children, and consequently how many of them become widows, it is not easy to see how society could exist, were no widows of any caste permitted again to enter on married life.

It is declared in the Hindu laws to be a crime for parents to sell their daughters to be married, or to accept any pecuniary consideration for giving them in marriage to any party whatever. But this law is little regarded. It is very common for parents to take all they can get in such cases, and for a pecuniary consideration they will often give their daughters in marriage to old men who are widowers, or to men who have already one or two wives. In this way young girls are often sacrificed for money to a wretched and miserable life by their selfish and unfeeling parents.

Parents generally marry their sons as well as their daughters when young, and in such cases the men and women are nearly of the same age. But sometimes boys, either from the poverty of their parents or from some other cause, grow up unmarried, and such men, whatever may be their age, will marry young girls. Among the brahmins, all the girls must be married before they are 11 years old, and as widows, however young they may be, cannot again enter the married state, all bachelors and widowers of this caste, if they wish to marry, whatever their age may be, can only marry young girls, mere children. This unreasonable custom is the cause of many unequal and incongruous connections — men 40, 50, 60 and more years old married to young girls. Such marriages and families can seldom be otherwise than unhappy.

POLYGAMY.

Polygamy is practised among all classes of the native population in India — among Hindus, Mohammedans, Parsees, and Jews. Among some classes the custom is, that if a man's first wife has no children he may take a second, and for the same reason a third, etc. And among some classes, if a man's wife has no son he may take a second wife. There may be other causes which are deemed sufficient for it.* Wealth and inclination generally govern the conduct of men in these matters more than any fixed rules.† The Koran allows any Mohammedan to marry four wives, and then to have as many concubines as he can maintain. But polygamy appears not to be more common among them than it is among the Hindus. The Parsees or Zoroastrians practise polygamy, but cases of it are not frequent. The Jews also in India practise it, and think they have sufficient authority for it in the example of the patriarchs and kings of the Old Testament. I have often had discussions with them upon this subject.

A peculiar kind of polygamy exists among the brahmins of Bengal. Bullalsen, a former Raja of Bengal, having observed that many of the brahmins had little regard to the shastras and religious rites and usages, in the hope of promoting learning and religion among them, divided them into several classes or orders. The first class was called *Kuleen* or the *Kuleen* brahmins, and was designed to embrace only those who were learned, pious, etc. But instead of continuing to be an Order of Merit, as was intended, it has become a mere hereditary distinction, a kind of hereditary nobility without any reference to the personal qualities in view of which it originated. This class claims and everywhere receives preëminence, and it is a great honor to be allied to them. The men of this class can marry into other divisions of the brahminical caste, who will often give large sums of money for the honor of such a connection, but the women or daughters of kuleen brahmins can marry only into their own class or order. In consequence of this strange usage, says Ward, "the sons of kuleens are generally preëngaged, while their un-

* The Institutes of Menu, which are the highest authority in such matters, say: — "A barren wife may be superseded by another in the eighth year; she whose children are all dead, in the tenth; she who brings forth only daughters, in the eleventh; she who speaks unkindly, without delay."

† I was once ascending the Ganges with some friends when one of our company who belonged to Calcutta, directed our attention to a large and beautiful house situated near the bank of the river, remarking that the resident was a son of the late king of Oude. After looking a while at the palace, the park, and other things, he pointed out some appurtenances, and said that those places were occupied by the harem. I inquired how many wives the owner had. My friend replied that he did not know the exact number, but there were about 80.

married daughters for want of young men of equal rank, become so numerous that husbands cannot be found for them; hence one kuleen brahmin often marries a number of wives of his own order. Each kuleen marries at least two wives; one the daughter of a brahmin of his own order, and the other of a shortry brahmin; the former he generally leaves at her father's, the other he takes to his own house. It is essential to the honor of a kuleen that he have one daughter, but by the birth of many daughters he sinks in respect; hence he dreads more than other Hindus the birth of daughters. Some inferior kuleens marry many wives. I have heard of persons having 120; many have 15 or 20, and others 40 or 50 each. Numbers procure a subsistence by this excessive polygamy; at their marriages they obtain large presents, and as often as they visit these wives they receive presents from the father, and thus having married into 40 or 50 families, a kuleen goes from house to house, and is fed, clothed, etc."* In this way Bullalsen's creation of an Order of Merit among the brahmins, has produced a state of monstrous polygamy, which has no equal in the history of human depravity.

The domestic habits of the Hindus and Mohammedans are such that it would be impossible to ascertain or definitely say what proportion of men have two or more wives, and in some districts the cases are much more frequent than in others. In some places the proportion of men who have two or more wives, may be 1 in 5, and in other places not more than 1 in 10. In this respect there is no difference between the native population in the territories under the English government, and in those which are subject to the native princes. When the East India Company began to acquire territory in India, and so have a native population under their government, Acts of Parliament were passed authorizing the inhabitants to live and act in accordance with their previously established laws and usages in civil and religious matters. The English government has always had the power to make any new laws for which there might appear to be occasion. But none have been enacted concerning polygamy, nor does it appear likely that any such will be enacted for some time to come. So the laws and usages previously existing are still in force, and they are administered by English

* Ward's View of the Hindus, vol. 1, p. 81, 82.

magistrates. Thus in Calcutta, Madras, and Bombay, which have belonged to the English for several generations, polygamy is practised as freely by the different classes and castes of the native population, as it would be if they were living under governments professing their own faith. And in the same manner polygamy with all its evils, personal, social, and moral, exists among more than 100 millions of people living under the British government. People of different religions and castes never intermarry with each other, and all questions and cases concerning marriage, inheritance, etc., are decided in the courts according to established laws and usages of the respective parties. Cases of this character, where the parties are Hindus, are decided according to the Hindu laws and usages, and where the parties are Mohammedans according to their laws and usages. So also with the Parsees, the Jews, etc. In cases affecting the validity of marriages, as cases concerning hereditary right to property, the question considered by the courts is, whether the marriage in its circumstances and connections was in accordance with the established usages of that class of people, and was then regarded by all interested as a proper and valid marriage. If it is decided to be of this character, then all questions depending upon the marriage or involved in it, are determined according to the laws and usages of the parties interested.

It has been mentioned that polygamy among the native population of India is protected by Acts of Parliament, and by the decisions of the highest courts. The marriage of a Hindu or a Mohammedan or a Jew in India with his second, third, or fourth wife, if it is performed according to the Hindu or Mohammedan or Jewish laws and usages, is as valid as his marriage with his first wife, as valid as the marriage of any European or American is in his own country. The children of each wife are equally legitimate. He cannot divorce either of his wives without due form of law, and the law is open to his wives for redress, if he should refuse to support them or their children.

CASTE.

The distinctions of *Caste* in India are so peculiar, and have existed so long, they have had so much influence upon the state and character of the people in time past, and still have so much, that they appear to deserve particular consideration.

The history of several ancient nations mention that the inhabitants were divided into different classes according to their occupations. "In Egypt the people are said to have been divided into 4 classes, namely, the priests, the military class, the artificers, and the husbandmen." "The Colchians and the Iberians were divided into 4 classes, whose rank and office were hereditary and unchangeable." In Persia, "Jamshed divided all the people into 4 classes." In these nations the divisions are ascribed to their government, and so like their other laws and usages, they perished in the changes of dynasties and the revolutions of time. Those who originated the distinctions of caste which have been perpetuated in India, whether they were princes or priests, or what is more probable, both combined, took what was for them, a wiser course. They inserted these distinctions in their sacred books, and so ascribed their origin and the laws for observing them to the Creator.

The Vedas and their expositors mention the existence and the comparative rank of the four original castes, and the Institutes of Menu and other works believed by the Hindus to be of divine origin, contain particular accounts of the origin and nature of these distinctions. The following are extracts from these works: —

"That the human race might be multiplied, Brahma caused the brahmins to proceed from his mouth, the kshatryas from his arms, the vaishyas from his thighs, and the shudras from his feet. To the brahmins he assigned the duties of reading the Vedas, of teaching them, of sacrificing, of alluring others to sacrifice, of giving alms if they be rich, and if indigent, of receiving gifts. — To defend the people, to sacrifice, to give alms, to read the Vedas, to shun the allurements of sensual gratification, are in a few words the duties of the kshatryas. — To keep herds of cattle, to bestow largesses, to sacrifice, to read the scriptures, to carry on trade, to lend money at interest, and to cultivate land, are prescribed to the vaishyas. — One principal duty the Supreme Ruler assigned to the shudras, namely, to serve the before-mentioned classes without depreciating their worth."

In the Bhagawat Gita, Krishna says, "Mankind was created by me, of four kinds, distinct in their principles, and in their duties." — "The duties of brahmins, kshatryas, vaishyas, and shudras are distributed agreeably to their natural characteristic qualities. The natural duties of the brahmins are subjugation of the mind and body, austerity, sanctity, forbearance, divine and human knowledge and faith. The duties of the kshatryas are heroism, energy, patience, policy, not fleeing in battle, generosity, aptitude for governing. The duties of the vaishyas are commerce, agriculture, and tending cattle. The duty of the shudras is to serve the other orders."

These extracts show that the Hindu sacred books teach that the distinctions of caste are of divine origin, and commenced with their creation. Such is the belief of all orthodox Hindus. They no more believe that the different castes into which they are divided, were originally of one common stock, and subsequently became separated into different castes as they now are, than we believe that camels, horses, goats, and hogs, were originally of one common stock, and that the differences we now see between them have all subsequently taken place. The Hindus all believe that the Creator of the human race, or different races as they regard them, was the founder of caste by separately creating each order. They also believe that he assigned to each caste its comparative rank, and its appropriate and particular duties. So there are no laws of higher origin or of more importance than those which pertain to caste.

The brahmins were to be treated with reverence almost equal to the gods, and with respect far greater than kings. Injuries inflicted upon them were to be punished with great severity, while the same crimes if committed by them were to be treated with great lenity, and for no crime whatever were they ever to be put to death, or reduced to slavery. Still the course of life prescribed for them was far from being one of ease and self-indulgence. A brahmin was to be emphatically a religious man. The first part of his life he was to be a student under the continual care of his spiritual guide, learning and reading the Vedas, and performing religious rites and ceremonies. In the second part he was to become a householder. In this period his duties were to read and teach the Vedas, to offer sacrifices, and to assist others to sacrifice, to receive gifts, and bestow alms. He may eat animal food if it has been offered in sacrifice, and this subject is mentioned in a manner which indicates a frequent practice. In all circumstances he is to be careful in sustaining his religious profession, to abstain from all amusements, and from all light conduct and frivolous conversation. And so he is to continue till the time for entering upon the third state, thus:—"When he perceives his muscles become flaccid, and his hair gray, and sees the child of his child, let him then seek refuge in a forest." He is to be clothed with the bark of trees, or the skin of a black antelope; he must not cut his hair or his nails, he must sleep on the bare ground, and "live without fire, without a mansion, wholly silent, feeding on roots and fruit." He must submit to many severe austerities,* and carefully perform all the required sacrifices and ceremonies. In the fourth, or last period or state of life, he is released from all the forms and ceremonies of religion; he may now cease to inflict acts of mortification upon himself, and devote his time to contemplation, and to meditation upon the Supreme Spirit. The abstinence and self-denial to be practised are still great, but they are not so severe as in the previous state. He may leave the forest and return to the abodes of civilized life. "Having abandoned all ceremonial acts, having expiated all his offences, having obtained a command over his organs, and having perfectly understood all the Vedas, he may become an anchorite in the house of his son, while the household affairs are conducted by his son." And thus he was to continue to the end of life.

The brahmins now seldom attempt to perform all these rites and to practise all these austerities. The rules of caste among them have changed in various ways, but they regard themselves as observing the most important and essential rules. They alone can possess and expound the Vedas, and they must officiate in all religious rites and ceremonies. They profess to obey their rules in respect to eating and drinking, and they have

* "In the hot season let him sit exposed to five fires, four blazing around him, with the sun above; in the rains let him stand uncovered, without even a mantle, where the clouds pour the heaviest showers; in the cold season let him wear humid vesture, and let him by degrees increase the austerity of his devotions."

great influence over all the other castes. In some districts they make one tenth or twelfth part of the people, but in others not more than one twentieth part. A small proportion of them understand the Sanscrit language and its literature, and nearly all are educated in the vernacular languages of their district. They are easy and polite in their manners, ready and fluent in conversation, and fond of discussion on religious and metaphysical subjects.

The kshatryas and vaishyas, as pure castes, are now declared by the brahmins to be extinct, and this is the general opinion among the Hindus.* A few families in some places claim to belong to these original castes, but their claims are not generally allowed, and it is certain that they do not retain and exercise the original rights of these castes, as reading the Vedas, offering sacrifices, etc. Only the brahmins now possess the Vedas, and officiate in religious rites and ceremonies.

Caste, in its nature and origin, is an essential part of the Hindu religion, and all nations and tribes not professing this faith, are called in their sacred books outcastes and polluted. Caste consists essentially in pretended and supposed *birth-purity*. It is strictly hereditary and never can be acquired. It is not properly of a moral nature, nor in any way connected with or dependent upon moral qualities. People may commit any kind of iniquity, may be guilty of falsehood, theft, lewdness, robbery, and murder, and they often are guilty of these crimes, are convicted of them and publicly punished for them, and yet do not lose caste. Caste appears not to have been designed to promote justice or purity or holiness, but by making fancied distinctions of different classes of the human race, and arbitrary rules concerning family connections and social intercourse, to elevate some of these classes and to depress others and to perpetuate this state, so that no vices could degrade the former, and no virtues elevate the latter.

The supposed purity of caste may be destroyed or impaired by a violation of its rules, and such violations are punished in various ways according to the nature of the offence. People may incur this evil by personally violating its rules, or by partici-

* Page 434.

pating knowingly or unknowingly with those who are transgressors. This liability to suffer for the transgression of others, makes people watchful over the conduct of one another. If there is any report or accusation against any one of having broken the rules of his caste, a meeting of the same caste-people is held to investigate the matter, and if he is found guilty, he is sentenced to some punishment. This punishment may be a fine or some penance, or entire exclusion from caste. The penalties are often heavy, humiliating, and severe, as the payment of large sums of money, difficult ceremonial ablutions, painful penances, humiliating confessions, eating and drinking things of a filthy and disgusting nature, but supposed to have some purifying efficacy. And the unhappy person is suspended from all the rights and privileges of caste till he has paid, or performed or suffered all the penalty. It is amazing to see what men will give, and do, and suffer to recover their standing in their caste. But then there is no punishment so great and so severe as exclusion from caste. According to the Hindu laws a man excluded from his caste loses all his marital, parental, social, and civil rights. He is to be expelled at once from his house and his home, to be disowned by his family and his friends, and to be driven from all society. He is to be regarded as dead, and funeral rites of a peculiar character are to be performed for him. His legal heirs take possession of his property as though he were dead. His family, his friends, and all his caste unite in executing the sentence which has been passed upon him. He can obtain no redress or sympathy by appealing to people of other castes, for the people of each caste always claim the right of managing such matters as they please, and one caste will not interfere with the proceedings of another caste. If he appealed to princes or to magistrates, they never interfered further than to ascertain that the proceedings had been according to the rules of caste; they never changed these rules — for they are believed to be of divine origin, and the duty of kings and princes are to govern their people according to these rules and laws.

The shudras, or fourth caste, are often called in the Institutes of Menu, "the servile class," and their state, civil, social, and religious, was extremely degraded. "Their duty was to serve the other classes (castes) without depreciating their worth."

They are not described as being the chattels or property of the other classes, though such appears to have been the state of some among them. They could acquire and hold property of any kind, and could dispose of it as they pleased. They could pursue the mechanical arts as joinery, masonry, etc. They might learn to read, to write, to paint, etc. Probably no kind of manual labor was prohibited. They could perform sacrifices but must not use the texts of the Vedas, nor the same ritual as the other castes. Brahmins were not allowed to teach them the Vedas, nor to assist them in sacrifice, nor to instruct them how to make any expiation for sin. To acquire the religious knowledge or to perform the religious rites of the other castes, was a crime.* The punishments to be inflicted upon shudras for various offences were far more severe than when committed by the other classes. Thus they were not only to be kept in greater ignorance, but to be punished more severely for their crimes.

The kshatryas and vaishyas having been destroyed or no longer existing as pure castes, all who are not brahmins, are regarded as belonging to the mixed castes (the offspring of unlawful connections), or to some of the numerous classes into which the shudras have become divided, or to those who are regarded as outcastes and included under the general name of pariars. Some of these classes have had for some generations, probably for some centuries, a different social and political position from what is assigned to them in their shastras. As the kshatryas and vaishyas, if still existing, are not recognized as pure castes, the ground they originally occupied in the social and political system must be occupied by the remaining castes. Many brahmins are now engaged in secular occupations. They

* "If a shudra gets by heart any part of the Vedas or the Shastras, the magistrates shall put him to death. If a shudra assumes the brahminical thread (the distinguishing badge of the brahmins) the magistrate shall fine him 800 puns of cowries. If a shudra shall perform the yog (a religious rite) the magistrate shall put him to death, or fine him 200 ashrafees."

"If a shudra shall presume to read any part of the Vedas or Shastras or Purans to a brahmin, a kshatrya, or a vaishya, the magistrate shall heat some bitter oil and pour it into that shudra's mouth; and if a shudra listens to the Vedas or Shastras, then the oil, heated as before, shall be poured into his ears, and anseez and wax shall be melted together, and the orifice of his ears shall be stopped therewith." — *Halhed's Gentoo Code.*

engage without religious scruples in nearly all kinds of government service. They have been ministers of State, counsellors, secretaries, judges, clerks, military officers, and common soldiers. In some districts they are divided into two classes, one class preparing themselves to obtain their livelihood by teaching religious duties and performing religious rites, and the other preparing themselves for secular employment. This last class have no hesitation about engaging in the service of Europeans, Mohammedans, or Hindus of a lower caste than themselves, if they are not required to do any thing contrary to their rules of caste.

So men of the lower castes have often been princes, generals, merchants, soldiers, etc., and have had brahmins in their employment. Still, whatever the business relations of the parties may be, each caste carefully observes the rules of its own order, and is expected carefully to avoid every thing which would be to the prejudice of the caste of the other party. There is thus mutual observance and forbearance, if not mutual respect.

Such was the state of the Hindus for 2,000 or 3,000 years when living under their own governments. Nor until recently was it materially different under the English government; for the policy they adopted was to govern their Hindu subjects according to Hindu laws and usages, and their Mohammedan subjects according to the Mohammedan laws and usages. And such continued to be their policy until 1836, when Lord William Bentinck, then governor-general, passed a law or caused one to be passed, that, "In any civil suit where the parties are of different religious persuasions, the laws of the Hindus, Mohammedans, or other religions, shall not be permitted to operate to deprive such party or parties of any property to which but for the operation of such laws they would have been entitled."

As this law was applicable only to Bengal, and some of its provisions appeared to be difficult or imperfect, it had not much influence. No further laws affecting caste were passed till 1850, when the Marquis of Dalhousie, then governor-general, passed the following: — "So much of any law or usage in force within the British territories as inflicts on any person forfeiture of rights or property, or may be held in any way to impair or affect any right of inheritance by reason of his or her renouncing, or having been excluded from the communion of any religion, or being deprived of caste, shall cease to be enforced as law in the courts of the East India Company, and in the courts established by the Royal Charter within the said territories." This law was designed to give equal toleration and protection to all classes of people. The Hindus remonstrated and protested, but all was in vain. The Act has become one of the laws of the country. No law in any country was ever more required, and no law ever produced more important results.

This law places all classes, Christians, Jews, Mohammedans, and Hindus, upon equal ground, permitting every man to profess and practise what religion he pleases, and to change his religion when he pleases, and retain his personal, family, and property rights. It was designed to confer upon the people of India the same liberty of conscience which the people in England and in the United States enjoy. And yet this law so reasonable and just, excited great alarm among the Hindus and Mohammedans, who regarded it as an uncalled for interference with their usages and rights, and designed to destroy the great bulwarks of their religion. Public meetings were held, earnest speeches were made, and exciting articles appeared in the native journals. Memorials were sent to the governor-general, and Court of Directors. And when these were found to be unavailing, a large sum of money was raised by subscription, and an English barrister of the supreme court in Calcutta was despatched with a memorial to England. In May, 1853, I saw this memorial (signed by more than 8,000 names) presented to the House of Lords by Lord Monteagle, who made a speech in favor of the memorialists. Lord Ellenborough (who had been governor-general of India) then made a speech, describing what would be the unhappy consequences of this law, and deprecating any changes in the religious laws and usages of the people of India. Earl Granville then made a speech in reply, and the memorial was then referred to the Committee of the House on the state of India. The prayer of the memorialists was not granted.

CUSTOMS AND MANNERS.

India, including a territory as large as all Europe south of the Baltic and Russia, or all the United States between the Mississippi and the Atlantic, extending through 26 degrees of latitude, containing 8 or 10 different nations, with as many different languages, and a population of 150 millions of inhabitants, must necessarily have great diversity of customs and manners. The difference between these nations in personal appearance, manners, and language, is nearly or quite as great as it is among the nations of Europe. The inhabitants of the northern parts are fairer than those in the Deckan and southern parts. Some people in the western and north-western provinces, as the Parsees, and Cashmerians, are but little darker than the inhabitants of the southern parts of Europe, while the natives of the Deckan, and the provinces south of it, are as dark and many of them darker than the mulattoes of the United States. Among the inhabitants of India are to be found people of every shade of complexion from a European or American of dark complexion to the common negro. But none of the inhabitants have the peculiar African features. They have black and straight hair, and dark eyes. People in the northern parts are of the average height of Europeans or Americans, but in the Deckan and in the provinces to the south of it, they are of less stature and lighter form. The Bengalees are not so large as the inhabitants of the north-west provinces, but are generally taller than the people on the eastern and western coast of the peninsula. They have generally, very dark complexion for that latitude; they are effeminate in their appearance, and timid and servile in their manners. The Teloogoos, the Tamulians, and the Canarese, are more timid and servile in their intercourse with Europeans, and with superiors among their own people, than the Mahrattas or the Gujerattees. The climate in the northern parts of India makes it necessary for the inhabitants to wear more clothing in the cool months than the inhabitants of the peninsula wear. The men wear turbans, pagotas, and caps of various kinds and shapes. Those of the rich are of fine cloth, and elegant shape, while the poor have, generally, only a few yards of coarse cloth wrapped round the head. The rich wear long garments, the upper part fitted to the body and confined with a girdle or sash, and the lower part hanging loosely. The Mohammedans and Parsees generally wear loose trousers; the Hindus wear a cloth wrapped round the body, fastened behind, and hanging loosely nearly to the feet. In the Deckan and the provinces south of it, the laboring classes generally wear but little clothing when in their ordinary occupation and in their houses. The shoes of all classes are commonly of clumsy make and appearance, and in the southern provinces are scarcely worn in the house. All classes, Mohammedans as well as Hindus, put off their shoes when they go into places of worship, or of any repute for sanctity. The women in the northern provinces are fairer and better looking than in the southern provinces. They also wear more clothing and adjust their dress with more taste and propriety, producing a more becoming and every way superior personal appearance. All classes of women are fond of ornaments. They wear jewels and rings in the ears and nose, rings on the fingers and toes, chains on the neck, and bracelets on their arms, their wrists, and their ankles. These ornaments are of gold, silver, precious stones, pearls, coral, ivory, etc., often amounting in value to hundreds, and sometimes to many thousands of dollars. They appear sometimes to be really burdened with their ornaments. They take great pains and manifest much pride in ornamenting their children, both girls and boys. Small children whose whole clothing did not cost a dollar, will often have on them ornaments worth $100. Children are often robbed and sometimes murdered to obtain their ornaments. A large part of the property of many people consists of jewelry. The dowry given with daughters in marriage consists to a great extent in articles of this character, and is regarded as the property of the wife. These articles are worn at marriages, holidays, and other festive occasions, and consisting, as they do, chiefly of gold and silver, they can be converted at any time into money, without much loss. A large part of the precious metals in the country is in jewelry, and the supposed possession and value of such property occasions much of the thieving, robbing, plundering, and murdering that take place. This fondness for ornaments, their extravagance in procuring them, and ostentation in using them, are the cause of many evils to their possessors and to the community, and they have been the subject of much censure and counsel, in the European and native papers, but hitherto apparently with little effect. These things will apparently be the principal objects of desire and attention among the females in India, as long as personal appearance shall continue to be the quality chiefly regarded. When education has produced a due appreciation of mental qualities in women, we may hope to see their excessive love of finery and pride of jewelry give place to more just views of character, and to the desired reformation of manners.

For greater security in times of danger, and for convenience in social intercourse and transactions of business, the agricultural population generally live in villages. The distinctions and rules of caste also make it necessary for people to live in villages, so that those of the same caste may live near each other, and so have opportunities and facilities for social intercourse, and for the mutual aid and protection which they require, but could not have if they lived in the dispersed state of the rural population of the United States. In some parts of the country the villages are surrounded with high walls, and entered through gates, which are closed or carefully guarded nights. Such walls have seldom been found necessary in the districts under the English government, and in many places they are becoming dilapidated. The houses are generally small, and badly constructed. They have seldom any glass windows, and the floors are commonly earth. Chairs and tables are seldom used, as people sit upon mats. Vessels for cooking and eating are of brass and copper, and those too poor to procure such, use coarse earthen vessels. In eating, their fingers serve for knives and forks. In some rural districts all the furniture in the houses would not upon an average exceed a few dollars' value. This furniture always includes one or more hand mills for grinding grain for the use of the family. Beds consist of a rude frame with a mat or mattrass upon them, or more frequently these are spread on the floor for the night and removed in the daytime. People generally make but little change in their dress for the night. Their practice of frequent bathing conduces to cleanliness and health. The villages generally have a few shops for the sale of grain, tobacco, coarse cloths, etc., and the large villages have appointed market-days or fairs, to which travelling traders, peddlers, and people from the hamlets resort. The villages generally contain one or two houses for travellers to lodge inside the gates, and so they have the same security as the inhabitants. The temple dedicated to the tutelary deity and containing his or her image, is generally just outside or inside the gate, and fronting it, so as to appear before people when going out or coming into the village.

In the large towns and old cities, the streets are generally narrow and crooked, few of them being wide enough or kept in a state to allow carriages of any kind to pass. Many of the houses are two and three stories high, built of brick or stones and lime, and the walls plastered on both sides. To Europeans they appear to be badly constructed, and as they have but little glass in the windows, the rooms appear to be dark, gloomy, inconvenient, and uncomfortable. The merchants and bankers generally occupy the principal street, and sometimes their shops and houses surround a public square. They sit cross-legged on carpets in their place of business on the floor, which is generally raised about two feet from the ground. They are commonly neat in their dress and personal appearance, and very courteous in their manners. They lend money to small traders, and to all classes of people, and the rate of interest and discount is generally high. They often make advances of money to the native princes upon a mortgage of the revenues of certain districts, or the taxes of a certain kind, and to the farmers and cultivators of the land upon the security of their crops. The bankers have much influence in the community, and they have often acted a conspicuous part in the political history of the country. Their general style of living is plain and frugal, but they expend money freely for ornaments, and also for the marriage of their children. They also sometimes spend large sums in going on pilgrimage to sacred places, in erecting temples, and in making tanks and large wells for public use. Such works are declared in the shastras to be very meritorious, and they procure a much desired reputation for the performer and his family. A rich man in India is expected to do far more for his family connections, and he generally does do more for them, than men in similar circumstances do for their relations and connections in the United States.

In Bengal, Gujerat, and the low grounds of the peninsula, rice is produced in large quantity. It is cooked in many different ways, and, mixed with sugar, butter, spices, and vegetables, forms the principal article of food. In the hilly and table-lands of the Deckan, and in the northern provinces of the country, wheat, rye, and other kinds of grain are produced and generally used. The people of India, when compared with the inhabitants of the United States, eat but little meat. The brahmins and jainas religiously abstain from meat of every kind.* They will not even eat eggs, saying there is the germ of life in them. Some classes will eat no meat but fish. The Jews and Mohammedans do not eat pork. Hindus of all classes abstain from eating beef, but the great body of them will eat fish, fowls, goats, and sheep. Still they use these kinds of food sparingly. Probably the rural population generally do not eat any kind of meat so often as once a week. In some instances people are so poor that they cannot procure meat. But people generally in the country districts could keep fowls if they wished to have them or their eggs for food, and the price of a sheep in the villages does not generally exceed half a dollar, and in some districts not more than 25 cents.

Water is the common drink at meals and other times. Tobacco is chewed and smoked, (used most in the latter way,) but the quality of the Indian plant is not so strong as American tobacco. All classes chew a pungent aromatic leaf called *betel* with *areca-nut*, lime, and spices, mixed together. These substances have some narcotic influence, but do not produce intoxication. The use of spirituous liquors is prohibited to the brahmins, and it is disreputable among all the higher classes.

* Some earnest advocates for the use of only vegetable food in this country, have confidently expressed the opinion that if men would use only vegetable food, they would gradually recover the patriarchal age. But unhappily for this opinion, no one has yet practised this mode of life long enough to prove by his own example, whether it is true or not. Now if the advocates of this opinion will only go to India, they can find thousands of people who have never eaten any kind of meat, nor did their ancestors eat any for more than 2,000 years past, and yet these classes of people do not live any longer than other classes who are in similar circumstances for preserving health, and who possess equal means for curing and avoiding diseases.

Some people, generally of the lower classes, use arrack and other kinds of intoxicating liquor, and some smoke, and in various ways use the intoxicating and stupefying vegetable called ganja, or Indian hemp (*cannabis sativa*). Opium is eaten and smoked, and a liquor made from it is drank, in the districts where it is produced. In the rural districts of the greater part of India, intemperance is uncommon, and it is chiefly seen in the cities and towns under the English government, where it has been introduced by a system of licensing persons to traffic in spirits. Drunkenness is most common in places which have grown up under the patronage and protection of the English government, where the European population is the largest, and their influence strongest, as in the cities of Calcutta, Madras, and Bombay, and at large military stations in the interior. The general opinion is that intemperance has been decreasing for some years past among the European population, while all admit that it has much increased among the native population since they came under English government. Temperance societies have been formed, and many natives as well as Europeans have united in efforts to prevent the spread of intemperance, and to remove and diminish the causes which sustain it.

The distinctions of caste are a great obstacle to free, social, and friendly intercourse. Among the wealthy it is a frequent practice and a work of great merit to give dinners to brahmins, but the person who gives the dinner, if he is not a brahmin, cannot eat with them or even be one of their company without eating. His presence in the company would pollute all the food, and make it unfit for any brahmin to eat. He can only look from some distance upon those who are feasting upon his liberality, and who will not allow him at whose expense they are eating, (and he may be their prince too,) to come near them, lest his touch should pollute the food they are eating. But among those of the same caste, eating together is a strong bond of union. Dinners are frequent and are regarded as evidence of good standing in the caste. While a man is under the censure of his caste, or any accusation of having violated any of its rules, he is excluded from all caste-dinners and ceremonies, and this is felt to be a great reproach and punishment. Dinners make an important part of family gatherings, and domestic and festive occasions, as marriages, etc. At such times the men and women always eat in separate places. People of all classes eat with their hands, using their fingers instead of knives, forks, and spoons. They sit on mats and carpets, and not in chairs or at tables.

The hunting of wild animals has always been one of the sports of India. The dreadful and much dreaded tiger, the noble and huge elephant, and the fearless lion are found in the forests, and hunting them has always been the favorite sport of the sovereigns of the country — a sport worthy of princes, kings, and emperors, if any kind of sport can have such a character.* Wild cattle, buffaloes, leopards, bears, wolves, several kinds of deer, wild hogs, etc., are found in different parts of the country, and are generally the property of any one who can kill them. Mock battles in illustration of wars and actions described in their sacred books are sometimes exhibited by princes on a large scale. Fights between animals, as elephants, lions, tigers, leopards, etc., are exhibited and draw great crowds of spectators. The amusements of the courts and kings in former times included dramatic exhibitions of a much higher character than any performances of this kind among the Hindus of the present age. There are 60 plays in the Sanscrit language. These exhibit more talent and taste than are to be found in similar works of any Asiatic nation ancient or modern, though they are inferior to the elaborated and finished dramas of Greece and Rome. These plays were performed in the royal palaces fitted up for the occasions before kings and their courts. Kalidas, the most celebrated of the Hindu dramatic writers, lived at the court of Vickramditya, who reigned in Awanti (the modern Oujein) about 50 years before the Christian era, and his plays appear to have

* But even in these kinds of sport the peculiarities of the southern Asiatic character were often conspicuous. The prince when on a hunting excursion would select his place and then send his servants and soldiers, often as numerous as a small army, to surround the land supposed to contain the game, and to urge it to the spot where the prince and his courtiers were waiting to shoot the animals as they passed a certain corner or reached a certain point. In this way the prince would have the honor and sport of killing all the game, unless he would permit his courtiers to assist him, while others would have all the labor and the danger of bringing it all to him to be shot, and then of escaping from them if attacked.

been performed before the prince and his court. The performers were men or women according to the respective parts, and the assemblies were of a mixed character. The parts of these plays and the manner in which they were performed, furnish an interesting picture of the ancient manners of the Hindus. They show that the exclusion of females from courts, assemblies, and public entertainments, was not the practice before the Mohammedan conquest. Among the ancient Hindus, women were permitted to appear freely and openly on public occasions. They assisted in dramatic exhibitions, and composed part of the assemblies which witnessed these amusements. They formed a part in marriage festivities and bridal processions. They attended public religious ceremonies and visited the temples whenever they pleased. And such continues to be the custom in some provinces, where the Hindus have retained their liberty and their power. Exhibitions or performances of a theatrical character are now very common in which one man is the principal speaker, aided by a few assistants and some musicians. In these performances females sometimes perform parts, but such parts are more frequently performed by men or boys in the dress of women.

No class of Asiatics ever dance for their own pleasure or amusement, but there are persons who are dancers by profession for the amusement of others.* These dancers are young women, and always supposed to be courtesans. They generally constitute a company of one, two, or three dancers with several musicians who stand behind them. All classes of people are very fond of these entertainments, and money is freely expended in supporting them. Among the rich they are often in large

* The southern Asiatics have no idea of pleasure in labor or exertion, unless in the excitement called forth by some great motive. They wonder much when they see English gentlemen and ladies appear to find pleasure in dancing. They often attend English balls as spectators, and when some of them after looking at the dancing for a while were asked what they thought of it, they replied that the English appeared to enjoy dancing, for if they did not find pleasure in it, they would not practise it, but they thought their own custom much better, namely, instead of laboring so hard and wearying and exhausting themselves by dancing, to hire persons whose professed business was dancing, and who could dance much better, and then sitting down themselves, or reclining on their couches at ease, look on and see them dance.

halls elegantly furnished with carpets, couches, mirrors, chandeliers, etc. The dress and performance of the dancers are said to be not ungraceful nor offensive to propriety or decency, but as the performers are always women of loose morals, such exhibitions cannot but have a licentious tendency. Indeed, it is said that the latter part of these entertainments is often designed and adapted to excite amorous passions and sometimes results in gross licentiousness. These amusements have an unhappy influence in promoting loose morals and in degrading the female character. The people are fond of chess,* cards, and some other games of skill. They also practise several games of chance and have various ways of gambling.

The Hindu festivals are numerous, and all are more or less religious in their character. In most of these, however, the religious part or rites occupy but a small portion of the time. The people on such occasions generally omit all labor, and putting on their best clothes ride out in carriages or walk about where the principal objects of attraction are:—to see curiosities and jugglers,† to procure fruits and sweetmeats, to reciprocate civilities and inquiries with friends, etc. In some instances, as on the Mohurrum, the chief festival of the Mohammedans in India, the people form long processions and proceed in order through the principal streets preceded by bands of music and carrying

* The invention of this celebrated game has been ascribed to the Hebrews, the Babylonians, and the Persians. But Sir W. Jones in his Dissertation "On the Indian Game of Chess," ascribes it to the Hindus.

† Jugglery has been practised in India from very remote antiquity, perhaps as early as it was in Egypt. The jugglers travel about over the country in companies, and exhibit their feats and arts in the private grounds of the wealthy, and in the public and open places of towns and cities, trusting to the generosity of spectators for compensation. They generally have snakes of poisonous or uncommon kinds, which are exhibited in various ways. Some of these snakes will raise their heads and move them slowly to the sound of a pipe, played by one of the company. They handle these snakes, even the most venomous kind, without fear or injury. It is said and doubtless truly, that the poisonous fangs have been extracted. This however does not always secure impunity, as such fangs in young snakes will sometimes grow again and inflict mortal wounds. These jugglers are remarkably expert in their feats of strength and agility, and in their tricks of deception. They are an ignorant and despised caste of people, and the general opinion of the other castes is that they worship evil spirits, and have the assistance of such beings in performing their feats and tricks.

banners, or something which represents the origin and occasion of the festival. There is very little intemperance on such days and rarely any rows or quarrels, or accidents or injuries.

The higher classes are very attentive to all the customs and usages of official and social intercourse, and great importance is given to such matters. At the durbars or levees of princes, the rank of every person who attends, is carefully determined, and each is seated according to his rank. The prince (raja, or emperor, or whatever he may be,) takes the seat assigned and prepared for him, which is the most conspicuous place. All pay their respects to him in succession, each presenting a gift called a *nuzzur*, for which he receives something, generally a dress, in return. The nuzzur generally consists of money, but may be of jewels, or some rare and curious article. People of rank are courteous and polite to all classes, and expect from others what they so freely give. Such is also the conduct and character of the lower classes. Indeed, there is more dignity, ease, and grace of manners, and a more careful observance of the civilities, rules, proprieties, and usages of official and social intercourse among all ranks and classes of people in India, than among the corresponding classes in Europe and America.

But it must be acknowledged that the Hindus are a very deceitful people, and often while apparently so civil, so kind, and benevolent, are in heart and in purpose, the very reverse of what they appear to be. They have great power of dissimulation and hypocrisy. Their language abounds in compliment, flattery, and assurances of good-will, which often deceive Europeans, though not each other, for among themselves all appear at once to understand just how much and how little such language and assurances mean, and what reliance can be put upon them. The Hindus are very discriminating judges of character, and are seldom deceived by Europeans, or by one another.

Perjury is fearfully common in the courts of justice. It is a frequent saying and a general opinion that men enough can be hired for a small sum to swear to their knowledge of things of which they know nothing, and to the truth of things which they know to be false. English magistrates of great experience in public business, have often declared that they could place but little reliance upon native testimony, especially upon that of the Hindus, unless it was corroborated by separate facts, and concurring circumstances. The native character appears to be equally depraved in respect to bribery. In the Hindu and Mohammedan governments, men holding official situations generally depended upon fees, bribes, and exactions, for compensation. Salaries were almost nominal, and yet government functionaries of all classes managed to accumulate large fortunes. Bribery and extortion in such governments were common, and the effects were very demoralizing and distressing. And bribery, notwithstanding all that can be done to prevent it, is yet not uncommon among the natives holding official situations under the English government. The Hindu sacred books justify falsehood, and even inculcate deceit in many specified cases. And such a code of morality, and the licentious character and immoral conduct of their gods, the objects of their worship and adoration, leave us little reason to expect much improvement in regard to telling the truth, till they have a purer code of morals, and begin to worship the Deity, whose actions are righteous, and whose attributes are holy.

BUDHISM.

Budhism has been mentioned as a form or system of religion which existed in India at an early period. The origin of this religion is involved in much obscurity. Some orientalists have been of the opinion that it preceded brahminism. But the more general opinion has been that it originated in some efforts to reform some of the brahminical doctrines, and became after a while a rival system. It was once the religion of some kingdoms in the valley of the Ganges, but after long struggles, it was expelled from all continental India, except Nepaul, where it is still the religion of the country, though in some places it is much mixed with brahminical superstitions. It is also the religion of the southern part of Ceylon, and of the countries east from India, as Burma, Siam, and China.

Budhism has differed much in its doctrines at different times, and also at the same time, as these have been set forth by its different professors. It is in vain to expect much truth, or reason, or consistency in such systems as Budhism and Brahminism, which were not only rival and conflicting systems, but the professors and followers of each could not agree upon its doctrines among themselves. It is enough to show the different doctrines, so far as these can now be ascertained, which were believed and professed among them.

The most ancient doctrines of Budhism appear to have been atheistical, holding that the material universe is eternal, and that all the changes which take place, are only the effect of the inherent and essential properties and qualities of matter. They professed to believe that the power of originating organization, and then of producing in these organized forms all the phenomena they exhibit, is inherent in matter, or nature as they call it, and that the agency which organized forms have in producing other forms, is the result of their inherent power, and requires no external aid or agent. To this supposed inherent and essential power of matter, they ascribe the origin and perpetuation of the human race and all other beings, as well as the changes which take place in inanimate and inorganic matter.

Some of the early Budhists appear to have believed in an infinite and self-existent Being, who created the material universe, or reduced its chaotic materials to form, and having communicated to them, or endowed them with all the various properties they now possess, again assumed a state of repose and unconcern about his works, and that the material universe by the operation and force of its communicated and now inherent power, continues and produces and exhibits all the endlessly diversified forms of existence and changes of matter, which compose the apparent world of life, action, and motion.

Of these pretended philosophers, one class believe in no Creator or Governor of the universe, and so are properly called atheists. The other class profess to believe in an eternal and self-existent Deity, who created the universe, or reduced it to its present state and order, but who has since exerted no agency in it, or superintendence over it. They appear to be of the opinion that the inherent powers of matter, or nature as they call it, in certain peculiarly combined organizations, produces consciousness, instinct, reason, volition, and the perception of moral relations and qualities. They appear to believe that in some inexplicable way, a kind of personal identity is acquired, and that the same being has successive states of existence, a kind of transmigration on the disorganization of one body into another. They believe that certain beings, called Budhas, have acquired the first rank in the scale of existence by a long course of virtuous actions and austerities in successive states of being or transmigrations.

The Budhists believe that the number of these Budhas who have thus raised themselves in the scale of beings is large,* and some of these at long intervals have appeared or become incarnate again and again in the world to reform mankind and restore religion to its original purity. Among the most distinguished of these incarnations was Gaudama, who appeared at several different times. His last appearance or incarnation was at Benares in the 6th century before the Christian era. He reformed Budhism, which had become very much corrupted, and taught the system as it now exists. He also established its rules of worship and its moral precepts. He is now regarded by the Budhists as the head of their religion and of the religious world, and to continue so (though long since passed into a higher state of existence) till he shall complete his allotted period which they generally hold to be 5,000 years.

In a religion so widely spread and where in its progress it must have come in conflict with previous forms of superstition, much difference in doctrine and practice might naturally be expected. The Budhists have a large body of literature which is as extravagant and absurd as the Purans. These works are in the Pali language which is the same with them in India, as the Sanscrit is with the brahmins. Pali appears to have been the language current in Magada, one of the ancient kingdoms on the Ganges where Gaudama was born and where Budhism was the prevailing religion for several centuries. Some of the kings of Magada were zealous in propagating this system.

The Budhists differ from the brahmins in some doctrines which each class regard as fundamental, and it does not appear

* Mr. Hodgson in his account of Budhism in Nepaul gives a list of 130 Budhas of the first class. — *Asiatic Researches*, vol. 16, p. 446.

strange that the two classes should call each other by odious names; that the brahmins shall call the Budhists atheists, and the Budhists should call the brahmins polytheists. The Budhists deny the authority of the Vedas and Purans and have their own sacred books. They believe in the primitive and natural equality of all mankind, and allow no distinctions of caste. Among the Budhists the priests can be from any class in the community. They must live in a state of celibacy and continence. They live together so far as their circumstances will permit, in monasteries, and are subject to particular rules of eating, sitting, bathing, and sleeping. They carry their respect for animal life much further than the brahmins, for they do not eat after noon, nor drink after dark for fear of swallowing minute insects. Some of them carry a brush with them to sweep places before they sit down, lest they should crush some living creatures. And some of them even keep a thin cloth over their mouths to prevent their taking in minute insects with their breath. As their priests can be from any class of the community, so they can at any time leave the priesthood, and resume their former place in the community. The difference between the priests of the two systems is much greater than between the laity. And some of these differences are of a nature to be peculiarly offensive to the brahmins.

The monuments of Budhism scattered over India show that its followers must once have been numerous, wealthy, and powerful. The cave-temples of Kennery in Salsette about 25 miles from Bombay, and of Karlee on the road from Bombay to Poona above the Ghats are Budhistical. Of the celebrated cave-temples of Elora, 16 miles north from Aurungabad some are Budhistical and some are brahminical, and some exhibit a mixture of both systems. Those last mentioned have the appearance of having been first made by the Budhists, and afterwards altered and appropriated to brahminical worship. Many Hindu temples exhibit evidence of their materials having previously been used in Budhist temples. The history of neither party furnishes any reliable accounts of the struggles between them, nor by what means the brahmins succeeded in triumphing over their enemies. For 2 or 3 centuries after the time of Gaudama, the Budhists were active and zealous in propagating their religion, and it was at that time carried into Ceylon, where the inhabitants had previously practised demonolatry, similar to the religion of the primitive inhabitants of India. Budhism continues to be the religion of the southern part of Ceylon, though many of the lower class still practise the worship of demons, which is often called devil-worship. From Ceylon Budhism was propagated eastwards to Burma, Siam, and China, and it is now supposed to be the religion of a larger number of the human family than any other system.

MOHAMMEDANS.

The Mohammedans of India are variously estimated at $\frac{1}{8}$, $\frac{1}{10}$, $\frac{1}{12}$ of the entire population of the country. This appears to be a small proportion when we consider the great number of this religion who immigrated into the country, their avowed purpose in conquering it, the long period they governed it, and the efforts they made to proselyte the inhabitants to their faith. And yet when we consider the population of India, commonly estimated at 150,000,000, the whole number of the Mohammedan population will probably amount to 15,000,000 or 18,000,000. They are most numerous in the valley of the Ganges, where their power was first established and the invaders and immigrants chiefly settled. In some districts in Bengal they make one fourth, and in a few places are said to make nearly one half of the population. In the southern parts of the peninsula their proportion is small; in some districts they are not more than 1 in 25 or 30 of the population. It has been estimated that half of the Mohammedan population of India are descendants of the conquerors and immigrants from Persia, Afghanistan, and Arabia, and half are the descendants of proselytes from Hinduism during the Mohammedan dynasties. As the conquerors and the subsequent immigrations were from Persia and Afghanistan, so the peculiar type of the religion they introduced and propagated, resembled what has existed in those countries far more than the pure and primitive form which has existed in Arabia.

Persian was the court language among the Mohammedan princes of India, and it still continues to be used among their descendants. But the language in general use among the Mohammedans is Hindustanee, which is formed of the language they brought with them into India, and of Hindee or Hinduee, the language they found in the valley of the Ganges where they first established their dominion, and which was the chief seat of their power. Hindustanee may be called the military language of India. It is easily acquired for colloquial purposes, and is the common medium of intercourse between Europeans and natives. It is easily combined with the vernacular languages, and so varies very considerably in different parts of India. The Mohammedan population is so much dispersed over the country, and their language is so easily acquired and already so much used, that some orientalists have urged the expediency and importance of making Hindustanee the *lingua franca* of the whole country. But this attempt is not likely to be made, and if made, would fail of success.

Some of the native princes are Mohammedans and a few of them, as the Nizam of Hydrabad, the Nabob of Lucknow, and some others, yet retain considerable territory and power. But these, through a failure of direct heirs to succeed them, or the mismanagement of their affairs, are diminishing in number, influence, and power, and it appears not unlikely that in a few years all will be divested of territorial possessions, and be reduced to a state of dependence upon the English for pensions and annuities to sustain some shadow of their former pageantry. The generally acknowledged principles of Mohammedan governments in matters of war, finance, the administration of justice, etc., are superior to those of the Hindus. But we look in vain for any evidence of their superiority in the state of their territories, which are generally in a bad state. Their misgovernment originates in part in the feelings of contempt they cherish towards all who are not of their faith, and the various offensive and oppressive ways in which they manifest these feelings.

Mohammedans in India all practise circumcision and attach great importance to it. The rite is generally performed by barbers, and it may be performed at any time before the 13th year.

They carefully abstain from eating pork. Their princes have often been intemperate, but the great body of the people, so far as I have seen them, do not use any kind of spirituous liquors, and drunkenness among them is disreputable and is seldom seen. I never heard of any Mohammedan being in any way engaged in trafficking in liquors. The general sentiment among them would not allow any one of their faith to follow such business in any place I knew. Polygamy is practised. Their domestic habits are such that it is difficult to know how far this custom exists. Their princes generally have several wives and concubines, but few of them have so many as their prophet Mohammed had. Wealthy men have generally more than one wife, and instances of polygamy are not unfrequent among the middling and lower classes. Perhaps taking all the population, one man in 5 or 6 may be a polygamist. But the custom prevails more in some provinces than in others. This custom has a very unhappy influence on families and on the general state of society. It is not a corruption of their system but an integral part of it. Mohammed himself practised it, and it has his authority in his example as well as in the doctrines he taught. So Mohammedanism can never be reformed so as to forbid polygamy, and this practice more than any thing else in the system is working the destruction of the countries and communities which profess this religion.

The Mohammedans have more intellectual character than the Hindus. This superiority appears to be the natural result of the more rational and consistent doctrines concerning God, his attributes, and his providence, contained in the Koran, than any doctrines found in the Hindu sacred books or in their worship. The object contemplated in religious worship must exert very considerable influence upon the mental character of any people, and when looking at the Hindu deities and at their rites and ceremonies, I have often wondered that the people who profess and practise such a religion do not become more stupid and dull of understanding than they are. The Mohammedans have generally more physical strength than the Hindus, which is owing probably in part to their northern origin, and in part to their eating more meat for food.

Mohammedans have generally a great contempt for the religion of the Hindus. They abhor it for its polytheism and idolatry. When I went to India the Koran had not, so far as I know, been printed in India. All copies of it were in manuscript and were scarce and costly. Some 10 or 12 years ago an attempt was made in Bombay to print the Koran in lithography and succeeded well. They were so pleased with these copies that other editions of different sizes were soon printed and many thousand copies were issued. They were purchased and carried or sent to be sold in Arabia, Persia, and other countries. For the last 10 years I was in India, as good a copy of the Koran could be purchased for one dollar as could be procured for 8 or 10 dollars for the first 10 years I was there. One rich man was so pleased with these printed copies that he printed an edition of 1,000 copies in beautiful style and distributed them. Rich men also often purchased a number of copies and distributed to people around, and sent them into those parts of the country where the Koran was supposed to be scarce. And such liberality and zeal have not been limited to Bombay. A native prince at Lucknow not long since expended $2,500 on an edition of the Koran in Arabic with a Hindustanee translation and commentary, which was designed for gratuitous circulation. Thus private zeal and liberality supplied the want of a Koran Society to furnish the destitute. I should not be surprised to hear of the formation of Koran Societies upon the plan, object, and agency of Bible Societies.

There is no priesthood among the Mohammedans in India. A man who can read and expound the Koran is called a Moolah. As people generally do not understand the language of the Koran (which is Arabic), they often assemble in the mosques and private houses to hear the Koran read and explained. Mohammedans fast during the month of Ramazan in India, as they do in Turkey and other countries. The fast consists in not eating or drinking any thing in the daytime. In the night they may eat and drink as much as they wish. Still this mode of fasting for a whole month is often a severe duty, and hard discipline. In many places are the tombs of reputed saints which are held in great veneration, and many people in their vicinity make vows to them. These saints have generally an anniversary or annual festival, when people assemble, often many thousands, to perform their vows and offer their prayers to the saints. These reputed saints occupy a place among the Mohammedans in India similar to what Romish saints have among the Roman Catholics in Europe. Mohammedanism in India consists much in local usages and popular superstitions, which have no authority in the Koran. Many go on pilgrimages to Mecca, and such as live to return are afterwards much respected among their people.

The Mohammedans are fond of religious discussion and controversy. Not restrained by any rules of caste, they can associate freely with Europeans. A few distinguished men among them have become Christians and honored their profession, but they are generally more opposed to Christianity than the Hindus. They have made considerable use of the press within a few years past for vindicating their religion and confirming the faith of their people. The most spirited controversy between Mohammedanism and Christianity has been in Northern India. Some able works have there been published on both sides, and the subject has excited much attention.

Christian writers on Mohammed have generally said that he performed no miracles and acknowledged in the Koran that he had not power to perform any, and they refer to places which are supposed to acknowledge or imply this want of power. But the Mohammedans do not admit that their prophet wanted this evidence of his mission's being divine. So far from this they believe that he performed many and wonderful miracles, and that signs and miracles and prodigies in testimony of his divine mission were frequently taking place around him. A work called the "Light of Mohammed," printed at Lucknow, at Agra, and at Carrapore, contains accounts of more such miracles and prodigies than all that are in the New Testament. Of this work 12 editions had been printed when I left India, and devout Mohammedans appeared to have entire confidence in its assertions and statements. Such views of Mohammed, of his mission and his works are more firmly and generally held by the Mohammedans in the northern parts of India, who have obtained their religion and their traditions from Persia, than in the southern parts where they have obtained their principles from Arabia.

The Mohammedan religion has made but little progress in India since the decline of their political power. Now and then some Hindu who has lost caste or is involved in trouble with his own people, will join the Mohammedans and become incorporated with them. According to the Hindu theory of caste, any person not a Hindu, whoever and whatever he may be, is lower than any Hindu who has always observed the rules of his caste. But practically the Mohammedans occupy a much higher social position even in the view of the Hindus themselves than the low caste Hindus. So when a Hindu of low caste becomes a member of the Mohammedan community, he rises in the social scale and in general respectability. Considering the state and circumstances of the low caste Hindus and the manner in which they are treated by the high castes, and that by becoming Mohammedans they at once come under their protection and often secure other advantages, as employment, relief from pecuniary embarrassment, a marriage connection, etc., (for the Mohammedans hold out these advantages to proselytes,) it appears strange that more Hindus do not become Mohammedans.

The progress of Christianity and other causes now in operation in India, will strongly affect the Mohammedans in common with all other classes of the native population, and when they see the Hindus losing all confidence in their sacred books, neglecting their idolatries and rites and ceremonies, some of them becoming Christians and others sinking into scepticism and indifference to all religion, it appears not unlikely that the Mohammedans may become animated with zeal for propagating their faith, and that this religion may spread faster than it ever did when urged on by all the force of political power and war against Hinduism in the state it then was. There is no prospect of Mohammedans again acquiring much political power in India, but considering the state of the native population and the various causes in operation affecting their religious character, it does not appear improbable that Mohammedanism may yet spread and become the religion of a much larger proportion of the people of the country before it shall be numbered one of the provinces of the kingdom of Immanuel, and its inhabitants become his obedient and happy subjects.

THE PARSEES.

The Parsees are a class of people who live chiefly in the western parts of India. Their number was found at the late census of Bombay, to be about 75,000 in that small island. They are also numerous in Gujerat, and a few are settled in most of the seaports and large cities in the southern countries of Asia. Their ancestors fled from Persia some centuries ago to escape the persecutions of the Mohammedans, and after wandering about for considerable time, became quietly settled in Gujerat. They are the most intelligent, wealthy, and enterprising of any class in the native population of India. The religion of their ancestors when they escaped from Persia, was the system of Zoroaster, the same as the religion of the ancient Persians, in the times of Cyrus and Xerxes. Their Scriptures are called the Zend Avesta, and are ascribed to Zoroaster. There has been much difference of opinion in respect to the time when he lived, how many there were of this name, and whether the work, called the Zend Avesta, was really written by any one of this name, or was not rather written long after the reputed epoch of any of the Zoroasters.

The Zend Avesta comprises several parts which are seldom used together. These are called the Vandidad, the Yasna or Izashne, and the Vispard. The Parsees appear generally to believe in two self-existent and eternal Beings, called Hormazd, the good deity, and Ahriman, the bad deity. The former produces all the good and the happiness that are in the world, and the latter produces all the evil and the misery that are in the world. Some believe that both these deities derive their being from one anterior, called Zarwan, though who and what this being was or is, they are not agreed. They believe in great numbers of good and evil angels, who have the power and the disposition to interfere in human affairs, and their religion consists in part of rites and supplications to procure the aid and protection of the one class, and of deprecations and other means to avert the power and displeasure of the other class. They have great reverence for fire, and they worship, gazing at the sun, moon, and stars, and often at fire wherever seen. Some among them say they contemplate the sun, moon, etc., only as symbols of the Deity, and that their worship is really aimed to the invisible, omnipresent, and omnipotent God. But probably many and perhaps most of them when gazing upon the sun in their worship, think of nothing beyond the visible object they are contemplating.

In their temples consecrated fire is kept continually burning. It is preserved with much care, and many rites and ceremonies are performed upon it and to it. Fragrant kinds of wood, gums, spices, etc., are thrown upon it, or offered to it. Their reverence for fire prevents their even using it for the self-indulgence of smoking tobacco, or any other substance. And as gunpowder can only be used in connection with fire, their reverence for this element prevents their using gunpowder for the destruction of human or of animal life. So they never become soldiers nor huntsmen. I am not aware that they ever make an image or symbol of any deity, and consecrating it, worship it as the Hindus prepare and worship the idols of their deities. But the Parsees address their prayers and praises to great numbers of supposed spiritual beings. They also address their prayers to created objects in such a way and spirit as appear clearly to deserve the name of religious homage.

The manner in which they dispose of their dead is peculiar. The Hindus generally burn their dead. The Mohammedans bury their dead. But the Parsees neither burn nor bury their dead. Large cemeteries are prepared with much labor and expense. They are open, (have no covering over them,) and are surrounded with high walls. They are intrusted to a particular class among them, and no others ever go into them. These persons take charge of all dead bodies, and perform the ceremonies of disposing of them. These bodies are carried into the cemeteries and deposited there, exposed to the sun, atmosphere, etc. The bodies of the wealthy are covered with a screen of brass wire, but the bodies of the common people have no covering put over them, and so are soon devoured by vultures, crows, etc., which may generally be seen in great numbers hovering over the cemeteries, and sitting on the walls. The bones are from time to time collected and put into a part of the cemetery till they are all decomposed. They attach great importance to their rites of burial.

Many of the Parsees are wealthy, have large and well-furnished houses, well-cultivated gardens, keep elegant carriages, etc. Women occupy a higher social position among them than among the Hindus or Mohammedans. Many women have some education, and the higher classes have shown a desire to have their daughters educated, and have established schools for this purpose. They have evinced more public spirit and liberality, and they associate with Europeans more than any other class of the native population.* A considerable number of them have been to Europe. Several Parsees have professed Christianity, and among the native ordained missionaries in India, are two well-educated and respectable men who were originally Parsees, but are in connection with the Free Church of Scotland in Bombay.

* The North American Review for July 1, 1851, contains a notice of Sir Jamsetjee Jejeebhoy, one of the Parsee merchants of Bombay. I was acquainted with Sir Jamsetjee, and saw many instances and monuments of his liberality. It has been lately stated in some of the Bombay journals, that the amount of his benefactions to public works and institutions, the cause of education, and to objects of charity and religion, has exceeded 1,000,000 dollars. And yet he is in possession of a princely fortune, all the result of his own industry and enterprise.

PART VI.

CHRISTIANITY IN INDIA.*

CHAPTER I.

THE SYRIAN CHURCHES OF MALABAR.

THE early history of Christianity in India is involved in much obscurity. Eusebius, the father of ecclesiastical history, says that "St. Bartholomew went to India." Socrates, who continued Eusebius's work, says, that in the division of the gentile world, which the apostles made among them, "India was assigned to St. Bartholomew." It appears uncertain, however, from his description of the country called India as contiguous to Ethiopia, what country was then intended by this name. And in another part of his work he says that India was not enlightened by the gospel till the reign of Constantine, or some time in the early part of the 4th century. There have also been many traditions in India that St. Thomas preached the gospel at different places in that country. Such have been the traditions of the Syrians or Nestorian Christians on the coast of Malabar, and these traditions have generally been believed by the Roman Catholic missionaries in India. But no mention is made of the tradition by Eusebius or Socrates, from which we may infer that they knew nothing of it, or if they did, that they had no confidence in it. Indeed, it is said that no mention of any such tradition is found in any of the Latin or Greek historians before the 14th century.

La Croze in his learned work called the History of Christianity in India, sums up these traditions thus: — "In the divis-

* An account of the Ecclesiastical Establishment for the European population has been given (see p. 308 and 358). This Part has respect to the propagation and state of Christianity among the native population.

ion of the world which was made by the Apostles, India fell to the lot of St. Thomas, who after having established Christianity in Arabia Felix and in the island of Socotra, proceeded to Cranganore, where the principal king of the country then resided. It was there that the fabulous adventures happened, of which we read in this Apostle's life, written by the pretended Abdias of Babylon. The Apostle having established many churches at Cranganore, proceeded to Quilon, a large city on the same coast where he converted many persons to the Christian faith. From this place he proceeded to the eastern coast, now called Coromandel, and lived for a while at Meliapore, a town now called by Europeans St. Thome, where he is said to have converted the king and all the people. Here a persecution arose, and the good Apostle was put to death by the idolaters, who were set on by their priests, the Brahmins."

Such is the sum of the traditions concerning St. Thomas in India, and they are generally believed by the Syrian Christians of Malabar and by Roman Catholics. But La Croze does not think them worthy of any credit. Some learned Roman Catholics in Europe do not put any confidence in these traditions. All ancient churches had strong motives, in their desires to sustain their comparative superiority, or at least their equality in rank, as well as to justify their doctrines and practices, to ascribe their origin, rules of discipline, etc., to the Apostles. And the reasons for their wishing for the reputation of having such an origin generally increased, as they departed more and more from the plain doctrines and simple usages of primitive Christianity. The best Protestant ecclesiastical historians say nothing concerning these traditions, from which it is evident they did not consider them as deserving any credit or consideration.

Christianity was early established in Egypt, and the church in Alexandria gloried in having been founded by St. Mark, and having him for her first bishop. There was then much commerce between Europe and India through Egypt, and many Christians would in this way visit the countries on the Red Sea and India. The people engaged in this commerce would soon become acquainted with the gospel, and considering the earnestness and ardor which then pervaded Christians generally, many would be likely soon to embrace it. At the Council of

Nice, in A. D. 325, Johannes, one of the bishops, signed his name as Bishop of Persia and India. There is not sufficient reason for believing that Christianity had made any considerable progress at that time in India; probably the territory designated by this name was the country adjoining Persia, perhaps on the Indus. There is evidence that the Syrian or Nestorian churches in Malabar were commenced as early as the 5th or 6th centuries, and perhaps before that time. The Mohammedan religion had its origin in the 7th century, and Mohammedans soon obtained possession of the countries separating India from Europe, and for a long period little was definitely known in Europe concerning the state of Christianity in the southern countries of Asia. In the 9th century there was an Armenian, some accounts describe him as a merchant and some describe him as a bishop, perhaps he united the business of the former with the dignity and office of the latter, who lived somewhere on the Malabar coast. He was a man of "immense wealth," and obtained large privileges from the kings of the country for the Christians. From this time they had some government of their own. Their chief is called *Raja* in the history of the country. This title would not necessarily imply that he was not dependent upon, or subordinate to, some king or prince of the country, though invested with power over the Christian population, somewhat like the state in which Christian communities have often been in Mohammedan countries, and now are in the Turkish dominions.

The Portuguese were surprised to find on their arriving in India a large body of people professing the Christian religion, and on inquiring into the state and faith of these Christians they were yet more surprised to find they were so heretical in their doctrines and discipline. They had never heard of the Pope, they knew nothing of the Latin language, and could trace their history for 1,300 years to the patriarch of Babylon, Seleucia, or Mosul, probably a succession of patriarchs, only having their residence in different places. At that time the Popes claimed to be the spiritual head of all the world, nor were they at all scrupulous in respect to means for enforcing obedience to their supremacy. The purpose of the court of Rome, as soon as the state and character of the Syrian Christians became known, was formed to bring them into subjection. The court of Lisbon and all the Portuguese ecclesiastics were expected to coöperate as good Catholics in using means in bringing about this great end. The Portuguese bishop and all his ecclesiastics said to the Malabar Christians, "Your church belongs to the Pope, and you must acknowledge him for your spiritual head." The Malabar Christians replied, "We never before heard of any Pope, and we have no need of him to govern us." Still they were disposed to treat the Romanists with kindness and in the spirit of Christian fellowship. They permitted them to preach in their churches, and they hoped to derive benefit in various ways from intercourse with them and from their power and influence with the princes of the country. The Romanists had only one object to accomplish, namely, to bring the Syrians into subjection to the Pope; and all their intercourse, and influence, and efforts were directed to this end. An ecclesiastic called Father Vincent opened a school called a college at Cranganore to spread the doctrines of his church. A similar school was subsequently opened at Voipecotta. These efforts very much disturbed and alarmed the Syrians, while yet they did not produce the effects which the Romanists expected. So some more decisive measures were deemed necessary, and various schemes were considered. As the Syrian bishop was the principal obstacle to their success, the Romanists resolved to remove him. He was arrested at Cochin, carried a prisoner to Goa, and thence sent to Portugal. It was their intention to send him to Rome. But soon after arriving in Lisbon, finding himself in a strange country and a prisoner in the hands of his enemies, his fortitude began to fail. He had an interview with one of the cardinals, to whom he so far acknowledged the supremacy of the Pope and promised to reform the churches under his spiritual jurisdiction that it was deemed expedient to send him back to India. The Romanists were fearful of the consequences of his being removed in the manner he was, and of his long absence from his people. Nor were their fears without some reason. The Syrians, deprived of their spiritual head, and fearful that yet more violent means would be used, took measures to procure another bishop from Mosul, and he arrived among them and entered upon the duties of his office before his predecessor returned from Portugal. A schism now took place among the Syrians. One party was supported by all the power and influence of the Portuguese, and the other contained the greater part of the Syrian Christians. In the progress and continuance of this schism, one Syrian bishop was seized and sent to Portugal and thence to Rome. This bishop appears to have been a man of weak character, if not of corrupt principles, and he is accused of having been sometimes guilty of much duplicity and hypocrisy. Another bishop was carried to Lisbon, and there died in prison. His only crime appears to have been a determination not to acknowledge the Pope's supremacy, nor to change the creed of his church to make it agree with the church of Rome. And for the same reasons another bishop was carried a prisoner to Goa and perished in the Inquisition. These aggressive measures were continued on the part of the Portuguese, and at a Provincial Council held in Goa in 1585, which the Syrians were summoned to attend, several decrees were passed concerning the state and doctrines of their church.

In 1599, Archbishop Menezes, having been for some time making previous arrangements among the Romanists and the Syrians, convoked the great synod of Diamper. At this synod the Archbishop presided, and among the decrees one was that "all the Syrian books on ecclesiastical subjects, that could be found, should be burned." This decree was immediately carried into effect, and even to this day "the Syrians say that while the books were burning, the Archbishop went round the church in procession chanting a song of triumph." Concerning the council at Diamper and other means used to bring these churches into subjection to the Pope, Mosheim in his history of the 16th century, says, "The Christians of St. Thomas who inhabited the coasts of India, suffered much from the methods employed by the Portuguese to engage them to embrace the doctrine and discipline of the Church of Rome, and to abandon the religion of their ancestors, which was much more simple and infinitely less absurd. The finishing stroke was put to the violence and brutality of these attempts by Don Alexis de Menezes, Archbishop of Goa, who about the conclusion of this century, calling the Jesuits to his assistance, obliged this unhappy and reluctant people to embrace the religion of Rome and to acknowledge the Pope's supreme jurisdiction, against both of which acts they had always expressed the utmost abhorrence. These violent councils and arrogant proceedings of Menezes and his associates were condemned by such of the Roman Catholics as were most remarkable for their equity and wisdom." *

The Syrian Christians appeared for a while to be astonished and bewildered by the violence of these proceedings, and the power apparently arrayed against them and liable to fall upon them, if they should incur its further displeasure. Some of the priests and churches continued in connection with Rome, using their liturgy in the Syrian language but altered and expurgated by Menezes. These have been called "the Syrio-Roman Christians," and are chiefly near the sea-coast. But many of the priests and churches refused to conform to this new order of doctrine and discipline, and have retained their ancient liturgy, rites, and ministry. These are called by their former name, "the Syrian Christians of Malabar."

For a long time little was known concerning these Christians in Europe or in America, and many yet living can remember the feelings of deep interest which were excited by Buchanan's account of them in 1807. The Church Missionary Society subsequently commenced a mission among them in the hope of effecting a reformation of doctrine and discipline. These efforts, however, have not produced the good results which were expected, these churches still retaining their long cherished forms, doctrines, rites, etc. Gibbon, near the close of the last century estimated the whole population of the Syrian Christians at 200,000. The Abbe Dubois was of the opinion they did not exceed 100,000 of whom two thirds were Romish Syrians. The Annals of the Propagation Society in a late No. say, that the Romish Syrio-Christians amount to nearly 100,000. The number of the original churches is about 50,000.

The liturgies of the Syrian Christians and their formularies of worship, and of their rites and ordinances, are in the ancient Syriac language, which very few among them understand, and it is not strange that early travellers among them should be mistaken in some matters, and so publish accounts of their doc-

* A particular account of these violent measures of Menezes is given by La Croze in his Histoire du Christianisme aux Indes. Also by Hough in his History of Christianity in India, who has given the Decrees of the Council of Diamper.

trines, etc., which further inquiry and research have shown to be in some respects incorrect. Their liturgies, formularies, etc., have been carefully examined and translated into English, by Dr. Mill, of Bishops College, and by Rev. J. Peet, who for many years lived among them. The following is given as a summary of the errors they contain.

"The principal errors of the Syrian Church may be enumerated under the following heads:—

1. Transubstantiation.

2. The sacrifice of the Mass, in which it is said that the priest offers Christ for the quick and the dead to give remission of pain and guilt.

3. Prayers for the dead.

4. Purgatory, or the possibility of transition from an unpardoned to a pardoned state between the period of death and judgment.

5. Worshipping the virgin Mary, supplicating her intercession, and observing a fast in her honor.

6. Worship of saints.

7. Prayers in an unknown tongue.

8. Extreme unction.

9. Attributing to the clergy the power to curse and destroy men's bodies and souls.

10. The having pictures in their churches representing God the Father.

11. Prayers to the altar and to the chancel.

Connected with these are the elevation of the host, the burning of incense and ringing of bells at the time of elevation, the priest receiving the host alone, etc."

These are certainly all very grave, and some of them fundamental errors, and they have formed a part of their doctrines, and been incorporated in their rules and worship of their church for some centuries, probably from their first settlement in India. Great changes are required to reform such errors, and to restore such a church to the purity and simplicity of the Gospel.

CHAPTER II.

ROMAN CATHOLIC MISSIONS AND CHURCH IN INDIA.

To spread a knowledge of the Romish faith, was one of the avowed objects of the Portuguese in prosecuting their voyages of discovery, and making their conquests in heathen countries. For this purpose missionaries of different orders, as Jesuits, Dominicans, etc., went out in their ships to remain in the countries discovered, and to convert the inhabitants to Christianity. Many people also of different trades and professions went out in these ships, and became permanent residents in the places of which the Portuguese took possession. Thus numerous colonies were formed. "Immediately on their taking possession of Goa, a church was dedicated to St. Catharine, who was solemnly chosen to be the patroness of the city, and the protectress of the Portuguese in India." Marriages between the Portuguese and the native inhabitants were encouraged by the Portuguese authorities, and they became frequent. It is said by one of the Portuguese historians in praise of Albuquerque, the greatest of all their viceroys in India, that he did much to promote intermarriages between his countrymen and the inhabitants of the country, and, as in all such cases the native party was always required to profess the Romish faith, the nominally Christian population in the Portuguese settlements was by these means greatly increased.

In 1542, the celebrated Francis Xavier reached Goa. He had acquired a high reputation for piety in Europe, and had long felt a strong desire to preach the Gospel in heathen countries. His conduct, on reaching the long-desired field of his future labor, was in accordance with his profession and character. He passed the first night alone in one of the churches that he might have all the time for undisturbed meditation and prayer. There were many priests and monks then in Goa, and all were under the superintendence of a bishop, but the state of religion was very low. Xavier's zeal and labors soon excited attention, and he had the satisfaction of seeing some reformation of manners, and better attendance upon the sacraments. Having spent a few months in Goa, he proceeded into the districts near Cape Comorin. The people here were pariars and fishermen. Some of them had been baptized by missionaries who had previously been among them, but the greater part were still heathen in profession, and all were much alike in practice. In a letter to some of his friends he wrote:—"You may judge what manner of life I lead here by what I relate to you. I am wholly ignorant of the language of the people, and they know as little of mine, and I have no interpreter. All I can perform is to baptize the children and serve the sick, an employment easily understood without the help of an interpreter, by only minding what they want." It appears from a further account, that he afterwards got the Lord's Prayer, the Ten Commandments, and some passages of Scripture translated into the language of the people, and these lessons he committed to memory. He says, "I went about with my bell in my hand and gathered all I met, both men and children, and instructed them in Christian doctrine as well as I could." His zeal and earnest affection towards them, so unlike any thing they had ever before seen, excited their attention and sympathy, and according to his views of conversion, his labors were accompanied with great success. In his account of his labors, he says that "in one month he baptized with his own hand 10,000 idolaters, and that not unfrequently in one day he baptized a well-peopled village." Having pursued his labors for some months in these districts, he returned to Goa, and wrote several very earnest letters to Europe, entreating that more missionaries might be sent to India. He preached in several places in the southern parts of the peninsula, when some events occurred which he thought were intimations from God that it was his duty to visit some countries further east. So he proceeded to Malacca, Amboyna, Ternate, and Japan, everywhere exhibiting his accustomed zeal. He continued his missionary labors in different places till his death in 1552, nearly 10 years from his arrival in India. He died in the island of Sancian, near the coast of China, but his body

43

was brought to Goa, and inclosed in a shrine in the church of Bom Jesus.*

In 1560, only 8 years after the death of Xavier, the Inquisition was established in Goa. The institution was on a large scale, having cells in the prison part of it sufficient for 200 criminals. It continued for more than 2 centuries, and its secret proceedings and public exhibitions showed a spirit of intolerance, persecution, and cruelty, to which heathenism can scarcely furnish any parallel.† In 1775 it was suppressed by royal edict from the king of Portugal. But in a few years it was restored, though in a somewhat modified form, and continued till 1812, when it was finally suppressed through the influence of the British government. The edifice soon fell to ruins, which have since been removed to be used for other purposes, so that only the place where the Inquisition once stood is now pointed out to the inquiring traveller. ‡

There is no part of the history of Romish missions in India, which exhibits scenes of more interest than some which occurred at Delhi. Acber, the greatest of all the Mogul emperors of India, and at that time the greatest monarch in the world, having become dissatisfied with Mohammedanism, the religion of his ancestors and of his country, sent a letter to the governor of

* In 1774, nearly 200 years after Xavier's death, Pope Benedict XIV. caused his name to be enrolled in the calendar of the saints, and gave him the title of "Protector of the Indies." From that time he has been regarded as the tutelar saint of Goa. When Dr. Buchanan was there in 1806, the Archbishop, referring to the long quiet the city had enjoyed, while most cities in India had been besieged, and many of them plundered, "ascribed the preservation of Goa to the prayers of St. Xavier." — "There is an old idol of Xavier near Cape Comorin, to which many Hindus as well Roman Catholics go on pilgrimage."— Thus Xavier has a place among the saints of the Romish Church and the gods of the heathen.

† The learned Mosheim says, "It may be affirmed from records of the highest credit and authority that the Inquisition erected by the Jesuits at Goa, and the penal laws they employed so freely in the propagation of the gospel, contributed much more than their arguments and exhortations, which were but sparingly used, to engage the Indians to embrace Christianity."

‡ Buchanan in his Christian Researches has given an account of the Inquisition at Goa, as it was in 1807. The best account I have seen is Dellon's *Relation de l'Inquisition de Goa.* Dr. Dellon was confined in the Inquisition for more than 2 years.

Goa, requesting that some qualified Christian teachers would come to him, assuring them of a safe journey and an honorable reception. He also requested that they would bring with them all the books of the law and the gospel, meaning complete copies of the Christian Scriptures.* This letter from the emperor naturally excited great attention at Goa. Three Romish priests were selected for this important mission, and they soon embarked for Surat. On arriving at Surat, the governor, who had received instructions from the emperor concerning them, received them with great respect and furnished them with an escort of cavalry to proceed to Delhi. The emperor received them with much honor, and offered them every thing they might require. "When an image of the crucifixion was exhibited, he showed his reverence for it by successively bowing, kneeling, and falling prostrate before it, thus conforming to the respective modes of the Mohammedan, Christian, and Hindu modes of worship. A richly ornamented image of Mary was then exhibited, and gazing upon it he declared it to be indeed a worthy representation of the Queen of Heaven. A book purporting to be the Bible in four different languages was then presented to him, which he received with great reverence, and kissing it placed it upon his head." Thus the Jesuits describe their first religious interview with him. They were greatly encouraged by these favorable indications, and requested the emperor to make arrangements for them to have a public discussion with the Moolahs upon the comparative merits of Christianity and Mohammedanism. The request was soon granted, and the Jesuits and the Moolahs had their discussion before the emperor and his court. The Jesuits in their accounts of this discussion describe their arguments as convincing and unanswerable, and probably the Moolahs said the same concerning their side of the cause. The emperor assured the priests privately that he was much pleased with their reasons and arguments, which encouraged them to hope that he would soon declare his conviction of the truth of Christianity. Considerable time passed without any thing more being said on the subject, and when the emperor again adverted to it he told them that one of the Moolahs had offered to bring their argu-

* For some account of Acber's religious principles, see p. 109 and 110.

ments for the truth of Christianity and against Mohammedanism, namely, that their religion was at first confirmed by miracles, and that these had never ceased to take place in their church, while no miracles were wrought at first to confirm the truth of the Koran, and none now took place among its followers — all such arguments and objections this Moolah offered to bring at once to a practical issue thus: — He would himself take the Koran in his hands, and calling upon Mohammed he would leap into a furnace, and either of the priests might take the Bible in his hands, and calling upon Jesus or Mary might leap into the furnace — both to do it at the same time before the emperor and his court. — The party whose religion was true, would come out of the furnace, himself and book safe and uninjured, and the party whose religion was false, would be consumed. — And then the emperor and his court would be satisfied whether Christianity or Mohammedanism is the true faith, and which will secure the salvation of mankind.

The Jesuits were much perplexed by this proposal, and they endeavored to satisfy the emperor that such a trial was not a proper way to ascertain the truth of a religion which had already abundant evidence in its favor, if men would only examine it, that they had exhibited the evidence once and were ready to do it again, and they solicited another public discussion. It was at length arranged that there should be another public discussion between the Jesuits and the Moolahs. This second discussion, like the former, took place before the emperor and his court. The Jesuits thought they had the advantage in reason and argument, but the result was no more satisfactory to the other party than the former discussion. The Moolahs all now declared that any further discussion or controversy was useless, and that it only remained to bring the great question in dispute at once to the practical issue which they formerly proposed, or for the priests to acknowledge the truth of the Koran. The emperor also intimated to the Jesuits that the offer of the Moolah appeared to be reasonable, especially as they believed that miracles still continued to take place in their church. The priests, however, were of a different opinion and declined accepting the offer.

These priests made a long sojourn at the court of Acber. He

treated them with much respect and gave them liberty freely to propagate their religious sentiments, assuring them of his protection of themselves and their proselytes. He had frequent conversations with them on religious subjects, but he gave them less and less reason to hope he would ever embrace Christianity. At length some public affairs required the emperor to proceed to Bengal, and the priests took leave of him and returned to Goa, having lived in Delhi for 12 years.

After an interval of 8 years, Acber again wrote to the governor of Goa, requesting that some Christian teachers might be sent to him. The request was answered and some priests proceeded to his court and were received with great respect. They were at first much encouraged by his inquiries and the spirit he manifested. But after a few interviews and conversations with them, the interest he manifested in religion diminished, and he apparently became indifferent on the subject. As they now seldom saw him, and their situation at court was becoming unpleasant, they left Delhi and returned to Goa. Still the emperor appears not to have continued in a state of indifference to religion, for after another interval of 4 years he again wrote to Goa for Christian teachers so earnestly and expressed such sentiments on the subject that, notwithstanding their former painful experience, another mission was sent to him. The members of this mission were at first more encouraged than either of their predecessors. But after a while on becoming more intimately acquainted with his habits and sentiments, they were disheartened and returned to Goa. This great emperor's religious principles have been the subject of much inquiry and doubt. In the early part of his life he appears to have been a sincere believer in the creed of his family and nation; then for some years to have been in doubt between Mohammedanism and Christianity, and in the last years of his life, excepting now and then seasons of doubt and anxiety concerning his own religious state, he was a deist, tolerating all the systems of religion professed in his empire, but not believing in the divine origin of any of them. These sceptical sentiments and the equal protection he extended to all classes of people without regard to their religious sentiments so long as they were good subjects, gave great offence to Moham-

43*

medans, but made his government popular among all his other subjects.

We cannot but admire the moral courage, the zeal and the perseverance of these Jesuits at the court of Acber. Had all the means and arguments they used for the conversion of the emperor and the introduction of Christianity at his court, been of a corresponding character, it appears not unlikely they might have witnessed very different results. Acber requested these Jesuits to prepare for his use a true history of Christ, and they prepared and presented to him a work which they declared in the preface was such as he had requested. They declared that the work "had been compiled from the Holy Gospels and other books of the prophets," such are their words. This work has been preserved, and it is as far from being a true History of Christ as the traditions and principles of the Roman Catholic Church are from being the doctrines contained in the New Testament. The strange stories and foolish legends contained in this work concerning Peter and Mary indicate that the Jesuits who compiled it, were more anxious to recommend Mary as the object of religious homage, and Peter and consequently the Pope, as the successor of Christ, than they were to exhibit the dignity, the grace, and the glory of the Redeemer and Saviour of sinners. Need we wonder that this great emperor and his learned Moolahs, after becoming acquainted with the traditions and doctrines, and the rites and usages of these Jesuits and their church, and supposing that this work was a true exhibition of Christianity, and that it showed only what was contained in the word of God,—need we wonder that such men should lose all respect for Christianity and manifest no desire for further inquiry?

The conversion of the natives to Christianity was pursued with vigor for more than 200 years from the arrival of the Portuguese in India. In all places subject to their power this work was favored by legislative enactments, and all in authority were enjoined and expected to use their influence in promoting it. Of Albuquerque, who was governor of all the Portuguese possessions in India, it is said that "he greatly favored intermarriages between the European settlers and the natives." The native party in all such cases must previously profess Christianity, and the offspring of all such connections would belong to the Christian community. The government appears to have been of the opinion that there would be no security for the continuance of their power, if their people did not embrace Christianity, and so come under the influence of the hierarchy.* Cottineau says, that "Mohammedans and Hindus were allowed to sojourn in Goa, but to exercise no public act of their religion." Another Roman Catholic historian says, that "no Hindu or Mohammedan was allowed to practise the rites of his religion publicly in any Portuguese settlement in India under pain of death." Probably the laws differed at different times. The same policy was probably pursued in their other possessions. He also says, that when "the Jesuits had converted a great part of the inhabitants of Salsette,† in order the better as they thought to detach the remainder of the inhabitants from the worship of idols, they destroyed all the temples and the pagodas."—"Nearly 1,200 temples were thus demolished, and the idols were broken to pieces." The same course was pursued in other places where it could prudently be done. Great numbers of priests, monks, and

* "Albuquerque viewed it as an essential object to attach the natives to his government, for which purpose he adopted a somewhat singular expedient. Having numerous female captives, some belonging to the first families in the country, he treated them in the most honorable manner; but not satisfied with this, he proceeded to arrange matrimonial connections between them and his Portuguese followers, without leaving them much choice on either side. It was made an absolute condition of the brides that they should embrace Christianity, an obstacle which was not found insurmountable, the prejudices of caste and religion being less deeply rooted there than in other parts of the East. A few such marriages being formed, the viceroy showed the parties peculiar favor, and bestowed upon the husbands some of his best appointments. The principal families finding themselves aggrandized by these connections, so far from objecting to them, gave their countenance to new matches. An odd story is told of a great number of weddings being celebrated at once with a splendid festival, when the lights being prematurely extinguished, it became difficult for the parties to recognize each other, and they fell into many mistakes. Next morning an investigation was proposed, but on mature reflection it was judged best that each should remain contented with the wife that had accidentally fallen to his lot, though different from the one to whom the church had united him, and the affair furnished to the army only an occasion of mirth."—*Murray's History of British India*, p. 127.

† An island or district near Goa, and not the one of this name near Bombay.

friars, as Jesuits, Dominicans, Capuchins, etc., engaged in this work. Money was freely expended in this cause, and thousands spent their lives in self-denying labors and sufferings to promote it. In all places subject to the Portuguese they could rely on the government for protection for themselves and their converts, and the power of government was often exerted to assist them in the dominions of the native princes. Of this influence the proceedings of Archbishop Menezes, in his aggressive measures upon the Syrian Church affords a striking example. Such was understood to be his connection with the Portuguese authorities and such was the support he was then receiving from them, that to resist him in any way appeared certain to incur their displeasure and all its dreaded consequences.

But the missionaries did not limit their labors for the conversion of the native population to the Portuguese possessions, nor to places where they could rely upon the protection and influence of government. They went into the territories of the native princes, but here they pursued a different course in carrying on the work of converting the people. The following extract is from the works of one who was himself a Roman Catholic missionary for more than 30 years in the southern parts of the peninsula, and must have been well informed on all such matters. Referring to the Jesuits, he says: —

"By degrees those missionaries introduced themselves into the inland country. They saw that in order to fix the attention of these people, gain their confidence and get a hearing, it was indispensably necessary to respect their prejudices and even to conform to their dress, their manner of living, and forms of society; in short, scrupulously to adopt the costumes and practices of the country. With this persuasion they at their first outset announced themselves as European brahmins, come from a distance of 5,000 leagues from the western part of the *Djamboody*, for the double purpose of imparting and receiving knowledge from their brother brahmins in India. Almost all these first missionaries were more or less acquainted with astronomy and medicine, the two sciences best calculated to ingratiate them with the natives of every description. After announcing themselves as brahmins they made it their study to imitate that tribe. They put on a Hindu dress of *cavy* or yellow color, the same as that used by the Indian religious teachers and penitents. They made frequent ablutions. Whenever they showed themselves in public, they applied to their foreheads, paste made of sandal-wood,* as used by the brahmins. They scrupulously abstained from every kind of animal food as well as from intoxicating liquors, entirely faring like brahmins, on vegetables and milk. It was by such a life of almost incredible privations and restraints that they insinuated themselves among these people. Fully aware of the unalterable attachment of the natives to their own usages and practices, they made it their principal study not to hurt their feelings by attacking all at once the superstitions with which most of their customs are infected. They judged it more prudent at the beginning to overlook many of them, and wait for a more favorable time to put the converts right on these subjects. Their color, their talents, their virtues, and above all their perfect disinterestedness rendered them acceptable even to the Hindu princes, who astonished at the novelty and singularity of these circumstances, bestowed their protection on these extraordinary men, and gave them full freedom to preach their religion and made proselytes to it." †

Of the missionaries thus engaged in propagating the Romish system in India, Robert de Nobili, who was a near relative of the Pope and a nephew of Cardinal Bellarmine, was the most remarkable. He and his companions assumed heathen and significant names, and did not scruple to add forgery and even perjury to their hypocrisy. In his History of Christianity in India, Hough says:—"Robert de Nobili pretended to belong to the highest order of brahmins, and to stop the mouths of his opposers, and particularly of those who treated his character of brahmin as a deception, he produced an old dirty parchment, on which he had forged in the ancient character, a deed showing that the brahmins of Rome were of much older date than those of India, and that the Jesuits of Rome descended in a direct line from the god Brahma. And when the authenticity of this smoky parchment was called in question by some Indian unbelievers, Robert de Nobili declared *upon oath* before the assembly of brahmins at Madura that he really derived his origin from the god Brahma."

* One of the distinguishing marks of the Hindu religion.

† Abbe Dubois, on the State of Christianity in India, p. 5 and 6.

Nobili and his associates used yet other means to establish their character as brahmins and the divine origin of the religion they taught. All the Hindus believe their Vedas to be the oldest and most sacred of all their religious books. These works are commonly reckoned 4 in number, and copies are very scarce. They are held in great veneration, only the brahmins being allowed to possess them, to read them, or even to hear them read. The Jesuits, finding that these books were regarded as the fountain of all divine knowledge, composed a work which they declared was one of the Vedas, in which they interwove an account of Christianity, its origin and doctrines, with much matter of a different character. The work exhibited much knowledge of the native language, and in the opinion of a distinguished orientalist, "it was written with consummate skill." It was composed in a style so closely resembling the true Vedas that many learned brahmins did not discover the forgery. The authors hoped in this way to show the truth of the Gospels and the divine origin of Christianity. This work was not known in Europe for many years. In 1761 it became known to Voltaire, who believing, or to affecting to believe, that it was a genuine Hindu Veda, and of contemporaneous origin with the other Vedas, used it to disprove the truth of the Scriptures, as though some of the facts, etc., contained in the Gospels concerning Jesus Christ were really contained in a heathen work written several centuries before Christ appeared in the world. Voltaire's arguments against Christianity excited much attention, and this pretended Veda was soon published at Paris. It was examined by M. Sonnerat, who satisfied the public that it was only a Veda in pretence, being in reality a work of recent origin, composed by some of the Jesuits in some of their missions in India. It was subsequently examined with much care by Mr. Ellis * of Madras, a distinguished orientalist, who showed the object and character of the work;—"that the Ezour Veda was purely a literary forgery, or rather as the object of the author or authors was not literary distinction—that it was a work of religious imposition without any parallel in the history of the world."

Concerning Nobili and the measures he and his associates

* Asiatic Researches, 14th vol. Art. 1st.

used to propagate Christianity in India, Mosheim, in his Ecclesiastical History, says: — "Considering on the one hand that the Indians beheld with an eye of prejudice and aversion all Europeans, and on the other that they held in the highest veneration the order of brahmins as descended from the gods, and that impatient of their rulers they paid an implicit and unlimited obedience to them alone, Nobili assumed the appearance and title of a brahmin that had come from a far country, and by besmearing his countenance and imitating the most austere and painful methods of living that the *sunyasees* (devotees) observed, he at length persuaded that credulous people that he was in reality a member of the venerable order of brahmins. By this stratagem he gained over to Christianity 12 eminent brahmins, whose example and influence engaged a prodigious number of the people to hear the instructions and receive the doctrine of the famous missionary."

These accounts show that these Romish missionaries, instead of converting the Hindus to Christianity, had themselves become Hindus and brahmins in profession and practice, and it would not be reasonable to expect that while they continued to sustain this character, they could effect any change by their labors or influence beyond some modification of Hinduism. And such was the result. When their conduct, the doctrines they taught, and the character of their proselytes became known, much dissatisfaction was felt among the Portuguese, "who accused these Jesuits of the most culpable indulgence in tolerating and winking at all kinds of idolatrous superstitions among their proselytes, and with having themselves rather become converts to the idolatrous worship of the Hindus, by conforming to many of their practices and superstitions, than making the Indians converts to the Christian religion." These complaints were made to the Pope, who was earnestly requested to interpose his authority. The Jesuits also sent deputations to Rome to explain their conduct and vindicate the course they had pursued. "This disgusting contest," says the Abbe Dubois, "which was carried on in several instances with much acrimony, lasted more than 40 years before it came to an end." The result of this controversy was that the Jesuits were censured by the Pope, who required them to refrain from certain specified rites and practices, and to carry out this reform among all their proselytes. The Jesuits complied with the decree of the Pope in respect to their own conduct, but they were able to effect only a partial reformation among their proselytes, of whom a large part preferred to continue as they were — a class of the Hindu population.

The great struggle between the English and the French for ascendency in India occurring just at this time, many Europeans found their way into different parts of the country, and the Hindus discovered to their great astonishment, "that those missionaries whom their color, their talents, and other qualities had induced them to regard as extraordinary beings, as men coming from another world, were in fact nothing else but disguised Feringas (Europeans), and that their country, their religion, and original education, were the same with those of the vile and contemptible Feringas, who had lately invaded their country. This event proved the last blow to the interests of the Romish religion in those provinces. No more conversions were made, and apostasy became almost general in several districts." Another important event also occurred at that time. The order of the Jesuits was suppressed and the proselytes became dependent, to a great extent, upon native priests who had been educated in India, who in education and Christian character were very inferior to their predecessors, who had but little influence over their countrymen that had assumed a Christian profession, and still less respect among those who still adhered to the Hindu system.

In the latter part of the last century, the Romish Christians in the southern parts of the peninsula were severely persecuted by the Mohammedan sovereign of Mysore. The following account is from the Abbe Dubois' Letters on Christianity in India: —

"When the late Tippoo Sultan sought to extend his own religious creed all over his dominions, and make by little and little all the inhabitants in Mysore converts to Islamism, he wished to begin this fanatical undertaking with the native Christians living in his country, as the most odious to him on the score of their religion. In consequence, in the year 1784, he gave secret orders to his officers in the different districts to make the most diligent inquiries after the places where Christians were to be found, and to cause the whole of them to be seized on the same day, and conducted under strong escorts to Seringapatam. This order was punctually carried into execution. Very few of them escaped, and I have it from good authority, that the aggregate number of persons seized in this manner amounted to more than 60,000.

"Some time after their arrival at Seringapatam, Tippoo ordered the whole to undergo the rite of circumcision and be made converts to Mohammedanism. The Christians were put together during the several days that the ceremony lasted; and O shame! O scandal!—will it be believed in the Christian world?—no one, not a single individual among so many thousands, had courage enough to confess in these trying circumstances, and become a martyr to his religion. The whole apostatized *en masse*, and without resistance or protestation, tamely underwent the operation of circumcision; no one among them possessing resolution enough to say, 'I am a Christian, and will die rather than renounce my religion.' So general a defection, so dastardly an apostasy is, I believe, unexampled in the annals of Christianity.

"After the fall of Tippoo Sultan, most of those apostates came back to be reconciled to their former religion, saying that their apostasy had been only external, and that they always kept in their hearts the true faith in Christ. About 2,000 of them fell in my way, and nearly 20,000 returned to the Mangalore district, from whence they had been carried away, and rebuilt there their former places of worship. God preserve them all from being exposed in future to the same trials, for should this happen, I have every reason (notwithstanding their solemn protestations when again reconciled to Christianity,) to apprehend the same sad results, that is to say, a tame submission and a general apostasy."

The Romish missionaries did not require their proselytes to renounce caste when they were baptized, nor to do any thing afterwards which was contrary to the rules and usages of caste. Indeed, some of these missionaries, as we have seen, pretended themselves to be brahmins, and they observed all the rules of caste which were necessary to sustain their assumed character. They refused to enter the houses of Hindus of low caste, or to administer to them the rites of the church. And to suit their system of proselyting to the prejudices of the Hindus, they had some missionaries who pretended to be of lower caste, and these could consistently associate with the Hindus and proselytes of low caste. In this way the new community formed under the teaching of the missionaries, appeared like a counterpart of brahminism, the proselytes retaining what they regarded as the most important and essential part of their national religion. Father Manduit, one of the missionaries, says:—"The catechist of low caste can never be employed to teach any of a caste above him. We must have pariar catechists to teach pariars, brahmin catechists to teach brahmins, etc." He describes his own conduct thus:—"Some time ago a catechist from the Madura mission, begged me to go to Poulour, there to baptize some pariar catechumens, and to hear the confession of some new neophytes of that caste. The fear that brahmins and shudras might come to learn the step I had taken, and thence look upon me as infamous and unworthy ever after of holding any intercourse with them, hindered me from going. The words of the holy Apostle Paul, which I had read that morning at the mass, determined me to take this resolution,—'Giving no offence to any one, that your ministry be not blamed.' 2 Cor. 6: 3. I therefore made these poor people go to a retired place about 3 leagues from here, where I myself joined them during the night, and with the most careful precautions there I baptized 9 of them."—"The poor pariars had not only separate catechists, but separate churches; and if they presumed to enter the church of a higher caste, they were driven out and well whipped. Even when they were dying, the Christian sunyasees (priests) refused to enter their dwellings; and the expiring person in nature's last agony, was dragged from his couch into the open air, or to a distant church that the sunyasee (priest), uncontaminated by entrance into the house, might, without contact, administer to him the last rites of the church."

These distinctions of caste have not been equally preserved in all parts of the country. In Bombay and its vicinity, a regard to caste among the Roman Catholics of Hindu origin, is chiefly limited to marriage connections. But in the southern parts of the peninsula, the distinctions of caste are nearly or quite as great and as rigidly adhered to, as they are among the Hindus.

They observe the rules of caste in respect to eating and drinking and social intercourse. The Christians of high caste must have preachers and catechists of high caste. They will not attend nor admit among them the instructions of any man of low caste, however well qualified he may be in learning, ability, and piety. The preacher and catechist of the pariars must himself be of the same caste, for no one of a higher caste will associate with them. In some places the churches are divided into two or three parts with separate doors for the different castes to enter and come out. In other places they have separate houses of worship, and if any man of low caste should enter a church of the high castes, the place would be regarded as polluted, and he would be at once expelled and severely punished.

In the southern part of India, I was several times in company with a large number of natives, who I supposed from their dress and appearance, were heathen and idolaters, but found on inquiry, that most of them were Roman Catholics. I learned in answer to my inquiries, that in their marriage connections, their eating and drinking, and in all their social and religious intercourse, they observed the rules of caste as much as the Hindus did. I asked them how they could all participate in the same sacraments, and yet preserve their rules of caste. They replied, that "their padre (priest) put his hands upon what was to be eaten and consecrated it, and then it became *prusad*, and could be taken and eaten by persons of different castes without their losing caste. This word *prusad* is the name given to food cooked in heathen temples, and then offered to the idols and consecrated with such rites that people of different castes can handle it and eat it and yet preserve their caste.

In other matters also they retain much of their former heathen customs. The Hindus are very fond of show and noise in their religion, and it is a frequent custom in some districts to put the idols of their gods on a car or carriage of some kind on festival days and then draw it about in procession. This usage has been retained by the Roman Catholics only substituting the images of their saints for the idols of the gods. In some places the same car is used on Hindu festival days for the idols of the gods, and on Romish festivals for the images of the saints. The Abbe Dubois in describing how Roman Catholics imitated the heathen in such things says:—"This Hindu pageantry is chiefly seen in the festivals celebrated by the native Christians. Their processions in the streets, always performed in the night time, have indeed been to me at all times a subject of shame. Accompanied with hundreds of tomtoms (small drums), trumpets, and all the discordant noisy music of the country, with numberless torches and fireworks — the statue of the saint placed on a car which is charged with garlands of flowers and other gaudy ornaments according to the taste of the country — the car slowly dragged by a multitude shouting all along the march — the congregation surrounding the car, all in confusion, several among them dancing or playing with small sticks or with naked swords — some wrestling, some playing the fool, all shouting or conversing with each other without any one exhibiting the least sign of respect or devotion. Such is the mode in which the Hindu Christians in the inland country celebrate their festivals. They are celebrated however with a little more decency on the coast. They are all exceedingly pleased with such a mode of worship, and any thing short of such pageantry, such confusion and such disorder would not be liked by them. I at several times strove to make those within my range sensible of the unreasonableness of so extravagant a worship, and how opposite it was to true piety; but my admonitions proving everywhere a subject of scandal rather than of edification among my hearers, who in several instances went so far as to suspect the sincerity of my faith, and to look upon me as a kind of freethinker and a dangerous innovator merely on account of my free remarks on the subject, I judged it more prudent to drop the matter and to overlook abuses it was out of my power to suppress." *

The Annals of the Propagation of the Faith, a Romish missionary magazine, contains many similar accounts in the journals and communications of the missionaries employed in India.

The facts which have been mentioned, and the extracts mostly from Roman Catholic writers, which have been given, show the kind of means used by the Romish missionaries to propagate Christianity in India, their example among the people, the doctrines they taught, and the superstitions they originated or tolerated. It must be obvious that, whatever might be the success

* Letters on Christianity in India, pp. 69, 70.

in the number of reported conversions, we could not expect a pure form of Christianity, or any enlightened religious community to be the result of such operations. The number of Roman Catholics in all India according to a late No. of the Annals of the Society for propagating the Faith is nearly 1,000,000. A small part of these are the descendants of Europeans settled in India, but the great body of them are the descendants of the mixed marriages of Europeans and natives, and the descendants of Hindus who became proselytes. The greater part of the Roman Catholic population in India are in the southern parts of the peninsula, which contain the Portuguese possessions and the Romish Syrian Christians. The number of these last mentioned is stated to be nearly 100,000. The number who still adhere to the ancient order, rites, etc., of the Syrian Church in India has been stated to be 50,000.

Goa, though now of little political or commercial importance, yet still retains much religious influence. There is here an Archbishop, always from Europe, and under him a large number of clergy, most of whom are persons born in the country and educated in Goa. There are 7 or 8 bishops or Apostolic Vicars in India, namely, 1 in Agra, 1 in Bombay, 1 in Calcutta, 1 in Madras, 1 in Pondicherry, 1 in Cochin or Verapoly, and 1 in Ceylon. These are always from Europe and have generally been Italians. A few of the priests are from Europe and live in the large cities, but the great part of them are natives and educated in the country. The education of this latter class is very limited. In Calcutta, Madras, Bombay, Pondicherry, and Goa, the Roman Catholic population includes many Europeans or descendants of Europeans and Indo-Britons, and the congregations in the churches exhibit every shade of complexion and every style of dress. But leaving the cities and large towns, the Roman Catholics, in complexion, dress, and personal appearance generally resemble the native population among whom they live. This is especially true of those living in the southern part of the peninsula.

To a devout Romanist the history and present state of the Roman Catholic religion in India, must be full of painful and melancholy interest. The first Portuguese ships that reached India, carried missionaries to communicate a knowledge of the

Gospel to the inhabitants. For 50 years the Portuguese power and possessions in India increased faster than those of any other European power. Indeed, the Portuguese possessions in India were greater in 20 years from their first sailing round the Cape of Good Hope, than those of the English were at the end of 100 years from their first reaching India. It was a professed object and leading policy of the Portuguese to bring all the native population in these possessions to embrace the Roman Catholic faith. In some of these possessions, and probably in all of them as soon as such a course could be safely pursued, when " the missionaries had converted the greater part of the inhabitants, in order to detach the remainder from the worship of idols, they destroyed all the temples and pagodas." In some of these places, and probably in all as soon as such a law could be prudently enforced, " Mohammedans and Hindus were allowed to sojourn, but were not permitted to perform any public acts of their religion." By such means the inhabitants generally became Christian in profession. Churches were erected, and colleges, monasteries, and nunneries were endowed. With the decline of the Portuguese power and the loss of their possessions, the population in such places dispersed. The churches, colleges, and monasteries were then generally neglected and fell to ruin. Many large ruins of such edifices I have seen in different parts of India. I have more than once seen the ruins of several large churches, where not a single Roman Catholic could be found, and their history could be learned only from the Hindu or Mohammedan inhabitants.

Great numbers of missionaries, as Jesuits, Franciscans, Dominicans, Capuchins, etc., engaged in the work of converting the inhabitants to the Romish faith in the Portuguese possessions and in the territories subject to the native princes. In some places the doctrines they inculcated and the policy they pursued, produced rather a modified form of heathenism than the pure and simple Christianity of the primitive churches.*

* The Abbe Dubois makes the following remarks, etc.: " During the long period I lived in India in the capacity of a missionary, I have made, with the assistance of a native missionary, in all between 200 and 300 converts of both sexes. Of this number two thirds were pariars or beggars, and the rest were composed of *shudras*, vagrants, and outcastes of several tribes, who being without resources, turned Christians in order to form new connections chiefly for

And whether such people are really in a more favorable state for embracing the truth than the heathen around them, remains to be seen. It is the opinion of the Abbe Dubois, who was a missionary among the Roman Catholics in India for more than 30 years, that they are not so numerous, or so intelligent, or so respectable now, as they were a century ago. The causes of their conversion and early increase, their decline and decrease, (if they have really decreased in number,) and their present ignorant and degraded state, are deserving the consideration of all professing Christians and philanthropists.

The great and besetting sin of the Roman Catholics in India is intemperance, and for this vice they are often and justly reproached by the Hindus and Mohammedans. It is probable that some of their ancestors were intemperate before they professed Christianity, as they belonged to low castes who indulge more or less in this practice. And those who were previously Mohammedans or high caste Hindus, and so not allowed by the principles of their religion to use spirituous liquors of any kind before their conversion, would be almost compelled by the usages of society to use them afterwards. Whatever the causes may be, the Roman Catholics in India are very intemperate, and they have suffered much from this vice. Still there is more domestic happiness among them than among the Hindu or Mohammedan population in corresponding circumstances. Polygamy is never allowed. The women dress more decently and have more their appropriate place in their families. More of them are educated, and they generally appear with more propriety and better manners in their intercourse with strangers and among their own people.

the purpose of marriage, or with some other interested views. Among them also are to be found some who believed themselves to be possessed with the devil, and who turned Christians after having been assured that on receiving baptism the unclean spirits would leave them and never return; and I will declare it with shame and confusion that I do not remember any one who may be said to have embraced Christianity from conviction and from quite disinterested motives. Among these new comers many apostatized and relapsed into paganism, finding that the Christian religion did not afford them the temporal advantages they had looked for in embracing it; and I am very ashamed that the resolution I have taken to tell the whole truth on this subject, forces me to make the humiliating avowal that those who continued Christians are the very worst among my flock."

One great defect, as all Protestants will believe, among the means which these missionaries used for the conversion of the native population and then for the instruction of their converts and churches in Christian doctrine, was the withholding from them, or rather not supplying them with, the Scriptures in their vernacular languages. No part of the Scriptures, so far as is now known, was ever published by the Roman Catholic missionaries in any of the languages of India. They were here able to carry out the orthodox doctrine of the Romish Church, of not allowing the common people (the laity) to have the word of God in their own language, and this not supplying them with the Scriptures has contributed in part to keep them in ignorance of Christian history, doctrine, and duty. Their ancestors retained the belief and the use of many of their heathen superstitions and rites when they professed Christianity, and their posterity now through several generations have never learned that these things are contrary to the precepts and the spirit of the religion they profess.

And yet the Roman Catholic population in India, even in their present ignorant and degraded state, present a very interesting view to the Christian and the philanthropist. They are nearly 1,000,000 in number, and though the greater part of them live in the peninsula, yet there are small communities of them scattered over all the country from Cape Comorin to Cashmere, and from the Indus to the Brahmaputra. These communities are made up of all the different nations, and some of them using all the different languages of India. They have all been baptized, they all bear the Christian name, they have some knowledge of Christian doctrines, as the Trinity, the crucifixion of Christ, a future resurrection and judgment, and they hope for salvation through Christ, though with only vague and indefinite views of his work and character. This profession and this knowledge, vague and obscure as it is, yet put them on very different ground from the Hindus and the Mohammedans. Should a Reformation like what occurred in Germany in the 16th century, take place among the Roman Catholics in India, should many of the priests and of the people be truly converted to God, the Scriptures in their own languages be freely supplied to them, and they all be stirred up to read, great indeed would be the effect not only through the 1,000,000 Roman Catholics, but through the 150,000,000 of Hindus and Mohammedans. And how soon in this way might hundreds of native missionaries be raised up to preach each in his own language the wonderful works and the yet more wonderful love of God. In this view of the Roman Catholic population of India I believe they have not received the attention from Protestants which their number, their circumstances, their character, and their relation to the native population of the country generally require.

CHAPTER III.

EARLY PROTESTANT MISSIONS.

The earliest Protestant mission in India was at Tranquebar on the Coromandel Coast. Baldæus and some others of the Dutch missionaries in Ceylon now and then visited the Dutch possessions of Tuticorin and Nagapatam on this coast; but their ministrations appear to have been limited to their countrymen and the native Christians in these places. Tranquebar became a Danish possession in 1621, but it was not till 80 years after this time that any measures were taken to convert the natives to the Christian religion. Dr. Lutkins, one of the chaplains of the king of Denmark, set before his Majesty the duty of converting the heathen in his eastern possessions to the Christian faith, and the king at once instructed him to take measures for doing it. After some inquiry, Ziegenbalg and Plutscho, two students at Halle, in Germany, were engaged and embarked for India in 1705. The manner in which they at first considered and engaged in this cause, and the spirit they everywhere manifested on the subject, showed their eminent qualifications for such an enterprise. They found much difficulty for a while in learning the Tamul language, as the natives there showed a jealousy of any European acquiring more than a colloquial use of it. Their brahmin teacher was much persecuted, "his enemies pursuing him from place to place, and persecuting him with great violence. At last they succeeded in getting him to Tanjore, where they accused him to the Raja of having betrayed their religion and revealed its most sacred mysteries to the missionaries. The Raja immediately loaded him with irons and threw him into prison where he lay for some months." The spiritual state of their own countrymen in India excited their sympathy, and they had one service a week with them, which some esteemed a great privilege. Seeing that some of the Europeans owned slaves, the missionaries obtained the consent of the masters that "these poor outcasts might meet for 2 hours daily for instruction." Thus it could again be said, "To the poor the gospel is preached." Nor did they hear in vain, for in less than a year from their arrival in India, "the missionaries had the satisfaction of baptizing five adult heathen slaves belonging to Danish masters. The services were publicly performed in the Danish church at Tranquebar after the candidates had been examined in all the Articles of the Christian Faith. They gave their answers with such readiness of mind as to put to shame many old persons who were present." In two years after their arrival they erected a church, and, at its dedication, "they preached both in Tamul and Portuguese to a crowded congregation of Christians, Hindus, and Mohammedans." The next month they baptized 9 adult Hindus, and again in less than a year several more were baptized. The native Christians were soon enough to form a respectable community. The missionaries were greatly encouraged with these indications of the blessing of God upon their labors. But the work of conversion did not proceed without exciting much persecution. "Some of the converts, like the primitive Christians, suffered the loss of all things, being turned out of their estates and banished from the society of kindred and friends. They were regarded as outcasts and the dregs of mankind. They were beaten with violence and in a few instances were put to death."

In 1708, Ziegenbalg visited Nagapatam, and "the Dutch magistrate sent through the country in all directions, inviting the most learned brahmins, sunyasees, etc., to a friendly conference with the missionary on religious subjects. A great assembly convened; the conference or discussion lasted for 5 days, and much information concerning the origin, history, doctrines, etc., of Christianity was diffused among the native population." In 1711 the translation of the New Testament into Tamul was completed. To print the Scriptures and other works they procured a press and types from Germany, but these types were found to be unsuitable and a font was cast at Tranquebar. The press proved a great help, and the New Testament and 32 Tamul works were printed in 2 or 3 years. Ziegenbalg's health having failed, in 1815 he embarked for Europe. His account of their missionary labors and the religion, etc., of the Hindus excited great attention in England and through Germany. Kings, princes, and prelates manifested an interest in the cause, and gave liberally to support it. The king of Denmark may be said to have originated the mission, and his well-known liberality and favor were in many ways of much advantage to them. In England Ziegenbalg had an interview with the king, with the prince of Wales, and several of the bishops and nobility.* The Society for Propagating the Gospel, and the Society for Promoting Christian Knowledge assisted the mission with money and materials for printing the Scriptures and other works. These things occurred nearly 150 years ago, and show that the *Spirit of Missions* is not of so recent origin as many have supposed.†

Ziegenbalg returned to India and resumed his labors as soon as his health would admit. The operations of the mission were carried on prudently and vigorously during his absence. M. Plutscho had some time previously returned to Europe in feeble health, but his place was well supplied by M. Grundler, who was every way a worthy associate of Ziegenbalg. But Ziegenbalg did not long survive his return. He died after an illness of a few weeks in Feb. 1719, at the early age of 36 years, of which

* George I. wrote to the missionaries in 1717 and again in 1727, acknowledging letters from them, and assuring them of the great interest he felt in their work. The Archbishop of Canterbury also wrote them several letters. — See *Christian Researches*, p. 120–125.

† The king appears to have taken a continued interest in this mission. Many years after Ziegenbalg was in England, 3 German missionaries remained a few days in London waiting for an opportunity to embark for India. "While in London they were introduced to the king, who discoursed with them for some time about the present state of the mission, the stipend of the missionaries, the languages they had learned, and other interesting matters relating to the work they had undertaken. When they took leave his Majesty ordered 180 crowns to be given to them."

he had spent 13 in India. The state of his mind in his sickness and death corresponded to his life. In view of the state of the mission and of the heathen he had a desire to live, but for himself only his desire was "rather to depart that he might be with Christ." In the full assurance of faith, says his biographer, he could adopt the language of the apostle, "I have fought a good fight, I have finished my course, I have kept the faith; henceforth there is laid up for me a crown of righteousness which the Lord the righteous Judge, shall give me at that day." At the time of Ziegenbalg's death, all the New Testament and the Old Testament to Ruth had been translated and printed in Tamul, the language there generally used by the natives. A Dictionary and Grammar had been prepared in the same language, and 32 works on Christian doctrine and duties for distribution and for use in the schools had been printed. Two churches had been erected. A seminary had been commenced for the education of catechists, and a native Christian community of 350 souls * had been converted from heathenism. The history of the propagation of Christianity shows few such men as Ziegenbalg; few have labored with such singleness of purpose, and seen their labors so much blessed; few were ever more beloved in life or lamented in death. And when the great Head of the church on earth was pleased to remove him to higher service in the temple above, the converts he had baptized, the seminary and schools he had established, the Scriptures he had translated, the dictionary, grammar, and numerous other works he had made, long continued to be witnesses of his ability, industry, zeal, and devotedness. By all these, though dead, he long continued, yea even to the present time has continued, to speak.

This mission after the death of Ziegenbalg was supplied with able laborers from Germany, and though subject to persecution from Romanists, Mohammedans, and Hindus, yet it continued to increase in the number of its converts and the general efficiency of its operations. Some of the catechists having become qualified for the ministry, were ordained and proved to be useful assistants. From some accounts of the schools it appears that a part of the scholars, at one time nearly half, were girls. Probably

* The number of these who were communicants is not given.

these belonged to the native Christian community. In 1750, three missionaries arrived, one of whom was Christian Frederick Schwartz, afterwards so celebrated for his long and successful labors in the missionary cause. In 1756, at the celebration of the jubilee or 50th anniversary of the mission, it is stated that more than 11,000 persons had been baptized, of whom many had adorned their profession, and died in the comfort of a good hope through grace. The state of piety in the Christian community at that time is described as very gratifying. The operations of the mission which had several stations, suffered much from the wars between the English and the French, and between these powers and the native princes. The Europeans engaged in these wars, by their drinking, fighting, and generally immoral conduct, (for so it appeared to the native population,) excited strong prejudice against Christianity in the minds of many Hindus and Mohammedans. An uncommon proportion of the German missionaries in India lived to be aged men, aged for Europeans in that climate, and this circumstance contributed much to promote the missionary cause. Schwartz was in the 48th year of his missionary labor when he died. Several of the native preachers and catechists lived to be aged. Some labored in the cause more than 50 years.*

Tranquebar was the original seat of the Protestant missions in India, and for 20 years or more the missionaries made that city their home. But the conversion of so many natives in Tranquebar, the visits of the missionaries to other cities, their tours through the provinces, the circulation of the Scriptures and tracts, and the labors of their native helpers, excited attention and inquiry in other places, and opened the way for enlarging their operations. In 1716, the missionaries of Tranquebar, encouraged by the English residents in Madras, opened a Tamul school there for native children, which was visited and examined from time to time, " when they never failed to preach to the heathen of the place. On these occasions they were always welcomed by the English." M. Schultze, one of them,

* In 1833, I became acquainted with a German missionary who was for some years a companion and fellow-laborer with Schwartz. When I last saw him he had been a missionary in India for 57 years, and he lived some years after that time.

mentions being at Madras in 1726, when "he was greatly encouraged by the governor and other gentlemen in authority, and preached to all classes, English, Germans, Portuguese, and Hindus." Circumstances were so favorable at Madras that Schultze, with the concurrence of his associate at Tranquebar, soon removed to Madras, which then became a station of the Danish mission. The Society for Promoting Christian Knowledge took him and the station under their patronage, and the governor, the members of council, and others liberally assisted in purchasing mission premises. In a few years 2 or 3 more missionaries joined him; their schools were prosperous; their catechists were diligent and zealous; and in 1736, only 9 years from the commencement of the mission, they had baptized 415 persons.

This Mission in Madras has continued under the charge of a succession of missionaries to the present time, and is now known as the Vepery Mission. In 1743 the health of Schultze became so much impaired that he was compelled to embark for Europe. The native Christian community then connected with the Mission, consisted of 619 souls, of whom 123 were communicants. This mission in its early history was much assisted by the English residents in Madras, and at one time the government gave them 500 pagodas or nearly $1,000 "by way of indemnity for what they had suffered in the war, and as a further benevolence towards relieving their present distresses, and the thorough reëstablishment of their mission." In 1761, a printing press was established in connection with the mission, which was in various ways of great advantage. A very considerable proportion of their converts had been previously Romanists. Among these was a priest, of the order of Dominican, a native of Portugal, whose name was De Costa. He held fast his Christian confession till his death, which occurred some years afterwards at Calcutta. In 1772, the journals of the missionaries contain the first mention that I have seen of the *cholera* in any history of India. In that year "it appeared first at Tripetty, a place among the hills north-west of Madras, whither innumerable multitudes went annually on pilgrimage from all parts of the Carnatic, especially from Madras. The great festival was held in the month of September, and this year one half of the vast concourse was swept away by this awful scourge."

An account of this mission published some years ago, stated that the whole number baptized since its origin was nearly 5,000, that many hundred children had received a good Christian education in its schools, and that its printing-press had been very useful in furnishing the Scriptures and other religious works in the native languages. The Christian community formed originally by this mission is now divided into 2 or 3 religious societies, each under the charge of different missionaries. Some are in connection with the Church of England, and some are in connection with the Lutheran Church.

Among the German and Danish missionaries to whom India is so much indebted, were many men of great ability, zeal, and piety. Ziegenbalg, who commenced the Tranquebar mission, deserves to be had in everlasting remembrance. Grundler was every way a worthy fellow-laborer and successor. The life and labors of Schwartz are well known. The English government in India employed him in important political transactions with the native princes. He was sent on an embassy to Hyder Ali, then in the height of his power. This powerful, haughty, and tyrannical prince, though himself a Mohammedan, had yet so great respect for Schwartz that he gave orders to all his officers to let the "*venerable* padre Schwartz go wherever he pleased in his army, his encampments, and the country around, when the war was raging with the English, and any European not in the prince's service found there, would have been instantly killed." In the political affairs of Tanjore, Schwartz acted an important part, rendering great services to the Raja, his family, and his subjects; and also to the English, and obtaining the approbation of all parties. The Raja showed his respect for him in various ways. "The funeral of Schwartz was delayed a little beyond the appointed time in consequence of Surfojee Raja wishing to look on him once more before the coffin was closed. Deeply was the prince affected at the sight of his guardian's corpse. He bedewed it with tears, covered it with a cloth of gold, and accompanied it to the grave." The Raja also erected a monument with a suitable inscription upon it, in the church at Tanjore, where Schwartz had so long and so successfully preached the gospel. The East India Company also showed their estimation of Schwartz's character and services by erecting a marble monument for him, in St. Mary's church, in Madras.

In the latter part of the last century the sources of support from Denmark and Germany gradually failed, and these missions became mostly dependent upon England. Of the original Danish and German missions there are now 7 stations connected with the Leipsic Missionary Society, which has 6 missionaries who have under their care about 3,000 native Christians. The Society for Propagating the Gospel in Foreign Parts, and the Society for Promoting Christian Knowledge (both Societies of the Church of England) assisted the Danish and German missions at different times. And when the original sources of support for these missions failed, the districts where they were, having in the mean time become subject to the English, it was natural these Societies should assume charge of these missions so far as was necessary for their support. So most of the native Christians formerly connected with the Danish and German missions, are now connected with the English Society for Propagating the Gospel in Foreign Parts.

Calcutta was not a place of any political or commercial importance under any native government. So there were no temples or mosques of any peculiar sanctity or antiquity in the city, or in its vicinity. Such a place and the population naturally gathered there, would in some respects be favorable for introducing Christianity. In 1732, some Dutch, Germans, and other foreigners, settled in Calcutta, applied to the missionaries in Tranquebar, to send them one or two missionaries, not only for the benefit of the natives, but also of themselves and their families, as they were destitute of the preaching and ordinances of the Gospel. The missionaries in Tranquebar, unable to spare any of their own number, sent the application to Germany, but no suitable persons inclined to this work could then be found. In 1753, the French under Count de Lally, having taken possession of Cuddalore, the Rev. John Kiernander, who had been a missionary in that place for some years, was compelled to leave, and seeing no prospect of being able to resume his labors, he proceeded to Calcutta. He found Lord Clive, then governor, and the members of the council cordially disposed to take him under their protection and to patronize his mission. He was also kindly received by the East India Company's chaplains, who obtained large donations and subscriptions for carrying on his missionary operations. He found in Calcutta several native Protestants from the southern provinces of India, and he had soon very considerable congregations in the Fort Church, which the governor and chaplains allowed him to use when it was not required for the religious services of the Europeans. Kiernander was soon joined by a Roman Catholic priest, who, renouncing the errors of his church, became a useful assistant in the missionary work. The congregation increased, and "during the first year he had 15 baptisms, among whom was one learned brahmin." The mission was encouraged and assisted by the European residents far beyond what was expected. Among those who supported it liberally, was Governor Vansittart, who had succeeded Lord Clive in this office.*

Mr. Kiernander's labors appear to have embraced different classes of people, but all equally in need of the Gospel. In 1766, only 8 years from his arrival in Calcutta, his church consisted of 189 communicants, of whom more than half were originally Romanists. Having acquired considerable property by his marriage in Calcutta, he began to erect a church, expecting it would cost about £2,500. But some unexpected difficulties occurred, and it was found when completed, that the cost had exceeded £7,000. This large and unexpected expense greatly embarrassed him, and deranged all his plans. At the dedication of this mission-church, the governor, the members of council, and many other Europeans high in authority were present, thus showing their respect for Mr. Kiernander, and the interest they felt in the cause. In 1767, of 36 converts in that year, 20 were previously Romanists, among whom was one priest, who proved to be a valuable assistant to Mr. K. in his

* Mr. Vansittart was Governor of Bengal for 5 years, when he returned to England. On returning to India, the ship in which he embarked, and all on board were lost; no tidings of them were ever heard after they sailed. Mr. V. was the father of the late Lord Bexley, who was for many years President of the British and Foreign Bible Society.

work. In the course of a few years, many more Romanists joined him, among whom were two more priests. One of these also became a useful fellow-laborer with Mr. K. This mission continued for many years in a prosperous state, and in 1778, the native Christian community embraced many families, and the communicants amounted to 200.

From this time the operations of the mission were less efficient, and its state began to decline. Unfavorable feelings towards all means for the introduction and propagation of Christianity in India, as dangerous to the stability and permanency of the English power in the country, now became more common, and for a while had much influence in Bengal. Mr. K. became too infirm from age to engage in active labors, or to superintend efficiently the operations of his mission. He also became pecuniarily involved, and so was unable to support, as he formerly did, the expenses of the mission.

In this view of the state of the mission, the Society for Promoting Christian Knowledge, which had at different times made some donations for the expenses of the mission, though nothing, so far as I can learn, for Mr. K.'s personal support, sent out the Rev. A. J. Clark, to take charge of it in 1787. Mr. C. was the first English missionary sent to India, and he soon left the missionary work and became one of the chaplains. From this time for several years there was no English missionary in Calcutta, or in any part of Bengal. Several chaplains superintended the mission in Calcutta, administering the ordinances, and superintending and directing the catechists and teachers. Among these chaplains were D. Brown, C. Buchanan, H. Martyn, T. Thomason, D. Corrie, and others, to whom the cause of religion among the European, as well as the native population in India is greatly indebted. Through the labors of these men, the cause of Christianity was sustained among the native population in Calcutta, and communities of native Christians were formed in Agra, Meerut, Cawnpore, Chunar, and other places, so that when the first missionaries of the Church Missionary Society arrived in India, they found that in these places much preparatory work had been done, and good foundations had been already laid for them to build upon. The labors of these good men are the more to be admired, as they were not required by any regulations of the government, and formed no part of their prescribed duty. And not only were these labors voluntary, and performed without any remuneration, but they required expenses for pundits and books to learn the native languages, and money for the support of catechists, school-teachers, and other operations. In the whole history of the propagation of Christianity in modern times, I know not where we can find more noble examples of Christian effort, liberality, and benevolence, than the names which have been mentioned, and some others like them among the East India Company's chaplains in India.

The first Protestant mission in Bombay was commenced by the American Board of Commissioners for Foreign Missions. In 1812, five missionaries, namely, Messrs. Hall, Judson, Newell, Nott, and Rice proceeded from the United States to Calcutta, with the intention to commence a mission somewhere in the East Indies. The governor-general of India would not allow them to remain in any part of the territory subject to the East India Company, and ordered them to leave the country immediately. In consequence of these peremptory orders they all left Calcutta, and Messrs. Hall and Nott proceeded to the western coast of India. On arriving in Bombay they found that the same peremptory orders from the governor-general had preceded them. Sir Evan Nepean, the governor of Bombay, was personally well disposed to them and to the missionary cause, but said that he did not feel he had any discretionary power to allow them to remain. But various causes delayed their departure, and they at length obtained permission to continue and pursue their missionary work. In 1813, some alterations favoring the introduction of Christianity into India were made in the East India Company's charter, and some other missionary societies soon commenced missions in the presidency of Bombay.

It has appeared proper to give this somewhat extended notice of the early missions in India, in the belief that they are not so well known as is desirable, and to show that modern missionary efforts commenced longer ago, and were prosecuted with more vigor than is generally supposed. The history and operations of the missionary societies, European and American, which are now engaged in propagating Christianity in India, are so well known that any detailed account of them here appears to be unnecessary. A brief statement of them, and a tabular view, showing the times when they were commenced, their stations, the number of their missionaries, schools, converts, etc., will be given. Also the results of the missionary enterprise, and some remarks and suggestions concerning ways and means of promoting the cause.

PRESENT STATE OF PROTESTANT MISSIONS IN INDIA.

The first Protestant missions in the southern countries of Asia, were commenced by the Dutch in Amboyna and Ceylon, and the next in the order of time, were the Danish and German mission, on the Coromandel Coast. These last-mentioned missions were assisted at different times by the Society for Propagating the Gospel and the Society for Promoting Christian Knowledge, in England. The first English missionaries who proceeded to India, were Dr. Carey and his associates in 1793. The exclusive policy of the East India Company for some time prevented the English missionary societies from engaging vigorously in propagating Christianity in India. The restrictions of this Company were removed by changes in the charter, when renewed by Parliament in 1813. From that time there has been a gradual increase in the missionary force in India. Missions have been commenced by societies of different denominations in the United Kingdom, and on the Continent of Europe, and in the United States of America. The stations of these missions were so much scattered over the country, and their operations, though communicated to their respective societies in Europe and the United States, and published in their reports, were yet often so little known to the Christian public in India that a collection of their statistics and more knowledge of their particular state became very desirable. This work was undertaken by the Rev. J. Mullens, in connection with the Calcutta Missionary Conference, and was accomplished to the satisfaction of all connected with the missionary cause. The statistics included Ceylon, as its missions are closely connected with those of India. The results were of a very encouraging character, and showed more progress and success than was generally expected. The statistics collected were published in tables which exhibited the names of the societies, the stations, and the missionaries, and the number of churches, communicants, catechists, schools, etc., connected with each mission. These tables show that in 1852, India (including Ceylon,) contained: —

The Agents of	22	Missionary Societies.
These Societies had	443	Missionaries;
Of whom	48	were Ordained Natives.
They had	698	Native licensed Preachers and Catechists.
There were	313	Missionary Stations.
And	331	Native Churches.
These Churches contained . . .	18,410	Communicants.
At these stations were . . .	112,191	Native Christians.
The Missionaries had	1,347	Vernacular Day Schools.
These Schools contained . . .	47,504	Boys.
They had	93	Boarding Schools,
And these Schools contained . .	2,414	Christian Boys.
They also superintended . . .	126	Superior English Day Schools.
In which were	14,562	Young Men and Boys.
They had also	347	Day School for Girls.
Which contained	11,549	Scholars.
And they had	102	Boarding Schools for Girls;
Which contained	2,779	Christian Girls.
They also maintained . . .	71	Regular Meetings in English for Europeans.

The tables are too numerous and extended to be all inserted here. Of the two following tables, the first exhibits the force of the principal missionary societies, and the second exhibits the summary of the missions in each Presidency and Ceylon. In the full tables of statistics, the missions of Ceylon are printed separately. In the first of these tables they are included. In the second table they appear by themselves.

PRINCIPAL MISSIONARY SOCIETIES IN INDIA AND CEYLON.

Societies.	Came to India.	Stations.	Preachers.		Native Churches.				Native Christians.	Boys' Schools.						Girls' Schools.				Eng. Chapels.
			Missionaries.	Native Catechists.	Number.	Admitted.	Excluded.	No. of Members.		Vernacular. Schs.	Vernacular. Boys.	Boarding. Schs.	Boarding. Boys.	English. Schs.	English. Boys.	Day. Schs.	Day. Girls.	Boarding. Schs.	Boarding. Girls.	
Church Miss. Society.	1815	61	95	136	60	209	53	5622	38,737	409	14,660	32	1,020	28	2,285	115	3,507	33	1,071	9
Soc. for Prop. Gospel.	1727	49	44	76	63	..	..	5025	25,498	173	4,525	17	400	9	390	50	1,343	13	284	4
London Miss. Society.	1805	27	55	173	29	127	9	1381	20,414	271	9,834	13	263	19	1,739	50	1,313	19	567	13
Wesleyan Miss. Society.	1814	32	36	26	42	139	6	1846	9,398	79	3,404	1	22	11	718	34	1,196	2	42	8
Americ. Board of Comr's.	1812	27	40	74	26	79	3	953	6,594	152	5,038	7	222	16	740	44	1,454	3	153	1
Baptist Miss. Society.	1793	27	33	86	52	141	93	1536	4,302	67	2,651	2	19	4	353	10	218	6	98	11
Free Church of Scotland.	1830	12	21	23	5	18	..	111	281	25	1,213	..	..	15	4,714	22	1,398	4	93	6
Estab. Church of Scotland.	1830	6	4	5	3	11	..	65	288	18	747	1	7	6	2,460	17	724	3	63	1
Basle Miss. Society.	1830	13	27	35	12	..	..	637	1,366	42	1,699	6	105	2	110	8	127	3	120	4
American Presbyterian Mission.	1834	9	27	16	8	18	..	151	407	17	706	3	48	10	963	2	63	3	62	6
Gen. Baptist Mission.	1822	5	8	13	4	24	10	256	750	6	81	2	100	..	..	1	4	2	79	2
American Baptist Mission.	1840	4	10	7	4	3	1	39	139	14	460	2	60	..	..	..	2	4	44	1

SUMMARY OF MISSIONS IN INDIA AND CEYLON.

Presidencies.	Stations.	Preachers.		Native Churches.				Native Christians.	Boys' Schools.						Girls' Schools.				English Chapels.
									Vernacular.		Boarding.		English.		Day.		Boarding.		
		Missionaries.	Native Catechists.	Number.	Admitted.	Excluded.	Number of Members.		Schools.	Boys.	Schools.	Boys.	Schools.	Boys.	Schools.	Girls.	Schools.	Girls.	
Bengal Presid'y.	89	103	130	87	229	127	3,500	14,778	140	6,470	22	790	22	6,005	24	669	29	830	21
Agra Presid'y.	29	66	49	22	69	16	678	2,032	61	3,707	10	191	22	1,754	10	242	10	175	14
Bombay Presid'y.	19	35	16	13	41	2	289	744	70	3,480	2	21	7	1,144	37	1,222	6	101	5
Madras Presid'y.	121	179	405	128	361	26	10,662	76,591	849	24,445	52	1,165	41	4,286	191	6,639	52	1,470	22
Ceylon.	55	60	98	81	132	11	3,281	18,046	227	9,402	7	247	34	1,373	85	2,747	5	203	9
Total . . .	313	443	698	331	832	182	18,410	112,191	1,347	47,504	93	2,414	126	14,562	347	11,519	102	2,779	71

Dr. W. Brown in his History of Missions, published in 1854, has given some later statistics and refers to numerous Reports, Journals, etc., for authority. He makes the whole number of communicants 21,299 which is a very considerable increase. Probably the catechists, schools, etc., had increased in equal proportion.

The 22 Missionary Societies engaged in propagating Christianity in India compose a part of nearly every Protestant church and denomination in Europe and America. They show an amount of talent, learning, wealth, and influence vastly exceeding what is generally supposed to be engaged in this cause. They show what a strong hold the cause of foreign missions has acquired upon the feelings of Christians. They show not only a conviction of the truth of Christianity, but of the duty of communicating a knowledge of it to the inhabitants of those countries who have hitherto remained ignorant of it. In the extent of their organization as well as in the learning, talent, wealth, influence, and piety they comprehend, they show that a late distinguished author had well considered this cause when he declared "the Spirit of Missions to be the Glory of the Age." *

Of the 443 missionaries, 48 (the number is greater now) were natives, born and most of them educated in the country. These have been ordained and are now laboring for the conversion of their countrymen. It must be obvious to all who have any acquaintance with India, that its population of 150,000,000 can never be evangelized by the direct labors of missionaries sent from Europe and America. The principal work of these missionaries must be to raise up and superintend a native agency. To prepare a suitably qualified agency to preach the gospel must require much time as well as great labor. Such agents must be converted from heathenism to Christianity, as well as be educated for the ministry. They must give evidence of having been called by God and renewed by his Spirit before they engage in this work. Now no human means can impart to them this essential part of their qualifications; God alone can give it. For this qualification in native agency, missionaries must look to Him who has commanded his Gospel to be preached to all the human family.

* John Foster.

Considering the time and labor necessary for preparing a native agency and the peculiar qualifications required for it, all must acknowledge that missionaries have made a good beginning. But they have done far more than to prepare these 48 ordained native missionaries. The course of preparation generally includes two previous states. When missionaries find young men who give evidence of piety and apparently possess natural talents for usefulness in the missionary work, they are first prepared for the class of assistants called catechists. This class contained 698 or more than 14 times the number of the ordained native missionaries. In this state they generally continue for some time, and some of them on account of their age or deficiency in strength of Christian character, or natural and acquired ability, continue in this class through life. But others, having approved themselves to the satisfaction of their teachers and employers for sufficient time, are licensed to preach. And such persons after sufficient trial and progress in Christian character and education are generally ordained. In the views of the missionary agency and operations which have been given, the licensed preachers are all included in the number of catechists. How large a part of these are licensed preachers, we have not the means of ascertaining.* While some of these are every year admitted into the class of ordained missionaries, their places are supplied, and more than supplied, by others admitted into the class of catechists.

In estimating the influence of the missionary stations in India it is necessary to consider their situation in respect to each other, and also to the whole country. These 331 stations are not like townships or parishes in America, where all might be included in a few districts or counties, but they are generally in large cities, where they are surrounded with a dense population, or in towns and villages 20, 30, and often 100 miles distant from each other. Thus situated, each becomes a centre of influence on the heathen population around it, and shedding their light on

* Since writing the above I have seen a statement that "the number of native preachers now in India is 551." If this number included the ordained native missionaries (as it probably did) it would still include a large proportion of those commonly called catechists in the class or division of licensed preachers.

the surrounding darkness, as they increase in number and influence they will gradually enlighten all the country.

These 331 churches are all in connection with the different Protestant missions. They are missionary churches, and do not include the churches composed of Europeans and under the pastoral care of the chaplains. Some of these mission churches are large, containing 200 or 300 members, but others are small, having been recently formed. If the whole number of communicants in the latest accounts (21,299) were divided by the number of churches, it would give an average of 64 members for each church. This number may appear small to people connected with the large churches in our cities. But there are more than this number of Congregational churches in New England, not one of which has so many members, though in some of these churches the Gospel has been preached and its ordinances administered for more than 100 years past, while in some of our States not half the Presbyterian churches have 64 members.

In most places where there is a church, there is a community of native Christians, who are not members of the church. Some of these are the children of pious parents, who have grown up and not yet given sufficient evidence of personal piety to be admitted members of the church. In some instances a man has become a member and his wife has not, and then a woman has become a member and her husband has not. Some are candidates for admission, and all have withdrawn from heathenism and belong to the native Christian community. This class of people generally attend upon the means of grace. They are nominally Christians, that is, they are Christians in the lower but not in the higher sense. Still compared with the heathen they are in an encouraging and hopeful state, and the number of them is yearly increasing. The number of this class at the beginning of 1852 was 112,191, and it is now probably much larger. In comparing the results of missionary operations with the number of agents employed, it should be remembered that a large part of this agency has been engaged in the cause but a few years. Some of them are yet occupied in learning the native languages, and others have just commenced their active labors. Some of the missions and many of the stations have been but recently commenced.

Another important fact is that a large part of these results have been realized within a few years past. And this is what might be expected in view of the state and character of the people and the circumstances of the missionaries. Christianity, as offered to the people of India, does not appear to be accompanied with those advantages of civilization which have often gained for it a favorable hearing, and to some extent a nominal and general reception among the aborigines of America, and the inhabitants of Africa and the islands of the Pacific. They have believed that the difference they saw between their own state and circumstances, and those of Christian nations, was to be ascribed to their different religions, and that the way to become like Christian nations was to renounce their own religion and become Christians — that in this way they might become civilized, learned, rich, and powerful. Every person who is well read in missionary history, knows that views of this nature have often had much influence at first in the spread of Christianity in the countries and places above referred to. And it is proper and right for missionaries to show to the people of such countries the advantages of Christian civilization. But the people of India are in such a state of civilization now that missionaries can show them no such advantages in connection with embracing Christianity. It is true that Christianity, if truly embraced, would gradually by its influence upon their moral and intellectual character, produce great and important changes in their social state and worldly circumstances. But these advantages would be realized slowly, and in a manner which they cannot now understand.

To some persons the number of native Christians in India may appear to be small. But let such remember that it is larger than the entire population of all the English territories in India was at the close of the first century of the East India Company,* which has always embodied the English power in India. But now the population in the territories subject to the English in India amount to 100,000,000, while their power extends indirectly over 50,000,000 more. Now while Christianity is in no way responsible for the means or the progress of the Brit-

* The East India Company commenced in A. D. 1600. So the close of its first century was the year 1700.

ish power in India, yet all Christians who take any part or feel any interest in the propagation of Christianity in that country, believe that these great political changes are preliminary and preparatory to the spread of the gospel. May we not therefore expect, since God has thus prepared the way in his providence, to see as much increase in the same time in the subjects of the kingdom of his grace? as much progress in the same time in the conversion of the people of India to Christianity?

The opinion is sometimes expressed that the missionary enterprise in India has proved to be a failure. Now in respect to all such assertions and opinions, two things may be observed: — First, they are made in a spirit of unfriendliness to this work, and of hostility to the cause. These opinions come from persons who have never given to the foreign missionary cause their sympathy, or their money, or their prayers. They have never cordially *wished* to see it in a prosperous state, or to hear of its success. They are wishing to find something to say against it. Secondly, when the authors of such assertions and opinions have given any facts or reasons for their support, it has been apparent that they were not sufficiently acquainted with the origin, history, and state of the different missions in India, to entitle their opinions to any confidence or consideration. The spirit of their remarks and opinions show the feelings in which they originated, and the errors in their statements show that they never looked for facts sufficient to verify or to correct them. Controversy with such persons and authors, so far as producing any conviction of their errors, or gaining their good-will and support of the cause, is of little use. They are generally incorrigible in their prejudices.

There is another class in the community who feel an interest in the foreign missionary cause, who contribute means liberally to promote it, who pray earnestly for its success, and who yet sometimes think the progress is very slow, and who not seeing the results they expected, are rather in a discouraged and dissatisfied than in a hopeful and thankful state of mind. For the encouragement of such and of all who may read this work, let us take a view of what has been done for the evangelization of India. And we cannot well appreciate what has been done without considering the state of India when the modern missionary operations were commenced there.

Results of the missionary enterprise include obstacles and difficulties which have been removed, as well as ground which has been acquired. Let us then look at some of the obstacles which formerly existed in India to the introduction and spread of Christianity, but which have been removed. Some of them will now be mentioned.

INDIA HAS BEEN OPENED FOR THE PROPAGATION OF CHRISTIANITY.

At the beginning of this century the only missionaries in India were Dr. Carey and his associates at Serampore, then recently arrived in the country, and struggling with many difficulties, and a few German or Danish missionaries on the Coromandel Coast. The general sentiment of the Europeans in India at that time was opposed to any interference with the religion of the native population. The governing authorities in India and in England partook largely of this spirit, and they were determined to exclude all missionaries from the territory subject to the East India Company, so that Dr. Carey and his associates were compelled to live under the protection of the king of Denmark, to whom Serampore then belonged. The first missionaries who went from America to India in 1812, found the country shut against them, and they were ordered by the governor-general of India to return home in the same ship which had brought them there. This order was avoided by one of them (Dr. Judson) proceeding to Burma, then beyond the power of the English government, and two others escaping to Bombay, where a similar order was at once given to them to leave India as soon as possible. It was not till the renewal of the East India Company's charter in 1813, that the Christian public in England, who had long been wishing to send missionaries to India, succeeded after a severe struggle in the Court of Directors and in Parliament, in opening India for the free propagation of the gospel. Thus only about 40 years ago not only were the inhabitants of India throughout almost the length and breadth of the country enveloped in the darkness of heathenism, but there was the determination of their rulers that they should continue in this state. But now the English government in India, instead of interposing its power to exclude missionaries from this country, permits them to proceed to any part of its territories which they may select for their residence and operations. All parts of India which are subject to the English (and these contain 100,000,000 of inhabitants), are as open for the free propagation of Christianity, by any proper means, as the United States are. In all these territories missionaries can circulate the Scriptures and any other religious books, and can preach all the principles of the gospel and against the rites and practices, and the superstitions and doctrines of Mohammedans and Hindus as much as they please, and yet be under the protection of English laws and English magistrates. Thus so far as the government is concerned, all external obstacles and internal restrictions are removed, the inhabitants of all classes are accessible, and missionaries are protected in the use of all proper ways and means in the prosecution of their work. Surely this is great progress. It is one of the triumphs of the missionary enterprise, and it has not been achieved without much effort and perseverance.

THE ENGLISH GOVERNMENT HAS WITHDRAWN ITS SUPPORT OF THE RELIGIONS OF INDIA.

The East India Company on assuming the possession of the country from Hindu and Mohammedan kings and princes, who had long supported their respective systems of religion and superstition, continued the policy of those governments, confirming their acts and administering their laws. Thus for some years the English government in India exhibited the strange and anomalous appearance of supporting Christianity for their countrymen, Hinduism for the Hindus, and Mohammedanism for the Mohammedans. They erected churches and supported chaplains for Christians; they repaired mosques for Mohammedans, and temples for Hindus; and they had several thousands of these with their moolahs and brahmins, their festivals, ceremonies, and worship under their care and superintendence.* These proceed-

* See pages 331–337.

ings were understood by the native population to show the approbation of the English government to each of these systems of religion, and that it was right for each class of people to follow their own religion. I have often heard brahmins and others argue earnestly from these proceedings that the English believed the Hindu and Mohammedan religions to be true, and to be good religions for those who practise them. I have seen brahmins in a time of drought spend a part of each day in prayers and ceremonies before, around, and over their idols to procure rain, and at the end of the drought they would make up their account for these idolatrous services and obtain payment for them at the English magistrate's office.

Now it often appeared to be of little use for missionaries to try to convince people of the falsehood of their religious systems, and the folly and iniquity of their idolatrous rites and worship, while they had before them such proceedings of the government, and obtained payments of money for their idolatrous rites and ceremonies. Happily these difficulties, long so embarrassing and discouraging and dishonorable to a Christian government, have been in a great degree removed, and there is reason to hope that the exceptionable things of this character which still continue, will erelong cease. And this great change in the policy of the government of India, is to be ascribed to the repeated and long-continued exertions of missionaries and others connected with the missionary cause in India and England. This change is one of the results of the missionary enterprise, and its importance cannot well be appreciated by those who have not seen the magnitude of the evil, the iniquity of various kinds connected with these systems of superstition, and the obstacles which they created in various ways to the spread of Christianity.

RECENT LAWS ON RELIGIOUS LIBERTY AND PROTECTION.

Another important change in favor of Christianity is in the laws securing liberty of conscience to all classes of the inhabitants. Some account of the peculiar laws or institution of the Hindus, called Caste, has been given in another part of this work.*

* Page 465–473.

If any Hindu violated the rules of caste, he was to be expelled from his house and his home, to be disowned by his family and his friends, and to lose all right to his property, hereditary or acquired. He was to be regarded as dead, and funeral ceremonies were to be performed for him. These rules of caste were the laws of the Hindu governments in India, and the English in succeeding to their power administered the laws which they found already established and in force. Thus the English courts administered the Hindu laws, and among them the rules of caste, for the Hindus. According to these laws, if any Hindu should become a Christian he was expelled from his caste and was exposed to the evils of being an *out-caste.* Many Hindus who became Christians suffered all the losses and evils of this unreasonable and unrighteous law. In such cases the law was regarded as so plain and its meaning as so explicit that the converts generally without any formal and judiciary proceedings submitted voluntarily to their losses and sufferings.

Such a law must necessarily be a great obstacle to the progress of Christianity. Missionaries and others who wished for the spread of the Gospel, used what means they could to effect some change. But the Hindus and Mohammedans were satisfied with these laws; not 1 among 100 of them wished for any change. In 1832 in the administration of Lord William Bentinck, a law was passed which was designed to secure liberty of conscience in Bengal. This law was limited in its operations to Bengal, and even there did not produce all the good effects expected from it. No further laws affecting caste were enacted till 1850, when the legislative council of India passed the following law:—"So much of any law or usage in force within the British territories, as inflicts on any person forfeiture of rights or property, or may be held in any way to impair or affect any right of inheritance, by reason of his or her renouncing or having been excluded from the communion of any religion or being deprived of caste, shall cease to be enforced as law in the courts of the East India Company, and in the courts established by the Royal Charter within the said territories." This law was designed to secure full liberty of conscience to all classes of people, to place Christians, Jews, Mohammedans, and Hindus on equal ground, permitting every man to profess what religion he pleases and to change his religion when he pleases, and yet enjoy the full protection of the laws. And yet the law gave great offence to the Hindus and Mohammedans, and they made vigorous and persevering but unavailing efforts to get it repealed.*

This law does not interfere with the caste of any class of people. Caste, with its social distinctions and religious observances, will continue just as long as the Hindus please to retain them. They will long continue to be a great obstacle to the progress of Christianity and civilization. But the rules of caste and the decisions of its members are no longer to be recognized as the laws of the land, and so no one can suffer so far as the law can protect him in his civil rights by disregarding them. The evils of caste will still be many, and the sufferings occasioned by it will be great, because they will be of such a nature that no law can remove them nor apply any remedy for them, any more than laws can provide a remedy for many social evils in the complicated relations of families and society.

The interpretation of the object and spirit of this law and the application of its principles by the courts, appear to have been very satisfactory to the friends of religious freedom. The importance of this law, applicable as it was at once to 100,000,000 of people in the English territory, and to be applied to 50,000,000 more as fast as they come under the English government, can scarcely be overestimated. The whole history of legislation does not contain a law which has produced more important consequences than will result from this enactment. And this law is one of the results of the missionary enterprise in India.

No one would expect, after considering the origin, nature, and influence of castes, to hear it had ever become an acknowledged and cherished feeling and usage in any Christian community. And yet the history of Christianity in India contains some painful chapters upon this subject. Unhappily there have been some mistaken opinions in respect to the existence and prevalence of caste in the mission churches of India, and so it appears expedient to give some account of it. The manner in which the distinctions of caste were treated by the Romish mis-

* See page 473.

sionaries, and how they were admitted into their churches and communities of native Christians, has been described.* The first Protestant missionaries appear to have had correct views of the nature of caste, and to have pursued a proper course in respect to it. Their rule was, "when any heathen embraced Christianity, he must renounce all superstitions connected with caste, for we admit no such distinctions, but teach them that in Christ they are all one, none having any preference before another." In the course of two or three generations the native Christian communities at some of their stations consisted chiefly of the descendants of their early converts, and many of these, though attending upon the instructions of the missionaries, yet not giving evidence of personal piety were not communicants; just as it is in many religious societies and congregations in America. From such communities, surrounded as they were by Hindus and Roman Catholics all carefully observing the rules of caste and attaching much importance to their observance, the missionaries found it difficult to exclude all the prejudices of caste. In their journals and correspondence they often spoke of their difficulties on this subject. These difficulties continued gradually to increase till they resulted in the observance and toleration of some distinctions among these Christian communities, corresponding somewhat to some of the rules of caste among the Hindus and Roman Catholics. But these distinctions observed in the Protestant communities, were regarded at first as merely of a civil and social character, and not as having their origin and observance in religion and morality.

These distinctions among the native Christians in the course of time became more and more like the distinctions of caste among the Hindus, and exerted a very unhappy influence. They regarded these distinctions as involving their personal, family, and social respectability in their own communities and in the view of the Hindus. Vigorous and persevering efforts have been made to reform these churches and to eradicate these distinctions from the native Christian communities, but the evils of admitting them, and then tolerating them so long, are found to

* See page 517–519.

be great, and not easily removed. Far the greater part of the native Christians formerly connected with Schwartz, and his predecessors and fellow-laborers, are now under the superintendence and care of English missionaries, and they are all agreed in regarding caste in all its principles, its spirit and its observances, as inconsistent with Christianity and not to be tolerated in Christian churches. In a few small communities of native Christians on the Coromandel Coast which have always been under German missionaries, some distinctions of caste are still tolerated. These communities contain in all about 3,000 souls, and they are chiefly the descendants of those who embraced Christianity 2 or 3 generations ago. They are connected with the Leipsic Missionary Society.

American missionaries in India have always required a renunciation of caste from their converts before admitting them to a profession of Christianity. And if at any time afterwards the spirit of caste became apparent in any of them, as it sometimes did, the missionaries have treated such members in the way of instruction, admonition, suspension, and excommunication, according to the nature and aggravation of their offences. The American missionaries in India can no more be justly charged with admitting and tolerating caste in their churches, than the ministers of Boston, New York, and Philadelphia can be justly charged with admitting and tolerating drunkenness.

POLYGAMY.

Polygamy is practised in India among the Hindus, the Mohammedans, the Zoroastrians, and the Jews. It is allowed and recognized by the Institutes of Menu, by the Koran, by the Zendavesta, and the Jews believe by their Scriptures — the Old Testament. It is recognized by all the courts in India — Native and English. The laws of the British Parliament recognize polygamy among all these classes, when the marriage connection has been formed according to the principles of their religion and to their established laws and usages. The marriage of a Hindu or a Mohammedan with his second or his third wife, is just as valid and as legally binding on all parties, as his marriage with his first wife, just as valid as the marriage of any Christian in the Church of England.

Polygamy then is one of the obstacles in India to the introduction of Christianity, and as it is not only part of the religion of the inhabitants, but is also recognized and protected by the legislative acts and legal decisions of the government, it becomes an important question in what way this obstacle can be met and the evil be removed.

Supposing now that any Hindu or Mohammedan or Jew, who has several wives to whom he has been legally married, should give evidence of piety and wish to make a public profession of Christianity, what shall be done in respect to his polygamy? In contracting these marriages he violated no laws of the country and no laws of God as he understood them, any more than Jacob or Elkanah did in marrying two wives, or than David did in marrying a yet larger number.* This man cannot divorce any of his wives, if he would; and it would be great injustice and cruelty to them and to their children, if he should. He cannot annul his legal obligations to provide for them. He is bound morally and legally to support them and to protect them while professing the Hindu or Mohammedan or Jewish religion, and his having become a Christian and embraced a purer faith, will not release him from these obligations in view of the English government and courts, or of the native population. Should he put them away or all but one, they will still be legally his wives and cannot be married to any other man. And further, they have done nothing to deserve such unkindness, cruelty, and disgrace at his hands.

There are other difficulties connected with native marriages. It has been already mentioned that such marriages are generally contracted by the parents and celebrated in accordance with the laws and usages of the country when the parties are young, often when they are mere children. But such marriages, though wholly the work of the parents, are yet valid and of legal obligation. Suppose a boy or a man who has been thus married, should become a Christian before the marriage is consummated, and the girl to whom he has been married remains a heathen,

* See Gen. 29 and 30 chap. 1 Sam. 1: 2. 2 Sam. 2: 2. 3: 2–5. 5: 12, 13. 12: 8, 24, 25. 2 Chron. 24 : 3.

must he acknowledge the marriage to be morally binding and take his wife? Suppose the woman becomes a Christian and the man continues to be a heathen, and on her arriving at a state of puberty he claims her to live with him. What shall she do? What shall her parents do, if they also have become Christians? Suppose again a man or a woman becomes a Christian and the other party refuses to fulfil the marriage contract, is the Christian party freed from the marriage obligation and at liberty to marry again? And supposing a man or a woman while living in the married state should become a Christian, and the other party for this reason abandons them or expels them and positively refuses to live any more with them, what is the innocent and suffering party to do? Must they continue single? Or are they at liberty to marry again? How far is 1 Cor. 7:15, applicable to such cases?

Some people in this country appear to be of the opinion that polygamy being contrary to the Christian dispensation, and contrary, as they think, to the well-being of families, as well as of general society and of nations, must be classed, wherever found, with theft, adultery, murder, etc., and that people in any country who have entered into this state, must have as clearly seen and known that they were doing wrong, as if they had been violating any of the Ten Commandments. But such were not the views of pious Jews in ancient times, as the cases of Jacob, Elkanah, and David clearly show, nor are such the views of Jews in modern times when they live in countries where they can follow their own usages and laws. Indeed, so far from viewing polygamy as morally wrong, they not unfrequently take a second or a third wife with much reluctance, and from a painful sense of duty to perpetuate their name, their family, and their inheritance.

Now what shall be done in respect to such persons when they give credible evidence of personal piety and seek admission into the Christian church? No case of this kind occurred in my own missionary experience. But some cases have occurred in India, and this difficulty will occur in numerous instances in the progress of the Gospel. The subject will also have the consideration and decision of the highest authority, ecclesiastical and judiciary, in India and in England. My opinion is that the general practice in missions in respect to such cases will be as follows:— When any man who has more than one wife to whom he has been legally married, wishes to be admitted into the Christian church, he will be required to make a free and full statement of his domestic relations. He will be permitted to retain his marital connection with all his wives and his parental relation to all his children, subject to the discipline of the church for the proper government of his household. Whether he may or may not, cohabit with his different wives, will be left I believe entirely to him and to them to act according to their views of duty. At the same time the nature of the married relation according to the Christian dispensation and the usage of the church, and the reason why such cases are for a while tolerated, will be fully explained. No man thus admitted while a polygamist can be ordained a Christian teacher.* In this way polygamy will have the testimony of the church against it, and as no Christian man can ever become a polygamist, all such cases will cease with the lives of those thus admitted.†

PREACHING.

There has seldom been much difference of opinion among missionaries and other Christians who reside in India in respect to the first and most important kind of agency to be employed in the propagation of the gospel in that country. This agency is acknowledged to be the preaching of the Gospel,—communicating a knowledge of the way of salvation, and of the doctrines and duties of Christianity by the voice of the living preacher. This is believed to be the divinely appointed means for convincing and converting sinners, whether they are Hindus and Mohammedans in India, or infidels and unconverted men in Christian countries. It must not, however, be understood that preaching the Gospel to a heathen population consists in delivering formal discourses on particular doctrines and duties to well-ordered and listening assemblies as in Christian lands. Preaching to the heathen of India has much more resemblance to the labors of John the Baptist and of Christ and his Apostles, as these are described in the New Testament. And no one will

* 1 Tim. 3: 2.

† Appendix C.

deny that their manner of preaching was good, was the very best for the circumstances and character of the people, and that the manner as well as the matter of their teaching was properly called "preaching the gospel." The preaching of our Saviour was, in conversations, discussions, exhortations, parables, and sometimes in extended discourses in the synagogues. It was suited to the state, circumstances, capacity, and character of the people. Sometimes he spoke to only a few individuals and even to only one person as to Nicodemus and the woman of Samaria, and at other times he addressed great multitudes.* He pursued his ministry in private houses, in the open fields, by the sea-side, in the synagogues and in the temples on the great festivals. His disciples proceeded in a similar manner while he was with them and also after his ascension to heaven.

So the missionary in India strives to communicate a knowledge of the gospel in conversations and discussions, in his own house, in school-houses, in the houses of the natives when he can gain admittance into them, in the highways and the byways, at their temples and to the multitudes who assemble at places of pilgrimage. He endeavors to adapt his language, his manner of illustration, and the truth he inculcates, to the capacities, the prejudices, and the errors of his hearers. Sometimes when addressing a crowd or an assembly he will see it best to propose some inquiry to awaken their attention, and then perhaps some discussion will ensue. And sometimes he will be interrupted by cavils and objections to which he must at once reply, or the hearers, believing he cannot reply, or is opposed to free discussion, will disperse. Of such trials and troubles, such hopes and disappointments, and such encouragements and discouragements, missionaries in India have abundant experience.

The opinion has sometimes been expressed that preaching the gospel can be of little use to the people of India till they are educated and more capable of understanding moral and religious truth. But to suppose that education must precede the preaching of the gospel in order to communicate to them a capacity to understand it, such an opinion is contrary to the general tenor and spirit of the Scriptures, to the practice of the Apostles, and to the experience of Christians in every age of

* John 3–7 chapters.

the world. The Scriptures always speak of mankind, whether heathen, or Jews, or nominal Christians, as having natural capacity to understand the Divine commands and to feel their obligations to obey them. The Hindus, though their minds are darkened by their pantheism and mysticism, and their moral sense obscured by their false philosophy, which often confounds natural appetites with moral qualities, and substitutes rites and ceremonies for moral duties, yet still retain power to understand the gospel and to feel its suitableness to their state and character. They can see and understand enough of the works of God in creation and providence, if they would only use their reason and obey the dictates of conscience, to convince them of the sin and folly of worshipping such beings as their deities are described to be in their sacred books. And further, they are conscious of being sinners, of deserving the divine displeasure, and of needing mercy, and so they can perceive the suitableness of the way of salvation through a Mediator.

Some have supposed that the Hindu religion with its pantheism, its polytheism, its mysticism, and its atheism, its cruel and horrid rites under the name of virtue, and its almost endless and absurdly significant ceremonies, must annihilate the natural perception of right and wrong, and leave people destitute of conscience till it could be supplied or resuscitated by instruction. But such is not the state of the Hindus, as I know from long residence among them and much intercourse with them. Nor is such the opinion of any missionary I have ever known, who had acquired their language and lived among them enough to form any opinion of their moral state or sense from his own observation and experience. If they cannot understand the evidences, the doctrines, and the duties of Christianity so well in their present state as they could if well educated, yet they can understand enough to become wise unto salvation through faith in Jesus Christ. There is therefore encouragement to preach the gospel to them as soon and as far as possible, and the question in each mission is how far its members shall devote their time to this work, and how far to preparing a native agency to do it.

The opinion I have sometimes heard expressed in this country that it must be useless, or nearly so, to try to make the people of India understand the nature of Christianity, the force of moral obligation, and their need of divine mercy, this opinion is not founded upon facts. If any system of error, superstition, and false philosophy, could reduce people to a state of mind in which they would become incapable of understanding the gospel, that system appears to be Hinduism. But constituted as man is, with the capacities and powers of a moral agent, and conscious as he is of being a sinner — of having done many things which he ought not to have done, and of not having done many things which he ought to have done, and of often seeing and approving the better course, and yet following the worse, he will retain, in all the possible states and circumstances where he has the free and voluntary exercise of his intellectual and moral faculties, the capacity to understand the gospel enough to feel its suitableness to his spiritual wants, and to experience its quickening power. In no part of the world is any portion of the human family so ignorant, so degraded, so debased, so mystified by error and superstition, as to exclude them from the "all nations" and the "every creature" contained in the last command of our Saviour to his disciples. — Matt. 28:19, and Mark 16:15.

The very singular political state of India and the circumstances of the English, the governing power in the country, have often made it apparently the duty of missionaries to engage in labors and duties not contemplated in their original object, and not making a part of their prescribed operations. The number of government chaplains would be sufficient for the spiritual instruction and pastoral care of all the European population in India, if they were so situated that they could attend regular services and stated ordinances. But the English population is so scattered over the country that many of them are to a great extent unsupplied with the regular ministration of the chaplains. There is also the class of people called Indo-Britons, who are much dispersed, and yet more imperfectly supplied with religious instruction than the scattered English population. Nominal Christians thus destitute of preaching and of the ordinances of the gospel, surrounded with a heathen population, and often setting a bad example before them, have appeared to have urgent claims upon missionaries. The immoral conduct of nominal Christians early produced in many places very unhappy prejudices against the doctrines and morality of Christianity; for the people of India regard all who come from Christian countries as Christians, and their conduct and character as exhibiting the doctrines and spirit of Christianity, just as we look upon all Turks as Mohammedans, and their conduct and character as exhibiting the principles and spirit of the Mohammedan religion. So strong and unhappy were these prejudices against Christianity that some of the early missionaries often expressed the opinion in their journals and correspondence that little success could be reasonably expected from efforts to convert the native population to Christianity so long as they had before them the unhappy conduct of so many professing Christians, and that the first duty of missionaries appeared to be to labor for the reformation of their own countrymen in India.

Motives of this character have induced missionaries in many places to engage in undertaking religious services in the English language for Europeans and Indo-Britons, sometimes only once and sometimes twice on the Sabbath. In a few instances preaching in English has become their principal work, and in such cases those for whose spiritual good they labored, assumed their support. These labors in many different places in the English language have been very useful, and have contributed largely to the improved state of religious principle and moral character now existing among these classes of people. American missionaries have engaged less in labors of this kind than English missionaries, partly because they have not been in places so much requiring such labors, and in part probably because such labors appeared to involve more departure from the object of their mission in the country.

At the time I left India in 1853, religious services were performed in the English language in more than 70 chapels by missionaries, on the Sabbath. In this way they have done and are doing a great and good work; a work apparently necessary to be done before the native population of India can be converted to Christianity. And a work in respect to its importance and magnitude which cannot be estimated by any who are not personally acquainted with the circumstances and character of Europeans in India, and their great power for good or evil over the inhabitants of the country.

TRANSLATIONS OF THE SCRIPTURES.

The Roman Catholic missionaries made no translations of the Scriptures in any of the languages of India. They wrote a work which they called Ezour Veda,* and then attempted to obtain for it the honor, the confidence, the currency, and the authority of a genuine Hindu work of this name. They expended money freely in erecting churches, colleges, and convents, but they made no versions of the Scriptures in any of the vernacular languages, and if any one of the 1,000,000 Roman Catholics in India and Ceylon has a copy of the word of God, he is indebted to the Protestants for it. To Protestants the ignorance and superstition of this class of people (so great that in some places they appear to be only one of the Hindu castes) do not appear strange in view of the circumstances in which they assumed the Christian profession, and in which they have always been kept by their spiritual guides. Their bishops and missionaries in India still pursue the same course. They will not supply their people with the Scriptures, and forbid them to receive copies from the Protestants.

The Dutch missionaries, wherever they introduced Christianity, translated the Scriptures into the vernacular language of the people. They appear to have relied more on catechetical and less on biblical instruction than English and American missionaries do. But the Scriptures were not withheld, nor concealed, nor sparingly and reluctantly supplied to the converts. In this respect the Dutch exhibited the genuine spirit of Protestantism.

In the Danish and German missions, which were the first Protestant missions on the continent in India, the translation of the Scriptures in Tamul was commenced as soon as the missionaries had sufficient knowledge of the language, and in a few years the native Christians had the whole Bible in their own tongue. All the different Protestant missions in India have felt it to be their duty to furnish the people of all classes, Hindus and Mohammedans as well as Christians, with the Scriptures in their own language. To make an intelligible and faithful trans-

* See p. 514.

lation of the Scriptures into any language, is a work of great difficulty and requiring much labor. The history of our English version clearly shows this fact. And this version was made into the language of a nation who had professed the Christian religion for many centuries, in the course of which their language had been acquiring the words, terms, and phrases which are necessary for describing the attributes and perfections of Jehovah, the doctrines and duties contained in his word, and the views of mind and affections of heart which constitute the experience and character of his sincere worshippers. No one who has not carefully examined our English version, especially the sacrifices, rites, and ceremonies of the Pentateuch, the symbols and figures of the prophets, and the condensed statements and description of doctrines and Christian affections in the epistles, can be aware how all the powers of the language were brought into requisition, and even then sometimes it became necessary to coin new terms and to use some already current in new senses to convey the meaning required. What then must be the difficulties of making an intelligible and faithful version of the Scriptures into the language of a heathen and idolatrous nation, a language comparatively destitute of religious words and phrases, and in which the few words and terms it may have, have senses and uses in accordance with their superstition and false religion. The words which suggest one meaning or idea to a Christian, will often suggest a very different one to a heathen; and language, used in describing the actions and perfections of Jehovah, is often referred to some heathen god, the most odious perhaps among all their deities.

The difficulties of making intelligible and faithful versions of the Scriptures into the languages of heathen nations, can be known only from experience. When missionaries and others living in India see how the meaning of language apparently plain and intelligible to every Christian, is yet often misunderstood by heathens, on account of their erroneous religious views, it becomes obvious that the language of heathen nations, especially if they are idolaters and polytheists, as really requires to be *Christianized* before it can become a proper medium for describing Christian doctrines, duties, and affections, as their conduct requires to be reformed, their minds to be enlightened, and their hearts to be purified before they can become the people of God, and worship him in spirit and in truth. But these difficulties have not deterred missionaries from translating the Scriptures into the languages of India. Nor should they, for they can be removed only by encountering them, struggling with them, and effecting the desired changes in them, and in the state and character of the people who use them. In this work the Bible Societies have rendered great assistance. There are 6 Bible Societies in India, (including Ceylon,) which are all connected with Bible Societies in Europe or America, and obtain liberal aid from them in money, printing materials, and Scriptures not published in the country. These Bible Societies in India have Committees of Management, and also Committees on Translations, consisting of men well acquainted with the native languages to whom all versions or revisions, and questions affecting translations of the Scriptures, are referred, and by whose opinions on such matters the Committees of Management are guided. Thus the Bombay Bible Society* has a Translation Committee for Scriptures in the Mahratta language, and another for Scriptures in the Gujerattee language — the two languages chiefly used in the Bombay Presidency. The Madras Bible Society has a Translation Committee for Scriptures in the Tamul language, another for Scriptures in Canarese, and another for Scriptures in Telugu, the three languages chiefly used in the Madras Presidency. So the Calcutta and other Bible Societies have their different Translation Committees. These Committees consist of the most competent men whose services can be engaged, and they are required to examine and approve, in a manner and to an extent satisfactory to the General Committee, all new translations and revisions of former translations before they can be printed. In this way all

* I was connected with this Society for 25 years, and for 13 years I was one of the Secretaries. I was a member of the Translation Committee for 20 years, and for 10 years I was its Secretary. For several of the last years of my residence in India, the preparation of a revised and complete edition of the Scriptures in Mahratta, (a language used by 8 or 10 millions of people,) was my principal work. In none of my labors for India did I ever feel a deeper interest, and upon no part of my missionary life can I look back with more satisfaction.

the means which the nature and circumstances of such works admit, are used to secure the correctness, suitableness, and faithfulness of the versions of the Scriptures printed by the Bible Societies in India.

Another object of the Bible Societies in India, is to keep each depository supplied as far as possible with the Scriptures in all the different languages in which they are likely to be required. I know of no sight more interesting than such a depository, in a city of half a million* of heathen and Mohammedans, containing the Scriptures in all the different languages in use among the people; such Scriptures to be sold as far as possible, and where this is not practicable, to be given to those who will preserve and read them. The Bible Societies in India endeavor to keep their depositories thus supplied, and with the aid of the British and Foreign Bible Society, and by freely coöperating with each other in printing and exchanging the Scriptures, they are able in a good degree to accomplish their object. Such depositories are monuments which show to heathen, Mohammedans, and Romanists, in what estimation Christians hold their Scriptures, while they invite all classes of people to search the Word of God that they may learn the truth and become "wise to salvation through faith in Jesus Christ."

The usual way of making a version of the Scriptures is first to translate and print one of the Gospels. The natives who read it, naturally inquire what the disciples of Christ did after he ascended to heaven; whether they obeyed his last command, and if so, what was the result. To such inquiries the Acts of the Apostles furnish the best reply, and this is generally the next book translated and printed. In India the next part to be translated would be Genesis, and perhaps Exodus to the ten commandments, to show the creation of the world, the origin of the human race, etc. The Hindu sacred books contain most absurd and unreasonable accounts of the creation of the universe, of the origin of mankind, of the distinction of castes, etc. Should the Scriptures be required for the use of converts, probably the book of Psalms, which is the great repository of devotional language and Christian experience, will be next trans-

* Calcutta, Madras, and Bombay have each more than this number.

lated and printed. In this way the different books which appear to be most needed and most suitable, are translated till the whole Bible is completed. A considerable part of what is printed, is given away in portions, and the copies of the New Testament printed and used are far more than of the whole Bible. It is always thought to be best to translate and print all the books of the Scriptures, and supply copies to all who wish for them. The Hindus restrict the possession and use of the Vedas to the brahmins. They alone have the right to interpret and explain these sacred books; and they are strictly forbidden to give them or to teach the language of them to the great body of the people, who are forbidden to possess or to read the Vedas, or even to hear them read. The Romish priests and missionaries have never given the Bible to their proselytes, and the great body of the native Roman Catholics in India are almost if not quite as ignorant of the Christian Scriptures, as the great body of the Hindus are of the Vedas. Protestant missionaries feel it their duty to translate all parts of the Scriptures, and though they do not regard all the different books as equally important, and do not use some parts separately, yet they include the whole in all bound copies of the Bible, and present these to all classes of people who wish to obtain them.

The whole Bible has been translated and printed in 10 different languages, and the New Testament has been translated and printed in 5 more languages in India.* The amount of talent and learning employed and of labor expended upon these versions, cannot possibly be appreciated nor well understood by persons not living in the country, or who have no experience in work of this kind. No one pretends that any of these versions are perfect; none are so sensible of their imperfection as those who have bestowed most labor upon them; and none are more

* To some persons this may appear to be a great number of languages for one country. But it need not appear so when the great extent and population of India are considered. Possibly education and social intercourse may hereafter be so much increased that some of these languages, in which the New Testament only has been printed, may not be perpetuated. But supposing there should be 15 different languages in which it is necessary to have distinct versions of the whole Bible, this will be only one version on an average, taking the whole country, for each 10,000,000 of its inhabitants.

ready and willing to consider every objection to them and every suggestion concerning them, and then bestow more labor upon them for their improvement. But though no one of the languages of India has yet a standard version of the Scriptures; a version satisfactory to all who use it, and to continue for generations without change, yet all has been done which the number and circumstances of missionaries in connection with the state of these languages and the character of the inhabitants could accomplish. A great work has been begun and much progress made in it, and a great blessing has been bestowed upon the people. May the former soon be completed, and the latter be realized and appreciated by the 150 millions of India, and all become able to read, each in his own language, of the wonderful works and the yet more wonderful love of God.

CHRISTIAN LITERATURE.

A civilized heathen nation or tribe in many respects presents a more encouraging field for the propagation of Christianity than an ignorant people, and yet there are some obstacles and difficulties in the former which are not to be encountered in the latter. In a civilized heathen nation or country, every kind of popular superstition and every form of error, iniquity, and depravity have become incorporated in their literature. The lullabies of the nursery, the stories of childhood, the dramas of the stage, the songs of the debauchee, the religious rites of the priest, and the discourses of the philosopher, all exhibit and in turn produce a corrupt taste, a polluted imagination, dissolute manners, a religion of frivolous ceremonies, and a vain and false philosophy. The popular mind appears to be preoccupied with the things contained in their literature, and to be thoroughly imbued with its spirit. Now this literature, these numerous works so closely interwoven with the history of their fabulous heroes and the exploits of their imaginary deities, cannot be destroyed. The only way to diminish their influence, and as far as possible to annihilate it, is to create a literature of a different character; a great, a difficult, and yet a necessary work, if the people are ever to change their religious principles and their moral character. The character and spirit of the Sanscrit and vernacular literature are such that education formerly appeared to be of little use except as a mere qualification for business, and so might just as well be limited to the objects for which it was wanted, as knowledge of the mechanical arts and skill in applying them are limited to the demand for them. And if this appeared to be the state of men in respect to education, how much more so in respect to women, who in oriental countries do not engage in business transactions requiring correspondence, numerical calculations, etc. It was often said by some who were well acquainted with the character of the indigenous literature, that it was not expedient to make any effort to promote native female education till there should be some works in the language which were worth reading, which would not be pernicious in their influence, and so be worse than to be ignorant of them.

The Boards or Councils of Education, which have been described,* have published some valuable works, as grammars, dictionaries, and other school-books to be used in the schools and colleges under their superintendence, and they have also published some useful works of general literature, as history, geography, chemistry, etc. By such publications they are performing good service in the cause of general education. But it has been one of the principles of these Boards, Councils, and Committees not to interfere in any way, in their course of education or in their publications, with the religious opinions and superstitions of any class of the native population. Their publications must contain nothing against Hinduism, or Mohammedanism, or Zoroastrianism. And some members of these bodies, being natives, are very careful that this rule shall be observed.

It must be evident that works prepared and published on such principles, however useful they might be in promoting education, would yet exert but little moral influence on the community, and effect but little, if any change in their religious principles and practices. They would leave the native population still under the undisputed influence of their systems of false religion and debasing superstition. A sound, moral, and Christian literature still remained to be supplied. Missionaries saw

* Page 317.

this necessity, and as there appeared to be no other way of supplying it, they engaged earnestly in this great work. Their efforts have been liberally supported by the Christian public in India, in England, and in America. There are now in India several Societies which are engaged in this good work, and they are liberally assisted by similar Societies in Europe and America. Some of the publications of these Societies are tracts, and small books for children, but others contain 400 and 500 pages each, and are in no way inferior in appearance to the publications of similar Societies in Europe and America. The series of the publications issued by some of these Societies now include nearly 100 works of different kinds. Some of these are translations, some are compilations, but more of them are original works, as such are more suited to the state and character of the people than mere translations of any European or American work. These publications are printed and bound in a neat and economical style, and they are circulated through all parts of India. They are carried by colporteurs into villages and neighborhoods, where the voice of the preacher has never been heard, and into many families from which he is excluded. The publications of these Societies now amount to several million copies.

For printing the Scriptures, tracts, Christian works, and school-books, there are now in India 25 printing establishments. Some of these have type-making and book-binding departments, and employ more than 100 men. Such printing establishments are essential to the efficiency and economy of missions, and they show the completeness of the means and operations of Missionary Societies for accomplishing the work in which they are engaged.

EDUCATION.

Among some heathen nations, as the aborigines of America, the inhabitants of the islands of the Pacific, and a large part of Africa, education in science and literature was unknown before missionaries went to them, as they have no science or literature, not even a written language. If such people are intellectually capable of apprehending the truths of Christianity, and morally capable of experiencing its enlightening and transforming power, yet the history of missions shows that while they continue in this state, their Christianity will bear little fruit, and cannot be expected long to continue in a pure state. In missionary operations among such tribes and nations, the importance of education has always been admitted by all Protestant denominations.

In the most civilized heathen nations, though some persons, according to the standard of education in such countries, may be highly educated, yet the great body of the people have no education, and many more have not enough to read the Scriptures, or any Christian work intelligibly. And further, education as it is conducted in such countries, is so much mixed up with error, superstition, and false philosophy, that the prejudices it produces sometimes appear to put people in a more unfavorable state for appreciating and embracing the Gospel, than if they were entirely uneducated. Such is the state and character of some classes of people in India. In commencing their operations, missionaries have generally seen the propriety and importance of establishing schools. One reason for them is to educate the minds of the people so that they may be more capable of understanding and appreciating the facts and evidences, the doctrines and duties of the Scriptures. Another reason for them is to increase the influence of missionaries with the people by communicating some advantages which they can appreciate, and by showing that Christianity rests upon an intelligent perception of its doctrines, and contains reasons for the performance of all its duties. And another reason for such education is in its procuring means and opening ways of access to the people, and opportunities for preaching to them. One great difficulty which missionaries often experience, is in obtaining access to people in circumstances where Christianity can be made the subject of communication, or consideration, or of conversation. People in their heathen state have no Sabbath when they meet together for worship. While heathen, and attached to their own superstitions, they will not leave their business and occupations, and assemble, to any considerable extent, to hear Christian instruction. Curiosity may induce some to go a few times, but this feeling is soon satisfied, and indifference, if not aversion, succeed. They have holidays enough and too many, but at such times they are generally intent upon keeping their holidays in their usual manner, which is generally very unfavorable to their hearing Christian instruction. Indeed, heathen holidays and festivals furnish much less favorable means and opportunities among a fixed population for communicating or hearing religious instruction, than is generally supposed. Missionaries also find it difficult to obtain suitable places for holding religious meetings. Their own houses (if they have any) may be inconvenient, or distant, or people may have some prejudice against assembling in them; the people may not have any suitable places for meeting, and be unwilling that their houses should be used in this way. In such circumstances, schools become very important as a medium of communication with different classes of people, with children and parents, and with men and women. And school-houses also become important as places for becoming acquainted with people for social intercourse and religious worship. School-houses become chapels under the control of missionaries. Their use for this purpose is often more important than for education. These reasons for making the education of the common people a part of missionary operations, are stronger in some heathen countries than in others, and I believe they can seldom if ever be adequately and fully appreciated by persons who have not themselves lived among a heathen population, and so had opportunities for becoming acquainted with their state and character.

Christian teachers should always be employed in mission schools if such can be obtained. But it will often be impossible to obtain such till a mission has made considerable progress and has competent teachers among its converts. But shall any mission ever employ heathen teachers in its schools? This question must be considered and decided in view of the character of the supposed teachers and the circumstances of a mission. In the mission schools in India the Scriptures are read, catechisms are taught and other Christian books are used. Missionaries have also opportunities of giving much religious instruction to the teachers, the scholars, and their parents. In such schools no heathen or nominal Christian teacher should be employed, if he is immoral in his conduct, or if he treats religion with levity, or ridicules any of the facts, or doctrines, or duties of Christianity, or actively opposes the teaching and influence of the missionaries. If Christian teachers cannot be obtained, and there are heathen teachers (I mean teachers who have not yet professed Christianity) of such a character as I have often known, I believe it may be expedient to employ them. Many such teachers have become converts, and then catechists and preachers of the Gospel.

The number of common free schools in all the missions in India and Ceylon at the latest accounts was 1,347, and the number of scholars in them was 47,504. These are all put down in the accounts as schools for boys. But where there are no schools expressly for girls, they are admitted into the schools for boys, that is, in such places the schools are common for both boys and girls, and in many of the schools for native Christians a considérable portion of the scholars are girls.

The general and inveterate prejudices against female education among the Mohammedan and Hindu population in India are well known. For a long time these prejudices were an effectual obstacle against all efforts to introduce female education. But by persevering and repeated efforts some schools expressly for girls were opened in some different missions, and now in nearly all the missions there are such schools. In some places girls and boys attend the same schools, especially where the scholars belong to native Christian families, but it has generally been found to be expedient to have schools expressly for girls. There are now in connection with the different missions 347 free common schools for girls in India, and the scholars in them amount to 11,549, a number which would have appeared incredible, had any one predicted it a few years ago.

In nothing have the native prejudices yielded more to European civilization and example than on the subject of female education. This department of education was commenced by missionaries, and for some years encountered strong prejudice and opposition. But the educated young men were at length able to see the advantages of it in some native girls, who had been educated in the mission schools, and also in the superiority of European females over their countrywomen of corresponding wealth and social position. These young men began to feel a desire that the girls to whom they had been betrothed in their childhood, and also that their sisters should be educated, and they commenced a few schools for this purpose. English ladies of rank, and gentlemen of high official and social position, encouraged this spirit and enterprise. Donations and subscriptions were freely made, and female schools were commenced in Calcutta, Madras, Bombay, and some other large cities. Commenced under such auspices, these schools were not likely to fail. Encouraged by their betrothed husbands and their brothers, many girls of the most respectable native families began to attend them. The scholars were soon numbered by hundreds and now amount to some thousands. The examinations are public and attended by English gentlemen and ladies of the highest rank. Prizes for improvement and good scholarship are given, and a zeal, interest, and liberality are manifested in the cause that would have appeared quite incredible a few years ago, to those acquainted only with the bigoted and apathetic Hindus as they then were. Some of the aged and more orthodox Hindus still retain their prejudices, and are much concerned at the changes they see taking place, and they sometimes predict the ruin of female virtue, and the disgrace of all respectable families. But the young men of the higher classes are carrying on this cause with prudence, energy, liberality, and success.

The government of India, aware of the changing state of native views and feelings and of the importance of this cause to the well-being of the native population, has recently included female education in their reformed system of education. In a late despatch from the Court of Directors to the governor-general of India in council, they say:—

"The importance of female education in India cannot be overrated; and we have observed with pleasure the evidence which is now afforded of an increased desire on the part of many of the natives of India to give a good education to their daughters. By this means a far greater proportion of impulse is imparted to the educational and moral tone of the people than by the education of men. We have already observed that schools for females are included among those to which grants in aid may be given, and we cannot refrain from expressing our cordial sympathy with the efforts which are being made in this direction. Our governor-general in council has declared in a communication to the government of Bengal that the government ought to give to native female education in India, its frank and cordial support, and in this we heartily concur."

How different from the state and prospect of India, when the missionaries could not find a native woman who could read, and when no man wished his wife or his daughter to learn to read, believing and frankly avowing his belief that it would be better for men and for families and for society, for all women to continue ignorant as they then were. Who can doubt that a new era has commenced in the social, moral, and intellectual state of India. A few years have seen changes on this subject, which considering the inveterate prejudices and peculiar character of the people we could scarcely expect to see in as many generations.

There is another class of missionary schools commonly called Boarding Schools, because the scholars are generally boarded on the mission premises, or receive some allowance for their support and live in families and in circumstances approved by the missionaries. These schools consist of orphans who have none to provide for them, or are the children of native Christians who are too poor or too ignorant to educate them, and in some instances of the children of respectable Hindus and Mohammedans who are willing they should conform to the rules of the schools. In these institutions the scholars are more separated from the Hindu and Mohammedan population, are brought more directly under Christian influence, and receive more religious instruction in public and in private. In most of these schools the English language is more or less taught, and in some of them the teaching is chiefly in English. The education which some such persons obtain, is of a high character, being designed to prepare them to become teachers, catechists, and preachers. These institutions are regarded as holding an important place in missionary operations, and some who were educated in them, have been very useful in the missionary work. It has generally been found expedient to have separate schools for boys and for girls. Sometimes they are in different parts of the same premises, but generally at different stations of the same mission. In the last missionary reports and published accounts, there were then 93 Boarding Schools for boys, containing 2,414 scholars; and 102 Boarding Schools for girls, containing 2,779 scholars. The principal reason for so many Boarding Schools for girls is that these schools furnish the only means in the country for female education of the higher kind, whereas many young men are educated in other institutions in the English language, science, and literature.

There is yet another class of educational institutions connected with missions in India, called English Schools, High Schools, Seminaries, and Colleges. In these institutions the English language, and general science and literature are taught in connection with Christianity and its evidences, its history, its doctrines, and its duties. Some of these schools are small, with only one teacher, while others are large, containing several hundred scholars, and a number of instructors. The instruction is generally gratuitous. In some schools the scholars pay admission fees, and for the use of books, and some of these schools or colleges, as they are called, have scholarships endowed for the support of a certain number of scholars. In Calcutta, Madras, Bombay, and in most of the large cities, are institutions of this character. In these cities the scholars generally belong to the middling and higher classes. In some of these institutions are scholars and classes, who would not compare unfavorably to those in the High Schools, and even in some of the Colleges in the United States.

The whole number of these English schools and institutions, connected with the different missions in India and Ceylon at the latest accounts, was 126, and the whole number of scholars in them was 14,562. English education has made more progress in Bengal, than in any other part of India. Some of the institutions for English education in all its various branches in Calcutta contain several hundred scholars, and it was recently stated on reliable authority that the number of scholars connected with these schools in that city and its vicinity exceeded 5,000. The policy of the English government in India in excluding all religious instruction from their system of education, and the spirit of natural and wide-spreading scepticism, resulting from that system, have excited strong interest for these institutions, and obtained much support for them. Many, who were Hindus and Mohammedans when they began their education in these institutions, became convinced of the truth of Christianity and openly professed their faith in Christ. Some such are now connected with the different missions, and are very usefully employed as ordained missionaries, licensed preachers, and catechists; some are filling important and responsible situations in the service of the government, and some are engaged in the pursuits of private business. A view of the government system of education and the results it has produced, and must naturally produce in the Hindu mind in respect to their sacred books, and a comparison of that system and its results with the system of education pursued in the different missions and the results of this system, are calculated to show the great importance of Christian education among the middle and higher classes of the native population. No one well acquainted with the native population can survey these numerous educational institutions, situated as they generally are in the great cities and large towns, containing so many students, all pursuing such a course of education without perceiving that this department of missionary operations is an agency of great influence, not only in subverting superstition and idolatry, but of diffusing sound religious knowledge and bringing very many to a saving acquaintance with divine truth.

NATIVE AGENCY.

It must be obvious to all who contemplate the magnitude of the missionary work in India — the evangelization of 150,000,000 — that it can never be accomplished by the direct personal labors of men sent from Europe and America. How is the great population of that country ever to hear the Gospel? The answer to this inquiry is obvious and easy to find. This great work must be accomplished chiefly by a native agency. It is by such an agency the great body of the people of India are to be converted to Christianity, and they must then have a native ministry.

The manner in which the East India Company acquired possession of that great country, and still holds and governs it, furnishes an appropriate illustration of the means by which its inhabitants are to be brought from their present state of superstition and idolatry into the kingdom and under the government of Emmanuel. The English acquired India by employing the inhabitants of the country to conquer it for them. The East India Company sent agents and officers to India, who enlisted the natives into their service, formed them into regiments, instructed them in military discipline, furnished them with weapons and showed them how to use them. These officers had then to retain the control of these regiments, support them and accompany, or rather lead them from province to province, and from one country to another. The sable regiments, thus enlisted, disciplined, and supported, have been seen following their English officers and marching under their banners not only in every part of India, but in Egypt, in Arabia, in Persia, in Afghanistan, in Mauritius, in Burma, in Java, and in China and its islands. Of the East India Company's military force probably at no time within a century past has more than one fourth, and sometimes not more than one eighth part been European, and all the rest have been natives of the country. A similar course has been pursued in the civil government of the country. Of the great number of men there employed in government business only a very small proportion, probably not 1 in 100, are sent from England. But these few employ, superintend, direct, and control the whole. To this system of policy, civil and military, wisely conceived and ably managed, England is indebted for the acquisition of her Asiatic possessions. And she could not now retain and govern her possessions in India by any civil agency and military force she could send from England. She can only retain and govern what she has acquired by continuing to employ the same agency under her control. And if the English had not pursued this course of policy, their possessions in India would now have consisted of some scattered forts here and there, and a few square miles of territory around them.

Now the Christians of America and Europe must pursue a somewhat analogous course in conquering India from the powers of darkness and bringing it under the dominion of Emmanuel. Missionaries must first be sent from Europe and America to preach the Gospel, but they should from the first have the work of preparing a native agency in view. Some missionary societies have made the preparation of such an agency a more prominent part of their operations than others. The number of their converts may not for a while have been large, yet they have acquired more influence in the native population. Of the ordained missionaries now in India about 50 are natives of the country, while the number of licensed preachers and catechists amounts to nearly or quite 700. These facts show that in some missions a good beginning has been made. While all missionaries are agreed that a native agency is very desirable, all do not attach equal importance to labors of this class of men. And there is some difference of opinion in respect to the best means of creating such agency.

Some missions have institutions in which pious young men, selected to become missionaries, catechists, etc., are educated expressly for this work. Other missions have seminaries, in some places called colleges, for general education in English science and literature as well as in the vernacular languages in connection with Christianity. These institutions are open to all classes of people upon the same terms. There are several such institutions of a high character and containing several hundred students in the large cities. In these institutions the students who have professed Christianity are formed into a theological class, and pursue an appropriate course of reading and instruction under the missionaries.

The climate of India furnishes strong reasons for raising up a native agency as soon as practicable. Though not so unhealthy as has been generally supposed, yet the climate will always be enervating and sickly to the European and American constitution.* Not only is life shorter and health more uncertain, but

* "It is generally believed that in this country [India] owing to the deadly climate the average duration of missionary life is 7 years, and many have come out as missionaries under the idea that they would be certain to meet with a premature death. But this is a great mistake. From a careful induction of the lives or services of 250 missionaries we have found that hitherto the average duration of missionary labor in India has been 16 years and 9 months each. It was doubtless much less at first, and numerous causes can be adduced in which young missionaries were cut off after a very short term of labor. But a better knowledge of the climate and of the precautions to be used against it, the use of airy dwelling-houses and light dress with other circumstances, have tended very much to reduce the injurious influence of the climate and preserve health, so that the average duration of life and labor is improving every year. As an illustration of this fact we may state that out of 147 missionaries laboring in In-

they have less energy of body and mind than in their native climate. And they can better perform the labor of qualifying a native agency than they can endure the fatigue and exposure of preaching to the native population in the only places and circumstances in which they can have access to them. It is impossible for missionaries to pursue their labors of itinerating and preaching in the cottages and hamlets and villages over a large part of India during much of the time in the hot months and in the rainy season. But such are the constitutions and habits of the natives that they could perform such missionary labors and yet suffer little inconvenience or injury to health from what has often cost Europeans sickness, sufferings, and death.

The nature and number of the languages of India furnish a strong reason for missionaries to prepare a native agency for their work. It has been said that missionaries have often failed in acquiring sufficient knowledge of the native languages to use them acceptably and intelligibly to the native population. But those who originated such an opinion, were mistaken. They were not competent judges themselves, and did not take the trouble to obtain the opinion of those who were competent. A few European missionaries have found a useful and what appeared to them an appropriate sphere of labor in preaching to their countrymen and Indo-Britons in English, or in teaching English science and literature in the mission seminaries. But I have known no American missionary, who has not acquired a knowledge of the native language of the people around him, and then made it the principal medium of his labors. Probably few Europeans or Americans acquire the exact pronunciation of the native languages, just as few foreigners ever acquire the exact pronunciation of all the words and sounds in the English language. Some of the native languages are difficult to acquire, and in most of these languages the first missionaries had to prepare grammars and dictionaries. Missionaries now have many and important facilities for acquiring the languages of India,

dia and Ceylon in 1830, fifty (we can give their names) are still laboring in health and usefulness, while of the 97 others who have since died or retired, 20 labored more than 20 years each. Several living missionaries have been in India more than 30 years. It is a remarkable fact that the average missionary life of 47 of the Tranquebar missionaries last century was 22 years each."—*Calcutta Review*, No. 31, p. 244.

compared with what their predecessors had. Still to acquire such a knowledge of any vernacular language as every missionary should have, requires considerable time and labor, and during all this time he must be supported from the funds of the society with which he is connected. Now a native missionary would not require this time, labor, and expense, and would yet be able to use his vernacular language in a more forcible, effectual, and acceptable manner, more suited to persons of every degree of capacity and measure of intelligence, than American or European missionaries are ever likely to acquire.

There is yet another reason in the languages of the people for a native agency. In most of the large cities the population is composed of different classes, and these classes have each their own language. Men of business early and easily acquire a knowledge of these different languages, and use them fluently as far as they have occasion. But the people of each class generally understand and use only their own hereditary language. Now a missionary has seldom time to acquire two or more languages so as to use them intelligibly and acceptably on religious subjects, and yet for want of understanding them, he often feels that he cannot improve the best opportunities and openings for usefulness. But a native missionary would not experience this difficulty, for such educated men generally understand all the languages used in the places where they live, and they can often apparently use one as well as another.

Another important reason for a native agency is its cheapness. The expense of one missionary's going to India and of his support there till he has become qualified for his work, is ordinarily enough to educate several native missionaries. And then the expense of one American or European missionary (including his family) when reduced to the lowest rate consistent with a due regard to health and usefulness, are ordinarily enough to support several native missionaries. The truth of this is well known to all who have any experience of living in India, and it corresponds to the systems of salaries and allowances in use in all missionary societies for their European and native agency.*

* It may not be improper to make a few remarks concerning the support of missionaries, thus incidentally brought into view. The expenses of living for Europeans or Americans in India in such circumstances as health requires, are

I often heard native missionaries preach to their countrymen, and I have never heard religious services of any kind and in any place with greater satisfaction. Their sermons and exhortations were sound in doctrine, appropriate in manner, and fervent in spirit. No one can hear them thus addressing their countrymen on the sin, folly, and absurdity of polytheism and idolatry, describing the character of Jehovah as displayed in his works and revealed in his word, inculcating the duty and obligation of all to love and serve him, setting forth his love for mankind as manifested in the way of salvation, and the love of Christ as exhibited in giving himself for an atoning sacrifice, and now exalted to be a Saviour, able, willing, and waiting to save all that come unto God through him, and then urging them to forsake their idolatry, turn to the true God, flee from the wrath to come,

generally rather large. Missionaries have now in nearly all places fixed salaries, but each missionary society has its own system of economy. Some missionaries have a fixed salary, designed for all their expenses in the same manner as salaries are in the United States. In some missions each missionary has a salary for personal and family expenses, but house-rent, travelling, etc., are extra charges. The expenses of living vary as much in different places as they do in this country, and this necessarily occasions a difference in salaries. But no missionary society gives any salary or allowance as compensation for labor or remuneration for services. The idea or principle of compensation has no place so far as I am aware in the system or economy of any mission in India. Salaries have always been fixed with a view to necessary and current expenses, and are never intended to exceed them.

I saw much of missionary operations in Bengal, Madras, Bombay, and Ceylon. The salaries of the European missionaries have generally been fixed by committees in India — men who are well acquainted with the climate, the circumstances, the duties and usefulness of missionaries, who feel a deep interest in the cause, and contribute liberally to promote it. Neither missions, nor committees, nor missionaries in India can be justly charged with extravagance in their expenditures. And yet the expense of one European or American missionary or family is as much as of several natives. This is not a matter of choice on the part of the former, but of necessity, if they have any regard to their usefulness, health, and life. For it is just as impossible for Europeans and Americans to live in the manner and circumstances of the people of that country, as it is for the latter to acquire the features and complexion of Europeans. A few Europeans have at different times endeavored to live like the native population on the ground of its being less expensive, of its affording better opportunities to exhibit the true spirit of Christianity, and in the hope of acquiring more social and personal influence. The result of such experiments have not been of a nature to encourage them.

and lay hold on eternal life by looking to Jesus as their Mediator and Saviour — no one can hear these native missionaries thus addressing their countrymen without being forcibly impressed with the great importance of a native ministry, and also with the importance of using all the means which appear likely by the blessing of God to secure such an agency in every mission as soon as possible.

GENERAL STATEMENTS AND REMARKS.

The question may naturally arise, what are the views of the native population generally concerning Christianity? Now the great body of the inhabitants have no clear and distinct views on the subject. They suppose that Europeans have some religion, and perhaps many of them have somewhere seen a church. But they have never heard a sermon preached, nor a word said on the subject of Christianity. They have never read any part of the Scriptures nor any Christian book, nor could they read them if they had them, for only a small proportion of the people are able to read. A view of the great extent of India, its great population, and the number and location of the missionaries, will show that such must be the general state of the people. It is melancholy to contemplate them in this state, but such is the fact.

There is another class or portion of them, who know that the religion of Europeans inculcates the existence and worship of only one God, that it forbids idolatry, and that it has its name from Jesus Christ who was in some way concerned, who performed some part they do not know what, in originating or establishing it. They suppose Christianity may be a good religion for those to whom it was given, and who have always practised it. But they do not suppose it claims to be the only true religion, and was designed for all mankind. Such persons have no knowledge of Christianity which impairs their confidence in their own system, nor have they generally any conviction of its truth which interferes with their observing all the principles and practices of their own religion. And they have not generally any prejudice against Christianity, unless what has been excited by the immoral conduct of some who profess it. For they do not know enough of Christianity, of its nature and doctrines, and its spirit and claims, to feel any prejudice against it.

There is another class or portion of the population who know more of Christianity, and are in a different state of mind in respect to it. They have perhaps been educated in some of the mission schools, or heard the Gospel preached, or read the Scriptures, or some Christian books, or have some acquaintance with the native Christians. In these, or some other ways, they have acquired considerable knowledge of Christianity, its history, its doctrines, and its duties. They have often more or less conviction of the truth of the Gospel, and of their duty to embrace it. They continue, however, to follow the Hindu religion, excusing themselves to their own consciences and to others as well as they can, for what they do. There are strong motives of a worldly nature to induce such persons to continue in their hereditary faith; at least not to renounce it, if they do not believe and practise it. If they should renounce their ancestral religion and embrace Christianity, they must incur sneering, reproach, and abuse. They must lose the good-will of their relatives and friends. They must break the rules of caste and become outcastes, and though the recent laws and decisions of the courts now protect such persons in the enjoyment of their personal and property rights, yet the circumstances of those who are expelled from their caste, who in the view of people generally become outcastes, are often very painful. In such cases there is often much suffering, which no law and no court can prevent, or relieve, or remove. The trials and sufferings which people often have to endure for breaking the rules of caste and becoming outcastes, cannot well be conceived by those who have not experienced them, or seen others actually enduring them. The members of the Madras Missionary Conference only expressed what many missionaries have seen, when they said, "Caste is one of the greatest obstacles to the progress of the Gospel in India." And again, "We have long regarded caste as a most formidable opponent of genuine Christianity, and a deadlier enemy in some respects to the souls of this people than even idolatry." Many of this class of people have peculiar claims on Christians for forbearance and sympathy, and for prayer to the God of all grace that they may be more enlightened and have strength of mind and purpose to act in accordance with their convictions of duty and to endure all its consequences.

There is another large and important class who regard Christianity and indeed all religion in a different light, and who are actuated by a different spirit. Many causes besides the means used to introduce and propagate Christianity, have been in operation for many years to undermine Hinduism. Some of the measures of the English government necessarily, though indirectly, have this influence. Foreign commerce, personal intercourse with foreigners, and the knowledge of foreign countries which the Hindus are acquiring in various ways, have a strong reflex influence upon their views of their own country, its government, religion, usages, and customs. Prominent among the causes which are coöperating to change the religious opinions and character of the Hindus, must be reckoned education in modern science and literature. It has been already stated that Christianity is excluded from the numerous colleges, seminaries, high schools and vernacular schools connected with the government.* But the Hindu sacred books are of such a character that education in modern science and literature must inevitably destroy all confidence in them and all respect for them.† There are now some hundreds of young men in Calcutta, Madras, Bombay, and other large cities, amounting probably to some thousands in all India, who through the influence of education and other causes have lost all confidence in Hinduism as the system was formerly taught and believed by the learned and is still practised by the mass of the people. It is not too much to say that hundreds of this class are as well educated for professions (were any professions open before them) and for social influence in India, as young men generally are for the professions and for social influence in this country when they graduate at our colleges. Their education has been of a different character. Few of them have learned Latin or Greek, but they generally understand and can fluently use 2 or 3 of the modern languages of India, and they have acquired a knowledge of the English language and its literature, or of Sanscrit, or of Persian, or of Arabic. The religious opinions of this class are generally deistical and are very freely and fearlessly avowed among themselves.

* Page 319.

† Page 320, 321.

This class of persons have clubs, associations, and societies for debates, discussions, and lectures, and among the subjects which engage their attention at such times, religion in some of its forms and claims has a prominent place. Christianity, as being the religion of the English (now the governing power of their country) and also of Europe, now containing the most highly civilized and powerful nations in the world, would naturally excite their curiosity, while its aggressive spirit and progressive state in their country excites feelings of opposition. Their libraries are well furnished with infidel and deistical works which have been procured from Europe and America. The historical facts and doctrines of the Bible, the ordinances of the Gospel, and certain parts and periods of the history of Christianity are made the subjects of inquiry, discussions, and lectures. At such times Christianity and all connected with it, the Scripture doctrines and characters, as well as parts of its history, are often treated with levity, scurrility, reviling, and blasphemy. To counteract the influence of such meetings where no one can speak for Christianity, missionaries appoint meetings for delivering lectures upon the facts, doctrines, and duties of the Scriptures, which they invite all the natives to attend, and also meetings for discussion in which they invite all to take a part. These meetings are often well attended. In some instances they have been continued once or twice a week for months and years, and the natives have often exhibited interest, zeal, and ability in the discussions. On such occasions they make a free use of the works of infidel writers, and the sneers, cavils, and arguments of deists in Europe and America are reproduced in India, to be there again answered and refuted.

The same class has also to a great extent the management and control of the native press in India. In their journals much appears of an infidel and scurrilous nature against Christianity, in perverted and distorted statements of its doctrines and duties, of its principles and its precepts, of the conduct and character of its professors, and of the ways and means used for propagating it. To counteract the influence of such attacks and statements, missionaries and friends of the missionary cause publish and support journals containing correct statements of

Christian doctrines, expositions of Scripture, religious intelligence, etc.

The following facts show the state of the native mind in India. The proprietor and editor of one of the oldest, best supported, and most ably managed newspapers in Bombay, some time ago expressed his views of the state of religion among all classes, and suggested what course should be pursued. After inserting two or three articles in his paper to prepare the minds of his readers, he said it was obvious to all that the state of religion was very sad and becoming worse, that all classes of people appeared to have lost all confidence in their sacred books; that Christians do not believe in their Bible, for they do not keep the Sabbath, many of them are intemperate, etc.; that the Jews, the Mohammedans, the Hindus, and the Zoroastrians do not believe in their respective sacred books, because if they do, they would not do so many things which are forbidden, and neglect to do so many that are commanded. He then proceeded to say that the sacred books of all these different classes of people may have been of divine origin, and when first given they may have been adapted to the then state and circumstances of the people, and have been very useful, but that they had become unsuitable to the present advanced state of knowledge and improved state of society, and that none of these sacred books could ever again have the confidence of their people, and become the rule of their faith and practice, and that if people should continue as they are, without any system of religion or standard of moral conduct, they would become worse and worse, and at length become depraved beyond recovery or endurance. He then suggested that a religious convention be held in Bombay, and that each class of people send a delegation of their learned and devout men with copies of their sacred books, and that the men of this convention should prepare from all these sacred books a *shastra* suited to the present state of the world, and adapted to all classes of people, and he expressed his belief that a shastra thus prepared and recommended would soon be generally adopted. In his next paper he proceeded to mention some of the doctrines which such a shastra should contain, and among these he said it should inculcate the existence of only one God, and the worship of him without any kind of idol or material symbol; and then he would have no distinctions of caste, which he thought was one of the great evils and absurd things in the Hindu religion.

Now these opinions and suggestions are chiefly remarkable, as exhibiting the state of the native mind. It is unnecessary to say that they are entirely subversive of Hinduism, involving the rejection of its sacred books as well as of its peculiar rites and its most cherished practices. The writer of these articles for the public was a respectable and well-educated Hindu, who had not renounced the principles or the practices of his hereditary faith, nor the rules of caste, and yet we see what a system of religion he was prepared to profess, if all the community would do the same. He was proprietor as well as editor of his paper, and so he had much interest in sustaining its popularity and increasing its circulation. Indeed, I was told that he had but little property besides his paper, and that he relied chiefly upon it for his support. He knew the state of religious opinion among the Hindus, and he was well assured that such opinions and suggestions would not be to the prejudice of his character, nor to the injury of his paper.

Now this man, the readers of his paper and the circle of his acquaintance show the state of hundreds and thousands in India, who are dissatisfied with the Hindu religion, and having no confidence in it would gladly embrace something more reasonable, more easily practised, and which they hope would exert a better influence upon society and the state and character of their nation. But they are not prepared to incur the reproach, the family and social troubles, and in some cases the loss of property, which would follow a renunciation of their ancestral faith and the rules of caste. And so they continue to be Hindus in name and profession, but sceptics in heart and libertines in practice, so far as they can be without reproach, persecution, loss of character and property.

It is now some years since a spirit of infidelity and scepticism began to take strong hold of the educated native mind in India. This spirit was first manifested in Calcutta, Madras, and Bombay, and it is making progress in all the large cities. Some persons when first awakened and enlightened to see the falsehood and absurdity of Hinduism, have continued their inquiries with more or less earnestness till they embraced Christianity in the full conviction of its being the only system of divine revelation. But many others have passed from a conviction of this falsehood of the Hindu religion into a state of scepticism and indifference to all religion, unless when the progress of Christianity now and then rouses them to oppose it.

There is yet another class of the native population which owes its origin to the influence of Christianity and other causes coöperating with it to change the religion of the country. They profess a system of reformed Hinduism. This class or sect originated many years ago, and for a while there were strong expectations that it would spread and have great influence upon the moral and intellectual character of the Hindus. Ram Mohun Roy, whose opinions and writings once excited much interest in America, was the principal agent in originating this Society, and in sustaining it while he lived. After his decease (which occurred in England in 1831), the Society declined, and for some years was apparently extinct. It was however resuscitated in 1839, and has been continued. The sect or denomination is not large, but it consists generally of men of intelligence, influence, and wealth. How far their efforts to reform the Hindu religion will succeed, and what form they will assume, remains to be seen.*

In the brief history and description of India, contained in this work, we have seen that the inhabitants for many centuries professed various forms of heathenism, as demonolatry, brahminism, and budhism.— That while professing these forms of religion, though they made progress in civilization, and their country became populous and wealthy, they yet made no progress in the knowledge of the true God, nor in any reasonable way of worshipping Him, "but became vain in their imaginations, and their foolish heart was darkened; professing themselves to be wise they became fools, and changed the glory of the uncorruptible God into an image made like to corruptible man, and to birds, and to four-footed beasts, and to creeping things."†— That the Mohammedans with the avowed object of converting the Hindus to their faith, invaded and overran the country, sub-

* For a more particular account of this Society, see Appendix D.

† Romans 1: 21–23.

dued the people, and used various means to effect their conversion. — That having been the predominant power in India for 7 or 8 centuries, their great empire fell to pieces, leaving nine tenths of the inhabitants still professing the religion of their ancestors. — That the time having arrived in the progress of maritime discovery and national intercourse, when the power and civilization of Europe must come into conflict with the power and civilization of the southern countries of Asia, the struggle for European ascendency and empire in India was between the English and the French — the former prospectively representing Protestantism with its civil and religious liberty, and the latter prospectively representing Romanism with its despotism and intolerance. — That in this great and long-continued struggle, the English were finally victorious, and from that time they have been extending their dominions and consolidating their power, till their Indian empire now holds the first place among the nations of Asia, and contains 100,000,000 of people. — That the English have suppressed many barbarous customs of heathenism and cruel rites of superstition, which had been long practised among the inhabitants. — That they have opened the country to the introduction and spread of Christianity. — That they have established the freedom of the press, and enacted laws securing equal rights and civil and religious liberty for all classes of people.

We have seen that the Romanists made long and vigorous efforts to introduce and propagate their religion, but without the success they expected. — That the different Protestant churches of Europe and America have entered vigorously upon the work of evangelizing the inhabitants. — That in removing difficulties, in creating means for acquiring the languages of the people, in making translations of the Scriptures, in preparing a Christian literature, in promoting general and special education, in preparing a native missionary agency, and in preaching the Gospel and gathering converts into churches — that in all these various ways, missionaries have done a great work, and that they and all the churches connected with them have reason, in view of the history and of the present state and prospect of this cause, to thank God and to take courage.

The future of India is to us unknown. But whatever may be

its political state and relations, we believe that it will one day become a province of the kingdom of Emmanuel. How soon it will become such, and what changes are to take place before it shall be included in the dominions of the Prince of Peace, we know not. How different has been the history of Christianity in all the countries of Christendom from what at different times was expected? How would the primitive Christians have been astonished, had any one speaking by the spirit of prophecy told them what would be the history of Christianity in all the countries where they were living? And how incredulous they would have been, had any one not inspired then expressed opinions of the future state of Christianity in those countries, corresponding to what has been its true state and history.

And whether the progress of Christianity in India is to be steadily onward till it shall supplant Hinduism, Mohammedanism, and other forms of error, and become the religion of the country; or Romanism is yet to revive, to put forth its power, renew its policy, and increase its votaries through the land; or the Mohammedans are to become animated with the spirit of proselytism, and attempt to accomplish by persuasion and policy what they failed to effect by force and power; or some reformed and philosophical system of Hinduism is to take the place of the present popular but absurd superstition; or general scepticism in respect to all revelation and indifference to all religion is to spread through the country; or some new form of error and delusion is yet to appear and for a while prevail;—these things are now beyond human knowledge. And happily our duty does not depend upon our knowing them. "Secret things belong to the Lord, but things which are revealed," whether in the word or in the providence of God, "belong to us." The history of the world from the days of the Apostles has never exhibited a more inviting and a more encouraging field for missionary enterprise than India now is. Should the masses of the Hindu population, through the progress of education and other causes, become excited and convinced of the falsehood and folly of the popular superstitions, and at the same time the Mohammedans and Romanists become animated with a spirit of proselytism, it is painful to contemplate what might be the results. Thus whether we look at the present state or not improbable contingencies of India, it is obvious that a great increase of the present missionary force is urgently required, and it is in the power as well as the duty of Christians to furnish it. A reference to the tables (pages 538, 539) which exhibit the state of the missions in India and Ceylon, will show that only *one fifth part* of this missionary force is from America, and that *five sixths* of it is from Europe. Now this is a much less proportion than is generally supposed in this country, and much less than we ought to have.

The following statement and appeal of the venerable Bishop of Calcutta to the people of England, is equally deserving the consideration of Christians in the United States:—

"What can exceed the inviting prospect which India presents? The fields white for the harvest, and awaiting the hand of the reaper! Nations bursting the intellectual sleep of 30 centuries! Superstitions no longer in the giant strength of youth, but doting to their fall! Britain placed at the head of the most extensive empire ever consigned to a western sceptre: that is, the only great power of Europe, professing the Protestant faith, intrusted with the thronging nations of Asia, whom she alone could teach! A paternal government employing every year of tranquillity in elevating and blessing the people, unexpectedly thrown upon its protection. No devastating plague, as in Egypt; no intestine wars; no despotic heathen or Mohammedan dominion prowling for its prey. But legislation going forth with her laws; science lighting her lamp; education scattering the seeds of knowledge; commerce widening her means of intercourse; the British power ever ready to throw her ægis of protection around the pious and discreet missionary.

"O where are the first propagators and professors of Christianity? Where are our martyrs and reformers? Where are the ingenuous, devoted, pious sons of our Universities? Where are our younger devoted clergy? Are they studying their ease? Are they resolved on a ministry, tame, ordinary, and agreeable to the flesh? Are they drivelling after minute literature, poetry, fame? Do they shrink from that toil and labor, which, as Augustine says, our Commander, *noster Imperator*, accounts most blessed? Let us unite in removing misconceptions; let us join in appealing to Societies; let us write to particular friends, and to public bodies; let us afford correct intelligible information. Let us send specific and individual invitations; and let us 'pray the Lord of the harvest that he would send forth more laborers into his harvest.'"

In view of the state of India and the other oriental countries, where God has been preparing the nations for the kingdom of the Redeemer, we may use the sublime prayer of the greatest of the English poets:—

"Come forth out of thy royal chambers, O Prince of all the kings of the earth, put on the visible robes of thy imperial Majesty; take up that unlimited sceptre which thy Almighty Father hath bequeathed thee, for now the voice of thy Bride calls thee, and all creatures sigh to be renewed." *

Our encouragement for making such supplications, and our assurance that our petitions are in accordance with the purposes of Jehovah, are found in many declarations of his Word, like the following:—

"From the rising of the sun to the going down of the same, my name shall be great among the Gentiles; and in every place incense shall be offered unto my name, and a pure offering; for my name shall be great among the Gentiles, saith the Lord of Hosts." †

And now in view of these promises, and of what we have seen and expect to see of their fulfilment, we close in the words of the Psalmist:—

"Blessed be the Lord God, the God of Israel, who only doeth wondrous things; and blessed be his glorious name forever and ever; and let the whole earth be filled with his glory; Amen, and Amen." ‡

* Milton's Works, p. 64. † Malachi, 1 ch., 11 v.
‡ Psalm 72, v. 18, 19.

APPENDIX.

A.—p. 357.

The State and Prospects of the English Language in India; read at a meeting of the American Oriental Society in New Haven, October 26, 1853. *By* D. O. ALLEN, D. D., *Missionary of the American Board in India.*

THE English language is our inheritance, and we expect to transmit it to our posterity. This inheritance, enriched as it is with the science and literature of the English nation for many centuries, we have reason to value very highly, and we naturally feel an interest in its extension in the world. It appears from the designs of Providence as developed in the course of events, that English is to be the language generally used in North America, and that in a few generations it will be vernacular over a larger part of the world and among a larger population than has ever yet used a common language. The state and prospects of North America, the extensive colonial possessions of England and her great and increasing dominions in southern Asia, are reasons for believing that the English language is hereafter to exert an influence in the world far beyond any other language, ancient or modern. To some this prospect has appeared so pleasing and gratifying that they are cherishing the opinion that the English language will be everywhere generally understood, and at a late public anniversary a popular orator chose for his subject—"The English the future universal language."

A large part—probably more than three fourths—of the population subject to the English government, live in India, and the English possessions in southern Asia appear likely to be yet further extended. It becomes therefore an interesting question, how far are these conquests likely to extend the knowledge and use of the English language in those countries? In examining this question, several facts and circumstances require to be taken into consideration.

1. The state of those countries when they became subject to the English Government. India and the other countries of southern Asia in which the English power has been, or appears likely to be, established and perpetuated, have been long reckoned among civilized nations. For many centuries—probably for more than two thousand years—they had regular governments, and their history embraces dynasties of powerful kings and emperors. For centuries they

have contained a large population, and they have well formed and some of them highly polished languages. They have some science, and the Sanscrit and Tamul languages especially have much literature, ancient and modern, sacred and profane, which they hold in great veneration, and to which they are strongly attached. In these respects the inhabitants of India and the other countries of southern Asia differ much from the aborigines of America, as well as of the islands of the Pacific and of Australia, where the inhabitants were comparatively few in number and scattered over a great extent of country, having no written language and no literature of any kind, with few of the comforts and conveniences and none of the arts and luxuries of civilized nations. To the conquerors of people of this character and in these circumstances, it appeared easier to communicate a knowledge of their own language than to acquire the languages of so many different uncivilized tribes, and then reduce them to system and order, and so make them a proper medium of communication for a Christian and civilized people.

2. Another means by which nations have extended their language with their power, has been by emigration to the conquered countries and permanent settlement in them. But in tropical climates the European constitution cannot endure the out-door labor, which is requisite in order to carry on the various necessary occupations of life. This is an established fact. The efforts of the Portuguese, the Spanish, and the Dutch to found colonies in different parts of southern Asia, and in eastern and western Africa, with the expectation that they would become self-perpetuating and increasing communities, and retain the complexion, language, religion, customs, and manners of their respective nations, have proved to be failures. Such colonies, in all instances, soon began to deteriorate. Some of them, of which great hopes were entertained, have become extinct, and in other places they have mingled with the indigenous population of the country, and are becoming assimilated to them in circumstances and character. The conquests of the English in southern Asia were subsequent to those of the nations above mentioned, and so, having the advantage of their experience, they have never attempted to found any colonies in their Asiatic possessions. The very low price of labor in all those countries is also one of the causes which have prevented emigration to them from England. Europeans could not subsist upon the common rate of wages in those countries, without adopting, to a great extent, the habits and customs of the inhabitants in respect to food, clothing, houses, etc.; and to do this would soon prove destructive to health and life. For these reasons, the English have never emigrated to any of their possessions in southern Asia so as to form any self-perpetuating community. Nor is it likely they will ever form any community there, which will use the English as their vernacular language. All classes of people who go from England to those countries, whether to engage in the service of the government, or for pursuits of private enterprise, intend at some future time to return to England, or go to some other congenial climate for their permanent home. Many situations can be filled only by those who have acquired a knowledge of one or two native languages, and who have shown their qualifications by examinations before committees appointed for this purpose; and Europeans generally learn enough of the language in use where they are, to hold communication with the people

in matters of business and in social and official intercourse. The native language thus becomes the medium of communication between the European and the native population; and it soon becomes as natural for Europeans to use the native language, in their intercourse with the people of the country, as it is for them to use the English language in their intercourse with the people of their own nation. Still, some natives acquire a colloquial knowledge of English, by hearing it used, and by using it in intercourse with Europeans before they have acquired any native language, and with some who are only transient residents in the country. The number of this class of natives is small, their pronunciation of English is bad, their use of it is ungrammatical, often scarcely intelligible, and their knowledge of it is very limited. From these statements and remarks it will be apparent that the people of India generally have not so many means and opportunities of acquiring a knowledge of the English language in connection with the government, or in matters of business, or in social intercourse, as might be naturally expected and have been generally supposed.

3. The languages of conquering nations have sometimes spread in their acquired possessions by intermarriages and a mixture of the nations or races. It was so with some nations which obtained possession of countries composing parts of the Roman empire. But the English language is not likely to spread much in India in this manner. Europeans differ so much and in so many ways from the inhabitants of the country, that intermarriages to any considerable extent are not likely ever to take place between them. In most places where Europeans have lived for any considerable time in southern Asia, there are some of a mixed race; and in India this class of people generally understand the English, and also some native language in use where they live. But this class is not large, nor are they likely to become numerous. They have not now, nor do they appear likely to acquire, a high social position, nor to exert much political influence. The name by which they are now generally known, is Indo-Briton. Some recent researches and statistics in connection with the renewal of the East India Company's charter by Parliament, do not exhibit this class of people in so favorable a state in respect to number, character, and prospects as was generally expected.

4. Another and yet more important cause affecting the state and prospects of the English language in India, is the regulations and policy of the government. In the Supreme Courts of Calcutta, Madras, and Bombay, the English language is used. But the jurisdiction of these Courts is limited to the above-mentioned cities and to such Europeans in other parts of the country as are not subject to military law. Much of the business in these Courts is transacted through interpreters. In the public offices also in these cities, the business, in its summary and written forms, is generally transacted and the records are kept, in the English language; and the work of this kind furnishes employment for many persons, as translators, copyists, etc. Hence a knowledge of English becomes a necessary qualification for employment in these offices. The situations (as they are called) in them are generally filled by natives of the country. But their knowledge of English is often very imperfect, being limited to the mere routine of business, while they seldom if ever use it in their families, or in social inter-

course, or in matters of business with their countrymen. In the seaports of southern Asia, the English language is used in correspondence, accounts, etc., in the European mercantile houses; and a considerable number of natives who understand English more or less, are thus employed. But the European merchants are a changing class of the population, and only a small part of the property and commerce of these cities is in their hands. When one leaves the large seaports, the business of all kinds with the native population and among them is found to be transacted in the language of their respective provinces. Whether in the political, or the military, or the financial, or the judicial departments, all business is transacted in the languages of the country, and the English language is only used by Europeans in their social intercourse, and in their business transactions with each other and with the government.

From the origin of the English power in India the importance of having some one language for general use through the country, has been a subject of much consideration and inquiry, and has engaged the attention of many learned men in the employment of the government, and of others connected with the cause of education and Christianity. The Mohammedan princes and emperors, who governed India for several centuries, retained the Persian language in use among themselves and in official transactions. The English, following the example of their predecessors, used the Persian in the courts and in their official transactions in Bengal and northern India for several years, and some learned men in government employment were of the opinion that it should be retained, and means be used to make it the common language of the country. Under the Mohammedan sovereigns, the Hindustanee became the common medium of intercourse among the great body of people professing their faith, and it made some progress among the Hindu population. Hindustanee may be called the military language of India. It is easily acquired for colloquial purposes, and is more used than any other by Europeans in their intercourse with the native population. For these reasons, some have been of the opinion that all lawful and proper means should be used to extend it, and make it the general language of all classes of people. Some have set forth the claims of the Sanscrit to become the general language of India, and some have been of the opinion that English — the language of the governing power of the country — should become the general language, and that the influence of the government in its official transactions, and in the patronage it bestows on education, should be directed to this end.

Each of these different languages has had able and learned advocates for its being made the *lingua franca* of India; but there are so many objections and obstacles in the way, that no one of them is likely to be adopted, or to secure much influence or effort for extending it. The need of any such general language, though experienced by Europeans who are often changing their places of residence, is not felt to much extent by the native population. Those living in the rural districts and villages, have seldom occasion to use any but their vernacular tongue, and those who live in the cities, easily acquire knowledge enough of the languages there used to transact their necessary business. To the educated natives of India the idea or plan of making any one language supersede those now in use, and so become the common language of the whole country, would appear as unreasonable, as it would appear to the educated people of Europe, were it proposed to select some language, as the English, or the French, or the German, and endeavor to make it supersede all the others, and so become the general and common language of all the people of Europe. Indeed, such a plan in India would in some respects appear more unreasonable, as the languages there have each generally its distinct and different alphabet. More extensive and accurate knowledge of the people and literature of India will show that the number of distinct languages is not so great as has been generally supposed—that some, which have been enumerated as different languages, are merely dialects, and of limited use. Some of these dialects will gradually disappear. The opinion which, after much discussion and consideration in the different Boards of Education, now generally prevails, is that it is not expedient to use any means with a view of making any one language common or general through the country—that the people of different parts of India who have distinct and well formed languages, as the Tamul, the Canarese, the Telugu, the Mahratta, the Gujeratee, the Bengalee, used each by a population of from seven or eight to twelve or fifteen millions, should retain each its own language, and that suitable and needed works on religion, science, and literature, either original or translated, should be prepared and printed, as soon as practicable, in the different languages. In this work of preparing such a native literature, very encouraging progress has been made in several languages.

We are now to consider the state and prospects of the English language in India as it is affected by education. From the commencement of the English power in India, a knowledge of both the English and native languages has been a valuable and important qualification for business, and so this acquisition has been an object of desire and exertion. The low price of labor in all southern Asia, compared with what it is in England, must always have made it pecuniarily an object for the English to employ the natives of the country in all kinds of work or business for which they could be found, or could become, qualified. And when the power of the English became permanently established, it was for their interest to encourage the acquisition of their language by the natives, that they might become qualified for service in the various departments of business. And as the power and dominions of the English have gradually increased from a few factories, or trading establishments, to the supremacy of India and the general control over a hundred and fifty millions of people, so there has been a constantly increasing demand for persons qualified for business by their knowledge of the English language. And as such qualifications were not common, and could not be acquired without much study and time, they have been generally well remunerated for their service. Every increase of the British dominions created more situations for which a knowledge of the English language was an indispensable qualification, and so there has been a constantly increasing demand for English education. Under the native governments, all situations were filled by natives, but as these provinces have come successively under the English government, all the more honorable and highly remunerating places have been filled by Europeans, and only those of the second or third rate are given to the natives. This change in the political state of the country, and the consequent proceedings of the governing power they feel very much, both in its humiliating influence upon their character and its impoverishing effect upon their circumstances; and many of them endeavor to acquire a knowledge of the English language in the hope that it will in some way be a qualification for business, or a recommendation for employment.

The educational institutions in which the English language is taught in India are of three kinds.

1. Private schools, or those which are supported by tuition. There have been several such in Calcutta, Madras, and Bombay. They have been supported chiefly by the higher classes of the native population, and many persons have been educated in them.

2. Schools connected with missionary and other benevolent societies. At most of the large missionary stations are schools of this character. Some of these have a large number of scholars, and good means of instruction. The primary object of such schools is moral and Scriptural education, with a view to prepare such persons, when educated, to become Christian teachers, catechists, and preachers among their countrymen. But these schools are generally open for all classes of people on such terms as induce Hindus and Mohammedans, as well as professed Christians, to become connected with them. Many who were Hindus and Mohammedans when they first entered these schools, became convinced, in the course of their education, of the truth of the Christian religion, publicly professed their faith in it, and are now in the employment of Missionary Societies, preaching the Gospel to their own people. Some of these are well educated, every way respectable in talents and character, and very useful in the work of promoting Christianity in India.

3. Schools supported by the government. The government, in its various departments, has occasion to employ a great number of people, and it is necessary, in order to fill particular situations and for the performance of some peculiar kinds of service, that a part of those to be employed should understand the English language. For this purpose the government appropriates very considerable sums from the revenues of the country to education, and the high schools contain means and facilities for learning English. The course of study in the English department of these schools is sufficient for acquiring a good knowledge of the language, and obtaining a very considerable acquaintance with its science and literature. Many who commence the study of English, finding it more difficult of acquisition than they expected, or not seeing so much prospect of employment as they had hoped for at first, become discouraged and abandon it. Many also acquire just knowledge enough of the language to converse in slow, familiar, and set phraseology, but not enough to use it easily and fluently, nor to understand it when so used by others, nor to read newspapers and common books with ease and intelligence. Such persons use the language no more than is necessary. They seldom attempt to read an English book, or to improve their knowledge of the language after leaving school. Indeed, many of them, when they succeed in obtaining employment, regard their object in acquiring the language as accomplished, and so retain only what they have occasion to

use as copyists, accountants, etc. But in these schools, some, though but a small part of those who commence the study of the language, acquire a correct use of it, become able to converse in it with ease and propriety, and obtain considerable knowledge of English science and literature. Yet even this class never, so far as I have known, use the English language in their families, and very seldom in any social intercourse or transactions of business, unless with Europeans.

The vernacular languages of India contain but little science or literature of any value, and something more than these languages contain is required for mental discipline and practical knowledge, in the course of education. The Sanscrit is closely connected with the languages now used in the country and has much ancient literature. But however useful the study of it may be for discipline of mind, and with reference to philology, ethnography, and other objects of antiquarian research, it contains but little practical science, or authentic history, or correct religious doctrine, and is nowhere now a vernacular language. In these circumstances, when education is to be extended beyond any vernacular language, the English — the language of the governing power of the country, with all its science and literature, and especially its numerous and excellent works on moral and religious subjects — has the first claims to attention.

In America and Europe the professions of theology, law, and medicine, furnish the great field of employment for the educated classes. These professions are equally open to all, and they require a large part — generally a majority — of those who obtain a collegiate or liberal education, to fill them. But these professions scarcely yet exist among the native population of India. There, educated men, who must engage in some business for support (and there are very few who are not in this state), generally look to the government for service, or to teaching, as their employment. In the altered political state and relations of the country — all the more honorable and lucrative situations being filled by Europeans — the higher classes of the native population find it exceedingly difficult to obtain any suitable occupation and means of respectable support, and so they naturally turn their thoughts to the study of the English language, in the hope that it will prove a qualification for business, or a recommendation for employment. This desire to learn English has been increasing for some years past, and probably the number now engaged in acquiring it, is three times as large as it was fifteen or twenty years ago. But, even at the present time, many who become thus educated, find it very difficult, and some find it impossible, to obtain such employment as they expected. The supply of such educated talent is increasing faster than the demand, and it will not be many years before the principal motives in which this strong desire for English education had its origin, will cease, or at least will exert less influence than they have had for some years past.

From the view which has been taken of the state of the English language in India, or southern Asia, it appears: That England has not founded, and is not likely to found, any colonies in any of those countries, and that there is no native community, nor any class of people, except the Indo-Britons, who use English as their vernacular language. — That the English people who go to India, expect to reside there only for a limited time, and then to go to some more congenial climate. — That while in India they generally learn enough of the native languages for social and official intercourse with the native population, and that the business of the government is chiefly transacted in the languages of the country. It also appears: That the English language is used in the Supreme Courts of Calcutta, Madras, and Bombay; and that in some of the government offices and mercantile houses, in the same cities, many natives more or less educated in the English language find employment. — That many among the native population have a strong desire to learn English, and are now engaged in the study of it, in private, missionary, and government schools and colleges. — That, of those who begin this study, many do not acquire sufficient knowledge for any practical purpose, and only a small part of them learn it thoroughly. — That when English education among the native population shall exceed the demand for it as a qualification for employment, then one of the principal motives for acquiring it will cease, and the desire now so strong will exert much less influence. — That the education of the great body of the people will always be in their respective vernacular languages, and that those languages will be improved and enriched by works of science and literature original and translated, in which encouraging progress has been made. — That the English language, including its science and literature, will generally be a branch of education in the high schools and colleges; and all who aspire to a liberal education, will be expected to have some knowledge of it. But that the English is not likely in any part of India or southern Asia to supersede the native languages, nor to become vernacular in any large community.

Appendix B. p. 433.

The following extract from an able article on Sanscrit literature in the Calcutta Review, confirms what has been said of its character, and may be interesting to some who are not acquainted with the language.

"1. The Sanscrit language contains *nothing of genuine history*, no national annals, no biography of eminent patriots, statesmen, warriors, philosophers, poets, or others, who have figured on the theatre of Indian life, public or private. Not a single page of pure historical matter unmixed with monstrous and absurd fable is extant, or probably was ever written in it. It supplies us with no assistance whatever in rescuing from eternal oblivion the worthies or the curses of past ages. It affords no certain clue to the discovery of even the origin of the races who first spoke or adopted it. Fabulous and extravagant legends are all, that in this class, it furnishes. European ingenuity, penetration, and perseverance may indeed by dint of hard and continued labor elicit a few isolated facts here and there, and comparison of dates and circumstances, rejecting the crudities and absurdities that have gathered round them, bring them to bear upon some point of ancient story, yet in the depths of obscurity. But nothing is certain; all is only a happy guess or probable inference at best. The very principle of historic narration appears either never to have entered into the minds of the early writers in this language, or else a base and selfish policy led them to falsify and obscure and mysticize all events in order to conceal their own usurpations, violence, and injustice.

2. Sanscrit literature presents us with nothing of geographical or statistical science. The true theory of the earth is not to be traced in it. Seas of milk, and curds, and spirit, and butter, and sugar-cane juice, with mountains 256,000 miles high bearing trees 8,000, or 9,000 miles tall; seas and continents ranged in succession round a central nucleus or navel, like the peels of an onion and other similar extravagancies and fooleries, form the staple of Sanscrit lore on those heads.

3. Cosmogony and geological science are precisely in the same condition of drivelling and hopeless allegory, out of which nothing can be drawn useful to any purpose under heaven.

4. Of natural history, the philosophy of nature and mechanical science (astronomy and geometry partially excepted), the Sanscrit exhibits nothing whatever; all is either impossible fable, or when natural and true, trivial, unscientific, and unarranged.

5. Hindu medical science is at zero. Empiricism rules the day. Anatomy is unknown. Pharmacy is little more than a knowledge of simples, united with absurd quackery.

6. The music of the Hindus is in an extremely backward state. A fantastic association with an ideal superstition has served with other causes to hinder its advancement as a science. As an art too, Hindu music is singularly rude; it knows nothing of harmony or counterpart. The Sanscrit musical shastras are numerous but of small value.

7. The same is the case with the other fine arts, as painting, architecture, and statuary. Books upon them are few and unimportant in character.

8. On the mechanical arts or handicrafts there are no express treatises; on some of them a few precepts of ordinary practice occur, as also on agriculture, etc., in general writings. Nothing in short can well be conceived poorer than Sanscrit literature in all the most important scientific or practical departments of knowledge. There is positively nothing to serve any other purpose of the European student but a not unnatural curiosity.

9. In every branch of experimental science or natural philosophy, Sanscrit is wholly wanting. The Hindu philosophers were rather poets than strict investigators of the system of things. They thought much and deeply but were ever fonder of chasing the phantoms of a speculative fancy, than of following the indications of nature. They loved more to indulge in abstraction and ingenious theories than to pursue experimental inquiries by a course of rigid induction. Their philosophy is therefore the philosophy of fancy, not of reality. It may be brilliant, captivating, and acute, ingenious and imposing; but it is after all, empty, impracticable, and useless; nay more, it is bewildering and injurious; it misleads and effeminates; it lowers the tone of the mind; it destroys the moral sense; it lays open to a thousand deceptions and aberrations, and it creates a taste which is incapable of relishing reality or moral truth.

10. In regard to mental and physical science, Sanscrit is nearly in the same

predicament. Plenty of mental *theory* indeed there is, but nothing of sound and vigorous reasoning; nothing of rigid analysis or accurate classification of mental phenomena. All is dreamy and visionary, fanciful and empirical assertion. The relation between cause and effect is utterly overlooked. The impossible and the absurd are treated with the gravity of serious philosophy and a positiveness only becoming those who deal in matters of fact.

11. The same may also be said of pneumatology, or the science of God. The psychology of man was never investigated by those who wrote in Sanscrit. The true principle of reasoning *a posteriori*, or from ascertained facts and observed phenomena alone, was never understood or adopted by them. They are ever afloat on a wide expanse of theory without chart, compass, or rudder; nay, without even a polestar to aid their navigation. Of matter and spirit, of mind and body, substance and form, nature and accident, indeed much, very much has been written, but to vastly little purpose notwithstanding. Six philosophical schools have put forth as many systems of things more or less symbolizing with the ancient systems of Greece and Rome, only with far less of either accuracy of investigation or vigor of conception. The Hindu mind has ever delighted in day-dreams and reveries; non-realities have had far more attractions for it than actualities; it has pleased and lost itself in a luxurious indulgence of an all-excursive fancy, that has soared far above all the coarse materialities of the actual world. In the history of no people has the scriptural allegation been more exactly verified than in that of the Hindus, that "man by wisdom knew not God." Not only are they in truth ignorant of God as to any really useful and practical purpose of philosophy, religion, or morals, but their so-called wisdom and beautiful science has itself been the cause of the density and perpetuation of that ignorance. They have reasoned or rather theorized, dreamt and disputed, talked and written of God and nature, matter and spirit, fate and will, action and passion, good and evil, till in the multitude of words they have wholly lost sight of the objects of inquiry. A blind fatality, a visionary system of unrealities, a thoughtless, objectless, passionless, soulless Deity, without qualification, without active intelligence or creative energy; an *atheistical* theology that identifies matter and spirit, God and nature, the human soul and the divine; a *suicidal* philosophy that destroys itself, a denial of the essential differences of things, an assertion of the intrinsic indifference of all acts and feelings which makes the character of an action depend upon *motive* of the performance, and the absolute dependence of every agent on a superior power — these and similar have been the conclusions arrived at by Hindu speculation. The Vedas themselves which are asserted to have proceeded immediately from the mouth of God, are a strange and heterogeneous assemblage of absurd physics and dreamy metaphysics, of fanciful philosophy and dreary superstition, of high-sounding invocations and petty prayers, of incantations for the injury or destruction of enemies, or the averting of personal evils, of recipes for sacrifices and the like. In them the elements are deified at the same time that the doctrine of the universal soul is asserted. These boasted Shastras are stuffed in fact with all manner of puerilities and inconsistencies, and are evidently a very crude digest as it were, of the odds and ends of mutually opposing theories, of airy visions and gross idol-

atries, containing neither true science, nor true ethics, nor elevated notions of God, or of his works and ways. Meanwhile as to practical religion, the bad passions and depraved tastes of effeminate and demoralized society have found their indulged and characteristic exercise and gratification in an idolatry more multiform and grotesque, more absurd and baseless, more cruel and disgusting, more corrupting and stupefying, more brutalizing and demoralizing, more injurious to social liberty, to domestic purity, to private virtue and to universal happiness than any other that ever existed. — *Calcutta Review*, No. 5, p. 12–14.

General Vans Kennedy in his learned work on Hindu Mythology, says, — "It must be admitted that the sacred Books of the Hindus contain neither geographical, nor chronological, nor historical information; that in them the use of numbers with respect both to time and place is extravagantly absurd, and that in their style and want of arrangement, they are not only deficient in the beauties by which the immortal works of Greece and Rome are distinguished, but even err against all principles of refined taste and classical composition."

In his View of Hindu Literature, the Rev. W. Ward says of Sanscrit poetry, — "It abounds in the most extravagant metaphors, and the most licentious images. Some allowance may be made for eastern manners, but granting every possible latitude, innumerable ideas are found in almost every poem which could have become familiar to the imagination only amidst a people, whose country was a brothel." Referring to Mr. W.'s opinion the Calcutta Review says, "This is strong language, but not too strong. It is impossible for a pure mind not to be perpetually shocked and revolted by the undisguised licentiousness, as it is for correct taste not to be offended and disgusted by the outrageous and childish extravagance of metaphoric ornaments with which all Hindu poetry is replete."

Appendix C. p. 554.

POLYGAMY.

The Calcutta Missionary Conference, consisting of the missionaries of the different Societies, which have missionaries in that city and its vicinity, after frequent consultations and much consideration on the subject of polygamy as it exists in India, were unanimous in the following opinions: —

"1. It is in accordance with the spirit of the Bible and the practice of the Protestant Church to consider *the State* as the proper fountain of legislation in all civil questions affecting marriage and divorce.

"2. The Bible being the true standard of morals, ought to be consulted in every thing which it contains on the subjects of marriage and divorce, and nothing determined contrary to its general principles.

"3. Married persons being both *Christians*, should not be divorced for any other cause than adultery. But if one of the parties be an *unbeliever*, and though not an adulterer, wilfully depart from and desert the other, a divorce may be properly sued for. They were of the opinion, however, that such liberty is allowable only in extreme cases, and where all known means of reconciliation after a trial of not less than one year have failed.

"4. Heathen and Mohammedan marriages and divorces, recognized by the laws of the country, are to be held valid. But it is strongly recommended that if either party before conversion have put away the other on slight ground, the divorced party should in all practicable and desirable cases, be taken back again.

"5. If a convert before becoming a Christian has married more wives than one, in accordance with the practice of the Jewish and primitive Christian Churches, he shall be permitted to keep them all; but such a person is not eligible to any office in the Church. In no other case is polygamy to be tolerated among Christians."

The Calcutta Christian Observer has contained at different times some well written articles upon these subjects. In a series of articles some years ago, the writer after fully establishing (as he believed) the intrinsic lawfulness of polygamy as it existed among the Jews of old, and as it now exists among the Hindus, Mohammedans, and Jews in India, proceeds thus to give his views of it in connection with the propagation of Christianity: —

"The previous lawfulness of polygamy abstractedly considered and the course actually adopted by the Almighty for its ultimate subversion suggest a *second* remark, that when a heathen man has been legally married (*i. e.* according to the laws of his own country and religion) to more than one wife, whether any distinction of grade or class of wife or concubine, etc., be observed or not, it does not appear that any thing in the character of polygamy itself or in the institution of Christianity, demands the putting away of any one or more of such women. They are his wives; he has promised them duty of marriage, support, and protection. He has no right to diminish aught of their just claims. The merciful provision of the law of Moses, in kindred cases, comes in support of my position. Exodus 21: 10, commands, even of a purchased slave whom her master has betrothed to himself, that "if he take unto himself another wife, her food, her raiment, and her duty of marriage shall he not diminish. And to apply the case to India: — What may be the precise law of the case I am not informed, but assuredly there would be great cruelty and hardship in a man, who becomes a Christian having several wives, dismissing all but one, who, even admitting that they *may* be legally put away, are by the usages of the country precluded from marrying another; and who, even if the husband continues to *support* them (the difficulty of doing which will certainly be much increased when the household is divided), are publicly disgraced and exposed, in deplorable moral ignorance, weakness, and strength of passion, to very strong temptations to pursue evil courses. Again, if there are children, whose shall they be? the father's? or the mother's? From one parent or the other they are certainly in this case to be separated. Whose control, instruction, and affectionate intercourse shall they continue to enjoy? Shall they be held legitimate or otherwise? If there are several wives, which shall be retained? The *first*, it may be replied; but by what law is she more a wife than the second, or the third? To these difficulties add the strong temptation held out to an insincere profession of Christianity for the mere purpose of getting rid of a wife or wives no longer loved, or whom the husband is weary of supporting, and it appears to me that a formidable mass of difficulties is raised against the position combated, sufficient to prove it absolutely untenable. Under the plea of a previous unlawfulness supported by no just reasoning and inculcated by no inspired Scriptures, helpless women legally united to men sacredly engaged to love, support, and protect them, are to be ejected from home, from the honors and comforts of wifedom and maternity, exposed to fearful temptations, cruel privations and self-denial, ignominy and solitariness, suffering a disruption of all the sweet ties of domestic intercourse and affection; the education of children is to be neglected, their filial attachments blighted, and a reward held out to the purest acts of injustice, of selfish cruelty and impious hypocrisy on the part of husbands and fathers.

"Let no Christian *after* he has been admitted into the Christian church, add unto his wives or support the practice of polygamy, however usual in his nation and country. But if already a polygamist, let him live, as the ancient patriarchs did, in the holy and faithful fulfilment of all the duties of marriage alike with all his wives legally such; let him not for a moment allow himself to entertain the monstrous and unnatural purpose of injuring those he loved and swore to love forever — who have lain in his bosom and become the mothers of his children and the partners of his joys and sorrows — by putting them away for no original or after fault of *theirs* upon *his* becoming a Christian. If they indeed should desert him, he is absolved by the same rules that apply to the case of a single heathen wife or husband voluntarily departing from a partner who has become a Christian, for then the act is theirs, not his. 'A brother or a sister is not under bondage in such cases.' But short of this, no legitimate ground appears to be left for supporting the ground I have thus endeavored to prove unscriptural and untenable.

"All the Calcutta missionaries, I believe, are firm in the persuasion not only that polygamy is highly inexpedient generally, but that it is, as such, a practice which the genius and tendency of Christianity are to abolish; not however by hastily and prematurely cutting off the allowance of it, and in so doing committing the greatest injustice against many helpless women, and violating the pure, benevolent, and peaceable spirit of Christ's religion, but by gradually elevating the human character among the neophytes, spiritualizing and refining its professors, and silently throwing into disuse that which like slavery for instance is so ill adapted in many respects to an advanced and cultivated society and to maturity of devotion and domestic enjoyment. The missionaries are of opinion that the very allowance, which God through Moses made for the Jews in their infant state as a people, is by parity of reason to be made now for polygamists, who from heathens become Christians; and they believe moreover that by 'the original law of marriage,' it must be as unlawful to abandon one wife as another, save for the cause of fornication." — *Calcutta Christian Observer*, vol. 4, pp. 91, 371 and 400.

The writer from whose articles in the Calcutta Christian Observer, these extracts are taken, had previously attempted to show that polygamy, as it existed among the Jews of old, was morally lawful, and by consequence that it is not morally wrong among the Jews, the Mohammedans, and the Hindus in modern times. The Jews practise polygamy in Mohammedan countries, and I believe wherever the laws allow them to do so, and they justify their conduct by reference to the examples of it contained in the Old Testament. Mohammed did not originate the custom in Arabia, for it had existed there for many centuries, probably from the time of the Jewish patriarchs.* He practised it himself and declared it to be lawful in the Koran. Polygamy has existed among the Hindus from an early period, probably as early as the days of Moses. There has been a disposition in this country to judge of polygamy, as it exists among Jews, Mohammedans, and Hindus, with great severity, and these views and feelings are likely to have some influence in considering and determining how such persons should be treated, if they wish to profess Christianity. Now if polygamy was not morally wrong, if the custom even had the divine approbation, among the Jews of old, it must follow I believe by consequence, that it is not intrinsically and morally wrong as it exists among the Jews, Mohammedans, and Hindus; and if it is not morally wrong among them, then the continuance of the relation (thus previously formed) after they have become Christians and the performance of all the obligations involved in the relation, cannot be morally wrong.

To those who have doubts in respect to the intrinsic moral lawfulness of polygamy as it existed among the ancient Jews, and who wish further to examine this subject, the consideration of the following extracts from a work called "*Thelyphthora*," published anonymously† many years ago in England, is recommended. The author of this work says:—

"The best and fairest, and indeed the only way, to get at the truth on this, as on every other occasion where religion is concerned, is to lay aside prejudice, from whatever quarter it may be derived, and to let the Bible speak for itself. Then we shall see that polygamy, notwithstanding the seventh commandment, was allowed by God himself, who, however others might mistake it, must infallibly know his own mind, be perfectly acquainted with his own will, and thoroughly understand his own law. If he did not intend to allow polygamy, but to prevent or condemn it, either by the seventh commandment, or by some other law, how is it possible that he should make laws for its *regulation*, any more than he should make laws for the regulation of *theft* or *murder*? How is it conceivable that he should give the least *countenance* to it, or so express his *approbation* as even to *work miracles* in support of it? For the making a woman *fruitful* who was naturally *barren*, must have been the effect of *supernatural* power. He *blessed*, and in a distinguished manner *owned*, the issue, and declared it legitimate to all intents and purposes. If this be not allowance, what is?

"As to the *first*, namely, his making laws for the regulation of polygamy, let us consider what is written in Exo. 21: 10. *If he* (*i. e.*, the husband) *take him another wife* (not, in so doing, he sins against the seventh commandment, recorded in the *preceding* chapter, but), *her food*, *her raiment*, (*i. e.*, of the first

* Gen. 20: 2, 5, 17. 26: 34. 28: 8, 9.

† This work, though published anonymously, was generally understood to be written by Rev. Martin Madan, Chaplain of the Lock Hospital in London.

wife), *and her duty of marriage, he shall not diminish.* Here God positively forbids a *neglect*, much more the *divorcing* or *putting away* the *first* wife, but charges no *sin* in taking the *second.*

"*2dly.* When Jacob married Rachel she was barren, and so continued for many years; but God did not leave this as a punishment upon her for marrying a man who had *another wife.* It is said, Gen. 30: 22, that *God remembered Rachel; and God hearkened unto her, and opened her womb, and she conceived and bare a son, and said, God hath taken away my reproach.* Surely this passage of Scripture ought to afford a complete answer to those who bring the words of the marriage bond, as cited by Christ, Matt. 19: 5.—*They twain shall be one flesh*—to prove polygamy sinful, and should lead us to construe them, as by this instance and many others the Lawgiver himself appears to have done; that is to say, where a woman, not betrothed to another man, unites herself in *personal knowledge* with the man of her choice, let that man's *situation* be what it may, *they twain shall be one flesh.* How, otherwise, do we find such a woman as Rachel united to Jacob, *who had a wife then living,* praying to God for a *blessing* on her intercourse with Jacob, and *God hearkening unto her, opening her womb,* removing her barrenness, and thus by miracle *taking away her reproach?* We also find the offspring legitimate, and inheritors of the land of Canaan; a plain proof that Joseph and Benjamin were *no bastards,* or born *out of lawful* marriage.* See a like palpable instance of God's miraculous blessing on polygamy in the case of Hannah, 1 Sam. i. and ii. These instances serve also to prove that, in God's account, the *second* marriage is just as valid as the *first,* and as obligatory; and that our making it less so, is contradictory to the Divine wisdom.

"*3dly.* God blessed and owned the issue. How eminently this was the case with regard to Joseph, see Gen. 49: 22–26; to Samuel, see 1 Sam. 3: 19. It was expressly commanded that a *bastard,* or son of a woman who was with child by *whoredom* (εκ πορνης, LXX.), should *not enter into the congregation of the Lord, even to his tenth generation* (Deut. 23: 2). But we find Samuel, the offspring of polygamy, ministering to the Lord in the tabernacle at Shiloh even in his *very childhood, clothed with a linen ephod, before Eli the priest.* See this whole history, 1 Sam. i. and ii. Who, then, can doubt of Samuel's legitimacy, and consequently of God's *allowance* of, and *blessing* on, polygamy? If such second marriage was, in God's account, null and void, as a sin against the *original* law of marriage, or the *seventh* commandment, or *any other* law of God, no mark of legitimacy could have been found on the issue; for a null and void marriage is tantamount to *no* marriage at all; and if no marriage, no legitimacy of the issue can possibly be. Instead of such a blessing as Hannah obtained, we

* If polygamy was unlawful, then Leah was the *only wife* of Jacob, and none but her children were *legitimate.* Rachel as well as Bilhah and Zilpah were merely *mistresses* and their children 6 in number were *bastards,* the offspring of *adulterous* connection. And yet there is no intimation of any such views and feelings in Laban's family, or in Jacob's family, or in Jewish history. Bilhah and Zilpah are called Jacob's *wives* (Gen. 37: 2). God honored the sons of Rachel, Bilhah, and Zilpah equally with the sons of Leah, made them the patriarchs of 7 of the tribes of the nation, and gave them equal inheritance in Canaan.—D. O. A.

should have found her and her husband Elkanah charged with adultery, dragged forth, and *stoned to death;* for so was adultery to be punished. All this furnishes us with a conclusive proof, that the having more than one wife with which a man cohabited, was not adultery in the sight of God; or, in other words, that it never was reckoned by him any sin against the *seventh* commandment, or the *original* marriage institution, or *any other law whatsoever.*

"4*thly.* But there is a passage (Deut. 21: 15) which is express to the point, and amounts to a demonstration of God's *allowance* of polygamy. *If a man have* TWO WIVES, *one* beloved *and another* hated, *and they have borne him children, both the* beloved *and the* hated; *and if the first-born be hers that was hated, then it shall be, when he maketh his sons to inherit that which he hath, that he may not make the son of the* beloved *first-born before the son of the* hated, *which is, indeed, the first-born, by giving him a double portion of all that he hath; for he is the beginning of his strength, and the right of the first-born is his.* On the footing of this law, the marriage of *both* women is *equally* lawful. God calls them both *wives* (for so the word נשים must be rendered in this place, as the context plainly shows), and he cannot be mistaken; if he *calls* them so, they certainly *were* so. If the *second* wife bore the *first* son, that son was to inherit before a son born *afterwards* of the *first* wife. Here the issue is expressly deemed *legitimate*, and inheritable to the *double portion of the first-born;* which could not be, if the *second* marriage were not deemed as lawful and valid as the *first.*

"5*thly.* To say that polygamy is sinful, is to make God the *author of sin;* for, not to forbid that which is evil, but even to countenance and promote it, is being so far the author of it, and accessory to it in the highest degree. And shall we dare to *say,* or even to *think,* that this is chargeable on Him who *is of purer eyes than to behold evil, and who cannot look on iniquity?* (Hab. 1: 13.) God forbid.

"When God is upbraiding David, by the prophet Nathan, for his ingratitude towards his Almighty benefactor (2 Sam. xii.), he does it in the following terms:—ver. 8,—*I gave thee thy master's house, and* THY MASTER'S WIVES *unto thy bosom, and I gave thee the house of Israel and Judah, and if that had been too little, I would moreover have given thee such and such things.*

"Can we suppose God giving *more wives* than *one* into David's bosom, who already had *more than one*, if it was *sin* in David to *take* them? Can we imagine that God would thus *transgress* (as it were) *his own commandment* in *one* instance, and yet so severely *reprove* and *chastise* David for breaking it in *another?* Is it not rather plain, from the whole transaction, that David committed *mortal sin* in taking another *living* man's wife, but not in taking the widows of the *deceased* Saul; and this, therefore, though the law of God condemned the *first*, yet it did not condemn the *second?*

"6*thly.* When David took the wife of Uriah, he was severely reprimanded by the prophet Nathan; but after Uriah's death, *he takes the same woman*, though he had other *wives* before, and no fault is found with him; nor is he charged with the least flaw or insincerity in his repentance on that account. The child which was the fruit of his intercourse with Bathsheba, during her husband Uriah's life, *God struck to death* with his own hand (2 Sam. 12: 15). Solomon, *born of the same woman, begotten by the same man*, in a state of *polygamy*, is acknowledged by God himself as David's lawful issue (1 Kings 5 : 5), and as such set upon his throne. The law which positively excluded *bastards*, or those born out of lawful wedlock, *from the congregation of the Lord, even unto the tenth generation* (Deut. 23 : 2), is wholly inconsistent with Solomon being employed *to build God's temple* — being *the mouth of the people to God in prayer* — and *offering sacrifices* in the *temple* at its *dedication* — unless David's marriage with Bathsheba was a *lawful marriage* — Solomon, the *lawful issue* of that marriage — consequently polygamy *no* sin, either against the primary institution of marriage, or against the seventh commandment. But so far from Solomon being under any disqualification from the *law* above mentioned, he is *appointed* by God himself *to build the temple* (1 Kings 8 : 19). *His prayer is heard, and the house is hallowed* (chap. 9 : 3), and *filled with such glory, that the priests could not stand to minister* (chap. 8 : 11). Solomon, therefore, as well as Samuel, stands as a demonstrable proof, that a child born under the circumstances of *polygamy* is no *bastard* — *God himself being the judge, whose judgment is according to truth.*

" A more striking instance of God's *thoughts* on the total difference between *polygamy* and *adultery*, does not meet us anywhere with more force and clearness in any part of the sacred history, than in the account which is given us of David and Bathsheba, and their issue.

" When David took Bathsheba, she was another man's wife ; the child which he begat upon her in that situation was begotten in *adultery* — *and the thing which David had done displeased the Lord* (2 Sam. 11 : 27). And what was the consequence ? We are told, 2 Sam. 12 : 1, *the Lord sent Nathan* the prophet *unto David.* Nathan opened his commission with a most beautiful parable descriptive of David's crime ; this parable the prophet applies to the conviction of the delinquent, sets it home upon his conscience, brings him to repentance, and the poor penitent finds mercy — his life is spared, ver. 13. Yet God will vindicate the honor of his moral government, and that in the most awful manner — the murder of Uriah is to be visited upon David and his house. *The sword shall never depart from thine house*, ver. 10. The *adultery* with Bathsheba was to be retaliated in the most aggravated manner. *Because thou hast despised me, and hast taken the wife of Uriah the Hittite to be thy wife, thus saith the Lord, I will raise up evil against thee out of thine own house, and I will take thy wives and give them unto thy neighbor before thine eyes ; and he shall lie with thy wives in sight of the sun ; for thou didst it secretly, but I will do this thing before all Israel, and before the sun.* All this was shortly fulfilled in the rebellion and incest of Absalom, chap. 16 : 21, 22. And this was done in the way of *judgment* on David for taking and defiling the wife of Uriah, and was included in the curses threatened (Deut. 28 : 30) to the despisers of God's laws.

" As to the issue of David's adulterous commerce with Bathsheba, it is written, 2 Sam. 12 : 15, *The Lord struck the child that Uriah's wife bare unto David, and it was very sick.* What a dreadful scourge this was to David, who could not but read his *crime* in his *punishment*, the following verses declare — wherein we find David almost frantic with grief. However, *the child's sickness was unto death*, for, ver. 18, *on the seventh day the child died.*

"Now, let us take a view of David's act of polygamy, when, after Uriah's death, he *added* Bathsheba to his *other* wives (ver. 24, 25). *And David comforted Bathsheba his wife, and went in unto her and lay with her, and she bare a son, and he called his name* (שלמה) Selomoh (that maketh *peace and reconciliation, or recompense*), and *the Lord loved him.* Again we find Nathan, who had been sent on the former occasion, sent also on this, but with a very *different* message. *And he* (the Lord) *sent by the hand of Nathan the prophet, and he called his name* JEDIDIAH (*Dilectus Domini*—Beloved of the Lord), *because of the Lord,*—*i. e.*, because of the favor God had towards him (ver. 24).

"Let any read onward through the whole history of Solomon; let them consider the instances of God's peculiar favor towards him already mentioned, and the many others that are to be found in the account we have of him; let them compare God's dealings with the *unhappy* issue of David's *adultery*, and this *happy* offspring of his *polygamy*, and if the *allowance* and *approbation* of the *latter* doth not as clearly appear as the *condemnation* and punishment of the *former*, surely all distinction and difference must be at an end, and the Scripture itself lose the force of its own evidence.

"*7thly.* I have mentioned the law being explained by the prophets. These were extraordinary messengers which God raised up and sent forth under a special commission, not only to foretell things to come, but to preach to the people, to hold forth the law, to point out their defections from it, and to call them to repentance, under the severest terms of God's displeasure unless they obeyed. Their commission, in these respects, we find recorded in Isa. 58: 1, *Cry aloud, spare not, lift up thy voice like a trumpet: Show my people their transgression, and the house of Jacob their sins.* This commission was to be faithfully executed at the peril of the prophet's own destruction, as appears from the solemn charge given to Ezekiel, chapter 3: 18, *When I say to the wicked, Thou shalt surely die, and thou givest him not warning, nor speakest to warn the wicked to save his life, the same wicked man shall die in his iniquity, but his blood will I require at thine hand.*

"These prophets executed their commissions very unfaithfully towards God and the people, as well as most dangerously for themselves, if polygamy was a *sin* against God's law, for is was the common practice of the whole nation, from the prince on the throne to the lowest of the people; and yet neither Isaiah, Jeremiah, nor any one of the prophets, bore the least testimony against it. They reproved them sharply and plainly for *defiling their neighbors' wives*, as Jer. 5: 8. 29: 23, in which fifth chapter we not only find the prophet bearing testimony against *adultery*, but against *whoredom* and *fornication* (ver. 7), for that they assembled themselves *by troops in the harlots' houses.* Not a word against *polygamy.* How is it possible, in any reason, to think that this, if a sin, should never be mentioned as such by God, by Moses, or any one of the prophets?*

* Some have considered Malachi 11: 14, 15, as a denunciation of polygamy. But a careful comparison of these verses with the 11th verse and with the state of the Jews at that time, as described in Ezra 10 and 11 chapters, and Nehemiah 13: 23-31, will show that the prophet had then no reference to polygamy, but was reproving the Jews for "having married the daughters of a strange god;" that is, heathen wives, which was strictly forbidden by the laws of Moses. Deut. 7: 3. Exo. 34: 16.—D. O. A.

"*Lastly.* In the Old Testament, polygamy was not only *allowed* in all cases, but in some *commanded.* Here, for example, is the law (Deut. 25 : 5–10), *If brethren dwell together, and one of them die and have no child, the wife of the dead shall not marry without unto a stranger: her husband's brother shall go in unto her, and take her to him to wife, and perform the duty of an husband's brother unto her. And it shall be that the first-born which she beareth shall succeed in the name of his brother which is dead, that his name be not put out of Israel*, etc.

"This law must certainly be looked upon as an *exception* from the general law (Lev. 18 : 16), and the reason of it appears in the law itself, namely, 'To preserve inheritances in the families to which they belonged.' . . . As there was no law against polygamy, there was nothing to exempt a *married* man from the obligation of marrying his brother's widow. . . . For, let us suppose that not only the surviving brother, but all the near kinsmen, to whom the marriage of the widow and the redemption of the inheritance belonged, were *married* men — if that exempted them from the obligation of this law — as they could not *redeem the inheritance* unless they *married the widow* (Ruth 4: 5) — the end of this important law must in many cases be defeated — the widow be tempted to marry a stranger — to put herself and the inheritance into his hands — and the whole reason assigned for the law itself, that of *raising up seed to the deceased*, to preserve the inheritance in his family, that *his name be not put out of Israel* — fall to the ground. For which weighty reasons, as there was evidently no law against polygamy, there could be no exemption of a man from the positive duty of this law *because he was married.* As we say, *Ubi cadit ratio, ibi idem jus.*" — Vol. i. pp. 108, 131, 260, 267; vol. ii. p. 244, 402.

Appendix D. p. 585.

An acquaintance with the Hindu sacred books will at once show that no one who has been educated in modern science and literature, can have any confidence in their divine origin. The accounts which the Purans give of the creation of the world, of the form of the earth, of different countries, of astronomy, philosophy, and many other subjects, are not only unreasonable and absurd, but are at variance with well-known facts. The same Purans contain accounts of the Hindu deities, describing their immoral conduct and odious character, and inculcating their worship by the performance of degrading rites and disgusting ceremonies. It was obvious to Europeans on becoming acquainted with the contents of these works, that the Hindus would believe them no longer than they continued in a state of ignorance of nearly all the world beyond their own country. It was evident that a knowledge of Christianity and of European science and literature would destroy all confidence in the popular superstitions of India, and leave the people in a state of scepticism, or lead them to embrace some system of religion founded on more reason and truth.

Such expectations have been realized. The progress of Christianity, the diffusion of general knowledge, and education in European science and literature aroused the native mind to inquiry and reflection, and many intelligent and discerning Hindus became satisfied that a large portion of their reputed sacred books had no just claim to divine authority. They saw that the Hindu religion, as exhibited in the popular creed and generally practised, was no longer credible and so must either be reformed or abandoned. The first man who took an open and public stand and fearlessly declared his views on this subject, was Ram Mohun Roy, who subsequently acquired much celebrity in India, Europe, and America as a Hindu reformer. He was a man of much general learning and had given special attention to the Vedas. In these works he found the doctrine of one God, "the God of the whole world," and believing this to be the basis and sum of all true religion, and the other doctrines and precepts of the Vedas to be sufficient for all the practical purposes of life, he fixed on them as being the original and genuine Hindu Scriptures, and rejected the Purans as mere human compositions, as legends, fables, and fictions. He felt a strong sympathy with his erring and deluded countrymen, and having, as he believed, found the truth, he determined to do what he could to communicate it to others. With much trouble and expense he collected the Upanishads (works containing extracts from the Vedas and commentaries upon their doctrines), translated them into the vernacular language, and circulated them. He incurred much censure from his family and friends and much obloquy from the native community, but he persevered year after year in what he felt was a good cause. He also published some other works, among which was one called "the Precepts of Jesus," or selections from the New Testament, all designed to enlighten and reform his countrymen. Other Hindus gradually embraced his views, and in 1830, in order to give public expression of their sentiments and to promote the reformation they had begun, they established what they called the *Brahm Sabha;* a regularly organized society with religious meetings, somewhat after the model of Christian assemblies, in which the Upanishads should be read and explained, and the worship of Brahm (the Supreme Being, not Brahma, the first of the Hindu Triad) should be performed with prayers and praise. These assemblies were not large, but their peculiar sentiments, the reputation for learning and piety of those who composed them, and the manner in which they conducted their worship, excited for a while much attention among the native population.

Ram Mohun Roy left India for England near the close of 1830. It was his intention to return and devote his life to the cause of reforming his countrymen; but he died in England in 1833. After his departure from India the Brahm Sabha gradually declined and little was heard of it for some years. In the mean time the causes and circumstances in which the Brahm Sabha originated, continued to operate with increasing force, and in 1839 it was resuscitated, or rather a new Society embracing its essential religious principles with a superior and more definite organization under a new name, the *Tattwabodhini Sabha,* was formed. One avowed object of this new society was to propagate their principles and to gain converts to their creed. For this purpose they established branch societies and opened schools in several large cities. They collected a library of religious works in the Sanscrit, Bengalee, and English languages. They obtained a printing-press (it was a donation from one of the members) and issued a journal containing the principles of the Society, and urging all Hindus to become members of it. They have professed to rely much upon the press for the propagation of their sentiments, and have published many works on religious subjects. Some of their works have been in Sanscrit, some have been in the vernacular languages, and some have been in English. They found great difficulty in determining what to select from the great mass of Hindu sacred writings for the basis of their faith, and also what to reject and what to reform and retain, of the popular superstitions, traditions, rites, and usages. On these subjects there was much difference of opinion among the members, and great interest was felt in their proceedings by some Europeans. In 1850, a work was published by authority, which contained a declaration of their principles and the creed of those who became members. This work is called *Brahm Dharma* or the Doctrines of Brahm, and calls the members *Brahmas* or worshippers of Brahm, the Supreme God. This class of religionists are also called in some works *Brahmists* which appears to be a more appropriate name. From this work it appears that they have constructed their religion upon a broader basis than the brahminical system. They say, "the doctrines of the Brahmas or spiritual worshippers of God, are founded upon a broader and more unexceptionable basis than the Scriptures of any single religious denomination in the earth. The volume of nature is open to all, and that volume contains a Revelation clearly teaching, in strong and legible characters, the great truths of religion and morality; giving as much knowledge of our state after death as is necessary for the attainment of future blessedness; yet adapted to the present state of our mental faculties. Now as the Hindu religion contains notions of God and of human duty, which coincide with that Revelation, we have availed ourselves of extracts from works which are great depositories of the national faith, and which have the advantage of national associations on their side, for disseminating the principles of pure religion among our countrymen."

They believe in the existence of beings whom they call gods, but do not recognize them as possessing any qualities, or having any agency in human affairs, which properly make them objects of religious worship. They appear to regard them as resembling the angels in the Jewish and Christian system.— "Brahm is the Supreme God of all the gods." — "The gods incessantly worship the Supreme Brahm." — "He is the Lord of the gods." — "All the gods offer him worship."

Idolatry is discarded in their creed, but is excused and defended in their works. Referring to some places in the Vedic writings, Ram Mohun Roy says: — "These as well as other texts of the same nature are not real commands but only direct those who are unfortunately incapable of adoring the invisible Supreme Being, to apply their minds to any visible object rather than allow them to remain idle." — "We come now to that part of the doctrines of the Vedas, which inculcates that those who cannot turn their minds to God in spirit, should worship him through the medium of matter. There are men of that grovelling class, whose minds are incapable of making a proper degree of exertion, and these are required not to lose themselves in the mazes of irreligion, the bane of society, but rather to fix their attention on some of the grandest objects of the world, and consider them to be so many manifestations of the supremacy of the only true God who pervades all creation; and to worship them as so animated by his influence that thus their minds may be gradually trained by spiritual intuition to the true mental adoration of the Supreme Being. Such injunctions were mercifully made for the benefit of the ignorant and untrained." — "The rites and ceremonies inculcated in the Vedas are intended to be preparatory to the spiritual worship of God, and are expressly declared to be useful to men who cannot raise their minds from nature up to nature's God." — The *Patrika* their authorized journal says, "We believe that *every kind of worshipper will have his own species of reward*, from the savage Polynesian, who addresses his ejaculations to a rude misshapen block of stone, to the Vedantist who adores God in spirit and in truth." This sentiment would excuse and justify nearly or quite all the kinds of idolatry and worship in India.

The Brahmists believe in the doctrine of transmigration, and that those who are not prepared for blessedness at death, must pass through successive births on the earth till they become prepared. Whether their views are that there are intervals of reward and punishment between these births, or that these births immediately succeed death as the reward and punishment of the previous birth, does not appear plain. — The *Patrika* says: "The man who is ignorant and impure gains not the rank (is not admitted to the presence) of Brahm at death, but returns to the world. The wise man having gained that dignity, is born no more. The man who in this world is able to know God, accomplishes the object of his birth; having perceived God, he is removed entirely from this world and dies no more." "Our religion inculcates that our good and bad actions shall all inevitably receive their proportionate reward and punishment, with the exception only of expiated sin, conformably to the exact extent which is necessary for the purpose of reformation and encouragement; that we shall thus have to pass a state of probation during successive lives of longer or shorter duration, until we are fitted by sacred knowledge and entire devotion to the divine will of God to enjoy that supreme felicity which may be said to be a participation of the divine nature."

The Brahmists retain the distinctions of caste in their system. It is not made prominent in their writings, but these contain nothing against caste, while they receive and declare their full belief in the Upanishads, which declare caste to be of divine origin. The members of the Dharma Sabha also carefully observe all the rules of caste among themselves and in their intercourse with others, and they have shown great zeal in opposing those who wish to weaken and destroy it. Their retaining and observing caste, shows that they have yet very inadequate views of the changes required to place the Hindus in the social, intellectual, and moral state which they profess to be seeking in this reformation.

The Brahm Dharma, which is the authorized exponent of their system of reformed Hinduism, contains the following: —

PRINCIPLES OF RELIGION.

"1. Before the production of this world there existed only the Supreme Brahm; nothing else existed whatsoever. He created all this.

"2. He is wisdom, eternity, joy, and goodness personified; the everlasting ruler of all; all-wise, without form, one only without a second, most wonderful in power.

"3. From his worship alone is happiness produced both here and hereafter.

"4. That worship consists in loving him and performing actions which give him pleasure."

The following is the Covenant of the Society for all who become members: —

"1. This day, the —— day of the month of ——, in the year ——, I adopt the religion of the worshippers of Brahm.

"2. I will live devoted to the worship of that one Supreme Brahm, who is the Creator, the Preserver, and the Destroyer of the universe; the cause of deliverance; all-wise; all-pervading; full of joy; the good; and without form. I will worship him with love and by doing things that will give him pleasure.

"3. I will worship no created thing as the Supreme Brahm, the Creator of all.

"4. Except on days of sickness or calamity, I will every day when my mind shall be at rest, in faith and love, fix my thoughts on the Supreme.

"5. I will live earnest in the practice of good deeds.

"6. I will endeavor to live free from evil deeds.

"7. If overcome by temptation I perchance do any thing evil, I will surely desire to be freed from it and be careful for the future.

"8. Every year and in all my worldly prosperity I will offer gifts to the Brahm Sumaj.

"O God, grant unto me strength that I may entirely observe this excellent religion."

The members of this Society carry their principles into effect by social religious worship. The following is a description of the manner in which their worship is conducted.

"The Society has from the first endeavored to consolidate itself and cultivate devout feelings among its members by the celebration of regular *worship*. For this purpose the followers of this doctrine, whether members of the Tattwabodhini Sabha or not, meet on Wednesday evenings as a *Brahm Sumaj* (an assembly of the worshippers of Brahm) at the premises of the Society in the Chitpore Road. Their long hall has been neatly fitted up with pews, rising backward from the centre to the two ends, and well lighted by chandeliers and wall-shades. In the middle of the hall upon a dais of grained marble sit the two pundits, the leaders in the worship, and in a recess immediately opposite to them are the musicians. The service commences with the reading of various passages from the Vedas. The *Gayutree** is then recited and meditated upon. A hymn from one of the Upanishads is then chanted by all present. An exposition of texts from

* Page 400, *note*.

the Vedas, or an essay on some branch of natural theology then follows. The president or some member of the Sabha then gives a short discourse, and the service closes with the singing of Brahmic hymns by the professional musicians, who accompany it with their instruments. The whole service occupies about an hour."

There are some things in this Society for reforming the Hindu religion (or rather the Hindus, for they do not profess to limit their principles to the original doctrines of the Hindus) which appear well. Their principles and their creed are avowed and published. Their house of worship is open for all, whether members of their Society or not, to meet and join with them. If there is any mystery or mysticism connected with them, it must be in their doctrines and not in their proceedings or practices. From 1846 to 1851, the average number of members of the Society in Calcutta exceeded 500. It is reported to have somewhat declined for 3 or 4 years past.

INDEX.

www.ingramcontent.com/pod-product-compliance
Lightning Source LLC
LaVergne TN
LVHW021100110826
845150LV00001B/133

* 9 7 8 1 4 2 5 5 6 6 1 4 2 *